THE BANNER OF TRUTH TRUST

Head Office
3 Murrayfield Road
Edinburgh, EH12 6EL
UK

North America Office
610 Alexander Spring Road
Carlisle, PA 17015
USA

banneroftruth.org

The Complete Works of Thomas Brooks first published in
6 volumes 1861-67
First Banner of Truth Trust reprint 1980
Reprinted 2001, 2024

*

ISBN
Vol I: 978 0 85151 303 4
6-volume set: 978 0 85151 302 7

*

Printed in the USA by
Versa Press Inc.,
East Peoria, IL

The Works of
THOMAS BROOKS

VOLUME I

EDITED WITH MEMOIR BY

Alexander B. Grosart

THE BANNER OF TRUTH TRUST

CONTENTS.

Chapter VIII.

PREFACE.

IT may surely be regarded as a favourable sign of the times, that so many reprints of the works of the thinkers of former days—laic and cleric—have been called for during the last ten years. It argues that while there may be many whose tastes incline them to 'milk for babes,' there are those who have appetites to relish, and stomachs to digest, 'stronger meat.' We have reference more immediately to the numerous and widely circulated republications of the elder Theologians of all shades of opinion on lesser matters: as well the acknowledged and famous, as the less known and hitherto uncollected and inedited. Of the former, suffice it to name Eden's 'Jeremy Taylor,' Napier's 'Isaac Barrow,' Wynter's 'Joseph Hall,' 'Thomas Goodwin' of this series; of the latter, our own 'Richard Sibbes,' and now 'Thomas Brooks,' with others in hand, together with the fine series of Commentaries being issued by our Publisher, and including such ripe and rare books as Airay on 'Philippians,' King on 'Jonah,' Stock and Torshell on 'Malachi,' Rainolds on 'Obadiah and Haggai,' Bernard and Fuller on 'Ruth,' Marbury on 'Obadiah and Habakkuk,' Hardy on '1st Epistle of St John,' Bayne on 'Ephesians,' and that *magnum opus*, Dr William Gouge on 'Hebrews.' It seems impossible that such intellectual and spiritual seed-corn as is treasured up in these early worthies can be sown thus broadcast, and yield an unbounteous harvest. Granted that, as with the sown grain, there is not a little of what is chaff, or,—speaking unmetaphorically,—that is tedious and attenuated, over-worded, effete, musty: yet the 'ingenuous' and thinking reader, like the kindly earth under supernal influences, assimilates the good and fruitful: and toward all the venerable writers, has a tender patience and charity and forgivingness, such as one feels for the garrulous 'white-head' that in other days wearied us in the chimney-corner, but, being gone, is remembered sacredly, pathetically, and with wet eyes.

We add Thomas Brooks to the 'Divines' of the 'Puritan Period' with no fear of contradiction when we claim for him a foremost place among the greatest of the later Puritans; meaning thereby those who were *in*-cluded, and, as Thomas Fuller would have said, *ex*-cluded also, by the 'Ejectment' of 1662. With the exception of John Bunyan, and perhaps, in separate minor works of Richard Baxter, no writer of the 17th century has been so *permanently* and widely and variously represented in the living Literature of the 18th and 19th as the author of 'Precious Remedies against Satan's Devices,' 'The Mute Christian under the Smarting Rod,' 'Apples of Gold,' and 'Heaven on Earth:' but, unfortunately, he has been mainly represented and known by these four treatises, whereas his other and numerous writings have the same merits—if the word be not chill and poor—with these; all passed through frequent editions in the outset, and have popularly gone out of sight, not as less weighty and vital, but capriciously and arbitrarily and mistakenly.

One immense advantage of Brooks over Sibbes is, that the whole of his many volumes, lesser and larger, were published by himself. He left nothing behind him to be thrust on the world as 'Remains' or *posthumous*—a healthy self-restraint and wisdom which it had been well if others, even of our most illustrious Divines, ancient and modern, had exercised.

In submitting this first collective edition of the 'Complete Works' of Brooks to the public, I beg attention to these six things:—

(*α*.) Our text, in every separate treatise and tractate, is based upon the last '*revised and corrected*' impression thereof *that passed under the eye of the author:* an explanatory 'Note' being prefixed to each, giving all needful information on the different editions. It may be mentioned that his collection of the original and early editions has cost the Editor fully £35, whereas the reprint will be furnished to the public for 25s.

(*β*.) The whole is *incorrupt, unmutilated, unchanged.* Of this, John Foster the 'Essayist' may be allowed to speak. Writing to a friend for the works of Howe, and preferring the old edition, he characteristically observes: 'In the *new* one, I recollect the Editor engaged, as a favour to the readers, to make—and I suppose he did make—some little tinkerings of the long, involved, and grotesquely constructed sentences: a thing sufficiently wanted, I allow, for it is quite wonderful that such a man as Howe should have bungled so sadly in the manner of sentence-making. But, nevertheless, I should prefer having his paragraphs just as he had made them, to *any* Editor's rectification of them: a preference, however, which cannot be supposed to be felt by any gentleman of the literary form of Burder and Hughes, the Editors and Correctors of Henry's Exposition.'[1] We offer no 'tinkerings,' no 'rectifications,' no 'corrections,' no 'improvements.' Even in bringing the old arbitrary orthography into accord with modern usage, we have duly noted all peculiar or transitive forms of words. So that Thomas Brooks is here given genuinely, as he himself published his writings. His style as a whole, however, is accurate, and compact, and modern-like, save in occasional quaintnesses and outspokenness.

(γ.) *The whole of the Bible-texts and references have been carefully verified.* Only those who have consulted the original editions are able to appreciate the toil involved in this: eighty per cent. at least being inaccurate. The important classical and patristic citations and allusions have similarly been verified and supplemented. This does not apply to the well-nigh innumerable anonymous 'anecdotes,' 'sayings,' 'readings;' though, even of those, a large proportion will be found to be traced and confirmed in our footnotes. Trite classical and other facts and names we have left as they occur.

(δ.) In response to the appeal of the lamented Herbert Coleridge and the 'Philological Society,' we have marked all Shakespearian and other noticeable words and phrases. As in Sibbes, a Glossary will furnish a Reference-Index thereto.

(ε.) For all foot-notes bearing my own initial, G., I am responsible: the rest belong to Brooks himself; and I take this opportunity of calling special attention to *them*. They consist, for the larger part, of the margin-notes of the original and early editions, and will always repay perusal. Very often it will be found that, by his multifarious reading, he gives point to some argument or appeal, or illustration, by a racy saying of Luther, or a felicitous bit from a Father, or some apt anecdote, or quaint, however unreal, opinion of old science, or a flash of wit or play upon a word. So that he will be a loser who passes by these notes, which are as the dust-of-gold of a rich and brilliant mind. Brooks himself attached no little importance to them. Thus, in his 'Word to the Reader,' prefixed to 'Precious Remedies,' he observes. 'If in thy reading thou wilt cast a serious eye upon the margin, thou wilt find many sweet and precious notes that will oftentimes give light to the things thou readest, and pay thee for thy pains with much comfort and profit.' (Our reprint, page 9.)

It only remains that I notice the one representative of an 'edition' of the Works of Brooks, and shew, by a recent reprint of a single book, how unworthily he has hitherto been edited.

(1.) The Rev. Charles Bradley, M.A., of Glasbury, Brecon, in 1824, issued two volumes (cr. 8vo.) containing, (1.) 'The Unsearchable Riches of Christ;' (2.) 'Remedies against Satan's Devices' [the golden Bible-

[1] Letter to the Rev. Joseph Hughes, in Foster's 'Life and Correspondence,' Vol. i. pp. 420, 421. (Ed. 1852.)

word 'precious' left out!]; (3.) 'A Treatise on Assurance' [*i. e.* Heaven on Earth]; (4.) 'The Mute Christian under the Smarting Rod;' (5.) 'Apples of Gold.'

This has long been out of print, so that we do no prejudice to existing interests when we characterise it as worthless, by its modernizations, and errors of omission and commission, beyond reckoning. A comparison of any single page with our text will reveal such tampering with what Brooks wrote as is most discreditable and vitiatory. It is sadly-amusive to observe the thin things that are deemed 'improvements' on our robust, outspoken Puritan.

(2.) The 'Cabinet of Jewels' was reprinted in a fair-looking volume, which bears the imprint, 'Huntly: published by Duncan Matheson. 1860.' If we err not, this is the earnest Revivalist and Missionary of Crimean celebrity. All honour to him as such, and all honour to his *motives* in re-issuing the precious book. But it swarms, as does Bradley, with blunders and 'corrections' (!) *e. g.*, the very *Errata* carefully prefixed by the author—not to specify others—are left unchanged; and so (to give a few specimens) we read 'fleshly joys' for Brooks's 'flashy joys' (page 22, line 4); saintly John Murcot of Dublin is transmogrified into 'John Marcol' (page 35, line 22); 'Assur's oppression' is spoken of instead of 'Asa's' (page 53, line 37); Rachel is made to cry out, 'Give me *water*' for 'Give me *children*' (page 75, line 2); and so throughout.

The same remarks, with but slight modification, are applicable to the many reprints of the 'Religious Tract Society' and other Publishers, who 'improve' and 'polish' into conformity with ideas of 'elegance' such as would have roused the rebuke of the fearless old preachers, who said what they meant, and meant to the letter, what they said.

I have, as in the case of Sibbes, very gratefully to record the kind help and sympathetic interest in our work shewn by many correspondents, sought and voluntary. I must specially name my excellent friend Joshua Wilson, Esq. of Nevil Park, Tunbridge Wells; John Bruce, Esq., London, the accomplished editor and biographer of the new Aldine 'Cowper,' and many other historico-biographic works; the Rev. R. Brook Aspland, M.A., London; the Rectors of St Thomas Apostles, and other of the London city churches; the Rectors and Curates of Newbury and other Churches in different Counties; the Rev. T. W. Davids, Colchester; the authorities of the British Museum; Williams' Library; Guildhall Library; the Bodleian, Oxford; the University Library, and various College Libraries, Cambridge; the Rev. J. E. B. Mayor, M.A., Cambridge, and the late Charles H. Cooper, Esq., Town Clerk, Cambridge,—together with very many to whom I am indebted for letters in answer to (I fear) troublesomely minute inquiries. I owe thanks also to 'Notes and Queries,' and other Literary Journals.

'For a conclusion of all by way of prefix'—here in part appropriating the words of Cawdrey and Palmer in the Epistle to their *Sabbatum Redivivum* (1645. Pt. I.)—I 'have but one word or two more to say, and that by way of earnest entreaty.' These 'Works,' reader! are full as the honey-comb of 'exceeding great and precious' TRUTH: no mere stately scholarliness, curious questioning, nice casuistry, windy phrases. Therefore, I pray 'That thou wilt do the Truth that right as to yield to and practise what thou art convinced of.' 'Consider' what I say, 'and the Lord give thee and me understanding and grace in all things through Jesus Christ. So prays,

Thine in Him,'

ALEXANDER B. GROSART.

308 UPPER PARLIAMENT STREET,
LIVERPOOL, *May* 1866.

MEMOIR OF THOMAS BROOKS.

IT is long since one said in his own quaintly-pensive way, 'Who knows whether the best men be known, or whether there be not more remarkable persons forgot, than any that stand remembered in the known account of Time?' Our endeavours towards elucidating the Lives of the Worthies embraced in these series of reprints, as well as the like experience of all who have sought to trace the footprints of shy, sequestered goodness, as distinguished from noisy and noised 'greatness,' so-called—satisfy us, that Sir Thomas Browne never wrote truer words.[1] Light—that shoots its silver arrows unbrokenly across the abysses between the sun and our earth, and yet ruffles not tiniest feather of bird's wing, or drop of dew in flower-cup—is a more potent thing than lightning; but, lacking the thunder-roar after it, in vulgar account is the weaker, albeit the thunder comes from no higher than the clouds. Similarly, the 'hidden ones'—who are really the '*best* men'—have been in by far too many cases outblazoned by your creature of circumstance. It needs a wider and intenser sky than ours to show some stars; and not until the 'new heavens' dome the 'new earth' will the truly 'great' names shine excellingly. RICHARD SIBBES, with rare fineness of thought and felicitousness of wording, has 'weighed' the two fames—and his 'counsel' may fittingly come in here. 'Let us commit the fame and credit,' says he, 'of what we are or do to God. *He will take care of that:* let us take care to be and to do as we should, and then *for noise and report*, let it be good or ill as God will send it. . . . *If we seek to be in the mouths of men, to dwell in the talk and speech of men*, God will abhor us. . . . Therefore let us labour to be good *in secret.* Christians should be as minerals, rich in the depth of the earth. That which is least seen is his (the Chris-

[1] Works by Wilkin, iii. page 492 (4 vols. 8vo, 1836).

tian's) riches. We should have our treasure deep; for the discovery of it, we should be ready when we are called to it; and for all other accidental things, let it fall out as God in his wisdom sees good. . . . *God will be careful enough to get us applause.* . . . As much reputation as is fit for a man will follow him, in being and doing what he should. *God will look to that.* Therefore we should not set up sails to our own meditations, that unless we be carried with the wind of applause, to be becalmed, and not go a whit forward; but we should be carried with the Spirit of God, and with a holy desire to serve God and our brethren, and to do all the good we can, *and* never care for the speeches of the world. . . . We shall have glory enough, and be known enough to devils, to angels, and men, *ere long.* Therefore, as Christ lived a hidden life—that is, He was not known what He was, that so He might work our salvation, so let us be content to be hidden ones. . . . THERE WILL BE A RESURRECTION OF CREDITS, as well as of bodies. We'll have glory enough BY-AND-BY.'[1]

In the cases of Sibbes himself, and Airay, and King, and Stock, and Torshell, and Bernard, and Marbury, and indeed nearly all, I have had to deplore the paucity of materials for anything like adequate Memoirs. But more than ever have I to do so in relation to THOMAS BROOKS. If a pun, that he himself would have relished, may be allowed, his memory has passed away like the 'summer *brooks.*' This is all the more regrettable, in that his books are vital and influential as at first—his name still a venerable and loved one to myriads. Only the other day we chanced upon a mission-volume that tells of strength and comfort gained from his words, away on the other side of that India which in his days was as dream-land, as wonder-land. I may as well give the pathetic little bit. Mrs Mason among the Karens writes: 'Two days passed when they came again, saying the money was all gone. At first I felt disposed to rebuke them, but turned to my closet for an hour, giving the time to prayer, *and to my dear little help-book "Precious Remedies against Satan's Devices."* In that time God taught me what to do, and strength was given for the day.'[2] Verily 'he, being dead, *yet speaketh.*'

Various explanations suggest themselves as to the absence of memorial of Brooks's outward-life.

(1.) It so happens that the 'Registers' of his University are singularly defective at the period of his attendance; so much so that even the sweet-natured Historian was moved to these severe censures: 'Hitherto we have given in the list of the yearly Commencers, but now must break off. Let Thomas Smith, University-Register, *bear the blame,*

[1] Works, Vol. I.; Memoir, pp. xxiii, xxiv.

[2] Civilizing Mountain Men, or Sketches of Mission Work among the Karens. By Mrs Mason, of Burmah. 1862. (Nisbet.)

who, about this year, entering into his office, *was so negligent* that, as one saith, *Cum fuit Academiæ a memoriâ, omnia tradidit oblivioni. I can hardly in-hold from inveighing on his memory, carelessness being dishonesty in public persons so entrusted.*'[1]

(2.) He was excluded from the 'Worthies' of Fuller by his rule, that 'the living' were 'omitted.'[2] How often the reader sighs over like dismissal of other names as still 'surviving.'[3]

(3.) The 'Fire' of London destroyed the MSS. of Ashe, and various fellow-labourers who had collected for the Lives of the elder and later Puritans, including 'The Ejected' of 1662.[4] Beyond all question Thomas Brooks held an honoured place therein. Then again the same 'Fire,' destroying the different Churches in which Brooks officiated, destroyed with them all their Registers and Records. So that Newcourt and other authorities are blank in respect of dates, and almost everything else. Add to all this, his own singularly reticent and modest 'hiding' of self—his absolute indifference to fame, other than the love of those who might 'profit' by his writings: and he yearned for that, as the close of his 'Epistles Dedicatory' shew.

As it is, after having expended fully the *maximum* of labour and '*painfulness*'—as the old Divines say,—in seeking to illumine the memory of this 'dead Saint,' I can only offer a *minimum* of result: and yet our little is relatively large to what has hitherto been known.

It is not ascertained in what city, town, or village Thomas Brooks was born: not even in what county. The very nativeness of his name has multiplied the difficulties of determining it. In 'this fair England' '*brooks*' flash by meadow and woodland everywhere; and as familiar and frequent is his name.[5] Certain turns of expression, certain apparently local words, occurring in his volumes, have made us feel assured that in this County or in that we should discover his family: but lo! the phrase and word proved to be common to many: and our toil went for nothing, save morsels of fact about others, unexpectedly turning up. From his 'Will'—which we have discovered, and print for the first time—we fondly hoped to trace him to Berkshire: but again were disappointed, spite of complete and carefully preserved 'Registers,' and all courtesy and helpfulness from their custodiers. From a 'Memorial' again, of Lancashire 'Worthies,' by the saintly Oliver Heywood—un-

[1] Fuller's 'History of the University of Cambridge,' page 208.

[2] *Ibid.*, page 207. [3] *Ibid.*, page 206.

[4] Brook, 'Lives of the Puritans,' vol. iii., *sub nominibus*.

[5] Mr Spurgeon plays on the name in his little volume of sentences from Brooks's writings, entitling it, 'Smooth Stones taken from Ancient Brooks. By the Rev. C. H. Spurgeon, of the Metropolitan Tabernacle. Being a Collection of Sentences, Illustrations, and Quaint Sayings, from the Works of that Renowned Puritan, Thomas Brooks.' (32mo, pp. xv. 296.)

published—which notices his death, in a little record that is useful, we half-anticipated to be able to claim him for it; but all inquiries leave us in uncertainty.[1] Besides, the orthography of the name confuses: for just as there were among Divines a John Howes as well as a John Howe, a John Owens as well as a John Owen, a Thomas Adam as well as a Thomas Adams, even a John Milton as well as *the* John Milton, so our Thomas Brooks is sometimes met with—even early—as now Thomas Brooke, and now Thomas Brookes and Brook—the penultimate being his own spelling on the title-page of 'Precious Remedies' [2d ed. 1653] and 'Unsearchable Riches' [1657, 1st ed.], though in the 'Epistles' he adheres to Brooks. Little do your arm-chair-easy critics know of the honest work spent in furnishing such 'Memoirs'—slight and unsatisfying though they be—as they magisterially discuss and dismiss with penurious thanks! Personally we have no plaint, much less complaint, to make: for our labours have been more than duly appreciated: but we feel constrained to remind those who may be tempted to regard a given 'Life' as insufficient, that in ninety-nine cases of a hundred what appears is as the one to the ninety-nine of anxious though fruitless inquiries.

The Manuscript 'entry' of Oliver Heywood referred to a short way back—and which will appear in its own place—gives his age at death as '72,' but by a clerical blunder probably, writes 1678 for 1680, the actual year of his decease. If 1680 was intended, then his birth-year must have been 1608—John Milton's also; if calculated from 1678, two years sooner, 1606. It seems likely that the former is the accurate date.

We are shut out from all insight into ancestry, parentage, and childhood, and 'boy' surroundings of our Worthy—whether he were of '*blue blood*' descent, or of a '*godly*' or worldly fatherhood and motherhood, whether 'in populous city pent,' or blown upon by the freshening influences of rural life. We do not know his 'School,' 'Schoolmasters,' or 'Schoolmates.' The whole 'make' of the man—as it is expressed in his Writings—warrants us in assuming that his 'home' was a '*church in the house*,' and his training the grave, serious, yet not morose but blithesome one, of the Puritans. By his '17th' year—at latest—the one University 'date' that survives through the heedlessness of that scion of the immortal Smiths rebuked by Fuller—he was at College, at '*Emmanuel*,' Cambridge. This was *the* Puritan College *par excellence:* the illustrious Founder of it—Sir Walter Mildmay—having been flouted by Elizabeth for his 'Puritan foundation.'[2] So that we

[1] For this we are indebted to the ever open stores of our good friend Joshua Wilson, Esq., of Nevil Park, Tunbridge Wells.

[2] Fuller tells the story pungently: 'Coming to Court after he had founded his College, the Queen told him, "Sir Walter, I hear you have erected a Puritan foundation." "No, Madam," saith he; "far be from me to countenance anything contrary to your established laws; but I have set an acorn which, when it becomes an oak, God alone knows

can scarcely err in finding in this choice confirmation of Puritan-parentage. The entry is as follows:[1]

'Thomas Brooks: matriculated as *pensioner* of Emanuel, July 7th 1625.'

'PENSIONER' must not be misunderstood as indicating narrow circumstances, much less poverty. John Milton was entered as 'pensioner,' only a few months previously, at a sister-college. There were four grades, the 'greater pensioner,' the 'lesser pensioner,' 'sizars,' and 'scholars.' These distinctions designate differing rank. All the first three lived as now we are accustomed to say on the Continent, *en pension, id est*, paid for their board and education, and in this respect were distinct from the *scholars* properly so called, who belonged to the foundation. The 'greater pensioners' or 'fellow commoners' paid most. They were (as they still are) the sons of noble or 'gentle' families, and had the privilege of dining at the upper table in the common hall along with the fellows. The 'sizars,' on the other hand, were poorer students; they paid least; and, though receiving the same education with the others, held a lower rank and had inferior accommodation. Intermediate between the 'greater pensioners' and the 'sizars' were the 'lower pensioners;' and it was (as it is still) to this class that the bulk of the students in all the colleges at Cambridge belonged.[2] By 'pensioner' after Brooks's name we are no doubt to understand 'lesser pensioner;' so that, as with the scrivener-father of the bard of 'Paradise Lost,' his parents were in good circumstances. When we know that Jeremy Taylor entered as *pauper scholaris*, and Sibbes as a 'sizar,' it had needed no vindication had Master Thomas Brooks taken his position in either class; but the matter-of-fact is as stated, and it is but right to state it. He must have been well born, and born as a 'gentleman.'

Brooks, in 'entering' Emanuel College on July 7th 1625, as above,

what will be the fruit thereof."' And the historian adds, 'Sure I am, at this day, it hath overshadowed all the University—more than a moiety of the present Masters of Colleges being bred therein.' As *before*, pp. 205, 206. For Full details on Sir Walter Mildmay, see Cooper's Athenæ Cantabrigienses, Vol. ii. pp. 51–55, 544. I cannot give this reference without paying a tribute of heartfelt regard to the just deceased senior author of this inestimable work, who, within a few days of his lamented death, dictated and even signed a letter bearing on my researches. Erudite, laborious, finely enthusiastic, ungrudging in communicating from his ample resources, all our Memoirs have been indebted to him. See finely touched estimate of him by Mr Mayor, reprinted from 'The Cambridge Papers of March 24. 1866,' in 'Notes and Queries,' March 31. 1866, pp. 253–54.

[1] Rev. J. E. B. Mayor, M.A., Librarian to the University of Cambridge, and the late Charles H. Cooper, Esq., to myself. Moreover, this one entry is all that the industry of Cole provides: Cole MSS. in British Museum, under 'Emanuel.'

[2] On all this cf. Masson's 'Life of Milton in Connection with the History of His Time,' particularly vol. i. pp. 88, 89. No one who seeks information on the period covered by the 'Life' of Milton, will fail to consult this treasure-house of materials.

had for Master that one of all the heads of Colleges, 'whose presence,' to quote the words of an unchallengeable authority—Professor David Masson—'was the most impressive.'[1] 'He was,' says Fuller—whose Churchism never for a moment hindered his generous recognition of worth and wit in whomsoever found—'the greatest pupil-monger in England in man's memory, having sixteen fellow-commoners, most heirs to fair estates, admitted in one year at Queen's College. As William the Popular of Nassau was said to have won a subject from the King of Spain to his own party every time he put off his hat, so was it commonly said in the College, that every time when Master Preston plucked off his hat to Dr Davenant, the College master, he gained a chamber or study for one of his pupils.'[2] He was pre-eminently a Puritan in its grandest and—at the time—reproached sense. Chosen 'Master' of Emanuel in 1622, he carried most of his pupils with him from Queen's thither; and as its Head, kept up the reputation of that House as the most Puritanical in the University. His 'Life' belongs to History: it yet remains unwritten, as, shame to Cambridge, his priceless Works remain to this day uncollected and inedited.[3] It was no common advantage to our student to have been placed under such a 'Master'; and his margin-references to 'Dr Preston,' and the same to 'Dr Sibbes,' together with occasional 'sayings' of the latter not met with elsewhere, assure us that he sat reverently at their feet.[4] His fellow-students at 'Emanuel'—assuming that he 'proceeded' through the ordinary *curriculum* of study—included Thomas Shepard, and John Cotton, and Thomas Hooker—afterwards the famous trio of New England 'Divines,' and spiritually the founders and fathers of Massachusetts. To the same College, earlier and later, belonged the holy Bedell, the many-sided Joseph Hall, the large-thoughted Ralph Cudworth, and these still lustrous Puritan 'Worthies'—Samuel Crooke, John Yates, John Stoughton, Ezekiel Culverwell, Stephen Marshall, Samuel Hudson, Nathanael Ward.[5] Elsewhere we have sketched his contemporaries in the University. Beginning with that name which overshadows all the rest—John Milton—the roll ends with Waller and Randolph.[6]

From the reasons assigned, it is our hap and mishap not to be able to

[1] Masson as before, p. 93.

[2] Fuller's Worthies: Northamptonshire; and Church History, *sub anno*, 1628; and also (from Masson as *supra*): Wood's Fasti, i. 333: Neal's History of the Puritans, ii. 193, *et seq.* Fuller was himself a student of Queen's before Preston had left it for Emanuel. On the whole position and subject of the Puritans, see that invaluable trans-Atlantic contribution to history, 'The Puritans: or the Church, Court, and Parliament of England, during the reigns of Edward VI. and Queen Elizabeth. By Samuel Hopkins. 3 vols. 8vo. (Boston, 1859–61).

[3] See our Memoir of Sibbes, vol. ii. pp. 51, 52, *et alibi.*

[4] See our Index, *sub-nominibus*, for these references.

[5] Cf. Brook's 'Lives of the Puritans,' *sub nominibus;* also Dr Sprague's 'Annals' of the American Pulpit, *ditto.*

[6] See our Memoir of Sibbes as before, pp. 52, 53, *et alibi.*

trace the 'progress' of Brooks. In all likelihood, he 'proceeded' from degree to degree, although in common with other of the Puritans, he places none on his title-pages, preferring the nobler designation, 'Preacher of the Gospel,' or 'Preacher of the Word.' Of his entire University course we have an incidental notice in one of those rare snatches of autobiography which occur in his writings. It occurs in a tractate, of which more anon, and runs thus: 'For a close of this branch. . . . I shall only say this: being compelled thereunto by some—that I do believe that I have spent more money at the University, and in helps to learning, than several of these petitioners are worth, though haply I have not been such a proficient as those that have spent less.' He adds: 'I am a lover of the tongues, and do by daily experience find, that knowledge in the original tongues is no small help for the understanding of Scripture,' &c.[1]

When Brooks left the University we cannot tell. The periods of residence and attendance varied; some being shorter and others longer. If he remained, as Sibbes and Gouge his contemporaries did, from nine to twelve years, adding the former to 1625, we are advanced to 1634; by the latter to 1637. He must have been 'licensed' or 'ordained' as a 'Preacher of the Gospel' by 1640 at latest. For in the tractate already quoted ['Cases Considered and Resolved'], which is dated 1653, he says, 'I am compelled to tell you that I have, by the gracious assistance of God, preached publicly, the Gospel, *above these thirteen years;* and the greatest part of those years I have spent in preaching the word in London, where God hath given me many precious seals of my ministry, which are now my comfort, and in the day of Christ will be my crown.'[2] At this time, too, he must have been involved in many labours; for in his 'Epistle' to 'the conscientious reader,' he thus appeals in regard to 'errata.' 'I desire that thou wouldst cast a mantle of love over the mistakes of the Printer, I having no opportunity to wait on the press, *by reason of my many engagements other ways.*'[3] How one wishes that the good man had had a little more communicative egotism, and confided to us when and where, before coming to London, and in London, he had 'preached the Word!' By 1648 he was Preacher of the Gospel at Thomas Apostles, London: such being his designation in the title-page of his first publication, viz., his Sermon, entitled 'The Glorious Day of the Saints' Appearance, calling for a glorious conversation from all Believers,' which was 'delivered . . . . at the interment of the corpse of that renowned Commander, Colonel Thomas Rainsborough, who was treacherously murdered at Doncaster, October 29. 1648, and honourably interred the 14th of November following, in the Chapel at Wapping, near London.' This 'Sermon' is

[1] 'Cases Considered and Resolved,' given *in extenso* in Appendix A to this Introduction.

[2] As before, page 8, 'a short Preamble.' [3] *Ibid.*, page 6.

on various accounts important and interesting biographically. It furnishes certain facts which must be brought together. First of all, he must by this time have won a commanding position, to have been appointed the 'Preacher' on so public and sorrowful an occasion. The honour came most unexpectedly, as was the giving of the Sermon to the public unintended by himself. On these two points in his 'Epistle' he thus speaks: 'When I preached upon the subject of the saints' glorious appearance at the last, He that knows all hearts and thoughts, knows that I had not the least thought to put it to press. And that, partly, because the meditations following were not the meditations of a week, no, nor of two days, but of some few hours: I having but short warning to provide; and other things falling in within the compass of that short time that did divert my thoughts some other ways. But mainly because of that little, little worth that is in it.' Then he continues: 'And yet, Right Honourable, *the intentions of some to put it to the press in case I would not consent to have it printed*—by which means truth and myself might have been co-partners in suffering—and the strong importunity of many precious souls, hath borne me down and subdued me to them.'[1] Again: It is dedicated to the 'Right Honourable Thomas, Lord Fairfax, Lord General of all the Parliament's Forces in England,' as to a friend and familiar, to whom it is his pride to 'testify,' not only to himself, 'but to all the world,' his 'thankful remembrance and due acknowledgment' of his Lordship's 'undeserved respect' towards him.'[2] In an age of venal flattery, the 'Epistles Dedicatory' of Brooks are throughout simple, plain-spoken, searching, direct as an old Hebrew prophet's 'burden:' hence this language certainly meant what it said. But specially one allusion is at once a key to other personal references scattered up and down his writings, and an explanation of how the years preceding 1640, as above, were occupied. Near the close of the Sermon,—and it is characteristic of the man, that only about a single page is devoted to Rainsborough himself,—he reveals 'service' with the lamented Commander. 'As for this thrice-honoured champion now in the dust: for his enjoyment of God, *from my own experience, being with him both at sea and land*, I have abundance of sweetness and satisfaction in my own spirit, which to me exceedingly sweetens so great a loss.'[3] I have said that this 'testimony' furnishes a key to other references. I allude to incidental intimations of his having been abroad. Thus, in the 'Epistle Dedicatory' to his 'Precious Remedies,' as one of the reasons for its publication he gives this: 'I have many precious friends *in several countries*, who are not a little desirous that my pen may reach them, now my voice cannot. *I have formerly been*, by the help of the mighty God of Jacob, *a weak instrument of good to them*, and cannot but hope and believe that the Lord

[1] Page 12. [2] Page 1. [3] Page 22.

will also bless those labours to them: they being in part the fruit of their desires and prayers, &c.[1] Again: In his 'Unsearchable Riches,' he thus barbs one of his many fearless rebukes: 'If you do not give them [ministers of the Gospel] honourable countenance, Jews and Turks, Papists and Pagans, will in the great day of account rise up against you and condemn you. *I could say much of what I have observed in other nations and countries* concerning this thing; but I forbear. Should I speak *what I have seen*, many professors [professing Christians] might well blush.'[2] Once more: 'In the 'Epistle Dedicatory' to his 'Heaven on Earth,' there occur these personal reminiscences, tantalizing by their very suggestiveness: '*I have observed* in some terrible storms *I have been in*, that the mariners' and the passengers' want of assurance, and of those other pearls of price that in this Treatise are presented to public view, hath caused their countenance to change,' &c. Then the 'Epistle' itself is addressed to 'The Right Honourable the Generals of the Fleets of the Commonwealth of England, and to those gallant Worthies (*my much honoured friends*), who, with the noble generals, have deeply jeoparded their lives unto many deaths, out of love to their country's good, and out of respect to the interest of Christ and the faithful people of this Commonwealth;' and of these,—besides the parenthesis italicized in the foregoing,—he assigns as one reason for so 'tendering' his volume to them. 'Because you are my friends, and that cordial love and friendship which I have found from you hath stamped in my affections a very high valuation of you.' Once more: a little further on, he says, 'I have been some years at Sea, and through grace I can say that I would not exchange my Sea experiences for England's riches. I am not altogether ignorant of the troubles, trials, temptations, dangers, and deaths, that do attend you.' In a margin-note at the close he adds, 'Had I a purse suitable to my heart, not a poor, godly soldier or sailor in England, who carries his life in one hand, but should have one of these books in the other.'[3] Further: In his 'London's Lamentations,' speaking of the wind, he observes: 'In some places of the world—where I have been—the motions of the wind are steady and constant, which mariners call their trade-wind.'[4] Besides these notices in his writings, by his 'Will,' which will be found in its own place, he leaves a 'legacy' to '*Vice-Admiral* Goodson's eldest daughter's son, that she had by her husband Captain Magger.'

Combining these various personal allusions,—which have hitherto been utterly overlooked,—it is plain that Brooks for 'some years' was 'at sea.' The question is, in what capacity? A consideration of the *facts* in the

[1] Our reprint, page 5.
[2] 1657, 1st edition, page 320.
[3] 2d edition, 1657, pp. 1, 4, 6, 27.
[4] Part II. page 21.

career of the two 'Commanders' named, viz., Colonel Rainsborough and Vice-admiral Goodson, with, by implication, a Captain Magger, lead me to the conclusion that he must have acted as 'chaplain,' both 'at Sea,' and 'on Land,' that is, in the Fleet and with the Army—alternating as the Commanders were then wont to do with the one and the other. My reasons are these, in brief: Colonel Rainsborough, with whom Brooks informs us he was 'at Sea and on Land,' is traceable on both by help of the 'State Papers.' He was the son of that William Rainsborough of the Navy, who was 'Captain' of the 'Marhonour' in 1635: of the 'Triumph' in the Fleet of the Earl of Nortumberland in 1636: 'admiral' of the Parliamentary Fleet which revolted in 1648, when the sailors seized their admiral and quietly put him ashore: and who survived the Restoration, and was imprisoned by Charles II. In all probability his son the 'Colonel' served under his father in the Navy; and the years 1635, *and* 1636 *on to* 1639–40, *thus correspond with the unaccounted for period of Brooks's life.* Then with reference to Brooks having also been 'with him on the Land,' our 'Colonel' is found on shore at the siege of Bristol, the surrender of Woodstock, the capture of Berkeley Castle, and elsewhere throughout the Civil War, until his 'death,' of which below.[1] Of Vice-admiral Goodson, very little remains; but as Captain William Goodson, he was commander and vice-admiral at Jamaica from 1655 to 1657, and received on 9th January 1658 an order for £500 from the Council of State, as a gratuity for his extraordinary services and expenses.[2] During these years, 1655–1658, Brooks could not be with Goodson; but he may have been in earlier years. It is a pity we have not fuller memoirs of those gallant sailor-soldiers and soldier-sailors, who emulated the brave deeds of Blake, and whose services on Sea and Land bear equally the impress of genius and devotion. I am not without hope that in the progress of the 'Calendars' of the Papers in our National Archives, light may yet

[1] I must here acknowledge the very great trouble taken by John Bruce, Esq., of London toward aiding my researches into this matter. It is to this not less willing than able gentleman I stand indebted for nearly all above *data*. Of Colonel Rainsborough's 'death'—celebrated by Brooks—it may be said that it was one of the saddest incidents of our Civil War. It occurred on the 29th October 1648. He had been sent by Cromwell to lay siege to Pontefract, and was lying at Doncaster on his way thither. A party of the Garrison, disguised as Parliament soldiers, entered Doncaster, deceived Rainsborough's men into the belief that they belonged to the Cromwellian army, penetrated into an inn where Rainsborough was lying, captured him in his bed, and on his making some resistance to being carried off, ran him through with their swords, and left him dead on the streets. The dastardly and bloody story is told as if it had been a gallant achievement, by Clarendon (Hist. Rebell., Book xi.), and as 'a murder or very questionable kind of homicide,' by Carlyle (Cromwell, iii. 420.) Brooks's Sermon will be given in Vol. VI.; and there further details may be looked for, including singular inedited broadsides issued on the day of the Funeral.

[2] 'Colonial Calendar,' 1574–1660, p. 462, and Mr Bruce to myself.

be shed on this altogether unrecognised portion of our Worthy's story. The dates and facts alike of the Rainsborough heroes accord with his allusions to what he had seen.

By 1648, Brooks—as we have found—was 'Preacher of the Gospel' at 'Thomas Apostles,' London. In the same year, '26th December,' and on the title-page of his second publication, viz., his first Sermon before the House of Commons, entitled, 'God's Delight in the Progress of the Upright, especially in Magistrates' Uprightness and constancy in ways of justice and righteousness in these Apostatizing Times, notwithstanding all discouragements, oppositions,' &c., he is still designated 'Preacher of the Gospel at Thomas Apostles;' so also, but in wording that reminds us of Richard Baxter's and other old title-pages, in his second sermon, of '8th October 1650,' viz., his 'Hypocrites Discovered,' in celebration of Cromwell's 'crowning victory' at Dunbar. He is therein described as 'Thomas Brooks, a weak and unworthy Teacher of the Gospel at Thomas Apostles, London.'

Of this first known 'benefice' or Church of Brooks, much curious antiquarian lore will be found in Newcourt's '*Repertorium Ecclesiasticum Parochiale Londinense*' (2 vols. folio, 1708); and thither our readers are referred.[1] But 'the Fire' of 1666 destroyed the whole Registers, and no trace of our Puritan Rector remains, save that by the courtesy of the present Incumbent of the united Parish, within whose bounds it stood, I learn a 'Mr Brooks' resided in one of the 'houses which belonged to the Church.'[2] As there was a 'parsonage-house' before the Fire, this was probably our Brooks.[3]

We cannot be far amiss in concluding that it was most probably to the impression made by his sermon for Rainsborough that Brooks owed his appointment to 'preach' before Parliament. The former sermon was delivered on 'November 14. 1648,' the latter in the succeeding month, 'December 26th.'

By 1652–53 Brooks had been transferred from 'Thomas Apostles' to 'Margaret's, Fish-street hill.' In his 'Precious Remedies' and in his 'Cases Considered and Resolved,' the title-pages (of 1652–53) designate him 'a willing Servant unto God, and the faith of his people, in the glorious Gospel of Christ at Margaret's, Fish-street hill,' and so through all his Writings up to 1662. It was not without opposition that our Worthy passed into this higher and wider sphere. The whole trying story is given by Brooks himself in the pamphlet already more than once quoted. It is printed *in extenso* in our Appendix to this our Memoir.[4] To it, therefore, all are referred. It is an invaluable

[1] See Vol. i. pp. 549–551. [2] Rev. L. B. White, M.A., *penes me*. May 27. 1861.

[3] Newcourt as before, page 551.

[4] See A; this tractate is exceedingly rare, and seems to have been unknown to previous writers, even to Calamy and Palmer. Hence the blunders corrected below.

contribution to his Biography and has many characteristic touches. It lies on the surface that the gist of the entire opposition lay in the Puritan-Rector's refusal—stern and fearless as that of Ambrose and John Calvin—to administer 'Baptism' and the 'Lord's Supper' to those palpably 'unworthy,'—a controversy which has a singular literature of its own from Brooks's treatise to the folio of William Morice, Esq., of Devon (1660), and the well-nigh innumerable polemics of Collinges, and Blake, and Drake, and Humphrey, and Saunders, and 'Tilenus before the Triers;' until in the next century it culminated in the 'dismissal' of Jonathan Edwards of America. Brooks's 'Cases Considered' did its work, and he kept his position. The 'Parish' of 'St Margaret's, Fish-street-hill,' was a populous and a 'burdensome' one. Full details will be found in Newcourt, but no memorial of Brooks.[1] The Church is memorable, as having been the spot 'where that fatal Fire first began that turned London into a ruinous heap.'[2]

What kind of 'preaching' the Parishioners got from their Pastor, his books attest. From 1652 onward these followed each other in rapid succession and with unflagging success. There was his 'Precious Remedies' in 1652; his 'Epistles' or 'Approbations' to Everard's 'Gospel-Treasury Opened,' and to the 'Works' of Dr Thomas Taylor, 1653; 'Heaven on Earth' in 1654; his 'Unsearchable Riches,' 'Apples of Gold,' and 'String of Pearls,' in 1657; his 'Epistle' to John Durant's '*Altum Silentium*,' in 1659; his 'Mute Christian' and 'Believer's Last Day his best Day,' 1660. In the last year—1660—his name stands beside that of THOMAS GOODWIN in the 'Renunciation and Declaration of the Ministers of Congregational Churches, *and Public Preachers*, of the same judgment, living in and about the city of London: against the late horrid insurrection and rebellion acted in the said City' (1661, 4to). In the same year also—1660—he preached the 'Sermons' that compose his 'Ark for all God's Noahs,' in the Church of St Olave's, Bread-street—Milton's street—where, as from the Epistle we learn, 'God blessed them then to those Christians that attended on his ministry.' Newcourt makes no mention of a St Olave's in 'Bread-street,' but probably it is intended by 'St Olave's, *Hart*-street.' Daniel Mills was the 'Rector,' who would cordially welcome Brooks as a 'Lecturer' to his

[1] Newcourt R. E. as before vol. i. pp. 405–407. Here under date '28th Septr. 1640' is entered 'Rob. Pory S. T. B.' as 'Rector,' '*mort. ult. Rectoris;*' then under date 18th August 1660, 'per resig. Pory, George Smalwood, A.M.;' and under 17th October 1662, 'per cess. Smalwood, Dav. Barton,' who, Newcourt adds, 'I suppose continued Rector here till his Church was burnt down in 1666.' Pory was no doubt the fellow-student and companion of Milton, and Newcourt may be accurate in regard to him; but Smalwood must have held some subordinate post, as it was on Brooks's 'Ejectment' or Resignation, not Smalwood's, this Barton succeeded. Newcourt in his High-Churchliness does not recognise Brooks at all; and here, as elsewhere, supplies from unnamed sources those whom he chooses to regard as the 'rightful' occupants. See our note [4] p. xxxiii.

[2] See B.

Church.[1] When, in 1662, he published his 'Ark for all God's Noahs in a gloomy stormy day,' he had to describe himself on its title-page as '*late* Preacher of the Gospel at Margaret's near Fish-street, and *still* Preacher of the Word in London, and Pastor of a Congregation there.' The little word '*late*,' and the other '*still*,' mark two events: the former, the 'Ejectment' of 1662; the latter, that while, with the illustrious 'two thousand' he had resigned 'St Margaret's' for 'conscience' sake,' he nevertheless did not and could not lay down his commission as a 'minister of the Gospel' and Servant of Christ. It needeth not that I tell the pathetic and heroic story of '*Black*' St Bartholomew's Day. It is as imperishable as is the fame of 'this England.' I simply say, that of the many noble and true men who all over the land stood faithful to their convictions, none was nobler, none worthier than the 'ejected' Rector of 'St Margaret's.' The closing portion of his 'Farewell Sermon,' and it has not a single bitter or controversial word, appears in all the 'Collections' of the 'Ejected' 'Farewell Sermons.' We give it in the Appendix to this our Memoir.[2] The 'Epistles' or 'Approbations' also, which appeared previous to 1662, follow the 'Farewell Sermon' there.[3] They may be compared with those of Sibbes. They pay worthy tribute to the worthy.

He had not himself alone to consider when he went out from 'St Margaret's.' He had married, probably many years before—though the date is not known—a daughter of the excellent John Burgess.[4] It

[1] [Cf. Newcourt R. E. as before, vol. i. pp. 510–512.] [2] See B. [3] See C.

[4] Calamy's 'Account,' p. 27; Continuation, pp. 28, 283. Calamy's 'Account' of Brooks lacks his usual carefulness. He describes 'St Margaret's, Fish-street hill' as 'St Mary Magdalen, Fish-street,' thus misreading 'St Mary' for 'St Magnus,' and also, if intending *it*, employing a name it did *not* bear until after the Fire in 1666, when being united thereto, the one name, 'St Magnus,' embraced both (Newcourt, as *supra*, p. 406). He has hereby misled Palmer (Nonc. Memorial, vol. i. p. 150), who enters Brooks as 'ejected from 'St Mary, Fish-street.' Further, Calamy had never seen 'Cases Considered and Resolved,' else he would not have made the following statements: 'About 1651 [1652–3] he was chosen by the majority of the Parishioners of St Mary Magdalen, Fish Street [*i. e.* St Margaret's] to be their minister; and he gathering a Church there in the congregational way, the rest of the Parish preferred a Petition against him to the Committee of ministers, and he published a Defence against their charges.' The 'Defence' in question is his 'Cases Considered and Resolved' (printed in our Appendix, A), and thereby it will be seen that it was not at all for the reason alleged he was opposed; and we have also shewn *above* that he prevailed and entered on possession of the Parish. His Church in the 'congregational way' was not 'commenced' for fully ten years subsequent, viz. on the 'Ejectment' of 1662, as told onward by us. The title-pages of Brooks's books issued from 1652 to 1662 attest that he was the 'clergyman' of St Margaret's up to 1662, and his subsequent title-pages similarly assert him to have been 'late' or 'formerly' thereof. Thus are Newcourt and Calamy alike, corrected and disproved. It is possible that while 'minister' of 'Margarets,' Brooks, in common with other of his brethren, had also a more select auditory elsewhere, to whom he held the office of 'pastor:' but we have no lights on the subject. Be this as it may, the 'Defence' had nothing to do with a church in the 'congregational way,' as Calamy affirms.

does not appear whether he had any family; but his wife—whose name was Martha—was indeed a 'help-meet,'—a woman of high-toned yet meekly tender *principle*, and all but the idol of her husband. She died in 1676, and her Funeral Sermon was preached by (probably) Dr John Collinges, of Norwich. Some extracts are added in our Appendix, from 'notes' which were no doubt furnished by Brooks himself.[1]

Thus self-placed, because conscience-placed, among the 'Ejected' of 1662, Brooks nevertheless remaining a Christ-anointed 'Preacher of the Gospel,' quietly continued his ministry within his Parish. Evidently, multitudes clave to their beloved and honoured Pastor, for to the praise of the laity be it said, the very life-blood of the different 'Churches' vacated by the 'two thousand' flowed into the humbler 'chapels' and 'conventicles' of the enforced Nonconformists. Brooks's 'chapel' occupied a site near his old Church in Fish-street, called the 'Pavement,' Moorfields. The only memorial that remains of it is preserved in certain MSS. in the custody of the Williams Library, London—drawn up by a Rev. Josiah Thompson—but it consists of a mere blundering transcript of Calamy's blunders.[2] He gives Brooks as the founder of the congregation, but dates it from 1660 or the Restoration, which is disproved by his preaching his 'Farewell Sermon' in St Margaret's in 1662.[3] Here our 'Confessor,' now growing old, continued his pristine unmistakeable, intense, powerful, and 'savoury' exhibition of Christ and 'The Gospel;' and as in brighter days, he issued volume upon volume, which bore the same characteristics and met with the same welcome as 'of old.' For proof, in his address to the 'Reader' prefixed to his 'Privy Key of Heaven' (1665), he was able to say gratefully, as one of the reasons for again publishing, 'That favour, that good acceptance and fair quarter, that my other poor labours have found, not only in this Nation but in other countries also, hath put me upon putting pen to paper once more.'[4] Even in the year of sore trial —1662—he could say, 'My former poor labours and endeavours have been acceptable to some of all ranks and degrees, and they have been blest to some of all ranks and degrees; and I have been encouraged, whetted, and stirred up by some on all hands, once more to cast

[1] See D. [2] See foot-note *supra* [4] p. xxxiii.

[3] The Thompson MSS. give details of the after-history of Brooks's congregation. Reeve continued only a few years: the 'rage' against Nonconformists flung him into Newgate with many others of the 'godly:' he died in 1686, never having recovered from the effects of his unrighteous imprisonment. He was succeeded in 1686 by Richard Taylor, who died in 1717; Mr Hall followed in 1718, and died in 1762; and he again was succeeded by Dr John Conder, grandfather, I believe, of the amiable poet Josiah Conder. Other particulars may be gleaned, but these must suffice: except perhaps this small bit of fact, viz., that the Rev. James Spong of London, whose congregation claims to represent Brooks'—has in his possession the Communion 'flagons' or cups, bearing an inscription to the effect that they were a gift to the church of Mr Thomas Brooks.'

[4] See *ante*.

in my net, and now I have done it.'[1] Thus was it unto the end: for in 1675, in the 'Epistle Dedicatory' to the 'Golden Key,' he uses much the same language: 'I must confess that that general acceptance that my former labours have found, both in the Nation and in foreign parts; and that singular blessing that has attended them from on high, hath been none of the least encouragements to me once more to cast in my mite into the common treasury.'[2] His 'Crown and Glory of Christianity,' a large massive quarto, appeared also in 1662; his 'Privy Key of Heaven,' and 'A Heavenly Cordial for the Plague,' in 1665; his 'Cabinet of Jewels,' in 1669; his 'London's Lamentations,' in 1670; and his 'Golden Key' and his 'Paradise Opened,' in 1676. He was ever 'about his Father's business;' his life a consecrated and burning, almost flaming one. Little casual references in 'Epistles Dedicatory' and otherwise, intimate engagements elsewhere, and 'absences' from 'the press' so as to be unable to correct errata. And so the Christ-like man went 'in and out,' a 'workman' needing not 'to be ashamed.' Through all the terrible 'Plague' year, which Defoe has made immortal he was at his post, winning thereby a golden word in the *Reliquiæ Baxterianæ*. After the equally appalling 'Fire,' he stood forth like another Ezekiel in his terrors, and yet soft as Jeremiah in his expostulations with the still careless, rejecting, neglecting. As he grew old he mellowed tenderly and winningly. He had 'troops of friends.' The 'Epistles Dedicatory' and incidental notices inform us of intimate fellowship with the foremost names of the period for worth and benevolence. Many made him their Almoner of 'monies,' especially during the dread '1662' and '1666.' His own circumstances placed him in comfort and ease.

Our Story of this venerable Puritan is well-nigh told. Behind the activities of his more public life there was a second marriage, as it would appear, about 1677–78. In his 'Will' he lovingly speaks of her as his 'dear and honoured wife whom God hath made all relations to meet in one.' Her name was Cartwright. Theirs was a brief union; she spring-young, he winter-old. He drew up his 'Last Testament' on March 20., 1680. It is a very characteristic document, repeating before-published quaint words.[3] It will be found in our Appendix. He died a little afterwards, viz. on September 27., aged 72.[4] John Reeve, his particular acquaintance and companion in sufferings, for conscience' sake, preached his 'Funeral Sermon.' It was published; and thus he sums up the character of the fine old man and 'faithful minister' of Jesus Christ:—

'Now, to close up, in commemoration of our dear friend deceased, who lived so desired, and died so lamented, I shall modestly and truly

[1] Ep. Dedy. to 'Crown of Glory,' pages 6, 7.

[2] Page 2. [3] See this Volume, page 455, *et alibi*. [4] See E.

offer some remarks about his personal and ministerial endowments to your view.

'First, For his personal endowments, he was certainly,

'1. *A person of a very sweet nature and temper:* so affable, and courteous, and cheerful, that he gained upon all that conversed with him; and if any taxed him with any pride or moroseness, or distantialness in his carriage, it must be only such as did not know him. He had so winning a way with him, he might bid himself welcome into whatsoever house he entered. Pride and moroseness are bad qualities for a man of his employ, and make men afraid of the ways of God, for fear they should never enjoy a good day after.

'2. *A person of a very great gravity:* and could carry a majesty in his face when there was occasion, and make the least guilt tremble in his presence with his very countenance. I never knew a man better loved, nor more dreaded. God had given him such a spirit with power, that his very frowns were darts, and his reproofs sharper than swords. He would not contemn familiarity, but hated that familiarity that bred contempt.

'3. *A person of a very large charity.* He had large bowels, and a large heart; a great dexterity in the opening of the bowels of others, as well as his own, to works of mercy, that I think I may say there is not a Church in England that hath more often and more liberal contributions for poor ministers and other poor Christians than this is, according to the proportion of their abilities.

'4. *A person of a wonderful patience.* Notwithstanding the many weaknesses and infirmities, which for a long time have been continually, without ceasing as it were, trying their skill to pull down his frail body to the dust, and at last effected it, yet I never heard an impatient word drop from him. When I came to visit him, and asked him, 'How do you, Sir?' he answered, 'Pretty well: I bless God I am well, I am contented with the will of my Father: my Father's will and mine is but one will.' It made me often think of that Isaiah xxxiii. 24, 'The inhabitant shall not say, I am sick: the people that dwell therein shall be forgiven their iniquity.' Sense of pardon took away sense of sickness.

'5. *A person of a very strong faith in the promises of both worlds:* and he could not be otherwise, being such a continual student in the Covenant. He feared nothing of himself or others, knowing the promise and oath of God would stand firm, and the Head of the Church would see to the safety of all his members, here and hereafter. Secondly, For his ministerial endowments, he was

'1. *An experienced minister.* From the heart to the heart; from the conscience to the conscience. He had a body of Divinity in his head, and the power of it upon his heart.

'2. *A laborious minister:* as his works in press and pulpit are undeniable witness of. To preach so often, and print so much, and yet not satisfied till he could imprint also his works upon the hearts of his people; which is the best way of printing that I know, and the greatest task of a minister of Christ.

'3. *He was a minister who delighted in his work.* It was his meat and drink to labour in that great work, insomuch that under his weakness he would be often preaching of little sermons—as he called them—to those that came to visit him, even when by reason of his distemper they were very hardly able to understand them.

'4. *He was a successful minister:* the instrument in the hand of God for the conversion of many souls about this City and elsewhere.

'5. *And now he is at rest.* And though he is gone, he is not lost; he is yet useful to the Church of God, and being dead he yet speaks by his example and writings, which were very profitable and spiritual.'

This modest, unexaggerated, heart-full portraiture is worthy of the man as the man was, with emphasis, worthy of it. It were to blur the sharp, nice lines to add of our own fainter and distant words. We deem them fitting close to our Memoir.

A single other sentence. There is no accredited portrait of Brooks. Granger mentions one as being on the title-page of his 'Unsearchable Riches,' but we have the whole of the editions, and there is no portrait whatever. Doubtless the Historian mis-remembered and was thinking of the small unsatisfactory miniature prefixed, along with numerous others, to some of the collections of the 'Farewell Sermons.' And so we introduce our Worthy and his Books: one who, while living, as 'ever under the great Task-master's eye,' wore in all simpleness and truth,

> 'The grand old name of gentleman,
> Defamed by every charlatan,
> And soiled with all ignoble use.'—[*In Memoriam*, c. x.]

ALEXANDER B. GROSART.

LIVERPOOL.

APPENDIX TO MEMOIR.

A.—Controversy on appointment to St Margaret's, Fish Street: See *ante*, pages xxxi, xxxiv, *et alibi*.

CASES
CONSIDERED and *RESOLVED*.
WHEREIN
All the tender godly conscientious Ministers in *England* (Whether for a Congregationall, or a Presbyteriall way) are concerned.
OR
Pills to Purge Malignants.
And all prophane, ignorant, and scandalous persons. (But more particularly Calculated for the Meridian of *Margarets* Fishstreet-hill) from those gross conceits that they have of their Children's right to Baptisme; and of their owne right to the Supper of the Lord, *&c.*
ALSO
Good Councell to bad men. Or friendly advise (in severall particulars) to unfriendly Neighbours.
By THOMAS BROOKS, a willing Servant unto God, and the Faith of his People, in the glorious Gospel of Christ, at *Margarets* Fishstreet-hill.

Mallem ruere cum Christo, quam regnare cum Cæsare. Luther.
Si veritas est causa discordiæ mori possum tacere non possum. Jerome.

LONDON:
Printed by *M. Simmons*, for *John Hancock* and are to be sold at the first Shop in *Popes-Head*-Alley, next to Cornhill 1653.

To the Conscientious Reader.

The world is full of books; and of how many may it be said, that they do but proclaim the vanity of the writer, and procure weariness, if not vexation, to the reader, in this knowing and censorious age! What I have written is out of faithfulness to Christ, and love to souls. If my pains shall prove advantageous for the internal and eternal good of any poor souls, I shall count it reward enough. I doubt not but those that are spiritual will find something of the Spirit in what follows, and for that cause will relish and love it, though others may therefore stand at the greater distance from it. Surely, where truth comes, the children of truth will entertain it, and ask nobody leave. In these days, they that have least right to ordinances do make the greatest noise in crying out for ordinances. God's ordinances are choice pearls, and yet too often cast before swine, which, doubtless, hath provoked the Lord to shed the blood of many among us who have unworthily drunk the blood of his Son, and trampled it under their feet as an unholy thing, Heb. x. 29. Though my candle be but little, yet I must not hide it under a bushel Though I have but one talent, yet I must not hide it in a napkin. I hope thou hast that anointing of the Spirit that will teach thee not to reject the fruit for the tree's sake; nor so much to mind the man as the matter. But, lest I should hold thee too long in the porch, I will briefly acquaint thee with the reasons that have induced me to present to the world what follows; and so draw to a close.

The reasons are these:

First, That the honour, truth, and ways of Christ, which I hope are dearer to me than my life, and which are struck at through my sides, may be vindicated, 1 Sam. ii. 30.

Secondly, That the mouth of iniquity, or, which is all one, that the foul mouths of profane, ignorant, malignant, and scandalous persons, may be effectually stopped, Ps. cvii. 42; Titus i. 11; Ps. lxiii. 11.

Thirdly, That the honest, just, and righteous proceedings of the Honourable Committee may be manifested, and not smothered by the false reports of any profane, malignant spirits that were present, who are apt and ready enough to call good evil, and evil good, light darkness, and darkness light, &c., Isa. v. 20.

Fourthly, That the importunate desires of several ministers and Christians may be satisfied, especially those to whom I preach, &c.

Fifthly, That my ministry and good name, which should be dearer to me than my life, may be vindicated, 2 Cor. x. 33. 'A good name is rather to be chosen than great riches, and loving favour rather than silver and gold,' Prov. xxii. 1. 'A good name is better than precious ointment,' saith Solomon, Eccles. vii. 1. The initial letter (ט) of the Hebrew word (טוב, *tob*) that in this text is rendered good, is bigger than ordinary, to shew the more than ordinary excellency of a good name amongst men. The moralists say of fame, or of a man's good name, *Omnia si perdas, famam servare memento; qua semel amissa postea nullus eris, i. e.* Whatsoever commodity you lose, be sure yet to preserve that jewel of a good name.[1] But if any shall delight to blot and blur my name, that their own may shine the brighter, I shall desire them frequently to remember a sweet saying of Austin: *Quisquis volens detrahit famæ meæ, nolens addit mercedi meæ,* He that willingly takes from my good name, unwillingly adds to my reward, Mat. v. 11, 12. The remembrance of this, and the bird in the bosom —conscience—singing, makes a heaven of joy in my heart, in the midst of all the trials that do attend me, 2 Cor. i. 12.

Sixthly, That others may be undeceived, who are apt enough to judge that there are other things, and worse things, charged upon me than indeed there is. And indeed, some say already that there were eighteen things, others that there were six-and-twenty things, charged against me; and all this to render my person and my doctrine contemptible in the world, &c., Jer. xx. 10, 11; Ps. xxxv. 11.

Seventhly, That the malignant and profane petitioners, and others of their stamp, may be either satisfied, convinced, and reformed, or

[1] The French have this proverb among them, That a good renown is better than a golden girdle. [For Omnia si perdas, &c., see Claudian, De Cons. Mall. Theod., v. 8.—G.]

that they may be found speechless, and without excuse in the day of Christ.

Eighthly, Because my case is a general case, and reaches all the godly, conscientious ministers in England, be they of one judgment or another. And clearly if, upon the following charge against me, the profane, ignorant, and malignant party should out and rout the godly ministers in the nations, I wonder where there would be found a conscientious minister that should not upon these grounds be outed and routed!

Reader, I desire that thou wouldst cast a mantle of love over the mistakes of the printer, I having no opportunity to wait upon the press, by reason of my many engagements other ways. I will not by any *prolepsis* detain thee at the door, but desire that the God of all consolations would bless thee with all external, internal, and eternal blessings, that thy actions may be prosperous, thy troubles few, thy comforts many, thy life holy, thy death happy, and thy soul lodged for ever in the bosom of Christ. So I remain

Thine, so far as thou art Christ's,

THOMAS BROOKS.

A SHORT PREAMBLE

That I intended to make before the Honourable Committee for Plundered Ministers, that Truth and myself might be the better vindicated and cleared.

GENTLEMEN,—It was a divine saying of Seneca, *Qui boni viri famam perdidit ne conscientiam perderet,* no man sets a better rate upon virtue than he that loseth a good name to keep a good conscience. He that hath a good conscience sits, Noah-like, quiet and still in the greatest combustions and distractions. *Conscientia pura semper secura,* a good conscience hath sure confidence; it makes a man as bold as a lion, Prov. xxviii. 1.

I remember Calvin, writing to the French king, saith that opposition is *evangelii genius,* the black angel that dogs the gospel at the heels. And certainly, where Christ is like to gain most, and Satan like to lose most, there Satan in his instruments will stir and rage most; yet, if every opposer of the gospel and the saints were turned into a devil, that old saying would be found true, *Veritas stat in aperto campo,* truth stands in the open fields, yea, and it will make those stand in whom it lives; yea, it will make them stand cheerfully, resolutely, and unmoveably, in the face of the greatest, highest, and hottest oppositions.

Concerning these profane, ignorant, malignant, and scandalous petitioners, I shall say, as Lactantius saith of Lucian, *Nec diis nec hominibus pepercit,* he spared neither God nor man. Such are these petitioners. It is said of Catiline, that he was *monstrum ex variis diversisque, inter se pugnantibus naturis conflatum,* a compound and bundle of warring lusts and vices. Such are these petitioners. Historians say that tigers rage and are mad when they smell the fragrancy of spices. Such are these petitioners, when they smell the fragrancy of the graces of God's Spirit in the principles and practices, in the lives and religious exercises, of the people of God.

Gentlemen, I am compelled to tell you that I have, by the gracious assistance of God, preached publicly the gospel above these thirteen years; and the greatest part of those years I have spent in preaching the word in London, where God hath given me many precious seals of my ministry, which are now my comfort, and in the day of Christ will be my crown. They are my 'living epistles,' they are my walking certificates, they are my letters testimonial, as Paul speaks, 2 Cor. iii. 1, 2. And yet, in all this time, none have shewed themselves so malicious, impudent, and ignorant, as to petition against me, as these that stand now before you; yet am I confident that this act of theirs shall work for my external, internal, and eternal good, Rom. viii. 28: and out of this eater, God will bring forth meat and sweetness to others also, Judges xiv. 14.

Gentlemen, I shall now trouble your patience no further, but come now to answer to the things that these profane, malignant petitioners have charged against me in their petition to this Honourable Committee.

To the Honourable Committee for Plundered Ministers,

The Humble Petition of the Parishioners of Margaret, New Fishstreet, London, whose Names are hereunto Subscribed;

Shewing,—That one Mr Thomas Brooks was, by order of your honours, dated the twenty-third of March 1651, appointed to preach for a month, next ensuing, as probationer, to the end that, upon the parishioners' and the said Mr Brooks's mutual trial of each other, the said Mr Brooks might continue, or your petitioners have some other to officiate amongst them.

Your petitioners are humbly bold to offer to your honours' consideration that they have had trial of the said Mr Brooks ever since your honours' order, but cannot find that comfort to their souls they hoped; nor indeed is the said Mr Brooks so qualified to your petitioners' understandings as to remain any longer with them. And further, your petitioners say that the said Mr Brooks refuseth to afford your petitioners the use of the ordinances of baptism and the Lord's supper, nor will he bury their dead.

The petitioners therefore humbly pray that your honours will be pleased to revoke your order, and give liberty to your petitioners for six months, to present a fit person to your honours to be their minister; and, in the mean time, that sequestrators may be appointed to provide for the service of the cure out of such money as shall arise for tithes out of the said parish. And, &c.

Queries upon the Malignants' Petition.

Gentlemen,—In their petition they say, that I was to 'preach a month as probationer, and after a mutual trial of each other, I might continue, or the petitioners have some other to officiate amongst them.' To this I say,

(1.) That I never had any such thing by one or other propounded to me, to preach amongst them as probationer. It was only thus propounded to me: That at a full meeting, I was chosen by the honest and well-affected of the parish to come and preach amongst them. And I did more than twice or thrice declare to them before I came, that if they did expect anything else of me, I would not come; only I did declare my willingness to receive any among them into fellowship with us that the Lord had taken into fellowship with himself, and that were willing to walk in gospel order.

(2.) I say, that had they propounded the business to me as it is presented in their petition, I would never have come upon such terms, and that upon several reasons, which here I shall omit.

(3.) I say, that they had a trial of me all the winter; I preached above twenty sermons on the lecture nights before this order was granted or desired. Therefore I know not to what purpose I should preach among them upon trial, when they had beforehand so large a trial of me.

(4.) I say, that these profane, malignant petitioners had neither a hand in choosing of me, nor yet hearts to make any trial of my ministry, so far as I can understand. And therefore they may well have a black brand put upon them, as men void of common honesty and ingenuity,[1] in abusing the honourable committee, and petitioning against me; whenas they were neither the major part of the parish by far, nor yet was the order of the committee granted to them; nor did the order of the committee give any power or liberty to these profane, malignant petitioners to choose some other to officiate, as they pretend. What greater dishonour and contempt can they cast upon the committee, than to declare to the world that they have given to them, that are so notoriously known for their profaneness and malignancy, an order to choose one to officiate amongst them!

In their petition they further say, 'That they have had trial of me ever since your honours' order.' This is as far from truth as the petitioners are from being real friends to the present authority of the nation; for it is notoriously known, that they use not to hear me but others, whose malignant principles and practices are most suitable to their own.

Further, they say, 'They cannot find that comfort to their souls they hoped.' Here give me leave to query: [1.] How they could have any comfort from my ministry that did not attend it? [2.] But grant they did, I query, Whether their want of comfort did not spring rather from their want of faith to close with the word, and to feed upon the word, and to apply the word to their own souls, than from any defect in my preaching? 'The word preached did not profit them, not being mixed with faith in them that heard it,' Heb. iv. 2. Faith and the word meeting make a happy mixture, a precious confection. When faith and the word is mingled together, then the word will be a word of power and life; then it will be a healing word, a quickening word, a comforting word, a saving word. Faith makes the soul fruitful;

[1] Ingenuousness.—G.

faith hath Rachel's eye and Leah's womb. Where faith is wanting, men's souls will be like the cypress; the more it is watered, the more it is withered. However, that tree that is not for fruit, is for the fire, Heb. vi. 8. Some say of king Midas—not true, but fabulous—that he had obtained of the gods, that whatsoever he touched should be turned into gold. I may truly say, in a spiritual sense, whatever faith touches it turns it into gold, into our good. A bee can suck honey out of a flower; so cannot a fly do. Faith will extract abundance of comfort out of the word, and gather one contrary out of another; honey out of the rock, Deut. xxxii. 36.[1] [3.] I query whether their not finding comfort by my ministry did not rather spring from a judicial act of God rather than from anything in my ministry. God many times punishes men's neglect of the means, and their despising the means, and their barrenness under the means, &c., by giving them up to a spirit of slumber, by shutting their eyes, and closing up their hearts, as you may see in that Isa. vi. 9, 10, 'And he said, Go and tell this people, Hear ye indeed, but understand not; and see ye indeed, but perceive not. Make the heart of this people fat, and make their ears heavy, and shut their eyes; lest they see with their eyes, and hear with their ears, and understand with their heart, and convert, and be healed.' A fat heart is a fearful plague. A fat heart is a most brutish and blockish heart, a heart fitted and prepared for wrath, Ps. cxix. 70. These four keys, say the Rabbins, God keeps under his own girdle: (1.) the key of the womb, (2.) the key of the grave, (3.) the key of the rain, (4.) the key of the heart. 'He openeth, and no man shutteth; and he shutteth, and no man openeth.'[2] [4.] I query whether their not finding of comfort did not spring from the wickedness and baseness of their own hearts, Isa. xxix. 13, 14; Ezek. xxxiii. 30–33; Mat. xv. 4–10. When men bring pride, and prejudice, and resolvedness to walk after the ways of their own hearts, let the minister say what he will (as they in Jer. xliv. 15, *et seq.*, which I desire you will turn to and read), it is no wonder that they can find no comfort in the word.[3] This is just as if the patient should cry out of the physician, Oh, he can find no comfort in anything he prescribes him, when he is resolved beforehand that he will rather die than follow his prescriptions. May not every one of these men's hearts say to him, as the heart of Apollodorus in the kettle, ἐγώ σοὶ τούτων αἰτία, it is I have been the cause of this? I judge they may; and if they will not now acknowledge it to their humiliation, they will at last be forced to acknowledge it to their confusion and destruction in that day wherein the great Searcher of hearts shall judge the souls of men. [5.] I query whether all the godly conscientious ministers of one judgment or another in all England would not be outed and routed if this plea of

[1] As Luther saith of prayer, so I may say of faith: it hath a kind of omnipotency in it; it is able to do all things. *Est quædam omnipotentia precum. Tantum possumus quantum credimus.*

[2] When she in Seneca was stricken with sudden blindness, she cried out of the light. So when God strikes profane men with spiritual blindness, then they cry out of the minister.

[3] The patient in Plutarch complained to his physician of his finger, when his liver was rotten. So many complain of the minister when their hearts are rotten. They complain they can find no comfort, when the fault lies in the baseness of their hearts.

profane, ignorant, malignant, and scandalous persons, that they cannot find no profit nor no comfort by their ministry, be admitted as a thing that has worth or weight in it, 1 Kings xxii. 8–29. Without doubt, if this would carry the day against a godly ministry, we should hear a cry from all parts of the nation where such men are, 2 Chron. xxxvi. 16, Oh! what shall we do with such preachers as these be? We can find no comfort, nor no profit by their ministry. We shall have none of these, but we will have such as will preach pleasing things, Lam. ii. 14. We will have common-prayer-book men, and such that will administer sacraments to us, as in former good days, wherein there was no such difference put between men and men, but all that would bring their twopences might come and be as welcome to the parson, if not more, as any Puritan or Roundhead of them all, Isa. xxx. 8–11. [6.] I query whether your not finding of comfort and profit by the word did not spring from Satan's blinding your eyes, and from his catching away the good seed out of your hearts. 'If our gospel be hid,' saith the apostle, 'it is hid to them that are lost; in whom the god of this world hath blinded the minds of them which believe not, lest the light of the glorious gospel of Christ, who is the image of God, should shine unto them,' 2 Cor. iv. 3, 4. Is it any wonder that profane, ignorant, scandalous persons can find no comfort by the word, whenas the devil hath shut their eyes with his black hand?[1] when he hath put a covering upon their eyes that they can't see any beauty, excellency, or glory in it? Gospel droppings have richly fallen among many, and yet, like Gideon's fleece, they are dry, because Satan hath blinded them, and catched away the good seed that was sown upon them: 'When any one heareth the word of the kingdom, and understandeth it not, then cometh the wicked one, and catches away[2] that which was sown in his heart' (or rather upon his heart); 'this is he which received seed by the wayside,' Mat. xiii. 19. [7.] I query whether your want of profit and comfort by the word did not spring from your want of interest in gospel consolations. Oh! it is not the hearing of gospel consolations that comforts, but the knowledge of a man's interest in them that cheers up the heart.[3] Ah! where is that word to be found in all the book of God that does evidence comfort,—which is children's bread,—to be of right belonging to profane, ignorant, malignant, and scandalous persons, as you can't but know yourselves to be, if conscience be in the least measure awakened. God hath all along in the Scripture made a separation between sin and comfort; and how then, can you expect comfort, who hold on in sinful ways, though love and wrath, life and death, heaven and hell, be often set before you? God is not prodigal of gospel consolations. They are the best and strongest wines in God's cellar, and reserved only for his best and dearest friends: Isa. xl. 1, 2, 'Comfort ye, comfort ye my people, saith your God: speak ye com-

[1] Satan is like the picture of the goddess that was so contrived that she frowned on men as they went into the temple, and smiled as they came out.

[2] ἁρπαζει α ἁρπαζω,—*Rapio*, He took it or snatched it by force or violence.

[3] It is interest in a pardon, a crown, an inheritance that comforts, and not the talking of them. So here. The very heathen could not have comfort nor quiet when they were under the rage of sinful lusts; therefore, when they knew not how to bridle them, they offered violence to nature, pulling out their own eyes, because they could not look upon a woman without lusting after her.

fortably to Jerusalem, and cry unto her that her warfare is accomplished, that her iniquity is pardoned,' &c. The Hebrew word that is here rendered *comfort* signifies first to repent, and then to comfort.[1] And certainly the sweetest joy is from the sourest tears. Tears are the breeders of spiritual joy. When Hannah had wept, she went away, and was no more sad. The bee gathers the best honey off the bitterest herbs. Christ made the best wine of water. The purest, the strongest, and most excellent joy is made of the waters of repentance. Ah ! lay your hands upon your hearts, and tell me whether you can look God in the face and say, Lord ! we are thine ; first, by purchase ; secondly, we are thine by choice ; thirdly, we are thine by conquest ; fourthly, we are thine by covenant ; fifthly, we are thine by marriage. Ah ! if you are not the Lord's in these respects, what minister on earth hath commission to comfort you ? Their commission is to read other lectures to profane, ignorant, scandalous persons, &c., than those of comfort and joy, as you may see in these scriptures, if you will but take the pains to read them : Ps. vii. 11, ix. 17, xi. 5, 6, xxxvii. 10–20, compared with Ps. lxxv. 8, cxlv. 20 ; Job xxi. 30 ? Prov. xi. 5, 21, 31, compared ; Prov. xii. 2, xiv. 9, xv. 29, xxi. 18, 27 ; Eccles. viii. 13 ; Isa. xi. 4, xiii. 11 ; Jer. xxv. 31 ; Ezek. iii. 18, 19 ; Nah. i. 3 ; Mal. iv. 3 ; Deut. xxviii. 15, *et seq.*; Lev. xxvi. 14, *et seq.* Ah ! did you but wisely consider the excellency of gospel-comforts above all other comforts in the world, you would not wonder at ministers giving them forth so sparingly to profane, ignorant, malignant, and scandalous persons ; for, first, gospel comforts are unutterable comforts, 1 Peter i. 8, Philip. iv. 4. Secondly, they are real, John xiv. 27 ; all others are but seeming comforts, but painted comforts. Thirdly, they are holy comforts, Isa. lxiv. 5, Ps. cxxxviii. 5 ; they flow from a Holy Spirit, and nothing can come from the Holy Spirit but that which is holy. Fourthly, they are the greatest and strongest comforts, Eph. vi. 17. Few heads and hearts are able to bear them, as few heads are able to bear strong wines. Fifthly, they reach to the inward man, to the soul, 2 Thes. ii. 17, the noble part of man. 'My soul rejoiceth in God my Saviour.' Our other comforts only reach the face ; they sink not so deep as the heart. Sixthly, they are the most soul-filling and soul-satisfying comforts, Ps. xvi. 11, Cant. ii. 3. Other comforts cannot reach the soul ; and therefore they cannot fill nor satisfy the soul. Seventhly, they comfort in saddest distresses, in the darkest night, and in the most stormy day, Ps. xciv. 19, Hab. iii. 17, 18. Eighthly, they are everlasting, 2 Thes. ii. 16. The joy of the wicked is but as a glass, bright and brittle, and evermore in danger of breaking ; but the joy of the saints is lasting.[2] *Æterna erit exultatio, quæ bono lætatur æterno,* their joy lasts for ever, whose object remains for ever. [8.] I query whether you, and men of your stamp, remaining under the power of your lusts, will ever say that you can

[1] נחמו נחמו, *nahhamu, nuhhamu,* from נחם *nahham,* which signifies first to repent (1 Sam. xv. 35), and then to comfort, because true comfort belongs only to the penitent. Divine comfort is a delicate thing, and it is not given to him that admits any other, saith Bernard. *Nulla verior miseria quam falsa lætitia* : There is no truer misory than false joy.—*Bernard.* *Nil nisi sanctum a sancto Spiritu prodire potest,* Neh. viii. 10. There have been those that have died under the strength and power of their joy.

[2] *Valde protestatus sum, me nolle sic satiari ab eo,* I said flatly that God should not put me off with these low things.—*Luther.*

find any comfort at all in any man's ministry, that is not a common-prayer-book man, or one that will give you and yours the sacraments, and lash at the power of godliness, and at the State in preaching and praying, &c. Doubtless under such a man's ministry, were he never so ignorant, scandalous, or profane, you would plead that you found much comfort to your souls, and that he was a man indeed for your money, &c. Well! if you have found no comfort under my ministry, yet my comfort is, that my reward is with the Lord, and my work with my God. My comfort is, that there are many hundreds in this city that have, and that do find comfort by the blessing and breathings of God upon my weak endeavours.[1]

Further, In their petition they say that 'I am not so qualified to their understandings as to remain any longer with them.'

To this I say, *First*, It is my joy and crown, that I am not so qualified as to please and content ignorant, profane, malignant, scandalous persons in their formality and impiety; remembering that he is the best preacher, *non qui aures tetigerit, sed qui cor pupugerit*, not that tickles the ear, but that breaks the heart. It is a comfort to me that I am no nearer that woe, Luke vi. 26, 'Woe be to you when all men speak well of you.' When one told Aristides that he had every man's good word, saith he, What evil have I done, that I should have every man's good word? *Male de me loquuntur, sed mali*, saith Seneca. It is sometimes more a shame than an honour to have the good word of profane, ignorant, scandalous persons. Latimer, in his last sermon before king Edward, saith, 'That he was glad when any objected indiscretion against him in his sermons; for by that he knew the matter was good, else they would soon have condemned that.' It was a notable saying of Salvian, *Mirum esset si hominibus loquentia de Deo verba non placeant,*[2] *quibus ipse forsitan Deus non placet:* it were very strange, saith he, if I should please a world of men, when God himself doth not give every man content. Luther, writing to his friend, hath this passage, 'My greatest fear is the praises of men, but my joy is in their reproaches and evil speeches.' It is certain that the praises of men, to many, are the basilisks that kill, the poison that destroys their immortal souls.

2. I say, if the understandings of ignorant, malignant, profane, and scandalous persons, should be the rule or standard by which the abilities or qualifications of such ministers, that are ministers, 'not of the letter, but of the spirit,' as the apostle speaks, 2 Cor. iii. 6, should be measured and tried; doubtless he that is no witch may easily conclude that there are no ministers in England qualified to their understandings, but such as are malignant, ignorant, profane, and scandalous as themselves; and such, without doubt, would be the only qualified men, to their understandings; as might be confirmed by a cloud of witnesses, Jer. v. 30, 31.

3. Though I am not qualified, as to their understandings, yet, through grace, I am qualified as to the understandings of those that are eminent both for piety and parts, and who have made trial of what is in me,

[1] I have read of one who cried out with a loud voice to Flavius Vespasianus, *Vulpem pilum mutare, non mores*, that the wolf might change his hair, but not his qualities. You know how to apply it, Isa. xlix. 4, 5.

[2] Qu. *verba placeant'?*—Ed.

and what the Lord hath done for me.[1] And though I am not so qualified as to gratify your lusts, yet it is joy and honour enough to me that the Lord hath so qualified me with gifts and graces as to make me instrumental to bring in souls to Christ, and to build up souls in Christ. In the day of account it will be made manifest that they have been the best, the wisest, and ablest preachers, who have brought most souls to Christ, and provoked most souls to walk with Christ, and cleave to Christ, and lift up Christ in this world, Prov. xi. 30. Through grace, I can say, with blessed Cooper, 'My witness is in heaven, that I have no such joy and pleasure as in doing the work of Christ, and in being serviceable to the honour of Christ, the interest of Christ, and the people of Christ.'[2]

4. If this plea of profane, ignorant, malignant, and scandalous persons should be admitted as authentic, doubtless all the godly, tender, conscientious ministers in the nation, that can't do as they would have them, would quickly be ejected. All the profane, ignorant, malignant, scandalous persons in the nation would soon cry out, as one man, Our ministers are not so qualified, to our understandings, as to remain any longer with us, *ergo*[3]—

5. It is to be remembered that, when the petitioners were several times pressed by the Committee to shew wherein I was not qualified for the work of the ministry, they all seemed to be dumb, and at very great loss, as not knowing what to answer;[4] but at last their malignant champion, after much pumping, gave this answer to the committee, That I was not so qualified, to their understandings, as to remain any longer among them, because I would not give them the sacraments, nor bury their dead; which put some rather upon smiling than upon answering. But at last a worthy member of that Committee made this answer, 'That they had both heard me and seen me in print, and so were best able to make a judgment of my abilities and fitness for the work of the ministry,' &c.[5] For a close of this branch of the petition, I shall only say this, being compelled thereunto by some, that I do believe that I have spent more money at the University, and in helps to learning, than several of these petitioners are worth, though, haply, I have not been so good a proficient as those that have spent less. I am a lover of the tongues, and do, by daily experience, find that knowledge in the original tongues is no small help for the understanding of Scripture, &c. Yet am I not kin to them that advance and lift up acquired gifts above the sweet sanctifying gifts and graces of the Spirit of Christ in the souls of his saints, as many have and do to this day. But cer-

[1] Chrysostom studied not *aures titillare*, but *corda pungere*, to tickle the ears of his hearers, but to prick and ravish their hearts.

[2] וְלֹקֵחַ, velokeakh, which signifies, by art and industry, to catch souls, as fowlers do to take birds.

[3] They that are wise cannot but observe much of this spirit upon all the profane, ignorant, and malignant persons in the nation.

[4] The petitioners seemed to be like those in Mat. xxii. 46, that were nonplussed by the question Christ put to them, &c.

[5] My first sermon, preached before the Parliament, was on the 26th December 1648. My second was preached on the 8th of October 1650, for that great victory the Lord of hosts gave our army over the Scots army in battle at Dunbar, Sept. 3. 1650, and both are printed by their order; besides my book called 'Precious Remedies against Satan's Devices,' which came forth this year, which some of them have seen.

tainly Christ will more and more cloud those that labour to cloud the shinings forth of his Spirit in the souls of his servants. Nor yet am I kin to Licinius, who held learning to be the commonwealth s rat's-bane. Neither am I kin to those that labour might and main the overthrow of learning, in order to their lifting up Jack Straw. It is sad when men are not so ingenuous as to favour that in others which they can't find in themselves.

Further, The petitioners say that I refuse to baptize their children, &c.

Ans. 1. This gives me leave to premise by the way that it is my judgment, upon many grounds moving me to it, that baptism is to be administered to the children of believing parents, who walk in the order of the gospel; and my practice herein doth answer to my judgment, as is well known to many.[1]

2. But, in the second place, I confess I have refused, and shall refuse, to baptize the children of profane, ignorant, malignant, and scandalous persons; and that upon these following grounds:[2]

[1.] Because I cannot find any warrant in my commission from Christ so to do. I do seriously profess that I have made a diligent search and strict inquiry into that commission that I have received from the Lord for the dispensing of holy things, and I cannot find anything in my commission that will bear me out in the baptizing the children of those parents that are profane, ignorant, malignant, scandalous, &c., and therefore I cannot do it, lest I should hear Christ and conscience sounding that sad word in my ears, 'Who hath required this at your hand?' Isa. i. 12.

[2.] Because such persons that are profane, ignorant, malignant, scandalous, &c., if they were now to be baptized themselves, ought not to be baptized, they having no right to baptism, as these scriptures in the margin do evidence;[3] therefore, such parents cannot justly, upon any Scripture account, challenge baptism for their children, who have no right to it themselves. All that know anything are not ignorant of this, that it is the parents' interest in the covenant that gives the child right to baptism. Now, how profane, ignorant, scandalous parents can give their children right to baptism, when they have no right to it themselves, is a thing that I am no ways able to reach, and a thing, I judge, too hard for any to prove, Hosea ii. 2, 3.

[3.] Because the children of parents, whereof neither can be judged to be a believer, ought not to be baptized till the child grow up to manifest his own faith, as these scriptures, among many others that might be produced, prove, Gen. xvii. 7–9; Acts ii. 39–41; 1 Cor. vii. 14, &c.

[4.] Because profane, ignorant, scandalous persons, &c., are visibly in covenant with Satan; and therefore to administer baptism, the seal of the covenant, to their children, upon their accounts who are visibly in covenant with Satan, cannot but be a notorious profan-

[1] Gen. xvii.; Acts ii. 38, 39; 1 Cor. vii. 14, &c.

[2] *Non parentum aut majorum authoritas, sed Dei docentis imperium*, the command of God must outweigh all authority and example of men.—*Jerome.*

[3] Mat. iii. 5–12; Mark i. 4, 5; Acts ii. 38, 41; Luke iii. 8; Acts xiii. 24; viii. 12, 31–40; x. 45–48; xviii. 8; xxii. 16, 17, &c.; so Ps. l. 16, 17.

ing of the ordinances; therefore I dare not do it.[1] Now, that such persons are visibly in covenant with Satan is clear: Isa. xxviii. 15, 'Because ye have said, We have made a covenant with death, and with hell are we at agreement; when the overflowing scourge shall pass through, it shall not come unto us: for we have made lies our refuge, and under falsehood have we hid ourselves.' Ver. 18, 'And your covenant with death shall be disannulled, and your agreement with hell shall not stand; when the overflowing scourge shall pass through, then ye shall be trodden down by it.' Not that they had formally made a covenant with Satan, but their ways and courses were such as did proclaim to the world that they had, as it were, formally made a covenant with hell and death. Therefore, to apply this blessed ordinance to their children, who are thus invisibly in covenant with Satan, and who are not capable thereof through want of divine warrant, cannot, doubtless, but be esteemed a high profaning of it.

[5.] Because I may not yield blind obedience, nor do anything doubtingly; both which I should do should I baptize their children, who are profane, ignorant, scandalous, mockers and scoffers at God and godliness, &c.

[6.] Because, by administering that holy ordinance to the children of profane, ignorant, scandalous persons, I shall make myself guilty of nourishing and cherishing in such wicked persons such vain opinions and conceits that cannot but be very prejudicial to their souls; as that they have a right to that precious ordinance, when they have none; that God hath taken their children into covenant, as well as the children of the best believers in the world, when he hath not; that God is more favourable and loving to them than indeed he is; and that their case is not so bad as some would make it, &c. All which opinions and conceits, with many more of the same stamp that might be named, cannot but prove many ways prejudicial to mens' immortal souls.

I shall forbear the laying down any more reasons why I have not, nor shall not, baptize their children who are profane, ignorant, malignant, scandalous, mockers and scoffers at God and godliness; judging that these may be sufficient to satisfy all intelligent men.[2]

Further, these petitioners say, that 'I will not give them the Lord's supper.'

Ans. Though I do give the Lord's supper to those to whom of right it belongs, yet I cannot, I dare not, give it to profane, ignorant, malignant, scandalous persons. I had, with Calvin, rather die, than that this hand of mine should give the things of God to the condemners of God. And with Chrysostom, I had rather give my life to a murderer, than Christ's body to an unworthy receiver; and had rather to suffer my own blood to be poured out like water, than to tender Christ's

[1] Isa. xxviii. 15, 18, כרתנו ברית, they cut a covenant with hell and death. In old time, men were wont to kill and cut asunder sacrificed beasts, and to pass between the parts divided, Gen. xv. 17; Jer. xxxiv. 18. The ceremony intended an imprecation that he might be cut in pieces, as that beast was, who should violate the covenant so made. The same rite was used among the heathenish Gentiles also, Rom. xiv. 23.

[2] If I partake in other men's sins, I must partake in their punishments, Rev. xviii. 4. Christians were wont to be of that courage that they feared nothing but sin. *Nil nisi peccatum timeo*, said Chrysostom.

blessed blood to any base liver; and that upon these following grounds:

[1.] Because such persons are excluded by the word of God from communion with believers in that glorious ordinance, as the Scriptures in the margin do evidence.[1]

[2.] Not only the Scriptures, but the very episcopal Rubric, for the administration of the communion, do exclude and shut out such persons from the supper of the Lord, in these words: 'They that intended to partake of the holy communion should signify their names afore to the curate; and if any of those be an open and notorious evil liver, so that the congregation is offended, or have done any wrong to his neighbour by word or deed, the curate having knowledge, shall call him and advertise him in any wise not to presume to the Lord's table until he hath openly declared himself to have truly repented, and amended his former naughty life, that the congregation may thereby be satisfied,' &c. As for the presbyterial way, you all know, that by their Directory and laws annexed, they must not receive any to the communion that are ignorant, scandalous, or profane in their conversation. So that the sum of what hath been said is this, that by the laws of God, and by the laws of episcopacy, and by the laws of presbytery, profane, ignorant, and scandalous persons are to be excluded from the supper of the Lord. *Ergo*—

[3.] Because the admitting of such as are profane, ignorant, scandalous, or that are scoffers and mockers of all goodness, &c., to the supper of the Lord, is the ready way to turn the house of God into a den of thieves, and to bring a dreadful doom both upon consenters and presumers, as the Scriptures in the margin will make good.[2] Not only the lack of the word and sacraments, saith Bilson, but the abuse of either, greatly hazards the weal of the whole church, Mat. vii. 6. If profane ones be allowed to defile the mysteries and assemblies of the faithful, and holy things be cast to dogs, it will procure a dreadful doom, as well to consentaries as presumers. *Ergo*—

[4.] Because there are many horrid sins in their coming to the supper of the Lord.

(1.) There is horrid pride, else no man in his wickedness would presume to taste of the tree of life. Yet pride cannot climb so high, but justice will sit above her.

(2.) There is rebellion and treason against the crown and dignity of Christ. Their hands and lips adore him, as Judas his did; but their hearts and lives abhor him.

(3.) There is theft and sacrilege. If the taking away of the communion cup or cloth, &c., be such horrible theft and sacrilege, surely it is far greater theft and sacrilege to take that bread and wine that is set apart, and sanctified by the Lord himself, for a holy use.[3]

[1] 2 Cor. vi. 14, *et seq.*; Philip. iii. 2; Mat. xv. 26; 1 Cor. v. 12, 13; Rev. xxii. 15, 21, 27. It is worse to admit a man openly polluted with sins, than a man bodily possessed with devils.—*Chrysostom.* The Thurians had a law, that whosoever went about to abolish an old law, should present himself with a rope about his neck before the people, that if his invention was not approved, he might presently be strangled. You know how to apply it.

[2] 1 Cor. xi. 27–30; Rev. ii. 12–16; 1 Cor. x. 3–9, 21, 22, compared; Neh. xiii. 18, 19.

[3] Possidonius reports, that all that took the gold of Tholosse [Colosse?] perished in

(4.) There is murder in the cruellest manner that can be; for they kill two at once—Christ, and their own souls, 1 Cor. xi. 27, 29, compared.

It was wickedness in Julian to throw his blood in the face of Christ; but for a wicked communicant to take Christ's own blood, as it were from his heart, and throw it into the face of Christ, is most abominable and damnable.

[5.] They want those qualifications that should fit them for this glorious ordinance. As,

(1.) Experimental knowledge.[1]

(2.) Faith, without which they cannot see Christ, nor receive Christ, nor feed upon Christ, nor apply Christ, nor seal to Christ.

(3.) Repentance from dead works.

(4.) New obedience.

(5.) Love to Christ and his children.

(6.) Holy thankfulness.

(7.) A spiritual appetite. All which are absolutely necessary to fit souls for the Lord's supper. *Ergo*—

[6.] Because such as are profane, scandalous, scoffers and mockers, &c., are not fit for civil society, how much less fit are they then for religious societies?[2] Men that love but their names and credits in the world, will shun the society of such vain persons; how much more, then, should men that love their Christ, and that love their precious souls, shun such society? Look, as shelves and sands do endanger the seaman, and as weeds endanger the corn, and bad humours the blood, and an infected house the neighbourhood, so does the society of evil men endanger good men. One said, 'As oft as I have been among wicked men, I returned home less a man than I was before.' Men that keep ill company are like those that walk in the sun, tanned insensibly. Eusebius reports of John the evangelist, that he would not suffer Cerinthus the heretic in the same bath with him, lest some judgment should abide them both. You may easily apply it to the point in hand. [Euseb., lib. iii. c. 25.]

[7.] Because such persons as are profane, scandalous, and wicked, &c., if they were in the church, they are by the word of God to be excommunicated, and cut off from visible union and communion with Christ and his church; therefore they are not to be admitted to the privileges of the church. That wickedness that is a sufficient ground for the casting them out if they were in, is a sufficient ground to keep them out from polluting the glorious ordinance of the Lord, 1 Cor. v.; 1 Tim. i. 19, 20; Mat. xviii. 15–18: 2 Thes. iii. 6; 1 Tim. vi. 3–5.

[8.] Because the supper of the Lord is a feast instituted by Christ only for his friends and children, for those that have received spiritual life from him, and that have union and communion with him, Mat. xxvi. 27–29; 1 Cor. x. 16, 17, &c.; Mat. iii. 12. But profane, igno-

the possession of it. Apply it. They may say with Henry the Seventh, 'The cup of life is made my death.

[1] A gracious soul may say, not only *Credo vitam æternam et edo vitam æternam,* I believe life eternal, but I receive life eternal.

[2] Read these scriptures: Prov. iv. 14–16; Eph. v. 14; 1 Cor. v. 9–11; 2 Tim. iii. 1–5. The heathen could say, *Qui æquo animo malis immiscetur, malus est,* he that is well contented to keep company with those that are naught, is himself made naught.

rant, malignant, scandalous persons, are chaff which the fan flings out of the floor. They be as dirt and dust which the besom sweeps out of the house, Luke xv. 8. They be as leaven, which, if let alone, sours the whole lump; and therefore must be purged out, 1 Cor. v. 6, 7. They be as thorns and briers, which must not stand in the midst of the corn, Heb. vi. 8, but must be stubbed up and burned. They be as open sepulchres, out of which proceeds nothing but noisome savours, Rom. iii. 13; Mat. iii. 7. They be as vipers, which must be shook off, as Paul shook off the viper that fastened upon his hand, Acts xxviii. 3–5. They be as ravenous wolves, which every careful, watchful shepherd must keep out of his fold, John x. 12. They be as swine, that will trample the choicest pearls under their feet, if they should be cast before them, Mat. vii. 6; therefore ministers must not hang gospel pearls in such swine's snouts, nor cast them under such swine's feet. The fouler the chest is, the more unfit it is to have a fair and precious garment put therein; and the filthier the soul is, the unfitter it is to receive in this holy sacrament. I have read of a jewel, that being put into a dead man's mouth, loseth all its virtue. Such a jewel is the supper of the Lord; it loseth its virtue when it is put in profane, ignorant, scandalous persons' mouths; who are dead God-wards, and dead heaven-wards, and dead holiness-wards, and dead Christwards.[1]

Lastly, these petitioners say, 'That I will not bury their dead.'

To this I shall give this short answer, that if they mean that I would bury their dead after the old fashion, I confess it; and shall only say, that it is most proper for the dead to bury the dead, as Christ speaks, Mat. viii. 22; my proper work being to preach the gospel. But if by burying their dead they mean that I will not accompany their corpse to the grave, being the last office of love that can be performed to the deceased person, it is notoriously false. All that know anything of the Scripture can't but know that there is nothing in all the book of God that will bear a minister out to bury the dead, as profane, ignorant, scandalous persons would have them buried; and therefore I don't, and I hope I shall never be so far left of God, as to conform to the superstitious desires and customs of vain men.[2]

Reader, for a close, thou mayest take notice, that though I was ready to give in the fore-named arguments, in answer to the objections made by the profane malignants in their petition against me, yet the Committee, in their wisdoms it seems, did not judge it meet so much as to ask me a reason why I did not baptize their children, give them the Lord's supper, and bury their dead;[3] they well knowing that there is nothing more ordinary than for those to be bawling and cry-

[1] The table of the Lord, saith Chrysostom, is that whereon the blessed carcase is laid; we must not suffer chattering jays to come thereunto, for only high-flying eagles are to feed thereupon.

[2] Nay, it is known to hundreds, that it is my practice, after the dead is buried, to preach to the people that are met upon that occasion, if so desired; many grounds moving me thereunto.

[3] Greater respect the honourable committee could not cast upon me, nor greater contempt upon the profane, malignant petitioners, than not to put me to answer to the things objected against me. One of these profane, malignant petitioners objected to me Judas his receiving the supper of the Lord, which I disproved; and yet this vain person, as I have been informed, boasted of victory.

ing out for ordinances that have no right to them; and that, if upon the non-giving of the ordinances to such profane persons, they should eject ministers out of their places, they should quickly eject all those in the nation that are most tender of the honour of Christ, and that have been some of their best friends in the worst times.

Before I give the counsel intended to the petitioners, I judge it useful, in several respects, to batter down that which most profane, ignorant, malignant, scandalous persons do count their stronghold, or their greatest argument to prove it lawful for them to receive the supper of the Lord, notwithstanding their profaneness and wickedness, and that is, 'That Judas was admitted to the Lord's supper, and that they are not worse than Judas, no, nor yet so bad.' *Ergo*—

Now for the casting down of this their imagined stronghold, for the despatching this their first-born, this their Goliath, consider with me these following things:

[1.] The Holy Ghost, by the evangelist John, doth punctually and expressly tell us, that Judas went out immediately after the sop. That this sop was no part of the sacramental supper, both fathers and schoolmen do agree; and many others in our own time, who are men of great piety and parts. *Ergo*[1]—

Did I know anything of weight that could be objected against this argument, I would be so faithful as to give an answer to it, as the Lord should enable me to do, but I know nothing that has that strength in it as to weaken the truth asserted.

[2.] Those to whom Christ gave the sacrament, he saith, without exception, 'This is my body which is given for you: this is the cup of the New Testament in my blood which is shed for you; and I will not drink henceforth of the fruit of the vine until that day I drink it new with you in my Father's kingdom.' Now I would willingly know how this can in the least measure stand with the wisdom, holiness, justice, righteousness, innocency, and integrity of Christ, to say this and promise this to Judas, whom he knew to be an hypocrite, reprobate, a devil, as himself calls him, John vi. 70, 71, xiii. 10, 11. If this be not to make Christ a false witness, a liar, a deceiver, &c., I know not anything.[2]

[3.] It is as clear as the sun, from that 22d of Luke, 28, 29, 30, that those to whom Christ gave the sacrament, were such as did continue with him in his temptations, and such as Christ did appoint to them a kingdom, and such as should sit upon thrones, &c., Mat. xxvi. 24, Mark xiv. 21, John vi. 70, Acts i. 25, 1 Cor. vi. 2, 3. Now, are there any so vain and foolish as to say that Judas did continue with him in his temptations? or that Christ did appoint to him any other kingdom than a kingdom of darkness? or that he shall sit on a throne to judge others, who shall at last be judged as a devil?

[4.] Judas was no ways capable of any of those noble ends and glorious uses for which the Lord Jesus appointed this sacrament, he having

[1] John xiii. 30. Hilary, Durand, Piscator, Beza, &c. Compare Mat. xxvi. and Mark xiv. together, and you shall find that neither of them do affirm that Judas was at the Lord's supper; therefore we have no ground to believe that Judas was at that blessed supper, Luke xxii. 19, 20; Mat. xxvi. 26–29.

[2] Were hypocrites and reprobates known to us, we ought to shut the door against them, and will Christ open it? Surely no.

no real love to Christ, no experimental knowledge of Christ, no faith to discern Christ, to apply Christ, to feed upon Christ, to seal to Christ, &c.[1] How could this ordinance strengthen grace in his heart, who was wholly void of grace? How could this ordinance confirm him in the love of God, who was at that very time under the greatest wrath of God? How could this ordinance seal up to him the pardon of his sins, who, notwithstanding all the hell-fire that Christ cast in his face, yet would hold on in his sins, and rather betray Christ into the hands of his enemies, and his own soul into the hand of Satan, than cease from doing wickedly, &c.[2] That little wisdom that is in man will work him to forbear his work and suspend his act where he sees his end will fail; and will not those treasures of wisdom that be in the Lord Jesus, Col. ii. 3, much more work him to suspend his work, where he sees plainly and clearly that his end will fail him, as in the case of Judas? Surely it will.

[5.] Consider seriously whether it be in any degree probable that Jesus Christ would give his blood to Judas, and yet not so much as lift up a prayer for Judas, John xvii. 9; that Christ would do the greater thing for Judas, and yet not do the lesser; that he should give his blood to Judas, and yet not spend a little of his breath to save Judas from wallowing in his blood for ever. Among men it would argue the greatest weakness that could be, to deny the least favour where they have shewed the greatest favour, &c.[3]

Well! but if, for argument's sake, we should grant that Judas did receive the Lord's supper, it will not from thence follow that it is lawful for those that are openly profane, wicked, scandalous, and malignant to receive it, and that upon these following grounds:

Reason 1. For that Judas was a close hypocrite, and carried his sin so secretly that nothing appeared openly against him for Christ yet to refuse him. Hypocrisy is spun of a fine thread, and not easily discerned: Mat. xxvi. 21, 22, And as they did eat, he said, 'Verily I say unto you, that one of you shall betray me. And they were exceeding sorrowful, and began every one of them to say unto him, Lord, is it I?' Sincere hearts are more jealous of themselves than of others, and will rather judge a thousand hypocrites to be saints, than one saint to be an hypocrite.[4]

Reason 2. Because Judas was a member of the church, and had done nothing openly that could cast him out; and by virtue of his membership he might justly claim it as his due, he being called into fellowship by Christ himself. Now, what advantage is this to such open profane wicked persons as *de jure* ought and *de facto* are excluded from the Lord's supper; as I have before clearly and fully proved?

Reason 3. Because in respect of wickedness and all profaneness they go beyond Judas. Judas was no drunkard, swearer, mocker, scoffer; he did not sin openly, and glory in his sin.[5] He did not by any open

[1] *Quod non actibus sed finibus pensantur officia*, duties are esteemed not by their acts, but by their ends. [2] Maximilian's motto was, *Tene mensuram, et respice finem.*

[3] *Sanguis Christi, clavis cœli*, Christ's blood is heaven's key; and so Judas would have found had Christ given it to him.

[4] *Secreta mea mecum*, my secret is with myself, is an Hebrew proverb. We are not to look to men's hearts, but to their lives and conversations, and, according as they are good or bad, so to proceed.

[5] Judas, as Tertullian thinks, was pretty honest till he carried the bag (it is hard to

way of wickedness sad and quench Christ's, his Spirit or disciples; he was so far from giving any scandal or offence to his fellow-disciples, that when Christ told them, 'One of you shall betray me,' they were all jealous of themselves, none of them were jealous of Judas: 'And they began every one of them to say unto him, Lord, is it I?' Judas betrayed Christ for thirty pieces of silver, but open, profane, wicked persons they betray Christ, his word, his people, and their own souls, for a thing of nought. They will transgress for a morsel of bread, as Solomon speaks, for a trifle, Isa. l. 1, 2, Prov. xxviii. 24. They will sell the greatest and the choicest things dog-cheap, even at the poorest and the lowest rate that the world, or the god of this world, shall bid.[1] Judas betrayed Christ once; and open, profane, wicked persons, by their open treasons and transgressions, do oftentimes in a day betray the crown, sceptre, and dignity of King Jesus. Judas plotted treason against Christ when he was in a low, afflicted, and despised condition; but such as are openly profane and wicked, they plot and act treason against Christ now he is exalted, crowned, and set down at the right hand of God in that glory and majesty that can neither be conceived nor expressed by any mortal creature. Judas betrays Christ, and is struck with dreadful horror and terror; but such as are openly wicked, they betray Christ, and yet joy in their transgressions, which are so many treasons against Christ. Judas betrays Christ, and yet justifies the innocency of Christ; he repents, and confesseth his sin; but such as are openly wicked, proceed from evil to evil, and yet, with the harlot, they wipe their mouths, and say, What evil have we done?[2]

Reason 4. Because Christ gave the blessed sacrament ministerially as he was man, leaving them a pattern to walk by that should come after him; and such was the carriage of Christ toward Judas all along.[3] Christ did not act toward Judas as he was an all-seeing God, nor as he was the heart-maker, the heart-searcher, the heart-observer, the heart-discoverer, but he acted towards him ministerially. Neither do I see how it could stand with the holiness, justice, faithfulness, and wisdom of Christ to give that holy ordinance to Judas, whom he knew as he was God, to be such a dog, a devil; considering how he had bound all his servants from casting pearls before swine. To affirm that Christ gave the sacrament to Judas, as he was God; what is this but to make Christ's practice fight against his own precepts, which for any to do is doubtless blasphemy in the highest degree.

And now I appeal to the consciences of all profane, wicked, malignant persons, whether they were not better a thousand times to be shut out from this glorious ordinance of the Lord's supper, till the Lord shall in mercy, if it be his good pleasure, fit them for it, than to think to get in at this door by making Judas the porter.

be in office, and not to put conscience out of office). Several other writers were of Tertullian's opinion concerning Judas.

[1] Cato hits M. Cœlis in the teeth with his baseness, that for a morsel of bread he would sell either his tongue or his silence.

[2] Isa. liii. 2, 3; Acts v. 30, 31; Rom. viii. 34; Eph. i. 20–23; Prov. xv. 21; Mat. xxvii 3–5; Prov. xxx. 20.

[3] Had Christ, as a God and searcher of the heart, kept out Judas from the passover, because he knew his heart was naught, he had left us a pattern to eject such as the church should be jealous of, that their hearts are not right before the Lord, when there is nothing detected.

I shall now address myself to give some good counsel to the petitioners; and so conclude.

GOOD COUNSEL TO BAD MEN; OR, FRIENDLY ADVICE TO UNFRIENDLY NEIGHBOURS AND THEIR ABETTORS.

YOUR petitioning against me to all understanding men was a compounded evil; an evil made up of pride, envy, malice, discontent, ignorance, &c. My counsel to you is to break off your sins by repentance, that it may go well with you for ever. If you will not, justice will be above you, and in the close you must lie down in sorrow. Tell me, can you dwell with the devouring fire? can you dwell with everlasting burnings? Dan. iv. 27, Isa. l. 11, xxxiii. 14. It was a good saying of Chrysostom, speaking of hell, *Ne quæramus ubi sit, sed quomodo illam fugiamus*, let us not seek where it is, but how we shall escape it.[1] Grievous is the torment of the damned for the bitterness of the punishments, but it is more grievous for the diversity of the punishments, but most grievous for the eternity of the punishments. Ah! consider before it be too late, what a sad thing it is for souls at last to have the gate of mercy, the gate of indulgence, the gate of hope, the gate of glory, shut upon them, Mat. xxv. 10. When a sinner is in hell, shall another Christ be found to die for him? or will the same Christ be crucified again? Oh, no! Oh that you were so wise and merciful to your own souls as to dwell upon these scriptures: John iii. 3, 'Jesus answered and said unto him, Verily, verily I say unto thee, Except a man be born again, he cannot see the kingdom of God.' Except men be first unmade, and then made up again by the Spirit and word, except the whole frame of their old conversation be dissolved and a better erected, there is no heaven to be had. Heaven is too holy and too hot to hold drunkards, revilers, mockers, and such like, as you may plainly see by comparing these scriptures together, 1 Cor. vi. 9, 10, Gal. v. 19–21, Jude 14, 15, Rev. xxi. 8, and xxii. 15. He that is truth itself, and cannot lie, hath said, 'Without holiness no man shall see God,' Heb. xii. 14.[2] This I am sure of, that all man's happiness here is his holiness, and his holiness shall hereafter be his happiness. You must in this life be holy, or in the life to come you shall never be happy. Seneca, a heathen man, saw so much excellency that morality put upon a man that he saith that *ipse aspectus boni viri delectat*, the very looks of a good man delights one. Oh! then, what a beauty and glory doth real sanctity put upon a man; 'it makes him more excellent than his neighbour,' as Solomon speaks, Prov. xii. 26. When Agesilaus heard the king of Persia styled the great king, saith he, 'I acknowledge none more excellent than myself, unless more righteous; none greater, unless better.' Ps. xvi. 3.

But to hasten towards a close, you may be very confident of these few things, which I desire, as you tender your own good, you would seriously consider.

[1] *Utinam ubique de gehenna dissereretur.* I could wish that men would discourse much and oft of hell.—Chrysostom.

[2] They were wont to say in former times, *Caius Seius bonus vir, sed Christianus*, Caius Seius was a good man, but he was a Christian. You may easily apply it, &c. Chrysostom calls some holy men of his time ἀγγιλοι, earthly angels.

[1.] That those ways of the flesh wherein now you walk will be bitterness in the latter end: Prov. xiv. 12, 'There is a way which seemeth right unto a man; but the end thereof are the ways of death.'[1] Though sin doth come sometimes clothed with a show of reason and religion, yet the end of it will be death. Sin at last will betray your souls into the hands of Satan, as Delilah did Samson into the hands of the Philistines.[2] Sin makes the soul black with filth and red with guilt; and then vengeance follows. The Rabbins were wont to tell scholars, to scare them from sin, that every sin made God's head ache; but without sound repentance you will at last find that every sin will make your hearts ache. Oh! then, when you are tempted to sin, you would say, as Demosthenes, the orator, did of the beautiful Lais, when he was asked an excessive sum of money to behold her: I will not, said he, buy repentance so dear. I am not so ill a merchant as to sell the eternal for the temporal.

[2.] You may be confident that all your oppositions one way or other against the ways of God, and against the people of God, is a fighting against God, who will be too hard for you when you have done your worst; and what you get you may put in your eyes, and weep it out again,[3] Acts v. 38, 39, ix. 4, 5. Those that strive for mastery with God, God will over-master with a witness: Isa. xxvii. 4, 'Who would set the briars and thorns against me in battle? I would go through them, I will burn them together.' God can nod a soul to hell; he can speak a soul miserable in a moment. Who ever stood out against him, and prospered? There is such a near union between God and his people, between God and his ways, that you cannot possibly oppose them but you oppose God himself, who can presently cause the greatest arm of human power to shrink up, as you may see in his dealing with Pharaoh, Haman, Belshazzar, and others, &c. Is a dry reed able to stand against a consuming fire? Is a worm able to overcome a lion? Is weakness able to overcome strength: 'Behold, the nations are as a drop of a bucket, and are counted as the small dust of the balance;' 'Behold, he taketh up the isles as a very little thing,' as the prophet Isaiah speaks, Isa. xl. 15. And what, then, is the poor creature, that he should fight against an almighty Creator? Cæsar told Metellus he could as easily destroy him as bid it be done. So can God. Who dares then engage against him?[4]

[3.] You may be confident, that though I hate your sins, yet I don't hate your persons. I am willing to live in love and peace with all men, so far as I may without sin; but I abhor compliancy with any man, to the dishonour of Christ, to the wounding of my conscience, to the profaning of holy things, or to the prejudice and disadvantage of the truth. It is below humanity to hate a man, whose nature and similitude he may behold in the humanity of Christ. *Deum odit qui*

[1] It was the saying of an ancient philosopher, Whosoever sinneth, doth in that decline from his purposed end, and is certainly deceived.

[2] Hark, scholar, said the harlot to Apuleius, it is but a bitter-sweet that you are so fond of. Ah! your scoffing and mocking will prove but a bitter-sweet at last.

[3] Constantine the Great's symbol [Qu. 'saying'?—G.] was *immedicabile vulnus ense rescindendum est*, when there is no hope of curing, men must fall a-cutting; and so will God deal with sinners' souls. Therefore, look about you, sinners.

[4] Said Caligula, speaking to the consuls, to think that I can kill you with a nod of my head; and can't God do it with as much ease?

hominem odit, he hateth God that hateth man. I must love men, but hate their vice. It is said of Ephesus, that they hated the deeds of the Nicolaitans; their errors, not their persons. So Jacob cursed the wrath of his sons, but blessed their persons. So Paul, 1 Cor. iv. 15, and so do I, through free mercy.[1]

[4.] You may be confident that I don't refuse the baptizing of your children, and the giving you the sacrament, &c., out of pride or envy, or upon any carnal account in the world, but only upon the grounds that I have before laid down. I take the Searcher of all hearts to witness, that I should much rejoice and bless the Lord if he would be pleased to work such a thorough work of grace upon all your hearts as that I might without sin dispense all the precious things of Christ to you. Ah! it is not a joy, but a real grief to my soul, that others have not that right, and can't come to those ordinances which God hath made so sweet and advantageous to me, and many others of the sons of Zion.

Oh! how willing should I be, and those that walk with me, to give you the right hand of fellowship, if we could but see that the Lord has taken you into fellowship with his blessed self, that so the ordinance might be a cordial, and not poison to you.[2]

I do profess before the Lord, that I do from my soul forgive you the wrong and injuries that you have done me, or attempted to do. God has been good to me, notwithstanding my failing towards him and my sins against him; and the sense of his love and rich goodness makes my bowels to yearn towards you.

Oh! it is a mercy more worth than a world to me that God hath given me such a frame of spirit as that I can pray for your souls, and weep over your sins, and that I am ready to serve you in all those ways wherein I may further the eternal welfare of your souls, &c. Make use of me in anything wherein I may serve you without sin; and see whether I shall not be willing to act for your good, notwithstanding all provocations to the contrary.[3]

[5.] For a close,—because I would not be over-tedious, I shall draw many things within a narrow compass,—you may be confident that my end in writing is your due conviction and satisfaction, that you may weigh my arguments, and clearly see that it is not will, nor humour, &c., but conscience, reason, and religion that acts me. If, notwithstanding what I have said, you shall continue in your malice, envy, hatred, &c., I shall have comfort in this, that I have in all faithfulness freed myself from being guilty of the blood of your souls; and

[1] Rom. xiv. 19; Heb. xii. 14. Luther said, that in the cause of God he was content, *totius mundi odium et impetum sustinere*, to undergo the hatred and violence of the whole world. The heathen orator could say, *A recta conscientia ne latum quidem unguem discedendum*, a man may not depart an hair's-breadth all his life long from the dictates of a good conscience.

[2] Cant. viii. 1; Ps. lxiii. 1–3; Rom. xiv. 1, and xv. 1; 1 John i. 3, 4; Luke xxiii. 24; Acts vii. 59, 60; Mat. vi. 12–15. Tully said of Cæsar, *Nihil oblivisci soles, nisi injurias*, that he forgat nothing but injuries.

[3] *Lilmod lelammed*, we therefore learn, that we may teach, is a proverb among the Rabbins. I could have dealt with you in another way, had I not intended the good of your souls. Jer. xliv. 15, *et seq*; Acts xx. 26, 27 Ezek. iii. 17–19; 1 Cor. ix. 20–22; John xii. 48; 2 Cor. v. 10; Rom. viii. 28; Micah vii. 8–10; Jer. xx. 9–12; Mal. iii. 17, 18; Isa. xlix. 4, 5.

in that I have declared to all the world my willingness to serve the interest of your souls in all things wherein I may without sin. And most confident I am, that if what I have written do not better you, it will be a witness against you when you and I shall meet before Christ's judgment-seat. And confident I am, that God will bring much good to me out of all the plots, designs, and actings that have been, or that shall be, by vain men against me. And confident I am, that the more you stir in any way of baseness or wickedness, the more the Lord will make you to stink, and the more contempt he will pour upon you, and the more bright he will cause my innocency to shine, and the more weighty shall be my crown in the day of Christ.

My desires for you before the Lord are these, that you may have such a sight of your sins as may work you to 'kiss the Son, lest he be angry, and you perish when his wrath is kindled but a little;' and that you may not trifle away the day of grace, and 'the things that belong to your eternal peace,' 'lest God should swear in his wrath that you shall never enter into his rest.'[1] Oh! that in the light of the Spirit you may see Christ to be the greatest good, the most desirable good, the most necessary good, the most suitable good, to be a total good, an only good, and an eternal good; that so your souls may in good earnest fall in love with Christ, and may cry out with that martyr, 'None but Christ, none but Christ.' Oh! none but Christ to save us, and none but Christ to rule us! none but Christ to justify us, and none but Christ to command us! Oh! that you may cease from doing evil, and learn to do well; that so you may be happy in life, blessed in death, and glorious in the morning of the resurrection, Isa. i. 16, 17.

B.—Close of Farewell Sermon; see page *ante* xxxi. From the Collection of 1662 (4to). The text is not given, nor the body of the Sermon, but only what follows:—

All that I shall do shall be to answer two or three queries, and then I shall leave a few legacies with you, that may speak when I am not advantaged to speak to you.

The first query is this, What should be the reason that men make such opposition against the gospel, against the plain, powerful, conscientious preaching of it? This is not the principal thing that I intend, and therefore I shall only touch upon the reason of it.

1. Men's hatred and opposition ariseth against the gospel because it doth discover their hidden works of darkness: John iii., 'They hate the light, lest their deeds should be reproved.' The gospel brings their deeds of darkness to light, and this stirs up a spirit of hatred and opposition against the gospel.

2. Ground is this: because sinners under the gospel, cannot sin at so

[1] Prayer is *porta cœli, clavis paradisi*, the gate of heaven, a key to let us in to paradise, Heb. iii. 7–12. *Nec Christus nec cœlum patitur hyperbolem*, a man cannot hyperbolise in speaking of Christ and heaven. *Omne bonum, in summo bono*, all good is in the chiefest good.

cheap a rate as otherwise they might do; the drunkard cannot be drunk at so cheap a rate; nor can the opposer and persecutor oppose and persecute at so cheap a rate as they might do where the gospel doth not shine in power and glory.

3. Because the gospel puts persons upon very hard service, upon very difficult work, pulling out a right eye, cutting off a right hand, offering up an Isaac, throwing overboard a Jonas, parting with bosom lusts and darling sins. Herod heard John Baptist gladly, till he came to touch his Herodias, and then off goes his head. As they say, John vi., 'This is a hard saying, and who can abide it?' and from that time they walked no more with him. This is a hard gospel indeed, and at this their blood riseth.

4. Because of the differing and distinguishing work that the gospel makes among the sons of men; it softens one, and hardens another that sits next to him; enlightens one, and strikes the other blind; it wins one and enrages the other. The same sun hath different effects on the objects on which it shineth. The gospel puts a difference between the precious and the vile; and this the vile cannot bear. It was never good days, say they, since such and such must be saints, and none else; we have as good hearts as any, and this enrageth them.

Lastly, It is from Satan. Satan knows that the very tendency of the gospel is to shake his kingdom about his ears. Satan and antichrist know that their kingdom must down by the power and light of the gospel; and therefore Satan and men of an antichristian spirit do all they can to oppose and shew their hatred against the everlasting gospel; and this makes them to be in such a rage against the gospel.

Query 2. When the gospel goes from a people, what goes? I shall give but a touch here.

1. When the gospel goes, peace, plenty, and trading go, 2 Chron. xv. 3, 5, 6, compared. Now for a long season Israel had been without the true God, and without a teaching priest. Why? They had priests; but they were Jeroboam's priests, as you may see, chap. xiii. 9, 'Have you not cast out the priests of the Lord, the sons of Aaron and the Levites, and have made you priests after the manner of the nations of other lands? so that whosoever comes to consecrate himself with a young bullock and seven rams, the same may be a priest of them that are no gods. A little business will buy a priesthood; and so they are said to be without the true God, without a teaching priest, and without law. Mark what follows: 'And in those times, there was no peace to him that went out, nor to him that came in; but great vexations were upon all the inhabitants of the country, and nation was destroyed of nation, and city of city, for God did vex them with all adversity.'

2. Safety and security goes when the gospel goes; so in the text but now cited. The ark was taken away, and when that was taken away, their strength and safety was gone. When the Jews rejected the gospel, the Romans came and took away both their place and nation: John xi. 48, 'If we let him thus alone, the Romans will come and take away both our place and nation.' About forty years after, Titus and Vespasian took away their city; they cried, 'If we let this man alone, the Romans will take away our nations.' And this was the ready way to bring the Romans upon them.

3. When the gospel goes, civil liberty goes. When the Jews slighted the gospel, and turned their backs upon it, they quickly became bond-slaves to the Romans.

4. When the gospel goes, the honour and glory, splendour and beauty of a nation goes. It is the gospel that is the honour and glory of a nation, and when that goes, all the glory goes. As old Eli said, when the ark was taken away, 'The glory is departed from Israel,' 1 Sam. iv. 32. Jer. ii. 11–13, 'Hath a nation changed their gods, which are yet no gods? but my people have changed their glory for that which doth not profit,' that is, the worship of God into the traditions of men. What is it that lifts up one nation above another but the gospel? Above all nations of the earth, England hath been lifted up to heaven.

5. When the gospel goes, all soul-happiness and blessedness goes. The gospel, you know, is the means appointed by God to bring souls to an acquaintance with Christ, to an acceptance of Christ, to an interest in Christ, to an assurance that he is theirs, and they are his. Now, when this goes, all soul-happiness and blessedness goes.

Lastly, When the gospel goes, the special presence of God goes, for that still goes with the gospel. There is a general presence of God, as the psalmist speaks, Ps. cxxxix., 'Where shall I go from thy Spirit? whither shall I fly from thy presence?' This presence of God reacheth from heaven to hell; in that sense, God is included in no place, not excluded out of any place. But, alas! what is this general presence? When the gospel goes, the special presence of God goes. This leads me by the hand to the third query.

Query 3. And that is this, Whether God will remove the gospel from England or no?

It is the fears of many; but I humbly suppose no. Whatsoever darkness may be upon it, yet that God will not remove it; and, if you please, I will offer a few things that signify something, as to my own satisfaction, and it may be so to you.

1. The rooting that it hath got in the hearts of sinners and saints, in the judgments, affections, and consciences, both of sinners and saints. Certainly it hath got so deep a root in the hearts of many thousands of saints and sinners, that it shall not be in the power of hell to raze it out.

2. The glorious anointings that are to be found upon many thousands of God's servants in this nation to preach the everlasting gospel, and who would be glad to preach upon the hardest terms, keeping God and a good conscience, to preach it freely, as the apostles of old did. And certainly God hath not laid in this treasure that it should be turned into a heap of confusion, but that it should serve to the end for which he laid it in.

3. The ineffectualness of all former attempts and designs to destroy the gospel. You know what endeavours of old there hath been to darken this sun, to put out the light of heaven, in the Marian days, and in other days since then; and yet it hath not been in prisons, racks, flames, pillories, nor anything else to extinguish the glory of it. And then,

4. All designs and attempts to extinguish the everlasting gospel have turned to the advancement, flourishing, and spreading of the gospel.

5. God never takes away the gospel from a people till the body of that people have thrust the everlasting gospel from them; when, indeed, they have been so bold as to thrust away the everlasting gospel, God hath been severe unto them; but till the body of a people have thrust away the everlasting gospel, God hath not taken it away from them. 2 Chronicles the 36th chapter and the 15th verse to the end, God sent his messengers early and late; they abused, and slighted, and scorned them, till there was no remedy. So in the 35th of Jeremiah from the 1st to the 12th; it is a famous text for this. So in the 13th chapter of the Acts and the 45th, 46th, and 47th verses, 'Because you have thought yourselves unworthy of salvation; lo, we turn to the Gentiles.' Till the Jews came to thrust away the everlasting gospel, the Lord continued it to them.

6. The spreading of the everlasting gospel is the special means appointed by God for the destruction of antichrist. First, He is to be consumed by the spirit of his mouth, then destroyed by the brightness of his coming; the spirit of faith and prayer in them that would be willing to lay down anything rather than part with the gospel. God will not put his blessed church to the blush; he will not make them ashamed of their confidence.

7. Are there not multitudes of the children of believers that fall under many promises? And will not God make good his engagements to them? 'I will circumcise your hearts, and the hearts of your seed; and the seed of the upright shall be blessed, &c.

8. The strange and wonderful affections and tenderness that God hath wrought in his children to the gospel; what meltings and mournings, and what a spirit of prayer hath God put upon his people!

9. There are many young tender plants and buds of grace, such in whom the Spirit of God hath stirred an hungering, thirsting, and longing after the great concerments of eternity. I would, upon these grounds, with others of the like import, hope and believe that the Lord will not remove his everlasting gospel, however he may correct his people for their trifling with and slighting the glorious gospel. I have several times thought what a day of darkness was upon the world, in respect of sin and superstition. When Christ brought the everlasting gospel, what a day of darkness and superstition was on the whole earth! But you know what the apostle speaks, 2 Cor. i. 21, 'For after that, in the wisdom of God, the world by wisdom knew not God, it pleased God, by the foolishness of preaching, to save them that believe.'

When it is nearest day, then it is darkest. There may be an hour of darkness that may be upon the gospel, as to its liberty, purity, and glory; and yet there may be a sunshining day ready to tread on the heels of it. And so much for the resolution of those queries.

I shall proceed, as I said, and leave some legacies with you, which may, by the finger of the Spirit, be made advantageous to you, whom we are not advantaged to speak unto you.

Legacy 1. The first legacy I would leave with you, shall be this: Secure your interest in Christ; make it your great business, your work, your heaven, to secure your interest in Christ. This is not an age, an hour, for a man to be between fears and hopes, between doubting and believing.

Take not up in a name to live, when you are dead God-ward and Christ-ward; take not up in an outward form, and outward privilege. They cried out, 'The temple of the Lord, the temple of the Lord,' that had no interest in, or love to, the Lord of the temple. Follow God, leave no means unattempted whereby your blessed interest may be cleared up.

Leg. 2. Make Christ and Scripture the only foundation for your souls and faith to build on: as the apostle saith, 1 Cor. iii. 11, 'Other foundations can no man lay than that which is laid, even Jesus Christ.' Isa. xxviii. 6, 'Behold, I lay in Zion for a foundation, a stone, a tried stone, a corner stone, a precious stone, a sure foundation,' Eph. ii. 10. Since it is a very dangerous thing, as much as your souls and eternity is worth, for you to build on anything beside Jesus Christ, many will say, Come, build on this authority and that, on this saying and that; but take heed.

Leg. 3. In all places and company, be sure to carry your soul preservative with you: go into no place or company, except you carry your soul preservations with you, that is, a holy care and wisdom. You know, in infectious times, men will carry outward preservatives with them; you had need to carry your preservatives about you, else you will be in danger of being infected with the ill customs and vanities of the times wherein you live, and that is a third.

Leg. 4. I would leave with you is this: Look that all within you rises higher and higher, by oppositions, threatenings and sufferings, that is, that your faith, your love, your courage, your zeal, your resolutions, and magnanimity rises higher by opposition and a spirit of prayer. Thus it did, Acts iv. 18–21, 29–31 compared; all their sufferings did but raise up a more noble spirit in them, they did but raise up their faith and courage. So Acts v. 40–42, they looked on it as a grace to be disgraced for Christ, and as an honour to be dishonoured for him. They say, as David, 'If this be to be vile, I will be more vile.' If to be found in the way of my God, to act for my God, to be vile, I will be more vile.

Leg. 5. Take more pains, and make more conscience of keeping yourselves from sin than suffering; from the pollutions and defilements of the day, than from the sufferings of the day. This legacy I would beg that you would consider; take more pains, and make more conscience of keeping yourselves from the evil of sin than the evil of punishment, from the pollutions and corruptions of the times than the sufferings of the times: Acts ii. 40, 'Save yourselves from this untoward generation.' Philip. ii. 15, 'The children of God must be harmless and blameless, without rebuke in the midst of a crooked and perverse generation.' Heb. xi. speaks full to the point in hand. Rev. iii. 4, 'Thou hast a few names even in Sardis that have not defiled their garments; and they shall walk with me in white: for they are worthy.' White was the habit of nobles, which imports the honour that God will put on those that keep their garments pure in a defiling day. Rev. xviii. 4, 'And I heard another voice from heaven, saying, Come out of her, my people, that ye be not partakers of her sins, and that ye receive not of her plagues.' If you will be tasting and sipping at Babylon's cup, you must resolve to receive more or less of Babylon's plagues.

Leg. 6. I would leave with you is this: Be always doing or receiving good. Our Lord and Master went up and down in this world doing good; he was still doing good to body and soul; he was acted by an untired power. Be still doing or receiving good. This will make your lives comfortable, your deaths happy, and your account glorious, in the great day of our Lord. Oh! how useless are many men in their generation! Oh! that our lips might be as so many honey-combs, that we might scatter knowledge!

Leg. 7. I would leave with you is this: Set the highest examples and patterns before your face of grace and godliness for your imitation. In the business of faith, set an Abraham before your eyes; in the business of courage, set a Joshua; in the business of uprightness, set a Job; of meekness, a Moses, &c. There is a disadvantage that redounds to Christians by looking more backwards than forwards. Men look on whom they excel, not on those they fall short of. Of all examples, set them before you that are most eminent for grace and holiness, for communion with God, and acting for God. Next to Christ, set the pattern of the choicest saints before you.

Leg. 8. Hold fast your integrity, and rather let all go than let that go. A man had better let liberty, estate, relations, and life go, than let his integrity go. Yea, let ordinances themselves go, when they cannot be held with the hand of integrity: Job xxvii. 5, 6, 'God forbid that I should justify you till I die. I will not remove my integrity from me; my righteousness I will hold fast, and I will not let it go: my heart shall not reproach me so long as I live.' Look, as the drowning man holds fast that which is cast forth for to save him, as the soldier holds fast his sword and buckler on which his life depends, so, saith Job, 'I will hold fast my integrity; my heart shall not reproach me. I had rather all the world should reproach me, and my heart justify me, than that my heart should reproach me, and all the world justify me.' That man will make but a sad exchange that shall exchange his integrity for any worldly concernment. Integrity maintained in the soul will be a feast of fat things in the worst of days; but let a man lose his integrity. and it is not in the power of all the world to make a feast of fat things in that soul.

Leg. 9. That I would leave with you is this: Let not a day pass over your head without calling the whole man to an exact account. Well, where have you been acting to-day? Hands, what have you done for God to-day? Tongue, what have you spoke for God to-day. This will be an advantage many ways unto you, but I can only touch on these legacies.

Leg. 10. Labour mightily for a healing spirit. This legacy I would leave with you as matter of great concernment. Labour mightily for a healing spirit. Away with all discriminating names whatever that may hinder the applying of balm to heal your wounds. Labour for a healing spirit. Discord and division become no Christian. For wolves to worry the lambs, is no wonder; but for one lamb to worry another, this is unnatural and monstrous. God hath made his wrath to smoke against us for the divisions and heart-burnings that have been amongst us. Labour for a oneness in love and affection with every one that is one with Christ. Let their forms be what they will, that which wins most upon Christ's heart, should win most upon ours, and that is his own grace and holiness. The question should be, What of the Father, what of the Son, what of the Spirit shines in this or that person? and accordingly let your love and your affections run out. That is the tenth legacy.

Leg. 11. Be most in the spiritual exercises of religion. Improve this legacy, for much of the life and comfort, joy and peace of your souls is wrapped up in it. I say, be most in the spiritual exercises of religion. There are external exercises, as hearing, preaching, praying, and conference; and there are the more spiritual exercises of religion, exercise of grace, meditation, self-judging, self-trial, and examination. Bodily exercise will profit nothing if abstracted from those more spiritual. The glory that God hath, and the comfort and advantage that will redound to your souls is mostly from the spiritual exercises of religion. How rare is it to find men in the work of meditation, of trial and examination, and of bringing home of truths to their own souls?

Leg. 12. Take no truths upon trust, but all upon trial, 1 Thes. v. 21, so 1 John iv. 1, Acts xvii. 11. It was the glory of that church, that they would not trust Paul himself; Paul, that had the advantage above all for external qualifications; no, not Paul himself. Take no truth upon trust; bring them to the balance of the sanctuary. If they will not hold weight there, reject them.

Leg. 13. The lesser and fewer opportunities and advantages you have in public to better and enrich your souls, the more abundantly address your souls to God in private: Mal. iii. 16, 17, 'Then they that feared the Lord, spake often one to another,' &c.

Leg. 14. Walk in those ways that are directly cross and contrary to the vain, sinful, and superstitious ways that men of a formal, carnal, lukewarm spirit walk in; this is the great concernment of Christians. But more of that by and by.

Leg. 15. Look upon all the things of this world as you will look upon them when you come to die. At what a poor rate do men look on the things of this world when they come to die! What a low value do men set upon the pomp and glory of it, when there is but a step between them and eternity! Men may now put a mask upon them, but then they will appear in their own colours. Men would not venture the loss of such great things for them did they but look on them now, as they will do at the last day.

Leg. 16. Never put off your conscience with any plea or with any argument that you dare not stand by in the great day of your account. It is dreadful to consider how many in these days put off their consciences. We did this and that for our families, they would have else perished. I have complied thus, and wronged my conscience thus, for this and that concernment. Will a man stand by this argument when he comes before Jesus Christ at the last day? Because of the souls of men, many plead this or that. Christ doth not stand in need of indirect ways to save souls; he hath ways enough to bring in souls to himself.

Leg. 17. Eye more, mind more, and lay to heart more, the spiritual and eternal workings of God in your souls, than the external providences of God in the world. Beloved, God looks that we should consider the operations of his hand; and the despising the works of his hands is so provoking to him that he threatens them to lead them into captivity for not considering of them. But above all look to the work that God is carrying on in your souls. Not a soul but he is carrying on some work or other in it, either blinding or enlightening, bettering or worstening; and therefore look to what God is doing in thy soul. All the motions of God within you are steps to eternity, and every soul shall be blessed or cursed, saved or lost to all eternity, not according to outward dispensations, but according to the inward operations of God in your souls. Observe what humbling work, reforming work, sanctifying work, he is about in thy spirit; what he is doing in that little world within thee. If God should carry on never so glorious a work in the world, as a conquest of the nations to Christ, what would it advantage thee if sin, Satan, and the world should triumph in thy soul, and carry the day there.

Leg. 18. Look as well on the bright side as on the dark side of the cloud; on the bright side of providence as well as on the dark side of providence. Beloved, there is a great weakness amongst Christians; they do so pore on the dark side of the providence as that they have no heart to consider of the bright side. If you look on the dark side of the providence of God to Joseph, how terrible and amazing was it! but if you look on the bright side, his fourscore years' reign, how glorious was it! If you look on the dark side of the providence of God to David, in his five years' banishment, much will arise to startle you; but if you turn to the bright side, his forty years' reign in glory, how amiable was it! Look on the dark side of the providence of God to Job, oh, how terrible was it in the first of Job! but compare this with the last of Job, where you have the bright side of the cloud, and there God doubles all his mercies to him. Consider the patience of Job, and the end that the Lord made with him. Do not remember the beginning only, for that was the dark side; but turn to the end of him, and there was his bright side. Many sins, many temptations, and much affliction would be prevented by Christians looking on the bright side of providence as well as on the dark.

Leg. 19. Keep up precious thoughts of God under the sourest, sharpest, and severest dispensations of God to you: Ps. xxii. 1–3, 'My God, my God, why hast thou forsaken me? why art thou so far from helping me, and from the words of my roaring? O my God, I cry in the daytime, but thou hearest not; and in the night season, and am not silent.' There was the psalmist under smart dispensations, but what precious thoughts had he of God after all: 'But thou art holy, O thou that inhabitest the praises of Israel: though I am thus and thus afflicted, yet thou art holy;' Ps. lxv. 5, 'By terrible things in righteousness wilt thou answer us, O God of our salvation.

Leg. 20. Hold on and hold out in the ways of well-doing, in the want of all outward encouragements, and in the face of all outward discouragements. It is nothing to hold out when we meet with nothing but encouragements; but to hold out in the face of all discouragements is a Christian duty: Ps. xliv., 'Though thou hast sore broken us in the place of dragons, and covered us with the shadow of death, yet have we not dealt falsely in thy covenant: our heart is not turned back, neither have we declined from thy ways.' It is perseverance that crowns all: 'Be thou faithful to the death, and I will give thee a crown of life,' Rev. ii. 10; 'And he that endureth to the end shall be saved,' Mat. xxiv. It is perseverance in well-doing that crowns all our actions. If you have begun in the Spirit, don't end in the flesh; do not go away from the Captain of your salvation; follow the Lamb, though others follow the beast and the false prophets.

Leg. 21. In all your natural, civil, and religious actions, let divine glory still rest on your souls, Rom. xiv. 7, 8, 1 Cor. x. 31. In all your bearings, in all your prayings, let the glory of Christ carry it; in all your closet duties, let the glory of Christ lie nearest your hearts.

Leg. 22. Record all special favours, mercies, providences, and experiences. It is true, a man should do nothing else, should he record all the favours and experiences of God towards him; and therefore my legacy is, record all special favours, peculiar experiences. Little do you know the advantage that will redound to your soul upon this account by recording all the experiences of the shinings of his face, of the leadings of his Spirit. Many a Christian loseth much by neglecting this duty.

Leg. 23. Never enter upon the trial of your estate, but when your hearts are at the best, and in the fittest temper. It is a great design of Satan, when the soul is deserted and strangely afflicted, to put the soul on trying work. Come, see what thou art worth for another world, what thou hast to shew for a better state, for an interest in Christ, a title for heaven. This is not a time to be about this work. Thy work is now to get off from this temptation, and therefore to pray and believe, and wait upon God, and to be found in all those ways whereby you may get off the temptation.

Leg. 24. Always make the Scripture, and not yourselves, nor your carnal reason, nor your bare opinion, the judges of your spiritual state and condition. I cannot see my condition to be good. I cannot perceive it. What! must your sense and your carnal reason be the judge of your spiritual state? Isa. viii. 20, 'To the law and to the testimony, if they speak not according to this rule, it is because there is no light, no morning in them;' John xii. 48, 'The word that I have spoken, the same shall judge you in the last day.' The Scripture is that which must determine the case in the great day, whether you have grace or no, or whether it be true or no.

Leg. 25. Make much conscience of making good the terms on which you closed with Christ. You know the terms, how that you would deny yourselves, take up his cross, and follow the Lamb wheresoever he should go. Now you are put to take up the cross, to deny yourselves, to follow the Lamb over hedge and ditch, through thick and thin. Do not turn your backs on Christ; the worst of Christ is better than the best of the world. Make conscience of making good your terms, to deny yourself, your natural self, your sinful self, your religious self, to follow him; and if you do so, oh! what an honour will it be to Christ, and advantage to your souls, and a joy to the upright!

Leg. 26. Walk by no rule but such as you dare die by and stand by in the great day of Jesus Christ. You may have many ways prescribed to worship by; but walk by none but such as you dare die by, and stand by, before Jesus Christ. Walk not by a multitude, for who dare stand by that rule when he comes to die?

Make not the example of great men a rule to go by, for who dare die by and stand by this in the great day of account. Do not make any authority that stands in opposition to the authority of Christ a rule to walk by, for who dare stand by this before Jesus Christ? Ah! sirs, walk by no rule but what you dare die by, and stand by at the great day.

Leg. 27. And lastly, sit down and rejoice with fear: Ps. ii., 'Let the righteous rejoice, but let them rejoice with fear.' Rejoice, that God hath done your souls good by the everlasting gospel; that he did not leave you till he brought you to an acceptance of, to a closing with, and a resignation of, your souls to Christ, and the clearing up of your interest in him. Rejoice, that you have had the everlasting gospel in so much light, purity, power, and glory, as you have had for many years together. Rejoice in the riches of grace that hath carried it in such a way towards you. And weep, that you have provoked God to take away the gospel, that you have no more improved it; that you have so neglected the seasons and opportunities of enriching your souls. When you should have come to church-fellowship, anything would turn you out of the way. Oh! sit down and tremble under your barrenness, under all your leanness. Notwithstanding all the cost and charge that God hath been at, that you have grown no more into communion with God, and conformity to God, and into the lively hope of the everlasting fruition of God. Here are your legacies, and the Lord make them to work in your souls, and then they will be of singular use to you, to preserve you so that you may give up your account before the great and glorious God with joy. Labour to make conscience of putting these legacies into practice, of sucking at these breasts, which will be of use to us, till we shall be gathered up into the fruition of God, where we shall need no more ordinances, no more preaching or praying.

C.—Introductory 'Epistles.' See *ante* page xxxiii.

I. 'The Gospel Treasury Opened, or the holiest of all unveiling; discovering yet more the riches of grace and glory to the vessels of mercy. Unto whom only it is given to know the mysteries of that kingdom and the excellency of Spirit, Power, Truth, above Letters, Forms, Shadows. In several Sermons, preached at Kensington and elsewhere,' by John Everard, D.D., deceased. 1679. (2d edition, 'very much enlarged'). 12mo. The following Epistle, entitled 'An Approbation,' is by Brooks, though good Matthew Barker adds his name also.

'The Publisher of this book is desirous that it might pass with some testimonial into the world; but it needs not testimony from man; for I find it impressed with such a divine image, and bearing such clear lineaments of heaven-born truths as testify it to be of God; and therefore strongly bespeaks us to receive it, as into our houses, so chiefly into our hearts. I dare assure thee, Reader, if thou hast received a spiritual relish, thou shalt taste much sweetness in it; and if thou canst rejoice to be "laid low," and made nothing, that God may be exalted and made "all in all," then shalt thou find here that which will help thy joy. And let me entreat thee, that as thou readest the book, to read also thine own heart; and by this thou mayest come to find thine heart in the book, and the book in thine heart, and [this] will make thee fall upon thy face with that idiot, and worship God and report, "God is in this word of a truth," 1 Cor. xiv. 25. Some are casting off the letter of

the Scriptures, others resting in it; some are despising ordinances, others are overvaluing them. I find the author walking warily betwixt both; giving due honour to the letter and to the form, while he is exalting the power and the Spirit incomparably above both; and thou shalt find him laying the axe of truth and the edge of the Spirit close to that cursed root of self-approbation in man, which is daily bringing forth such bitter fruits in his heart, in his life, and in the world; and yet remains unseen and untouched in the hearts of many that would be thought to be arrived at the brink of perfection, while they scarce understand wherein the great imperfection of the natural man doth lie.

Some expressions in thy reading may seem harsh or obscure to thee, as they did to me; but read it over and over with prayer, strongly desirous to be taught of God; and in reading be not weary, but blow and take breath, and at it again: and thou, comparing one place with another, wilt clearly see what the author means, and shalt find his whole discourse to have a sacred tendency to lay man low, and so to put him into a rich capacity of coming in to the nearest fellowship with God. So that while some seek to build up themselves upon the deceitful foundation of corrupted nature, and struggle, though in vain, in the light and power of it, to advance towards perfection; he is planting his spiritual artillery against it, to throw it into the dust, so that man may come to be surely rooted and bottomed upon the righteousness, power, and wisdom of Jesus Christ; which is the only foundation that God hath laid, and the gospel revealed.

And in some things thou must give him a latitude to his judgment, as thou desirest by thine own in others. If thou findest some truths delivered and enforced with re-iterated expressions, consider they were delivered for the most part in several congregations; so that in some particulars the same things may be reinforced, but yet with more lustre, to make truth more clear. Thou hast them as they were preached and pressed in sermons to the capacity and conscience of his auditors, and taken from his mouth by a Notary; yet afterwards owned and approved by himself, he desiring to peruse them, they lying with him three or four months, and compared with his own notes. Read, consider, and try 'and hold fast that which is good.'

THO. BROOKS.
M. BARKER.

March 26, 1653.

II. 'ALTUM SILENTIUM, or Silence the Duty of Saints. By John Durant, 12mo. 1659.

TO THE READER.—Christian Friend,—The book of Job (saith Augustine) is the afflicted man's Scripture; and I may say this little book is the afflicted man's duty. A little pearl may be of great price; and such is this little treatise that now is put into thy hand.

The waves did but lift Noah's ark nearer to heaven; and the higher the waters rose, the nearer the ark was lifted up to heaven: sometimes such an operation afflictions have upon Noahs, upon preachers of righteousness; and if they have not had the same operation upon the author of the ensuing discourse, I am much mistaken. Afflictions to some are like the prick at the nightingale's breast, that awakes her, and puts her upon her sweet and delightful notes; and whether they have not had such an operation upon the worthy author, I will leave the reader to judge. The more precious odours and the purest spices are beaten and bruised, the sweeter scent and savour they send abroad. Had not God bruised to death one of the choicest and sweetest flowers in the author's garden, he had not sent abroad this sweet and savoury sermon.

We try metal by knocking it; if it sound well, then we like it well. That is a tried Christian, a thorough Christian indeed, that gives a pleasant sound when under the knocking hand of God. If thou layest thine ear, thy heart, close to the following tract, thou wilt hear such a sound as will be sweeter to thee than the honey or the honey-comb.

That Christian is worth a world who, under the sorest and sharpest afflictions, is like the stone in Thracia, that neither burneth in the fire nor sinketh in the water; whose silence and patience is invincible and impregnable. None are such an honour to God, such a glory to the gospel, such a shame to Satan, and such a wonder to the world as these; who can lay their hands upon their mouths when God's rod lays heavy upon their backs. That this is every Christian's duty and glory is fully and sweetly evinced in the following discourse.

Happy are we when God's corrections are our instructions, his lashes our lessons, his scourges our schoolmasters, his chastisements our advertisements. And to note this, the Hebrews and Greeks both express chastening and teaching by one and the same word, (מוסר, *παιδεία*), [margin, Isa. xxxvi. 9; Ps. xciv. 12; Prov. iii. 12, 13; chap. vi. 23], because the latter is the true end of the former, according to that in the proverb, Smart makes wit, and vexation gives understanding. That this happiness the reader may attain to, is the thing endeavoured by the author.

Reader, thou hast much wrapped up in a little; it is more to be admired than to have Homer's Iliads compressed in a nutshell; it is a mourning sermon, and mourning should be plain. The reverend author knew right well, that it was better to present truth in her native plainness than to hang her ears with counterfeit pearls. He knew that the king of Nineveh was a king as well in his sackcloth, as in his royal robes. The author is known to be a master-workman, and one that could easily shoot his arrows over his hearers' heads [margin, See his precious works in print, and then judge], but he had rather shoot them into his hearers' hearts. He dares not affect sublime notions, obscure expressions, which are but mysterious nothings. He dares not do as many, who make plain truths difficult, and easy truths hard; and so darken counsel by words without knowledge, Job xxxviii. 2. If thou will but taste and try, thou wilt find this little treatise to be a heavenly honey-hive to thy soul.

If thou shalt say, Oh! it is sweet, it is seasonable, it is suitable to my condition, and to God's dispensations abroad in the world; but why have we no more of this sweet wine, no more of this water of life, no more of these clusters of Canaan? I must tell thee, that the honoured author buried his dear and hopeful daughter on the Friday, and preached this sermon on the Sabbath day following; and therefore there has been more cause to bless the Lord, and admire the Lord for his goodness, assistance, and presence with the author, that has enabled him to bring forth a truth of so great weight and concernment to us, even then, when he was under such sore and sharp rebukes of God. It is not every one's happiness to have such a presence of God with them, when the rod of God is heavy upon them.

Reader, the point insisted on is a point of special use to Christians; especially to such as are under the afflicting hand of God, whether in spirituals or temporals; and if storms should fall upon us from abroad or at home, it will be found (in the use of it) more worth than gold. I have read of the stone Garamantides, that had drops of gold in it: many a golden drop wilt thou find in the following lines. As Moses laid up the manna in the golden pot, and as Alexander kept Homer's Iliad in a cabinet embroidered with gold, so do thou lay up this sermon in the golden cabinet of thy heart. If troubles at present are not upon thee, yet thou must remember that thou art born to them, as the sparks fly upwards [margin, Job v. 7; John xvi. ult. 14; Acts xxi. 22]. God had but one Son without sin, he hath no son without sorrow; he had but one without corruption, he hath none without correction; he scourges every son whom he receives; he can quickly turn thy summer day into winter night, and then this sermon may be to thee a suitable and invaluable mercy. I shall only take leave to hint a few things to the author, my reverend brother, and to my dear sister, his virtuous yoke-fellow, who are above all others concerned in this sharp and sweet dispensation, and so conclude.

First, That well-grounded hope, confidence, and assurance, that you and others had of the buddings and blossomings of grace in her, in her tender age, and of her being now at rest in the bosom of the Father, should not only quiet and silence you, but also joy and rejoice you [margin, Heb. xi. 4]. Why may you not think that you hear her, though dead, yet speaking thus unto you?

> Where God has stamp'd his image upon a mite,
> 'Tis meet that God should have his right:
> After a few years past, a wearied breath
> I have exchanged for a happy death.
> Short was my life, the longer is my rest;
> God takes them soonest whom he loveth best.
> She that is born to-day, and dies to-morrow,
> Loses some hours of joy, but years of sorrow;
> Other diseases often come to grieve us,
> Death strikes but once, and that stroke relieves us:
> Therefore (my parents dear), take heed of weeping cross,
> And mind my happiness more than your own great loss.
> This is all I'll say to make the reckoning even,
> Your dearest mercy is not too good for heaven.
> Hasten to me, where now I am possess'd
> With joys eternal, in Christ my only rest.

Secondly, The designs of God in all the sharp afflictions he exercises his children with, as (1.) the purging away of their sins, Isa. i. 25; (2.) the making of them more partakers of his holiness, Heb. xii. 10; (3.) the trial of their graces, Job xxiii. 10; (4.) the communication of more of himself and of his love to their souls, Hosea i. 14; (5.) the multiplying of their spiritual experiences, 2 Cor. i. 4, 5; (6.) the crucifying of their hearts to the world, and the world to their hearts, Gal. vi. 14 [margin, *Nam finis dat amabilitatem et facilitatem mediis*]; (7.) to draw them to look and fix their souls upon the great concernment of another world, John xiv. 1–3; (8.) that heaven may be the more sweet and precious to them at last, 2 Cor. iv. 16–18, Rom. viii. 17, 18; how sweet is a calm after a storm, and summer days after long winter nights; (9.) to make them more and more conformable to Christ their head, Rom. viii. 17; (10.) that sinners may at the last be found dumb and speechless, 1 Peter iv. 17, 18. Now, is there not enough in these glorious ends and designs of God to make his people sit mute under the sharpest trials? Surely there is. Why then don't they sit silent before the Lord?

Thirdly, All the mercies you enjoy, were first the Lord's before they were yours, and always the Lord's more than they were yours, 1 Chron. xxix. 14. 'All things come of thee, and of thine own have we given thee.' The sweet of mercy is yours, but the sovereign right to dispose of your mercies is the Lord's. *Quicquid es debes creanti; quicquid potes, debes redimenti* (Bern), whatsoever thou art, thou owest to him that made thee; and whatsoever thou hast, thou owest to him that redeemed thee. Say, as Jerome adviseth a friend of his (in the like case), Thou hast taken away whom thou hast given me: I grieve not that thou hast taken them, but praise the Lord that was pleased to give them. You think it but just and reasonable that men should deal with their own as they please; and is it not much more just and reasonable that God should do with his own as he pleases?

Fourthly, That God that has taken one, might have taken all; there are several left, though one be taken. Job, you know, was a nonsuch in his generation, and yet the sentence of death was passed upon all his children at a clap; and under this said clap Job does not blaspheme, but bless; he does not murmur, but worships; he accuses not God, but clears God of injustice under saddest and severest strokes of justice, Job i. Geographers write that the city of Syracuse in Sicily is so curiously situated, that the sun is never out of sight: though one mercy be gone, yet you have several that remain, and this should make you mute.

Themistocles invited many philosophers to supper; the owner sends for one half of those necessaries that he was using. Can you endure this disgrace? said the philosophers. Yes, said he, very well, for he might have sent justly for them all. The application is easy. Oh! let not nature do more than grace.

Fifthly and lastly, Under sharp afflictions, we ought carefully to look that natural afflictions don't hinder the exercise of gracious dispositions. Though we may weep, yet we may not weep out either the eye of faith, or the eye of hope [margin, 1 Thes. iv. 13]: though you may water your flowers, yet you may not drown your flowers. They that wept, yea, that wept much, yet said, The will of the Lord be done [margin, Acts xxi. 13, 14]. Jacob doated too much upon his Joseph, and his affections were too strong for his judgment, when, upon the sight of the bloody coat, he refused to be comforted, and said, I will go down into the grave unto my son, mourning [margin, Gen. xxxvii. 33–35]. And David was too fond of his son Absalom, when, like a puny baby, he wept and said, O my son Absalom! my son! my son! Absalom! would God I had died for thee, O Absalom, my son! my son! [margin, 2 Sam. xviii. 32, 33]. The Egyptians mourned for Jacob seventy days, but Joseph (though he had more cause) mourned but seven days; because he had more grace, and better hopes of Jacob's eternal welfare, than the infidels had. In the midst of all your tears, keep up the exercise of grace, and then you shall not mourn that you have mourned.

That your own is no sooner in your hand, is only from the remissness and dilatoriness of him into whose hands you had ordered the copy.

To conclude: that you and I, and all others (into whose hands this sermon may fall) may live up, and live out, the following discourse, under all the changes that has or shall pass upon us, is the earnest desire and hearty prayer of him who is your entire friend and servant in our dearest Lord.

THO. BROOKS.

III. The 'Epistle' prefixed to the 'Works' of Dr Thomas Taylor, of 'Aldermanbury, London,' (folio, 1653), bears the name of Brooks, only in common with Gouge and Calamy, Jackson, Ashe, Caryl, Manton, Greenhill, Strong, Griffith, Venning, and Jemmat. The first signature is that of Dr William Gouge; and probably the 'Epistle' was drawn up by him, and simply signed by the others. Yet does there seem touches from the hand of Brooks.

IV. 'GOSPEL FEAR; or the Heart trembling at the Word of God evidenceth a blessed frame of spirit. Delivered in several Sermons from Isa. lxvi. 2, and 2 Kings xxii. 14. By Jeremiah Burroughes.[1] "His mercy is on them that fear him from generation to generation," Luke i. 50. "Work out your own salvation with fear and trembling," Philip. ii. 12. London: Printed by J. D. for B. Aylmer at the three Pigeons in Cornhill. 1674.' 12mo.

TO THE READER.—Christian Reader,—These following sermons are the labours of that prince of preachers, Mr Jer. Burroughs, who is now a shining sun in that upper world. But they that are taken out of this valley of Baca, and carried up by troops of glorious angels into the highest heaven, stand in no need of the praises of men, having the fruition of the eternal God. And therefore I shall wheel about to these choice sermons that are here presented to thine eyes.[2] In

1 Died Nov. 14. 1646.—G.

2 Chrysostom, in his learned oration compiled upon the death [of] Philogonius. Melanchton saith of Pomeranus, He was the grammarian; of himself, that he was the logician; of

the three first thou wilt find this great and glorious truth, viz., that a heart trembling at God's word is very precious in God's eyes,—Heb. vi. 10; Isa. lxii. 6; Ezek. xxxvi. 37,—clearly opened, fully proved, and sweetly and faithfully improved, so as that, by a blessing from on high, it may contribute greatly to the internal and eternal welfare of thy precious and immortal soul. Concerning the Word, premise this with me, viz. that in these six following acceptations the word is taken in the blessed Scriptures, (1.) By the Word is sometimes meant the whole Scriptures, Old and New Testament. (2.) By the Word is meant our Lord Jesus Christ, who is the spirit, life, and soul of the word, John i. (3.) By the Word is sometimes meant the commands of the word, Heb. i. (4.) By the Word is sometimes meant the threatenings of God. (5.) By the Word is sometimes meant the precious promises: Ps. cxix. 49, 'Remember the word unto thy servant, upon which thou hast caused me to hope.' God is not unrighteous to forget, yet we must, as his remembrancers, put his promises in suit. (6.) By the Word is sometimes meant those holy prophecies which are scattered up and down in the Scriptures, Jude 14. The word thus considered occasioned one Baldusgar, a famous minister in Germany, to say, *Veniat, veniat verbum Domini et submittemus illi sexcenta, si nobis essent, colla*, let the word of the Lord come, let it come, saith he; we will submit to it if we had many hundred necks to put under it. The design of the worthy author in this little piece is, to win and work the reader to submit to the Word, to be guided by the Word, to prize the Word, to lay up the Word, and to live out the Word in a conversation becoming the gospel. The Jewish Rabbins were wont to say, that upon every letter of the law there hangs mountains of profitable matter. I am sure in the following discourse thou wilt find even mountains of heavenly matter hanging upon all the main particulars that this blessed author offers to thy serious consideration in this small treatise. Here you have Homer's Iliads in a nutshell; much choice matter in a little room. It is said of Cæsar, *Major fuit cura Cæsari libellorum quam purpuræ*, he had greater care of his books than of his royal robes; for, swimming through the waters to escape his enemies, he carried his books in his hand above the waters, but lost his robes. But what are Cæsar's books to God's books? or to this little book that is now put into thy hand? Surely the word of the Lord is very sweet to all those gracious souls who make conscience of trembling at it, Ps. xix. 10; cxix. 103; Job xxiii. 12; Cant. ii. 3. Luther said he could not live in paradise, if he might, without the Word, *at cum verbo etiam in inferno facile est vivere*, but with the Word he could live in hell itself.[1] The philosopher gave thanks that he was born in the time of true philosophy. Ah! how happy are we that are born in such a time wherein the Lord doth *effundere Spiritum*, pour forth his Spirit, not by drops, as in the time of the Law, but showers down of his gifts and graces, as was most evident in the author of this following piece. Not only the day-star, but the Sun of righteousness was risen upon that people that had once the happiness to sit under the author's ministry; neither is it a small part of this world's happiness that they are blessed with his most excellent labours to this very day. One cannot say of any divine thing, that it is his own properly till in his heart. I can say of a bird, or of this or that, it is my own when in my hand; but I cannot say God is mine till in my heart, or that Christ is mine till in my heart, or that the Spirit is mine till in my heart, or that grace is mine till in my heart, or that the word is mine till in my heart. 'I have kept thy word in my heart, that I may not sin against thee,' saith David, Ps. cxix. 11; and therefore, reader, it highly concerns thee to get that word into

Justus Ionius, that he was the orator; but of Luther he was *omnia in omnibus*, all in all. Adam in *vit. Luther*, p. 170. The application is easy.

[1] *Sacræ Scripturæ tuæ sunt sanctæ deliciæ meæ.*—Augustine. Dolphins, they say, love music; so do gracious souls love the music of the word.

thy heart that is here presented to thine eye. Ah! Christians, your hearts are never in so good a frame, so safe a frame, so sweet a frame, so happy a frame, so gospel a frame, as when they are in a trembling frame; and therefore make this little piece your delightful companion till your hearts are brought into such a blessed frame, &c.

Obj. But may not reprobates and devils tremble at the word? did not Belshazzar tremble at the handwriting? did not Felix tremble at the word preached by Paul? and is it not said that the devils believe and tremble? Dan. v. 5, 6; Acts xxiv. 24, 25; James ii. 19.

Ans. 1. Wicked men and devils may tremble at the judgments denounced in the word, but they tremble not at the offence committed against the holy commandments of God, as sincere Christians do: Ezra x. 3, Shechaniah said, 'We have trespassed against our God; let us make a covenant with our God according to the counsel of my Lord, and of those that tremble at the commandments of God.' The commandments discovering their sin, they tremble who before were hardened in their practice of marrying with the Canaanites; but we hear nothing, we find nothing of this in Belshazzar, or Felix, or the devils. But,

Ans. 2. Secondly, I answer, the wicked tremble, but never mend their ways. Pharaoh trembles, but never mends. Saul trembles, but never mends. Belshazzar trembles, but never mends. Felix trembles, but never mends; and devils tremble, but never mend. But Paul trembles, and cries out, 'Lord, what wilt thou have me to do?' And the jailor trembles, and cries out, 'Sirs, what must I do to be saved?' Acts ix. 4–6; xvi. 29, 30. But,

Ans. 3. Thirdly, The trembling of the wicked drives them further and further off from God, and off from duty; as you see in Saul, who, under his tremblings, runs to a witch; but gracious tremblings draw the soul nearer and nearer to God, as you see in Jehoshaphat, who feared and set himself to seek the Lord, and proclaimed a fast throughout all Judah, 2 Chron. xxiii. 3. The saints, under all their holy tremblings, they follow after God as the people followed after Saul's tremblings, 1 Sam. xiii. 7. But,

Ans. 4. Fourthly, The godly tremble, and mourn and tremble. Their trembling hearts are broken hearts, and their broken hearts are trembling hearts; they look upon sin and tremble, and they look upon sin and mourn, Isa. lxvi. 2; Jer. ix. 1, 2; Ps. cxix. 136: Jer. xxv. 13, 17, 'But if ye will not hear it, my soul shall weep in secret places for your pride, and mine eyes shall weep sore and run down with tears,' &c. The wicked tremble, but, under all their tremblings, their hearts are as dry and hard as rocks, yea, harder than the very rocks: Jer. v. 3, 'They made their faces harder than a rock; they have refused to return,' Ezek. iii. 7–9; Jer. vii. 26. Pharaoh trembled, but yet was hardened; the devils tremble, but yet are hardened. If one penitent tear could purchase heaven, hell could not afford that one tear. Repenting tears are precious; they are, saith Gregory, 'the fat of the sacrifice;' and, as Basil saith, 'the medicine of the soul;' and, as Bernard, 'the wine of angels.' But these are only to be found among those choice souls who make conscience of trembling at God's word, and who enjoy that choice tenderness of heart that is in this little treatise drawn to the life. Verily we cannot meet on this side hell with a worse temper of spirit than that which inclines a sinner to drop counterfeit tears, and to despise the forbearance of God, and to kick against the bowels of his goodness, Rom. ii. 4, as that profane Arian did who was executed at Harwich, concerning whom Mr Greenham acquainteth us with this strange and prodigious narration. This hellish heretic, saith he—for so were the deniers of Christ's divinity accounted of in those days, whatever thoughts men have of them now—a little before he was executed, afforded a few whorish tears, asking whether he might be saved by Christ or no? when one told him that if he truly repented, he should surely not perish, he breaks out into this speech, Nay, if your Christ be so easy to be entreated indeed as you say, then I defy him, and care not for him. Oh horrible blasphemy, and desperate wickedness! for a man to draw himself back from repentance by that very cord of love whereby he should have been drawn to it.[1] But,

Ans. 5. Fifthly and lastly, The hearts of wicked men and devils only tremble upon the account of punishment and the judgment to come, Acts xxiv. 25; Mat. viii. 28, 29. As a malefactor trembleth before the judge, and under the sense of his doom; but a child of God trembles under the sense of God's goodness and kindness to him: Hosea iii. 7, 'And shall fear the Lord and his goodness;' or, as some sense it, 'they shall fear the Lord because of his goodness.' The Hebrew is, 'they shall fear *to* the Lord *pavebunt ad Dominum*, that is, trembling they shall make haste to him as frighted doves do to their columbaries. See Hosea xi. 11. Look! as holy tremblings and gladness are consistent together, Ps. ii. 11; and as a holy fear and joy are consistent together, as you see in those good women who went from Christ's sepulchre with fear and great joy, Mat. xxviii. 8, a strange composition of two contrary passions, but frequently found in the best hearts; so a holy love and trembling are consistent together.[2] A child whose heart is full of love to his father, when he looks upon him as offended or grieved, he trembles, like that poor woman, Mark v. 33, who, fearing that she had offended Christ in her approaching to him, came trembling, but yet with a heart full of love to Christ. So here, when a child of God fixes one eye upon the holiness and justice of God, he trembles; and when, at the same time, he fixes his other eye upon the patience, the goodness, the graciousness, and readiness of God to forgive as a father, he loves and joys; but now all the tremblings of the wicked are from apprehensions of wrath to come, and from a hansel[3] of hell in their consciences on this side hell. These five things I thought to hint at, that the reader may be the better able to grapple with the same objection when he meets with it in this little piece.

The dew of heaven hath richly fallen among many, and yet, like Gideon's fleece, they are dry when all the regions about them are wet, Judges vi. 37–40; and is it not so with many in these days, who sit under gospel droppings, and who have the labours of many famous men put every day into their hands? and yet how are their souls like the mountains of Gilboa, upon which there fell neither dew nor rain! This is and this must be for a lamentation, 2 Sam. i. 21. If the books of the law chance to fall upon the ground, the Jews' custom is presently to proclaim a fast. Ah, friends! what cause have we to fast and mourn, when we see the word preached, printed, offered, to fall upon the ground, and to be trampled upon, as it is this day by atheists, papists, Socinians, and other vain persons! &c. The Jews have a law which enjoins them to take up any paper which they see lying on the ground; and the reason is, lest haply the word of God be written in the paper and ignorantly trodden under foot. Though Christians ought to be free from such superstitious curiosities, yet they ought to be very careful that the least tittle of the word, the least truth revealed in the word, be not trodden under foot either by themselves or others; considering its excellency and usefulness as a guide, a light, to lead us through the wilderness of this world to the heavenly Canaan: Prov. vi. 22, 'When thou goest, it shall lead thee; when thou sleepest, it shall keep thee; when thou awakest, it shall talk with thee.' That is, according to the gloss of the Rabbinical interpreters, when thou goest, it shall lead thee, viz. in thy passage through this world; when thou sleepest, it shall keep thee, viz. when thou liest down in the grave; and when thou awakest, it shall talk with thee, viz. when thou art awakened at the glorious resurrection. But, that I may not

[1] Mr Greenham in his treatise, entitled A sweet Comfort for an afflicted Conscience on Prov. xviii. 14. [2] God loves at once familiarity and fear. [3] Earnest, foretaste.—G.

make the porch too large, I shall hasten to a close. There are three sorts of persons, above all others, that I would seriously recommend this treatise to.

(1.) First, Those that do tremble at the word, and those that have soft and tender hearts; for these will find choice comforts, special encouragements, and singular supports to cheer and bear up their hearts in their greatest trials, inward or outward, or in the worst of times.

(2.) Secondly, Those that are bold sinners, secure sinners, stupid sinners, insensible sinners; for these will find variety of arguments to awaken them, to startle them, to soften them, and to work them into a trembling frame and a tender frame, with singular directions and counsel how to obtain those spiritual frames which are infinitely more worth than all those crowns and kingdoms that men are this day contending for in blood.

(3.) Thirdly, Those that are under many fears, and doubts, and disputes in their own hearts, whether they do tremble at this word or no, and whether they have a tender heart or no; for I dare venture to say that such persons will find in this treatise those blessed truths that will, by a blessing from on high, scatter their fears, resolve their doubts, and put a happy issue to all their disputes.

Reader, When thou hast once seriously read over this little treatise, I cannot but judge that thou wilt readily conclude with me, viz. That the two special points here handled, viz. our trembling at God's word, and a tender heart, are, (1.) Two great and weighty points. (2.) Two very noble and necessary points, which all should labour to know and understand who would be blessed here and happy hereafter. (3.) Two seasonable and suitable points to the days and times wherein we live, which abound with all sorts of sins, and which are attended with the sorest of spiritual judgments, such as blindness, hardness, insensibleness. (4.) Two important points that have singular other points wrapped up in the womb of them, and that are dependent upon them. (5.) Two points that are not every day handled in the pulpit, nor sent unto the press.

Reader, The importunity of a worthy friend hath prevailed with me to give thee the trouble of reading this epistle. And now I shall conclude with a few words of counsel: (1.) Let him that casts his eye on this book not borrow it, but buy it; (2.) seriously read it; (3.) highly prize it; (4.) earnestly pray over it; (5.) endeavour to have his heart and life made conformable to the matter contained in it; (6.) to lay it up among his choicest treasures; and (7.) when he is in the mount, to remember him who unfeignedly and earnestly desires that this little piece may be highly blessed to the writer, reader, and hearer: and so I shall take leave and rest,

Thy real friend and soul's servant,

THOMAS BROOKS.

D.—Mrs Brooks. (See *ante*, p. xxxiv).

The following is the title-page of the Funeral Sermon of the first Mrs Brooks:—

STRENGTH
IN
Weakness.

A
SERMON
Preached at the FUNERAL of
Mrs. MARTHA BROOKS,
Late WIFE to
Mr. THO. BROOKS Minister of the Gospel in *London;*
Who Departed this Life *June* 20. 1676.

To which are Added
Some EXPERIENCES of the Grace and Dealings of
GOD, Observed and Gathered by a near Relation of
the said Mrs. *Brooks*.

By J.C. a Friend of the Deceased, and her Surviving Husband.

2 COR. 12. 10.
—Ὅταν γὰρ ἀσθενῶ, τότε δυνατός εἰμι.

HEB. 11. 34.
Ἐνεδυναμώθησαν ἀπὸ ἀσθενείας.—

LONDON,
Printed for *John Hancock* at the Three Bibles in *Popes-Head Alley, Cornhill.* 1676. [4to.]

We give the 'Notes' that were furnished by, no doubt, Brooks.

A short account of some of the choice experiences, blessed discoveries, and gracious evidences, of Mrs Martha Brooks, who fell asleep in Jesus, June 20. 1676. Drawn up by a near relation, that best understood her spiritual estate and condition.

It is long since that the Lord made it the day of his power—Ps. cx. 3—upon her soul. Many years ago, the great and glorious God, by his Spirit and power, by his word and rod, brought her from under the power, use, and dominion of sin and Satan, 1 Thes. i. 5; Prov. xxix. 15, and brought her off from restings or stayings upon her own righteousness—which she daily looked upon to be but filthy rags, and as a menstruous cloth—and brought her into fellowship and communion with himself, his Son, and his blessed Spirit, &c., Rom. vi. 14; Acts xxvi. 18; Isa. lxiv. 6; John i. 3, 4; 2 Cor. xiii. 14.

To make a full narration of these great things, would make this little piece to swell beyond its due proportion; and though it might please some, yet it might dissatisfy others; and therefore I shall do little more than hint at things, that so I may bring all I intend to say into a narrow compass.

Should I say all I could,

First, About her knowledge and acquaintance with Christ, when and where should I make an end? Only this I may say: 1, her knowledge was inward; 2, it was affectionate; 3, experimental; 4, humbling; 5, growing; 6, communicative; 7, practical, Job xxii. 21; John xvii. 3, vii. 17, xiii. 1.

Secondly, Should I say all I could about her high approbation of Christ,—

Acts iv. 12; 1 Tim. i. 15; Col. i. 19, i. 2, 3; Acts v. 31; Col. ii. 6; Rom. vii. 12; Ps. cxix. 72; Rev. iii. 19; Dan. ix. 14; Neh. ix. 33—when and where should I make an end? Only this I may hint: 1, that she highly approved of the person of Christ as the most suitable good in heaven or earth to her soul; 2, she highly approved of the personal excellencies of Christ as the most transcendent excellencies; 3, she highly approved of Christ in all his offices, both kingly, prophetical, and priestly; 4, she highly approved of all the precious things of Christ, as his day, his laws, his worship, his ordinances, his ways, his saints; 5, she highly approved of the rebukes, of the severe rebukes, of Christ, knowing that they were the fruits of his love, and that he was holy and wise, just and righteous, in all his rebukes, &c.

Thirdly, About her choice and election of Christ to be her Head and Husband, Cant. ii. 16; Deut. xxvi. 17, her Sovereign and Saviour; upon choice she would have none but Christ to save her, nor none but Christ to rule her.

Fourthly, About her reception of Christ, Job i. 12; Ps. xxiv. 7–10: 1, in all his offices; 2, into every room of her soul; 3, once for all; 4, upon his own gospel terms, Mat. xvi. 24.

Fifthly, About her high, her very high, estimation of Christ, 1 Peter ii. 7, she prized above all her duties, above all her privileges, above all her graces, above all her outward contentments, and above all her spiritual enjoyments; he was to her the chiefest of ten thousand, Cant. v. 10; Ps. xlv. 2; Mat. xiii. 26; Prov. viii. 11; Philip. iii. 8; he was fairer than the children of men; he was the pearl of price in her eye; he was more precious than rubies to her soul. She looked upon all things as nothing in comparison of Christ; she had rather have one Christ than a thousand worlds.

Sixthly, About her marriage union and communion with Christ, of which freely and frequently she discoursed both with ministers and Christians throughout her sickness. Her marriage union with Christ was breasts of consolation and wells of salvation to her, Cant. iii. 11; Hosea ii. 18–20; 2 Cor. xi. 2; Ps. lxvi. 11, xii. 3. Throughout her nine months' sickness by these she did live, and in these things were the life of her spirit, Isa. xxxviii. 16.

Seventhly, About her trustings and cleavings to Christ as the ivy cleaves to the oak, the child to the mother, or as the wife cleaves to the husband. In all her ups and downs, she would be still hanging upon Christ, and cleaving to Christ, John xiii. 15; Acts xi. 23; Ruth i. 14; Gen. ii. 24.

Eighthly, About her thirstings, breathings, and longings, after higher, clearer, and fuller enjoyments of Christ, she could never have enough of Christ, Ps. xlii. 1, 2, lxiii.; Mal. i. 2, 3; Ps. lxxxiv., xxvii. 4, 8, nor enough of his presence, nor enough of his Spirit, nor enough of his grace, nor enough of his manifestations, nor enough of his consolations; the constant cry of her soul was, More of Christ! more of Christ! O more of Christ!

Ninthly, About her sad lamenting and bewailing the withdrawings of Christ, Cant. v. 6; Isa. viii. 17, 7; Micah vii. 8, 9, 2. There were no days so sad, so dark, so gloomy, so grievous, so afflictive to her, as those days wherein he that should comfort her soul stood afar off, Lam. xvi. The shinings of Christ's face made a heaven in her heart; and the hidings of his face was her only hell. Let whoso would frown, if Christ did but smile, all was well.

Tenthly, About her sympathising with Christ in all the dishonours that were done to his name, his person, his day, his offices, his ordinances, his ways, his saints; and it was a grief to her to see others grieving of Christ, Ps. cxix. 53, cxxxvi.; Jer. ix. 1, 2; Ezek. ix. 4, 6; 1 Peter ii. 4, 7, 8. Other men's sins were matter of her sorrow; the sins of others hath cost her many a prayer, many a sigh, many a tear, and many a groan. Now, should I say all I could upon these ten particulars, when should I make an end? and therefore I must satisfy myself and the reader with a-hinting at things.

Her whole life (human frailties excepted) since God made it the day of his power upon her soul, was a daily walking with God; and all the days that ever passed over her head, there was none for delight, pleasure, profit, comfort, content, boldness, and satisfaction, to those wherein she walked most evenly, most closely, and most exactly with God, Gen. v. 22, vi. 9, xvii. 1; Ps. cxix., cxii. 44, 45; Acts xxiv. 16; Heb. xiii. 18.

Concerning Sin. 1. Sin of all burdens was her greatest, Ps. xxxviii. 4, xl. 12. 2. Her hatred and indignation against sin was universal, Ps. cxix. 104, 128; Isa. ii. 20, xxx. 22; Hosea xiv. 8; Ps. cxix. 176. 3. Her whole life was a daily conflicting with sin, Rom. vii. 23, 24; Ps. xvii. 4. She had rather be rid of all her sins, than be rid of all her troubles, sorrows, trials, bodily ailments, Job vii. 20, 21, xxxiv. 31, 32; Hosea xiv. 2. Others are all for the removing of the judgments and afflictions they are under, Exod. viii. 8; Num. xxi. 6, 7; Jer. xxx. 15. 5. She durst not allow herself in any known sin, much less in a course or way of sin, Ps. cxix. 1, 3; Rom. vii. 15; 1 John iii. 9; Prov. xvi. 17. 6. Her greatest conflict was with heart sins, secret sins, spiritual sins, invisible sins; sins that lie most hid and remote from the eyes of the world, Ps. xix. 12, cxix., cxiii. 'I hate vain thoughts:' secret self-love, secret pride, secret unbelief, secret hypocrisy, secret murmurings, secret carnal confidence, &c., 2 Chron. xxxii. 25; 2 Cor. vii. 1, did sit saddest upon her spirit. 7. There was an irreconcilable opposition in her soul against sin; she could not, she would not, she durst not upon any terms in the world, admit of any truce or reconciliation with sin, 1 Kings xiv. 30; Rom. vii. 23; Gal. v. 17; Rom. vi. 6; Ps. li. 2, 7, &c. 8. Her daily slips and falls did daily produce more soul-loathings, soul-humiliation, self-judging, self-abasement, self-abhorrency, Ezek. xvi. 61, 63; 2 Cor. vii. 11; Ps. xviii. 9. Her constant desires and earnest endeavours were to avoid and shun all known appearances of sin, Gen. xxxix. 12; 2 Cor. viii. 20, 21; 1 Cor. ix. 11–15; 1 Thes. v. 22; Jude 23; Exod. xxiii. 7; Deut. xii. 30; Prov. v. 8. 10. And, lastly, she set herself, her soul, her greatest strength against her bosom sins, her constitution sins, her most powerful and most prevalent sins; she set herself most against right-eye sins, and right-hand sins.

Concerning closet-prayer. I never knew any woman spend more time in her closet, nor keep more private days to God than she did. The duties of her closet were her meat and drink, and she was always best when she was most with God in a corner. She has many a whole day been pouring out her soul before God in her closet, for the nation, for Sion, and the great concerns of her own soul, when them about her did judge it more expedient that she had been in her bed, by reason of some bodily infirmity that did hang upon her; but the divine pleasures that she took in her closet did drown the sense of pain. Secret enjoyments of God makes heavy afflictions light, long afflictions short, and bitter afflictions sweet, Isa. xxxiii. 24, 2 Cor. iv. 16–18. She found by frequent experience that closet-duties were mighty enriching, soul-fattening, soul-strengthening, soul-nourishing; and this endeared her to her closet.

Concerning ordinances. All that did thoroughly know her did know, 1, that she greatly loved the ordinances in the power and purity; 2, that she highly prized them; 3, that she made improvements of them, &c., endeavouring, according to her measure received, so to live as that she might reflect honour and glory upon the ordinances; 4, she made conscience of one ordinance as well as another, Luke i. 5, 6; she did not as some, cry up some ordinances and cry down others, nor keep close to some, and live in the neglect of others; 5, she ran all hazards in times of dangers to enjoy the ordinances, and chose rather with Moses to suffer afflictions with the people of God, than to enjoy the pleasures of sin, which were but for a season, Heb. xi. 24–27. 6. I never knew any Christian under such a load of weaknesses strive and labour to enjoy the ordinances as she did the three last years before her death.

Concerning her love to the saints. First, It was sincere for the image of God, of Christ, of grace, and holiness, 1 John iii. 14, 18; 1 John v. 1. The image of God was the loadstone that drew out her love to the saints.

2. It was universal, to one Christian as well as another, to all as well as any, to poor Lazarus as well as rich Abraham, to an afflicted and despised Job as well as to an admired David, to an afflicted Jacob as well as to a raised Joseph, Neh. i. 15; Col. i. 4; Philip. iv. 21; 1 Peter ii. 17.

3. It was an extensive love; it extended to those that were remote in respect of place, as well as to those that were near, to those saints whose faces she never saw, as well as to those whose faces she daily beheld; and all upon the serious reports of the grace of God that has been sparkling and shining in them, Rom. v. 26.

4. It was a fervent love, an active love, a love that put her upon doing, upon acting for them, and distributing to them according to her ability and their necessity, 1 Peter i. 22; Acts xi. 28–30; 1 Peter iv. 11. Her love was not a cold, idle, lazy love, like theirs in James ii. 14–17.

5. It was a constant love, a permanent love, 1 Cor. xiii. 8, Heb. xiii. 1: 'Let brotherly love continue,' 1 John iv. 16, Prov. xvii. 17. It was a love like that of Christ, who loved his to the end, John xiii. 1, xv. 12. Look, as our love must be sincere without hypocrisy, so it must be constant without deficiency. That love was never true that is not constant. True love, like the pulse, will still be beating, it will still be working, and turning out to the person beloved.

6. She loved, honoured, and prized them most and best in whom the spiritual and supernatural causes of love did most shine and sparkle, Ps. xv. 4, xvi. 3, xlv. 13, cxix. 119. Such saints as were magnificent in grace, noble in grace, glorious in grace, wonderful in grace, had most of her heart, and were most honoured and prized by her; she loved them best that were best.

Concerning the signal and blessed presence of God with her throughout her nine months' sickness. This divine presence with his sick and weak handmaid did manifest itself several ways; at first by preserving her eminently from sinning under her sufferings, as she would often say, Though I groan, yet I bless God I do not grumble. I remember what Job, Jeremiah, and Jonah said and did in the days of their sore sufferings; but God stood by his poor handmaid, and greatly armed her against those particular sins that an afflicted state lays the afflicted open to. Secondly, this glorious presence of God was manifested by keeping up in her daily exercise of those particular graces that was to be acted in an afflicted condition, as faith, hope, patience, self-denial, contentation and submission. Thirdly, this gracious presence of God did manifest itself by enabling his weak and sick handmaid in all her continued weakness to be still a-justifying of God, and crying out, The Lord is righteous, the Lord is righteous; he is holy and just, he can do me no wrong, he will do me no wrong. Though the cup be bitter to the flesh, yet it is a cup that my Father hath put into my hand, and therefore I will drink it, and lay my hand upon my mouth, and be silent at my Father's foot, Lam. i. 18; Ps. cxix. 75; Gen. xviii. 25; John xviii. 11; Lam. iii. 26–28; Rev. xx. 2.

Fourthly, This gracious presence of God was signally manifested in the chaining up of Satan; for the greatest part of her sickness, her body being very low, her spirits low, and her strength low, and by reason of her great and many weaknesses, she was cast unavoidably under great indispositions, both as to civil and sacred things; the greater was the mercy in God's chaining up of Satan; and if now and then Satan began to be busy, the Lord quickly rebuked him, and laid a law of restraint upon him. Fifthly, this gracious presence of God was signally manifested in keeping down and in keeping off the fears and terrors of death. She could all along cast the gauntlet to death, and say with the apostle, 'O death, where is thy sting? O grave, where is thy victory?' &c.,

1 Cor. xv. 55–57. Death is the king of terrors, as Job speaks, Job xviii. 14, Heb. ii. 14, 15, and the terror of kings, as the philosopher speaks; and yet the great and blessed God took away the dread and terror of death from her. If you ask those that lie under the fears and terrors of death, they will tell you that deliverance from those fears and terrors would be a heaven on this side heaven unto them. I could greatly enlarge, but that both the press and the bookseller calls aloud upon me to conclude.

The design of these few hints is to comfort and encourage relations and friends to write after this blessed copy and example of that dear servant of Christ who hath now exchanged earth for heaven, a wilderness for a paradise, a sick-bed for a royal throne, pains, strong and long pains, for everlasting pleasures, and the presence of poor, frail, sinful mortals for the presence of God, Christ, angels, and the spirits of just men made perfect, Ps. xvi. 11, Heb. xii. 22, 23.

E.—WILL. See *ante* page xxxv.

EXTRACTED from the PRINCIPAL REGISTRY of HER MAJESTY'S COURT OF PROBATE.

(In the Prerogative Court of Canterbury.)

DEATH IS A FALL that came in by a Fall: that statute Law of Heaven 'Dust thou art and to dust thou shalt returne' will first or last take hold of all mortalls; the core of that apple that Adam eat in Paradise will choke us all round one by one; there is not one man living that shall not see death; though all men shall not meete in Heaven, nor in Hell, yet all men shall meete in the grave whether wee and all a[re] going. To prevent ill consequences and the mischiefes that follow without making a Will and to sett my house in order I doo make this short following Will. First I bequeath unto my loveing Couson Mistress Elenor Crith, fifty pounds which I will that my Executrix pay within a twelve moneths after my death. I give to Vice Admirall Goodsons eldest daughters sonne that shee had by her husband, Captain Magger[1] twenty five pounds but in case of his Mortallity to what child shee pleaseth. I will and bequeath unto her sister Maryes eldest child twenty five pounds both of which summes my Executrix is to pay within a yeare after my death. Item I give my studdy of bookes to be sold by my Couson Ford and my couson Henry Goodman and Master Crouch; and the money thence ariseing to be equally divided into foure proportions, one for my couson Martha Wright, another for Mary Wright, the other two for Roger Timborland's two children which he had by my couson Joan, as soon as the sale is made[2] my Will is that my Executrix pay it into my couson Martha and Mary Wright, and to Master Collins of Newbury I give for the use of the other two; And should it soo happen that either of the Girls should dye before age or marriage, that then the surviving sister should have her sisters loss, and in case of both their Mortallities before age or Marriage that then Master Collins gives the money to Ministers and Ministers Widows that hee and Master Woodbridge the minister is acquainted with[3] Item that one hundred pounds that I have upon Master John Juxon and

[1] Query—the shipwright and purveyor of wood to the Navy frequently mentioned in the 'Calendar' of Charles II. [1660–1667], who was termed Robert Magore?—G.

[2] Mr Mayor of the University Library, Cambridge, informs me that there was a 'printed catalogue' of Brooks's Library issued for the sale. I have not been so fortunate as to trace it.—G.

[3] Benjamin Woodbridge, M.A., was the venerable 'Ejected' of Newbury in 1662. See Palmer's 'Nonconformist's Memorial,' vol. i. pp. 290, 291.—G.

that is now in the hand of Master Shepheard be delivered into the hands of my honoured Father[1] Master Thomas Cartwright And that the money upon that Bond to paye in as he is able into the hands of my Father Master Thomas Cartwright And my Will is that this Money so paid in be by my Father Cartwright and my Couson Ford and my Couson Henry Goodman distributed amongst such ministers and ministers Widows as they think meete Item I give to my deare and honoured Mother Mistress Patience Cartwright my Sedan: And all the rest my real and personal Estate I give unto my deare and honoured Wife [in] whom God hath made all relations to meet in one.[2] I doo ordaine my said Wife to be sole Executrix of this my last Will and Testament and my honoured Father Master Thomas Cartwright the only Overseer and Assistant to my Executrix In witnesses hereof I putt my hand and seale the day and year under written—THOMAS BROOKS—March the twenty seventh one thousand six hundred and Eighty—Witness Edward Wylde—Henry Chandler—Tho. Cartwright.—

Probatum apud London fuit hujusmodi Testamentum coram Venerabili viro Domino Thoma Lyton Milite, Legum Doctore, Surrogato Venerabilis et egregij viri Domini Leolini Jenkins Militis, Legum etiam Doctoris, Curiæ Prærogativæ Cantuariensis Magistri Custodis sive Commissarij legitime constituti, decimo quinto die mensis Octobris Anno Domini Millesimo sexcentesimo Octogesimo; Juramento Patienciæ Brooks Relictæ dicti defuncti et Executricis in hujusmodi Testamento nominat; Cui commissa fuit Administratio omnium et singulorum bonorum, jurium et creditorum dicti defuncti, de bene et fideliter Administrando eadem ad sancta Dei Evangelia in debita Juris forma Jurat.

[1] Father-in-law.—G.

[2] *Mrs Brooks.* In accord with this loving mention of his second as before of his first wife, I add here the second 'Dedication' of Brooks's funeral sermon by John Reeve, M.A. [See *ante* page xxxv.] It is as follows:—

'To my honoured and worthy friend, Mrs Patience Brooks, the relict of that faithful pastor deceased, J. R. wisheth external, internal, and eternal happiness. The loss of a Christian friend is a great loss, much more of a Christian relation, and yet more of such a near relation, most of all of such a relation as was both a loving husband and a spiritual guide. These twisted sorrows, like a four-fold cord, are not easily broken loose from. I cannot but condole with you in your affliction, and pray for great supports for you under so great a trial. You have need of patience, and that patience itself should be more patient. It is a Father's rod in a Father's hand, and, though smarting, yet instructive and medicinal. Let not time but grace overcome your sorrow. Then will you approve yourself a Christian indeed, and do more than others. I need not use arguments to you that are so well skilled in your duty through grace. The indefatigable pains you have taken to write from your husband's mouth such large and frequent meditations and divine truths which were continually dropping from his lips under his weakness, they cannot but make an extraordinary deep impression of themselves upon your heart. You are much admired—I don't flatter you, but commend you—for your excessive love and tenderness to him under all those infirmities he so quietly submitted himself to, your cheerfulness under the hardest services, that none but yourself could have gone through with so much content to him; and your perseverance in it to the last, speaks a rejoicing to your conscience, and may be an alleviation of your grief. And it is to be observed that God foresaid what must be provided him, a loving wife, and a skilful and careful nurse, to be his consort and comfort. And now he is at rest, be you at rest; and let the love you bear him rejoice in his present discharge from sin and sorrow. We must not dispute Providence, but submit. I have been bold, without your leave, to affix your name to your husband's memorials. Accept the service as from one that honours you, and shall upon all occasions approve himself your very entire friend and servant in the Lord, JOHN REEVE.'

PRECIOUS REMEDIES.

NOTE.

The editions of 'Precious Remedies,' from its original publication in 1652, have been very numerous. The '2d' was issued in 1653, 'corrected and enlarged.' For many years reprints followed in rapid succession, more numerous indeed than at first sight appears, *e.g.* those of 1661 and 1669, though distinct impressions, being without designation as new editions. The '7th' appeared in 1671, the '8th' in 1676, and the '9th' in 1682. Our text is that of the '8th,' collated with the 1st and 2d. The '8th' was chosen, as having been the last during the author's own lifetime: but the collation was found necessary, inasmuch as Brooks, after a '2d' and usually '*corrected*' and '*enlarged*' edition, seems to have allowed his books to be reprinted without further oversight. Thus in our text (page 11) for 'Dan's adder' it misprints 'Pan's adder,' and so on in a multitude of like cases in all the after-editions of all his writings. Hence the later editions prove much more incorrect than the earlier, especially in the textual and marginal references, &c., and a recurrence to the original or early '*corrected*' edition often enables us to see the source of the error. The title-page of the '8th' edition is given below. G.

PRECIOUS

REMEDIES

AGAINST

Satan's Devices:

OR,

SALVE for { Believers and Unbelievers } SORES.

Being a Companion for those that are in Christ, or out of Christ; that slight or neglect Ordinances, under a pretence of living above them; that are growing (in Spirituals) or decaying; that are Tempted, or Deserted; Afflicted or opposed; that have Assurance, or that want Assurance, *&c.*

By *Thomas Brooks*, formerly a willing Servant unto God, and the Faith of his People, in the glorious Gospel of Christ at St. *Margarets Fishstreet-hill.*

The Eighth Edition.

Ephes. 6. 11.

Put on the whole Armour of God, that ye may be able to stand against the wiles of the Devil.

LONDON

Printed for *John Hancock*, and are to be sold at the three Bibles, the first shop in *Popes-head Alley*, next to *Cornhill.* 1676.

THE EPISTLE DEDICATORY.

To his most dear and precious ones, the sons and daughters of the Most High God, over whom the Holy Ghost hath made him a Watchman.

Beloved in our dearest Lord, Christ, the Scripture, your own hearts, and Satan's devices, are the four prime things that should be first and most studied and searched. If any cast off the study of these, they cannot be safe here, nor happy hereafter. It is my work as a Christian, but much more as I am a Watchman, to do my best to discover the fulness of Christ, the emptiness of the creature, and the snares of the great deceiver;[1] which I have endeavoured to do, in the following Discourse, according to that measure of grace which I have received from the Lord. God once accepted a handful of meal for a sacrifice [Lev. ii. 2, v. 12], and a gripe[2] of goat's hair for an oblation; and I know that you have not so 'learned the Father,' as to despise 'the day of small things' [Zech. iv. 10].

Beloved, Satan being fallen from light to darkness, from felicity to misery, from heaven to hell, from an angel to a devil, is so full of malice and envy that he will leave no means unattempted, whereby he may make all others eternally miserable with himself; he being shut out of heaven, and shut up 'under the chains of darkness till the judgment of the great day' [Jude 6], makes use of all his power and skill to bring all the sons of men into the same condition and condemnation, with himself. Satan hath cast such sinful seed into our souls, that now he can no sooner tempt, but we are ready to assent; he can no sooner have a plot upon us, but he makes a conquest of us. If he doth but shew men a little of the beauty and bravery[3] of the world, how ready are they to fall down and worship him!

Whatever sin the heart of man is most prone to, that the devil will help forward. If David be proud of his people, Satan will provoke him to number them, that he may be yet prouder, 2 Samuel xxiv.

If Peter be slavishly fearful, Satan will put him upon rebuking and

[1] If a minister had as many eyes as Argus, to watch, and as many heads as Typheus, to dispose, and as many hands as Briareus, to labour, he might find employment enough for them all. [(1.) Argus, surnamed Panoptes, all-seeing. Cf. Æschylus, *Prom.* Apollod. Ov. *ll. cc.* (2.) *Typheus*, *i.e.* Typhœus. Cf. Pindar. *Pyth.* i. 31; viii. 21; Ol. iv. 12. (3.) *Briareus*, *i.e.* Ægæon. Cf. Apollod. i. 9, § 1; Hesiod, Theog. 957.—G.]

[2] Gripe or 'handful.' Cf. Exod. xxv. 4; xxxv. 26.—G.

[3] Finery.—G.

denying of Christ, to save his own skin, Mat. xvi. 22, chap. xxvi. 69–75. If Ahab's prophets be given to flatter, the devil will straightway become a lying spirit in the mouths of four hundred of them, and they shall flatter Ahab to his ruin, 1 Kings xxii. If Judas will be a traitor, Satan will quickly enter into his heart, and make him sell his master for money, which some heathens would never have done, John xiii. 2. If Ananias will lie for advantage, Satan will fill his heart that he may lie, with a witness, to the Holy Ghost, Acts v. 3. Satan loves to sail with the wind, and to suit men's temptations to their conditions and inclinations. If they be in prosperity, he will tempt them to deny God, Prov. xxx. 9; if they be in adversity, he will tempt them to distrust God; if their knowledge be weak, he will tempt them to have low thoughts of God; if their conscience be tender, he will tempt to scrupulosity; if large, to carnal security; if bold-spirited, he will tempt to presumption; if timorous, to desperation; if flexible, to inconstancy; if stiff, to impenitency, &c.

From the power, malice, and skill of Satan, doth proceed all the soul-killing plots, devices, stratagems, and machinations, that be in the world. Several devices he hath to draw souls to sin, and several plots he hath to keep souls from all holy and heavenly services, and several stratagems he hath to keep souls in a mourning, staggering, doubting, and questioning condition.

He hath several devices to destroy the great and honourable, the wise and learned, the blind and ignorant, the rich and the poor, the real and the nominal saints.

One while he will restrain from tempting, that we may think ourselves secure, and neglect our watch; another while he will seem to fly, that he may make us proud of the victory; one while he will fix men's eyes more on others' sins than their own, that he may puff them up; another while he may fix their eyes more on others' graces than their own, that he may overwhelm them, &c.

A man may as well tell the stars, and number the sands of the sea, as reckon up all the Devices of Satan; yet those which are most considerable, and by which he doth most mischief to the precious souls of men, are in the following Treatise discovered, and the Remedies against them prescribed.

Beloved, I think it necessary to give you and the world a faithful account of the reasons moving me to appear in print, in these days, wherein we may say, there was never more writing and yet never less practising, and they are these that follow, &c.

Reason 1. *First,* Because Satan hath a greater influence upon men, and higher advantages over them (having the wind and the hill, as it were), than they think he hath, and the knowledge of his high advantage, is the highway to disappoint him, and to render the soul strong in resisting, and happy in conquering, &c.

Reason 2. Your importunity, and the importunity of many other 'precious sons of Sion,' Lam. iv. 2, hath after much striving with God, my own heart, and others, made a conquest of me, and forced me to do that at last, which at first was not a little contrary to my inclination and resolution, &c.

Reason 3. The strange opposition that I met with from Satan, in the study of this following discourse, hath put an edge upon my spirit, knowing that Satan strives mightily to keep those things from seeing the light, that tend eminently to shake and break his kingdom of darkness, and to lift up the kingdom and glory of the Lord Jesus Christ, in the souls and lives of the children of men, &c.[1]

Reason 4. Its exceeding usefulness to all sorts, ranks, and conditions of men in the world. Here you have salve for every sore, and a plaster for every wound, and a remedy against every disease, especially against those that tend most to the undoing of souls, and the ruin of the State, &c.

Reason 5. I know not of any one or other that have writ of this subject; all that ever I have seen have only touched upon this string, which hath been no small provocation to me, to attempt to do something this way, that others, that have better heads and hearts, may be the more stirred to improve their talents in a further discovery of Satan's *Devices*, and in making known of such choice *Remedies*, as may enable the souls of men to triumph over all his plots and stratagems,[2] &c.

Reason 6. I have many precious friends in several countries, who are not a little desirous that my pen may reach them, now my voice cannot. I have formerly been, by the help of the mighty God of Jacob, a weak instrument of good to them, and cannot but hope and believe that the Lord will also bless these labours to them; they being, in part, the fruit of their desires and prayers, &c.

Reason 7. Lastly, Not knowing how soon my glass may be out, and how soon I may be cut off by a hand of death, from all opportunities of doing further service for Christ or your souls in this world, I was willing to sow a little handful of spiritual seed among you; that so, when I put off this earthly tabernacle, my love to you, and that dear remembrance of you, which I have in my soul, may strongly engage your minds and spirits to make this book your companion, and under all external or internal changes, to make use of this heavenly salve, which I hope will, by the blessing of the Lord, be as effectual for the healing of all your wounds, as their looking up to the brazen serpent was effectual to heal theirs that were bit and stung with fiery serpents. I shall leave this book with you as a legacy of my dearest love, desiring the Lord to make it a far greater and sweeter legacy than all those carnal legacies are that are left by the high and mighty ones of the earth to their nearest and dearest relations, &c.

Beloved, I would not have affection carry my pen too much beyond my intention. Therefore, only give me leave to signify my desires for you, and my desires to you, and I shall draw to a close.

My desires for you are, 'That he would grant you, according to the riches of his glory, to be strengthened with might by his Spirit in the

[1] Pirates make the strongest and the hottest opposition against those vessels that are most richly laden. So doth Satan, that arch-pirate, against those truths that have most of God, Christ, and heaven in them.

[2] Brooks overlooked the remarkable '*Stratagema*' of Acontius, which, previous to 'Precious Remedies,' had been translated by no less a man than John Goodwin into English, and by others into almost every European language.—G.

inner man; that Christ may dwell in your hearts by faith, that ye, being rooted and grounded in love, may be able to comprehend with all saints what is the breadth, and length, and depth, and height; and to know the love of Christ that passeth knowledge, that ye might be filled with all the fulness of God,' Eph. iii. 16–19; and 'That ye might walk worthy of the Lord unto all pleasing, being fruitful in every good work, and increased in the knowledge of God, strengthened with all might according to his glorious power, unto all patience and long-suffering, with joyfulness,' Col. i. 10, 11; 'That ye do no evil,' 2 Cor. xiii. 7; 'That your love may abound yet more and more in knowledge, and in all judgment;' 'That ye may approve things that are excellent, that ye may be sincere, and without offence till the day of Christ,' Philip. i. 27, iv. 1; and that 'our God would count you worthy of this calling, and fulfil all the good pleasure of his goodness, and the work of faith with power;' 'That the name of our Lord Jesus Christ may be glorified in you, and ye in him, according to the grace of our God and the Lord Jesus Christ,' 2 Thes. i. 11, 12. And that you may be eminent in sanctity, sanctity being Zion's glory, Ps. xciii. 5; that your hearts may be kept upright, your judgments sound, and your lives unblameable. That as ye are now 'my joy,' so in the day of Christ you may be 'my crown;' that I may see my labours in your lives; that your conversation may not be earthly, when the things you hear are heavenly; but that it may be 'as becomes the gospel,' Philip. i. 9, 10. That as the fishes which live in the salt sea yet are fresh, so you, though you live in an uncharitable world, may yet be charitable and loving; That ye may, like the bee, suck honey out of every flower; that ye may shine in a sea of troubles, as the pearl shines in the sky, though it grows in the sea; that in all your trials you may be like the stone in Thracia, that neither burneth in the fire nor sinketh in the water; That ye may be like the heavens, excellent in substance and beautiful in appearance; that so you may meet me with joy in that day wherein Christ shall say to his Father, 'Lo, here am I, and the children that thou hast given me,' Isa. viii. 18.

My desires to you are, That you would make it your business to study Christ, his word, your own hearts, Satan's plots, and eternity, more than ever; That ye would endeavour more to be inwardly sincere than outwardly glorious; to live, than to have a name to live; That ye would labour with all your might to be thankful under mercies, and faithful in your places, and humble under divine appearances, and fruitful under precious ordinances; That as your means and mercies are greater than others', so your account before God may not prove a worse than others'; That ye would pray for me, who am not worthy to be named among the saints, that I may be a precious instrument in the hand of Christ to bring in many souls unto him, and to build up those that are brought in in their most holy faith; and 'that utterance may be given to me, that I may make known all the will of God,' Eph. vi. 19; That I may be sincere, faithful, frequent, fervent, and constant in the work of the Lord, and that my labour be not in vain in the Lord; that my labours may be accepted in the Lord and his saints, and I may daily see the travail of my soul, &c.

But, above all, pray for me, that I may more and more find the power and sweet of those things upon my own heart, that I give out to you and others; that my soul be so visited with strength from on high, that I may live up fully and constantly to those truths that I hold forth to the world; and that I may be both in life and doctrine 'a burning and a shining light,' that so, when the Lord Jesus shall appear, 'I may receive a crown of glory which he shall give to me in that day, and not only to me, but to all that love his appearance,' &c., John v. 35 and 2 Tim. i. 8.

For a close, remember this, that your life is short, your duties many, your assistance great, and your reward sure; therefore faint not, hold on and hold up, in ways of well-doing, and heaven shall make amends for all.

I shall now take leave of you, when my heart hath by my hand subscribed, that I am,

Your loving pastor under Christ, according to all pastoral affections and engagements in our dearest Lord,

THOMAS BROOKS.

A WORD TO THE READER.

Dear Friend!—Solomon bids us buy the truth (Prov. xxiii. 23), but doth not tell us what it must cost, because we must get it though it be never so dear. We must love it both shining and scorching.[1] Every parcel of truth is precious, as the filings of gold; we must either live with it, or die for it. As Ruth said to Naomi, 'Whither thou goest I will go, and where thou lodgest I will lodge, and nothing but death shall part thee and me,' Ruth i. 16, 17; so must gracious spirits say, Where truth goes I will go, and where truth lodges I will lodge, and nothing but death shall part me and truth.[2] A man may lawfully sell his house, land, and jewels, but truth is a jewel that exceeds all price, and must not be sold; it is our heritage: 'Thy testimonies have I taken as an heritage for ever,' Ps. cxix. 111. It is a legacy that our forefathers have bought with their bloods, which should make us willing to lay down anything, and to lay out anything, that we may, with the wise merchant in the Gospel (Mat. xiii. 45), purchase this precious pearl, which is more worth than heaven and earth, and which will make a man live happily, die comfortably, and reign eternally.[3]

And now, if thou pleasest, read the work, and receive this counsel from me.

First, Thou must know that every man cannot be excellent, that yet may be useful. An iron key may unlock the door of a golden treasure, yea (*ferrum potest quod aurum non potest*), iron can do some things that gold cannot, &c.

Secondly, Remember, it is not hasty reading, but serious meditating upon holy and heavenly truths, that makes them prove sweet and profitable to the soul.[4] It is not the bee's touching of the flower that gathers honey, but her abiding for a time upon the flower that draws out the sweet. It is not he that reads most, but he that meditates most, that will prove the choicest, sweetest, wisest, and strongest Christian, &c.

Thirdly, Know that it is not the knowing, nor the talking, nor the

[1] Multi amant veritatem lucentem, oderunt redarguentem.
[2] Si veritas est causa discordiæ, mori possum, tacere non possum.—*St Jerome.*
[3] Veritas vincit. Truth at last triumphs.
[4] It is a law among the Persees [Parsees] in India, to use premeditation in what they are to do, that if it be bad, to reject it, if good, to act it.

reading man, but the doing man, that at last will be found the happiest man.[1] "If you know these things, blessed and happy are you if you do them." "Not every one that saith, Lord, Lord, shall enter into the kingdom of heaven, but he that doth the will of my Father that is in heaven," John xvi. 14, Mat. vii. 21. Judas called Christ Lord, Lord, and yet betrayed him, and is gone to his place. Ah! how many Judases have we in these days, that kiss Christ, and yet betray Christ; that in their words profess him, but in their works deny him; that bow their knee to him, and yet in their hearts despise him; that call him Jesus, and yet will not obey him for their Lord.

Reader, If it be not strong upon thy heart to practise what thou readest, to what end dost thou read? To increase thy own condemnation?[2] If thy light and knowledge be not turned into practice, the more knowing man thou art, the more miserable man thou wilt be in the day of recompense; thy light and knowledge will more torment thee than all the devils in hell. Thy knowledge will be that rod that will eternally lash thee, and that scorpion that will for ever bite thee, and that worm that will everlastingly gnaw thee; therefore read, and labour to know, that thou mayest do, or else thou art undone for ever.[3] When Demosthenes was asked, what was the first part of an orator, what the second, what the third? he answered, Action; the same may I say. If any should ask me, what is the first, the second, the third part of a Christian? I must answer, Action; as that man that reads that he may know, and that labours to know that he may do, will have two heavens—a heaven of joy, peace, and comfort on earth, and a heaven of glory and happiness after death.

Fourthly and lastly, If in thy reading thou wilt cast a serious eye upon the margent,[4] thou wilt find many sweet and precious notes, that will oftentimes give light to the things thou readest, and pay thee for thy pains with much comfort and profit. So desiring that thou mayest find as much sweetness and advantage in reading this Treatise as I have found, by the over-shadowings of heaven, in the studying and writing of it, I recommend thee 'to God, and to the word of his grace, which is able to build thee up, and to give thee an inheritance among them which are sanctified,' Acts xx. 32. And rest, reader,

Thy soul's servant in every office of the gospel,

THOMAS BROOKS.

[1] It was a good saying of Justin Martyr, *Non in verbis, sed in factis res nostræ religionis consistunt.*—[Apolog. 22.—G.]

[2] The heathen philosopher, Seneca, liked not such as are *semper victuri*, always about to live, but never begin.—[*De vita beata, et alibi.*—G.]

[3] God loves, saith Luther, *curistas*, not *quæristas*, the runner, not the questioner. . . . Pacunius hath an elegant saying: I hate, saith he, the men that are idle in deed, and philosophical in word, &c.

[4] Margin; transferred here and throughout in our edition to the foot of page.—G.

PRECIOUS REMEDIES AGAINST SATAN'S DEVICES.

Lest Satan should get an advantage of us: for we are not ignorant of his devices.—2 Cor. II. 11.

In this fifth verse, the apostle shews, that the incestuous person had by his incest sadded those precious souls that God would not have sadded.[1] Souls that walk sinfully are Hazaels to the godly, 2 Kings viii. 12, *et seq.*, and draw many sighs and tears from them. Jeremiah weeps in secret for Judah's sins, Jer. ix. 1; and Paul cannot speak of the belly-gods with dry eyes, Philip. iii. 18, 19. And Lot's righteous soul was burdened, vexed, and racked by the filthy Sodomites, 2 Peter ii. 7, 8.[2] Every sinful Sodomite was a Hazael to his eyes, a Hadad-rimmon to his heart, Zech. xii. 11. Gracious souls use to mourn for other men's sins as well as their own, and for their souls and sins who make a mock of sin, and a jest of damning their own souls. Guilt or grief is all that gracious souls get by communion with vain souls, Ps. cxix. 136, 158.

In the 6th verse, he shews that the punishment that was inflicted upon the incestuous person was sufficient, and therefore they should not refuse to receive him who had repented and sorrowed for his former faults and follies. It is not for the honour of Christ, the credit of the gospel, nor the good of souls, for professors to be like those bloody wretches, that burnt some that recanted at the stake, saying, 'That they would send them into another world whiles they were in a good mind.'[3]

In the 7th, 8th, 9th, and 10th verses, the apostle stirs up the church to forgive him, to comfort him, and to confirm their love towards him, lest he should be 'swallowed up with over much sorrow,' Satan going about to mix the detestable darnel, Mat. xiii. 25, of desperation with the godly sorrow of a pure penitent heart. It was a sweet saying of one, 'Let a man grieve for his sin, and then joy for his grief.'[4] That sorrow for sin that keeps the soul from looking towards the mercy-

[1] 'Saddened.'—G.

[2] καταπονούμενον, ἐβασάνιζεν.

[3] [Foxe.] Acts and Mon. fol. 1392 [Cf. Under Cranmer and Recantation, ed. 1631. Vol. iii. 667, 668.—G.]

[4] Doleat et de dolore gaudeat.—*Jerome.*

seat, and that keeps Christ and the soul asunder, or that shall render the soul unfit for the communion of saints, is a sinful sorrow.

In the 11th verse, he lays down another reason to work them to shew pity and mercy to the penitent sinner, that was mourning and groaning under his sin and misery; *i. e.* lest Satan should get an advantage of us: for we are not ignorant of his devices. A little for the opening of the words

Lest Satan should get an *advantage* of us; lest Satan over-reach us. The Greek word πλεονεκτηθῶμεν, signifieth to have more than belongs to one. The comparison is taken from the greedy merchant, that seeketh and taketh all opportunities to beguile and deceive others. Satan is that wily merchant, that devoureth, not widows' houses, but most men's souls.

'We are not ignorant of Satan's *devices*,' or plots, or machinations, or stratagems, Νοήματα. He is but a titular Christian that hath not personal experience of Satan's stratagems, his set and composed machinations, his artificially moulded methods, his plots, darts, depths, whereby he outwitted our first parents, and fits us a pennyworth still, as he sees reason.

The main observation that I shall draw from these words is this:

Doct. That Satan hath his several devices to deceive, entangle, and undo the souls of men.

I shall, 1. Prove the point.

2. Shew you his several devices; and,

3. The remedies against his devices.

4. How it comes to pass that he hath so many several devices to deceive, entangle, and undo the souls of men.

5. I shall lay down some propositions concerning Satan's devices.

I. For the *proof of the point*, take these few Scriptures: Eph. vi. 11, 'Put on the whole armour of God, that ye may be able to stand against the *wiles* of the devil.' The Greek word that is here rendered 'wiles,' is a notable emphatical word.

(1.) It signifies such snares as are laid behind one, such treacheries as come upon one's back at unawares. It notes the methods or waylayings of that old subtle serpent, who, like Dan's adder 'in the path,' biteth the heels of passengers, and thereby transfuseth his venom to the head and heart.[1] The word Μεθοδείας signifies an ambushment or stratagem of war, whereby the enemy sets upon a man *ex insidiis*, at unawares.[2]

(2.) It signifies such snares as are set to catch one in one's road. A man walks in his road, and thinks not of it; on the sudden he is catched by thieves, or falls into a pit, &c.

(3.) It signifies such as are purposely, artificially, and craftily set for the taking the prey at the greatest advantage that can be. The Greek μεθοδείας, being derived from μετὰ and ὁδὸς, signifies properly a waylaying, circumvention, or going about, as they do which seek after

[1] Cf. Genesis xlix. 17. Misprinted originally 'Pan's,' and so has been usually transmitted.—G.

[2] Spelled 'anawares,' which is to be noted along with the earlier form 'anonywar.' Cf. Richardson *sub voce*.—G.

their prey. Julian, by his craft, drew more from the faith than all his persecuting predecessors could do by their cruelty. So doth Satan more hurt in his sheep's skin than by roaring like a lion.

Take one scripture more for the proof of the point, and that is in 2 Tim. ii. 26, 'And that they might recover themselves out of the snare of the devil, who are taken captive by him at his will.' The Greek word that is here rendered recover themselves, Ἀνανήψωσιν, signifies to awaken themselves. The apostle alludeth to one that is asleep or drunk, who is to be awakened and restored to his senses; and the Greek word that is here rendered 'taken captive,' signifies to be taken alive, ἐζωγρημένοι. The word is properly a warlike word, and signifies to be taken alive, as soldiers are taken alive in the wars, or as birds are taken alive and ensnared in the fowler's net. Satan hath snares for the wise and snares for the simple; snares for hypocrites, and snares for the upright; snares for generous souls, and snares for timorous souls; snares for the rich, and snares for the poor; snares for the aged, and snares for youth, &c. Happy are those souls that are not taken and held in the snares that he hath laid![1]

Take one proof more, and then I will proceed to the opening of the point, and that is in Rev. ii. 24, 'But unto you I say, and unto the rest in Thyatira, as many as have not this doctrine, and which have not known the depths of Satan, as they speak, I will put upon you no other burden but to hold fast till I come.' Those poor souls called their opinions the depths of God, when indeed they were the depths of Satan. You call your opinions depths, and so they are, but they are such depths as Satan hath brought out of hell. They are the whisperings and hissings of that serpent, not the inspirations of God.

II. Now, the second thing that I am to shew you is, his *several devices;* and herein I shall first shew you the several devices that he hath to draw the soul to sin. I shall instance in these twelve, which may bespeak our most serious consideration.

His first device to draw the soul to sin is,

Device (1). *To present the bait and hide the hook;* to present the golden cup, and hide the poison; to present the sweet, the pleasure, and the profit that may flow in upon the soul by yielding to sin, and by hiding from the soul the wrath and misery that will certainly follow the committing of sin. By this device he took our first parents: Gen. iii. 4, 5, 'And the serpent said unto the woman, Ye shall not surely die: for God doth know, that in the day ye eat thereof, then your eyes shall be opened; and ye shall be as gods, knowing good and evil.' Your eyes shall be opened, and you shall be as gods! Here is the bait, the sweet, the pleasure, the profit. Oh, but he hides the hook,—the shame, the wrath, and the loss that would certainly follow![2]

There is an opening of the eyes of the mind to contemplation and joy, and there is an opening of the eyes of the body to shame and

[1] Cf. [Daniel] Pareus *in loc.* 1 Tim. iv. 1. [Works, 3 vols. folio, 1647.—G.]

[2] So to reduce Dr [Rowland] Taylor, martyr, they promised him not only his pardon, but a bishopric. Acts & Mon. fol. i. 86. [Foxe. ed. 1631. Vol. iii. p. 176.—G.] . . . . Inest peccatum cum delectaris: regnat si consentis. [Augustine in Ps. l.—G.]

confusion. He promiseth them the former, but intends the latter, and so cheats them—giving them an apple in exchange for a paradise, as he deals by thousands now-a-days. Satan with ease puts fallacies upon us by his golden baits, and then he leads us and leaves us in a fool's paradise. He promises the soul honour, pleasure, profit, &c., but pays the soul with the greatest contempt, shame, and loss that can be. By a golden bait he laboured to catch Christ, Mat. iv. 8, 9. He shews him the beauty and the bravery of a bewitching world, which doubtless would have taken many a carnal heart; but here the devil's fire fell upon wet tinder, and therefore took not. These tempting objects did not at all win upon his affections, nor dazzle his eyes, though many have eternally died of the wound of the eye, and fallen for ever by this vile strumpet the world, who, by laying forth her two fair breasts of profit and pleasure, hath wounded their souls, and cast them down into utter perdition. She hath, by the glistering of her pomp and preferment, slain millions; as the serpent Scytale,[1] which, when she cannot overtake the fleeing passengers, doth, with her beautiful colours, astonish and amaze them, so that they have no power to pass away till she have stung them to death. Adversity hath slain her thousand, but prosperity her ten thousand.[2]

Now, the remedies against this device of the devil are these:

Remedy (1). *First, Keep at the greatest distance from sin, and from playing with the golden bait that Satan holds forth to catch you;* for this you have Rom. xii. 9, 'Abhor that which is evil, cleave to that which is good.' When we meet with anything extremely evil and contrary to us, nature abhors it, and retires as far as it can from it. The Greek word that is there rendered 'abhor,' is very significant; it signifies to hate it as hell itself, to hate it with horror.[3]

Anselm used to say, 'That if he should see the shame of sin on the one hand, and the pains of hell on the other, and must of necessity choose one, he would rather be thrust into hell without sin, than to go into heaven with sin,' so great was his hatred and detestation of sin. It is our wisest and our safest course to stand at the farthest distance from sin; not to go near the house of the harlot, but to fly from all appearance of evil, Prov. v. 8, 1 Thes. v. 22. The best course to prevent falling into the pit, is to keep at the greatest distance; he that will be so bold as to attempt to dance upon the brink of the pit, may find by woful experience that it is a righteous thing with God that he should fall into the pit. Joseph keeps at a distance from sin, and from playing with Satan's golden baits, and stands. David draws near, and plays with the bait, and falls, and swallows bait and hook with a witness. David comes near the snare, and is taken in it, to

[1] Scytale: Solinus, c. xxvii. and xl.—G.

This world at last shall be burnt for a witch, saith one. . . . Multi amando res noxias sunt miseri, habendo miseriores.—*Aug*[*ustine*] in Ps xvi. Many are miserable by loving hurtful things, but they are more miserable by having them. . . . Men had need pray with Bernard, Da Domine ut sic possideamus temporalia, ut non perdamus æterna. Grant us, Lord, that we may so partake of temporal felicity, that we may not lose eternal.

[3] *ἀποστυγοῦντες.* The simple verb imports extreme detestation, which is aggravated by the composition.—*Chrys*[*ostom*].

the breaking of his bones, the wounding of his conscience, and the loss of his God.[1]

Sin is a plague, yea, the greatest and most infectious plague in the world; and yet, ah! how few are there that tremble at it, that keep at a distance from it! 1 Cor. v. 6, 'Know ye not that a little leaven leaveneth the whole lump?' As soon as one sin had seized upon Adam's heart, all sin entered into his soul and overspread it. How hath Adam's one sin spread over all mankind! Rom. v. 12, 'Wherefore as by one man sin entered into the world, and death by sin, and so death passed upon all men, for that all have sinned.' Ah, how doth the father's sin infect the child, the husband's infect the wife, the master's the servant! The sin that is in one man's heart is able to infect a whole world, it is of such a spreading and infectious nature.[2]

The story of the Italian, who first made his enemy deny God, and then stabbed him, and so at once murdered both body and soul,[3] declares the perfect malignity of sin; and oh! that what hath been spoken upon this head may prevail with you, to stand at a distance from sin!

The second remedy is,

Remedy (2). To consider, *That sin is but a bitter sweet.* That seeming sweet that is in sin will quickly vanish, and lasting shame, sorrow, horror, and terror will come in the room thereof: Job xx. 12–14, 'Though wickedness be sweet in his mouth, though he hide it under his tongue, though he spare it, and forsake it not, but keep it still within his mouth, yet his meat in his bowels is turned, it is the gall of asps within him.' Forbidden profits and pleasures are most pleasing to vain men, who count madness mirth, &c. Many long to be meddling with the murdering morsels of sin, which nourish not, but rent and consume the belly, the soul, that receives them. Many eat that on earth that they digest in hell. Sin's murdering morsels will deceive those that devour them. Adam's apple was a bitter sweet; Esau's mess was a bitter sweet; the Israelites' quails a bitter sweet; Jonathan's honey a bitter sweet; and Adonijah's dainties a bitter sweet. After the meal is ended, then comes the reckoning. Men must not think to dance and dine with the devil, and then to sup with Abraham, Isaac, and Jacob in the kingdom of heaven; to feed upon the poison of asps, and yet that the viper's tongue should not slay them.[4]

When the asp stings a man, it doth first tickle him so as it makes him laugh, till the poison, by little and little, gets to the heart, and

[1] It was a divine saying of a heathen, 'That if there were no God to punish him, no devil to torment him, no hell to burn him, no man to see him, yet would he not sin for the ugliness and filthiness of sin, and the grief of his own conscience.'—*Seneca.* [De Beneficiis, l. iv. 28, and often in his 'Letters.' Cf. *sub Conscientia.*—G.]

[2] Sin is like those diseases that are called by physicians, *corruptio totius substantiæ.*

[3] Told in Wanley's *Wonders*, with authorities, b. iv. c xii.—G.

[4] When the golden bait is set forth to catch us, we must say as Demosthenes the orator did of the beautiful Lais, when he was asked an excessive sum of money to behold her, 'I will not buy repentance so dear;' I am not so ill a merchant as to sell eternals for temporals. If intemperance could afford more pleasure than temperance Heliogabalus should have been more happy than Adam in paradise.—*Plutarch.*

then it pains him more than ever it delighted him. So doth sin; it may please a little at first, but it will pain the soul with a witness at last; yea, if there were the least real delight in sin, there could be no perfect hell, where men shall most perfectly be tormented with their sin.

The third remedy against this device of Satan is,

Remedy (3). Solemnly to consider, *That sin will usher in the greatest and the saddest losses that can be upon our souls.* It will usher in the loss of that divine favour that is better than life, and the loss of that joy that is unspeakable and full of glory, and the loss of that peace that passeth understanding, and the loss of those divine influences by which the soul hath been refreshed, quickened, raised, strengthened, and gladded, and the loss of many outward desirable mercies, which otherwise the soul might have enjoyed.[1]

It was a sound and savoury reply of an English captain at the loss of Calais, when a proud Frenchman scornfully demanded, When will you fetch Calais again, replied, When your sins shall weigh down ours.[2] Ah, England! my constant prayer for thee is, that thou mayest not sin away thy mercies into their hands that cannot call mercy mercy, and that would joy in nothing more than to see thy sorrow and misery, and to see that hand to make thee naked, that hath clothed thee with much mercy and glory.

The fourth remedy against this device of Satan is,

Remedy (4). Seriously to consider, *That sin is of a very deceitful and bewitching nature.*[3] Sin is from the greatest deceiver, it is a child of his own begetting, it is the ground of all the deceit in the world, and it is in its own nature exceeding deceitful. Heb. iii. 13, 'But exhort one another daily, while it is called To-day, lest any of you be hardened through the deceitfulness of sin.' It will kiss the soul, and pretend fair to the soul, and yet betray the soul for ever. It will with Delilah smile upon us, that it may betray us into the hands of the devil, as she did Samson into the hands of the Philistines. Sin gives Satan a power over us, and an advantage to accuse us and to lay claim to us, as those that wear his badge; it is of a very bewitching nature, it bewitches the soul, where it is upon the throne, that the soul cannot leave it, though it perish eternally by it.[4] Sin so bewitches the soul, that it makes the soul call evil good, and good evil; bitter sweet and sweet bitter, light darkness and darkness light; and a soul thus bewitched with sin will stand it out to the death, at the sword's point with God; let God strike and wound, and cut to the very bone, yet the bewitched soul cares not, fears not, but will still hold on in a course of wickedness, as you may see in Pharaoh, Balaam, and Judas. Tell the bewitched soul that sin is a viper that will certainly kill when it is not killed, that sin often kills

[1] Isa. lix. 2, Ps. li. 12, Isa. lix. 8, 2 Chron. xv. 3, 4, Jer. xvii. 18, Jer. v. 2.

[2] Quando peccata vestra erunt nostris graviora.

[3] In Sardis there grew an herb, called *Appium Sardis*, that would make a man lie laughing when he was deadly sick; such is the operation of sin.

[4] Which occasioned Chrysostom to say, when Eudoxia the empress threatened him, Go tell her, 'Nil nisi peccatum timeo,' I fear nothing but sin.

secretly, insensibly, eternally, yet the bewitched soul cannot, nor will not, cease from sin.

When the physicians told Theotimus that except he did abstain from drunkenness and uncleanness, &c., he would lose his eyes, his heart was so bewitched to his sins, that he answers, 'Then farewell sweet light;'[1] he had rather lose his eyes than leave his sin. So a man bewitched with sin had rather lose God, Christ, heaven, and his own soul than part with his sin. Oh, therefore, for ever take heed of playing or nibbling at Satan's golden baits.

The second device of Satan to draw the soul to sin is,

Device (2). *By painting sin with virtue's colours.* Satan knows that if he should present sin in its own nature and dress, the soul would rather fly from it than yield to it; and therefore he presents it unto us, not in its own proper colours, but painted and gilded over with the name and show of virtue, that we may the more easily be overcome by it, and take the more pleasure in committing of it. Pride, he presents to the soul under the name and notion of neatness and cleanliness, and covetousness (which the apostle condemns for idolatry) to be but good husbandry;[2] and drunkenness to be good fellowship, and riotousness under the name and notion of liberality, and wantonness as a trick of youth, &c.

Now, the remedies against this device of Satan are these,

Remedy (1). *First,* consider, *That sin is never a whit the less filthy, vile, and abominable, by its being coloured and painted with virtue's colours.* A poisonous pill is never a whit the less poisonous because it is gilded over with gold; nor a wolf is never a whit the less a wolf because he hath put on a sheep's skin; nor the devil is never a whit the less a devil because he appears sometimes like an angel of light. So neither is sin any whit the less filthy and abominable by its being painted over with virtue's colours.

The second remedy against this device of Satan is,

Remedy (2). *That the more sin is painted forth under the colour of virtue, the more dangerous it is to the souls of men.* This we see evident in these days, by those very many souls that are turned out of the way that is holy—and in which their souls have had sweet and glorious communion with God—into ways of highest vanity and folly, by Satan's neat[3] colouring over of sin, and painting forth vice under the name and colour of virtue. This is so notoriously known that I need but name it. The most dangerous vermin is too often to be found under the fairest and sweetest flowers, and the fairest glove is often drawn upon the foulest hand, and the richest robes are often put upon the filthiest bodies. So are the fairest and sweetest names upon the greatest and the most horrible vices and errors that be in the world. Ah! that we had not too many sad proofs of this amongst us.[4]

[1] Vale lumen amicum.—*Ambrose.*

[2] 'Thrift,' 'economy.'—G.

[3] Careful, clever.—G.

[4] Turpiora sunt vitia quæ virtutum specie celantur.—*Jer*[*ome.*] . . . . Thus the *Illuminates* (as they called themselves) a pestilent sect in Arragon, professing and affecting in themselves a kind of angelic purity, fell suddenly to the justifying of bestiality, as many have done in these days.

The third remedy against this device of Satan is,

Remedy (3). *To look on sin with that eye [with] which within a few hours we shall see it.* Ah, souls! when you shall lie upon a dying bed, and stand before a judgment-seat, sin shall be unmasked, and its dress and robes shall then be taken off, and then it shall appear more vile, filthy, and terrible than hell itself; then, that which formerly appeared most sweet will appear most bitter, and that which appeared most beautiful will appear most ugly, and that which appeared most delightful will then appear most dreadful to the soul.[1] Ah, the shame, the pain, the gall, the bitterness, the horror, the hell that the sight of sin, when its dress is taken off, will raise in poor souls! Sin will surely prove evil and bitter to the soul when its robes are taken off. A man may have the stone who feels no fit of it. Conscience will work at last, though for the present one may feel no fit of accusation. Laban shewed himself at parting. Sin will be bitterness in the latter end, when it shall appear to the soul in its own filthy nature. The devil deals with men as the panther doth with beasts; he hides his deformed head till his sweet scent hath drawn them into his danger. Till we have sinned, Satan is a parasite; when we have sinned, he is a tyrant.[2] O souls! the day is at hand when the devil will pull off the paint and garnish that he hath put upon sin, and present that monster, sin, in such a monstrous shape to your souls, that will cause your thoughts to be troubled, your countenance to be changed, the joints of your loins to be loosed, and your knees to be dashed one against another, and your hearts to be so terrified, that you will be ready, with Ahithophel and Judas,[3] to strangle and hang your bodies on earth, and your souls in hell, if the Lord hath not more mercy on you than he had on them. Oh! therefore, look upon sin now as you must look upon it to all eternity, and as God, conscience, and Satan will present it to you another day!

The fourth remedy against this device of Satan is,

Remedy (4.) Seriously to consider, *That even those very sins that Satan paints, and puts new names and colours upon, cost the best blood, the noblest blood, the life-blood, the heart-blood of the Lord Jesus.*[4] That Christ should come from the eternal bosom of his Father to a region of sorrow and death; that God should be manifested in the flesh, the Creator made a creature; that he that was clothed with glory should be wrapped with rags of flesh; he that filled heaven and earth with his glory should be cradled in a manger; that the power of God should fly from weak man, the God of Israel into Egypt; that the God of the law should be subject to the law, the God of the circumcision circumcised, the God that made the heavens

[1] Tacitus speaks of Tiberius, that when his sins did appear in their own colours, they did so terrify and torment him that he protested to the Senate that he suffered daily. [*Ann.* vi. 51.—G.]

[2] Satan, that now allures thee to sin, will ere long make thee to see that *peccatum est deicidium*, sin is a murdering of God; and this will make thee murder two at once, thy soul and thy body, unless the Lord in mercy holds thy hands.

[3] 2 Sam. xvii. 23, and Mat. xxvii. 5.—G.

[4] Una guttula plus valet quam cœlum et terra.—*Luther; i.e.* one little drop (speaking of the blood of Christ) is more worth than heaven and earth.

working at Joseph's homely trade; that he that binds the devils in chains should be tempted; that he, whose is the world, and the fulness thereof, should hunger and thirst; that the God of strength should be weary, the Judge of all flesh condemned, the God of life put to death; that he that is one with his Father should cry out of misery, 'My God, my God, why hast thou forsaken me?' Mat. xxvii. 46; that he that had the keys of hell and death at his girdle should lie imprisoned in the sepulchre of another, having in his lifetime nowhere to lay his head, nor after death to lay his body; that that head, before which the angels do cast down their crowns, should be crowned with thorns, and those eyes, purer than the sun, put out by the darkness of death; those ears, which hear nothing but hallelujahs of saints and angels, to hear the blasphemies of the multitude; that face, that was fairer than the sons of men, to be spit on by those beastly wretched Jews; that mouth and tongue, that spake as never man spake, accused for blasphemy; those hands, that freely swayed the sceptre of heaven, nailed to the cross; those feet, 'like unto fine brass,' nailed to the cross for man's sins; each sense annoyed: his feeling or touching, with a spear and nails; his smell, with stinking flavour, being crucified about Golgotha, the place of skulls; his taste, with vinegar and gall; his hearing, with reproaches, and sight of his mother and disciples bemoaning him; his soul, comfortless and forsaken; and all this for those very sins that Satan paints and puts fine colours upon! Oh! how should the consideration of this stir up the soul against it, and work the soul to fly from it, and to use all holy means whereby sin may be subdued and destroyed![1]

After Julius Cæsar was murdered, Antonius brought forth his coat, all bloody and cut, and laid it before the people, saying, 'Look, here you have the emperor's coat thus bloody and torn:' whereupon the people were presently in an uproar, and cried out to slay those murderers; and they took their tables and stools that were in the place, and set them on fire, and run to the houses of them that had slain Cæsar, and burnt them. So that when we consider that sin hath slain our Lord Jesus, ah, how should it provoke our hearts to be revenged on sin, that hath murdered the Lord of glory, and hath done that mischief that all the devils in hell could never have done?[2]

It was good counsel one gave, 'Never let go out of your minds the thoughts of a crucified Christ.'[3] Let these be meat and drink unto you; let them be your sweetness and consolation, your honey and your desire, your reading and your meditation, your life, death, and resurrection.

The third device that Satan hath to draw the soul to sin is,

[1] One of the Rabbins, when he read what bitter torments the Messias should suffer when he came into the world, cried out, *Veniat Messias et ego non videam*, *i.e.* Let the Messias come, but let not me see him! Dionysius being in Egypt at the time of Christ's suffering, and seeing an eclipse of the sun, and knowing it to be contrary to nature, cried out, *Aut Deus naturæ patitur, aut mundi machina dissolvitur*, Either the God of nature suffers, or the frame of the world will be dissolved.

[2] It is an excellent saying of Bernard, *Quanto pro nobis vilior, tanto nobis charior*. The more vile Christ made himself for us, the more dear he ought to be to us.

[3] *Nolo vivere sine vulnere cum te video vulneratum.* O my God! as long as I see thy wounds, I will never live without wounds, said Bonaventura.

Device (3). *By extenuating and lessening of sin.* Ah! saith Satan, it is but a little pride, a little worldliness, a little uncleanness, a little drunkenness, &c. As Lot said of Zoar, 'It is but a little one, and my soul shall live,' Gen. xix. 20. Alas![1] saith Satan, it is but a very little sin that you stick so at. You may commit it without any danger to your soul. It is but a little one; you may commit it, and yet your soul shall live.

Now the remedies against this device of Satan are these:

Remedy (1). First, Solemnly consider, *That those sins which we are apt to account small, have brought upon men the greatest wrath of God,* as the eating of an apple, gathering a few sticks on the Sabbath day, and touching of the ark. Oh! the dreadful wrath that these sins brought down upon the heads and hearts of men![2] The least sin is contrary to the law of God, the nature of God, the being of God, and the glory of God; and therefore it is often punished severely by God; and do not we see daily the vengeance of the Almighty falling upon the bodies, names, states, families, and souls of men, for those sins that are but little ones in their eyes? Surely if we are not utterly left of God, and blinded by Satan, we cannot but see it. Oh! therefore, when Satan says it is but a little one, do thou say, Oh! but those sins that thou callest little, are such as will cause God to rain hell out of heaven upon sinners as he did upon the Sodomites.

The second remedy against this device of Satan is,

Remedy (2). Seriously to consider, *That the giving way to a less sin makes way for the committing of a greater.* He that, to avoid a greater sin, will yield to a lesser, ten thousand to one but God in justice will leave that soul to fall into a greater. If we commit one sin to avoid another, it is just we should avoid neither, we having not law nor power in our own hands to keep off sin as we please; and we, by yielding to the lesser, do tempt the tempter to tempt us to the greater. Sin is of an encroaching nature; it creeps on the soul by degrees, step by step, till it hath the soul to the very height of sin.[3] David gives way to his wandering eye, and this led him to those foul sins that caused God to break his bones, and to turn his day into night, and to leave his soul in great darkness. Jacob and Peter, and other saints, have found this true by woful experience, that the yielding to a lesser sin hath been the ushering in of a greater. The little thief will open the door, and make way for the greater, and the little wedge knocked in will make way for the greater. Satan will first draw thee to sit with the drunkard, and then to sip with the drunkard, and then at last to be drunk with the drunkard. He will first draw thee to be unclean in thy thoughts, and then to be unclean in thy looks, and then to

[1] Brooks uses 'alas' much as Sibbes does. Cf. glossary to each, *sub voce.*—G.

[2] Draco, the rigid lawgiver, being asked why, when sins were not equal, he appointed death to all, answered, he knew that all sins were not equal, but he knew the least deserved death. So, though the sins of men be not all equal, yet the least of them deserves eternal death.

[3] Ps. cxxxvii. 9, 'Happy shall he be that taketh and dasheth thy little ones against the stones.' Hugo's gloss is pious, &c., *Sit nihil in te Babylonicum,* Let there be nothing in thee of Babylon; not only the grown men, but the little ones must be dashed against the stones; not only great sins, but little sins must be killed, or they will kill the soul for ever.

be unclean in thy words, and at last to be unclean in thy practices. He will first draw thee to look upon the golden wedge, and then to like the golden wedge, and then to handle the golden wedge, and then at last by wicked ways to gain the golden wedge, though thou runnest the hazard of losing God and thy soul for ever; as you may see in Gehazi, Achan, and Judas, and many in these our days. Sin is never at a stand: Ps. i. 1, first ungodly, then sinners, then scorners. Here they go on from sin to sin, till they come to the top of sin, viz. to sit in the seat of scorners, or as it is in the Septuagint—τῶν λοιμῶν—to affect the honour of the chair of pestilence.

Austin, writing upon John, tells a story of a certain man, that was of an opinion that the devil did make the fly, and not God. Saith one to him, If the devil made flies, then the devil made worms, and God did not make them, for they are living creatures as well as flies. True, said he, the devil did make worms. But, said the other, if the devil did make worms, then he made birds, beasts, and man. He granted all. Thus, saith Austin, by denying God in the fly, became to deny God in man, and to deny the whole creation.[1]

By all this we see, that the yielding to lesser sins, draws the soul to the committing of greater.[2] Ah! how many in these days have fallen, first to have low thoughts of Scripture and ordinances, and then to slight Scripture and ordinances, and then to make a nose of wax of Scripture and ordinances, and then to cast off Scripture and ordinances, and then at last to advance and lift up themselves, and their Christ-dishonouring and soul-damning opinions, above Scripture and ordinances. Sin gains upon man's soul by insensible degrees: Eccles. x. 13, 'The beginning of the words of his mouth is foolishness, and the end of his talking is mischievous madness.' Corruption in the heart, when it breaks forth, is like a breach in the sea, which begins in a narrow passage, till it eat through, and cast down all before it. The debates of the soul are quick, and soon ended, and that may be done in a moment that may undo a man for ever. When a man hath begun to sin, he knows not where, or when, or how he shall make a stop of sin. Usually the soul goes on from evil to evil, from folly to folly, till it be ripe for eternal misery. Men usually grow from being naught to be very naught, and from very naught to be stark naught, and then God sets them at nought for ever.

Remedy (3). The third remedy against this third device that Satan hath to draw the soul to sin, is solemnly to consider, *That it is sad to stand with God for a trifle.* Dives would not give a crumb, therefore he should not receive a drop, Luke xvi. 21. It is the greatest folly in the

[1] An Italian having found his enemy at advantage, promised him if he would deny his faith, he would save his life. He, to save his life, denied his faith, which having done, he stabbed him, rejoicing that by this he had at one time taken revenge both on body and soul. [See authorities, Note 8, page 14.—G.]

[2] A young man being long tempted to kill his father, or lie with his mother, or be drunk, he thought to yield to the lesser, viz. to be drunk, that he might be rid of the greater; but when he was drunk, he did both kill his father, and lie with his mother. [Related, with authorities, in Wanley's *Wonders*, book iv. c. xviii.: probably a reference to an extraordinary legend of Judas Iscariot. See Mrs Jameson's *Sacred and Legendary Art*, vol. i. p. 235; but cf. the old Italian legend of St John Chrysostom, *ibid.*, p. 317.—G.]

world to adventure the going to hell for a small matter. 'I tasted but a little honey,' said Jonathan, 'and I must die,' 1 Sam. xiv. 29. It is a most unkind and unfaithful thing to break with God for a little. Little sins carry with them but little temptations to sin, and then a man shews most viciousness and unkindness, when he sins on a little temptation. It is devilish to sin without a temptation; it is little less than devilish to sin on a little occasion. The less the temptation is to sin, the greater is that sin.[1] Saul's sin in not staying for Samuel, was not so much in the matter, but it was much in the malice of it; for though Samuel had not come at all, yet Saul should not have offered sacrifice; but this cost him dear, his soul and kingdom.

It is the greatest unkindness that can be shewed to a friend, to adventure the complaining, bleeding, and grieving of his soul upon a light and a slight occasion. So it is the greatest unkindness that can be shewed to God, Christ, and the Spirit, for a soul to put God upon complaining, Christ upon bleeding, and the Spirit upon grieving, by yielding to little sins. Therefore, when Satan says it is but a little one, do thou answer, that often times there is the greatest unkindness shewed to God's glorious majesty, in the acting of the least folly, and therefore thou wilt not displease thy best and greatest friend, by yielding to his greatest enemy.

Remedy (4). The fourth remedy against this device of Satan, is seriously to consider, *That there is great danger, yea, many times most danger, in the smallest sins.* 'A little leaven leaveneth the whole lump,' 1 Cor. v. 6. If the serpent wind in his head, he will draw in his whole body after. Greater sins do sooner startle the soul, and awaken and rouse up the soul to repentance, than lesser sins do. Little sins often slide into the soul, and breed, and work secretly and undiscernibly in the soul, till they come to be so strong, as to trample upon the soul, and to cut the throat of the soul. There is oftentimes greatest danger to our bodies in the least diseases that hang upon us, because we are apt to make light of them, and to neglect the timely use of means for removing of them, till they are grown so strong that they prove mortal to us. So there is most danger often in the least sins. We are apt to take no notice of them, and to neglect those heavenly helps whereby they should be weakened and destroyed, till they are grown to that strength, that we are ready to cry out, the medicine is too weak for the disease; I would pray, and I would hear, but I am afraid that sin is grown up by degrees to such a head, that I shall never be able to prevail over it; but as I have begun to fall, so I shall utterly fall before it, and at last perish in it, unless the power and free grace of Christ doth act gloriously, beyond my present apprehension and expectation. The viper is killed by the little young ones that are nourished and cherished in her belly: so are many men eternally killed and betrayed by the little sins, as they call them, that are nourished in their own bosoms.[2]

[1] It was a vexation to king Lysimachus, that his staying to drink one small draught of water lost him his kingdom; and so it will eternally vex some souls at last that for one little sin, compared with great transgressions, they have lost God, heaven, and their souls for ever. [Plutarch. Cf. Bp. Jeremy Taylor, vol. iv. p. 457 (Eden).—G.]

[2] Cæsar was stabbed with bodkins. Pope Adrian was choked with a gnat. A

I know not, saith one, whether the maintenance of the least sin be not worse than the commission of the greatest: for this may be of frailty, that argues obstinacy. A little hole in the ship sinks it; a small breach in a sea-bank carries away all before it; a little stab at the heart kills a man; and a little sin, without a great deal of mercy, will damn a man.[1]

Remedy (5). The fifth remedy against this device of Satan, is solemnly to consider, *That other saints have chosen to suffer the worst of torments, rather than they would commit the least sin, i. e.* such as the world accounts.[2] So as you may see in Daniel and his companions, that would rather choose to burn, and be cast to the lions, than they would bow to the image that Nebuchadnezzar had set up. When this *pecchaddillo*,[3] in the world's account, and a hot fiery furnace stood in competition, that they must either fall into sin, or be cast into the fiery furnace, such was their tenderness of the honour and glory of God, and their hatred and indignation against sin, that they would rather burn than sin; they knew that it was far better to burn for their not sinning, than that God and conscience should raise a hell, a fire in their bosoms for sin.[4]

I have read of that noble servant of God, Marcus Arethusius, minister of a church in the time of Constantine, who in Constantine's time had been the cause of overthrowing an idol's temple; afterwards, when Julian came to be emperor, he would force the people of that place to build it up again. They were ready to do it, but he refused; whereupon those that were his own people, to whom he preached, took him, and stripped him of all his clothes, and abused his naked body, and gave it up to the children, to lance it with their pen-knives, and then caused him to be put in a basket, and anointed his naked body with honey, and set him in the sun, to be stung with wasps. And all this cruelty they shewed, because he would not do anything towards the building up of this idol temple; nay, they came to this, that if he would do but the least towards it, if he would give but a halfpenny to it, they would save him. But he refused all, though the giving of a halfpenny might have saved his live; and in doing this, he did but live up to that principle that most Christians talk of, and all profess, but few come up to, viz., that we must choose rather to suffer the worst of torments that men and devils can invent and inflict, than to commit the least sin, whereby God should be dishonoured, our consciences wounded, religion reproached, and our own souls endangered.

scorpion is little, yet able to sting a lion to death. A mouse is but little, yet killeth an elephant, if he gets up into his trunk. The leopard being great, is poisoned with a head of garlic. The smallest errors prove many times most dangerous. It is as much treason to coin pence as bigger pieces.

[1] One little miscarriage doth, in the eyes of the world, overshadow all a Christian's graces, as one cloud doth sometimes overshadow the whole body of the sun.

[2] Melius mori fame quam Idolothytis vesci.—*Augustine.* It is better to die with hunger, than to eat that which is offered to idols.

[3] The early form of this at the time scarcely accepted word; but the context indicates a reminiscence of Boskierus (*Codrus Evang.*), who uses the term and preceding illustrations of little sins.—G.

[4] Many heathens would rather die than cozen or cheat one another, so faithful were they one to another. Will not these rise in judgment against many professors in these days, who make nothing of over-reaching one another?

Remedy (6). The sixth remedy against this device of Satan is, seriously to consider, *That the soul is never able to stand under the guilt and weight of the least sin, when God shall set it home upon the soul.* The least sin will press and sink the stoutest sinner as low as hell, when God shall open the eyes of a sinner, and make him see the horrid filthiness and abominable vileness that is in sin. What so little, base, and vile creatures as lice or gnats, and yet by these little poor creatures, God so plagued stout-hearted Pharaoh, and all Egypt, that, fainting under it, they were forced to cry out, 'This is the finger of God,' Exod. viii. 16, x. 19. When little creatures, yea, the least creatures, shall be armed with a power from God, they shall press and sink down the greatest, proudest, and stoutest tyrants that breathe.[1] So when God shall cast a sword into the hand of a little sin, and arm it against the soul, the soul will faint and fall under it. Some, who have but projected adultery, without any actual acting it; and others, having found a trifle, and made no conscience to restore it, knowing, by the light of natural conscience, that they did not do as they would be done by; and others, that have had some unworthy thought of God, have been so frightened, amazed, and terrified for those sins, which are small in men's account, that they have wished they had never been; that they could take no delight in any earthly comfort, that they have been put to their wits' end, ready to make away themselves, wishing themselves annihilated.[2]

Mr Perkins mentions a good man, but very poor, who, being ready to starve, stole a lamb, and being about to eat it with his poor children, and as his manner was afore meat, to crave a blessing, durst not do it, but fell into a great perplexity of conscience, and acknowledged his fault to the owner, promising payment if ever he should be able.

Remedy (7). The seventh remedy against this device is, solemnly to consider, *That there is more evil in the least sin than in the greatest affliction;* and this appears as clear as the sun, by the severe dealing of God the Father with his beloved Son, who let all the vials of his fiercest wrath upon him, and that for the least sin as well as for the greatest.

'The wages of sin is death,' Rom. vi. 23; of sin indefinitely, whether great or small.[3] Oh! how should this make us tremble, as much at the least spark of lust as at hell itself; considering that God the Father would not spare his bosom Son, no, not for the least sin, but would make him drink the dregs of his wrath!

And so much for the remedies that may fence and preserve our souls from being drawn to sin by this third device of Satan.

[1] The tyrant Maximinus, who had set forth his proclamation engraven in brass for the utter abolishing of Christ and his religion, was eaten of lice. [Maximinus II., Euseb. H. E. viii. 14, ix. 2, &c.—G.]

[2] *Una guttula malæ conscientiæ totum mare mundani gaudii absorbet; i.e.* one drop of an evil conscience swallows up the whole sea of worldly joy. How great a pain, not to be borne, comes from the prick of this small thorn, said one.

[3] Death is the heir of the least sin; the best wages that the least sin gives his soldiers is, death of all sorts. In a strict sense, there is no sin little, because no little God to sin against.

The fourth device that Satan hath to draw the soul to sin is,

Device (4). *By presenting to the soul the best men's sins, and by hiding from the soul their virtues; by shewing the soul their sins, and by hiding from the soul their sorrows and repentance:* as by setting before the soul the adultery of David, the pride of Hezekiah, the impatience of Job, the drunkenness of Noah, the blasphemy of Peter, &c., and by hiding from the soul the tears, the sighs, the groans, the meltings, the humblings, and repentings of these precious souls.

Now, the remedies against this device of the devil are these:

Remedy (1). The first remedy against this device of Satan is, seriously to consider, *That the Spirit of the Lord hath been as careful to note the saints' rising by repentance out of sin, as he hath to note their falling into sins.* David falls fearfully, but by repentance he rises sweetly: 'Blot out my transgressions, wash me throughly from my iniquity, cleanse me from my sin; for I acknowledge my transgressions, and my sin is ever before me. Purge me with hyssop, and I shall be clean; wash me, and I shall be whiter than snow; deliver me from blood-guiltiness, O God, thou God of my salvation.' It is true, Hezekiah's heart was lifted up under the abundance of mercy that God had cast in upon him; and it is as true that Hezekiah humbled himself for the pride of his heart, so that the wrath of the Lord came not upon him, nor upon Jerusalem, in the days of Hezekiah. It is true, Job curses the day of his birth, and it is as true that he rises by repentance: 'Behold, I am vile,' saith he; 'what shall I answer thee? I will lay my hand upon my mouth. Once have I spoken, but I will not answer; yea twice, but I will proceed no further. I have heard of thee by the hearing of the ear, but now mine eye seeth thee; wherefore, I abhor myself, and repent in dust and ashes,' Job xl. 4, 5; xlii. 5, 6.[1] Peter falls dreadfully, but rises by repentance sweetly; a look of love from Christ melts him into tears. He knew that repentance was the key to the kingdom of grace. As once his faith was so great that he leapt, as it were, into a sea of waters to come to Christ; so now his repentance was so great that he leapt, as it were, into a sea of tears, for that he had gone from Christ. Some say that, after his sad fall, he was ever and anon weeping, and that his face was even furrowed with continual tears. He had no sooner took in poison but he vomited it up again, ere it got to the vitals; he had no sooner handled this serpent but he turned it into a rod to scourge his soul with remorse for sinning against such clear light, and strong love, and sweet discoveries of the heart of Christ to him.[2]

Clement notes that Peter so repented, that all his life after, every night when he heard the cock crow, he would fall upon his knees, and, weeping bitterly, would beg pardon of his sin.[3] Ah, souls, you can easily sin as the saints, but can you repent with the saints!

[1] Tertullian saith that he was (*nulli rei natus nisi pœnitentiæ*) born for no other purpose but to repent.

[2] Luther confesses that, before his conversion, he met not with a more displeasing word in all his study of divinity than *repent*, but afterward he took delight in the word. *Pœnitens de peccato dolet et de dolore gaudet*, to sorrow for his sin, and then to rejoice in his sorrow.

[3] In Hefele's *Patrum Apostolicarum Opera*. 1847. 8vo.—G.

Many can sin with David and Peter, that cannot repent with David and Peter, and so must perish for ever.

Theodosius the emperor, pressing that he might receive the Lord's supper, excuses his own foul fact by David's doing the like; to which Ambrose replies, Thou hast followed David transgressing, follow David repenting, and then think thou of the table of the Lord.[1]

Remedy (2). The second remedy against this device of Satan is, solemnly to consider, *That these saints did not make a trade of sin.* They fell once or twice, and rose by repentance, that they might keep the closer to Christ for ever. They fell accidentally, occasionally, and with much reluctancy;[2] and thou sinnest presumptuously, obstinately, readily, delightfully, and customarily. Thou hast, by thy making a trade of sin, contracted upon thy soul a kind of cursed necessity of sinning, that thou canst as well cease to be, or cease to live, as thou canst cease to sin. Sin is, by custom, become as another nature to thee, which thou canst not, which thou wilt not lay aside, though thou knowest that if thou dost not lay sin aside, God will lay thy soul aside for ever; though thou knowest that if sin and thy soul do not part, Christ and thy soul can never meet. If thou wilt make a trade of sin, and cry out, Did not David sin thus, and Noah sin thus, and Peter sin thus? &c. No; their hearts turned aside to folly one day, but thy heart turns aside to folly every day, 2 Peter ii. 14, Prov. iv. 16; and when they were fallen, they rise by repentance, and by the actings of faith upon a crucified Christ;[3] but thou fallest, and hast no strength nor will to rise, but wallowest in sin, and wilt eternally die in thy sins, unless the Lord be the more merciful to thy soul. Dost thou think, O soul! this is good reasoning? Such a one tasted poison but once, and yet narrowly escaped; but I do daily drink poison, yet I shall escape. Yet such is the mad reasoning of vain souls. David and Peter, &c., sinned once foully and fearfully; they tasted poison but once, and were sick to death; but I taste it daily, and yet shall not taste of eternal death. Remember, O souls! that the day is at hand when self-flatterers will be found self-deceivers, yea, self-murderers.

Remedy (3). The third remedy against this device of Satan is, seriously to consider, *That though God doth not, nor never will, disinherit his people for their sins, yet he hath severely punished his people for their sins.* David sins, and God breaks his bones for his sin: 'Make me to hear joy and gladness, that the bones which thou hast broken may rejoice,' Ps. li. 8. 'And because thou hast done this, the sword shall never depart from thy house, to the day of thy death,' 2 Sam. xii. 10. Though God will not utterly take from them his loving-kindness, nor suffer his faithfulness to fail, nor break his covenant, nor alter the thing that is gone out of his mouth, yet will he 'visit their transgression with a rod, and their iniquity with stripes,'

[1] Theodoret, Hist. l. iv. c. xvii.

[2] The saints cannot sin (*voluntate plena sed semi-plena*) with a whole will, but, as it were, with a half will, an unwilling willingness; not with a full consent, but with a dissenting consent.

[3] Though sin do (*habitare*) dwell in the regenerate, as Austin notes, yet it doth not (*regnare*) reign over the regenerate; they rise by repentance.

Ps. lxxxix. 30, 35. The Scripture abounds with instances of this kind. This is so known a truth among all that know anything of truth, that to cite more scriptures to prove it would be to light a candle to see the sun at noon.[1]

The Jews have a proverb, 'That there is no punishment comes upon Israel in which there is not one ounce of the golden calf;' meaning that that was so great a sin, as that in every plague God remembered it; that it had an influence into every trouble that befell them. Every man's heart may say to him in his sufferings, as the heart of Apollodorus in the kettle, 'I have been the cause of this.'[2] God is most angry when he shews no anger. God keep me from this mercy; this kind of mercy is worse than all other kind of misery.

One writing to a dead friend hath this expression: 'I account it a part of unhappiness not to know adversity; I judge you to be miserable, because you have not been miserable.'[3] It is mercy that our affliction is not execution, but a correction.[4] He that hath deserved hanging, may be glad if he scape with a whipping. God's corrections are our instructions, his lashes our lessons, his scourges our schoolmasters, his chastisements our advertisements;[5] and to note this, both the Hebrews and the Greeks express chastening and teaching by one and the same word (*Musar*, *Paideia*[6]), because the latter is the true end of the former, according to that in the proverb, 'Smart makes wit, and vexation gives understanding.' Whence Luther fitly calls affliction 'The Christian man's divinity.'[7] So saith Job (chap. xxxiii. 14–19), 'God speaketh once, yea, twice, yet man perceiveth it not. In a dream, in a vision of the night, when deep sleep falleth upon men, in slumberings upon the bed; then he openeth the ears of men, and sealeth their instruction, that he may withdraw man from his purpose, and hide pride from man. He keepeth back his soul from the pit, and his life from perishing by the sword.' When Satan shall tell thee of other men's sins to draw thee to sin, do thou then think of the same men's sufferings to keep thee from sin. Lay thy hand upon thy heart, and say, O my soul! if thou sinnest with David, thou must suffer with David, &c.

Remedy (4). The fourth remedy against this device of Satan is, solemnly to consider, *That there are but two main ends of God's recording of the falls of his saints.*

And the one is, to keep those from fainting, sinking, and despair, under the burden of their sins, who fall through weakness and infirmity.

And the other is, that their falls may be as landmarks to warn others that stand, to take heed lest they fall. It never entered into the

[1] Josephus reports that, not long after the Jews had crucified Christ on the cross, so many of them were condemned to be crucified, that there were not places enough for crosses, nor crosses enough for the bodies that were to be hung thereon. [The Jewish War and Antiq.—G.]

[2] The tyrant of Cassandreia.—G.

[3] *Qui non est cruciatus non est Christianus*, saith Luther, There is not a Christian that carries not his cross.

[4] Ps. xciv. 12; Prov. iii. 12, 13, 16; Obad. 6, 13; Isa. ix. 1, *et seq.*

[5] Admonitions.—G.

[6] That is, מוּסָר, Prov. iii. 11; and *παιδεία*, Heb. xii. 5, 7, 8, 11.—G.

[7] Theologium Christianorum. . . . . Afflictiones Benedictiones, Afflictions are blessings.—*Bernard.*

heart of God to record his children's sins, that others might be encouraged to sin, but that others might look to their standings, and to hang the faster upon the skirts of Christ, and avoid all occasions and temptations that may occasion the soul to fall, as others have fallen, when they have been left by Christ. The Lord hath made their sins as landmarks, to warn his people to take heed how they come near those sands and rocks, those snares and baits, that have been fatal to the choicest treasures, to wit, the joy, peace, comfort, and glorious enjoyments of the bravest spirits and noblest souls that ever sailed through the ocean of this sinful troublesome world; as you may see in David, Job, Peter, &c. There is nothing in the world that can so notoriously cross the grand end of God's recording of the sins of his saints, than for any from thence to take encouragement to sin; and wherever you find such a soul, you may write him Christless, graceless, a soul cast off by God, a soul that Satan hath by the hand, and the eternal God knows whither he will lead him.[1]

The fifth device that Satan hath to draw the soul to sin is,

Device (5). *To present God to the soul as one made up all of mercy.* Oh! saith Satan, you need not make such a matter of sin, you need not be so fearful of sin, not so unwilling to sin; for God is a God of mercy, a God full of mercy, a God that delights in mercy, a God that is ready to shew mercy, a God that is never weary of shewing mercy, a God more prone to pardon his people than to punish his people; and therefore he will not take advantage against the soul; and why then, saith Satan, should you make such a matter of sin?

Now the remedies against this device of Satan are these:

Remedy (1). The first remedy is, seriously to consider, *That it is the sorest judgment in the world to be left to sin upon any pretence whatsoever.* O unhappy man! when God leaveth thee to thyself, and doth not resist thee in thy sins.[2] Woe, woe to him at whose sins God doth wink. When God lets the way to hell be a smooth and pleasant way, that is hell on this side hell, and a dreadful sign of God's indignation against a man; a token of his rejection, and that God doth not intend good unto him. That is a sad word, 'Ephraim is joined to idols: let him alone,' Hosea iv. 17; he will be uncounsellable and incorrigible; he hath made a match with mischief, he shall have his bellyful of it; he falls with open eyes, let him fall at his own peril. And that is a terrible saying, 'So I gave them up unto their own hearts' lusts, and they walked in their own counsels,' Ps. lxxxi. 12. A soul given up to sin, is a soul ripe for hell, a soul posting to destruction. Ah Lord! this mercy I humbly beg, that whatever thou givest me up to, thou wilt not give me up to the ways of my own heart; if thou wilt give me up to be afflicted, or tempted, or reproached, &c., I will patiently sit down, and say, It is the Lord; let him do with me what seems good in his own eyes. Do anything

[1] I have known a good man, saith Bernard, who, when he heard of any that had committed some notorious sin, he was wont to say with himself, '*Ille hodie et ego cras,*' he fell to-day, so may I to-morrow.

[2] *Humanum est peccare, diabolicum perseverare, et angelicum resurgere.—Aug*[*ustine*]; *i.e.* It is a human thing to fall into sin, a devilish to persevere therein, and an angelical or supernatural to rise from it.

with me, lay what burden thou wilt upon me, so thou dost not give me up to the ways of my own heart.[1]

Remedy (2). The second remedy against this device of Satan is, solemnly to consider, *That God is as just as he is merciful.* As the Scriptures speak him out to be a very merciful God, so they speak him out to be a very just God. Witness his casting the angels out of heaven, 2 Peter ii. 4–6, and his binding them in chains of darkness[2] till the judgment of the great day; and witness his turning Adam out of paradise, his drowning of the old world, and his raining hell out of heaven upon Sodom; and witness all the crosses, losses, sicknesses, and diseases, that be in the world; and witness Tophet, that was prepared of old; witness his 'treasuring up of wrath against the day of wrath, unto the revelation of the just judgments of God; but above all, witness the pouring forth of all his wrath upon his bosom Son, when he did bear the sins of his people, and cried out, 'My God, my God, why hast thou forsaken me?' Mat. xxvii. 46.

Remedy (3). The third remedy against this device of Satan is, seriously to consider, *That sins against mercy will bring the greatest and sorest judgments upon men's heads and hearts.* Mercy is Alpha, Justice is Omega. David, speaking of these attributes, placeth mercy in the foreward, and justice in the rearward, saying, 'My song shall be of mercy and judgment,' Ps. ci. 1. When mercy is despised, then justice takes the throne.[4] God is like a prince, that sends not his army against rebels before he hath sent his pardon, and proclaimed it by a herald of arms: he first hangs out the white flag of mercy; if this wins men in, they are happy for ever; but if they stand out, then God will put forth his red flag of justice and judgment; if the one is despised, the other shall be felt with a witness.[5]

See this in the Israelites. He loved them and chose them when they were in their blood, and most unlovely. He multiplied them, not by means, but by miracle; from seventy souls they grew in few years to six hundred thousand; the more they were oppressed, the more they prospered. Like camomile, the more you tread it, the more you spread it; or to a palm-tree, the more it is pressed, the further it spreadeth; or to fire, the more it is raked, the more it burneth. Their mercies came in upon them like Job's messengers, one upon the neck of the other: He put off their sackcloth, and girded them with gladness, and 'compassed them about with songs of deliverance;' he 'carried them on the wings of eagles;' he kept them 'as the apple of his eye,' &c.[6] But they, abusing his mercy, became the greatest objects of his wrath. As I know not the man that can reckon up

[1] *A me, me salva Domine;* Deliver me, O Lord, from that evil man myself.—*Aug*[*ustine*].

[2] God hanged them up in gibbets, as it were, that others might hear and fear, and do no more so wickedly. [3] Cf. Rom. ii. 5; but it is the sinner, not God.—G.

[4] *Quanto gradus altior, tanto casus gravior;* the higher we are in dignity, the more grievous is our fall and misery.

[5] *Deus tardus est ad iram, sed tarditatem gravitate pœnæ compensat;* God is slow to anger, but he recompenseth his slowness with grievousness of punishment. If we abuse mercy to serve our lust, then, in Salvian's phrase, God will rain hell out of heaven, rather than not visit for such sins.

[6] Ps. xxxii. 7; Exod. xix. 4; Deut. xxxii. 10.—G.

their mercies, so I know not the man that can sum up the miseries that are come upon them for their sins. For as our Saviour prophesied concerning Jerusalem, 'that a stone should not be left upon a stone,' so it was fulfilled forty years after his ascension, by Vespasian the emperor and his son Titus, who, having besieged Jerusalem, the Jews were oppressed with a grievous famine, in which their food was old shoes, old leather, old hay, and the dung of beasts. There died, partly of the sword and partly of the famine, eleven hundred thousand of the poorer sort; two thousand in one night were embowelled; six thousand were burned in a porch of the temple; the whole city was sacked and burned, and laid level to the ground; and ninety-seven thousand taken captives, and applied to base and miserable service, as Eusebius and Josephus saith.[1] And to this day, in all parts of the world, are they not the off-scouring of the world? None less beloved, and none more abhorred, than they.[2]

And so Capernaum, that was lifted up to heaven, was threatened to be thrown down to hell. No souls fall so low into hell, if they fall, as those souls that by a hand of mercy are lifted up nearest to heaven. You slight souls that are so apt to abuse mercy, consider this, that in the gospel days, the plagues that God inflicts upon the despisers and abusers of mercy are usually spiritual plagues; as blindness of mind, hardness of heart, benumbedness of conscience, which are ten thousand times worse than the worst of outward plagues that can befall you. And therefore, though you may escape temporal judgments, yet you shall not escape spiritual judgments: 'How shall we escape, if neglect so great salvation?' Heb. ii. 3,[3] saith the apostle. Oh! therefore, whenever Satan shall present God to the soul as one made up all of mercy, that he may draw thee to do wickedly, say unto him, that sins against mercy will bring upon the soul the greatest misery; and therefore whatever becomes of thee, thou wilt not sin against mercy, &c.

Remedy (4). The fourth remedy against this device of Satan, is seriously to consider, *That though God's general mercy be over all his works, yet his special mercy is confined to those that are divinely qualified.*[4] So in Exodus xxxiv. 6, 7, 'And the Lord passed by before me, and proclaimed, The Lord, the Lord God, merciful and gracious, longsuffering, and abundant in goodness and truth, keeping mercy for thousands, forgiving iniquity, transgression, and sin, and that will by no means clear the guilty.' Exodus xx. 6, 'And shewing mercy unto thousands of them that love me, and keep my command-

[1] Vespasian brake into their city at Kedron, where they took Christ, on the same feast day that Christ was taken; he whipped them where they whipped Christ; he sold twenty Jews for a penny, as they sold Christ for thirty pence.—*S. Andr. Cat.* [*Sic* in all editions; but qu. St Augustine, De Civitate Dei?—G.]

[2] Men are therefore worse, because they ought to be better; and shall be deeper in hell, because heaven was offered unto them; but they would not. *Ingentia beneficia, flagitia, supplicia.* Good turns aggravate unkindnesses, and men's offences are increased by their obligations. [Eusebius, Eccl. Hist. *sub* Jerusal. Josephus, Jewish War, Book vi. 5, *et alibi.*—G.]

[3] ἀμελήσαντες. Shift off, disregard.

[4] Augustus, in his solemn feasts, gave trifles to some, but gold to others that his heart was most set upon. So God, by a hand of general mercy, gives these—poor trifles—outward blessings, to those that he least loves; but his gold, his special mercy, is only towards those that his heart is most set upon.

ments.' Ps. xxv. 10, 'All the paths of the Lord are mercy and truth, unto such as keep his covenant, and his testimonies.' Ps. xxxii. 10, 'Many sorrows shall be to the wicked; but he that trusteth in the Lord, mercy shall compass him about.' Ps. xxxiii. 18, 'Behold, the eye of the Lord is upon them that fear him, upon them that hope in his mercy.' Ps. ciii. 11, 'For as the heaven is high above the earth, so great is his mercy toward them that fear him.' Ver. 17, 'But the mercy of the Lord is from everlasting to everlasting upon them that fear him.' When Satan attempts to draw thee to sin by presenting God as a God all made up of mercy, oh then reply, that though God's general mercy extend to all the works of his hand, yet his special mercy is confined to them that are divinely qualified, to them that love him and keep his commandments, to them that trust in him, that by hope hang upon him, and that fear him; and that thou must be such a one here, or else thou canst never be happy hereafter; thou must partake of his special mercy, or else eternally perish in everlasting misery, notwithstanding God's general mercy.

Remedy (5). The fifth remedy against this device of Satan is, solemnly to consider, *That those that were once glorious on earth, and are now triumphing in heaven, did look upon the mercy of God as the most powerful argument to preserve them from sin, and to fence their souls against sin, and not as an encouragement to sin.* Ps. xxvi. 3–6, 'For thy loving-kindness is before mine eyes, and I have walked in thy truth; I have not sat with vain persons, neither will I go in with dissemblers. I have hated the congregation of evil-doers, and will not sit with the wicked.' So Joseph strengthens himself against sin from the remembrance of mercy: 'How then can I,' saith he, 'do this great wickedness, and sin against God?' Gen. xxxix. 9. He had fixed his eye upon mercy, and therefore sin could not enter, though the irons entered into his soul; his soul being taken with mercy, was not moved with his mistress's impudence. Satan knocked oft at the door, but the sight of mercy would not suffer him to answer or open. Joseph, like a pearl in a puddle, keeps his virtue still.[1] So Paul, 'Shall we continue in sin, that grace may abound? God forbid. How shall we that are dead to sin, live any longer therein?' Rom. vi. 1, 2. There is nothing in the world that renders a man more unlike to a saint, and more like to Satan, than to argue from mercy to sinful liberty; from divine goodness to licentiousness. This is the devil's logic, and in whomsoever you find it, you may write, 'This soul is lost.' A man may as truly say, the sea burns, or fire cools, as that free grace and mercy should make a soul truly gracious to do wickedly. So the same apostle, 'I beseech you therefore, brethren, by the mercies of God, that ye present your bodies a living sacrifice, holy, acceptable unto God, which is your reasonable service,' Rom. xii. 1. So John, 'These things I write unto you, that ye sin not,' 1 John ii. 1, 2. What was it that he wrote? He wrote, 'That we might have fellowship with the Father and his Son; and that the blood of Christ cleanseth us

[1] The stone called *Pontaurus*, is of that virtue, that it preserves him that carries it from taking any hurt by poison. The mercy of God in Christ to our souls is the most precious stone or pearl in the world, to prevent us from being poisoned with sin.

from all sin, and that if we confess our sin, he is just and faithful to forgive us our sins; and that if we do sin, we have an advocate with the Father, Jesus Christ the righteous.' These choice favours and mercies the apostle holds forth as the choicest means to preserve the soul from sin, and to keep at the greatest distance from sin; and if this won't do it, you may write the man void of Christ and grace, and undone for ever.

The sixth device that Satan hath to draw the soul to sin is,

Device (6). *By persuading the soul that the work of repentance is an easy work, and that therefore the soul need not make such a matter of sin.* Why! Suppose you do sin, saith Satan, it is no such difficult thing to return, and confess, and be sorrowful, and beg pardon, and cry, 'Lord, have mercy upon me;' and if you do but this, God will cut the score,[1] and pardon your sins, and save your souls, &c.

By this device Satan draws many a soul to sin, and makes many millions of souls servants or rather slaves to sin, &c.

Now, the remedies against this device of Satan are these that follow:

Remedy (1). The first remedy is, seriously to consider, *That repentance is a mighty work, a difficult work, a work that is above our power.* There is no power below that power that raised Christ from the dead, and that made the world, that can break the heart of a sinner or turn the heart of a sinner. Thou art as well able to melt adamant, as to melt thine own heart; to turn a flint into flesh, as to turn thine own heart to the Lord; to raise the dead and to make a world, as to repent. Repentance is a flower that grows not in nature's garden. 'Can the Ethiopian change his skin, or the leopard his spots? then may ye also do good, that are accustomed to do evil,' Jer. xiii. 23. Repentance is a gift that comes down from above.[2] Men are not born with repentance in their hearts, as they are born with tongues in their mouths:[3] Acts v. 31, 'Him hath God exalted with his right hand to be a Prince and a Saviour, for to give repentance to Israel, and forgiveness of sins.' So in 2 Tim. ii. 25, 'In meekness instructing them that oppose themselves; if God peradventure will give them repentance to the acknowledging of the truth.' It is not in the power of any mortal to repent at pleasure.[4] Some ignorant deluded souls vainly conceit that these five words, '*Lord! have mercy upon me,*' are efficacious to send them to heaven; but as many are undone by buying a counterfeit jewel, so many are in hell by mistake of their repentance. Many rest in their repentance, though it be but the shadow of repentance, which caused one to say, 'Repentance damneth more than sin.'

[1] The reference is to the 'scored' or notched sticks by which debt accounts were recorded anciently.—G.

[2] Fallen man hath lost (*imperium suum* and *imperium sui*) the command of himself, and the command of the creatures. And certainly he that cannot command himself cannot repent of himself.

[3] *Da pœnitentiam et postea indulgentiam*, said dying Fulgentius.

[4] It was a vain brag of king Cyrus, that caused it to be written upon his tombstone, πάντα ποιεῖν δυνάμην, I could do all things; so could Paul too, but it was 'through Christ, which strengthened him.' [Cf. Arrian vi. 29: Plutarch, *Alexander*, 69.—G.]

Remedy (2). The second remedy against this device of Satan is, solemnly to consider *of the nature of true repentance.* Repentance is some other thing than what vain men conceive.[1]

Repentance is sometimes taken, in a more strict and narrow sense, for godly sorrow; sometimes repentance is taken, in a large sense, for amendment of life. Repentance hath in it three things, viz.:

The act, subject, terms.

(1.) *The formal act of repentance is a changing and converting.* It is often set forth in Scripture by turning. 'Turn thou me, and I shall be turned,' saith Ephraim; 'after that I was turned, I repented,' saith he, Jer. xxxi. 18. It is a turning from darkness to light.

(2.) *The subject changed and converted, is the whole man;* it is both the sinner's heart and life: first his heart, then his life; first his person, then his practice and conversation. 'Wash ye, make you clean,' there is the change of their persons; 'Put away the evil of your doings from before mine eyes; cease to do evil, learn to do well,' Isa. i. 16; there is the change of their practices. So 'Cast away,' saith Ezekiel, 'all your transgresssions whereby you have transgressed;' there is the change of the life; 'and make you a new heart and a new spirit,' xviii. 30; there is the change of the heart.

(3.) *The terms of this change and conversion, from which and to which both heart and life must be changed; from sin to God.* The heart must be changed from the state and power of sin, the life from the acts of sin, but both unto God; the heart to be under his power in a state of grace, the life to be under his rule in all new obedience; as the apostle speaks, 'To open their eyes, and to turn them from darkness to light, and from the power of Satan unto God,' Acts xxvi. 18. So the prophet Isaiah saith, 'Let the wicked forsake their ways, and the unrighteous man his thoughts, and let him return unto the Lord,' lv. 7.

Thus much of the nature of evangelical repentance. Now, souls, tell me whether it be such an easy thing to repent, as Satan doth suggest. Besides what hath been spoken, I desire that you will take notice, that repentance doth include turning from the most darling sin. Ephraim shall say, 'What have I to do any more with idols?' Hosea xiv. 8. Yea, it is a turning from all sin to God: Ezek. xviii. 30, 'Therefore I will judge you, O house of Israel, every one of you according to his ways, saith the Lord God. Repent, and turn yourselves from your transgresssons; so iniquity shall not be your ruin.

[1] The Hebrew word for repentance is תשובה, from שוב, which signifies to return, implying a going back from what a man had done. It notes a turning or converting from one thing to another, from sin to God. The Greeks have two words by which they express the nature of repentance, one is μεταμέλειν, which signifies to be careful, anxious, solicitous, after a thing is done; the other word, μετάνοια, is *resipiscentia*, after-wit, or after-wisdom, the mind's recovering of wisdom, or growing wiser after our folly. Ab. *ἄνοια dementia, et μετὰ post*, it being the correction of men's folly, and returning *ad sanam mentem.* True repentance is a thorough change both of the mind and manners; *optima et optissima pœnitentia est nova vita*, saith Luther, which saying is an excellent saying. Repentance *for* sin is nothing worth without repentance *from* sin. If thou repentest with a contradiction, saith Tertullian, God will pardon thee with a contradiction; if thou repentest and yet continuest in thy sin, God will pardon thee, and yet send thee to hell; there is a pardon with a contradiction. Negative goodness serves no man's turn to save him from the axe.

Herod turned from many, but turned not from his Herodias, which was his ruin. Judas turned from all visible wickedness, yet he would not cast out that golden devil covetousness, and therefore was cast into the hottest place in hell. He that turns not from every sin, turns not aright from any one sin. Every sin strikes at the honour of God, the being of God, the glory of God, the heart of Christ, the joy of the Spirit, and the peace of a man's conscience; and therefore a soul truly penitent strikes at all, hates all, conflicts with all, and will labour to draw strength from a crucified Christ to crucify all. A true penitent knows neither father nor mother, neither right eye nor right hand, but will pluck out the one and cut off the other. Saul spared but one Agag, and that cost him his soul and his kingdom, 1 Sam. xv. 9. Besides, repentance is not only a turning from all sin, but also a turning to all good; to a love of all good, to a prizing of all good, and to a following after all good: Ezek. xviii. 21, 'But if the wicked will turn from all the sins that he hath committed, and keep all my statutes, and do that which is lawful and right, he shall surely live, he shall not die;' that is, only negative righteousness and holiness is no righteousness nor holiness.[1] David fulfilled *all* the will of God, and had respect unto *all* his commandments, and so had Zacharias and Elizabeth. It is not enough that the tree bears not ill fruit; but it must bring forth good fruit, else it must be 'cut down and cast into the fire,' Luke xiii. 7. So it is not enough that you are not thus and thus wicked, but you must be thus and thus gracious and good, else divine justice will put the axe of divine vengeance to the root of your souls, and cut you off for ever. 'Every tree that bringeth not forth good fruit is hewed down and cast into the fire,' Mat. iii. 10. Besides, repentance doth include a sensibleness of sin's sinfulness, how opposite and contrary it is to the blessed God. God is light, sin is darkness; God is life, sin is death; God is heaven, sin is hell; God is beauty, sin is deformity.

Also true repentance includes a sensibleness of sin's mischievousness; how it cast angels out of heaven, and Adam out of paradise; how it laid the first corner stone in hell, and brought in all the curses, crosses, and miseries, that be in the world; and how it makes men liable to all temporal, spiritual, and eternal wrath; how it hath made men Godless, Christless, hopeless, and heavenless.

Further, true repentance doth include sorrow for sin, contrition of heart. It breaks the heart with sighs, and sobs, and groans, for that a loving God and Father is by sin offended, a blessed Saviour afresh crucified, and the sweet comforter, the Spirit, grieved and vexed.

Again, repentance doth include, not only a loathing of sin, but also a loathing of ourselves for sin. As a man doth not only loathe poison, but he loathes the very dish or vessel that hath the smell of the poison; so a true penitent doth not only loathe his sin, but he loathes himself,

[1] It is said of Ithacus, that the hatred of the Priscilian heresy was all the virtue that he had. The evil servant did not riot out his talent, Mat. xxv. 18. Those reprobates, Mat. xxiii. 2, robbed not the saints, but relieved them not; for this they must eternally perish.

the vessel that smells of it; so Ezek. xx. 43, 'And there shall ye remember your ways and all your doings, wherein ye have been defiled; and ye shall loathe yourselves in your own sight for all your evils that ye have committed.' True repentance will work your hearts, not only to loathe your sins, but also to loathe yourselves.[1]

Again, true repentance doth not only work a man to loathe himself for his sins, but it makes him ashamed of his sin also: 'What fruit have ye of those things whereof ye are now ashamed?' saith the apostle, Rom. vi. 21. So Ezekiel, 'And thou shalt be confounded, and never open thy mouth any more, because of thy shame, when I am pacified toward thee for all that thou hast done, saith the Lord God,' xxxvi. 32. When a penitential soul sees his sins pardoned, the anger of God pacified, the divine justice satisfied, then he sits down and blushes, as the Hebrew hath it, as one ashamed. Yea, true repentance doth work a man to cross his sinful self, and to walk contrary to sinful self, to take a holy revenge upon sin, as you may see in Paul, the jailor, Mary Magdalene, and Manasseh. This the apostle shews in 2 Cor. vii. 10, 11: 'For godly sorrow worketh repentance never to be repented of; but the sorrow of the world worketh death. For behold the self-same thing, that ye sorrowed after a godly sort, what carefulness it wrought in you, yea, what clearing of yourselves, yea, what indignation, yea, what fear, yea, what vehement desire, yea, what zeal, yea, what revenge.'[2] Now, souls, sum up all these things together, and tell me whether it be such an easy thing to repent as Satan would make the soul to believe, and I am confident your heart will answer that it is as hard a thing to repent as it is to make a world, or raise the dead.

I shall conclude this second remedy with a worthy saying of a precious holy man: 'Repentance,' saith he, 'strips us stark naked of all the garments of the old Adam, and leaves not so much as a shirt behind.' In this rotten building it leaves not a stone upon a stone. As the flood drowned Noah's own friends and servants, so must the flood of repenting tears drown our sweetest and most profitable sins.

Remedy (3). The third remedy against this device of Satan is seriously to consider, *That repentance is a continued act.* The word *repent* implies the continuation of it.[3] True repentance inclines a man's heart to perform God's statutes always, even unto the end. A true penitent must go on from faith to faith, from strength to strength; he must never stand still nor turn back. Repentance is a grace, and must have its daily operation as well as other graces. True repentance is a continued spring, where the waters of godly sorrow are

[1] True repentance is a sorrowing for sin, as it is *offensivum Dei, aversivum a Deo.* This both comes from God, and drives a man to God, as it did the church in the Canticles, and the prodigal: Ezek. xiii. 22, 23.

[2] Quantum displicet Deo immunditia peccati, in tantum placet Deo erubescentia pœnitentis.—*Ber*[*nard*]: *i. e.* So much the more God hath been displeased with the blackness of sin, the more will he be pleased with the blushing of the sinner. They that do not burn now in zeal against sin, must ere long burn in hell for sin.

[3] Anselm in his Meditations confesseth, that all his life was either damnable for sin committed, or unprofitable for good omitted; at last concludes, *Quid restat, O peccator, nisi ut in tota vita tua deplores totam vitam tuam,* Oh, what then remains but in our whole life to lament the sins of our whole life.

always flowing: 'My sins are ever before me,' Ps. li. 3. A true penitent is often casting his eyes back to the days of his former vanity, and this makes him morning and evening to 'water his couch with his tears.' 'Remember not against me the sins of my youth,' saith one blessed penitent; and 'I was a blasphemer, and a persecutor, and injurious,' saith another penitent.[1] Repentance is a continued act of turning, a repentance never to be repented of, a turning never to turn again to folly. A true penitent hath ever something within him to turn from; he can never get near enough to God; no, not so near him as once he was; and therefore he is still turning and turning that he may get nearer and nearer to him, that is his chiefest good and his only happiness, *optimum maximum*, the best and the greatest.[2] They are every day a-crying out, 'O wretched men that we are, who shall deliver us from this body of death!' Rom. vii. 24. They are still sensible of sin, and still conflicting with sin, and still sorrowing for sin, and still loathing of themselves for sin. Repentance is no transient act, but a continued act of the soul. And tell me, O tempted soul, whether it be such an easy thing as Satan would make thee believe, to be every day a-turning more and more from sin, and a-turning nearer and nearer to God, thy choicest blessedness. A true penitent can as easily content himself with one act of faith, or one act of love, as he can content himself with one act of repentance.

A Jewish Rabbi, pressing the practice of repentance upon his disciples, exhorting them to be sure to repent the day before they died, one of them replied, that the day of any man's death was very uncertain. 'Repent, therefore, every day,' said the Rabbi, 'and then you shall be sure to repent the day before you die.' You are wise, and know how to apply it to your own advantage.

Remedy (4). The fourth remedy against this device of Satan is solemnly to consider, *That if the work of repentance were such an easy work as Satan would make it to be, then certainly so many would not lie roaring and crying out of wrath and eternal ruin under the horrors and terrors of conscience, for not repenting; yea, doubtless, so many millions would not go to hell for not repenting, if it were such an easy thing to repent.*[3] Ah, do not poor souls under horror of conscience cry out and say, Were all this world a lump of gold, and in our hand to dispose of, we would give it for the least drachm of true repentance! and wilt thou say it is an easy thing to repent? When a poor sinner, whose conscience is awakened, shall judge the exchange of all the world for the least drachm of repentance to be the happiest exchange that ever sinner made, tell me, O soul, is it good going to hell? Is it good dwelling with the devouring fire, with everlasting burnings? Is it good to be for ever separated

[1] Ps. vi. 6, xxv. 7, 1 Tim. i. 13.—G.

[2] It is truly said of God, that he is *Omnia super omnia.*

[3] If thou be backward in the thoughts of repentance, be forward in the thoughts of hell, the flames whereof only the streams of the penintent eye can extinguish.—*Tertul-[lian]*. Oh, how shalt thou tear and rend thyself! how shalt thou lament fruitless repenting! What wilt thou say? Woe is me, that I have not cast off the burden o sin; woe is me, that I have not washed away my spots, but am now pierced with mine iniquities; now have I lost the surpassing joy of angels!—*Basil.*

from the blessed and glorious presence of God, angels, and saints, and to be for ever shut out from those good things of eternal life, which are so many, that they exceed number; so great, that they exceed measure; so precious, that they exceed all estimation? We know it is the greatest misery that can befall the sons of men; and would they not prevent this by repentance, if it were such an easy thing to repent as Satan would have it? Well, then, do not run the hazard of losing God, Christ, heaven, and thy soul for ever, by hearkening to this device of Satan, viz., that it is an easy thing to repent, &c. If it be so easy, why, then, do wicked men's hearts so rise against them that press the doctrine of repentance in the sweetest way, and by the strongest and the choicest arguments that the Scripture doth afford? And why do they kill two at once: the faithful labourer's name and their own souls, by their wicked words and actings, because they are put upon repenting, which Satan tells them is so easy a thing? Surely, were repentance so easy, wicked men would not be so much enraged when that doctrine is, by evangelical considerations, pressed upon them.

Remedy (5). The fifth remedy against this device of Satan is seriously to consider, *That to repent of sin is as great a work of grace as not to sin.*[1] By our sinful falls the powers of the soul are weakened, the strength of grace is decayed, our evidences for heaven are blotted, fears and doubts in the soul are raised (will God once more pardon this scarlet sin, and shew mercy to this wretched soul?), and corruptions in the heart are more advantaged and confirmed; and the conscience of a man after falls is the more enraged or the more benumbed. Now for a soul, notwithstanding all this, to repent of his falls, this shews that it is as great a work of grace to repent of sin as it is not to sin. Repentance is the vomit of the soul; and of all physic, none so difficult and hard as it is to vomit. The same means that tends to preserve the soul from sin, the same means works the soul to rise by repentance when it is fallen into sin. We know the mercy and loving-kindness of God is one special means to keep the soul from sin; as David spake, 'Thy loving-kindness is always before mine eyes, and I have walked in thy truth, and I have not sat with vain persons, neither will I go in with dissemblers. I have hated the congregation of evil doers, and will not sit with the wicked,' Ps. xxvi. 3–5. So by the same means the soul is raised by repentance out of sin, as you may see in Mary Magdalene, who loved much, and wept much, because much was forgiven her, Luke vii. 37–39, &c. So those in Hosea, 'Come, let us return unto the Lord; for he hath torn, and he will heal; he hath smitten, and he will bind us up. After two days he will revive us, in the third day he will raise us up, and we shall live in his sight, or before his face,' Hos. vi. 1, 2; as the Hebrew [לפניו] hath it, *i.e.* in his favour. Confidence in God's mercy and love, that he would heal them, and bind up their wounds, and revive their dejected spirits, and cause them to live in his favour, was that which did work their hearts to repent and return unto him.

[1] Yet it is better to be kept from sin than cured of sin by repentance, as it is better for a man to be preserved from a disease than to be cured of the disease.

I might further shew you this truth in many other particulars, but this may suffice: only remember this in the general, that there is as much of the power of God, and love of God, and faith in God, and fear of God, and care to please God, zeal for the glory of God, 2 Cor. vii. 11, requisite to work a man to repent of sin, as there is to keep a man from sin; by which you may easily judge, that to repent of sin is as great a work as not to sin. And now tell me, O soul, is it an easy thing not to sin? We know then certainly it is not an easy thing to repent of sin.

Remedy (6). The sixth remedy against this device of Satan is, seriously to consider, *That he that now tempts thee to sin upon this account, that repentance is easy, will, ere long, to work thee to despair, and for ever to break the neck of thy soul, present repentance as the difficultest and hardest work in the world;* and to this purpose he will set thy sins in order before thee, and make them to say, 'We are thine, and we must follow thee.'[1] Now, Satan will help to work the soul to look up, and see God angry; and to look inward, and to see conscience accusing and condemning; and to look downwards, and see hell's mouth open to receive the impenitent soul: and all this to render the work of repentance impossible to the soul. What, saith Satan, dost thou think that that is easy which the whole power of grace cannot conquer while we are in this world? Is it easy, saith Satan, to turn from some outward act of sin to which thou hast been addicted? Dost thou not remember that thou hast often complained against such and such particular sins, and resolved to leave them? and yet, to this hour, thou hast not, thou canst not? What will it then be to turn from every sin? Yea, to mortify and cut off those sins, those darling lusts, that are as joints and members, that be as right hands and right eyes? Hast thou not loved thy sins above thy Saviour? Hast thou not preferred earth before heaven? Hast thou not all along neglected the means of grace? and despised the offers of grace? and vexed the Spirit of grace? There would be no end, it I should set before thee the infinite evils that thou hast committed, and the innumerable good services that thou hast omitted, and the frequent checks of thy own conscience that thou hast contemned; and therefore thou mayest well conclude that thou canst never repent, that thou shalt never repent. Now, saith Satan, do but a little consider thy numberless sins, and the greatness of thy sins, the foulness of thy sins, the heinousness of thy sins, the circumstances of thy sins, and thou shalt easily see that those sins that thou thoughtest to be but motes, are indeed mountains; and is it not now in vain to repent of them? Surely, saith Satan, if thou shouldest seek repentance and

[1] Beda tells of a certain great man that was admonished in his sickness to repent, who answered that he would not repent yet; for if he should recover, his companions would laugh at him; but, growing sicker and sicker, his friends pressed him again to repent, but then he told them it was too late. *Quia jam judicatus sum et condemnatus:* For now, said he, I am judged and condemned.

As one *Lamachus*, a commander, said to one of his soldiers that was brought before him for a misbehaviour, who pleaded he would do so no more, saith he, *Non licet in bello bis peccare*, no man must offend twice in war; so God will not suffer men often to neglect the day of grace.

grace with tears, as Esau, thou shalt not find it; thy glass is out, thy sun is set, the door of mercy is shut, the golden sceptre is taken in, and now thou that hast despised mercy, shalt be for ever destroyed by justice. For such a wretch as thou art to attempt repentance, is to attempt a thing impossible. It is impossible that thou, that in all thy life couldst never conquer one sin, shouldst master such a numberless number of sins; which are so near, so dear, so necessary, and so profitable to thee, that have so long bedded and boarded with thee, that have been old acquaintance and companions with thee. Hast thou not often purposed, promised, vowed, and resolved to enter upon the practice of repentance, but to this day couldst never attain it? Surely it is in vain to strive against the stream, where it is so impossible to overcome; thou art lost and cast for ever; to hell thou must, to hell thou shalt. Ah, souls! he that now tempts you to sin, by suggesting to you the easiness of repentance, will at last work you to despair, and present repentance as the hardest work in all the world, and a work as far above man as heaven is above hell, as light is above darkness. Oh that you were wise, to break off your sins by timely repentance.[1]

Now the seventh device that Satan hath to draw the soul to sin is,

Device (7). *By making the soul bold to venture upon the occasions of sin.* Saith Satan, You may walk by the harlot's door, though you won't go into the harlot's bed; you may sit and sup with the drunkard, though you won't be drunk with the drunkard; you may look upon Jezebel's beauty, and you may play and toy with Delilah, though you do not commit wickedness with the one or the other; you may with Achan handle the golden wedge, though you do not steal the golden wedge, &c.

Now the remedies against this device of the devil are these:

Remedy (1). The first remedy is, solemnly *to dwell upon those scriptures that do expressly command us to avoid the occasions of sin, and the least appearance of evil:* 1 Thes. v. 22, 'Abstain from all appearance of evil.' Whatsoever is heterodox, unsound, and unsavoury, shun it, as you would do a serpent in your way, or poison in your meat.[2]

Theodosius tare the Arian's arguments presented to him in writing, because he found them repugnant to the Scriptures; and Austin retracted even ironies only, because they had the appearance of lying.

When God had commanded the Jews to abstain from swine's flesh, they would not so much as name it, but in their common talk would call a sow another thing. To abstain from all appearance of evil, is to do nothing wherein sin appears, or which hath a shadow of sin. Bernard glosseth finely, 'Whatever is of evil show,[3] or of ill report, that he may neither wound conscience nor credit.' We must shun and be shy of the very show and shadow of sin, if either we tender our credit abroad, or our comfort at home.

[1] Repentance is a work that must be timely done, or utterly undone for ever. *Aut pœnitendum aut pereundum.*

[2] Epiphanius saith that in the old law, when any dead body was carried by any house, they were enjoined to shut their doors and windows.

[3] *Quicquid est male coloratum.*

It was good counsel that Livia gave her husband Augustus: 'It behoveth thee not only not to do wrong, but not to seem to do so,' &c.: so Jude 23, 'And others save with fear, pulling them out of the fire, hating even the garment spotted by the flesh.' It is a phrase taken from legal uncleanness, which was contracted by touching the houses, the vessels, the garments, of unclean persons.[1] Under the law, men might not touch a menstruous cloth, nor God would not accept of a spotted peace-offering. So we must not only hate and avoid gross sins, but everything that may carry a savour or suspicion of sin; we must abhor the very signs and tokens of sin. So in Prov. v. 8, 'Remove thy way far from her, and come not nigh the door of her house.' He that would not be burnt, must dread the fire; he that would not hear the bell, must not meddle with the rope.[2] To venture upon the occasion of sin, and then to pray, 'Lead us not into temptation,' is all one as to thrust thy finger into the fire, and then to pray that it might not be burnt So, in Prov. iv. 14, 15, you have another command: 'Enter not into the path of the wicked, and go not in the way of evil men: avoid it, and pass not by it, turn from it, and pass away.' This triple gradation of Solomon sheweth with a great emphasis, how necessary it is for men to flee from all appearance of sin, as the seaman shuns sands and shelves, and as men shun those that have the plague-sores running upon them. As weeds do endanger the corn, as bad humours do endanger the blood, or as an infected house doth endanger the neighbourhood; so doth the company of the bad endanger those that are good. Entireness[3] with wicked consorts is one of the strongest chains of hell, and binds us to a participation of both sin and punishment.

Remedy (2). The second remedy against this device of Satan is, solemnly to consider, *That ordinarily there is no conquest over sin, without the soul turns from the occasion of sin.* It is impossible for that man to get the conquest of sin, that plays and sports with the occasions of sin. God will not remove the temptation, except you turn from the occasion. It is a just and righteous thing with God, that he should fall into the pit, that will adventure to dance upon the brink of the pit, and that he should be a slave to sin, that will not flee from the occasions of sin. As long as there is fuel in our hearts for a temptation, we cannot be secure. He that hath gunpowder about him had need keep far enough off from sparkles. To rush upon the occasions of sin, is both to tempt ourselves, and to tempt Satan to tempt our souls. It is very rare that any soul plays with the occasions of sin, but that soul is ensnared by sin.[4] It is seldom that God keeps that soul from the acts of sin, that will not keep off from the occasions of sin. He that adventures upon the occasions of sin is as he that would quench the fire with oil, which is a fuel to maintain it, and

[1] Socrates speaks of two young men that flung away their belts, when, being in an idol's temple, the lustrating water fell upon them, detesting, saith the historian, the garment spotted by the flesh. [The ecclesiastical historian, *not* the philosopher.—G.]

[2] One said, As oft as I have been among vain men, I returned home less a man than I was before.

[3] Friendship.—G.

[4] The fable saith, that the butterfly asked the owl how she should deal with the fire which had singed her wings, who counsels her not to behold so much as its smoke.

increase it. Ah, souls, often remember how frequently you have been overcome by sin, when you have boldly gone upon the occasions of sin; look back, souls, to the day of your vanity, wherein you have been as easily conquered as tempted, vanquished as assaulted, when you have played with the occasions of sin. As you would for the future be kept from the acting of sin, and be made victorious over sin, oh! flee from the occasions of sin.

Remedy (3). The third remedy against this device of Satan is, seriously to consider, *That other precious saints, that were once glorious on earth, and are now triumphing in heaven, have turned from the occasion of sin, as hell itself;* as you may see in Joseph, Gen. xxxix. 10, 'And it came to pass, as she spake to Joseph day by day, that he hearkened not unto her, to lie by her, or to be with her.'[1] Joseph was famous for all the four cardinal virtues, if ever any were. In this one temptation you may see his fortitude, justice, temperance, and prudence, in that he shuns the occasion: for he would not so much as be with her. And that a man is indeed, that he is in a temptation, which is but a tap to give vent to corruption. The Nazarite might not only not drink wine, but not taste a grape, or the husk of a grape. The leper was to shave his hair, and pare his nails. The devil counts a fit occasion half a conquest, for he knows that corrupt nature hath a seed-plot for all sin, which being drawn forth and watered by some sinful occasion, is soon set a-work to the producing of death and destruction. God will not remove the temptation, till we remove the occasion. A bird whiles aloft is safe, but she comes not near the snare without danger. The shunning the occasions of sin renders a man most like the best of men. A soul eminently gracious, dares not come near the train, though he be far off the blow. So Job xxxi. 1, 'I have made a covenant with mine eyes; why then should I think upon a maid?'[2] I set a watch at the entrance of my senses, that my soul might not by them be infected or endangered. The eye is the window of the soul, and if that should be always open, the soul might smart for it. A man may not look intently upon that, that he may not love entirely. The disciples were set a-gog, by beholding the beauty of the temple. It is best and safest to have the eye always fixed upon the highest and noblest objects: as the mariner's eye is fixed upon the star, when their hand is on the stern. So David, when he was himself, he shuns the occasion of sin: Ps. xxvi. 4, 5, 'I have not sat with vain persons, neither will I go in with dissemblers; I have hated the congregation of evil doers, and will not sit with the wicked.'

Stories speak of some that could not sleep when they thought of the trophies of other worthies, that went before them. The highest and choicest examples are to some, and should be to all, very quickening and provoking; and oh that the examples of those worthy saints, David, Joseph, and Job, might prevail with all your souls to shun and

[1] There are stories of heathens that would not look upon beauties, lest they should be ensnared. Democritus plucked out his own eyes to avoid the danger of uncleanness.

[2] ברית ברתי, I cut a covenant. In making covenants, it was a custom among the Jews to cut some beast or other in pieces, and so walk between the pieces, to signify that they desired God to destroy them that should break the covenant.

avoid the occasions of sin! Every one should strive to be like to them in grace, that they desire to be equal with in glory. He that shooteth at the sun, though he be far short, will shoot higher than he that aimeth at a shrub. It is best, and it speaks out much of Christ within, to eye the highest and the worthiest examples.

Remedy (4). The fourth remedy against this device of Satan is, solemnly to consider, *That the avoiding the occasions of sin, is an evidence of grace, and that which lifts up a man above most other men in the world.*[1] That a man is indeed, which he is in temptation; and when sinful occasions do present themselves before the soul, this speaks out both the truth and the strength of grace; when with Lot, a man can be chaste in Sodom, and with Timothy can live temperate in Asia, among the luxurious Ephesians; and with Job can walk uprightly in the land of Uz, where the people were profane in their lives, and superstitious in their worship; and with Daniel be holy in Babylon; and with Abraham righteous in Chaldea; and with Nehemiah, zealous in Damasco, &c. Many a wicked man is big and full of corruption, but shews it not for want of occasion; but that man is surely good, who in his course will not be bad, though tempted by occasions. A Christless soul is so far from refusing occasions when they come in his way, that he looks and longs after them, and rather than he will go without them he will buy them, not only with love or money, but also with the loss of his soul. Nothing but grace can fence a man against the occasions of sin, when he is strongly tempted thereunto. Therefore, as you would cherish a precious evidence in your own bosoms of the truth and strength of your graces, shun all sinful occasions.

The eighth device that Satan hath to draw the soul to sin, is,

Device (8). *By representing to the soul the outward mercies that vain men enjoy, and the outward miseries that they are freed from, whilst they have walked in the ways of sin.* Saith Satan, Dost thou see, O soul, the many mercies that such and such enjoy, that walk in those very ways that thy soul startles to think of, and the many crosses that they are delivered from, even such as makes other men, that say they dare not walk in such ways, to spend their days in sighing, weeping, groaning, and mourning? and therefore, saith Satan, if ever thou wouldst be freed from the dark night of adversity, and enjoy the sunshine of prosperity, thou must walk in their ways.[2]

By this stratagem the devil took those in Jer. xliv. 16–18, 'As for the word that thou hast spoken unto us in the name of the Lord, we will not hearken unto thee: but we will certainly do whatsoever thing goeth forth of our mouth, to burn incense unto the queen of heaven, and to pour out drink-offerings unto her, as we have done, we, and our fathers, our kings, and our princes, in the cities of Judah, and

[1] Plutarch saith of Demosthenes, that he was excellent at praising the worthy acts of his ancestors, but not so at imitating them. Oh that this were not applicable to many professors in our times!

[2] It was a weighty saying of Seneca, *Nihil est infelicius eo, cui nil unquam contigit adversi*, there is nothing more unhappy than he who never felt adversity. Some of the heathens would be wicked as their gods were, counting it a dishonour to their god to be unlike him.—*Lactantius.*

in the streets of Jerusalem: for then had we plenty of victuals, and were well, and saw no evil. But since we left off to burn incense to the queen of heaven, and to pour out drink-offerings unto her, we have wanted all things, and have been consumed by the sword and by the famine.' This is just the language of a world of ignorant, profane, and superstitious souls in London, and England, that would have made them a captain to return to bondage, yea, to that bondage that was worse than that the Israelites groaned under. Oh, say they, since such and such persons have been put down, and left off, we have had nothing but plundering and taxing, and butchering of men, &c.; and therefore we will do as we, and our kings, and nobles, and fathers have formerly done, for then had we plenty at home, and peace abroad, &c., and there was none to make us afraid.[1]

Now the remedies against this device of Satan are these that follow:

Remedy (1). The first remedy is, solemnly to consider, *That no man knows how the heart of God stands by his hand.* His hand of mercy may be towards a man, when his heart may be against that man, as you may see in Saul and others; and the hand of God may be set against a man, when the heart of God is dearly set upon a man, as you may see in Job and Ephraim.[2] The hand of God was sorely set against them, and yet the heart and bowels of God were strongly working towards them. No man knoweth either love or hatred by outward mercy or misery; for all things come alike to all, to the righteous and to the unrighteous, to the good and to the bad, to the clean and to the unclean, &c. The sun of prosperity shines as well upon brambles of the wilderness as fruit-trees of the orchard; the snow and hail of adversity lights upon the best garden as well as the stinking dunghill or the wild waste. Ahab's and Josiah's ends concur in the very circumstances. Saul and Jonathan, though different in their natures, deserts, and deportments, yet in their deaths they were not divided. Health, wealth, honours, &c., crosses, sicknesses, losses, &c., are cast upon good men and bad men promiscuously. 'The whole Turkish empire is nothing else but a crust, cast by heaven's great housekeeper to his dogs.'[3] Moses dies in the wilderness as well as those that murmured. Nabal is rich, as well as Abraham; Ahithophel wise, as well as Solomon; and Doeg honoured by Saul, as well as Joseph was by Pharaoh. Usually the worst of men have most of these outward things; and the best of men have least of earth, though most of heaven.

Remedy (2). The second remedy against this device of Satan is, seriously to consider, *That there is nothing in the world that doth so*

[1] It is said of one of the emperors, that Rome had no war in his days, because it was plague enough to have such an emperor. You are wise, and know how to apply it. [The allusion, no doubt, is to Charles I., and the agitation for the Restoration of Charles II Cromwell died Sept. 3. 1658.—G.]

[2] Tully judged the Jews' religion to be naught, because they were so often overcome, and impoverished, and afflicted; and the religion of Rome to be right, because the Romans prospered and became lords of the world; and yet, though the Romans had his hand, yet the Jews had his heart, for they were dearly beloved though sorely afflicted. [Brooks's reference is found in Cicero, in Orat. Pro L. Flacco 28.—G.]

[3] Nihil est nisi mica panis.—*Luther.*

provoke God to be wroth and angry, as men's taking encouragement from God's goodness and mercy to do wickedly. This you may see by that wrath that fell upon the old world, and by God's raining hell out of heaven upon Sodom and Gomorrah. This is clear in Jeremiah xliv., from ver. 20 to ver. 28. The words are worthy of your best meditation. Oh that they were engraven in all your hearts, and constant in all your thoughts! Though they are too large for me to transcribe them, yet they are not too large for me to remember them. To argue from mercy to sinful liberty, is the devil's logic, and such logicians do ever walk as upon a mine of gunpowder ready to be blown up. No such soul can ever avert or avoid the wrath of God. This is wickedness at the height, for a man to be very bad, because God is very good. A worse spirit than this is not in hell. Ah, Lord, doth not wrath, yea, the greatest wrath, lie at this man's door? Are not the strongest chains of darkness prepared for such a soul? To sin against mercy is to sin against humanity. It is bestial; nay, it is worse. To render good for evil is divine, to render good for good is human, to render evil for evil is brutish; but to render evil for good is devilish; and from this evil deliver my soul, O God.[1]

Remedy (3). The third remedy against this device of Satan is, solemnly to consider, *That there is no greater misery in this life, than not to be in misery; no greater affliction, than not to be afflicted.* Woe, woe to that soul that God will not spend a rod upon! This is the saddest stroke of all, when God refuses to strike at all: Hos. iv. 17, 'Ephraim is joined to idols; let him alone.' 'Why should you be smitten any more? you will revolt more and more,' Isa. i. 5. When the physician gives over the patient, you say, 'Ring out his knell, the man is dead.' So when God gives over a soul to sin without control, you may truly say, 'This soul is lost,' you may ring out his knell, for he is twice dead, and plucked up by the roots. Freedom from punishment is the mother of security, the step-mother of virtue, the poison of religion, the moth of holiness, and the introducer of wickedness. 'Nothing,' said one, 'seems more unhappy to me, than he to whom no adversity hath happened.' Outward mercies ofttimes prove a snare to our souls. 'I will lay a stumbling-block,' Ezek. iii. 20. Vatablus his note there is, 'I will prosper him in all things, and not by affliction restrain him from sin.'[2] Prosperity hath been a stumbling-block, at which millions have stumbled and fallen, and broke the neck of their souls for ever.[3]

Remedy (4). The fourth remedy against this device of Satan is, seriously to consider, *That the wants of wicked men, under all their outward mercy and freedom from adversity, is far greater than all their outward enjoyments.* They have many mercies, yet they want more than they enjoy; the mercies which they enjoy are nothing to the

[1] Such souls make God a god of *clouts*, one that will not do as he saith; but they shall find God to be as severe in punishing as he is to others gracious in pardoning. Good turns aggravate unkindnesses, and our guilt is increased by our obligations.

[2] Faciam ut omnia habeat prospera; calamitatibus eum a peccato non revocabo. [Annot. in Lib. Vet. Test. Paris, 1557.—G.]

[3] *Religio peperit divitias, et filia devoravit matrem*; religion brought forth riches, and the daughter soon devoured the mother, saith Augustine.

mercies they want. It is true, they have honours and riches, and pleasures and friends, and are mighty in power; their seed is established in their sight with them, and their offspring before their eyes: 'Their houses are safe from fear, neither is the rod of God upon them;' 'They send forth their little ones like a flock, and their children dance. They take the timbrel and harp, and rejoice at the sound of the organ;' 'They spend their days in wealth, their eyes stand out with fatness, they have more than heart can wish: and they have no bands in their death, but their strength is firm; they are not in trouble as other men,' as David and Job speak.[1] Yet all this is nothing to what they want.[2] They want interest in God, Christ, the Spirit, the promises, the covenant of grace, and everlasting glory; they want acceptation and reconciliation with God; they want righteousness, justification, sanctification, adoption, and redemption; they want the pardon of sin, and power against sin, and freedom from the dominion of sin; they want that favour that is better than life, and that joy that is unspeakable and full of glory, and that peace that passes understanding, and that grace, the least spark of which is more worth than heaven and earth; they want a house that hath foundations, whose builder and maker is God; they want those riches that perish not, the glory that fades not, that kingdom that shakes not. Wicked men are the most needy men in the world, yea, they want those two things that should render their mercies sweet, viz., the blessing of God, and content with their condition, and without which their heaven is but hell on this side hell.[3] When their hearts are lifted up and grown big upon the thoughts of their abundance, if conscience does but put in a word and say, It is true, here is this and that outward mercy. Oh, but where is an interest in Christ? Where is the favour of God? Where are the comforts of the Holy Ghost? Where are the evidences for heaven? &c. This word from conscience makes the man's countenance to change, his thoughts to be troubled, his heart to be amazed, and all his mercies on the right hand and left to be as dead and withered. Ah, were but the eyes of wicked men open to see their wants under their abundance, they would cry out and say, as Absalom did, 'What are all these to me so long as I cannot see the king's face?' 2 Sam. xiv. 24, 33. What is honour, and riches, and the favour of creatures, so long as I want the favour of God, the pardon of my sins, an interest in Christ, and the hopes of glory! O Lord, give me these, or I die; give me these, or else I shall eternally die.

Remedy (5). The fifth remedy against this device of Satan is, solemnly to consider, *That outward things are not as they seem, and are esteemed.* They have, indeed, a glorious outside, but if you view

[1] Cf. Psalm xlix. 11, lxxiii. 7; Job xxi. 12, &c., &c.—G.

[2] Men that enjoy all worldly comforts may truly say, *Omnes humanæ consolationes sunt desolationes.*

[3] *Nec Christus nec cœlum patitur hyperbolem*, neither Christ nor heaven can be hyperbolised. A crown of gold cannot cure the headache, nor a velvet slipper cannot ease the gout; no more can honour or riches quiet and still the conscience. The heart of man is a three-square triangle, which the whole round circle of the world cannot fill, as mathematicians say, but all the corners will complain of emptiness, and hunger for something else.

their insides, you will easily find that they fill the head full of cares, and the heart full of fears. What if the fire should consume one part of my estate, and the sea should be a grave to swallow up another part of my estate! what if my servants should be unfaithful abroad, and my children should be deceitful at home! Ah, the secret fretting, vexing, and gnawing that doth daily, yea hourly, attend those men's souls whose hands are full of worldly goods!

It was a good speech of an emperor, 'You,' said he, 'gaze on my purple robe and golden crown, but did you know what cares are under it, you would not take it up from the ground to have it.' It was a true saying of Augustine on the 26th Psalm, 'Many are miserable by loving hurtful things, but they are more miserable by having them.'[1] It is not what men enjoy, but the principle from whence it comes, that makes men happy. Much of these outward things do usually cause great distraction, great vexation, and great condemnation at last, to the possessors of them. If God gives them in his wrath, and do not sanctify them in his love, they will at last be witnesses against a man, and millstones for ever to sink a man in that day when God shall call men to an account, not for the use, but for the abuse of mercy.

Remedy (6). The sixth remedy against this device of Satan is, seriously to consider *the end and the design of God in heaping up mercy upon the heads of the wicked, and in giving them a* quietus est, *rest and quiet from those sorrows and sufferings that others sigh under.* David, in Psalm lxxiii. 17–20, shews the end and design of God in this. Saith he, 'When I went into the sanctuary of God, then I understood their end: surely thou didst set them in slippery places, thou castedst them down into destruction. How are they brought into desolation as in a moment: they are utterly consumed with terrors. As a dream, when one awaketh, so, O Lord, when thou awakest, thou shalt despise their image.'[2] So in Ps. xcii. 7, 'When the wicked spring as grass, and when all the workers of iniquity do flourish, it is that they shall be destroyed for ever.' God's setting them up, is but in order to his casting them down; his raising them high, is but in order to his bringing them low: Exod. ix. 16, 'And in very deed, for this cause have I raised thee up, for to shew in thee my power, and that my name may be declared throughout all the earth.' I have constituted and set thee up as a butt-mark,[3] that I may let fly at thee, and follow thee close with plague upon plague, till I have beaten the very breath out of thy body, and got myself a name, by setting my feet upon the neck of all thy pride, power, pomp, and glory. Ah, souls, what man in his wits would be lifted up that he might be cast down; would be set higher than others, when it is but

[1] Multi amando res noxias sunt miseri, habendo miseriores.—*Augustine* on Psalm xxvi.—G.

[2] Valens, the Roman emperor, fell from being an emperor to be a footstool to Sapor, king of Persia. Dionysius, king of Sicily, fell from his kingly glory to be a schoolmaster. The brave Queen Zenobia was brought to Rome in golden chains. Valens, an emperor, Belisarius, a famous general, Henry the Fourth, Bajazet, Pythias, great Pompey, and William the Conqueror, these, from being very high, were brought very low; they all fell from great glory and majesty to great poverty and misery.

[3] Arrow-mark or target.—G.

in order to his being brought down lower than others? There is not a wicked man in the world that is set up with Lucifer, as high as heaven, but shall with Lucifer be brought down as low as hell. Canst thou think seriously of this, O soul, and not say, O Lord, I humbly crave that thou wilt let me be little in this world, that I may be great in another world; and low here, that I may be high for ever hereafter.[1] Let me be low, and feed low, and live low, so I may live with thee for ever; let me now be clothed with rags, so thou wilt clothe me at last with thy robes; let me now be set upon a dunghill, so I may at last be advanced to sit with thee upon thy throne. Lord, make me rather gracious than great, inwardly holy than outwardly happy, and rather turn me into my first nothing, yea, make me worse than nothing, rather than set me up for a time, that thou mayest bring me low for ever.

Remedy (7). The seventh remedy against this device of Satan is solemnly to consider, *That God doth often most plague and punish those whom others think he doth most spare and love;* that is, God doth plague and punish them most with spiritual judgments—which are the greatest, the sorest, and the heaviest—whom he least punishes with temporal punishments.[2] There are no men on earth so internally plagued as those that meet with least external plagues. Oh the blindness of mind, the hardness of heart, the searedness of conscience, that those souls are given up to, who, in the eye of the world, are reputed the most happy men, because they are not outwardly afflicted and plagued as other men. Ah, souls, it were better that all the temporal plagues that ever befell the children of men since the fall of Adam should at once meet upon your souls, than that you should be given up to the least spiritual plague, to the least measure of spiritual blindness or spiritual hardness of heart, &c. Nothing will better that man, nor move that man, that is given up to spiritual judgments. Let God smile or frown, stroke or strike, cut or kill, he minds it not, he regards it not; let life or death, heaven or hell, be set before him, it stirs him not; he is mad upon his sin, and God is fully set to do justice upon his soul. This man's preservation is but a reservation unto a greater condemnation; this man can set no bounds to himself; he is become a brat of fathomless perdition; he hath guilt in his bosom and vengeance at his back wherever he goes. Neither ministry nor misery, neither miracle nor mercy, can mollify his heart, and if this soul be not in hell, on this side hell, who is?[3]

Remedy (8). The eighth remedy against this device of Satan is, *To dwell more upon that strict account that vain men must make for all that good that they do enjoy.*[4] Ah! did men dwell more

[1] Da Domine, ut sic possideamus temporalia, ut non perdamus æterna. Grant us, Lord, that we may so partake of temporal felicity, that we may not lose eternal.—*Bernard.*

[2] Psalm lxxxi. 12, lxxviii. 26–31, cvi. 15. He gave them their requests, but sent leanness into their soul. It is a heavy plague to have a fat body and a lean soul; a house full of gold, and a heart full of sin.

[3] It is better to have a sore than a seared conscience. It is better to have no heart than a hard heart, no mind than a blind mind.

[4] In this day men shall give an account (De bonis commissis, de bonis dimissis, de malis commissis, de malis permissis) of good things committed unto them, of good things

upon that account that they must ere long give for all the mercies that they have enjoyed, and for all the favours that they have abused, and for all the sins they have committed, it would make their hearts to tremble and their lips to quiver, and rottenness to enter into their bones; it would cause their souls to cry out, and say, Oh that our mercies had been fewer and lesser, that our account might have been easier, and our torment and misery, for our abuse of so great mercy, not greater than we are able to bear. Oh cursed be the day wherein the crown of honour was set upon our heads, and the treasures of this world were cast into our laps; oh cursed be the day wherein the sun of prosperity shined so strong upon us, and this flattering world smiled so much upon us, as to occasion us to forget God, to slight Jesus Christ, to neglect our souls, and to put far from us the day of our account!

Philip the Third of Spain, whose life was free from gross evils, professed, 'That he would rather lose his kingdom than offend God willingly;' yet being in the agony of death, and considering more thoroughly of his account he was to give to God, fear struck into him, and these words brake from him: 'Oh! would to God I had never reigned. Oh that those years that I have spent in my kingdom, I had lived a solitary life in the wilderness! Oh that I had lived a solitary life with God! How much more securely should I now have died! How much more confidently should I have gone to the throne of God! What doth all my glory profit me, but that I have so much the more torment in my death?' God keeps an exact account of every penny that is laid out upon him and his, and that is laid out against him and his; and this in the day of account men shall know and feel, though now they wink and will not understand. The sleeping of vengeance causeth the overflowing of sin, and the overflowing of sin causeth the awakening of vengeance. Abused mercy will certainly turn into fury. God's forbearance is no quittance. The day is at hand when he will pay wicked men for the abuse of old and new mercies. If he seem to be slow, yet he is sure. He hath leaden heels, but iron hands. The farther he stretcheth his bow, or draweth his arrow, the deeper he will wound in the day of vengeance. Men's actions are all in print in heaven, and God will, in the day of account, read them aloud in the ears of all the world, that they may all say Amen to that righteous sentence that he shall pass upon all despisers and abusers of mercy.[1]

The ninth device that Satan hath to draw the soul to sin is,

Device (9). *By presenting to the soul the crosses, losses, reproaches, sorrows, and sufferings that do daily attend those that walk in the ways of holiness.* Saith Satan, Do not you see that there are none in the world that are so vexed, afflicted, and tossed, as those that walk more circumspectly and holily than their neighbours?

neglected by them, of evil committed by them, and of evils suffered [allowed] by them. In die judicii plus valebit conscientia pura, quam marsupia plena; then shall a good conscience be more worth than all the world's good.—*Bernard.*

[1] Hierom [Jerome] still thought that voice was in his ears (*Surgite mortui et venite ad judicium*), Arise, you dead, and come to judgment. As oft as I think on that day, how doth my whole body quake, and my heart within me tremble.

They are a byword at home, and a reproach abroad; their miseries come in upon them like Job's messengers, one upon the neck of another, and there is no end of their sorrows and troubles. Therefore, saith Satan, you were better walk in ways that are less troublesome, and less afflicted, though they be more sinful; for who but a madman would spend his days in sorrow, vexation, and affliction, when it may be prevented by walking in the ways that I set before him?

Now the remedies against this device of Satan are these:

Remedy (1). The first remedy against this device of Satan is, solemnly to consider, *That all the afflictions that do attend the people of God, are such as shall turn to the profit and glorious advantage of the people of God.* They shall discover that filthiness and vileness in sin, that yet the soul hath never seen.

It was a speech of a German divine[1] in his sickness, 'In this disease I have learned how great God is, and what the evil of sin is; I never knew to purpose what God was before, nor what sin meant, till now.' Afflictions are a crystal glass, wherein the soul hath the clearest sight of the ugly face of sin. In this glass the soul comes to see sin to be but a bitter-sweet; yea, in this glass the soul comes to see sin not only to be an evil, but to be the greatest evil in the world, to be an evil far worse than hell itself.

Again, They shall contribute to the mortifying and purging away of their sins, Isa. i. 15, and xxvii. 8, 9. Afflictions are God's furnace, by which he cleanses his people from their dross. Affliction is a fire to purge out our dross, and to make virtue shine; it is a potion to carry away ill humours, better than all the *benedictum medicamentum,* as physicians call them.[2] Aloes kill worms; colds and frosts do destroy vermin; so do afflictions the corruptions that are in our hearts. The Jews, under all the prophet's thunderings, retained their idols; but after their Babylonish captivity, it is observed, there have been no idols found amongst them.

Again, Afflictions are sweet preservatives to keep the saints from sin, which is a greater evil than hell itself. As Job spake, 'Surely it is meet to be said unto God, I have borne chastisement, I will not offend any more: That which I see not, teach thou me; if I have done iniquity, I will do no more. Once have I spoken foolishly, yea, twice, I will do so no more,' Job xxxiv. 31, 32. The burnt child dreads the fire. Ah! saith the soul under the rod, sin is but a bitter-sweet; and for the future I intend, by the strength of Christ, that I will not buy repentance at so dear a rate.[3]

The Rabbins, to scare their scholars from sin, were wont to tell them, 'That sin made God's head ache;' and saints under the rod have found by woful experience, that sin makes not only their heads, but their hearts ache also.

Augustine, by wandering out of his way, escaped one that lay in

[1] Gaspar Olevianus (1586).—G.

[2] In times of peace our armour is rusty, in time of war it is bright.

[3] Salt brine preserves from putrefaction, and salt marshes keep the sheep rom the rot: so do afflictions the saints from sin. The ball in the Emblem saith, *Percussa surgo,* the harder you beat me down in affliction, the higher I shall bound in affection towards heaven and heavenly things.

wait to mischief him.[1] If afflictions did not put us out of our way, we should many times meet with some sin or other that would mischief our precious souls.

Again, They will work the saints to be more fruitful in holiness: Heb. xii. 10, 11, 'But he afflicts us for our profit, that we might be partakers of his holiness.' The flowers smell sweetest after a shower; vines bear the better for bleeding; the walnut-tree is most fruitful when most beaten. Saints spring and thrive most internally when they are most externally afflicted. Afflictions are called by some 'the mother of virtue.' Manasseh his chain was more profitable to him than his crown. Luther could not understand some Scriptures till he was in affliction. The Christ-cross is no letter, and yet that taught him more than all the letters in the row. God's house of correction is his school of instruction.[2] All the stones that came about Stephen's ears did but knock him closer to Christ, the corner-stone. The waves did but lift Noah's ark nearer to heaven; and the higher the waters grew, the more near the ark was lifted up to heaven. Afflictions do lift up the soul to more rich, clear, and full enjoyments of God:[3] Hosea ii. 14, 'Behold, I will allure her into the wilderness, and speak comfortably to her'; (or rather, as the Hebrew hath it); 'I will earnestly or vehemently speak to her heart.'[4] God makes afflictions to be but inlets to the soul's more sweet and full enjoyment of his blessed self. When was it that Stephen saw the heavens open, and Christ standing at the right hand of God, but when the stones were about his ears, and there was but a short step betwixt him and eternity? And when did God appear in his glory to Jacob, but in the day of his troubles, when the stones were his pillows, and the ground his bed, and the hedges his curtains, and the heavens his canopy? Then he saw the angels of God ascending and descending in their glistering robes. The plant in Nazianzen grows with cutting; being cut, it flourisheth; it contends with the axe, it lives by dying, and by cutting it grows.[5] So do saints by their afflictions that do befall them; they gain more experience of the power of God supporting them, of the wisdom of God directing them, of the grace of God refreshing and cheering them, and of the goodness of God quieting and quickening of them, to a greater love to holiness, and to a greater delight in holiness, and to a more vehement pursuing after holiness.

I have read of a fountain, that at noonday is cold, and at midnight it grows warm; so many a precious soul is cold God-wards, and heaven-wards, and holiness-wards, in the day of prosperity; that grow warm God-wards and heaven-wards, and holiness-wards, in the midnight of adversity.

Again, Afflictions serve to keep the hearts of the saints humble and

[1] Confessions.—G.

[2] Schola crucis, schola lucis.

[3] Cf. 'Epistle' prefixed to Durant's *Altum Silentium*, by Brooks.—G.

[4] ודברתי . . . על לבה *Vedibbartignal libbab.*

[5] It is reported of Tiberius the emperor, that passing by a place where he saw a cross lying in the ground upon a marble stone, and causing the stone to be digged up, he found a great deal of treasure under the cross. So many a precious saint hath found much spiritual and heavenly treasure under the crosses they have met withal.

tender: Lam. iii. 19, 20, 'Remembering my affliction and my misery, the wormwood and the gall. My soul hath them still in remembrance, and is humbled in me,' or bowed down in me, as the original hath it.[1] So David, when he was under the rod, could say, 'I was dumb, I opened not my mouth; because thou didst it,' Ps. xxxix. 4.

I have read of one [Gregory Nazianzen], who, when anything fell out prosperously, would read over the Lamentation of Jeremiah, and that kept his heart tender, humbled, and low. Prosperity doth not contribute more to the puffing up the soul, than adversity doth to the bowing down of the soul. This the saints by experience find; and therefore they can kiss and embrace the cross, as others do the world's crown.[2]

Again, They serve to bring the saints nearer to God, and to make them more importunate and earnest in prayer with God. 'Before I was afflicted, I went astray; but now have I kept thy word.' 'It is good for me that I have been afflicted, that I might learn thy statutes.' 'I will be to Ephraim as a lion, and as a young lion to the house of Judah. I, even I, will tear and go away: I will take away, and none shall rescue him.' 'I will go and return to my place, till they acknowledge their offence, and seek my face: in their affliction they will seek me early.' And so they did. 'Come,' say they, 'and let us return unto the Lord: for he hath torn, and he will heal us; he hath smitten, and he will bind us up. After two days he will revive us: in the third day he will raise us up, and we shall live in his sight.'[3] So when God had hedged up their way with thorns, then they say, 'I will go and return to my first husband; for then was it with me better than now,' Hosea ii. 6, 7. Ah the joy, the peace, the comfort, the delight, and content that did attend us, when we kept close communion with God, doth bespeak our return to God. 'We will return to our first husband; for then was it with us better than now.'

When Tiribazus, a noble Persian, was arrested, he drew out his sword, and defended himself; but when they told him that they came to carry him to the king, he willingly yielded.[4] So, though a saint may at first stand a little out, yet when he remembers that afflictions are to carry nearer to God, he yields, and kisses the rod. Afflictions are like the prick at the nightingale's breast, that awakes her, and puts her upon her sweet and delightful singing.

Again, Afflictions they serve to revive and recover decayed graces; they inflame that love that is cold, and they quicken that faith that is decaying, and they put life into those hopes that are withering, and spirits into those joys and comforts that are languishing.[5] Musk, saith one, when it hath lost its sweetness, if it be put into the sink amongst filth it recovers it. So do afflictions recover and revive de-

[1] יתשוח from שוח.

[2] The more precious odours and the purest spices, are beaten and bruised, the sweeter scent and savour they send abroad. So do saints when they are afflicted.

[3] Ps. cxix. 67, 71. Hosea v. 14, 15; vi. 1, 2.

[4] Cf. Diodorus xv. 8–11: Plutarch, *Artaxerxes*, 24, 27, 29.—G.

[5] Most men are like a top, that will not go unless you whip it, and the more you whip it the better it goes. You know how to apply it. They that are in adversity, saith Luther, do better understand Scriptures; but those that are in prosperity, read them as a verse in Ovid. Bees are killed with honey, but quickened with vinegar. The honey of prosperity kills our graces, but the vinegar of adversity quickens our graces.

cayed graces. The more saints are beaten with the hammer of afflictions, the more they are made the trumpets of God's praises, and the more are their graces revived and quickened. Adversity abases the loveliness of the world that might entice us; it abates the lustiness of the flesh within, that might incite us to folly and vanity; and it abets the spirit in his quarrel to the two former, which tends much to the reviving and recovering of decayed graces. Now, suppose afflictions and troubles attend the ways of holiness, yet seeing that they all work for the great profit and singular advantage of the saints, let no soul be so mad as to leave an afflicted way of holiness, to walk in a smooth path of wickedness.

Remedy (2). The second remedy against this device of Satan is, solemnly to consider, *that all the afflictions that do befall the saints, do only reach their worser part; they reach not, they hurt not, their noble part, their best part.* All the arrows stick in the target, they reach not the conscience: 1 Peter iii. 13, 'And who shall harm you, if ye be followers of that which is good,' saith the apostle. That is, none shall harm you. They may thus and thus afflict you, but they shall never harm you.[1]

It was the speech of an heathen, whenas by the tyrant he was commanded to be put into a mortar, and to be beaten to pieces with an iron pestle, he cries out to his persecutors, 'You do but beat the vessel, the case, the husk of Anaxarchus, you do not beat me.' His body was to him but as a case, a husk; he counted his soul himself, which they could not reach. You are wise, and know how to apply it.

Socrates said of his enemies, 'They may kill me, but they cannot hurt me.' So afflictions may kill us, but they cannot hurt us; they may take away my life, but they cannot take away my God, my Christ, my crown.

Remedy (3). The third remedy against this device of Satan is, seriously to consider, *That the afflictions that do attend the saints in the ways of holiness, are but short and momentary.* 'Sorrow may abide for a night, but joy comes in the morning,' Ps. xxx. 5. This short storm will end in an everlasting calm, this short night will end in a glorious day, that shall never have end.[2] It is but a very short time between grace and glory, between our title to the crown and our wearing the crown, between our right to the heavenly inheritance and our possession of the heavenly inheritance. Fourteen thousand years to the Lord is but as one day. What is our life but a shadow, a bubble, a flower, a post, a span, a dream? &c. Yea, so small a while doth the hand of the Lord rest upon us, that Luther cannot get diminutives enough to extenuate it, for he calls it a very little cross that we bear, το πικρον μικρον. The prophet in Isaiah xxvi. 20, saith the indignation doth not (*transire*) pass, but (*pertransire*) over-pass. The sharpness, shortness, and suddenness of it is set forth by

[1] The Christian soldier shall ever be master of the day. *Mori posse, vinci non posse,* said Cyprian to Cornelius; he may suffer death, but never conquest.

[2] There are none of God's afflicted ones that have not their *lucida intervalla,* intermissions, respites, and breathing whiles, under their short and momentary afflictions. When God's hand is on thy back, let thy hand be on thy mouth, for though the affliction be sharp, it shall be but short.

the travail of a woman, John xvi. 21. And that is a sweet scripture, 'For ye have need of patience, that after ye have done the will of God, ye might receive the promise.' 'For yet a little while, he that shall come will come, and will not tarry,' Heb. x. 36, 37. *Tantillum tantillum adhuc pusillum.* A little, little, little while.[1]

When Athanasius's friends came to bewail him, because of his misery and banishment, he said, 'It is but a little cloud, and will quickly be gone.'[2] It will be but as a day before God will give his afflicted ones beauty for ashes, the oil of gladness for the spirit of heaviness; before he will turn all your sighing into singing, all your lamentations into consolations, your sackcloth into silks, ashes into ointments, and your fasts into everlasting feasts, &c.

Remedy (4). The fourth remedy against this device of Satan, is seriously to consider, *That the afflictions that do befall the saints are such as proceed from God's dearest love.*[3] 'As many as I love, I rebuke and chasten,' Rev. iii. 19. Saints, saith God, think not that I hate you, because I thus chide you. He that escapes reprehension may suspect his adoption. God had one Son without corruption, but no son without correction. A gracious soul may look through the darkest cloud, and see a God smiling on him. We must look through the anger of his correction to the sweetness of his countenance; and as by the rainbow we see the beautiful image of the sun's light in the midst of a dark and waterish cloud.

When Munster lay sick, and his friends asked him how he did and how he felt himself, he pointed to his sores and ulcers, whereof he was full, and said, 'These are God's gems and jewels, wherewith he decketh his best friends, and to me they are more precious than all the gold and silver in the world.' A soul at first conversion is but rough cast; but God by afflictions doth square and fit, and fashion it for that glory above, which doth speak them out to flow from precious love; therefore the afflictions that do attend the people of God should be no bar to holiness, nor no motive to draw the soul to ways of wickedness.

Remedy (5). The fifth remedy against this device of Satan is, solemnly to consider, *That it is our duty and glory not to measure afflictions by the smart but by the end.* When Israel was dismissed out of Egypt, it was with gold and ear-rings, Exod. xi. 3; so the Jews were dismissed out of Babylon with gifts, jewels, and all necessary utensils, Ezra i. 7–11. Look more at the latter end of a Christian than the beginning of his affliction. Consider the patience of Job, and what end the Lord made with him. Look not upon Lazarus lying at Dives's door, but lying in Abraham's bosom. Look not to the beginning of Joseph, who was so far from his dream, that the sun and moon should reverence him, that for two years he was cast where he could see neither sun, moon, nor stars; but behold him at last made ruler over Egypt. Look not upon David, as there was but a step between him and death, nor as he was envied by some, and slighted and

[1] Ἔτι γὰρ μικρὸν ὅσον ὅσον. [2] Nubecula est, cito transibit.—*Athanasius.*

[3] Austin asketh, *Si amatur quo modo infirmatur*, If he were beloved, how came he to be sick? So are wicked men apt to say, because they know not that corrections are pledges of our adoption, and badges of our Sonship. God had one Son without sin, but none without sorrow.—[Augustine on Rev. iii. 19.—G.]

despised by others; but behold him seated in his royal throne, and dying in his bed of honour, and his son Solomon and all his glistering nobles about him. Afflictions, they are but as a dark entry into your Father's house; they are but as a dirty lane to a royal palace. Now tell me, souls, whether it be not very great madness to shun the ways of holiness, and to walk in the ways of wickedness, because of those afflictions that do attend the ways of holiness.[1]

Remedy (6). The sixth remedy against this device of Satan is, seriously to consider, *That the design of God in all the afflictions that do befall them, is only to try them; it is not to wrong them, nor to ruin them, as ignorant souls are apt to think.* 'He knoweth the way that I take: and when he hath tried me, I shall come forth as gold,' saith patient Job, xxiii. 10. So in Deut. viii. 2, 'And thou shalt remember all the way which the Lord thy God led thee these forty years in the wildernesss, to humble thee, and to prove thee, to know what was in thy heart, whether thou wouldst keep his commandments or no.' God afflicted them thus, that he might make known to themselves and others what was in their hearts. When fire is put to green wood, there comes out abundance of watery stuff that before appeared not; when the pond is empty, the mud, filth, and toads come to light.[2] The snow covers many a dunghill, so doth prosperity many a rotten heart. It is easy to wade in a warm bath, and every bird can sing in a sunshine day, &c. Hard weather tries what health we have; afflictions try what sap we have, what grace we have. Withered leaves soon fall off in windy weather, rotten boughs quickly break with heavy weights, &c. You are wise, and know how to apply it.

Afflictions are like pinching frosts, that will search us; where we are most unsound, we shall soonest complain, and where most corruptions lie, we shall most shrink. We try metal by knocking; if it sound well, then we like it. So God tries his by knocking, and if under knocks they yield a pleasant sound, God will turn their night into day, and their bitter into sweet, and their cross into a crown; and they shall hear that voice, 'Arise, and shine; for the glory of the Lord is risen upon thee, and the favours of the Lord are flowing in on thee,' Isa. lx. 1.[3]

Remedy (7). The seventh remedy against this device of Satan is, solemnly to consider, *That the afflictions, wrath, and misery that do attend the ways of wickedness, are far greater and heavier than those are that do attend the ways of holiness.*[4] Oh, the galling, girding, lashing, and gnawing of conscience, that do attend souls

[1] Afflictions, they are but our Father's goldsmiths, who are working to add pearls to our crowns. Tiberius saw paradise when he walked upon hot burning coals. Herodotus said of the Assyrians, Let them drink nothing but wormwood all their life long; when they die, they shall swim in honey. You are wise, and know how to apply it.

[2] The king of Aracam, in Scaliger, tries her whom he means to marry by sweating. If they be sweet, he marries them; if not, then he rejects them. You may easily make the application.

[3] Dunghills raked send out a filthy steam, ointments a sweet perfume. This is applicable to sinners and saints under the rod.

[4] Sin oftentimes makes men insensible of the wrath of the Almighty. Sin transforms many a man, as it were, into those bears in Pliny, that could not be stirred with the sharpest prickles; or those fishes in Aristotle, that though they have spears thrust into their sides, yet they awake not. [*Bears*: Pliny, lib. viii. c. 54.—G.]

in a way of wickedness! 'The wicked,' saith Isaiah, 'are like the troubled sea, when it cannot rest, whose waters cast up mire and dirt.' 'There is no peace to the wicked, saith my God.'[1] There are snares in all their mercies, and curses and crosses do attend all their comforts, both at home and abroad. What is a fine suit of clothes with the plague in it? and what is a golden cup when there is poison at the bottom? or what is a silken stocking with a broken leg in it? The curse of God, the wrath of God, the hatred of God, and the fierce indignation of God, do always attend sinners walking in a way of wickedness. Turn to Deut. xxviii., and read from ver. 15 to the end of the chapter, and turn to Levit. xxvi., and read from ver. 14 to the end of that chapter, and then you shall see how the curse of God haunts the wicked, as it were a fury, in all his ways. In the city it attends him, in the country hovers over him; coming in, it accompanies him; going forth, it follows him, and in travel it is his comrade. It fills his store with strife, and mingles the wrath of God with his sweetest morsels. It is a moth in his wardrobe, murrain among his cattle, mildew in the field, rot among sheep, and ofttimes makes the fruit of his loins his greatest vexation and confusion. There is no solid joy, nor lasting peace, nor pure comfort, that attends sinners in their sinful ways.[2] There is a sword of vengeance that doth every moment hang over their heads by a small thread;[3] and what joy and content can attend such souls, if the eye of conscience be but so far open as to see the sword? Ah! the horrors and terrors, the tremblings and shakings, that attend their souls!

The tenth device that Satan hath to draw the soul to sin is,

Device (10). *By working them to be frequent in comparing themselves and their ways with those that are reputed or reported to be worse than themselves.* By this device the devil drew the proud pharisee to bless himself in a cursed condition, 'God, I thank thee that I am not as other men are, extortioners, unjust, adulterers, or even as this publican, &c., Luke xviii. 11. Why, saith Satan, you swear but pretty oaths, as 'by your faith and troth,' &c., but such and such swear by wounds and blood; you are now and then a little wanton, but such and such do daily defile and pollute themselves by actual uncleanness and filthiness; you deceive and overreach your neighbours in things that are but as toys and trifles, but such and such deceive and overreach others in things of greatest concernment, even to their ruin and undoings; you do but sit, and chat, and sip with the drunkard, but such and such sit and drink and are drunk with the drunkard; you are only a little proud in heart and habit, in looks and words, &c.

Now the remedies against this device of the devil are these:

Remedy (1). The first remedy against this device of Satan is, solemnly to consider this, *That there is not a greater nor a clearer argument to prove a man a hypocrite, than to be quick-sighted abroad and blind at home,* than to see 'a mote in another man's eye,

[1] Isa. lvii. 20, and xlviii. 22.

[2] Sin brings in sorrow and sickness, &c. The Rabbins say, that when Adam tasted the forbidden fruit, his head ached. Sirens are said to sing curiously while they live, but to roar horribly when they die. So do the wicked.

[3] Allusion is to Damocles.—G.

and not a beam in his own eye,' Mat. vii. 3, 4; than to use spectacles to behold other men's sins rather than looking-glasses to behold his own; rather to be always holding his finger upon other men's sores, and to be amplifying and aggravating other men's sins than mitigating of his own, &c.[1]

Remedy (2). The second remedy against this device of Satan is, *To spend more time in comparing of your internal and external actions with the Rule, with the Word, by which you must be judged at last, than in comparing of yourselves with those that are worse than yourselves.*[2] That man that, comparing his self with others that are worse than himself, may seem, to himself and others, to be an angel; yet, comparing himself with the word, may see himself to be like the devil, yea, a very devil. 'Have not I chosen twelve, and one of you is a devil?' John vi. 70. Such men are like him, as if they were spit out of his mouth.

Satan is called 'the god of this world,' 2 Cor. iv. 4, because, as God at first did but speak the word, and it was done, so, if the devil doth but hold up his finger, give the least hint, they will do his will, though they undo their souls for ever. Ah, what monsters would these men appear to be, did they but compare themselves with a righteous rule, and not with the most unrighteous men; they would appear to be as black as hell itself.

Remedy (3). The third remedy against this device of Satan is, seriously to consider, *That though thy sins be not as great as others, yet without sound repentance on thy side and pardoning mercy on God's, thou wilt be as certainly damned as others, though not equally tormented with others.*[3] What though hell shall not be so hot to thee as others, yet thou must as certainly to hell as others, unless the glorious grace of God shines forth upon thee in the face of Christ. God will suit men's punishments to their sins; the greatest sins shall be attended with the greatest punishments, and lesser sins with lesser punishments. Alas, what a poor comfort will this be to thee when thou comest to die, to consider that thou shalt not be equally tormented with others, yet must be for ever shut out from the glorious presence of God, Christ, angels, and saints, and from those good things of eternal life, that are so many that they exceed number, so great that they exceed measure, so precious that they exceed estimation! Sure it is, that the tears of heaven[4] are not sufficient to bewail the loss of heaven; the worm of grief gnaws as painful as the fire burns. If those souls, Acts xx. 37, wept because they should see Paul's face no more, how deplorable is the eternal deprivation of the beatifical vision![5]

[1] History speaks of a kind of witches that, stirring abroad, would put on their eyes, but returning home they boxed them up again. So do hypocrites.

[2] The nearer we draw to God and his word, the more rottenness we shall find in our bones. The more any man looks into the body of the sun, the less he seeth when he looks down again. It is said of the basilisk, that if he look into a glass he presently dieth; so will sin, and a sinner (in a spiritual sense), when the soul looks into the word, which is God's glass, &c.

[3] As in heaven one is more glorious than another, so in hell one shall be more miserable than another.—*August*[*ine*].

[4] Qu, 'hell'?—G.

[5] The gate of indulgence, the gate of hope, the gate of mercy, the gate of glory, the gate of consolation, and the gate of salvation, will be for ever shut against them, Mat. xxv. 10.

But this is not all: thou shalt not be only shut out of heaven, but shut up in hell for ever; not only shut out from the presence of God and angels, &c., but shut up with devils and damned spirits for ever; not only shut out from those sweet, surpassing, unexpressible, and everlasting pleasures that be at God's right hand, but shut up for ever under those torments that are ceaseless, remediless, and endless.[1] Ah, souls, were it not ten thousand times better for you to break off your sins by repentance, than to go on in your sins till you feel the truth of what now you hear?

The God of Israel is very merciful. Ah, that you would repent and return, that your souls might live for ever! Remember this, grievous is the torment of the damned, for the bitterness of the punishments, but most grievous for the eternity of the punishments. For to be tormented without end, this is that which goes beyond the bounds of all desperation. Ah, how do the thoughts of this make the damned to roar and cry out for unquietness of heart, and tear their hair, and gnash their teeth, and rage for madness, that they must dwell in 'everlasting burnings' for ever![2]

The eleventh device that Satan hath to draw the soul to sin is,

Device (11). *By polluting and defiling the souls and judgments of men with such dangerous errors, that do in their proper tendency tend to carry the souls of men to all looseness and wickedness, as woful experience doth abundantly evidence.* Ah, how many are there filled with these and such like Christ-dishonouring and soul-undoing opinions, viz., that ordinances are poor, low, carnal things, and not only to be lived above, but without also; that the Scriptures are full of fallacies and uncertainties, and no further to be heeded than they agree with that spirit that is in *them;* that it is a poor, low thing, if not idolatry too, to worship God in a Mediator; that the resurrection is already past; that there was never any such man or person as Jesus Christ, but that all is an allegory, and it signifies nothing but light and love, and such good frames born in men; that there is no God nor devil, heaven nor hell, but what is within us; that there is no sin in the saints, they are under no law but that of the Spirit, which is all freedom; that sin and grace are equally good, and agreeth to his will,—with a hundred other horrid opinions, which hath caused wickedness to break in as a flood among us, &c.

Now the remedies against this device of Satan are those that follow:

Remedy (1). The first remedy against this device of Satan is, solemnly to consider, *That an erroneous, vain mind is as odious to God as a vicious life.*[3] He that had the leprosy in his head was to be pronounced utterly unclean, Levit. xiii. 44. Gross errors make the heart foolish, and render the life loose, and the soul light in the eye of God. Error spreads and frets like a gangrene, and renders the soul a leper in the sight of God.[4]

[1] It was a good saying of Chrysostom, speaking of hell: *Ne quæramus ubi sit, sed quomodo illam fugiamus*, let us not seek where it is, but how we shall escape it.

[2] Surely one good means to escape hell is to take a turn or two in hell by our dail meditations.

[3] A blind eye is worse than a lame foot.

[4] The breath of the erroneous is infectious, and, like the dogs of *Congo,* they bite though they bark not.

It was God's heavy and dreadful plague upon the Gentiles, to be given up to a mind void of judgment, or an injudicious mind, or a mind rejected, disallowed, abhorred of God, or a mind that none have cause to glory in, but rather to be ashamed of, Rom. i 28. I think that in these days God punisheth many men's former wickednesses by giving them up to soul-ruining errors. Ah, Lord, this mercy I humbly beg, that thou wouldst rather take me into thine own hand, and do anything with me, than give me up to those sad errors to which thousands have married their souls, and are in a way of perishing for ever.[1]

Remedy (2). The second remedy against this device of Satan is, *To receive the truth affectionately, and let it dwell in your souls plenteously.*[2] When men stand out against the truth, when truth would enter, and men bar the door of their souls against the truth, God in justice gives up such souls to be deluded and deceived by error, to their eternal undoing: 2 Thes. ii. 10–12, 'Because they received not the love of the truth, that they might be saved, God shall send them strong delusions (or, as the Greek hath it, "the efficacy of error," ἐνεργείαν πλάνης), that they should believe a lie; that they all might be damned who believed not the truth, but had pleasure in unrighteousness.' Ah, sirs, as you love your souls, do not tempt God, do not provoke God, by your withstanding truth and out-facing truth, to give you up to believe a lie, that you may be damned. There are no men on earth so fenced against error as those are that receive the truth in the love of it. Such souls are not 'easily tossed to and fro, and carried about with every wind of doctrine by the sleight of men and cunning craftiness, wherein they lie in wait to deceive,' Eph. iv. 14.[3] It is not he that receives most of the truth into his head, but he that receives most of the truth affectionately into his heart, that shall enjoy the happiness of having his judgment sound and clear, when others shall be deluded and deceived by them, who make it their business to infect the judgments and to undo the souls of men.

Ah, souls, as you would not have your judgments polluted and defiled with error, 'Let the word of the Lord,' that is more precious than gold, yea than fine gold, 'dwell plenteously in you,' Col. iii. 16.[4] It is not the hearing of truth, nor the knowing of truth, nor the commending of truth, nor the talking of truth, but the indwelling of truth in your souls, that will keep your judgments chaste and sound, in the midst of all those glittering errors that betray many souls into his hands, that can easily 'transform himself into an angel of light,' 2 Cor. xi. 14, that he may draw others to lie in chains of darkness with him for ever.[5] Oh, let not the word be a stranger, but make it your choicest familiar! Then will you be able to stand in the day wherein

[1] Through animosity to persist in error is diabolical; it were best that we never erred; next to that, that we amended our error.

[2] The greatest sinners are sure to be the greatest sufferers.

[3] ἐν τῇ κυβείᾳ, Gr., signifies cogging with a die; such sleights as cheaters and false gamesters use at dice.

[4] ἐνοικείτω, *i. e.* indwell in you as an ingrafted word incorporated into your souls, so concocted and digested by you, as that you turn it into a part of yourselves.

[5] They must needs err that know not God's ways, yet can they not wander so wide as to miss of hell.

many shall fall on your right hand, and on your left, by the subtlety of those that shall say, 'Lo, here is Christ, or lo, there is Christ.'

There was more wit than grace in his speech that counselled his friends, 'Not to come too nigh unto truth, lest his teeth should be beaten out with its heels.' Ah, souls, if truth dwell plenteously in you, you are happy; if not, you are unhappy under all your greatest felicity.[1]

'It is with truth,' saith Melancthon, 'as it is with holy water, every one praised it, and thought it had some rare virtue in it; but offer to sprinkle them with it, and they will shut their eyes, and turn away their faces from it.'

Remedy (3). The third remedy against this device of Satan is, solemnly to consider, *That error makes the owner to suffer loss.* All the pains and labour that men take to defend and maintain their errors, to spread abroad and infect the world with their errors, shall bring no profit, nor no comfort to them in that day, wherein 'every man's work shall be made manifest, and the fire shall try it of what sort it is,' as the apostle shews in that remarkable scripture, 1 Cor. iii. 11–15. Ah, that all those that rise early and go to bed late, that spend their time, their strength, their spirits, their all, to advance and spread abroad God-dishonouring and soul-undoing opinions, would seriously consider of this, that they shall lose all the pains, cost, and charge that they have been, or shall be at, for the propagating of error; and if they are ever saved, it shall be by fire, as the apostle there shews. Ah, sirs, Is it nothing to lay out your money for that which is not bread? and your strength for that which will not, which cannot, profit you in the day that you must make up your account, and all your works must be tried by fire?[2] Ah, that such souls would now at last 'buy the truth, and sell it not,' Prov. xxiii. 23. Remember you can never over-buy it, whatsoever you give for it; you can never sufficiently sell it, if you should have all the world in exchange for it.

It is said of Cæsar, that 'he had greater care of his books than of his royal robes,' for, swimming through the waters to escape his enemies, he carried his books in his hand above the waters, but lost his robes.[3] Ah, what are Cæsar's books to God's books? Well, remember this, that one day, yea, one hour spent in the study of truth, or spreading abroad of truth, will yield the soul more comfort and profit, than many thousand years spent in the study and spreading abroad of corrupt and vain opinions, that have their rise from hell, and not from heaven, from the god of this world and not from that God that shall at last judge this world, and all the corrupt opinions of men.

Remedy (4). The fourth remedy against this device of Satan is, *To hate, reject, and abominate all those doctrines and opinions that are contrary to godliness, and that open a door to profaneness,*[4] *and all*

[1] *Veritas vincit*, Truth at last triumphs. *Veritas stat in aperto campo*, Truth stands in the open fields; ay, and it makes those souls stand in whom it dwells, when others fall as stars from heaven.

[2] Error as a glass is bright, but brittle, and cannot endure the hammer, or fire, as gold can, which, though rubbed or melted, remains firm and orient.

[3] Major fuit cura Cæsari libellorum quam purpuræ.

[4] One old piece of gold is worth a thousand new counters, and one old truth of God

such doctrines and opinions that require men to hold forth a strictness above what the Scripture requireth; and all such doctrines and opinions that do advance and lift up corrupted nature to the doing of supernatural things, which none can do but by that supernatural power that raised Christ from the grave; and such opinions that do lift our own righteousness in the room of Christ's righteousness, that place good works in the throne of Christ, and makes them co-partners with Christ, &c. And all those opinions and doctrines that do so set up and cry up Christ and his righteousness, as to cry down all duties of holiness and righteousness, and all those doctrines and opinions that do make the glorious and blessed privileges of believers in the days of the gospel to be lesser, fewer, and weaker, than they were in the time of the law. Ah, did your souls arise with a holy hatred, and a strong indignation against such doctrines and opinions, you would stand when others fall, and you would shine as the sun in his glory, when many that were once as shining stars may go forth as stinking snuffs.[1]

Remedy (5). The fifth remedy against this device of Satan is, *To hold fast the truth.* As men take no hold on the arm of flesh till they let go the arm of God, Jer. xvii. 5, so men take no hold on error till they have let go their hold of truth, therefore hold fast the truth, 2 Tim. i. 13, and Titus i. 9. Truth is thy crown, hold fast thy crown, and let no man take thy crown from thee. Hath not God made truth sweet to thy soul, yea, sweeter than honey, or the honeycomb? and wilt not thou go on to heaven, feeding upon truth, that heavenly honeycomb, as Samson did of his honeycomb.[2] Ah, souls, have you not found truth sweetening your spirits, and cheering your spirits, and warming your spirits, and raising your spirits, and corroborating your spirits? Have not you found truth a guide to lead you, a staff to uphold you, a cordial to strengthen you, and a plaster to heal you? And will not you hold fast the truth? Hath not truth been your best friend in your worst days? Hath not truth stood by you when friends have forsaken you? Hath not truth done more for you than all the world could do against you, and will you not hold fast the truth?[3] Is not truth your right eye, without which you cannot see for Christ? And your right hand, without which you cannot do for Christ? And your right foot, without which you cannot walk with Christ? And will you not hold fast truth? Oh! hold fast the truth in your judgments and understandings, in your wills and affections, in your profession and conversation.

Truth is more precious than gold or rubies, 'and all the things thou canst desire are not to be compared to her,' Prov. iii. 15.[4] Truth is that heavenly glass wherein we may see the lustre and

is more than a thousand new errors. True hatred is εἰς το γενος, to the whole kind; it is sad to frown upon one error and smile upon another.

[1] Gideon had seventy sons, and but one bastard, and yet that bastard destroyed all the rest (Judges viii. 18, *et seq.*). One turn may bring a man quite out of the way.

[2] The priests of Mercury, when they ate their figs and honey, cried out (γλυκῦ ἡ ἀλήθεια), Sweet is truth.

[3] It is with truth as with some plants, which live and thrive but in warm climates.

[4] Said of 'wisdom.'—G.

glory of divine wisdom, power, greatness, love, and mercifulness. In this glass you may see the face of Christ, the favour of Christ, the riches of Christ, and the heart of Christ, beating and working sweetly towards your souls. Oh! let your souls cleave to truth, as Ruth did to Naomi, Ruth i. 15, 16, and say, 'I will not leave truth, nor return from following after truth; but where truth goes I will go, and where truth lodgeth I will lodge; and nothing but death shall part truth and my soul.'[1] What John said to the church of Philadelphia I may say to you, 'Hold fast that which thou hast, that no man take thy crown,' Rev. iii. 11. The crown is the top of royalties: such a thing is truth: 'Let no man take thy crown.' 'Hold fast the faithful word,' as Titus speaks, chap. i. 9.[2] You were better let go anything than truth; you were better let go your honours and riches, your friends and pleasures, and the world's favours; yea, your nearest and dearest relations, ay, your very lives, than to let go truth. Oh, keep the truth, and truth will make you safe and happy for ever. Blessed are those souls that are kept by truth.

Remedy (6). The sixth remedy against this device of Satan is, *To keep humble.* Humility will keep the soul free from many darts of Satan's casting, and erroneous snares of his spreading. As low trees and shrubs are free from many violent gusts and blasts of wind which shake and rend the taller trees, so humble souls are free from those gusts and blasts of error that rend and tear proud, lofty souls. Satan and the world have least power to fasten errors upon humble souls. The God of light and truth delights to dwell with the humble; and the more light and truth dwells in the soul, the further off darkness and error will stand from the soul. The God of grace pours in grace into humble souls, as men pour liquor into empty vessels; and the more grace is poured into the soul, the less error shall be able to overpower the soul, or to infect the soul.[3]

That is a sweet word in Psalm xxv. 9, 'The meek' (or the humble) 'will he guide in judgment, and the meek will he teach his way.'[4] And certainly souls guided by God, and taught by God, are not easily drawn aside into ways of error. Oh, take heed of spiritual pride! Pride fills our fancies, and weakens our graces, and makes room in our hearts for error. There are no men on earth so soon entangled, and so easily conquered by error, as proud souls. Oh, it is dangerous to love to be wise above what is written, to be curious and unsober in your desire of knowledge, and to trust to your own capacities and abilities to undertake to pry into all secrets, and to be puffed up with a carnal mind. Souls that are thus a-soaring up above the bounds and limits

[1] Though I cannot dispute for the truth, yet I can die for the truth, said that blessed martyr.

[2] Ἀντεχόμενοι, Hold fast as with tooth and nail, against these that would snatch it from us.

[3] I have read of one who, seeing in a vision so many snares of the devil spread upon the earth, he sat down mourning, and said within himself, *Quis pertransiet ista*, who shall pass through these? whereunto he heard a voice answering, *Humilitas pertransiet*, humility shall pass through them.

[4] Ps. xxv. 9, ענוים, Gnanavim, from ענה, Gnanah, which signifies the humble or afflicted. The high tide quickly ebbs, and the highest sun is presently declining. You know how to apply it.

of humility, usually fall into the very worst of errors, as experience doth daily evidence.[1]

Remedy (7). The seventh remedy against this device of Satan is, solemnly to consider, *The great evils that errors have produced.* Error is a fruitful mother, and hath brought forth such monstrous children as hath set towns, cities, and nations on fire.[2] Error is that whorish woman that hath cast down many, wounded many, yea, slain many strong men, many great men, and many learned men, and many professing men in former times and in our time, as is too evident to all that are not much left of God, destitute of the truth, and blinded by Satan. Oh, the graces that error hath weakened, and the sweet joys and comforts that error hath clouded, if not buried! Oh, the hands that error hath weakened, the eyes that error hath blinded, the judgments of men that error hath perverted, the minds that error hath darkened, the hearts that error hath hardened, the affections that error hath cooled, the consciences that error hath seared, and the lives of men that error hath polluted! Ah, souls! can you solemnly consider of this, and not tremble more at error than at hell itself? &c.

The twelfth device that Satan hath to draw the soul to sin is,

Device (12). *To affect*[3] *wicked company, to keep wicked society.* And oh! the horrid impieties and wickedness that Satan hath drawn men to sin, by working them to sit and associate themselves with vain persons.

Now, the remedies against this device of the devil are these:

Remedy (1). The first remedy against this device of Satan is, *To dwell, till your hearts be affected, upon those commands of God that do expressly require us to shun the society of the wicked*: Eph. v. 11, 'And have no fellowship with the unfruitful works of darkness, but rather reprove them;' Prov. iv. 14–16, 'Enter not into the path of the wicked, and go not in the way of evil men. Avoid it, pass not by it, turn from it, and pass away.' 1 Cor. v. 9–11, 2 Thes. iii. 6, Prov. i. 10–15. Turn to these Scriptures, and let your souls dwell upon them, till a holy indignation be raised in your souls against fellowship with vain men. 'God will not take the wicked by the hand,' as Job speaks, xxxiv. 20, xxx. 24. Why then should you? God's commands are not like those that are easily reversed, but they are like those of the Medes, that cannot be changed. If these commands be not now observed by thee, they will at last be witnesses against thee, and millstones to sink thee, in that day that Christ shall judge thee.[4]

Remedy (2). The second remedy against this device of Satan is, seriously to consider, *That their company is very infectious and dangerous,* as is clear from the scripture above mentioned. Ah, how many have lost their names, and lost their estates, and strength, and God, and heaven, and souls, by society with wicked men! As ye shun a stinking carcase, as the seaman shuns sands and rocks, and shelves,[5] as ye shun those that have the plague-sores running upon them, so

1 The proud soul is like him that gazed upon the moon, but fell into the pit.

2 Errors in conscience produce many great evils, not only *ad intra*, in men's own souls, but also *ad extra*, in human affairs.

3 'Choose.'—G.

4 Non parentum aut majorum authoritas, sed Dei docebit imperium.—*Jerome*. The commands of God must outweigh all authority and example of men.

5 'Shoals.'—G.

should you shun the society of wicked men. As weeds endanger the corn, as bad humours endanger the blood, or as an infected house the neighbourhood, so doth wicked company the soul,[1] Prov. xiii. 20.

Bias, a heathen man, being at sea in a great storm, and perceiving many wicked men in the ship, called upon the gods: 'Oh, saith he, forbear prayer, hold your tongues; I would not have the gods take notice that you are here; they sure will drown us all if they should.' Ah, sirs, could a heathen see so much danger in the society of wicked men, and can you see none?

Remedy (3). The third remedy against this device of Satan is, *To look always upon wicked men, under those names and notions that the Scripture doth set them out under.* The Scripture calls them lions for their fierceness, and bears for their cruelty, and dragons for their hideousness, and dogs for their filthiness, and wolves for their subtleness. The Scripture styles them scorpions, vipers, thorns, briers, thistles, brambles, stubble, dirt, chaff, dust, dross, smoke, scum, as you may see in the margin.[2] It is not safe to look upon wicked men under those names and notions that they set out themselves by, or that flatterers set them out by; this may delude the soul, but the looking upon them under those names and notions that the Scripture sets them out by, may preserve the soul from frequenting their company and delighting in their society. Do not tell me what this man calls them, or how such and such count them; but tell me how doth the Scripture call them, how doth the Scripture count them? As Nabal's name was, so was his nature, 1 Sam. xxv. 25, and as wicked men's names are, so are their natures. You may know well enough what is within them, by the apt names that the Holy Ghost hath given them.[3]

Remedy (4). The fourth remedy against this device of Satan, is, solemnly to consider, *That the society and company of wicked men have been a great grief and burden to those precious souls that were once glorious on earth, and are now triumphing in heaven:* Ps. cxx. 5, 6, 'Woe is me, that I dwell in Meshech, that I sojourn in the tents of Kedar! My soul hath long dwelt with him that hateth peace.' So Jeremiah, 'Oh that I had in the wilderness a lodging-place of wayfaring men, that I might leave my people, and go from them! for they be all adulterers, an assembly of treacherous men,' Jer. ix. 2. So they 'vexed Lot's righteous soul by their filthy conversation,' 2 Pet. ii. 7;[4] they made his life a burden, they made death more desirable to him than life, yea, they made his life a lingering death. Guilt or grief is all the good gracious souls get by conversing with wicked men.[5]

[1] Eusebius reports of John the Evangelist, that he would not suffer Cerinthus, the heretic, in the same bath with him, lest some judgment should abide them both.—*Euseb.* l. iii. cap. 25. [Cf. Note in Sibbes, vol. vii. 603.—G.] A man that keepeth ill company is like him that walketh in the sun, tanned insensibly.

[2] 2 Tim. iv. 17, Isa. xi. 7, Ezek. iii. 10, Mat. vii. 6, Rev. xxii. 15, Luke xiii. 32, Isa. x. 17, Ezek. ii. 6, Judges ix. 14, Job xxi. 18, Ps. lxxxiii. 13, Ps. xviii. 42, Ezek. xxii. 18, 19, Isa. lxv. 5, Ezek. xxiv. 6.

[3] Lactantius says of Lucian (*nec diis, nec hominibus pepercit*), he spared neither God nor man; such monsters are wicked men, which should render their company to all that have tasted of the sweetness of divine love, a burden and not a delight.

[4] Vide Bezam, *i. e.* the Annott. of Beza, *in loc.*—G.

[5] O Lord, let me not go to hell, where the wicked are; for Lord, thou knowest I never

The second thing to be shewed is,

The several devices that Satan hath, as to draw souls to sin, so to keep souls from holy duties, to hinder souls in holy services, and to keep them off from religious performances.

'And he shewed me Joshua the high priest standing before the angel of the Lord, and Satan standing at his right hand to resist him,' Zech. iii. 1.

The truth of this I shall shew you in the following particulars:

The first device that Satan hath to draw souls from holy duties, and to keep them off from religious services, is,

Device (1). *By presenting the world in such a dress, and in such a garb to the soul, as to ensnare the soul, and to win upon the affections of the soul.* He represents the world to them in its beauty and bravery,[1] which proves a bewitching sight to a world of men.[2] (It is true, this took not Christ, because Satan could find no matter in him for his temptation to work upon.) So that he can no sooner cast out his golden bait, but we are ready to play with it, and to nibble at it; he can no sooner throw out his golden ball, but men are apt to run after it, though they lose God and their souls in the pursuit. Ah! how many professors in these days have for a time followed hard after God, Christ, and ordinances, till the devil hath set before them the world in all its beauty and bravery, which hath so bewitched their souls that they have grown to have low thoughts of holy things, and then to be cold in their affections to holy things, and then to slight them, and at last, with the young man in the Gospel, to turn their backs upon them. Ah! the time, the thoughts, the spirits, the hearts, the souls, the duties, the services, that the inordinate love of this wicked world doth eat up and destroy, and hath ate up and destroyed. Where one thousand are destroyed by the world's frowns, ten thousand are destroyed by the world's smiles. The world, siren-like, it sings us and sinks us; it kisses us, and betrays us, like Judas; it kisses us and smites us under the fifth rib, like Joab. The honours, splendour, and all the glory of this world, are but sweet poisons, that will much endanger us, if they do not eternally destroy us.[3] Ah! the multitude of souls that have surfeited of these sweet baits and died for ever.

Now the remedies against this device of Satan are these,

Remedy (1). The first remedy against this device of Satan is, *To dwell upon the impotency and weakness of all these things here below.* They are not able to secure you from the least evil, they are not able to procure you the least desirable good. The crown of gold cannot cure the headache, nor the velvet slipper ease the gout, nor the jewel about the

loved their company here, said a gracious gentlewoman, when she was to die, being in much trouble of conscience.

[1] 'Finery.'—G.

[2] The beauty of the world foils a Christian more than the strength; the flattering sunshine more than the blustering storm. In storms we keep our garments close about us [as in the fable of the sun and wind.—G.].

[3] The inhabitants of Nilus are deaf by the noise of the waters; so the world makes such a noise in men's ears, that they cannot hear the things of heaven. The world is like the swallows' dung, that put out Tobias his eyes. The champions could not wring an apple out of Milo's hand by a strong hand, but a fair maid, by fair means, got it presently.

neck cannot take away the pain of the teeth. The frogs of Egypt entered into the rich men's houses of Egypt, as well as the poor. Our daily experience doth evidence this, that all the honours, riches, &c., that men enjoy, cannot free them from the cholic, the fever, or lesser diseases.[1] Nay, that which may seem most strange is, that a great deal of wealth cannot keep men from falling into extreme poverty: Judges i. 6, you shall find seventy kings, with their fingers and toes cut off, glad, like whelps, to lick up crumbs under another king's table; and shortly after, the same king that brought them to this penury, is reduced to the same poverty and misery. Why then should that be a bar to keep thee out of heaven, that cannot give thee the least ease on earth?

Remedy (2). The second remedy against this device of Satan is, *To dwell upon the vanity of them as well as upon the impotency of all worldly good.* This is the sum of Solomon's sermon, 'Vanity of vanities, and all is vanity.' This our first parents found, and therefore named their second son Abel, or vanity. Solomon, that had tried these things, and could best tell the vanity of them, he preacheth this sermon over again and again, 'Vanity of vanities, and all is vanity.' It is sad to think how many thousands there be that can say with the preacher, 'Vanity of vanities, all is vanity,' nay, swear it, and yet follow after these things as if there were no other glory, nor felicity, but what is to be found in these things they call vanity.[2] Such men will sell Christ, heaven, and their souls for a trifle, that call these things vanity, but do not cordially believe them to be vanity, but set their hearts upon them as if they were their crown, the top of all their royalty and glory. Oh let your souls dwell upon the vanity of all things here below, till your hearts be so throughly convinced and persuaded of the vanity of them, as to trample upon them, and make them a footstool for Christ to get up, and ride in a holy triumph in your hearts.[3]

Chrysostom said once, 'That if he were the fittest in the world to preach a sermon to the whole world, gathered together in one congregation, and had some high mountain for his pulpit, from whence he might have a prospect of all the world in his view, and were furnished with a voice of brass, a voice as loud as the trumpets of the archangel, that all the world might hear him, he would choose to preach upon no other text than that in the Psalms,' O mortal men, how long will ye love vanity, and follow after leasing? Ps. iv. 2.

[1] The prior in Melancthon rolled his hand up and down in a basinful of angels, thinking thereby to have charmed his gout, but it would not do. Nugas the Scythian, despising the rich presents and ornaments that were sent unto him by the emperor of Constantinople, asked whether those things could drive away calamities, diseases, or death.

[2] Gilemex, king of Vandals, led in triumph by Belisarius, cried out, 'Vanity of vanity, all is vanity.' The fancy of Lucian, who placeth Charon on the top of an high hill, viewing all the affairs of men living, and looking on their greatest cities as little birds' nests, is very pleasant.

[3] Oh the imperfection, the ingratitude, the levity, the inconstancy, the perfidiousness of those creatures we most servilely affect. Ah, did we but weigh man's pain with his payment, his crosses with his mercies, his miseries with his pleasures, we should then see that there is nothing got by the bargain, and conclude, 'Vanity of vanities, all is vanity.'

Tell me, you that say all things under the sun are vanity, if you do really believe what you say, why do you spend more thoughts and time on the world, than you do on Christ, heaven, and your immortal souls? Why do you then neglect your duty towards God, to get the world? Why do you then so eagerly pursue after the world, and are so cold in your pursuing after God, Christ, and holiness? Why then are your hearts so exceedingly raised, when the world comes in, and smiles upon you; and so much dejected, and cast down, when the world frowns upon you, and with Jonah's gourd withers before you?

Remedy (3). The third remedy against the device of Satan is, *To dwell much upon the uncertainty, the mutability, and inconstancy of all things under the sun.* Man himself is but the dream of a dream, but the generation of a fancy, but an empty vanity, but the curious picture of nothing, a poor, feeble, dying flash. All temporals are as transitory as a hasty headlong current, a shadow, a ship, a bird, an arrow, a post that passeth by. 'Why shouldst thou set thine eyes upon that which is not?' saith Solomon, Prov. xxiii. 5. And saith the apostle, 'The fashion of this world passeth away,'[1] 1 Cor. vii. 31. Heaven only hath a foundation, earth hath none, 'but is hanged upon nothing,' as Job speaks, xxvi. 7. The apostle willed Timothy to 'charge rich men that they be not high-minded, nor put their trust in uncertain riches,' 1 Tim. vi. 17.[2] They are like bad servants, whose shoes are made of running leather, and will never tarry long with one master.[3] As a bird hoppeth from tree to tree, so do the honours and riches of this world from man to man, Let Job and Nebuchadnezzar testify this truth, who fell from great wealth to great want. No man can promise himself to be wealthy till night; one storm at sea, one coal of fire, one false friend, one unadvised word, one false witness, may make thee a beggar and a prisoner all at once. All the riches and glory of this world is but as smoke and chaff that vanisheth; 'As a dream and vision in the night, that tarrieth not,' Job xx. 8. 'As if a hungry man dreameth, and thinketh that he eateth, and when he awaketh his soul is empty; and like a thirsty man which thinketh he drinketh, and behold when he is awaked, his soul is faint,' as the prophet Isaiah saith, chap. xxix. 8. Where is the glory of Solomon? the sumptuous buildings of Nebuchadnezzar? the nine hundred chariots of Sisera? the power of Alexander? the authority of Augustus, that commanded the whole world to be taxed? Those that have been the most glorious, in what men generally account glorious and excellent, have had inglorious ends; as Samson for strength, Absalom for favour, Ahithophel for policy, Haman for favour, Asahel for swiftness, Alexander for great conquest, and yet after twelve years poisoned. The same you may see in the four mighty kingdoms, the Chaldean, Persian, Grecian, and

[1] 1 Cor. vii. 31 intimateth, that there is nothing of any firmness, or solid consistence, in the creature.

[2] Riches were never true to any that trusted to them; they have deceived men, as Job's brook did the poor travellers in the summer season.

[3] A phrase meaning, he is given to rambling about. See Halliwell and Wright *sub voce.*—G.

Roman: how soon were they gone and forgotten![1] Now rich, now poor, now full, now empty, now in favour, anon out of favour, now honourable, now despised, now health, now sickness, now strength, now weakness. Oh, let not these uncertain things keep thee from those holy services and heavenly employments, that may make thee happy for ever, and render thy soul eternally blessed and at ease, when all these transitory things shall bid thy soul an everlasting farewell.[2]

Remedy (4). The fourth remedy against this device of Satan is, seriously to consider, *That the great things of this world are very hurtful and dangerous to the outward and inward man, through the corruptions that be in the hearts of men.* Oh, the rest, the peace, the comfort, the content that the things of this world do strip many men of! Oh, the fears, the cares, the envy, the malice, the dangers, the mischiefs, that they subject men to![3] They oftentimes make men carnally confident.[4] The rich man's riches are a strong tower in his imagination. 'I said in my prosperity I should never be moved,' Ps. xxx. 6. They often swell the heart with pride, and make men forget God, and neglect God, and despise the rock of their salvation. When Jeshurun 'waxed fat, and was grown thick, and covered with fatness, then he forgot God, and forsook God that made him, and lightly esteemed the rock of his salvation,' as Moses spake, Deut. xxxii. 15. Ah, the time, the thoughts, the spirits, that the things of the world consume and spend! Oh, how do they hinder the actings of faith upon God! how do they interrupt our sweet communion with God! how do they abate our love to the people of God! and cool our love to the things of God! and work us to act like those that are most unlike to God! Oh, the deadness, the barrenness that doth attend men under great outward mercies![5] Oh, the riches of the world chokes the word; that men live under the most soul-searching, and soul-enriching means with lean souls. Though they have full purses, though their chests are full of silver, yet their hearts are empty of grace. In Genesis xiii. 2, it is said, that 'Abraham was very rich in cattle, in silver, and in gold.' According to the Hebrew (*Chabbedgh*) it is 'Abraham was very weary;' to shew that riches are a heavy burden, and a hindrance many times to heaven, and happiness.[6]

[1] The most renowned Frederick lost all, and sued to be made but sexton of the church that himself had built. · I have read of a poor fisherman, who, while his nets were a-drying, slept upon the rock, and dreamed that he was made a king, on a sudden starts up, and leaping for joy, fell down from the rock, and in the place of his imaginary felicities loses his little portion of pleasures.

[2] The pomp of this world John compareth to the moon, which *crescit et decrescit*, increaseth and decreaseth, Apoc. xii. 1.

[3] Henry the Second hearing Mentz his chief city to be taken, used this blasphemous speech: I shall never, saith he, love God any more, that suffered a city so dear to me to be taken from me.

[4] When one presented Antipater, king of Macedonia, with a book treating on happiness, his answer was (*οὐ σχολάζω*), I have no leisure.

[5] That four good mothers beget four bad daughters: great familiarity begets contempt, truth hatred, virtue envy, riches ignorance; a French proverb.

[6] Ponacrites bestowed five talents for a gift upon one Anacreon, who for two nights after was so troubled with care how to keep them, and how to bestow them, as he carried them back again to Ponacrites, saying, they were not worth the pains which he had already taken for them. [Query Polycrates?—G.]

King Henry the Fourth asked the Duke of Alva if he had observed the great eclipse of the sun, which had lately happened; No, said the duke, I have so much to do on earth, that I have no leisure to look up to heaven. Ah, that this were not true of most professors in these days. It is very sad to think, how their hearts and time is so much taken up with earthly things, that they have scarce any leisure to look up to heaven, or to look after Christ, and the things that belong to their everlasting peace.

Riches, though well got, yet are but like to manna; those that gathered less had no want, and those that gathered more, it was but a trouble and annoyance to them. The world is troublesome, and yet it is loved; what would it be if it were peaceable? You embrace it, though it be filthy; what would you do if it were beautiful? You cannot keep your hands from the thorns; how earnest would you be then in gathering the flowers?[1] The world may be fitly likened to the serpent Scytale, whereof it is reported, that when she cannot overtake the flying passengers, she doth with her beautiful colours so astonish and amaze them, that they have no power to pass away, till she hath stung them.[2] Ah, how many thousands are there now on earth, that have found this true by experience, that have spun a fair thread to strangle themselves, both temporally and eternally, by being bewitched by the beauty and bravery of this world.[3]

Remedy (5). The fifth remedy against this device of Satan is, to consider, *That all the felicity of this world is mixed.* Our light is mixed with darkness, our joy with sorrow, our pleasures with pain, our honour with dishonour, our riches with wants. If our lights be spiritual, clear, and quick, we may see in the felicity of this world our wine mixed with water, our honey with gall, our sugar with wormwood, and our roses with prickles.[4] Sorrow attends worldly joy, danger attends worldly safety, loss attends worldly labours, tears attend worldly purposes. As to these things, men's hopes are vain, their sorrow certain and joy feigned. The apostle calls this world 'a sea of glass,' a sea for the trouble of it, and glass for the brittleness and bitterness of it.[5] The honours, profits, pleasures, and delights of the world are true gardens of Adonis, where we can gather nothing but trivial flowers, surrounded with many briers.

Remedy (6). The sixth remedy against this device of Satan is, *To get better acquaintance and better assurance of more blessed and glorious things.*[6] That which raised up their spirits, Heb. x. and xi., to trample upon all the beauty, bravery, and glory of the world, was the acquaintance with, 'and assurance of better and more durable

[1] A recollection of Augustine.—G.

[2] Sicily is so full of sweet flowers that dogs cannot hunt there. And what do all the sweet contents of this world, but make us lose the scent of heaven!

[3] *Scytale:* Solinus cxxvii., xl.—G.

[4] Hark, scholar, said the harlot to Apuleius, it is but a bitter sweet you are so fond of. Surely all the things of this world are but bitter sweets.

[5] Qu. *not* this world? Cf. Rev. iv. 6, xv. 2, xxi. 18.—G.

[6] Let heaven be a man's object, and earth will soon be his abject. Luther being at one time in some wants, it happened that a good sum of money was unexpectedly sent him by a nobleman of Germany, at which, being something amazed, he said, I fear that God will give me my reward here, but I protest I will not be so satisfied.

things.' 'They took joyfully the spoiling of their goods, knowing in themselves that they had in heaven a better and a more durable substance.' 'They looked for a house that had foundations, whose builder and maker was God.' 'And they looked for another country, even an heavenly.' 'They saw him that was invisible, and had an eye to the recompence of reward.' And this made them count all the glory and bravery of this world to be too poor and contemptible for them to set their hearts upon. The main reason why men doat upon the world, and damn their souls to get the world, is, because they are not acquainted with a greater glory. Men ate acorns, till they were acquainted with the use of wheat. Ah, were men more acquainted with what union and communion with God means, what it is to have 'a new name, and a new stone, that none knows but he that hath it,' Rev. ii. 17; did they but taste more of heaven, and live more in heaven, and had more glorious hopes of going to heaven, ah, how easily would they have the moon under their feet.

It was an excellent saying of Lewis of Bavyer, emperor of Germany, 'Such goods are worth getting and owning, as will not sink or wash away if a shipwreck happen, but will wade and swim out with us.'[1] It is recorded of Lazarus, that after his resurrection from the dead, he was never seen to laugh, his thoughts and affections were so fixed in heaven, though his body was on earth, and therefore he could not but slight temporal things, his heart being so bent and set upon eternals. There are goods for the throne of grace, as God, Christ, the Spirit, adoption, justification, remission of sin, peace with God, and peace with conscience; and there are goods of the footstool, as honours, riches, the favour of creatures, and other comforts and accommodations of this life. Now he that hath acquaintance with, and assurance of the goods of the throne, will easily trample upon the goods of the footstool. Ah that you would make it your business, your work, to mind more, and make sure more to your own souls, the great things of eternity, that will yield you joy in life and peace in death, and a crown of righteousness in the day of Christ's appearing, and that will lift up your souls above all the beauty and bravery of this bewitching world, that will raise your feet above other men's heads. When a man comes to be assured of a crown, a sceptre, the royal robes, &c., he then begins to have low, mean, and contemptible thoughts of those things that before he highly prized. So will assurance of more great and glorious things breed in the soul a holy scorn and contempt of all these poor, mean things, which the soul before did value above God, Christ, and heaven, &c.

Remedy (7). The seventh remedy against this device of Satan is, seriously to consider, *That true happiness and satisfaction is not to be had in the enjoyment of worldly good.* True happiness is too big and too glorious a thing to be found in anything below that God that

[1] *Hujusmodi comparandæ sunt opes quæ cum naufrago simul enatent.* There is, saith Augustine, *bona throni*, goods of the throne; and there are *bona scabelli*, goods of the footstool. When Basil was tempted with money and preferment, saith he, Give me money that may last for ever, and glory that may eternally flourish; for the fashion of this world passeth away, as the waters of a river that runs by a city.

is a Christian's *summum bonum*, chiefest good.[1] The blessed angels, those glistering courtiers, have all felicities and blessedness, and yet have they neither gold, nor silver, nor jewels, nor none of the beauty and bravery of this world. Certainly if happiness was to be found in these things, the Lord Jesus, who is the right and royal heir of all things, would have exchanged his cradle for a crown; his birth chamber, a stable, for a royal palace; his poverty for plenty; his despised followers for shining courtiers; and his mean provisions for the choicest delicates, &c. Certainly happiness lies not in those things that a man may enjoy, and yet be miserable for ever. Now a man may be great and graceless with Pharaoh, honourable and damnable with Saul, rich and miserable with Dives, &c.: therefore happiness lies not in these things. Certainly happiness lies not in those things that cannot comfort a man upon a dying bed. Is it honours, riches, or friends, &c., that can comfort thee when thou comest to die? Or is it not rather faith in the blood of Christ, the witness of the Spirit of Christ, the sense and feeling of the love and favour of Christ, and the hopes of eternally reigning with Christ? Can happiness lie in those things that cannot give us health, or strength, or ease, or a good night's rest, or an hour's sleep, or a good stomach? Why, all the honours, riches, and delights of this world cannot give these poor things to us, therefore certainly happiness lies not in the enjoyment of them, &c.[2] And surely happiness is not to be found in those things that cannot satisfy the souls of men. Now none of these things can satisfy the soul of man. 'He that loveth silver shall not be satisfied with silver, nor he that loveth abundance with increase; this is also vanity,' said the wise man, Eccles. v. 10. The barren womb, the horse leech's daughter, the grave and hell, will as soon be satisfied, as the soul of man will by the enjoyment of any worldly good. Some one thing or other will be for ever wanting to that soul that hath none but outward good to live upon. You may as soon fill a bag with wisdom, a chest with virtue, or a circle with a triangle, as the heart of man with anything here below. A man may have enough of the world to sink him, but he can never have enough to satisfy him, &c.

Remedy (8). The eighth remedy against this device of Satan is, solemnly to consider, *Of the dignity of the soul.* Oh, the soul of man is more worth than a thousand worlds! It is the greatest abasing of it that can be to let it doat upon a little shining earth, upon a little painted beauty and fading glory, when it is capable of union with Christ, of communion with God, and of enjoying the eternal vision of God.

Seneca could say, 'I am too great, and born to greater things, than that I should be a slave to my body.'[3] Oh! do you say my soul is

[1] True happiness lies only in our enjoyment of a suitable good, a pure good, a total good, and an eternal good; and God is only such a good, and such a good can only satisfy the soul of man. Philosophers could say, that he was never a happy man that might afterwards become miserable.

[2] Gregory the Great used to say, He is poor whose soul is void of grace, not whose coffers are empty of money. *Anima rationalis cœteris omnibus occupari potest, impleri non potest;* the reasonable soul may be busied about other things, but it cannot be filled with them.

[3] Epistle xiv.—G.

too great, and born to greater things, than that I should confine it to a heap of white and yellow earth.[1]

I have been the longer upon the remedies that may help us against this dangerous device of Satan, because he doth usually more hurt to the souls of men by this device than he doth by all other devices. For a close, I wish, as once Chrysostom did, that that sentence, Eccles. ii. 11, 'Then I looked on all the works that my hands had wrought, and on the labour that I had laboured to do, and behold all was vanity and vexation of spirit, and there was no profit under the sun,' were engraven on the door-posts into which you enter, on the tables where you sit, on the dishes out of which you eat, on the cups out of which you drink, on the bed-steads where you lie, on the walls of the house where you dwell, on the garments which you wear, on the heads of the horses on which you ride, and on the foreheads of all them whom you meet, that your souls may not, by the beauty and bravery of the world, be kept off from those holy and heavenly services that may render you blessed while you live, and happy when you die; that you may breathe out your last into his bosom who lives for ever, and who will make them happy for ever that prefer Christ's spirituals and eternals above all temporal transitory things.

Device (2.) The second device that Satan hath to draw the soul from holy duties, and to keep them off from religious services, is, *By presenting to them the danger, the losses, and the sufferings that do attend the performance of such and such religious services.* By this device Satan kept close those that believed on Christ from confessing of Christ: in John xii. 42, 'Nevertheless among the chief rulers also many believed on him; but because of the Pharisees they did not confess him, lest they should be put out of the synagogue.' I would walk in all the ways of God, I would give up myself to the strictest way of holiness, but I am afraid dangers will attend me on the one hand, and losses, and happily such and such sufferings on the other hand, saith many a man. Oh, how should we help ourselves against this temptation and device of Satan!

Now the remedies against this device of Satan are these that follow.

Remedy (1). The first remedy against this device of Satan is to consider, *That all the troubles and afflictions that you meet with in a way of righteousness shall never hurt you, they shall never harm you.* 'And who is he that shall harm you, if you be followers of that which is good?' saith the apostle, *i.e.* none shall harm you, 1 Pet. iii. 13.[2] Natural conscience cannot but do homage to the image of God stamped upon the natures, words, works, and life of the godly; as we may see in the carriage of Nebuchadnezzar and Darius towards Daniel. All

[1] Plutarch tells of Themistocles, that he accounted it not to stand with his state to stoop down to take up the spoils the enemies had scattered in flight; but saith to one of his followers, Δύνασαι σὺ, γὰρ οὐκ εἶ Θεμιστοκλῆς, You may, for you are not Themistocles. Oh what a sad thing it is that a heathen should set his feet upon those very things that most professors set their hearts, and for the gain of which, with Balaam, many run the hazard of losing their immortal souls for ever.

[2] *Nemo proprie læditur nisi a seipso,* Nobody is properly hurt but by himself, and his own fault.

afflictions and troubles that do attend men in a way of righteousness can never rob them of their treasure, of their jewels. They may rob them of some light slight things, as the sword that is by their side, or the stick in their hand, or of the flowers or ribbons that be in their hats.[1] The treasures of a saint are the presence of God, the favour of God, union and communion with God, the pardon of sin, the joy of the Spirit, the peace of conscience, which are jewels that none can give but Christ, nor none can take away but Christ. Now why should a gracious soul keep off from a way of holiness because of afflictions, when no afflictions can strip a man of his heavenly jewels, which are his ornaments and his safety here, and will be his happiness and glory hereafter? Why should that man be afraid, or troubled for storms at sea, whose treasures are sure in a friend's hand upon land? Why, a believer's treasure is always safe in the hands of Christ; his life is safe, his soul is safe, his grace is safe, his comfort is safe, and his crown is safe in the hand of Christ.[2] 'I know him in whom I have believed, and that he is able to keep that which I have committed unto him until that day,' saith the apostle, 2 Tim. i. 12. The child's most precious things are most secure in his father's hands; so are our souls, our graces, and our comforts in the hand of Christ.

Remedy (2). The second remedy against this device of Satan is to consider, *That other precious saints that were shining lights on earth, and are now triumphing in heaven, have held on in religious services, notwithstanding all the troubles and dangers that have surrounded them.*[3] Nehemiah and Ezra were surrounded with dangers on the left hand and on the right, and yet, in the face of all, they hold on building the temple and the wall of Jerusalem. So Daniel, and those precious worthies, Ps. xliv. 19, 20, under the want of outward encouragements, and in the face of a world of very great discouragements, their souls clave to God and his ways. 'Though they were sore broken in the place of dragons, and covered with the shadow of death, yea, though they were all the day long counted as sheep for the slaughter, yet their hearts were not turned back, neither did their steps decline from his ways.' Though bonds and imprisonments did attend Paul and the rest of the apostles in every place, yet they held on in the work and service of the Lord; and why, then, should you degenerate from their worthy examples, which is your duty and your glory to follow? 2 Cor. vi. 5, Heb. xi. 36.

Remedy (3). The third remedy against this device of Satan is,

[1] Gordius, that blessed martyr, accounted it a loss to him not to suffer many kinds of tortures. He saith tortures are but tradings with God for glory. The greater the combat is, the greater is the following reward. [For above of Gordius, cf. Clarke's 'Martyrologie,' 1677 folio, pages 54, 55.—G.]

[2] That was a notable speech of Luther, Let him that died for my soul see to the salvation of it.

[3] Wil. Fowler (martyr) said that heaven should as soon fall as I will forsake my profession, or budge in the least degree from it. So Santus being under as great torments as you have read of, cries out, *Christianus sum*, I am a Christian. No torments could work him to decline the service of God. I might produce a cloud of witnesses; but if those do not work you to be noble and brave, I am afraid more will not. [For Fowler see Clarke's 'Martyrologie,' as before, pp. 450, 451, and for Sanctus [*not* Santus] page 31.—G.]

solemnly to consider, *That all the troubles and dangers that do attend the performance of all holy duties and heavenly services are but temporal and momentary, but the neglect of them may lay thee open to all temporal, spiritual, and eternal dangers.* 'How shall we escape, if we neglect so great salvation?' Heb. ii. 3. He saith not, if we reject or renounce so great salvation. No; but if we neglect, or shift off so great salvation, how shall we escape?[1] That is, we cannot by any way, or means, or device in the world, escape. Divine justice will be above us, in spite of our very souls. The doing of such and such heavenly services may lay you open to the frowns of men, but the neglect of them will lay you open to the frowns of God; the doing of them may render you contemptible in the eyes of men, but the neglect of them may render you contemptible in the eyes of God; the doing of them may be the loss of thy estate, but the neglect of them may be the loss of God, Christ, heaven, and thy soul for ever; the doing of them may shut thee out from some outward temporal contents, the neglect of them may shut thee out from that excellent matchless glory 'that eye hath not seen, nor ear heard, neither hath it entered into the heart of men,' Isa. lxiv. 4. Remember this, there is no man that breathes but shall suffer more by neglecting those holy and heavenly services that God commands, commends, and rewards, than possibly he can suffer by doing of them.[2]

Remedy (4). The fourth remedy against this device of Satan is, to consider, *That God knows how to deliver from troubles by troubles, from afflictions by afflictions, from dangers by dangers.* God, by lesser troubles and afflictions, doth oftentimes deliver his people from greater, so that they shall say, We had perished, if we had not perished;[3] we had been undone, if we had not been undone; we had been in danger, if we had not been in danger. God will so order the afflictions that befall you in the way of righteousness, that your souls shall say, We would not for all the world but that we had met with such and such troubles and afflictions; for surely, had not these befallen us, it would have been worse and worse with us. Oh the carnal security, pride, formality, dead-heartedness, lukewarmness, censoriousness, and earthliness that God hath cured us of, by the trouble and dangers that we have met with in the ways and services of the Lord!

I remember a story of a godly man, that as he was going to take shipping for France, he broke his leg; and it pleased Providence so to order it, that the ship that he should have gone in, at that very instant was cast away, and not a man saved; so by breaking a bone, his life was saved.[4] So the Lord many times breaks our bones, but it is in order to the saving of our lives and our souls for ever. He gives us a portion that makes us heart-sick, but it is in order to the making us perfectly well, and to the purging of us from those ill humours that

[1] ἀμελήσαντες. Disregard, not care for it.

[2] Francis Xavorias [Xavier.—G.] counselled John the Third, king of Portugal, to meditate every day a quarter of an hour upon that text, 'What shall it profit a man to gain the whole world, and lose his soul!'

[3] Periissem nisi periissem.

[4] The 'breaking of his leg' on the way saved the life of the saintly Bernard Gilpin from being sacrificed by Bonner. See Memoir of Dr Airay, prefixed to his 'Philippians,' in the series of 'Commentaries' issued by the Publisher of this,—G.

have made our heads ache, and God's heart ache, and our souls sick, and heavy to the death, &c. Oh therefore let no danger or misery hinder thee from thy duty.[1]

Remedy (5). The fifth remedy against this device of Satan is, solemnly to consider, *That you shall gain more in the service of God, and by walking in righteous and holy ways, though troubles and afflictions should attend you, than you can possibly suffer, or lose, by your being found in the service of God.* 'Godliness is great gain,' 1 Tim. vi. 6. Oh, the joy, the peace, the comfort, the rest, that saints meet with in the ways and service of God! They find that religious services are not empty things, but things in which God is pleased to discover his beauty and glory to their souls. 'My soul thirsts for God,' saith David, 'that I might see thy beauty and thy glory, as I have seen thee in thy sanctuary,' Ps. lxiii. 2. Oh, the sweet looks, the sweet words, the sweet hints, the sweet joggings, the sweet influences, the sweet love-letters, that gracious souls have from heaven, when they wait upon God in holy and heavenly services, the least of which will darken and outweigh all the bravery and glory of this world, and richly recompense the soul for all the troubles, afflictions, and dangers that have attended it in the service of God.[2] Oh, the saints can say under all their troubles and afflictions, that they have meat to eat, and drink to drink, that the world knows not of; that they have such incomes, such refreshments, such warmings, &c., that they would not exchange for all the honours, riches, and dainties of this world. Ah, let but a Christian compare his external losses with his spiritual, internal, and external gain, and he shall find, that for every penny that he loses in the service of God, he gains a pound; and for every pound that he loses, he gains a hundred; for every hundred lost, he gains a thousand. We lose pins in his service, and find pearls; we lose the favour of the creature, and peace with the creature, and haply the comforts and contents of the creature, and we gain the favour of God, peace with conscience, and the comforts and contents of a better life. Ah, did the men of this world know the sweet that saints enjoy in afflictions, they would rather choose Manasseh's iron chain than his golden crown; they would rather be Paul a prisoner, than Paul rapt up in the third heaven. For 'light afflictions,' they shall have 'a weight of glory;' for a few afflictions, they shall have these joys, pleasures, and contents, that are as the stars of heaven, or as the sands of the sea that cannot be numbered; for momentary afflictions, they shall have an eternal crown of glory.[3] 'It is but winking, and

[1] Non essem ego salvus nisi ista periissent.—*Anaxagoras.* Had not these things perished, I could not have been safe, said this phliosopher, when he saw great possessions that he had lost.

[2] Tertul [lian], in his book to the martyrs, hath an apt saying (*Negotiatio est aliquid amittere ut majora lucreris*), *i. e.* that's right and good merchandise, when something is parted with to gain more. He applieth it to their sufferings, wherein, though the flesh lost something, yet the spirit got much more.

[3] When the noble General Zedislaus had lost his hand in the wars of the king of Poland, the king sent him a golden hand for it. What we lose in Christ's service he will make up, by giving us some golden mercies. Though the cross be bitter, yet it is but short; a little storm, as one said of Julian's persecution, and an eternal calm follows.

thou shalt be in heaven presently,' said the martyr.[1] Oh, therefore, let not afflictions or troubles work thee to shun the ways of God, or to quit that service that should be dearer to thee than a world, yea, than thy very life, &c.

The third device that Satan hath to hinder souls from holy and heavenly services, and from religious performances, is,

Device (3). *By presenting to the soul the difficulty of performing them.* Saith Satan, it is so hard and difficult a thing to pray as thou shouldst, and to wait on God as thou shouldst, and to walk with God as thou shouldst, and to be lively, warm, and active in the communion of saints, as thou shouldst, that you were better ten thousand times to neglect them, than to meddle with them; and doubtless by this device Satan hath and doth keep off thousands from waiting on God, and from giving to him that service that is due to his name.

Now, the remedies against this device of Satan are these:

Remedy (1). The first remedy against this device of Satan is, *To dwell more upon the necessity of the service and duty, than on the difficulty that doth attend the duty.* You should reason thus with your souls: O our souls, though such and such services be hard and difficult, yet are they not exceeding necessary for the honour of God, and the keeping up his name in the world, and the keeping under of sin, and the strengthening of weak graces, and so the reviving of languishing comforts, and for the keeping clear and bright your blessed evidences, and for the scattering of your fears, and for the raising of your hopes, and for the gladding the hearts of the righteous, and stopping the mouths of unrighteous souls, who are ready to take all advantages to blaspheme the name of God, and throw dirt and contempt upon his people and ways. Oh, never leave thinking on the necessity of this and that duty, till your souls be lifted up far above all the difficulties that do attend religious duties.[2]

Remedy (2). The second remedy against this device of Satan is, solemnly to consider, *That the Lord Jesus will make his services easy to you, by the sweet discovery of himself to your souls, whilst you are in his service.* 'Thou meetest him that rejoiceth and worketh righteousness, those that remember thee in thy ways,' as the prophet Isaiah saith, Isa. lxiv. 5.[3] If meeting with God, who is goodness itself, beauty itself, strength itself, glory itself, will not sweeten his service to thy soul, nothing in heaven or earth will.

Jacob's meeting with Rachel, and enjoying of Rachel, made his hard service to be easy and delightful to him; and will not the soul's enjoying of God, and meeting with God, render his service to be much more easy and delightful? Doubtless it will. The Lord will give that

[1] Paulisper O senex, oculos claude, nam statim lumen Dei videbis.—*Sozomen*, lib. ii. cap. ii.—G.

[2] The necessity of doing your duty appears by this, that you are his servants by a threefold right; you are his servants (*jure creationis, jure sustentationis, jure redemptionis*) by right of creation, and by right of sustentation, and by right of redemption.

[3] פגעת, *Paganta*, is diversely taken; but most take the word here, to meet a soul with those bowels of love and tenderness as the father of the prodigal met the prodigal with. God is *Pater miserationum*, he is all bowels; he is swift to shew mercy, as he is slow to anger.

sweet assistance by his Spirit and grace, as shall make his service joyous and not grievous, a delight and not a burden, a heaven and not a hell, to believing souls.[1] The confidence of this divine assistance raised up Nehemiah's spirit far above all those difficulties and discouragements that did attend him in the work and service of the Lord, as you may see in Nehemiah ii. 19, 20, 'But when Sanballat the Horonite, and Tobiah the servant, the Ammonite, and Geshem the Arabian, heard it, they laughed us to scorn, and despised us, and said, What is this thing that ye do? will ye rebel against the king? Then answered I them, and said unto them, The God of heaven, he will prosper us; therefore we his servants will arise and build: but you have no right, nor portion, nor memorial, in Jerusalem.' Ah, souls, while you are in the very service of the Lord, you shall find by experience, that the God of heaven will prosper you, and support you, and encourage and strengthen you, and carry you through the hardest service, with the greatest sweetness and cheerfulness that can be. Remember this, that God will suit your strength to your work, and in the hardest service you shall have the choicest assistance.

Remedy (3). The third remedy against this device of Satan is, *To dwell upon the hard and difficult things that the Lord Jesus hath passed through for your temporal, spiritual, and eternal good.* Ah, what a sea of blood, a sea of wrath, of sin, of sorrow and misery, did the Lord Jesus wade through for your internal and eternal good![2] Christ did not plead, This cross is too heavy for me to bear; this wrath is too great for me to lie under; this cup, which hath in it all the ingredients of divine displeasure, is too bitter for me to sup off,[3] how much more to drink the very dregs of it? No, Christ stands not upon this; he pleads not the difficulty of the service, but resolutely and bravely wades through all, as the prophet Isaiah shews: 'The Lord God hath opened my ear, and I was not rebellious, neither turned away my back. I gave my back to the smiters, and my cheeks to them that plucked off the hair; I hid not my face from shame and spitting,' chap. l. 6. Christ makes nothing of his Father's wrath, the burden of your sins, the malice of Satan, and the rage of the world, but sweetly and triumphantly passes through all. Ah, souls! if this consideration will not raise up your spirits above all the discouragements that you meet with, to own Christ and his service, and to stick and cleave to Christ and his service, I am afraid nothing will. A soul not stirred by this, not raised and lifted up by this, to be resolute and brave in the service of God, notwithstanding all dangers and difficulties, is a soul left of God to much blindness and hardness.[4]

[1] Luther speaks excellently to Melancthon, who was apt to be discouraged with doubts and difficulties, and fear from foes, and to cease the service they had undertaken. 'If the work be not good, why did we ever own it? If it be good, why should we ever decline it? Why, saith he, should we fear the conquered world, that have Christ the conqueror on our side'? [From the Reformer's Letters during the diet of Augsburg, A.D. 1530. Cf. D'Aubigné, Hist. of Ref.; c. xiv. § 10, c. 6.—G.]

[2] It is not fit, since the Head was crowned with thorns, that the members should be crowned with rosebuds, saith Zanch[ius].

[3] Qu. 'sip of'?—ED.

[4] Godfrey of Bullen [Bouillon], first king of Jerusalem, refused to be crowned with a crown of gold, saying, it became not a Christian there to wear a crown of gold, where Christ for our salvation had sometime worn a crown of thorns. [Cf. Tasso.—G.]

Remedy (4). The fourth remedy against this device of Satan is to consider, *That religious duties, holy and heavenly exercises, are only difficult to the worse, to the ignoble, part of a saint.* They are not to the noble and better part of a saint, to the noble part, the soul, and the renewed affections of a saint. Holy exercises are a heavenly pleasure and recreation, as the apostle speaks: 'I delight in the law of God, after the inward man: with my mind I serve the law of God, though with my flesh the law of sin,' Rom. vii. 22. To the noble part of a saint, Christ's 'yoke is easy, and his burden is light,' Mat. xi. 30.[1] All the commands and ways of Christ (even those that tend to the pulling out of right eyes and cutting off of right hands) are joyous, and not grievous, to the noble part of a saint.[2] All the ways and services of Christ are pleasantness, in the abstract, to the better part of a saint. A saint, so far as he is renewed, is always best when he sees most of God, when he tastes most of God, when he is highest in his enjoyments of God, and most warm and lively in the service of God. Oh, saith the noble part of a saint, that it might be always thus! Oh that my strength were the strength of stones, and my flesh as brass, that my worser part might be more serviceable to my noble part, that I might act by an untired power in that service, that is a pleasure, a paradise, to me.

Remedy (5). The fifth remedy against this device of Satan is, solemnly to consider, *That great reward and glorious recompence that doth attend those that cleave to the service of the Lord in the face of all difficulties and discouragements.* Though the work be hard, yet the wages is great. Heaven will make amends for all. Ay, one hour's being in heaven will abundantly recompense you for cleaving to the Lord and his ways in the face of all difficulties. This carried the apostle through the greatest difficulties. He had an eye 'to the recompence of reward;' he looked for 'a house that had foundations, whose builder and maker was God,' and for 'a heavenly country.' Yea, this bore up the spirit of Christ in the face of all difficulties and discouragements: 'Looking unto Jesus, the author and finisher of our faith; who, for the joy that was set before him, endured the cross, despising the shame, and is set down at the right hand of the throne of God,' Heb. xii. 2.[3]

Christians that would hold on in the service of the Lord, must look more upon the crown than upon the cross, more upon their future glory than their present misery, more upon their encouragements than upon their discouragements. God's very service is wages; his ways are strewed with roses, and paved 'with joy that is unspeakable and full of glory,' and with 'peace that passeth understanding.' Some degree of comfort follows every good action, as heat accompanies fire,

[1] χρηστος, *i.e.* my yoke is a benign, a gracious, a pleasant, a good, and a gainful yoke, opposed to πονηρὸς, painful, tedious.

[2] As every flower hath its sweet savour, so every good duty carries meat in the mouth, comfort in the performance of it.

[3] Basil speaks of some martyrs that were cast out all night naked in a cold, frosty time, and were to be burned the next day, how they comforted themselves in this manner: The winter is sharp, but paradise is sweet; here we shiver for cold, but the bosom of Abraham will make amends for all.

as beams and influences issue from the sun: 'Moreover, by them is thy servant warned, and in keeping of them there is great reward,' Ps. xix. 11. Not only for keeping, but in keeping of them, there is great reward.[1] The joy, the rest, the refreshing, the comforts, the contents, the smiles, the incomes[2] that saints now enjoy in the ways of God, are so precious and glorious in their eyes, that they would not exchange them for ten thousand worlds. Ah! if the vails[3] be thus sweet and glorious before pay-day comes, what will be that glory that Christ will crown his saints with for cleaving to his service in the face of all difficulties; when he shall say to his Father, 'Lo, here am I, and the children which thou hast given me,' Isa. viii. 18. If there be so much to be had in a wilderness, what then shall be had in paradise? &c.

The fourth device that Satan hath to keep souls off from holy exercises, from religious services, is,

Device (4). *By working them to make false inferences from those blessed and glorious things that Christ hath done.* As that Jesus Christ hath done all for us, therefore there is nothing for us to do but to joy and rejoice. He hath perfectly justified us, and fulfilled the law, and satisfied divine justice, and pacified his Father's wrath, and is gone to heaven to prepare a place for us, and in the mean time to intercede for us; and therefore away with praying, and mourning, and hearing, &c. Ah! what a world of professors hath Satan drawn in these days from religious services, by working them to make such sad, wild, and strange inferences from the sweet and excellent things that the Lord Jesus hath done for his beloved ones.

Now, the remedies against this device are these:

Remedy (1). The first remedy against this device of Satan is, *To dwell as much on those scriptures that shew you the duties and services that Christ requires of you, as upon those scriptures that declare to you the precious and glorious things that Christ hath done for you.*[4] It is a sad and dangerous thing to have two eyes to behold our dignity and privileges, and not one to see our duties and services. I should look with one eye upon the choice and excellent things that Christ hath done for me, to raise up my heart to love Christ with the purest love, and to joy in Christ with the strongest joy, and to lift up Christ above all, who hath made himself to be my all; and I should look with the other eye upon those services and duties that the Scriptures require of those for whom Christ hath done such blessed things, as upon that of the apostle: 'What, know ye not that your body is the temple of the Holy Ghost, which is in you, which ye have of God? and ye are not your own: for ye are bought with a price; therefore glorify God in your body, and in your spirit, which are God's,' 1 Cor. vi. 19, 20. And that: 'Therefore, my beloved brethren, be ye stedfast, unmoveable, always abounding in the work of the Lord, knowing that your labour

[1] This is *præmium ante præmium*, a sure reward of well doing; *in* doing thereof, not only *for* doing thereof, there is great reward, Ps. xix. 11.

[2] 'In-comings.'—G.

[3] 'Gratuities.'—G.

[4] Tertullian hath this expression of the Scriptures: *Adoro plenitudinem Scripturarum*, I adore the fulness of the Scripture. Gregory calls the Scripture, *Cor et animam Dei*, the heart and soul of God; and who will not then dwell in it?

is not in vain in the Lord,' 1 Cor. xv. 58. And that: 'And let us not be weary in well-doing, for in due season we shall reap if we faint not,' Gal. vi. 9. And that of the apostle: 'Rejoice always,' 1 Thes. v. 16, and 'Pray without ceasing,' 1 Thes. v. 17. And that in the Philippians, 'Work out your own salvation with fear and trembling,' ii. 12; and that, 'This do till I come,' 1 Tim. iv. 13; and that, 'Let us consider one another, to provoke one another to love, and to good works, not forsaking the assembling of ourselves together, as the manner of some is, but exhorting one another, and so much the more as you see the day approaching,' Heb. x. 24, 25. Now, a soul that would not be drawn away by this device of Satan, he must not look with a squint eye upon these blessed scriptures, and abundance more of like import, but he must dwell upon them; he must make these scriptures to be his chiefest and his choicest companions, and this will be a happy means to keep him close to Christ and his service in these times, wherein many turn their backs upon Christ, under pretence of being interested in the great glorious things that have been acted by Christ, &c.[1]

Remedy (2). The second remedy against this device of Satan is, to consider, *That the great and glorious things that Jesus Christ hath done, and is a-doing for us, should be so far from taking us off from religious services and pious performances, that they should be the greatest motives and encouragements to the performance of them that may be, as the Scriptures do abundantly evidence.* I will only instance in some, as that, 'That we, being delivered out of the hands of our enemies, might serve him without fear, in holiness and righteousness before him all the days of our lives,' 1 Peter ii. 9, Luke i. 74, 75. Christ hath freed you from all your enemies, from the curse of the law, the predominant damnatory power of sin, the wrath of God, the sting of death, and the torments of hell; but what is the end and design of Christ in doing these great and marvellous things for his people? It is not that we should throw off duties of righteousness and holiness, but that their hearts may be the more free and sweet in all holy duties and heavenly services.[2] So the apostle, 'I will be their God, and they shall be my people:' 'And I will be a Father unto you, and ye shall be my sons and daughters, saith the Lord Almighty.' Mark what follows: 'Having therefore these promises, dearly beloved, let us cleanse ourselves from all filthiness of the flesh and spirit, perfecting holiness in the fear of the Lord,' 2 Cor. vi. 17, 18, chap. vii. 1 compared. And again: 'The grace of God that bringeth salvation hath appeared to all men, teaching us that, denying all ungodliness and worldly lusts, we should live soberly, righteously, and godly in this present world, looking for that blessed hope, and the glorious appearing of the great God and our Saviour Jesus Christ, who gave himself for us, that he might redeem us from all iniquity, and

[1] The Jews were much in turning over the leaves of the Scripture, but they did not weigh the matter of them: John v. 39, 'You search the Scriptures.' Greek there seemeth to be indicative rather than imperative.

[2] This I am sure of, that all man's happiness here is his holiness, and his holiness shall hereafter be his happiness. Christ hath therefore broke the devil's yoke from off our necks, that his Father might have better service from our hearts.

purify us unto himself a peculiar people, zealous of good works,' Titus ii. 12–14. Ah, souls! I know no such arguments to work you to a lively and constant performance of all heavenly services, like those that are drawn from the consideration of the great and glorious things that Christ hath done for you; and if such arguments will not take you and win upon you, I do think the throwing of hell fire in your faces will never do it.[1]

Remedy (3). The third remedy against this device of Satan is, seriously to consider, *That those precious souls which Jesus Christ hath done and suffered as much for as he hath for you, have been exceeding active and lively in all religious services and heavenly performances.*[2] He did as much and suffered as much for David as for you, and yet who more in praying and praising God than David? 'Seven times a day will I praise the Lord,' Ps. cxix. 174. Who more in the studying and meditating on the word than David? 'The law is my meditation day and night,' Ps. cxix. 97. The same truth you may run and read in Jacob, Moses, Job, Daniel, and in the rest of the holy prophets and apostles, for whom Christ hath done as much for as for you. Ah, how have all those worthies abounded in works of righteousness and holiness, to the praise of free grace? Certainly Satan hath got the upper hand of those souls that do argue thus. Christ hath done such and such glorious things for us, therefore we need not make any care and conscience of doing such and such religious services as men say the word calls for. If this logic be not from hell, what is? Ah, were the holy prophets and apostles alive to hear such logic come out of the mouths of such as profess themselves to be interested in the great and glorious things that Jesus Christ hath done for his chosen ones, how would they blush to look upon such souls! and how would their hearts grieve and break within them to hear the language and to observe the actings of such souls.[3]

Remedy (4). The fourth remedy against this device of Satan is, seriously to consider this, *That those that do not walk in the ways of righteousness and holiness, that do not wait upon God in the several duties and services that are commanded by him, cannot have that evidence to their own souls of their righteousness before God, of their fellowship and communion with God, of their blessedness here, and their happiness hereafter, as those souls have, that love and delight in the ways of the Lord, that are always best when they are most in the works and service of the Lord.*[4] 'Little children,' saith

[1] *Tace, lingua; loquere, vita*, talk not of a good life, but let thy life speak. Your actions in passing pass not away; for every good work is a grain of seed for eternal life.

[2] The saints' motto in all ages hath been *Laboremus*, let us be doing. God loves. *Curristas*, not *Quæristas*, the runner, not the questioner or disputer, saith Luther.

[3] The day is at hand when God will require of men, *Non quid legerint, sed quid egerint. nec quid dixerint, sed quomodo vixerint.* He that talks of heaven, but doth not the will of God, is like him that gazed upon the moon, but fell into the pit.

[4] Certainly it is one thing to judge by our graces, another thing to rest or put our trust in them. There is a great deal of difference betwixt declaring and deserving. As David's daughters were known by their garments of divers colours, so are God's children by their piety and sanctity. A Christian's emblem should be an house walking towards heaven. High words surely make a man neither holy nor just; but a virtuous life, a circumspect walking, makes him dear to God. A tree that is not fruitful is for the fire. Christianity is not a talking, but a walking with

the apostle, 'let no man deceive you: he that doth righteousness is righteous, even as he is righteous,' 1 John iii. 7. 'In this,' saith the same apostle, 'the children of God are manifest, and the children of the devil; whosoever doth not righteousness is not of God, neither he that loveth not his brother,' ver. 10. 'If ye know that he is righteous,' saith the same apostle, 'ye know that every one that doth righteousness, is born of him. He that saith, I know him, and keepeth not his commandments, is a liar, and the truth is not in him. But whosoever keepeth his word, in him verily is the love of God perfected: hereby know we that we are in him. He that saith he abideth in him, ought himself also to walk, even as he walked.' 'If we say that we have fellowship with him, and walk in darkness, we lie, and do not the truth; but if we walk in the light, as he is in the light, we have fellowship one with another; and the blood of Jesus Christ cleanseth us from all sin,' saith the same apostle, 1 John ii. 4–6, and i. 6, 7. So James ii. 14, 20, 'What doth it profit, my brethren, though a man say he hath faith, and have no works; can faith save him?' *i. e.* it cannot. 'For as the body without spirit is dead, so faith without works is dead also.' To look after holy and heavenly works, is the best way to preserve the soul from being deceived and deluded by Satan's delusions, and by sudden flashes of joy and comfort; holy works being a more sensible[1] and constant pledge of the precious Spirit, begetting and maintaining in the soul more solid, pure, clear, strong, and lasting joy. Ah souls! As you would have in yourselves a constant and a blessed evidence of your fellowship with the Father and the Son, and of the truth of grace, and of your future happiness, look that you cleave close to holy services; and that you turn not your backs upon religious duties.

Remedy (5). The fifth remedy against this device of Satan is, solemnly to consider, *That there are other choice and glorious ends for the saint's performance of religious duties, than for the justifying of their persons before God, or for their satisfying of the law or justice of God, or for the purchasing of the pardon of sin, &c. viz., to testify their justification.*[2] 'A good tree cannot but bring forth good fruits,' Mat. vii. 17, to testify their love to God, and their sincere obedience to the commands of God; to testify their deliverance from spiritual bondage, to evidence the indwellings of the Spirit, to stop the mouths of the worst of men, and to glad those righteous souls that God would not have sadded. These, and abundance of other choice ends there be, why those that have an interest in the glorious doings of Christ, should, notwithstanding that, keep close to the holy duties and religious services that are commanded by Christ. And if these considerations will not prevail with you, to wait upon God in holy and heavenly

God, who will not be put off with words; if he miss of fruit, he will take up his axe, and then the soul is cut off for ever.—[Query, 'horse'? But prefixed to a volume of 1656, called 'Sacred Principles, Services and Soliloquies, or a Manual of Devotions,' is a singular frontispiece, having this very emblem of a 'house' ascending upward, representative, as explained in quaint accompanying verse, of the Church. So that the mixed metaphor belongs to the period.—G.]

[1] 'Conscious.'—G.

[2] It is a precious truth, never to be forgotten, *Quod non actibus, sed finibus pensantur officia*, that duties are esteemed not by their acts, but by their ends.

duties. I am afraid if one should rise from the dead, his arguments would not win upon you, but you would hold on in your sins, and neglect his service, though you lost your souls for ever, &c.[1]

The fifth device Satan hath to draw souls off from religious services, and to keep souls off from holy duties, is,

Device (5). *By presenting to them the paucity and poverty of those that walk in the ways of God, that hold on in religious practices.* Saith Satan, Do not you see that those that walk in such and such religious ways are the poorest, the meanest, and the most despicable persons in the world? This took with them in John vii. 47–49, 'Then answered the pharisees, Are ye also deceived? Have any of the rulers, or of the pharisees, believed on him? But this people who knoweth not the law are cursed.'

Now the remedies against this device are these that follow:

Remedy (1). The first remedy against this device of Satan is, to consider, *That though they are outwardly poor, yet they are inwardly rich.* Though they are poor in temporals, yet they are rich in spirituals.[2] The worth and riches of the saints is inward. 'The King's daughter is all glorious within,' Ps. xlv. 13. 'Hearken, my beloved brethren, hath not God chosen the poor of this world, rich in faith, and heirs of the kingdom which he hath promised to them that love him?' saith James ii. 5. 'I know thy poverty, but thou art rich,' saith John to the church of Smyrna,' Rev. ii. 4. What though they have little in possession, yet they have a glorious kingdom in reversion. 'Fear not, little flock, it is your Father's pleasure to give you a kingdom,' Luke xii. 32. Though saints have little in hand, yet they have much in hope. You count those happy, in a worldly sense, that have much in reversion, though they have little in possession; and will you count the saints miserable because they have little in hand, little in possession, though they have a glorious kingdom in reversion of this? I am sure the poorest saint that breathes will not exchange, were it in his power, that which he hath in hope and in reversion, for the possession of as many worlds as there be stars in heaven, or sands in the sea, &c.

Remedy (2). The second remedy against this device of Satan is, to consider, *That in all ages God hath had some that have been great, rich, wise, and honourable, that have chosen his ways, and cleaved to his service in the face of all difficulties.* Though not many wise men, yet some wise men; and though not many mighty, yet some mighty have; and though not many noble, yet some noble have. Witness Abraham, and Jacob, and Job, and several kings, and others that the Scriptures speak of. And ah! how many have we among ourselves, whose souls have cleaved to the Lord, and who have swum to his service through the blood of the slain, and who have not counted

[1] *Finis movet ad agendum*, the end moves to doing. *Tene mensuram et respice finem*, keep thyself within compass, and have an eye always to the end of thy life and actions, was Maximilian the emperor's motto.

[2] Do not you see, saith Chrysostom, the places where treasures are hid, are rough and overgrown with thorns? Do not the naturalists tell you, that the mountains that are big with gold within, are bare of grass without? Saints have, as scholars, poor commons here, because they must study hard to go to heaven.

their lives dear unto them, that they and others might enjoy the holy things of Christ, according to the mind and heart of Christ, &c.[1]

Remedy (3). The third remedy against this device of Satan is, solemnly to consider, *That the spiritual riches of the poorest saints do infinitely transcend the temporal riches of all the wicked men in the world; their spiritual riches do satisfy them; they can sit down satisfied with the riches of grace that be in Christ, without honours, and without riches*, &c.[2] 'He that drinks of that water that I shall give him, shall thirst no more,' John iv. 13. The riches of poor saints are durable; they will bed and board with them; they will go to the prison, to a sickbed, to a grave, yea, to heaven with them. The spiritual riches of poor saints are as wine to cheer them, and as bread to strengthen them, and as cloth to warm them, and as armour to protect them. Now, all you that know anything, do know that the riches of this world cannot satisfy the souls of men, and they are as fading as a flower, or as the owners of them are, &c.[3]

Remedy (4). The fourth remedy against this device is, seriously to consider, *That though the saints, considered comparatively, are few; though they be 'a little, little flock,' 'a remnant,' 'a garden enclosed,' 'a spring shut up, a fountain sealed;' though they are as 'the summer gleanings;' though they are 'one of a city, and two of a tribe;'*[4] *though they be but a handful to a houseful, a spark to a flame, a drop to the ocean, yet consider them simply in themselves, and so they are an innumerable number that cannot be numbered.* As John speaketh: 'After this I beheld, and lo, a great multitude which no man could number, of all nations, and kindreds, and peoples, and tongues, stood before the throne, and before the Lamb, clothed with white robes, and palms in their hands,' Rev. vii. 9. So Matthew speaks: 'And I say unto you, that many shall come from the east and west, and shall sit down with Abraham, Isaac, and Jacob in the kingdom of heaven,' Mat. viii. 11. So Paul: 'But ye are come unto mount Sion, and unto the city of the living God, the heavenly Jerusalem, and to an innumerable company of angels, to the general assembly and church of the first-born, which are written in heaven, and to God the judge of all, and to the spirits of just men made perfect,' Heb. xii. 22.[5]

Remedy (5). The fifth remedy against this device of Satan is, seriously to consider, *That it will be but as a day before these poor despised saints shall shine brighter than the sun in his glory.* It will not be long before you will wish, Oh! that we were now among the poor, mean despised ones in the day that God comes to make up his jewels! It will not be long before these poor few saints shall be lifted up upon their thrones to judge the multitude, the world, as the apostle speaks: 'Know ye not that the saints shall judge the world?' 1 Cor. vi. 2. And in that

[1] Good nobles, saith one, are like black swans; and [are] thinly scattered in the firmament of a State, even like stars of the first magnitude: yet some God hath had in all ages, as might be shewed out of histories.

[2] Alexander's vast mind inquired if there were any more worlds to conquer.

[3] Crassus was so rich that he maintained an army with his own revenues; yet he, his great army, with his son and heir, fell together, and left his great estate to others.

[4] Luke xii. 32, Isaiah i. 9, Canticles iv. 12, Judges viii. 2, and Jeremiah iii. 14.—G.

[5] When Fulgentius saw the nobility of Rome sit mounted in their bravery, it mounted his meditations to the heavenly Jerusalem.

day, oh! how will the great and the rich, the learned and the noble, wish that they had lived and spent their days with these few poor contemptible creatures in the service of the Lord! Oh! how will this wicked world curse the day that ever they had such base thoughts of the poor mean saints, and that their poverty became a stumbling-block to keep them off from the ways of sanctity.[1]

I have read of Ingo, an ancient king of the Draves, who, making a stately feast, appointed his nobles, at that time pagans, to sit in the hall below, and commanded certain poor Christians to be brought up into his presence-chamber, to sit with him at his table, to eat and drink of his kingly cheer; at which many wondering, he said, 'He accounted Christians, though never so poor, a greater ornament to his table, and more worthy of his company, than the greatest peers unconverted to the Christian faith; for when these might be thrust down to hell, those might be his consorts and fellow-princes in heaven.' You know how to apply it. Although you see the stars sometimes by their reflections in a puddle, or in the bottom of a well, ay, in a stinking ditch, yet the stars have their situation in heaven. So, though you see a godly man in a poor, miserable, low, despised condition for the things of this world, yet he is fixed in heaven, in the region of heaven: 'Who hath raised us up,' saith the apostle, 'and made us sit together in heavenly places in Christ Jesus.' Oh! therefore, say to your own souls, when they begin to decline the ways of Sion because of the poverty and paucity of those that walk in them, The day is at hand when those few, poor, despised saints shall shine in glory, when they shall judge this world, and when all the wicked of this world will wish that they were in their condition, and would give ten thousand worlds, were it in their power, that they might but have the honour and happiness to wait upon those whom for their poverty and paucity they have neglected and despised in this world.

Remedy (6). The sixth remedy against this device of Satan is, solemnly to consider, *That there will come a time, even in this life, in this world, when the reproach and contempt that is now cast upon the ways of God, by reason of the poverty and paucity of those that walk in those ways, shall be quite taken away, by his making them the head that have days without number been the tail, and by his raising them up to much outward riches, prosperity, and glory, who have been as the outcast because of their poverty and paucity.*[2] John,

[1] Mr Fox being once asked whether he knew a certain poor man who had received succour of him in time of trouble, he answered, I remember him well. I tell you I forget lords and ladies to remember such. So will God deal by his poor saints. He will forget the great and mighty ones of the world to remember his few poor despised ones. Though John the Baptist was poor in the world, yet the Holy Ghost calls him the greatest that was born of woman. Ah, poor saints, men that know not your worth, cannot have such low thoughts of you, but the Lord will have as high.

[2] These following scriptures do abundantly confirm this truth: Jer. xxxi. 12; Isa. xxx. 28, lxii. 8, 9; Joel ii. 28, 24; Micah iv. 6; Amos ix. 18, 14; Zech. viii. 12; Isa. xli. 18, 19, lv. 18, lxvi. 6, 7, lxv. 21, 22, lxi. 4, lx. 10; Ezek. xxxvi. 10. Only take these two cautions: 1. That in these times the saints' chiefest comforts, delights, and contents will consist in their more clear, full, and constant enjoyment of God. 2. That they shall have such abundant measure of the Spirit poured out upon them, that their riches and outward glory shall not be snares unto them, but golden steps to a richer living in God.

speaking of the glory of the church, the new Jerusalem that came down from heaven, Rev. xxi. 24, tells us, 'That the nations of them which are saved shall walk in the light of it, and the kings of the earth do bring their glory into it.' So the prophet Isaiah, 'They shall bring their sons from far, and their silver and their gold with them. For brass I will bring gold, and for iron I will bring silver, and for wood brass, and for stones iron,' chap. lx. 17. And so the prophet Zechariah speaks: chap. xiv. 14, 'And the wealth of all the heathen round about shall be gathered together, gold, and silver, and apparel, in great abundance.' The Lord hath promised that 'the meek shall inherit the earth,' Mat. v. 5; and 'heaven and earth shall pass away, before one jot or one tittle of his word shall pass unfulfilled,' ver. 18. Ah, poor saints! now some thrust sore at you, others look a-squint upon you, others shut the door against you, others turn their backs upon you, and most of men (except it be a few that live much in God, and are filled with the riches of Christ) do either neglect you or despise you because of your poverty; but the day is coming when you shall be lifted up above the dunghill, when you shall change poverty for riches, your rags for robes, your reproach for a crown of honour, your infamy for glory, even in this world.

And this is not all, but God will also mightily increase the number of his chosen ones, multitudes shall be converted to him: 'Who hath heard such a thing? who hath seen such things? shall the earth be made to bring forth in one day? or shall a nation be born at once? for as soon as Sion travailed, she brought forth children. And they shall bring all your brethren for an offering unto the Lord, out of all nations, upon horses, and in chariots, in litters, and upon mules, and upon swift beasts, to my holy mountain Jerusalem, saith the Lord; as the children of Israel bring an offering in a clean vessel into the house of the Lord,' Isa. lxvi. 8, 19, 20. Doth not the Scripture say, that 'the kingdoms of this world must become the kingdoms of our Lord'? Rev. xi. 15. Hath not God given to Christ 'the heathen, and the uttermost parts of the earth for his possession'? Ps. ii. 8. Hath not the Lord said, that in 'the last days the mountain of the Lord's house shall be lifted up above the hills, and shall be established in the top of the mountains, and all nations shall flow unto it,' Isa. ii. 2 and liv. 14 and lxi. 9. Pray, read, and meditate upon Isa. lx. and lxvi. and ii. 1–5, and there you shall find the multitudes that shall be converted to Christ. And oh! that you would be mighty in believing; and, in wrestling with God, that he would hasten the day of his glory, that the reproach that is now upon his people and ways may cease!

The sixth device that Satan hath to keep souls off from religious services is,

Device (6). *By presenting before them the examples of the greatest part of the world, that walk in the ways of their own hearts, and that make light and slight of the ways of the Lord.*[1] Why, saith Satan, do not you see that the great and the rich, the noble and the honourable, the learned and the wise, even the greatest number of men, never trouble themselves about such and such ways, and why then should

[1] John vii. 48, 49, 1 Cor. i. 26, 28, Micah vii. 2–4.

you be singular and nice? You were far better do as the most do, &c.

Now, the remedies against this device are these:

Remedy (1). The first remedy against this device of Satan is, solemnly to consider *Of those scriptures that make directly against following the sinful examples of men.* As that in Exodus, 'Thou shalt not follow a multitude to do evil, neither shalt thou speak in a cause to decline after many to wrest judgment,' chap. xxiii. 2. The multitude generally are ignorant, and know not the way of the Lord, therefore they speak evil of that they know not. They are envious and maliciously bent against the service and way of God, and therefore they cannot speak well of the ways of God: 'This way is everywhere spoken against,' saith they, Acts xxviii. 22. So in Num. xvi. 21, 'Separate from them, and come out from among them.' So the apostle, 'Have no fellowship with the unfruitful works of darkness,' Eph. v. 11. So Solomon, 'Enter not into the way of the wicked; forsake the foolish, and live,' Prov. iv. 14 and ix. 6. They that walk with the most shall perish with the most.[1] They that do as the most shall ere long suffer with the most. They that live as the most, must die with the most, and to hell with the most.

Remedy (2). The second remedy against this device of Satan is, seriously to consider, *That if you will sin with the multitude, all the angels in heaven and men on earth cannot keep you from suffering with the multitude.* If you will be wicked with them, you must unavoidably be miserable with them.[2] Say to thy soul, O my soul! if thou wilt sin with the multitude, thou must be shut out of heaven with the multitude, thou must be cast down to hell with the multitude: 'And I heard a voice from heaven saying, Come out of her, my people, that ye be not partakers of her sins, and that ye receive not of her plagues,' Rev. xviii. 4. Come out in affection, in action, and in habitation, for else the infection of sin will bring upon you the infliction of punishment. So saith the wise man, 'He that walketh with wise men shall be wise, but a companion of fools shall be destroyed,' or as the Hebrew hath it, 'shall be broken in pieces,' Prov. xiii. 20.[3] Multitudes may help thee into sin, yea, one may draw thee into sin, but it is not multitudes that can help thee to escape punishments; as you may see in Moses and Aaron, that were provoked to sin by the multitude, but were shut out of the pleasant land, and fell by a hand of justice as well as others.

Remedy (3). The third remedy against this device of Satan is, solemnly to consider, *The worth and excellency of thy immortal soul.* Thy soul is a jewel more worth than heaven and earth. The loss of thy soul is incomparable, irreparable, and irrecoverable; if that be lost, all is lost, and thou art undone for ever. Is it madness and folly in a man to kill himself for company, and is it not greater madness or folly to break the neck of thy soul, and to damn it for company?

[1] The way to hell is broad and well beaten. The way to be undone for ever is to do as the most do. *Argumentum turpissimum est turba*, the multitude is the weakest and worst argument, saith Seneca. [*De Vita Beata*, ii.—G.]

[2] Sin and punishment are linked together with chains of adamant. Of sin we may say as Isidore doth of the serpent, *Tot dolores quot colores*, so many colours, so many dolours.

[3] ירוע, *Jeroange*, from רוע, *Ruange*, to be naught.

Suspect that way wherein thou seest multitudes to walk; the multitude being a stream that thou must row hard against, or thou wilt be carried into that gulf out of which angels cannot deliver thee. Is it not better to walk in a straight way alone, than to wander into crooked ways with company? Sure it is better to go to heaven alone than to hell with company.

I might add other things, but these may suffice for the present; and I am afraid, if these arguments do not stir you, other arguments will work but little upon you.[1]

The seventh device that Satan hath to keep souls off from holy exercises, from religious services, is,

Device (7). *By casting in a multitude of vain thoughts, whilst the soul is in seeking of God, or in waiting on God;* and by this device he hath cooled some men's spirits in heavenly services, and taken off, at least for a time, many precious souls from religious performances. I have no heart to hear, nor no heart to pray, nor no delight in reading, nor in the society of the saints, &c. Satan doth so dog and follow my soul, and is still a-casting in such a multitude of vain thoughts concerning God, the world, and my own soul, &c., that I even tremble to think of waiting upon God in any religious service. Oh! the vain thoughts that Satan casts in do so distaste my soul, and so grieve, vex, perplex, and distract my soul, that they even make me weary of holy duties, yea, of my very life. Oh! I cannot be so raised and ravished, so heated and melted, so quickened and enlarged, so comforted and refreshed, as I should be, as I might be, and as I would be in religious services, by reason of that multitude of vain thoughts, that Satan is injecting or casting into my soul, &c.[2]

Now, the remedies against this device of Satan are these:

Remedy (1). The first remedy against this device of Satan is, *To have your hearts strongly affected with the greatness, holiness, majesty, and glory of that God before whom you stand, and with whom your souls do converse in religious services.* Oh! let your souls be greatly affected with the presence, purity, and majesty of that God before whom thou standest. A man would be afraid of playing with a feather, when he is speaking with a king. Ah! when men have poor, low, light, slight, &c., thoughts of God, in their drawing near to God, they tempt the devil to bestir himself, and to cast in a multitude of vain thoughts to disturb and distract the soul in its waiting on God. There is nothing that will contribute so much to the keeping out of vain thoughts, as to look upon God as an omniscient God, an omnipresent God, an omnipotent God, a God full of all glorious perfections, a God whose majesty, purity, and glory will not suffer him to behold the least iniquity.[3] The reason why the blessed saints and glorious angels in heaven have not so much as one vain thought is, because

[1] What wise man would fetch gold out of a fiery crucible, hazard his immortal soul, to gain the world, by following a multitude in those steps that lead to the chambers of death and darkness?

[2] *Vellem servire Domino, sed cogitationes non patiuntur*; Lord, now how fain would I serve thee, and vain thoughts will not suffer me!

[3] When Pompey could not keep his soldiers in the camp by persuasion, he cast himself all along in the narrow passage that led out of it, and bid them go if you will, but you must first trample upon your general; and the thoughts of this overcame them. You are wise, and know how to apply it to the point in hand.

they are greatly affected with the greatness, holiness, majesty, purity, and glory of God.

Remedy (2). The second remedy against this device of Satan is, *To be peremptory in religious services, notwithstanding all those wandering thoughts the soul is troubled with.* This will be a sweet help against them: for the soul to be resolute in waiting on God, whether it be troubled with vain thoughts or not;[1] to say, Well I will pray still, and hear still, and meditate still, and keep fellowship with the saints still. Many precious souls can say from experience, that when their souls have been peremptory in their waiting on God, that Satan hath left them, and hath not been so busy in vexing their souls with vain thoughts. When Satan perceives that all those trifling vain thoughts that he casts into the soul do but vex the soul into greater diligence, carefulness, watchfulness, and peremptoriness in holy and heavenly services, and that the soul loses nothing of his zeal, piety, and devotion, but doubles his care, diligence, and earnestness, he often ceases to interpose his trifles and vain thoughts, as he ceased to tempt Christ, when Christ was peremptory in resisting his temptations.

Remedy (3). The third remedy against this device of Satan is, to consider this, *That those vain and trifling thoughts that are cast into our souls, when we are waiting upon God in this or that religious service, if they be not cherished and indulged, but abhorred, resisted, and disclaimed, they are not sins upon our souls, though they may be troubles to our minds; they shall not be put upon our accounts, nor keep mercies and blessings from being enjoyed by us.* When a soul in uprightness can look God in the face, and say, Lord, when I approach near unto thee, there be a world of vain thoughts crowd in upon me, that do disturb my soul, and weaken my faith, and lessen my comfort and spiritual strength. Oh, these are my clog, my burden, my torment, my hell! Oh, do justice upon these, free me from these, that I may serve thee with more freeness, singleness, spiritualness, and sweetness of spirit.[2] These thoughts may vex that soul, but they shall not harm that soul, nor keep a blessing from that soul. If vain thoughts resisted and lamented could stop the current of mercy, and render a soul unhappy, there would be none on earth that should ever taste of mercy, or be everlastingly happy.

Remedy (4). The fourth remedy against this device of Satan is, solemnly to consider, *That watching against sinful thoughts, resisting of sinful thoughts, lamenting and weeping over sinful thoughts, carries with it the sweetest and strongest evidence of the truth and power of grace, and of the sincerity of your hearts, and is the readiest and the surest way to be rid of them*, Ps. cxxxix. 23. Many low and carnal considerations may work men to watch their words, their lives, their actions; as hope of gain, or to please friends, or to get a name in the world, and many other such like considerations. Oh! but to watch

[1] It is a rule in the civil law, *Nec videtur actum, si quid supersit quod agatur*, nothing seems to be done, if there remains aught to be done. *Si dixisti, Sufficit, periisti*, if once thou sayest it is enough, thou art undone, saith Augustine.

[2] It is not Satan casting in of vain thoughts that can keep mercy from the soul, or undo the soul, but the lodging and cherishing of vain thoughts: 'O Jerusalem, how long shall vain thoughts lodge within thee?' Jer. iv. 14; Heb. 'in the midst of thee.' They pass through the best hearts, they are lodged and cherished only in the worst hearts.

our thoughts, to weep and lament over them, &c., this must needs be from some noble, spiritual, and internal principle, as love to God, a holy fear of God, a holy care and delight to please the Lord, &c.[1] The schools do well observe, that outward sins are of greater infamy, *majoris infamiæ;* but inward heart sins are of greater guilt, *majoris reatus;* as we see in the devil's. There is nothing that so speaks out a man to be thoroughly and kindly wrought upon, as his having his thoughts to be 'brought into obedience,' as the apostle speaks, 2 Cor. x. 4, 5. Grace is grown up to a very great height in that soul where it prevails, to the subduing of those vain thoughts that walk up and down in the soul.[2] Well! though you cannot be rid of them, yet make resistance and opposition against the first risings of them. When sinful thoughts arise, then think thus, The Lord takes notice of these thoughts; 'he knows them afar off,' as the Psalmist speaks, Ps. xxxviii. 6. He knew Herod's bloody thoughts, and Judas his betraying thoughts, and the Pharisees' cruel and blasphemous thoughts afar off.[3] Oh! think thus: All these sinful thoughts, they defile and pollute the soul, they deface and spoil much of the inward beauty and glory of the soul. If I commit this or that sin, to which my thoughts incline me, then either I must repent or not repent; if I repent, it will cost me more grief, sorrow, shame, heart-breaking, and soul-bleeding, before my conscience will be quieted, divine justice pacified, my comfort and joy restored, my evidences cleared, and my pardon in the court of conscience sealed, than the imagined profit or seeming sensual pleasure can be worth: 'What fruit had you in those things whereof you are now ashamed,' Rom. vi. 21.[4]

If I never repent, oh! then my sinful thoughts will be scorpions that will eternally vex me, the rods that will eternally lash me, the thorns that will everlastingly prick me, the dagger that will be eternally a-stabbing me, the worm that will be for ever a-gnawing me! Oh! therefore, watch against them, be constant in resisting them, and in lamenting and weeping over them, and then they shall not hurt thee, though they may for a time trouble thee. And remember this, he that doth this doth more than the most glistering and blustering hypocrite in the world doth.[5]

Remedy (5). The fifth remedy against this device of Satan is, *To labour more and more to be filled with the fulness of God, and to be enriched with all spiritual and heavenly things.* What is the reason that the angels in heaven have not so much as an idle thought? It is because they are filled with the fulness of God, Eph. iii. 19.[6] Take it for an experienced truth, the more the soul is filled with the fulness of God and enriched with spiritual and heavenly things, the less room

[1] Thoughts are the first-born, the blossoms of the soul, the beginning of our strength, whether for good or evil, and they are the greatest evidences for or against a man that can be.

[2] Ps. cxxxix. 23; Isa. lix. 7, lxvi. 18; Mat. ix. 4, xii. 25.

[3] Zeno, a wise heathen, affirmed God even beheld the thoughts. Mat. xv. 15-18.

[4] Tears instead of gems were the ornaments of David's bed when he had sinned; and so they must be thine, or else thou must lie down in the bed of sorrow for ever.

[5] Inward bleeding kills many a man; so will sinful thoughts, if not repented of.

[6] The words are an Hebraism. The Hebrews, when they would set out many excellent things, they add the name of God to it: city of God, cedars of God, wrestlings of God. So here, 'That ye may be filled with the fulness of God.'

there is in that soul for vain thoughts. The fuller the vessel is of wine, the less room there is for water. Oh, then, lay up much of God, of Christ, of precious promises, and choice experiences in your hearts, and then you will be less troubled with vain thoughts. 'A good man, out of the good treasure of his heart, bringeth forth good things,' Mat. xii. 35.

Remedy (6). The sixth remedy against this device of Satan is, *To keep up holy and spiritual affections; for such as your affections are, such will be your thoughts.* 'Oh how I love thy law! it is my meditation all the day,' Ps. cxix. 97. What we love most, we most muse upon. 'When I awake, I am still with thee,' Ps. cxxxix., &c. That which we much like, we shall much mind. They that are frequent in their love to God and his law, will be frequent in thinking of God and his law: a child will not forget his mother.

Remedy (7). The seventh remedy against this device of Satan is, *To avoid multiplicity of worldly business.* Oh let not the world take up your hearts and thoughts at other times. Souls that are torn in pieces with the cares of the world will be always vexed and tormented with vain thoughts in all their approaches to God.[1] Vain thoughts will be still crowding in upon him that lives in a crowd of business. The stars which have least circuit are nearest the pole; and men that are least perplexed with business are commonly nearest to God.

The eighth device that Satan hath to hinder souls from religious services, from holy performances, is,

Device (8). *By working them to rest in their performances; to rest in prayer, and to rest in hearing, reading, and the communion of saints,* &c. And when Satan hath drawn the soul to rest upon the service done, then he will help the soul to reason thus: Why, thou wert as good never pray, as to pray and rest in prayer; as good never hear, as to hear and rest in hearing; as good never be in the communion of saints, as to rest in the communion of saints. And by this device he stops many souls in their heavenly race, and takes off poor souls from those services that should be their joy and crown, Isa. lviii. 1–3, Zech. vii. 4–6, Mat. vi. 2, Rom. i. 7.

Now the remedies against this device are these:

Remedy (1). The first remedy against this device of Satan is, *To dwell much upon the imperfections and weaknesses that do attend your choicest services.* Oh the spots, the blots, the blemishes that are to be seen on the face of our fairest duties![2] When thou hast done all thou canst, thou hast need to close up all with this, 'Oh enter not into judgment with thy servant, O Lord,' Ps. cxliii. 2, for the weaknesses that cleave to my best services. We may all say with the church, 'All our righteousnesses are as a menstruous cloth.' Isa. lxiv. 6. If God should be strict to mark what is done amiss in our best actions, we are undone. Oh the water that is mingled with our wine, the dross that cleaves unto our gold!

[1] 2 Tim. ii. 4, ἐμπλέκεται, is entangled; it is a comparison which St Paul borroweth from the custom of the Roman empire, wherein soldiers were forbidden to be proctors of other men's causes, to undertake husbandry or merchandise.

[2] Pride and high confidence is most apt to creep in upon duties well done, saith one.

Remedy (2). The second remedy against this device of Satan is, to consider *The impotence and inability of any of your best services, divinely to comfort, refresh, and bear your souls up from fainting, and sinking in the days of trouble, when darkness is round about you, when God shall say to you, as he did once to the Israelites,* 'Go and cry unto the gods that you have chosen; let them save you in the time of your tribulation,' Judges x. 14. So, when God shall say in the day of your troubles, Go to your prayers, to your hearing, and to your fasting, &c., and see if they can help you, if they can support you, if they can deliver you.[1] If God in that day doth but withhold the influence of his grace, thy former services will be but poor cordials to comfort thee; and then thou must and will cry out, Oh, 'none but Christ, none but Christ.' Oh my prayers are not Christ, my hearing is not Christ, my fasting is not Christ, &c. Oh! one smile of Christ, one glimpse of Christ, one good word from Christ, one nod of love from Christ in the day of trouble and darkness, will more revive and refresh the soul than all your former services, in which your souls rested, as if they were the bosom of Christ, which should be the only centre of our souls. Christ is the crown of crowns, the glory of glories, and the heaven of heavens.

Remedy (3). The third remedy against this device of Satan is, solemnly to consider, *That good things rested upon will as certainly undo us, and everlastingly destroy us, as the greatest enormities that can be committed by us.* Those souls that after they have done all, do not look up so high as Christ, and rest, and centre alone in Christ, laying down their services at the footstool of Christ, must lie down in sorrow; their bread is prepared for them in hell. 'Behold, all ye that kindle a fire, compass yourselves with the sparks: and walk in the light of your fire, and in the sparks ye have kindled. This shall ye have at mine hands; ye shall lie down in sorrow,' Isa. l. 11. Is it good dwelling with everlasting burnings, with a devouring fire? If it be, why then rest in your duties still; if otherwise, then see that you centre only in the bosom of Christ.

Remedy (4). The fourth remedy against this device of Satan is, *To dwell much upon the necessity and excellency of that resting-place that God hath provided for you.* Above all other resting-places himself is your resting-place; his free mercy and love is your resting-place; the pure, glorious, matchless, and spotless righteousness of Christ is your resting-place. Ah! it is sad to think, that most men have forgotten their resting-place, as the Lord complains: 'My people have been as lost sheep, their shepherds have caused them to go astray, and have turned them away to the mountains: they are gone from mountain to hill, and forgotten their resting-place,' Jer. l. 6. So poor souls that see not the excellency of that resting-place that God hath appointed for their souls to lie down in, they wander from mountain to hill, from one duty to another, and here they will rest and there they will rest; but souls that see the excellency of that resting-place that God hath provided for them, they will say, Farewell prayer, farewell hearing, farewell fasting, &c., I will rest no more in you, but now I will rest

[1] *Omne bonum in summo bono,* all good is in the chiefest good. *Nec Christus, nec cœlum patitur hyperbolem.*

only in the bosom of Christ, the love of Christ, the righteousness of Christ.

III. The third thing to be shewed is,

The several devices that Satan hath to keep souls in a sad, doubting, questioning, and uncomfortable condition.

Though he can never rob a believer of his crown, yet such is his malice and envy, that he will leave no stone unturned, no means unattempted, to rob them of their comfort and peace, to make their life a burden and a hell unto them, to cause them to spend their days in sorrow and mourning, in sighing and complaining, in doubting and questioning. Surely we have no interest in Christ; our graces are not true, our hopes are the hopes of hypocrites; our confidence is our presumption, our enjoyments are our delusions, &c.[1]

I shall shew you this in some particulars, &c.

Device 1. The first device that Satan hath to keep souls in a sad, doubting, and questioning condition, and so making their life a hell, is, *By causing them to be still poring and musing upon sin, to mind their sins more than their Saviour; yea, so to mind their sins as to forget, yea, to neglect their Saviour;* that, as the Psalmist speaks, 'The Lord is not in all their thoughts,' Ps. x. 4. Their eyes are so fixed upon their disease, that they cannot see the remedy, though it be near; and they do so muse upon their debts, that they have neither mind nor heart to think of their Surety, &c.[2]

Now the remedies against this device are these.

Remedy (1). The first remedy is for weak believers to consider, *That though Jesus Christ hath not freed them from the presence of sin, yet he hath freed them from the damnatory power of sin.* It is most true that sin and grace were never born together, neither shall sin and grace die together; yet while a believer breathes in this world, they must live together, they must keep house together. Christ in this life will not free any believer from the presence of any one sin, though he doth free every believer from the damning power of every sin. 'There is no condemnation to them that are in Christ Jesus, who walk not after the flesh, but after the Spirit,' Rom. viii. 1. The law cannot condemn a believer, for Christ hath fulfilled it for him; divine justice cannot condemn him, for that Christ hath satisfied; his sins cannot condemn him, for they in the blood of Christ are pardoned; and his own conscience, upon righteous grounds, cannot condemn him, because Christ, that is greater than his conscience, hath acquitted him.[3]

Remedy (2). The second remedy against this device of Satan is, to

[1] Blessed Bradford, in one of his epistles, saith thus, 'O Lord, sometime methinks I feel it so with me, as if there were no difference between my heart and the wicked. I have a blind mind as they, a stout, stubborn, rebellious hard heart as they,' and so he goes on, &c [A frequent plaint by this holy man. See his 'Writings,' consisting mainly of 'Letters,' by Townsend (Parker Society), 1853.—G.]

[2] A Christian should wear Christ in his bosom as a flower of delight, for he is a whole paradise of delight. He that minds not Christ more than his sin, can never be thankful and fruitful as he should.

[3] *Peccata enim non nocent, si non placent*, my sins hurt me not, if they like me not. Sin is like that wild fig-tree, or ivy in the wall; cut off stump, body, bough, and branches, yet some strings or other will sprout out again, till the wall be plucked down.

consider, *That though Jesus Christ hath not freed you from the molesting and vexing power of sin, yet he hath freed you from the reign and dominion of sin.* Thou sayest that sin doth so molest and vex thee, that thou canst not think of God, nor go to God, nor speak with God.[1] Oh! but remember it is one thing for sin to molest and vex thee, and another thing for sin to reign and have dominion over thee. 'For sin shall not have dominion over you, for ye are not under the law, but under grace,' Rom. vi. 14. Sin may rebel, but it shall never reign in a saint. It fareth with sin in the regenerate as with those beasts that Daniel speaks of, 'that had their dominion taken away, yet their lives were prolonged for a season and a time,' Dan. vii. 12.

Now sin reigns in the soul when the soul willingly and readily obeys it, and subjects to its commands, as subjects do actively obey and embrace the commands of their prince. The commands of a king are readily embraced and obeyed by his subjects, but the commands of a tyrant are embraced and obeyed unwillingly. All the service that is done to a tyrant is out of violence, and not out of obedience. A free and willing subjection to the commands of sin speaks out the soul to be under the reign and dominion of sin; but from this plague, this hell, Christ frees all believers.[2] Sin cannot say of a believer as the centurion said of his servants, 'I bid one Go, and he goeth; and to another, Come, and he cometh; and to another, Do this, and he doth it,' Mat. viii. 9. No! the heart of a saint riseth against the commands of sin; and when sin would carry his soul to the devil, he hales his sin before the Lord, and cries out for justice. Lord! saith the believing soul, sin plays the tyrant, the devil in me; it would have me to do that which makes against thy holiness as well as against my happiness; against thy honour and glory, as my comfort and peace; therefore do me justice, thou righteous Judge of heaven and earth, and let this tyrant sin die for it, &c.

Remedy (3). The third remedy against this device of Satan is, *Constantly to keep one eye upon the promises of remission of sin, as well as the other eye upon the inward operations of sin.* This is the most certain truth, that God would graciously pardon those sins to his people that he will not in this life fully subdue in his people. Paul prays thrice, *i.e.* often, to be delivered from the thorn in the flesh. All he can get is, 'My grace is sufficient for thee,' 2 Cor. xii. 9; I will graciously pardon that to thee that I will not conquer in thee, saith God. 'And I will cleanse them from all their iniquity, whereby they have sinned against me, and whereby they have transgressed against me. I, even I, am he that blotteth out thy transgressions for mine own sake, and will not remember thy sins,'[3] Jer. xxxiii. 8, Isa.

[1] The primitive Christians chose rather to be thrown to lions without than left to lusts within. *Ad leones magis quam leonem*, saith Tertullian. [Often in his famous 'Apology.'—G.]

[2] It is a sign that sin hath not gained your consent, but committed a rape upon your souls, when you cry out to God. If the ravished virgin under the law cried out, she was guiltless, Deut. xxii. 27; so when sin plays the tyrant over the soul, and the soul cries out, it is guiltless; those sins shall not be charged upon the soul.

[3] Isa. xliv. 22, Micah vii. 18, 19, Col. ii. 13, 14. The promises of God are a precious book, every leaf drops myrrh and mercy. Though the weak Christian cannot open, read, and apply them, Christ can and will apply them to their souls. מחה, an Hebrew

xliii. 25. Ah! you lamenting souls, that spend your days in sighing and groaning under the sense and burden of your sins, why do you deal so unkindly with God, and so injuriously with your own souls, as not to cast an eye upon those precious promises of remission of sin which may bear up and refresh your spirits in the darkest night, and under the heaviest burden of sin?

Remedy (4). The fourth remedy against this device of Satan is, *To look upon all your sins as charged upon the account of Christ, as debts which the Lord Jesus hath fully satisfied;* and indeed, were there but one farthing of that debt unpaid that Christ was engaged to satisfy, it would not have stood with the unspotted justice of God to have let him come into heaven and sit down at his own right hand. But all our debts, by his death, being discharged, we are freed, and he is exalted to sit down at the right hand of his Father, which is the top of his glory, and the greatest pledge of our felicity: 'For he hath made him to be sin for us that knew no sin, that we might be made the righteousness of God in him,' saith the apostle, 2 Cor. v. 21.[1] All our sins were made to meet upon Christ, as that evangelical prophet hath it: 'He was wounded for our transgressions, he was bruised for our iniquities, the chastisement of our peace was upon him, and with his stripes we are healed. All we like sheep have gone astray, we have turned every one to his own way, and the Lord hath laid on him the iniquity of us all;' or, as the Hebrew hath it, 'He hath made the iniquity of us all to meet in him,' Isa. liii. 5, 6. In law, we know that all the debts of the wife are charged upon the husband. Saith the wife to one and to another, If I owe you anything, go to my husband. So may a believer say to the law, and to the justice of God, If I owe you anything, go to my Christ, who hath undertaken for me. I must not sit down discouraged, under the apprehension of those debts, that Christ, to the utmost farthing, hath fully satisfied. Would it not argue much weakness, I had almost said much madness, for a debtor to sit down discouraged upon his looking over those debts that his surety hath readily, freely, and fully satisfied? The sense of his great love should engage a man for ever to love and honour his surety, and to bless that hand that hath paid the debt, and crossed the books, &c. But to sit down discouraged when the debt is satisfied, is a sin that bespeaks repentance.[2]

Christ hath cleared all reckoning betwixt God and us. You remember the scapegoat. Upon his head all the iniquities of the children of Israel, and all their transgressions in all their sins, were confessed and put, and the goat did bear upon him all their iniquities, &c., Lev. xvi. 21. Why! the Lord Jesus is that blessed scapegoat, upon whom all our sins were laid, and who alone hath carried 'our sins away into the land of forgetfulness, where they shall never be remembered more.'[3]

participle, and notes a constant, a continued act of God. I, I am he, blotting out thy transgressions to day and to-morrow, &c.

[1] Christ was *peccatorum maximus*, the greatest of sinners by imputation and reputation.

[2] Christ hath the greatest worth and wealth in him. As the worth and value of many pieces of silver is in one piece of gold, so all the excellencies scattered abroad in the creatures are united in Christ. All the whole volume of perfections which are spread through heaven and earth are epitomised in him.

[3] Christ is *canalis gratiæ*, the channel of grace from God.

A believer, under the guilt of his sin, may look the Lord in the face, and sweetly plead thus with him: It is true, Lord, I owed thee much, but thy Son was my ransom, my redemption. His blood was the price; he was my surety and undertook to answer for my sins; I know thou must be satisfied, and Christ hath satisfied thee to the utmost farthing: not for himself, for what sins had he of his own? but for me; they were my debts that he satisfied for; be pleased to look over the book, and thou shalt find that it is crossed by thy own hand upon this very account, that Christ hath suffered and satisfied for them.[1]

Remedy (5). The fifth remedy against this device of Satan is, solemnly to consider, *Of the reasons why the Lord is pleased to have his people exercised, troubled, and vexed with the operations of sinful corruptions;* and they are these: partly to keep them humble and low in their own eyes;[2] and partly to put them upon the use of all divine helps, whereby sin may be subdued and mortified; and partly, that they may live upon Christ for the perfecting the work of sanctification; and partly, to wean them from things below, and to make them heart-sick of their absence from Christ, and to maintain in them bowels of compassion towards others that are subject to the same infirmities with them; and that they may distinguish between a state of grace and a state of glory, and that heaven may be more sweet to them in the close. Now doth the Lord upon these weighty reasons suffer his people to be exercised and molested with the operations of sinful corruptions? Oh then, let no believer speak, write, or conclude bitter things against his own soul and comforts, because that sin troubles and vexes his righteous soul, &c.; but lay his hand upon his mouth and be silent, because the Lord will have it so, upon such weighty grounds as the soul is not able to withstand.[3]

Remedy (6). The sixth remedy against this device of Satan is, solemnly to consider, *That believers must repent for their being discouraged by their sins.* Their being discouraged by their sins will cost them many a prayer, many a tear, and many a groan; and that because their discouragements under sin flow from ignorance and unbelief. It springs from their ignorance of the richness, freeness, fulness, and everlastingness of God's love; and from their ignorance of the power, glory, sufficiency, and efficacy of the death and sufferings of the Lord Jesus Christ; and from their ignorance of the worth, glory, fulness, largeness, and completeness of the righteousness of Jesus Christ; and from their ignorance of that real, close, spiritual, glorious, and inseparable union that is between Christ and their precious souls. Ah! did precious souls know and believe the truth of these things as they should, they would not sit down dejected and overwhelmed under the sense and operation of sin, &c.[4]

[1] The bloods of Abel, for so the Hebrew hath it, as if the blood of one Abel had so many tongues as drops, cried for vengeance against sin; but the blood of Christ cries louder for the pardon of sin.

[2] Augustine saith, that the first, second, and third virtue of a Christian is humility. [Cf. under Humilitas in Conf., and De C. D. Epist. 56 ad Diosc.—G.]

[3] *Lilme Blelammed*, we therefore learn, that we may teach, is a proverb among the Rabbins. After the Trojans had been wandering and tossing up and down the Mediterranean sea, as soon as they espied Italy, they cried out with exulting joy, Italy, Italy! So will saints when they come to heaven.

[4] God never gave a believer a new heart that it should always lie a-bleeding, and that it should always be rent and torn in pieces with discouragements.

The second device that Satan hath to keep souls in a sad, doubting, and questioning condition is,

Device (2). *By working them to make false definitions of their graces.* Satan knows, that as false definitions of sin wrong the soul one way, so false definitions of grace wrong the soul another way.

I will instance only in faith: Oh how doth Satan labour might and main to work men to make false definitions of faith! Some he works to define faith too high, as that it is a full assurance of the love of God to a man's soul in particular, or a full persuasion of the pardon and remission of a man's own sins in particular. Saith Satan, What dost thou talk of faith? Faith is an assurance of the love of God, and of the pardon of sin; and this thou hast not; thou knowest thou art far off from this; therefore thou hast no faith. And by drawing men to make such a false definition of faith, he keeps them in a sad, doubting, and questioning condition, and makes them spend their days in sorrow and sighing, so that tears are their drink, and sorrow is their meat, and sighing is their work all the day long, &c.

The philosophers say there are eight degrees of heat; we discern three. Now, if a man should define heat only by the highest degree, then all other degrees will be cast out from being heat. So if men shall define faith only by the highest degrees, by assurance of the love of God, and of the pardon of his sins in particular, what will become of lesser degrees of faith?

If a man should define a man to be a living man, only by the highest and strongest demonstrations of life, as laughing, leaping, running, working, walking, &c., would not many thousands that groan under internal and external weaknesses, and that cannot laugh, nor leap, nor run, nor work, nor walk, be found dead men by such a definition, that yet we know to be alive? It is so here, and you know how to apply it, &c.

Now the remedies against this device are these:

Remedy (1). The first remedy against this device of Satan is, solemnly to consider, *That there may be true faith, yea, great measures of faith, where there is no assurance.* The Canaanite woman in the Gospel had strong faith, yet no assurance that we read of. 'These things have I written unto you,' saith John, 'that believe on the name of the Son of God, that ye may know that ye have eternal life, and that ye may believe on the name of the Son of God,' 1 John v. 13. In these words you see that they did believe, and had eternal life, in respect of the purpose and promise of God, and in respect of the seeds and beginnings of it in their souls, and in respect of Christ their head, who sits in heaven as a public person, representing all his chosen ones, 'Who hath raised us up together, and made us sit together in heavenly places in Christ Jesus,' Eph. ii. 6; and yet they did not know that they had eternal life. It is one thing to have a right to heaven, and another thing to know it; it is one thing to be beloved, and another thing for a man to know that he is beloved. It is one thing for God to write a man's name in the book of life, and another thing for God to tell a man that his name is written in the book of life; and to say to him, Luke x. 20, 'Rejoice, because thy name is written in heaven.' So Paul, 'In whom ye also trusted, after ye heard the word of truth, the gospel of your salvation:

in whom also, after ye believed, ye were sealed with that Holy Spirit of promise,' Eph. i. 13. So Micah: 'Rejoice not against me, O my enemy: for when I shall fall, I shall rise; when I shall sit in darkness, the Lord shall be a light unto me. I will bear the indignation of the Lord, because I have sinned,' &c., or, 'the sad countenance of God,' as the Hebrew hath it, Micah vii. 8, 9. This soul had no assurance, for he sits in darkness, and was under the sad countenance of God; and yet had strong faith, as appears in those words, 'When I fall, I shall rise; when I sit in darkness, the Lord shall be a light unto me.' He will bring me forth to the light, and I shall behold his righteousness. And let this suffice for the first answer.[1]

Remedy (2). The second remedy against this device of Satan is, solemnly to consider, *That God in the Scripture doth define faith otherwise.* God defines faith to be a receiving of Christ—'As many as received him, to them he gave this privilege, to be the sons of God,' John i. 12. 'To as many as believed on his name,' Acts xi. 23—to be a cleaving of the soul unto God, though no joy, but afflictions, attend the soul. Yea, the Lord defines faith to be a coming to God in Christ, and often to a resting and staying, rolling of the soul upon Christ. It is safest and sweetest to define as God defines, both vices and graces. This is the only way to settle the soul, and to secure it against the wiles of men and devils, who labour, by false definitions of grace, to keep precious souls in a doubting, staggering, and languishing condition, and so make their lives a burden, a hell, unto them.[2]

Remedy (3). The third remedy against this device of Satan is, seriously to consider this, *That there may be true faith where there is much doubtings.* Witness those frequent sayings of Christ to his disciples, 'Why are ye afraid, O ye of little faith?'[3] Persons may be truly believing who nevertheless are sometimes doubting. In the same persons that the fore-mentioned scriptures speak of, you may see their faith commended and their doubts condemned, which doth necessarily suppose a presence of both.

Remedy (4). The fourth remedy against this device of Satan is, solemnly to consider, *That assurance is an effect of faith; therefore it cannot be faith.* The cause cannot be the effect, nor the root the fruit. As the effect flows from the cause, the fruit from the root, the stream from the fountain, so doth assurance flow from faith. This truth I shall make good thus:

The assurance of our salvation and pardon of sin doth primarily arise from the witness of the Spirit of God that we are the children of God, Eph. i. 13; and the Spirit never witnesseth this till we are believers: 'For we are sons by faith in Christ Jesus,' Gal. iv. 6. Therefore assurance is not faith, but follows it, as the effect follows the cause.

Again, no man can be assured and persuaded of his salvation till he be united to Christ, till he be ingrafted into Christ; and a man cannot be ingrafted into Christ till he hath faith. He must first be ingrafted into Christ by faith before he can have assurance of his salvation; which doth clearly evidence, that assurance is not faith, but an effect and fruit of faith, &c.

[1] So those in Isa. l. 10 had faith, though they had no assurance.

[2] Mat. xi. 28, John vi. 37, Heb. vii. 25, 26. [3] Mat. vi. 30, xiv. 31, xvi. 8; Luke xii. 28.

Again, faith cannot be lost, but assurance may; therefore assurance is not faith.[1] Though assurance be a precious flower in the garden of a saint, and is more infinitely sweet and delightful to the soul than all outward comforts and contents; yet it is but a flower that is subject to fade, and to lose its freshness and beauty, as saints by sad experience find, &c.

Again, a man must first have faith before he can have assurance, therefore assurance is not faith. And that a man must first have faith before he can have assurance, is clear by this, a man must first be saved before he can be assured of his salvation; for he cannot be assured of that which is not. And a man must first have a saving faith before he can be saved by faith, for he cannot be saved by that which he hath not; therefore a man must first have faith before he can have assurance, and so it roundly follows that assurance is not faith, &c.[2]

The third device that Satan hath to keep the soul in a sad, doubting, and questioning condition is,

Device (3). *By working the soul to make false inferences from the cross actings of Providence.* Saith Satan, Dost thou not see how Providence crosses thy prayers, and crosses thy desires, thy tears, thy hopes, thy endeavours?[3] Surely if his love were towards thee, if his soul did delight and take pleasure in thee, he would not deal thus with thee, &c.

Now, the remedies against this device are these:

Remedy (1). The first remedy against this device of Satan is, solemnly to consider, *That many things may be cross to our desires that are not cross to our good.* Abraham, Jacob, David, Job, Moses, Jeremiah, Jonah, Paul, &c., met with many things that were contrary to their desires and endeavours, that were not contrary to their good; as all know that have wisely compared their desires and endeavours and God's actings together. Physic often works contrary to the patients' desires, when it doth not work contrary to their good.

I remember a story of a godly man, who had a great desire to go to France, and as he was going to take shipping he broke his leg; and it pleased Providence so to order it, that the ship that he should have gone in at that very same time was cast away, and not a man saved; and so by breaking a bone his life was saved. Though Providence did work cross to his desire, yet it did not work cross to his good, &c.[4]

Remedy (2). The second remedy against this device of Satan is, solemnly to consider, *That the hand of God may be against a man, when the love and heart of God is much set upon a man.* No man can conclude how the heart of God stands by his hand. The hand of God was against Ephraim, and yet his love, his heart, was dearly set upon Ephraim: 'I have surely heard Ephraim bemoaning himself thus: Thou hast chastised me, and I was chastised, as a bullock unaccustomed

[1] Ps. li. 12, xxx. 6, 7; Cant. v. 6; Isa. viii. 17.

[2] There is many thousand precious souls, of whom this world is not worthy, that have the faith of reliance, and yet want assurance and the effects of it; as high joy, glorious peace, and vehement longings after the coming of Christ.

[3] Ps. lxxvii. 7, *et seq.*, xxxi. 1, *ult.*, lxxiii. 2, 23.

[4] The Circumcellians being not able to withstand the preaching and writing of Augustine, sought his destruction, having beset the way he was to go to his visitation, but by God's providence he, missing his way, escaped the danger. [See *ante*, Conf.—G.]

to the yoke. Turn thou me, and I shall be turned; for thou art the Lord my God. Surely, after that I was returned, I repented; and after that I was instructed, I smote upon my thigh; I was ashamed, yea, even confounded, because I did bear the reproach of my youth. Ephraim is my dear Son, he is a pleasant child; for since I spake against him, I do earnestly remember him still. Therefore my bowels are troubled for him; I will surely have mercy upon him, saith the Lord,' Jer. xxxi. 18–20.[1]

God can look sourly, and chide bitterly, and strike heavily, even where and when he loves dearly. The hand of God was very much against Job, and yet his love, his heart, was very much set upon Job, as you may see by comparing chaps. i. and ii. with xli. and xlii. The hand of God was sore against David and Jonah, when his heart was much set upon them. He that shall conclude that the heart of God is against those that his hand is against, will condemn the generation of the just, whom God unjustly would not have condemned.

Remedy (3). The third remedy against this device of Satan, is, to consider, *That all the cross providences that befall the saints are but in order to some noble good that God doth intend to prefer*[2] *upon them.* Providence wrought cross to David's desire, in taking away the child sinfully begotten, but yet not cross to more noble good; for was it not far better for David to have such a legitimate heir as Solomon was, than that a bastard should wear the crown, and sway the sceptre?

Joseph, you know, was sold into a far country by the envy and malice of his brethren, and afterwards imprisoned because he would not be a prisoner to his mistress's lusts; yet all these providences did wonderfully conduce to his advancement, and the preservation of his father's family, which was then the visible church of Christ. It was so handled by a noble hand of providence, that what they sought to decline,[3] they did promote. Joseph was therefore sold by his brethren that he might not be worshipped, and yet he was therefore worshipped because he was sold.[4]

David was designed to a kingdom, but oh! the straits, troubles, and deaths that he runs through before he feels the weight of the crown; and all this was but in order to the sweetening of his crown, and to the settling of it more firmly and gloriously upon his head. God did so contrive it that Jonah's offence, and those cross actings of his that did attend it, should advantage that end which they seemed most directly to oppose. Jonah he flies to Tarshish, then cast into the sea, then saved by a miracle. Then the mariners, as it is very probable, who cast Jonah into the sea, declared to the Ninevites what had happened; therefore he must be a man sent of God, and that his threatenings must be believed and hearkened to, and therefore they must repent and humble themselves, that the wrath threatened might not be executed, &c.[5]

Remedy (4). The fourth remedy against this device of Satan is,

[1] God's providential hand may be with persons when his heart is set against them. God's providential hand was for a time with Saul, Haman, Asshur, and Jehu, and yet his heart was set against him. 'No man knoweth love or hatred by all that is before him,' Eccles. ix. 1, 2. [2] = confer.—G. [3] 'Lower' = injure.—G.

[4] Cf. Genesis xxxvii. 7, &c.—G.

[5] The motions of divine providence are so dark, so deep, so changeable, that the wisest and noblest souls cannot tell what conclusions to make.

seriously to consider, *That all the strange, dark, deep, and changeable providences that believers meet with, shall further them in their way to heaven, in their journey to happiness.* Divine wisdom and love will so order all things here below, that they shall work for the real, internal, and eternal good of them that love him. All the rugged providences that David met with, did contribute to the bringing of him to the throne; and all the rugged providences that Daniel and the 'three children' met with, did contribute to their great advancement. So all the rugged providences that believers meet with, they shall all contribute to the lifting up of their souls above all things, below God. As the waters lifted up Noah's ark nearer heaven, and as all the stones that were about Stephen's ears did but knock him the closer to Christ, the corner-stone, so all the strange rugged providences that we meet with, they shall raise us nearer heaven, and knock us nearer to Christ, that precious corner-stone.[1]

The fourth device that Satan hath to keep souls in a sad, doubting, and questioning condition is,

Device (4). *By suggesting to them that their graces are not true, but counterfeit.* Saith Satan, All is not gold that glitters, all is not free grace that you count grace, that you call grace. That which you call faith is but a fancy, and that which you call zeal, is but a natural heat and passion; and that light you have, it is but common, it is short, to what many have attained to that are now in hell, &c. Satan doth not labour more mightily to persuade hypocrites that their graces are true when they are counterfeit, than he doth to persuade precious souls that their graces are counterfeit, when indeed they are true, and such as will abide the touchstone of Christ, &c.[2]

Now the remedies against this device are these:

Remedy (1). The first remedy against this device of Satan is, seriously to consider, *That grace is taken two ways.*

[1.] It is taken for *the gracious good-will and favour of God,* whereby he is pleased of his own free love to accept of some in Christ for his own. This, some call the first grace, because it is the fountain of all other graces, and the spring from whence they flow, and it is therefore called grace, because it makes a man gracious with God, but this is only in God.

[2.] Grace is taken for *the gifts of grace,* and they are of two sorts, common or special.

Some are common to believers and hypocrites, as a gift of knowledge, a gift of prayer, &c.

Some are special graces, and they are proper and peculiar to the saints, as faith, humility, meekness, love, patience, &c., Gal. v, 22, 23.

Remedy (2). The second remedy against this device of Satan is, wisely to consider, *The differences betwixt renewing grace and restraining grace, betwixt sanctifying grace and temporary grace*; and this I will shew you in these ten particulars.

[1.] True grace *makes all glorious within and without*: 'The King's

[1] Orosius, speaking of Valentinian, saith: He that for Christ's name's sake had lost a tribuneship, within a while after succeeded his persecutor in the empire.

[2] Yet it must be granted that many a fair flower may grow out of a stinking root, and many sweet dispositions and fair actions may be where there is only the corrupt root of nature.

daughter is all glorious within; her raiment is of wrought gold,' Ps. xlv. 13. True grace makes the understanding glorious, the affections glorious. It casts a general glory upon all the noble parts of the soul: 'The King's daughter is all glorious within.' And as it makes the inside glorious, so it makes the outside glorious: 'Her clothing is of wrought gold.' It makes men look gloriously, and speak gloriously, and walk and act gloriously, so that vain souls shall be forced to say that these are they that have seen Jesus.[1] As grace is a fire to burn up and consume the dross and filth of the soul, so it is an ornament to beautify and adorn the soul. True grace makes all new, the inside new and the outside new: 'If any man be in Christ, he is a new creature,' 2 Cor. v. 17,[2] but temporary grace doth not this. True grace changes the very nature of a man. Moral virtue doth only restrain or chain up the outward man, it doth not change the whole man. A lion in a grate is a lion still; he is restrained, but not changed, for he retains his lion-like nature still. So temporary graces restrain many men from this and that wickedness, but it doth not change and turn their hearts from wickedness. But now true grace, that turns a lion into a lamb, as you may see in Paul, Acts ix., and a notorious strumpet into a blessed and glorious penitent, as you may see in Mary Magdalene, &c., &c., Luke vii.[3]

[2.] *The objects* of true grace are *supernatural.* True grace is conversant about the choicest and the highest objects, about the most soul-ennobling and soul-greatening objects, as God, Christ, precious promises that are more worth than a world, and a kingdom that shakes not, a crown of glory that withers not, and heavenly treasures that rust not. The objects of temporary grace are low and poor, and always within the compass of reason's reach.[4]

[3.] True grace enables a Christian, *when he is himself, to do spiritual actions with real pleasure and delight,* To souls truly gracious, Christ's yoke 'is easy, and his burden is light;' 'his commandments are not grievous, but joyous.' 'I delight in the law of God after the inward man,' saith Paul.[5] The blessed man is described by this, that he 'delights in the law of the Lord,' Ps. i. 2. 'It is joy to the just to do judgment,' saith Solomon, Prov. xxi. 15. To a gracious soul, 'All the ways of the Lord are pleasantness, and his paths are peace, Prov. iii. 17; but to souls that have but temporary grace, but moral virtues, religious services are a toil, not a pleasure; a burden, and not a delight. 'Wherefore have we fasted,' say they, 'and thou seest not? Wherefore have we afflicted our souls, and thou takest no knowledge?' Isa. lviii. 3, &c. 'Ye have said,' say those in Malachi, 'It is vain to serve God; and what profit is it that we have kept his ordinances, and that we have walked mournfully before the Lord of hosts?' Mal. iii. 14. 'When will the new moon be gone,' say those in Amos, 'that we may sell corn, and the Sabbath, that we may set forth wheat, making the ephah small,

[1] God brings not a pair of scales to weigh our graces, but a touchstone to try our graces. Purity, preciousness, and holiness is stamped upon all saving graces, Acts xv. 9, 2 Peter iv. 1, Jude 20.

[2] *καινη κτισις*, a new creation: new Adam, new covenant, new paradise, new Lord, new law, new hearts, and new creatures go together.

[3] It seems right to question this admittedly common mode of speaking of Mary of Magdala. It is not certain that the two were identical.—G.

[4] 2 Cor. iv. 18. Prov. xiv. A saint hath his feet where other men's heads are, Mat. vi.

[5] Mat. xi. 30; 1 John v. 3; Rom. vii. 22.

and the shekel great, and falsifying the balances by deceit,' Amos viii. 5.

[4.] True grace makes *a man most careful, and most fearful of his own heart.*[1] It makes him most studious about his own heart, informing that, examining that, and watching over that; but temporary grace, moral virtues, make men more mindful and careful of others, to instruct them and counsel them, and stir up them, and watch over them, &c. Which doth with open mouth demonstrate that their graces are not saving and peculiar to saints, but that they are temporary, and no more than Judas, Demas, and the pharisees had, &c.

[5.] Grace will *work a man's heart to love and cleave to the strictest and holiest ways and things of God, for their purity and sanctity, in the face of all dangers and hardships.* 'Thy word is very pure, therefore thy servant loveth it,' Ps. cxix. 140. Others love it, and like it, and follow it, for the credit, the honour, the advantage that they get by it; but I love it for the spiritual beauty and purity of it. So the psalmist, 'All this is come upon us; yet have we not forgotten thee, neither have we dealt falsely in thy covenant. Our heart is not turned back, neither have our steps declined from thy way: though thou hast sore broken us in the place of dragons, and covered us with the shadows of death,' Ps. xliv. 17–19. But temporary grace, that will not bear up the soul against all oppositions and discouragements in the ways of God, as is clear by their apostasy in John vi. 60, 66, and by the stony grounds falling away, &c., Mat. xiii. 20, 21.[2]

[6.] True grace will *enable a man to step over the world's crown, to take up Christ's cross; to prefer the cross of Christ above the glory of this world.* It enabled Abraham, and Moses, and Daniel, with those other worthies in Heb. xi., to do so.

Godfrey of Bullen [Bouillon], first king of Jerusalem, refused to be crowned with a crown of gold, saying, 'That it became not a Christian there to wear a crown of gold, where Christ had worn a crown of thorns.' Oh! but temporary grace cannot work the soul to prefer Christ's cross above the world's crown; but when these two meet, a temporary Christian steps over Christ's cross to take up, and keep up, the world's crown. 'Demas hath forsaken us to embrace this present world,' 2 Tim. iv. 10. So the young man in the Gospel had many good things in him; he bid fair for heaven, and came near to heaven; but when Christ set his cross before him, he steps over that to enjoy the world's crown, Mat. xix. 19-22. When Christ bid him, 'go and sell all that he had, and give to the poor,' &c., 'he went away sorrowful, for he had great possessions.' If heaven be to be had upon no other terms, Christ may keep his heaven to himself, he will have none, &c.[3]

[7.] Sanctifying grace, renewing grace, *puts the soul upon spiritual duties, from spiritual and intrinsecal motives,* as from the sense of divine love, that doth constrain the soul to wait on God, and to act for

[1] Ps. li. 10, and cxix. 36, 80, and cxxxix. 23, and lxxxvi. 11.

[2] Grace is a panoply against all trouble, and a paradise of all pleasures.

[3] Few are of Jerome's mind, that had rather have St Paul's coat with his heavenly graces, than the purple of kings with their kingdoms. The king of Navarre told Beza, that in the cause of religion he would launch no further into their sea, than he might be sure to return safe to the haven. [Henry IV., afterwards the Apostate from Protestantism.—G.]

God;[1] and the sense of the excellency and sweetness of communion with God, and the choice and precious discoveries that the soul hath formerly had of the beauty and glory to [*sic*] God, whilst it hath been in the service of God. The good looks, the good words, the blessed love-letters, the glorious kisses, and the sweet embraces that gracious souls have had from Christ in his service, do provoke and move them to wait upon him in holy duties. Ah! but restraining grace, temporary grace, that puts men upon religious duties only from external motives, as the care of the creature, the eye of the creature, the rewards of the creature, and the keeping up of a name among the creatures, and a thousand such like considerations, as you may see in Saul, Jehu, Judas, Demas, and the scribes and pharisees, &c.[2]

The abbot in Melancthon lived strictly, and walked demurely, and looked humbly, so long as he was but a monk, but when, by his seeming extraordinary sanctity, he got to be abbot, he grew intolerable proud and insolent; and being asked the reason of it, confessed, 'That his former lowly look was but to see if he could find the keys of the abbey.' Such poor, low, vain motives work temporary souls to all the service they do perform, &c.

[8.] Saving grace, renewing grace, will *cause a man to follow the Lord fully in the desertion of all sin, and in the observation of all God's precepts.* Joshua and Caleb followed the Lord fully,[3] Num. xiv. 24; Zacharias and Elizabeth were righteous before God, and walked in all the commandments and ordinances of the Lord blameless, Luke i. 5, 6. The saints in the Revelation are described by this, that 'they follow the Lamb whithersoever he goes,' Rev. xiv. 4; but restraining grace, temporary grace, cannot enable a man to follow the Lord fully. All that temporary grace can enable a man to do, is to follow the Lord partially, unevenly, and haltingly, as you may see in Jehu, Herod, Judas, and the scribes and pharisees, who paid tithe of 'mint, and anise, and cummin, but omitted the weighty matters of the law, judgment, mercy, and faith,' &c., Mat. xxiii. 23.

True grace works the heart to the hatred of all sin, and to the love of all truth; it works a man to the hatred of those sins that for his blood he cannot conquer, and to loathe those sins that he would give all the world to overcome, Ps. cxix. 104, 128.[4] So that a soul truly gracious can say, Though there be no one sin mortified and subdued in me, as it should, and as I would, yet every sin is hated and loathed by me. So a soul truly gracious can say, Though I do not obey any one command as I should, and as I would, yet every word is sweet, every command of God is precious, Ps. cxix. 6, 119, 127, 167. I dearly prize and greatly love those commands that I cannot obey; though there be

[1] As what I have, if offered to thee, pleaseth not thee, O Lord, without myself, so the good things we have from thee, though they may refresh us, yet they satisy us not without thyself.—*Bern*[*ard*].

[2] It is an excellent speech of Bernard, *Bonus es Domine animæ quærenti; quid invenienti?* Good art thou, O Lord, to the soul that seeks thee, what art thou then to the soul that finds thee?

[3] וימלא, hath fulfilled after me. A metaphor taken from a ship under sail, that is strongly carried with the wind, as fearing neither rocks nor sands.

[4] I had rather go to hell pure from sin, than to heaven polluted with that filth, saith Anselm. *Da quod jubes et jube quod vis,* Give what thou commandest, and command what thou wilt. [Augustine.—G].

many commands that I cannot in a strict sense fulfil, yet there is no command I would not fulfil, that I do not exceedingly love. 'I love thy commandments above gold, above fine gold:' 'My soul hath kept thy testimonies, and I love them exceedingly,' Ps. cxix. 117, and xcix. 7.

[9.] True grace *leads the soul to rest in Christ, as in his* summum bonum, *chiefest good.* It works the soul to centre in Christ, as in his highest and ultimate end. 'Whither should we go? thou hast the words of eternal life,' John vi. 68. 'My beloved is white and ruddy, the chiefest of ten thousand; I found him whom my soul loved, I held him and would not let him go,' Cant. v. 10, iii. 4. That wisdom a believer hath from Christ, it leads him to centre in the wisdom of Christ, 1 Cor. i. 30; and that love the soul hath from Christ, it leads the soul to centre in the love of Christ; and that righteousness the soul hath from Christ, it leads the soul to rest and centre in the righteousness of Christ, Philip. iii. 9.[1] True grace is a beam of Christ, and where it is, it will naturally lead the soul to rest in Christ. The stream doth not more naturally lead to the fountain, nor the effect to the cause, than true grace leads the soul to Christ. But restraining grace, temporary grace, works the soul to centre and rest in things below Christ. Sometimes it works the soul to centre in the praises of the creature; sometimes to rest in the rewards of the creature: 'Verily they have their reward,' saith Christ, Mat. vi. 1, 2: and so in an hundred other things. &c., Zech. vii. 5, 6.

[10.] True grace will *enable a soul to sit down satisfied and contented with the naked enjoyments of Christ.* The enjoyment of Christ without honour will satisfy the soul; the enjoyment of Christ without riches, the enjoyment of Christ without pleasures, and without the smiles of creatures, will content and satisfy the soul. 'It is enough; Joseph is alive,' Gen. xlv. 28. So saith a gracious soul, though honour is not, and riches are not, and health is not, and friends are not, &c., it is enough that Christ is, that he reigns, conquers, and triumphs. Christ is the pot of manna, the cruse of oil, a bottomless ocean of all comfort, content, and satisfaction. He that hath him wants nothing; he that wants him enjoys nothing.[2] 'Having nothing,' saith Paul, 'and yet possessing all things,' 2 Cor. vi. 10. Oh! but a man that hath but temporary grace, that hath but restraining grace, cannot sit down satisfied and contented, under the want of outward comforts.[3] Christ is good with honours, saith such a soul; and Christ is good with riches, and Christ is good with pleasures, and he is good with such and such outward contents. I must have Christ and the world, or else with the young man in the Gospel, in spite of my soul, I shall forsake Christ to follow the world. Ah! how many shining professors be there in the world, that cannot sit down satisfied and contented, under the want of this or that outward comfort and content, but are like bedlams, fretting

[1] Grace is that star that leads to Christ; it is that cloud and pillar of fire that leads the soul to the heavenly Canaan, where Christ sits chief.

[2] *Cui cum paupertate bene convenit, pauper non est,* saith Seneca, a contented man cannot be a poor man. [Epistle i. and *De Constantia Sapientis,* vi.—G].

[3] Charles the Great his motto was, *Christus regnat, vincit, triumphat.* And so it is the saints.' St Austin upon Ps. xii. brings in God rebuking a discontented Christian thus: What is thy faith? have I promised thee these things? What! wert thou made a Christian that thou shouldst flourish here in this world?

and vexing, raging and madding,[1] as if there were no God, no heaven, no hell, nor no Christ to make up all such outward wants to souls. That a soul truly gracious can say, in having nothing I have all things, because I have Christ; having therefore all things in him, I seek no other reward, for he is the universal reward. Such a soul can say, Nothing is sweet to me without the enjoyment of Christ in it; honours, nor riches, nor the smiles of creatures, are not sweet to me no farther than I see Christ, and taste Christ in them.[2] The confluence of all outward good cannot make a heaven of glory in my soul, if Christ, who is the top of my glory, be absent; as Absalom said, 'What is all this to me so long as I cannot see the king's face?' 2 Sam. xiv. 32. So saith the soul, why do you tell me of this and that outward comfort, when I cannot see his face whom my soul loves? Why, my honour is not my Christ, nor riches is not Christ, nor the favour of the creature is not Christ; let me have him, and let the men of this world take the world, and divide it amongst themselves; I prize my Christ above all, I would enjoy my Christ above all other things in the world; his presence will make up the absence of all other comforts, and his absence will darken and embitter all my comforts; so that my comforts will neither taste like comforts, nor look like comforts, nor warm like comforts, when he that should comfort my soul stands afar off, &c., Lam. i. 16. Christ is all and in all to souls truly gracious, Col. iii. 11. We have all things in Christ, and Christ is all things to a Christian. If we be sick, he is a physician; if we thirst, he is a fountain; if our sins trouble us, he is righteousness; if we stand in need of help, he is mighty to save; if we fear death, he is life; if we be in darkness, he is light; if we be weak, he is strength; if we be in poverty, he is plenty; if we desire heaven, he is the way. The soul cannot say, this I would have, and that I would have; but saith Christ, it is in me, it is in me eminently, perfectly, eternally.[3]

The fifth device that Satan hath to keep souls in a sad, doubting, and questioning condition is,

Device (5). *By suggesting to them, That that conflict that is in them, is not a conflict that is only in saints, but such a conflict that is to be found in hypocrites and profane souls;* when the truth is, there is as much difference betwixt the conflict that is in them, and that which is in wicked men, as there is betwixt light and darkness, betwixt heaven and hell.[4] And the truth of this I shall evidence to you in the following particulars:

[1.] *The whole frame of a believer's soul is against sin.* Understanding, will, and affection, all the powers and faculties of the soul are in

[1] Going about as 'mad.'—G.

[2] Content is the deputy of outward felicity, and supplies the place where it is absent. As the Jews throw the book of Esther to the ground before they read it, because the name of God is not in it, as the Rabbins have observed; so do saints in some sense those mercies wherein they do not read Christ's name, and see Christ's heart. [With reference to the throwing down of the book of Esther, see Trapp's quaint remarks on it, under Esther i. 1.—G].

[3] Luther said, he had rather be in hell with Christ, than in heaven without him. None but Christ, none but Christ, said Lambert, lifting up his hands and his fingers' end flaming. [Clarke's 'Martyrologie,' as before, *sub nomine*.—G].

[4] John viii. 44, the devil is a liar, and the father of it. The devil's breasts (saith Luther) are very fruitful with lies.

arms against sin. A covetous man may condemn covetousness, and yet the frame and bent of his heart may be to it; a proud person may condemn pride, and yet the frame of his spirit may be to it; and the drunkard may condemn drunkenness, and yet the frame of his spirit may be to it; a man may condemn stealing and lying, and yet the frame of his heart may be to it.[1] 'Thou that preachest a man should not steal, dost thou steal? Thou that sayest a man should not commit adultery, dost thou commit adultery? thou that abhorrest idols, dost thou commit sacrilege? Thou that makest thy boast of the law, through breaking the law dishonourest thou God?' Rom. ii. 21–23. But a saint's will is against it. 'The evil that I would not do, that I do;' and his affections are against it, 'What I hate, I do,' Rom. vii. 19, 20.

[2.] A saint *conflicts against sin universally, the least as well as the greatest;* the most profitable and the most pleasing sin, as well as against those that are less pleasing and profitable. He will combat with all, though he cannot conquer one as he should, and as he would. He knows that all sin strikes at God's holiness, as well as his own happiness; at God's glory, as well as at his soul's comfort and peace.[2]

He knows that all sin is hateful to God, and that all sinners are traitors to the crown and dignity of the Lord Jesus. He looks upon one sin, and sees that that threw down Noah, the most righteous man in the world, and he looks upon another sin, and sees that that cast down Abraham, the greatest believer in the world, and he looks upon another sin, and sees that that threw down David, the best king in the world, and he looks upon another sin, and sees that that cast down Paul, the greatest apostle in the world. He sees that one sin threw down Samson, the strongest man in the world; another cast down Solomon, the wisest man in the world; and another Moses, the meekest man in the world; and another sin cast down Job, the patientest man in the world; and this raiseth a holy indignation against all, so that nothing can satisfy and content his soul but a destruction of all those lusts and vermin that vex and rack his righteous soul. It will not suffice a gracious soul to see justice done upon one sin, but he cries out for justice upon all. He would not have some crucified and others spared, but cries out, Lord, crucify them all, crucify them all. Oh! but now the conflict that is in wicked men is partial; they frown upon one sin and smile upon another; they strike at some sins yet stroke others; they thrust some out of doors but keep others close in their bosoms; as you may see in Jehu, Herod, Judas, Simon Magus, and Demas. Wicked men strike at gross sins, such as are not only against the law of God, but against the laws of nature and nations, but make nothing of less sins; as vain thoughts, idle words, sinful motions, petty oaths, &c.

[1] It was a good saying of him [Augustine, *Conf*—G.] that said, *Domine libera me a malo homine, me ipso*, Lord, deliver me from an ill man, myself. Austin complains, That men do not tame their beasts in their own bosoms.

[2] Ps. cxix. 104, I hate every false way; *sinethi*, from שׂנא, which signifies to hate with a deadly and irreconcileable hatred. He knows that all the parts of the old man hath, and doth play the part of a treacherous friend and a friendly traitor; therefore he strikes at all. The greater the combat is, the greater shall be the following rewards, saith Tertullian. True hatred is πρὸς τὰ γένη, against the whole kind. Plutarch reports of one who would not be resolved of his doubts, because he would not lose the pleasure in seeking for resolution. So wicked men will not be rid of some sins, because they would not lose the seeming pleasure of sinning.

They fight against those sins that fight against their honour, profits, pleasures, &c., but make truce with those that are as right hand and as right eyes to them, &c.

[3.] *The conflict that is in a saint, against sin, is maintained by several arguments:* by arguments drawn from the love of God, the honour of God, the sweetness and communion with God, and from the spiritual and heavenly blessings and privileges that are conferred upon them by God, and from arguments drawn from the blood of Christ, the glory of Christ, the eye of Christ, the kisses of Christ, and the intercession of Christ, and from arguments drawn from the earnest of the Spirit, the seal of the Spirit, the witness of the Spirit, the comforts of the Spirit. Oh! but the conflict that is in wicked men is from low, carnal, and legal arguments, drawn from the eye, ear, or hand of the creature, or drawn from shame, hell, curses of the law, &c., 2 Cor. xii. 7-9.[1]

[4.] The conflict that is in saints is *a constant conflict.* Though sin and grace were not born in the heart of a saint together, and though they shall not die together, yet, whilst a believer lives, they must conflict together. Paul had been fourteen years converted, when he cried out, 'I have a law in my members rebelling against the law of my mind, and leading me captive to the law of sin,' Rom. vii. 2, 3.

Pietro Candiano, one of the dukes of Venice, died fighting against the Nauratines with the weapons in his hands. So a saint lives fighting and dies fighting, he stands fighting and falls fighting, with his spiritual weapons in his hands.[2] But the conflict that is in wicked men is inconstant: now they fall out with sin, and anon they fall in with sin; now it is bitter, anon it is sweet; now the sinner turns from his sin, and anon he turns to the wallowing in sin, as the swine doth to the wallowing in the mire, 2 Pet. ii. 19, 20. One hour you shall have him praying against sin, as if he feared it more than hell, and the next hour you shall have him pursuing after sin, as if there were no God to punish him, no justice to damn him, no hell to torment him.

[5.] The conflict that is in the saints, *is in the same faculties;* there is the judgment against the judgment, the mind against the mind, the will against the will, the affections against the affections, that is, the regenerate part against the unregenerate part, in all the parts of the soul; but now, in wicked men, the conflict is not in the same faculties, but between the conscience and the will. The will of a sinner is bent strongly to such and such sins, but conscience puts in and tells the sinner, God hath made me his deputy, he hath given me a power to hang and draw, to examine, scourge, judge and condemn, and if thou dost such and such wickedness, I shall be thy jailor and tormenter. I do not bear the rod nor the sword in vain, saith conscience; if thou sinnest, I shall do my office, and then thy life will be a hell: and this raises a tumult in the soul.[3]

[1] Though to be kept from sin brings comfort to us, yet for us to oppose sin from spiritual and heavenly arguments, and God to pardon sin, that brings most glory to God.

[2] It was an excellent saying of Eusebius Emesenus, Our fathers overcame the torrents of the flames, let us overcome the fiery darts of vices. Consider that the pleasure and sweetness that follows victory over sin, is a thousand times beyond that seeming sweetness that is in sin.

[3] A heathen could say, their soul is in a mutiny; a wicked man is not friends with himself, he and his conscience are at difference.—*Arist*[*otle*].

[6.] The conflict that is in the saints, *is a more blessed, successful, and prevailing conflict.* A saint, by his conflict with sin, gains ground upon his sin: 'They that are Christ's,' saith the apostle, 'have crucified the world with the affections and lusts,' Gal. v. 24. Christ puts to his hand and helps them to lead captivity captive, and to set their feet upon the necks of those lusts that have formerly trampled upon their souls and their comforts. As the house of Saul grew weaker and weaker, and the house of David stronger and stronger, so the Lord, by the discoveries of his love, and by the influences of his Spirit, he causeth grace, the nobler part of a saint, to grow stronger and stronger, and corruption, like the house of Saul, to grow weaker and weaker. But sin in a wicked heart gets ground, and grows stronger and stronger, notwithstanding all his conflicts. His heart is more encouraged, emboldened, and hardened in a way of sin, as you may see in the Israelites, Pharaoh, Jehu, and Judas, who doubtless found many strange conflicts, tumults, and mutinies in their souls, when God spake such bitter things against them, and did such justice upon them, 2 Tim. iii. 13.[1]

But remember this by way of caution: Though Christ hath given sin its death-wound, by his power, Spirit, death, and resurrection, yet it will die but a lingering death.[2] As a man that is mortally wounded dies by little and little, so doth sin in the heart of a saint. The death of Christ on the cross was a lingering death, so the death of sin in the soul is a lingering death; now it dies a little, and anon it dies a little, &c., as the psalmist speaks, 'Slay them not, lest my people forget: scatter them by thy power; and bring them down, O Lord our shield,' Ps. lix. 11. He would not have them utterly destroyed, but some relics preserved as a memorial. So God dealeth in respect of sin; it is wounded and brought down, but not wholly slain; something is still left as a monument of divine grace, and to keep us humble, wakeful, and watchful, and that our armour may be still kept on, and our weapons always in our hands.

The best men's souls in this life hang between the flesh and the spirit, as it were like Mahomet's tomb at Mecca, between two loadstones; like Erasmus, as the papists paint him, betwixt heaven and hell; like the tribe of Manasseh, half on this side of Jordan, in the land of the Amorites, and half on that side, in the Holy Land; yet, in the issue, they shall overcome the flesh, and trample upon the necks of their spiritual enemies.[3]

The sixth device that Satan hath to keep souls in a sad, doubting, questioning condition is,

Device (6). *By suggesting to the soul, that surely his estate is not*

[1] These two, grace and sin, are like two buckets of a well, when one is up, the other is down. They are like the two laurels at Rome, when one flourishes the other withers. The more grace thrives in the soul, the more sin dies in the soul. From naught they grow to be very naught, and from very naught to be stark naught. Lactant[ius] said of Lucian, *Nec Diis, nec hominibus pepercit*, he spared neither God nor man.

[2] Mortification is a continued act, it is a daily dying to sin, 'I die daily.' A crucified man will strive and struggle, yet, in the eyes of the law, and in the account of all that see him, he is dead. It is just so with sin.

[3] There is no such pleasure, saith Cyprian, as to have overcome an offered pleasure; neither is there any greater conquest than that that is gotten over a man's corruptions. The Romans lost many a battle, and yet in the issue were conquerors in all their wars; it is just so with the saints.

good, because he cannot joy and rejoice in Christ as once he could; because he hath lost that comfort and joy that once was in his spirit. Saith Satan, Thou knowest the time was when thy heart was much carried out to joying and rejoicing in Christ; thou dost not forget the time when thy heart used to be full of joy and comfort; but now, how art thou fallen in thy joys and comforts! Therefore, thy estate is not good; thou dost but deceive thyself to think that ever it was good, for surely if it had, thy joy and comfort would have continued. And hereupon the soul is apt to take part with Satan, and say, It is even so; I see all is naught, and I have but deceived my own soul, &c.

Now the remedies against this device are these:

Remedy (1). The first remedy against this device of Satan is, to consider, *That the loss of comfort is a separable adjunct from grace.* The soul may be full of holy affections when it is empty of divine consolations.[1] There may be, and often is, true grace, yea, much grace, where there is not a drop of comfort, nor dram of joy. Comfort is not of the being, but of the well-being, of a Christian. God hath not so linked these two choice lovers together, but that they may be put asunder. That wisdom that is from above will never work a man to reason thus: I have no comfort, therefore I have no grace; I have lost that joy that once I had, therefore my condition is not good, was never good, &c. But it will enable a man to reason thus: Though my comfort is gone, yet the God of my comfort abides; though my joy is lost, yet the seeds of grace remain. The best men's joys are as glass, bright and brittle, and evermore in danger of breaking.[2]

Remedy (2). The second remedy against this device of Satan is, solemnly to consider, *That the precious things that thou still enjoyest are far better than the joys and comforts that thou hast lost.* Thy union with Christ, thy communion with Christ, thy sonship, thy saintship, thy heirship, thou still enjoyest by Christ, are far better than the comforts thou hast lost by sin. What though thy comforts be gone, yet thy union and communion with Christ remains, Jer. xxxi. 18, 19, 20. Though thy comforts be gone, yet thou art a son, though a comfortless son; an heir, though a comfortless heir; a saint, though a comfortless saint. Though the bag of silver, thy comforts, be lost, yet the box of jewels, thy union with Christ, thy communion with Christ, thy sonship, thy saintship, thy heirship, which thou still enjoyest, is far better than the bag of silver thou hast lost; yea, the least of those precious jewels is more worth than all the comforts in the world. Well! let this be a cordial to comfort thee, a star to lead thee, and a staff to support thee, that thy box of jewels are safe, though thy bag of silver be lost.[3]

Remedy (3). The third remedy against this device of Satan is, to consider, *That thy condition is no other than what hath been the condition of those precious souls whose names were written upon the heart of Christ, and who are now at rest in the bosom of Christ.* One day

[1] Ps. lxiii. 1, 2, 8, Isa. l. 10, Micah vii. 8, 9, Ps. xlii. 5.

[2] Spiritual joy is a sun that is often clouded; though it be as precious a flower as most paradise affords, yet it is subject to fade and wither.

[3] When one objected to Faninus his cheerfulness to Christ's agony and sadness, he answered, Christ was sad, that I might be merry; he had my sins, and I have his righteousness. [Clarke's 'Martyrologie,' as before, *sub nomine.*—G.]

you shall have them praising and rejoicing, the next day a-mourning and weeping. One day you shall have them a-singing, 'The Lord is our portion;' the next day a-sighing and expostulating with themselves, 'Why are ye cast down, O our souls?' 'Why is our harp turned to mourning? and our organ into the voice of them that weep?' &c.[1]

Remedy (4). The fourth remedy against this device of Satan is, solemnly to consider, *That the causes of joy and comfort are not always the same.* Happily, thy former joy and comfort did spring from the witness of the Spirit, he bearing witness to thy soul, that thy nature was changed, thy sins pardoned, thy soul reconciled, &c.[2] Now, the Spirit may, upon some special occasion, bear witness to the soul, that the heart of God is dearly set upon him, that he loves him with an everlasting love, &c., and yet the soul may never enjoy such a testimony all the days of his life again. Though the Spirit be a witnessing Spirit, it is not his office every day to witness to believers their interest in God, Christ, heaven, &c.

Or, happily, thy former joy and comfort did spring from the newness and suddenness of the change of thy condition. For a man in one hour to have his night turned into day, his darkness turned into light, his bitter into sweet, God's frowns into smiles, his hatred into love, his hell into a heaven, must greatly joy and comfort him.[3] It cannot but make his heart to leap and dance in him, who, in one hour, shall see Satan accusing him, his own heart condemning him, the eternal God frowning upon him, the gates of heaven barred against him, all the creation standing armed, at the least beck of God, to execute vengeance on him, and the mouth of the infernal pit open to receive him. Now, in this hour, for Christ to come to the amazed soul, and to say to it, I have trod the wine-press of my Father's wrath for thee; I have laid down my life a ransom for thee; by my blood I have satisfied my Father's justice, and pacified his anger, and procured his love for thee; by my blood I have purchased the pardon of thy sins, thy freedom from hell, and thy right to heaven; oh! how wonderfully will this cause the soul to leap for joy!

Remedy (5). The fifth remedy against this device of Satan is, to consider, *That God will restore and make up the comforts of his people.*[4] Though thy candle be put out, yet God will light it again, and make it burn more light than ever. Though thy sun for the present be clouded, yet he that rides upon the clouds shall scatter those clouds, and cause the sun to shine and warm thy heart as in former days, as the psalmist speaks: 'Thou which hast shewed me great and sore troubles, shalt

[1] Ps. li. 12, xxx. 6, 7; Job xxiii. 6, 8, 9, 30, 31; Lamen. i. 16, Mat. xxvii. 46, Ps. xlii. 5, Lament. v. 15.

[2] The Spirit doth not every day make a feast in the soul; he doth not make every day to be a day of weaving the wedding robes.

[3] A pardon given unexpectedly into the hand of a malefactor, when he is on the last step of the ladder, ready to be turned off, will cause much joy and rejoicing. The newness and suddenness of the change of his condition will cause his heart to leap and rejoice; yet, in process of time, much of his joy will be abated, though his life be as dear to him still as ever it was.

[4] Hudson the martyr, deserted at the stake, went from under his chain, and, having prayed earnestly, was comforted immediately, and suffered valiantly. So Mr Glover, when he was within sight of the stake, cried out to his friend, He is come, he is come, meaning the Comforter that Christ promised to send. [On Thomas Hudson, see Clarke's 'Martyrologie,' as before, pp. 498, 499; on Glover, *ibid.* pp. 460–61.—G.]

quicken me again, and shalt bring me up again from the depths of the earth. Thou shalt increase my greatness, and comfort me on every side,' Ps. lxxi. 20, 21. God takes away a little comfort, that he may make room in the soul for a greater degree of comfort. This the prophet Isaiah sweetly shews: 'I have seen his ways, and will heal him; I will lead him also, and restore comforts unto him, and to his mourners,' Isa. lvii. 18. Bear up sweetly, O precious soul! thy storm shall end in a calm, and thy dark night in a sunshine day; thy mourning shall be turned into rejoicing, and the waters of consolation shall be sweeter and higher in thy soul than ever;[1] the mercy is surely thine, but the time of giving it is the Lord's. Wait but a little, and thou shalt find the Lord comforting thee on every side.

The seventh device that Satan hath to keep souls in a sad, doubting, and questioning condition, is,

Device (7). *By suggesting to the soul his often relapses into the same sin which formerly he hath pursued with particular sorrow, grief, shame, and tears, and prayed, complained, and resolved against.* Saith Satan, Thy heart is not right with God; surely thy estate is not good; thou dost but flatter thyself to think that ever God will eternally own and embrace such a one as thou art, who complainest against sin, and yet relapsest into the same sin; who with tears and groans confessest thy sin, and yet ever and anon art fallen into the same sin.

I confess this is a very sad condition for a soul after he hath obtained mercy and pity from the Lord, after God hath spoken peace and pardon to him, and wiped the tears from his eyes, and set him upon his legs, to return to folly.[2] Ah! how do relapses lay men open to the greatest afflictions and worst temptations! How do they make the wound to bleed afresh! How do they darken and cloud former assurances and evidences for heaven! How do they put a sword into the hand of conscience to cut and slash the soul! They raise such fears, terrors, horrors, and doubts in the soul, that the soul cannot be so frequent in duty as formerly, nor so fervent in duty as formerly, nor so confident in duty as formerly, nor so bold, familiar, and delightful with God in duty as formerly, nor so constant in duty as formerly. They give Satan an advantage to triumph over Christ; they make the work of repentance more difficult; they make a man's life a burden, and they render death to be very terrible unto the soul, &c.

Now the remedies against this device are these:

Remedy (1). The first remedy against this device of Satan is, solemnly to consider, *That there are many scriptures that do clearly evidence a possibility of the saints falling into the same sins whereof they have formerly repented.* 'I will heal their backslidings, I will love them freely: for mine anger is turned away from them,' saith the Lord by the prophet Hosea, chap. xiv. 4. So the prophet Jeremiah speaks: 'Go and proclaim these words toward the north, and say, Return, thou backsliding Israel, saith the Lord, and I will not cause mine anger to fall upon you: for I am merciful, saith the Lord, and I

[1] See Ps. cxxvi. 6, and xlii. 7, 8.

[2] A backslider may say, *Opera et impensa periit*, all my pains and charge is lost.

will not keep mine anger for ever. Turn, O backsliding Israel, saith the Lord; for I am married unto you: and I will take you one of a city, and two of a family, and I will bring you to Zion,' chap. iii. 12, 14. So the psalmist: 'They turned back, and dealt unfaithfully with their fathers; they were turned aside like a deceitful bow.' And no wonder, for though their repentance be never so sincere and sound, yet their graces are but weak, and their mortification imperfect in this life. Though by grace they are freed from the dominion of sin, and from the damnatory power of every sin, and from the love of all sin, yet grace doth not free them from the seed of any one sin; and therefore it is possible for a soul to fall again and again into the same sin. If the fire be not wholly put out, who would think it impossible that it should catch and burn again and again?[1]

Remedy (2). The second remedy against this device of Satan is, seriously to consider, *That God hath nowhere engaged himself by any particular promise, that souls converted and united to Christ shall not fall again and again into the same sin after conversion.* I cannot find in the whole book of God where he hath promised any such strength or power against this or that particular sin, as that the soul should be for ever, in this life, put out of a possibility of falling again and again into the same sins; and where God hath not a mouth to speak, I must not have a heart to believe. God will graciously pardon those sins to his people that he will not in this life effectually subdue in his people. I would go far to speak with that soul that can shew me a promise, that when our sorrow and grief hath been so great, or so much, for this or that sin, that then God will preserve us from ever falling into the same sin. The sight of such a promise would be as life from the dead to many a precious soul, who desires nothing more than to keep close to Christ, and fears nothing more than backsliding from Christ.[2]

Remedy (3). The third remedy against this device of Satan is, seriously to consider, *That the most renowned and now crowned saints have, in the days of their being on earth, relapsed into one and the same sin.*[3] Lot was twice overcome with wine; John twice worshipped the angel; Abraham did often dissemble, and lay his wife open to adultery to save his own life, which some heathens would not have done: 'And it came to pass, when God caused me to wander from my father's house, that I said unto her, This is thy kindness which thou shalt shew unto me; at every place whither we shall come, say of me, as he is my brother,' Gen. xx. 13. David in his wrath was resolved, if ever man was, that he would be the death of Nabal, and all his innocent family; and after this he fell into the foul murder of Uriah. Though Christ told his disciples that his 'kingdom was not of this world,' yet again, and again, and again, three several times they

[1] The sin of backsliding is a soul-wounding sin, 'I will heal their backsliding.' You read of no arms for the back, though you do for the breast. When a soldier bragged too much of a great scar in his forehead, Augustus Cæsar (in whose time Christ was born) asked him if he did not get it as he looked back when he fled.

[2] In some cases the saints have found God better than his word. He promised the children of Israel only the land of Canaan, but besides that he gave them two other kingdoms which he never promised. And to Zacharias he promised to give him his speech at the birth of the child, but besides that he gave him the gift of prophecy.

[3] A sheep may often slip into a slough, as well as a swine.

would needs be on horseback; they would fain be high, great, and glorious in this world. Their pride and ambitious humour put them, that were but as so many beggars, upon striving for pre-eminence and greatness in the world, when their Lord and Master told them three several times of his sufferings in the world, and of his going out of the world. Jehoshaphat, though a godly man, yet joins affinity with Ahab, 2 Chron. xviii. 1–3, 30, 31; and though he was saved by a miracle, yet soon after he falls into the same sin, and 'joins himself with Ahaziah king of Israel, who did very wickedly,' 2 Chron. xx. 35–37. Samson is by the Spirit of the Lord numbered among the faithful worthies, yet he fell often into one gross sin, as is evident, Heb. xi. 32. Peter, you know, relapsed often, and so did Jonah; and this comes to pass that they may see their own inability to stand, to resist or overcome any temptation or corruptions, Jude 14, 15, 16.[1] And that they may be taken off from all false confidences, and rest wholly upon God, and only upon God, and always upon God; and for the praise and honour of the power, wisdom, skill, mercy, and goodness of the physician of our souls, that can heal, help, and cure when the disease is most dangerous, when the soul is relapsed, and grows worse and worse, and when others say, 'There is no help for him in his God,' and when his own heart and hopes are dying.[2]

Remedy (4). The fourth remedy against this device of Satan is, to consider, *That there are relapses into enormities, and there are relapses into infirmities.* Now it is not usual with God to leave his people frequently to relapse into enormities; for by his Spirit and grace, by his smiles and frowns, by his word and rod, he doth usually preserve his people from a frequent relapsing into enormities; yet he doth leave his choicest ones frequently to relapse into infirmities (and of his grace he pardons them in course), as idle words, passion, vain thoughts, &c.[3] Though gracious souls strive against these, and complain of these, and weep over these, yet the Lord, to keep them humble, leaves them frequently to relapse into these; and these frequent relapses into infirmities shall never be their bane, because they be their burden.

Remedy (5). The fifth remedy against this device of Satan is, to consider, *That there are involuntary relapses, and there are voluntary relapses.* Involuntary relapses are, when the resolution and full bent of the heart is against sin, when the soul strives with all its might against sin, by sighs and groans, by prayers and tears, and yet out of weakness is forced to fall back into sin, because there is not spiritual strength enough to overcome. Now, though involuntary relapses must humble us, yet they must never discourage nor defect us; for God will freely and readily pardon those, in course. Voluntary relapses are, when the soul longs and loves to 'return to the flesh-pots of Egypt,' Exod. xvi. 3; when it is a pleasure and a pastime to a man to return

[1] Perhaps the prodigal sets out unto us a Christian relapse, for he was a son before, and with his father, and then went away from him, and spent all; and yet he was not quite undone, but returned again.

[2] The prodigal saw the compassion of his father the greater, in receiving him after he had run away from him.

[3] Relapses into enormities are *peccata vulnerantia et divastantia*, wounding and wasting sins; therefore the Lord is graciously pleased to put under his everlasting arms, and stay his chosen ones from frequent falling into them.

to his old courses, such voluntary relapses speak out the man blinded, hardened, and ripened for ruin, &c.[1]

Remedy (6). The sixth remedy against this device of Satan is, to consider, *That there is no such power, or infinite virtue, in the greatest horror or sorrow the soul can be under for sin, nor in the sweetest or choicest discoveries of God's grace and love to the soul, as for ever to fence and secure the soul from relapsing into the same sin.* Grace is but a created habit, that may be prevailed against by the secret, subtle, and strong workings of sin in our hearts; and those discoveries that God makes of his love, beauty, and glory to the soul, do not always abide in their freshness and power upon the heart; but by degrees they fade and wear off, and then the soul may return again to folly, as we see in Peter, who, after he had a glorious testimony from Christ's own mouth of his blessedness and happiness, labours to prevent Christ from going up to Jerusalem to suffer, out of bare slavish fears that he and his fellows could not be secure, if his Master should be brought to suffer, Mat. xvi. 15–19, and ver. 22–24. And again, after this, Christ had him up into the mount, and there shewed him his beauty and his glory, to strengthen him against the hour of temptation that was coming upon him; and yet, soon after he had the honour and happiness of seeing the glory of the Lord (which most of his disciples had not), he basely and most shamefully denies the Lord of glory, thinking by that means to provide for his own safety;[2] and yet again, after Christ had broke his heart with a look of love for his most unlovely dealings, and bade them that were first acquainted with his resurrection to 'go and tell Peter that he was risen,' Mark xvi. 7; I say, after all this, slavish fears prevail upon him, and he basely dissembles, and plays the Jew with the Jews, and the Gentile with the Gentiles, to the seducing of Barnabas, &c., Gal. ii. 11–13.

Yet, by way of caution, know, it is very rare that God doth leave his beloved ones frequently to relapse into one and the same gross sin; for the law of nature is in arms against gross sins, as well as the law of grace, so that a gracious soul cannot, dares not, will not, frequently return to gross folly. And God hath made even his dearest ones dearly smart for their relapses, as may be seen by his dealings with Samson, Jehoshaphat, and Peter. Ah, Lord! what a hard heart hath that man, that can see thee stripping and whipping thy dearest ones for their relapses, and yet make nothing of returning to folly, &c.

The eighth device that Satan hath to keep souls in a sad, doubting, and questionable condition, is,

Device (8). *By persuading them that their estate is not good, their hearts are not upright, their graces are not sound, because they are so followed, vexed, and tormented with temptations.* It is his method, first to weary and vex thy soul with temptations, and then to tempt the soul, that surely it is not beloved, because it is so much tempted. And by this stratagem he keeps many precious souls in a sad, doubting,

[1] There is a great difference between a sheep that by weakness falls into the mire, and a swine that delights to wallow in the mire; between a woman that is forced, though she strives and cries out, and an alluring adulteress.

[2] Christ upbraided his disciples for their unbelief and hardness of heart, who had seen his glory, 'as the glory of the only begotten Son of God, full of grace and truth.'

and mourning temper many years, as many of the precious sons of Sion have found by woful experience, &c.[1]

Now the remedies against this device are these:

Remedy (1). The first remedy against this device of Satan is, solemnly to consider, *That those that have been best and most beloved, have been most tempted by Satan.* Though Satan can never rob a Christian of his crown, yet such is his malice, that he will therefore tempt, that he may spoil them of their comforts. Such is his enmity to the Father, that the nearer and dearer any child is to him, the more will Satan trouble him, and vex him with temptations. Christ himself was most near and most dear, most innocent and most excellent, and yet none so much tempted as Christ. David was dearly beloved, and yet by Satan tempted to number the people.[2] Job was highly praised by God himself, and yet much tempted; witness those sad things that fell from his mouth, when he was wet to the skin. Peter was much prized by Christ; witness that choice testimony that Christ gave of his faith and happiness, and his shewing him his glory in the mount, and that eye of pity that he cast upon him after his fearful fall, &c., and yet tempted by Satan. 'And the Lord said, Simon, Simon, behold, Satan hath desired to have you, that he may sift you as wheat: but I have prayed for thee, that thy faith fail thee not,' &c., Luke xxii. 31, 32.

Paul had the honour of being exalted as high as heaven, and of seeing that glory that could not be expressed; and yet he was no sooner stepped out of heaven, but he is buffeted by Satan, 'lest he should be exalted above measure,' 2 Cor. xii. 2, 7. If these, that were so really, so gloriously, so eminently beloved of God, if these, that have lived in heaven, and set their feet upon the stars, have been tempted, let no saints judge themselves not to be beloved, because they are tempted. It is as natural for saints to be tempted, that are dearly beloved, as it is for the sun to shine, or a bird to sing. The eagle complains not of her wings, nor the peacock of his train, nor the nightingale of her voice, because these are natural to them; no more should saints of their temptations, because they are natural to them. 'For we wrestle not against flesh and blood, but against principalities, against powers, against the rulers of the darkness of this world, against spiritual wickedness in high places,' Eph. vi. 12.

Remedy (2). The second remedy against this device of Satan is, to consider, *That all the temptations that befall the saints shall be sanctified to them by a hand of love.* Ah! the choice experiences that the saints get of the power of God supporting them, of the wisdom of God directing them (so to handle their spiritual weapons, their graces, as not only to resist, but to overcome), of the mercy and goodness of the Lord pardoning and succouring of them. And therefore, saith Paul, 'I received the messenger of Satan for to buffet me, lest I should be exalted, lest I should be exalted above measure,' 2 Cor. xii. 7.[3] Twice

[1] He may so tempt as to make a saint weary of his life: Job x. 1, 'My soul is weary of my life.'

[2] Pirates do not use to set upon poor empty vessels—[See 'Ep. Dedicatory.'—G.]; and beggars need not fear the thief. Those that have most of God, and are most rich in grace, shall be most set upon by Satan, who is the greatest and wisest pirate in the world.

[3] Vide Bezam, Grotium, et Estium [on the passage.—G.].

in that verse; he begins with it, and ends with it. If he had not been buffeted, who knows how his heart would have swelled; he might have been carried higher in conceit, than before he was in his ecstasy. Temptation is God's school, wherein he gives his people the clearest and sweetest discoveries of his love;[1] a school wherein God teaches his people to be more frequent and fervent in duty. When Paul was buffeted, then he prayed thrice, *i. e.* frequently and fervently; a school wherein God teaches his people to be more tender, meek, and compassionate to other poor, tempted souls than ever; a school wherein God teaches his people to see a greater evil in sin than ever, and a greater emptiness in the creature than ever, and a greater need of Christ and free grace than ever; a school wherein God will teach his people that all temptations are but his goldsmiths, by which he will try and refine, and make his people more bright and glorious. The issue of all temptations shall be to the good of the saints, as you may see by the temptations that Adam and Eve, and Christ and David, and Job and Peter and Paul met with. Those hands of power and love, that bring light out of darkness, good out of evil, sweet out of bitter, life out of death, heaven out of hell, will bring much sweet and good to his people, out of all the temptations that come upon them.

Remedy (3). The third remedy against this device of Satan is, wisely to consider, *That no temptations do hurt or harm the saints, so long as they are resisted by them, and prove the greatest afflictions that can befall them.* It is not Satan's tempting, but your assenting; not his enticing, but your yielding, that makes temptations hurtful to your soul. If the soul when it is tempted resists temptation, and saith with Christ, 'Get thee behind me, Satan,' Mat. xvi. 23; and with that young convert, 'I am not the man I was,'—*ego non sum ego*—or as Luther counsels all men to answer all temptations with these words—*Christianus sum*—I am a Christian. If a man's temptation be his greatest affliction, then is the temptation no sin upon his soul, though it be a trouble upon his mind. When a soul can look the Lord in the face, and say, Ah, Lord! I have many outward troubles upon me, I have lost such and such a near mercy, and such and such desirable mercies; and yet thou that knowest the heart, thou knowest that all my crosses and losses do not make so many wounds in my soul, nor fetch so many sighs from my heart, tears from my eyes, as those temptations do that Satan follows my soul with! When it is thus with the soul, then temptations are only the soul's trouble, they are not the soul's sin.

Satan is a malicious and envious enemy. As his names are, so is he; his names are all names of enmity; the accuser, the tempter, the destroyer, the devourer, the envious man; and this malice and envy of his he shews sometimes by tempting men to such sins as are quite contrary to the temperature of their bodies, as he did Vespasian and Julian, men of sweet and excellent natures, to be most bloody murderers.[2] And sometimes he shews his malice by tempting men to such things as will

[1] Luther said, there were three things that made a preacher, meditation, prayer, and temptation.

[2] Sometimes he shews his malice by letting those things abide by the soul, as may most vex and plague the soul, as Gregory observes in his leaving of Job's wife, which was not out of his forgetfulness, carelessness, or any love or pity to Job, but to vex and torment him, and to work him to blaspheme God, despair, and die, &c.

bring them no honour nor profit, &c. 'Fall down and worship me.' Mat. iv. 9, to blasphemy, and atheism, &c., the thoughts and first motions whereof cause the heart and flesh to tremble. And sometimes he shews his malice by tempting them to those sins which they have not found their natures prone to, and which they abhor in others. Now, if the soul resists these, and complains of these, and groans and mourns under these, and looks up to the Lord Jesus to be delivered from these, then shall they not be put down to the soul's account, but to Satan's, who shall be so much the more tormented, by how much the more the saints have been by him maliciously tempted, &c.

Make present and peremptory resistance against Satan's temptations, bid defiance to the temptation at first sight. It is safe to resist, it is dangerous to dispute. Eve lost herself and her posterity by falling into lists[1] of dispute, when she should have resisted, and stood upon terms of defiance with Satan. He that would stand in the hour of temptation must plead with Christ, 'It is written.' He that would triumph over temptations must plead still, 'It is written.[2] Satan is bold and impudent, and if you are not peremptory in your resistance, he will give you fresh onsets. It is your greatest honour, and your highest wisdom, peremptorily to withstand the beginnings of a temptation, for an after-remedy comes often too late.

Mrs Catherine Bretterege once, after a great conflict with Satan, said, 'Reason not with me, I am but a weak woman; if thou hast anything to say, say it to my Christ; he is my advocate, my strength, and my redeemer, and he shall plead for me.'[3]

Men must not seek to resist Satan's craft with craft, *sed per apertum Martem*, but by open defiance. He shoots with Satan in his own bow, who thinks by disputing and reasoning to put him off. As soon as a temptation shews its face, say to the temptation, as Ephraim to his idols, 'Get you hence, what have I any more to do with you?' Hosea xiv. 8. Oh! say to the temptation, as David said to the sons of Zeruiah, 'What have I to do with you?' 2 Sam. xvi. 10. You will be too hard for me. He that doth thus resist temptations, shall never be undone by temptations, &c.[4]

Make strong and constant resistance against Satan's temptations. Make resistance against temptations by arguments drawn from the honour of God, the love of God, your union and communion with God; and from the blood of Christ, the death of Christ, the kindness of Christ, the intercession of Christ, and the glory of Christ; and from the voice of the Spirit, the counsel of the Spirit, the comforts of the Spirit, the presence of the Spirit, the seal of the Spirit, the whisperings of the Spirit, the commands of the Spirit, the assistance of the Spirit, the witness of the Spirit; and from the glory of heaven, the excellency of grace,

[1] 'Artifices.' Cf. Halliwell, *sub voce*.—G.

[2] When Constantine the emperor was told that there was no means to cure his leprosy but by bathing his body in the blood of infants, he presently answered, *Malo semper ægrotare quam tali remedio convalescere*, I had rather not be cured than use such a remedy.

[3] See 'Two Funeral Sermons for Mrs Catherine Bretterege;' the one by W. Harrison, the other by W. Legh. 1605.'—G.

[4] I have read of one, who, being tempted with offers of money to desert Christ, gave this excellent answer: Let not any man think that he will embrace other men's goods to forsake Christ, who hath forsaken his own proper goods to follow Christ.

the beauty of holiness, the worth of the soul, and the vileness or bitterness and evil of sin—the least sin being a greater evil than the greatest temptation in the world.

And look that you make constant resistance, as well as strong resistance; be constant in arms. Satan will come on with new temptations when old ones are too weak.[1] In a calm prepare for a storm. The tempter is restless, impudent, and subtle; he will suit his temptations to your constitutions and inclinations. Satan loves to sail with the wind. If your knowledge be weak, he will tempt you to error; if your conscience be tender, he will tempt you to scrupulosity and too much preciseness, as to do nothing but hear, pray, read, &c.; if your consciences be wide and large, he will tempt you to carnal security; if you are bold-spirited, he will tempt you to presumption; if timorous, to desperation; if flexible, to inconstancy; if proud and stiff, to gross folly; therefore still fit for fresh assaults, make one victory a step to another. When you have overcome a temptation, take heed of unbending your bow, and look well to it, that your bow be always bent, and that it remains in strength. When you have overcome one temptation, you must be ready to enter the list[2] with another. As distrust in some sense is the mother of safety, so security is the gate of danger. A man had need to fear this most of all, that he fears not at all. If Satan be always roaring, we should be always a-watching and resisting of him. And certainly he that makes strong and constant resistance of Satan's temptations, shall in the end get above his temptations, and for the present is secure enough from being ruined by his temptations, &c.

For a close of this, remember, that it is dangerous to yield to the least sin to be rid of the greatest temptation. To take this course were as if a man should think to wash himself clean in ink, or as if a man should exchange a light cross, made of paper, for an iron cross, which is heavy, toilsome, and bloody. The least sin set home upon the conscience, will more wound, vex, and oppress the soul, than all the temptations in the world can; therefore never yield to the least sin to be rid of the greatest temptation.[3] Sidonius Apollinarius relateth how a certain man named Maximus, arriving at the top of honour by indirect means, was the first day very much wearied, and fetching a deep sigh, said, 'Oh, Damocles! how happy do I esteem of thee, for having been a king but the space of a dinner! I have been one whole day, and can bear it no longer.'[4] I will leave you to make the application.

IV. The fourth thing to be shewed is,

The several ways and devices that Satan hath to destroy and ensnare all sorts and ranks of men in the world.

I shall begin with the honourable and the great, and shew you the devices that Satan hath to destroy them. I will only instance in those that are most considerable.

Device (1). His first device to destroy *the great and honourable of*

[1] Luke iv. 13, 'And when the devil had ended all the temptation, he departed from him for a season.' Christ had no rest until he was exactly tried with all kinds of temptations. [Calvin *in loc.*—G.]

[2] 'Course.'—G.

[3] He that will yield to sin to be rid of temptation, will be so much the more tempted, and the less able to withstand temptations.

[4] *Opera:* Sidonius C. S. Apollinaris, *sub nomine* (Paris, 1652, by Sirmond).—G.

the earth is, *By working them to make it their business to seek themselves, to seek how to greaten themselves, to raise themselves, to enrich themselves, to secure themselves*, &c., as you may see in Pharaoh, Ahab, Rehoboam, Jeroboam, Absalom, Joab, Haman, &c.[1] But were the Scripture silent, our own experiences do abundantly evidence this way and method of Satan to destroy the great and the honourable; to bury their names in the dust, and their souls in hell, by drawing them wholly to mind themselves, and only to mind themselves, and in all things to mind themselves, and always to mind themselves. 'All,' saith the apostle, 'mind themselves,' Philip. ii. 21. All comparatively, in respect of the paucity of others, that let fall their private interests, and drown all self-respects in the glory of God and the public good, &c.

Now the remedies against this device are these,

Remedy (1). The first remedy against this device of Satan is, solemnly to consider, *That self-seeking is a sin that will put men upon a world of sins, upon sins not only against the law of God, the rules of the gospel, but that are against the very laws of nature, that are so much darkened by the fall of man.*[2] It puts the Pharisees upon opposing Christ, and Judas upon betraying Christ, and Pilate upon condemning Christ. It puts Gehazi upon lying, and Balaam upon cursing, and Saul and Absalom upon plotting David's ruin. It put Pharaoh and Haman upon contriving ways to destroy those Jews that God did purpose to save by his mighty arm. It puts men upon using wicked balances, and the bag of deceitful weights. It puts men upon ways of oppression, and 'selling the righteous for silver, and the poor for a pair of shoes,' &c., Amos ii. 6. I know not any sin in the world but this sin of self-seeking will put men upon it, though it be their eternal loss.

Remedy (2). The second remedy against this device of Satan is, seriously to consider, *That self-seeking doth exceedingly abase a man.* It strips him of all his royalty and glory. Of a lord it makes a man become a servant to the creature, ay, often to the worst of creatures; yea, a slave to slaves, as you may see in Judas, Demas, Balaam, and the Scribes and Pharisees.[3] Self-seekers bow down to the creatures, as Gideon's many thousands bowed down to the waters. Self-seeking will make a man say anything, do anything, and be anything, to please the lusts of others, and to get advantages upon others. Self-seeking transforms a man into all shapes and forms; now it makes a man appear as an angel of light, anon as an angel of darkness.[4] Now self-seekers are seemingly for God, anon they are openly against God; now you shall have them crying, 'Hosanna in the highest,' and anon, 'Crucify him, crucify him;' now you shall have them build with the saints, and anon you shall have them plotting the overthrow of the saints, as those self-seekers did in Ezra and Nehemiah's time. Self-seekers are the basest of all persons. There is no service so base, so

[1] Self-seeking, like the deluge, overthrows the whole world.

[2] Self-love is the root of the hatred of others, 2 Tim. iii. 2. First, lovers of themselves, and then fierce, &c. The naturalists observe, that those beasts which are most cruel to others are most loving to their own.

[3] A self-seeker is a Cato without, but a Nero within. Domitian would seem to love them best whom he willed least should live, and that is the very temper of self-seekers.

[4] It was death in Moses' rites to counterfeit that ceremonial and figurative ointment, Ex. xxx. What shall it then be to counterfeit the spirit of life and holiness!

poor, so low, but they will bow to it. They cannot look neither above, nor beyond their own lusts, and the enjoyment of the creature, Rom. i. 25. These are the prime and ultimate objects of their intendments.

It is said of Tiberius, 'that whilst Augustus ruled, he was no way tainted in his reputation, and that while Drusus and Germanicus were alive, he feigned those virtues which he had not, to maintain a good opinion of himself in the hearts of the people; but after he had got himself out of the reach of contradiction and controlment, there was no fact in which he was not faulty, no crime to which he was not accessory.' My prayer shall be, that Tiberius his spirit may not be found in any of our rulers, lest it prove their ruin, as it did his; and that wherever it is, it may be detected, loathed, and ejected, that so neither the state nor souls may be ruined by it, &c.

Remedy (3). The third remedy against this device of Satan is, solemnly *To dwell upon those dreadful curses and woes that are from heaven denounced against self-seekers.* 'Woe unto them that join house to house, that lay field to field, till there be no place, that they may be placed alone in the midst of the earth,' Isa. v. 8. So Habakkuk, ii. 6, 9–12, 'Woe to him that increaseth that which is not his, and to him that ladeth himself with thick clay!' 'Woe to him that coveteth an evil covetousness to his house, that he may set his nest on high, that he may be delivered from the power of evil! Thou hast consulted shame to thy house by cutting off many people, and hast sinned against thy soul. For the stone shall cry out of the wall, and the beam out of the timber shall answer it. Woe to him that buildeth a town with blood, and establisheth a city by iniquity!' The materials of the house built up by oppression shall come as joint witnesses. The stones of the wall shall cry, 'Lord, we were built up by blood and violence; and the beam shall answer, True, Lord, even so it is.' The stones shall cry, Vengeance, Lord! upon these self-seekers! and the beam shall answer, Woe to him, because he built his house with blood![1] So Isaiah, 'Woe unto them that decree unrighteous decrees, and that write grievousness which they have prescribed; to turn aside the needy from judgment, and to take away the right from the poor of my people, that widows may be their prey, and that they may rob the fatherless,' Isa. x. 1, 2. So Amos, 'Woe unto them that are at ease in Zion, and trust in the mountain of Samaria, which are named chief of the nations, to whom the house of Israel came; that put far away the evil day, and cause the seat of violence to come near; that lie upon beds of ivory, and stretch themselves upon their couches, and eat the lambs out of the flock, and the calves out of the middle of the stall; that drink wine in bowls, and anoint themselves with the chief ointments: but they are not grieved for the afflictions of Joseph,' Amos vi. 1, 3–6. So Micah, 'Woe to them that devise iniquity, and work evil upon their beds! when the morning is light, they practise it, because

[1] Crassus, a very rich Roman, and a great self-seeker, for greedy desire of gold, he managed war against the Parthians, by whom both he and thirty thousand Romans were slain. And because the barbarians conjectured that he made this assault upon them for their gold, therefore they melted gold, and poured it into his dead body, saying, *Satura te auro*, Satisfy thyself with gold. [The above was done by Orodes, who said, 'Sate thyself now with that metal of which in life thou wert so greedy.'—*Dion. Cass.* xl. 27; *Florus*, iii. 11.—G.]

it is in the power of their hand. And they covet fields, and take them by violence, and houses, and take them away. So they oppress a man and his house, even a man and his heritage,' Micah ii. 1, 2.

By these scriptures, you see that self-seekers labour like a woman in travail, but their birth proves their death, their pleasure their pain, their comforts their torment, their glory their shame, their exaltation their desolation. Loss, disgrace, trouble and shame, vexation and confusion, will be the certain portion of self-seekers.

When the Tartarians had taken in battle the Duke of Muscovia, they made a cup of his skull, with this inscription, 'All covet, all lose.'[1]

Remedy (4). The fourth remedy against this device of Satan is, solemnly to consider, *That self-seekers are self-losers and self-destroyers.* Absalom and Judas seek themselves, and hang themselves. Saul seeks himself, and kills himself. Ahab seeks himself, and loses himself, his crown and kingdom. Pharaoh seeks himself, and overthrows himself and his mighty army in the Red Sea. Cain sought himself, and slew two at once, his brother and his own soul. Gehazi sought change of raiment, but God changed his raiment into a leprous skin. Haman sought himself, and lost himself. The princes and presidents sought themselves, in the ruin of Daniel, but ruined themselves, their wives and children. That which self-seekers think should be a staff to support them, becomes by the hand of justice an iron rod to break them; that which they would have as springs to refresh them, becomes a gulf utterly to consume them. The crosses of self-seekers shall always exceed their mercies: their pain their pleasure; their torments their comforts. Every self-seeker is a self-tormentor, a self-destroyer; he carries a hell, an executioner, in his own bosom, &c.[2]

Remedy (5). The fifth remedy against this device of Satan is, *To dwell much upon the famous examples of those worthy saints that have denied themselves and preferred the public good before their own particular advantage.*[3] As Moses, 'And the Lord said unto Moses, Let me alone, that I may destroy them, and blot out their name from under heaven: and I will make of thee a nation mightier and greater than they,' Deut. ix. 14. Oh! but this offer would not take with Moses, he being a man of a brave public spirit. It is hot in his desires and prayers that the people might be spared and pardoned; saith he, 'Pardon, I beseech thee, the iniquity of this people, unto the greatness of thy mercy, and as thou hast forgiven this people from Egypt until now. And the Lord said, I have pardoned according to thy word,' ix. 26, *et seq.* Ah! should God make such an offer to many that write themselves Moses, and are called by many, Moses, I am afraid they would prefer their own advantage above the public good; they would not care what become of the people, so they and theirs might be made great and

[1] Tacitus the Roman emperor's word was, *Sibi bonus, aliis malus,* He that is too much for himself, fails to be good to others.

[2] Adam seeks himself, and loses himself, paradise, and that blessed image that God had stamped upon him. Lot seeks himself, Gen. xiii. 10, 11, and loses himself and his goods. Peter seeks to save himself, and miserably loses himself. Hezekiah, in the business of the ambassadors, seeks himself, and lost himself and his life too, had not God saved him by a miracle.

[3] It is good to be of his opinion and mind, who was rather willing to beautify Italy than his own house. The ancients were wont to place the statues of their princes by their fountains, intimating they were (or at least should be) fountains of the public good.

glorious in the world; they would not care so they might have a Babel built for them, though it was upon the ashes and ruin of the people. Baser spirits than these are not in hell; no, not in hell; and I am sure there are no such spirits in heaven. Such men's hearts and principles must be changed, or they will be undone for ever. Nehemiah was a choice soul, a man of a brave public spirit, a man that spent his time, his strength, and his estate, for the good and ease of his people. 'Moreover,' saith he, 'from the time that I was appointed to be their governor in the land of Judah, from the twentieth year even unto the two and thirtieth year of Artaxerxes the king, that is, twelve years, I and my brethren have not eaten the bread of the governor. Yea, also I continued in the work of this wall: and all my servants were gathered hither unto the work. Moreover, there were at my table an hundred and fifty of the Jews and rulers, besides those that came unto us from among the heathen that are about us. Now, that which was prepared for me daily was one ox, and six choice sheep; also fowls were prepared for me, and once in ten days store of all sorts of wine: yet for all this required I not the bread of the governor, because the bondage was heavy upon the people. Think upon me, O my God, for good, according to all that I have done for this people,' Neh. v. 14–19. So Daniel was a man of a brave public spirit: 'Then the presidents and princes sought to find occasion against Daniel concerning the kingdom; but they could find no occasion nor fault; forasmuch as he was faithful, neither was there any error or fault found in him. Then said these men, We shall not find any occasion against this Daniel, except we find it against him concerning the law of his God,' Daniel vi. 4, 5.[1]

Christ had a public spirit, he laid out himself, and laid down himself for a public good. Oh! never leave looking and meditating upon these precious and sweet examples till your souls are quickened and raised up, to act for the public good, more than for your own particular advantage. Many heathens have been excellent at this.[2]

Macrobius writes of Augustus Cæsar, in whose time Christ was born, that he carried such an entire and fatherly affection to the commonwealth, that he called it *filiam suam*, his own daughter; and therefore refused to be called *Dominus*, the lord or master of his country, and would only be called *Pater patriæ*, father of his country, because he governed it not by fear, *per timorem, sed per amorem*, but by love; the senate and the people of Rome jointly saluting him by the name of *Pater patriæ*, father of his country. The people very much lamented his death, using that speech, 'Would he had never been born, or never died.'[3]

So Marcus Regulus, to save his country from ruin, exposed himself to the greatest sufferings that the malice and rage of his enemies could inflict.

So Titus and Aristides, and many others, have been famous for their preferring the public good above their own advantage. My prayer is,

[1] A certain great emperor coming into Egypt, to shew the zeal he had for the public good, saith to the Egyptians, Draw from me as from your river Nilus. The Counsellor saith, a statesman should be thus tripartited: his will to God, his love to his master, his heart to his country, his secret to his friend, his time to business.

[2] Solomon's tribunal was underpropped with lions, to shew what spirit and metal a magistrate should be made of.

[3] *Utinam aut non nasceretur, aut [non] moreretur.*

and shall be, that all our rulers may be so spirited by God, that they may be willing to be anything, to be nothing, to deny themselves, and to trample their sinful selves under feet, in order to the honour of God, and a public good; that so neither saints nor heathens may be witnesses against them in that day, wherein the hearts and practices of all the rulers in the world shall be open and bare before him that judges the world in righteousness and judgment.

Remedy (6). The sixth remedy against this device of Satan is, seriously to consider, *That self is a great let to divine things; therefore the prophets and apostles were usually carried out of themselves, when they had the clearest, choicest, highest, and most glorious visions.* Self-seeking blinds the soul that it cannot see a beauty in Christ, nor an excellency in holiness; it distempers the palate that a man cannot taste sweetness in the word of God, nor in the ways of God, nor in the society of the people of God. It shuts the hand against all the soul-enriching offers of Christ; it hardens the heart against all the knocks and entreaties of Christ; it makes the soul as an empty vine, and as a barren wilderness: 'Israel is an empty vine, he bringeth forth fruit to himself,' Hosea x. 1. There is nothing that speaks a man to be more empty and void of God, Christ, and grace, than self-seeking. The Pharisees were great self-seekers, and great undervaluers of Christ, his word and Spirit. There is not a greater hindrance to all the duties of piety than self-seeking. Oh! this is that that keeps many a soul from looking after God and the precious things of eternity. They cannot wait on God, nor act for God, nor abide in those ways wherein they might meet with God, by reason of self. Self-seeking is that which puts many a man upon neglecting and slighting the things of his peace. Self-seekers will neither go into heaven themselves, nor suffer others to enter, that are ready to take the kingdom by violence, as you may see in the Scribes and Pharisees. Oh! but a gracious spirit is acted quite other ways, as you may see in that sweet scripture, Cant. vii. 13, 'At our gates are all manner of pleasant fruits, new and old, which I have laid up for thee, O beloved.' All the church hath and is, is only for him. Let others bear fruit to themselves, and lay up for themselves, gracious spirits will hide for Christ and lay up for Christ.[1] All the divine endeavours and productions of saints fall into God's bosom, and empty themselves into his lap. As Christ lays up his merits for them, his graces for them, his comforts for them, his crown for them, so they lay up all their fruits, and all their loves, all their graces, and all their experiences, and all their services, only for him who is the soul of their comforts, and the crown and top of all their royalty and glory, &c.

The second device that Satan hath to ensnare and destroy the great and honourable of the earth is,

Device (2). *By engaging them against the people of the Most High, againt those that are his jewels, his pleasant portion, the delight of his eye and the joy of his heart.* Thus he drew Pharaoh to engage against the children of Israel, and that was his overthrow, Exod. xiv. So he

[1] Self-seekers, with Esau, prefer a mess of pottage above their birthright, and with the men of Shechem, esteem the bramble above the vine, the olive, and the fig-tree, yea, empty things above a full Christ, and base things above a glorious Christ. The saints' motto is, *Propter te, Domine, propter te.* The saints' motto is, *Non nobis, Domine.*

engaged Haman against the Jews, and so brought him to hang upon that gallows that he had made for Mordecai, Esther vii. So he engaged those princes and presidents against Daniel, which was the utter ruin of them and their relations, Dan. vi. So in Rev. xx. 7–9, 'And when the thousand years are expired, Satan shall be loosed out of his prison. And he shall go out to deceive the nations which are in the four quarters of the earth, Gog and Magog, to gather them together to battle, whose number is as the sand of the sea. And they went up upon the breadth of the earth, and compassed the camp of the saints about, and the beloved city; and fire came down from heaven and consumed them.'

Now the remedies against this device are these:

Remedy (1). The first remedy against this device of Satan is, solemnly to consider, *That none have engaged against the saints, but have been ruined by the God of saints.* Divine justice hath been too hard for all that have opposed and engaged against the saints, as is evident in Saul, Pharaoh, Haman, &c: 'He reproved kings for their sakes, saying, Touch not mine anointed, nor do my prophets no harm,' Ps. cv. 15. When men of Balaam spirits and principles have been engaged against the saints, how hath the angel of the Lord met them in the way, and justled their bones against the wall! how hath he broke their backs and necks, and by his drawn sword cut them off in the prime of their days, and in the height of their sins![1] Ah! what a harvest hath hell had in our days, of those who have engaged against the Lamb, and those that are called chosen and faithful! Ah! how hath divine justice poured out their blood as water upon the ground! how hath he laid their honour and glory in the dust, who, in the pride and madness of their hearts, said, as Pharaoh, 'We will pursue, we will overtake, we will divide the spoil, our lusts shall be satisfied upon them. We will draw our sword, our hand shall destroy them,' Exod. xv. 9. In the things wherein they have spoken and done proudly, justice hath been above them. History abounds in nothing more than in instances of this kind, &c.

Remedy (2). The second remedy against this device of Satan is, *To dwell some time every morning upon the following scriptures, wherein God hath engaged himself to stand by his people and for his people, and to make them victorious over the greatest and wisest of their enemies.*[2] Associate yourselves, saith the Lord by the prophet, 'O ye people, and ye shall be broken in pieces; and give ear, all ye of far countries: gird yourselves, and ye shall be broken in pieces. Take counsel together, and it shall come to nought; speak the word, and it shall not stand: for God is with us.' 'Fear not, thou worm Jacob, and ye men of Israel: I will help thee, saith the Lord, and thy Redeemer, the holy One of Israel. Behold, I will make thee a new sharp threshing instrument having teeth: thou shalt thresh the mountains, and beat them small, and shalt make the hills as chaff. Thou shalt fan them, and the wind shall carry them away, and the whirlwind shall scatter them, and thou shalt rejoice in the Lord, and shalt glory in the holy One of Israel.' 'No weapon that is formed against thee shall

[1] As they said once of the Grecians in the epigram, whom they thought invulnerable, We shoot at them, but they fall not down; we wound them, and not kill them, &c. *Tanto plus gloriæ referemus, quoniam eo plures superabimus.* The number of opposers makes the Christian's conquest the more illustrious, said Pedarelus in Erasmus.

[2] *Occidi poterant, sed vinci non poterant,* said Cyprian of the Christians in his time.

prosper, and every tongue that shall rise against thee in judgment thou shalt condemn. This is the heritage of the servants of the Lord, and their righteousness is of me, saith the Lord.' 'Now also many nations are gathered together against thee that say, Let us be defiled, and let our eye look upon Sion. But they know not the thoughts of the Lord, neither understand they his counsel; for he shall gather them as sheaves into the floor. Arise and thresh, O daughter of Sion: I will make thy horn iron, and I will make thy hoof brass, and thou shalt beat in pieces many people, and I will consecrate their gain unto the Lord, and their substance unto the Lord of the whole earth.' 'Behold, I will make Jerusalem a cup of trembling unto all the people round about, when they shall be in the siege, both against Judah and against Jerusalem. And in that day will I make Jerusalem a burdensome stone for all people: all that burden themselves with it shall be cut in pieces, though all the people of the earth be gathered together against it.'[1]

Remedy (3). The third remedy against this device of Satan is, to consider, *That you cannot engage against the saints, but you must engage against God himself, by reason of that near and blessed union that is between God and them.* You cannot be fighters against the saints, but you will be found in the casting up of the account to be fighters against God himself.[2] And what greater madness than for weakness itself to engage against an almighty strength! The near union that is between the Lord and believers, is set forth by that near union that is betwixt a husband and his wife. 'They two shall be one flesh. This is a great mystery: but I speak concerning Christ and the church; we are members of his body, of his flesh, and of his bones,' saith the apostle, Eph. v. 32. This near union is set forth by that union that is between the head and the members, which make up one body, and by that union that is betwixt the graff and the stock, which are made one by insition.[3] The union between the Lord and a believer is so near, that you cannot strike a believer, but the Lord is sensible of it, and takes it as done to himself. 'Saul, Saul, why persecutest thou me?' Acts ix. 4; and 'in all their afflictions he was afflicted,' &c., Isa. lxiii. 9. Ah, souls! who ever engaged against God and prospered? who ever took up the sword against him but perished by it? God can speak you to hell and nod you to hell at pleasure. It is your greatest concernment to lay down your weapons at his feet, and to 'Kiss the Son, lest he be angry, and you perish in the midway,' Ps. ii. 12.

Remedy (4). The fourth remedy against this device of Satan is, solemnly to consider, *That you are much engaged to the saints, as instruments for the mercies that you do enjoy, and for the preventing and removing of many a judgment that otherwise might have been your ruin before this day.* Were it not for the saints' sake, God would quickly make the heavens to be as brass and the earth as iron; God would quickly strip thee of thy robes and glory, and set thee upon the dunghill with Job. They are the props that bear the world from falling about thy ears, and that keep the iron rod from breaking of thy bones.

[1] Isa. viii. 9, 10; xli. 14, 15, and liv. 17; Micah iv. 11–13; Zech. xii. 2, 3.—G.

[2] Acts v. 39. It seems to be drawn from the fable of the giants, which were said to make war with the gods.

[3] The soul's happiness consists not in anything, but in its union with God; nor its misery lies not so much in anything, as in its disunion from God.

'Therefore he said that he would destroy them, had not Moses his chosen stood before him in the breach, to turn away his wrath, lest he should destroy them,' Ps. cvi. 23.

Ah! had not the saints many a time cast themselves into the breach betwixt God's wrath and you, you had been cut off from the land of the living, and had had your portion with those whose names are written in the dust.[1] Many a nation, many a city, and many a family, is surrounded with blessings for the Josephs' sakes that live therein, and are preserved from many calamities and miseries for the Moseses', the Daniels', the Noahs', and the Jobs' sakes, that dwell amongst them. That is a sweet word, Prov. x. 25, 'As the whirlwind passeth, so is the wicked no more: but the righteous is an everlasting foundation, or is the foundation of the world.'[2] The righteous is the foundation of the world, which but for their sakes would soon shatter and fall to ruin. So the psalmist: Ps. lxxv. 3, 'The earth and all the inhabitants thereof are dissolved: I bear up the pillars of it. Selah.'

The emperor Marcus Antoninus being in Almany[3] with his army, was enclosed in a dry country by his enemies, who so stopped all the passages that he and his army were like to perish for want of water. The emperor's lieutenant seeing him so distressed, told him that he had heard that the Christians could obtain any thing of their God by their prayers, whereupon the emperor, having a legion of Christians in his army, desired them to pray to their God for his and the army's delivery out of that danger, which they presently did, and presently a great thunder fell amongst the enemies, and abundance of water upon the Romans, whereby their thirst was quenched, and the enemies overthrown without any fight.[4][5] I shall close up this last remedy with those sweet words of the psalmist: 'In Judah is God known; his name is great in Israel. In Salem also is his tabernacle, and his dwelling-place in Zion. There brake he the arrows of the bow, the shield, and the sword, and the battle. Selah,' Ps. lxxvi. 1–3.

Secondly, Satan hath his devices to ensnare and destroy *the learned and the wise*, and that sometimes *by working them to pride themselves in their parts and abilities; and sometimes by drawing them to rest upon their parts and abilities; and sometimes by causing them to make light and slight of those that want their parts and abilities, though they excel them in grace and holiness; and sometimes by drawing them to engage their parts and abilities in those ways and things that make against the honour of Christ, the joy of the Spirit, the advancement of the gospel, and the liberty of the saints, &c.*[6][7]

Now the remedies against this device are these.

Remedy (1). The first remedy against this device of Satan is, seriously to consider, *That you have nothing but what you have received, Christ*

[1] *Hic homo potuit apud Deum quod voluit*, said one concerning Luther. He could have what he would of God. Prayer is *Porta cœli, clavis paradisi*, the gate of heaven, a key to let us into paradise. When the danger is over, the saint is forgotten, is a French proverb, and that which many saints in England have found by experience.

[2] יסוד עולם *Jsodh Gnolam* from *Jasedh*.

[3] Germany.—G.

[4] The famous mythical 'Thundering Legion.'—G.

[5] Mary, Queen of Scots, that was mother to King James, was wont to say, That she feared Mr Knox's prayers more than an army of ten thousand men.

[6] John v. 44; 1 Kings xxii. 22–25: 1 Cor. i. 18–29.

[7] The truth of this you may see in the learned Scribes and Pharisees.

being as well the fountain of common gifts as of saving grace. 'What hast thou,' saith the apostle, 'that thou hast not received? And if thou hast received it, why dost thou glory as though thou hadst not received it?' 1 Cor. iv. 7.[1] There are those that would hammer out their own happiness, like the spider climbing up by the thread of her own weaving. Of all the parts and abilities that be in you, you may well say as the young man did of his hatchet, 'Alas, master! it was but borrowed,' 2 Kings vi. 5. Alas, Lord! all I have is but borrowed from that fountain that fills all the vessels in heaven and on earth, and it overflows. My gifts are not so much mine as thine: 'Of thine own have we offered unto thee,' said that princely prophet, &c., 1 Chron. xxix. 14.

Remedy (2). The second remedy against this device of Satan is, solemnly to consider, *That men's leaning and trusting to their own wits, parts, and abilities, have been their utter overthrow and ruin;* as you may see in Ahithophel, and those presidents and princes that engaged against Daniel, and in the Scribes and Pharisees. God loves to confute men in their confidences.[2] He that stands upon his parts and abilities, doth but stand upon a quicksand that will certainly fail him. There is nothing in the world that provokes God more to withdraw from the soul than this; and how can the soul stand, when his strength is departed from him? Everything that a man leans upon but God, will be a dart that will certainly pierce his heart through and through. Ah! how many in these days have lost their estates, their friends, their lives, their souls, by leaning upon their admired parts and abilities! The saints are described by their leaning upon their beloved, the Lord Jesus, Cant. viii. 5. He that leans only upon the bosom of Christ, lives the highest, choicest, safest, and sweetest life. Miseries always lie at that man's door that leans upon anything below the precious bosom of Christ; such a man is most in danger, and this is none of his least plagues, that he thinks himself secure. It is the greatest wisdom in the world to take the wise man's counsel: 'Trust in the Lord with all thine heart, and lean not to thine own understanding,' Prov. iii. 5.

Remedy (3). The third remedy against this device of Satan is, to consider, *That you do not transcend others more in parts and abilities, than they do you in grace and holiness.* There may be, and often is, great parts and abilities, where there is but little grace, yea, no grace; and there may be, and often is, a great deal of grace, where there is but weak parts and abilities.[3] You may be higher than others in gifts of knowledge, utterance, learning, &c., and those very souls may be higher than you in their communion with God, in their delighting in God, in their dependence upon God, in their affections to God, and in their humble, holy, and unblameable walking before God.[4] Is it folly and madness in a man, to make light and slight of another, because he is

[1] *Quicquid es debes creanti; quicquid potes debes redimenti*, said Bernard. Whatsoever thou art, thou owest to him that made thee; and whatsoever thou hast, thou owest to him that redeemed thee.

[2] General councils were seldom successful, because men came with confidence, leaning to their own understanding, and seeking for victory rather than verity, saith one.

[3] Judas and the Scribes and Pharisees had great parts, but no grace. The disciples had grace, but weak parts.

[4] Luke xi. 1; xxiv. 19–28.

not so rich in lead or iron as he, when he is a thousand thousand times richer in silver and gold, in jewels and in pearls, than he? And is it not madness and folly with a witness, in those that have greater parts and abilities than others, to slight them upon that account, when that those very persons that they make light and slight of have a thousand times more grace than they? And yet, ah! how doth this evil spirit prevail in the world!

It was the sad complaint of Austin in his time: 'The unlearned,' saith he, 'rise up and take heaven by violence, and we with all our learning are thrust down to hell.'[1] It is sad to see how many of the rabbis of these times do make an idol of their parts and abilities, and with what an eye of pride, scorn, and contempt do they look upon those that want their parts, and that do not worship the idol that they have set up in their own hearts. Paul, who was the great doctor of the Gentiles, did wonderfully transcend in all parts and abilities the doctors and rabbis of our times, and yet, ah! how humbly, how tenderly, how sweetly, doth he carry himself towards the meanest and the weakest! 'To the weak I became as weak, that I might win the weak: I am made all things to all men, that I might by all means save some,' 1 Cor. ix 22. 'Who is weak, and I am not weak? Who is offended, and I burn not? Wherefore, if meat make my brother to offend, I will eat no flesh while the world standeth, lest I make my brother to offend,' 1 Cor. viii. 13. But, ah! how little of this sweet spirit is to be found in the doctors of our age, who look sourly and speak bitterly against those that do not see as they see, nor cannot speak as they speak. Sirs! the Spirit of the Lord, even in despised saints, will be too hard for you, and his appearance in them, in these latter days, will be so full of spiritual beauty and glory, as that they will darken that, that you are too apt to count and call your glory. The Spirit of the Lord will not suffer his choicest jewel grace to be always buried under the straw and stubble of parts and gifts, Isa. lx. 13–17.

Remedy (4). The fourth remedy against this device of Satan is, to consider, *That there is no such way for men to have their gifts and parts blasted and withered, as to pride themselves in them, as to rest upon them, as to make light and slight of those that want them, as to engage them against those persons, ways, and things, that Jesus Christ hath set his heart upon.* Ah! how hath God blasted and withered the parts and abilities of many among us, that have once been famous shining lights![2] How is their sun darkened, and their glory clouded! 'How is the sword of the Lord upon their arm, and upon their right eye! how is their arm clean dried up, and their right eye utterly darkened!' as the prophet speaks, Zech. xi. 17. This is matter of humiliation and lamentation. Many precious discerning saints do see this, and in secret mourn for it; and oh! that they were kindly sensible of God's withdrawing from them, that they may repent, keep humble, and carry it sweetly towards God's jewels, and lean only upon the Lord,

[1] Surgunt indocti et rapiunt cœlum, et nos cum doctrina nostra detrudimur in gehennam. [More accurately as follows: 'Surgunt indocti et cœlum rapiunt, et nos cum doctrinis nostris sine corde, ecce ubi volutamur in carne et sanguine.' Confess. l. viii. c. 8.—G.]

[2] Becanus saith, that the tree of knowledge bears many leaves, and little fruit. Ah! that it were not so with many in these days, who once did outshine the stars, &c.

and not upon their parts and understanding, that so the Lord may delight to visit them with his grace at such a rate as that their faces may shine more gloriously than ever, and that they may be more serviceable to the honour of Christ, and the faith of the saints, than formerly they have been, &c.

Thirdly, Satan hath his devices to destroy the saints; and one great device that he hath to destroy the saints is,

By working them first to be strange, and then to divide, and then to be bitter and jealous, and then 'to bite and devour one another,' Gal. v. 15. Our own woful experience is too great a proof of this. The Israelites in Egypt did not more vex one another than Christians in these days have done, which occasioned a deadly consumption to fall upon some.[1]

Now the remedies against this device are these:

Remedy (1). The first remedy against this device of Satan is, *To dwell more upon one another's graces than upon one another's weaknesses and infirmities.* It is sad to consider that saints should have many eyes to behold one another's infirmities, and not one eye to see each other's graces, that they should use spectacles to behold one another's weaknesses, rather than looking-glasses to behold one another's graces.[2]

Erasmus tells of one who collected all the lame and defective verses in Homer's works, but passed over all that was excellent. Ah! that this were not the practice of many that shall at last meet in heaven, that they were not careful and skilful to collect all the weaknesses of others, and to pass over all those things that are excellent in them. The Corinthians did eye more the incestuous person's sin than his sorrow, which was like to have drowned him in sorrow.

Tell me, saints, is it not a more sweet, comfortable, and delightful thing to look more upon one another's graces than upon one another's infirmities? Tell me what pleasure, what delight, what comfort is there in looking upon the enemies, the wounds, the sores, the sickness, the diseases, the nakedness of our friends? Now sin, you know, is the soul's enemy, the soul's wound, the soul's sores, the soul's sickness, the soul's disease, the soul's nakedness; and ah! what a heart hath that man that loves thus to look! Grace is the choicest flower in all a Christian's garden; it is the richest jewel in all his crown; it is his princely robes; it is the top of royalty; and therefore must needs be the most pleasing, sweet, and delightful object for a gracious eye to be fixed upon. Sin is darkness, grace is light; sin is hell, grace is heaven; and what madness is it to look more at darkness than at light, more at hell than at heaven![3]

Tell me, saints, doth not God look more upon his people's graces than upon their weaknesses? Surely he doth. He looks more at David's and Asaph's uprightness than upon their infirmities, though they were great and many. He eyes more Job's patience than his passion. 'Re-

[1] If we knock, we break. Dissolution is the daughter of dissension.

[2] Flavius Vespasian, the emperor, was more ready to conceal the vices of his friends than their virtues. Can you think seriously of this, Christians, that a heathen should excel you, and not blush?

[3] *Non gens, sed mens, non genus sed genius,* Not race or place, but grace truly sets forth a man.

member the patience of Job,' not a word of his impatience, James v. 11. He that drew Alexander whilst he had a scar upon his face, drew him with his finger upon the scar. God puts his fingers upon his people's scars, that no blemish may appear. Ah! saints, that you would make it the top of your glory in this, to be like your heavenly Father. By so doing, much sin would be prevented, the designs of wicked men frustrated, Satan outwitted, many wounds healed, many sad hearts cheered, and God more abundantly honoured, &c.[1]

Remedy (2). The second remedy against this device of Satan is, solemnly to consider, *That love and union makes most for your own safety and security.* We shall be *insuperabiles* if we be *inseparabiles*, invincible if we be inseparable. The world may frown upon you, and plot against you, but they cannot hurt you. Unity is the best bond of safety in every church and commonwealth.[2]

And this did that Scythian king in Plutarch represent lively to his eighty sons, who, being ready to die, he commanded a bundle of arrows fast bound together to be given to his sons to break; they all tried to break them, but, being bound fast together, they could not; then he caused the band to be cut, and then they broke them with ease. He applied it thus: 'My sons, so long as you keep together, you will be invincible; but if the band of union be broke betwixt you, you will easily be broken in pieces.'[3]

Pliny writes of a stone in the island of Scyros, that if it be whole, though a large and heavy one, it swims above water, but being broken, it sinks.[4] So long as saints keep whole, nothing shall sink them; but if they break, they are in danger of sinking and drowning, &c.

Remedy (3). The third remedy against this device of Satan is, *To dwell upon those commands of God that do require you to love one another.* Oh! when your hearts begin to rise against each other, charge the commands of God upon your hearts, and say to your souls, O our souls! hath not the eternal God commanded you to love them that love the Lord? And is it not life to obey, and death to rebel?[5] Therefore look that you fulfil the commands of the Lord, for his commands are not like those that are easily reversed; but they are like those of the Medes, that cannot be changed. Oh! be much in pondering upon these commands of God. 'A new commandment I give unto you, that ye love one another, as I have loved you, that ye also love one another,' John xiii. 34. It is called a new commandment, because it is renewed in the gospel, and set home by Christ's example, and because it is rare, choice, special, and remarkable above all others.[6]

[1] Sin is Satan's work, grace is God's work; and is it not most meet that the child should eye most and mind most his father's work?

[2] There was a temple of Concord amongst the heathens; and shall it not be found among Christians, that are temples of the Holy Ghost?

[3] Pancirollus [Guy] saith, that the most precious pearl among the Romans was called *unio*, union.

[4] Lib. xxxvi. c. 26, and elsewhere: no doubt a volcanic, porous product.—G.

[5] To act, or run cross to God's express command, though under pretence of revelation from God, is as much as a man's life is worth, as you may see in that sad story, 1 Kings xiii. 24.

[6] Some conceive it to be an Hebraism, in which language *new*, *rare*, and *excellent*, are synonimals.

'This is my commandment, That ye love one another, as I have loved you.' 'These things I command you, that ye love one another.' 'Owe no man any thing, but love one another: for he that loveth another, hath fulfilled the law.' 'Let brotherly love continue.' 'Love one another, for love is of God, and every one that loveth is born of God, and knoweth God.' 'See that ye love one another with a pure heart fervently.' 'Finally, be ye all of one mind, having compassion one of another. Love as brethren, be pitiful, be courteous.' 'For this is the message that ye heard from the beginning, that we should love one another.' 'And this is his commandment, that we should believe on the name of his Son Jesus Christ, and love one another, as he gave us commandment.' 'Beloved, if God so loved us, we ought to love one another.'[1] Oh! dwell much upon these precious commands, that your love may be inflamed one to another.

In the primitive times, it was much taken notice of by the heathens, that in the depth of misery, when fathers and mothers forsook their children, Christians, otherwise strangers, stuck one to another, whose love of religion proved firmer than that of nature. Ah! that there were more of that spirit among the saints in these days. The world was once destroyed with water for the heat of lusts, and it is thought it will be again destroyed with fire for the coldness of love.[2]

Remedy (4). The fourth remedy against this device of Satan is, *To dwell more upon these choice and sweet things wherein you agree, than upon those things wherein you differ.* Ah! did you but thus, how would sinful heats be abated, and your love raised, and your spirits sweetened one to another. You agree in most, you differ but in a few; you agree in the greatest and weightiest, as concerning God, Christ, the Spirit, the Scripture, &c. You differ only in those points that have been long disputable amongst men of greatest piety and parts. You agree to own the Scripture, to hold to Christ the head, and to walk according to the law of the new creature.[3] Shall Herod and Pilate agree? Shall Turks and pagans agree? Shall bears and lions, tigers and wolves, yea, shall a legion of devils, agree in one body? And shall not saints agree, who differ only in such things as have least of the heart of God in them, and that shall never hinder your meeting in heaven? &c.

Remedy (5). The fifth remedy against this device of Satan is, solemnly to consider, *That God delights to be styled* Deus pacis, *the God of peace; and Christ to be styled* Princeps pacis, *the Prince of peace, and King of Salem, that is, King of peace; and the Spirit is a Spirit of peace.* 'The fruit of the Spirit is love, joy, peace,' Gal. v 22. Oh! why then should not the saints be children of peace? Certainly, men of froward, unquiet, fiery spirits, cannot have that sweet evidence of their interest in the God of peace, and in the Prince of peace, and in the Spirit of

[1] John xv. 12, 17; Rom. xiii. 8; Heb. xiii. 1; 1 John iv. 7; 1 Peter i. 22, and iii. 8; 1 John iii. 11, 23; iv. 11.—G.

[2] The ancients use to say commonly, that Alexander and Ephestion [*i. e.* Hephaestion] had but one soul in two distinct bodies, because their joy and sorrow, glory and disgrace, was mutual to them both. [Cf. Note on above frequently recurring saying, in Sibbes, Vol. II., page 194: where the reference is misprinted to page 35 for page 37.—G.].

[3] What a sad thing was it that a heathen should say, No beasts are so mischievous to men as Christians are one to another.

peace, as those precious souls have that follow after the things that make for love and peace. The very name of peace is sweet and comfortable; the fruit and effect thereof pleasant and profitable, more to be desired than innumerable triumphs; it is a blessing that ushers in a multitude of other blessings,[1] 2 Cor. xiii. 11; Isa. ix. 6.

The ancients were wont to paint peace in the form of a woman, with a horn of plenty in her hand.[2] Ah! peace and love among the saints, is that which will secure them and their mercies at home; yea, it will multiply their mercies; it will engage the God of mercy to crown them with the choicest mercies; and it is that that will render them most terrible, invincible, and successful abroad. Love and peace among the saints is that which puts the counsels of their enemies to a stand, and renders all their enterprises abortive; it is that which doth most weaken their hands, wound their hopes, and kill their hearts, &c.

Remedy (6). The sixth remedy against this device of Satan is, *To make more care and conscience of keeping up your peace with God.* Ah! Christians, I am afraid that your remissness herein is that which hath occasioned much of that sourness, bitterness, and divisions that be among you.[3] Ah! you have not, as you should, kept up your peace with God, and therefore it is that you do so dreadfully break the peace among yourselves. The Lord hath promised, 'That when a man's ways please him, he will make his enemies to be at peace with him,' Prov. xvi. 7. Ah! how much more then would God make the children of peace to keep the peace among themselves, if their ways do but please him! All creatures are at his beck and check. Laban followed Jacob with one troop. Esau met him with another, both with hostile intentions; but Jacob's ways pleasing the Lord, God by his mighty power so works that Laban leaves him with a kiss, and Esau met him with a kiss; he hath an oath of one, tears of the other, peace with both. If we make it our business to keep up our league with God, God will make it his work and his glory to maintain our peace with men; but if men make light of keeping up their peace with God, it is just with God to leave them to a spirit of pride, envy, passion, contention, division, and confusion, to leave them 'to bite and devour one another, till they be consumed one of another,'[4] &c.

Remedy (7). The seventh remedy against this device of Satan is, *To dwell much upon that near relation and union that is between you.* This consideration had a sweet influence upon Abraham's heart: 'And Abraham said unto Lot, Let there be no strife, I pray thee, between me and thee, and between my herdsmen and thy herdsmen; for we are brethren,' Gen. xiii. 8.[5] That is a sweet word in the psalmist, 'Behold, how good and how pleasant it is for brethren to live together in unity,'

[1] *Ubi pax ibi Christus, quia Christus pax*, where peace is, there is Christ, because Christ is peace. *Dulce nomen pacis*, said the orat[illegible].

[2] The Grecians had the statue of Peace, with Pluto, the god of riches, in her arms.

[3] There is no fear of knowing too much, but there is much fear in practising too little.

[4] Pharnaces sent a crown to Cæsar at the same time he rebelled against him; but he returned the crown and this message back, *Faceret imperata prius*, let him return to his obedience first. There is no sound peace to be had with God or man, but in a way of obedience. [Pharnaces II. Appian, *Mithr.* 120; Dion. Cass. xlii. 45–48; Plutarch, *Cæsar*, 50; *Suet. Jul.* 35.—G.]

[5] מריבה, Oh! let there be no bitterness between us, for we are brethren.

Ps. cxxxiii. 1. It is not *good and not pleasant,* or *pleasant and not good,* but *good and pleasant.* There be some things that be *bona sed non jucunda,* good and not pleasant, as patience and discipline; and there be some things that are pleasant but not good, as carnal pleasures, voluptuousness, &c. And there are some things that are neither good nor pleasant, as malice, envy, worldly sorrow, &c.; and there are some things that are both good and pleasant, as piety, charity, peace, and union among brethren; and oh! that we could see more of this among those that shall one day meet in their Father's kingdom and never part. And as they are brethren, so they are all fellow-members: 'Now ye are the body of Christ, and members in particular,' 1 Cor. xii. 27. And again: 'We are members of his body, of his flesh, and of his bones,' Eph. v. 30. Shall the members of the natural body be serviceable and useful to one another, and shall the members of this spiritual body cut and destroy one another? Is it against the law of nature for the natural members to cut and slash one another?[1] And is it not much more against the law of nature and of grace for the members of Christ's glorious body to do so? And as you are all fellow-members, so you are fellow-soldiers under the same Captain of salvation, the Lord Jesus, fighting against the world, the flesh, and the devil. And as you are all fellow-soldiers, so you are all fellow-sufferers under the same enemies, the devil and the world. And as you are all fellow-sufferers, so are you fellow-travellers towards the land of Canaan, 'the new Jerusalem that is above.' 'Here we have no abiding city, but we look for one to come.' The heirs of heaven are strangers on earth. And as you are all fellow-travellers, so are you all fellow-heirs of the same crown and inheritance.[2]

Remedy (8). The eighth remedy against this device of Satan is, *To dwell upon the miseries of discord.* Dissolution is the daughter of dissension. Ah! how doth the name of Christ, and the way of Christ, suffer by the discord of saints! How are many that are entering upon the ways of God hindered and sadded, and the mouths of the wicked opened, and their hearts hardened against God and his ways, by the discord of his people! Remember this, the disagreement of Christians is the devil's triumph; and what a sad thing is this, that Christians should give Satan cause to triumph![3]

It was a notable saying of one, 'Take away strife, and call back peace, lest thou lose a man, thy friend; and the devil, an enemy, joy over you both,' &c.

Remedy (9). The ninth remedy against this device of Satan is, seriously to consider, *That it is no disparagement to you to be first in seeking peace and reconcilement, but rather an honour to you, that you have begun to seek peace.* Abraham was the elder, and more worthy than Lot, both in respect of grace and nature also, for he was uncle unto Lot, and yet he first seeks peace of his inferior, which God hath

[1] The parti-coloured coats were characters of the king's children: so is following after peace now.

[2] Rev. xii. 7, 8; Heb. ii. 10; Rev. ii. 10; John xv. 19, 20; Heb. xii. 14, xiii. 4; Rom. viii.15–17.

[3] Our dissensions are one of the Jews' greatest stumbling-blocks. Can you think of it, and your hearts not bleed?

recorded as his honour.[1] Ah ! how doth the God of peace, by his Spirit and messengers, pursue after peace with poor creatures. God first makes offer of peace to us : 'Now then we are ambassadors for Christ, as though God did beseech you by us : we pray you in Christ's stead, be ye reconciled to God,' 2 Cor. v. 20. God's grace first kneels to us, and who can turn their backs upon such blessed and bleeding embracements, but souls in whom Satan the god of this world kings it? God is the party wronged, and yet he sues for peace with us at first : 'I said, Behold me, behold me, unto a nation that was not called by my name,' Isa. lxv. 1.[2] Ah ! how doth the sweetness, the freeness, and the riches of his grace break forth and shine upon poor souls. When a man goes from the sun, yet the sunbeams follow him ; so when we go from the Sun of righteousness, yet then the beams of his love and mercy follow us. Christ first sent to Peter that had denied him, and the rest that had forsaken him : 'Go your ways, and tell his disciples and Peter, that he goeth before you into Galilee : there shall ye see him, as he said unto you,' Mark xvi. 7. Ah ! souls, it is not a base, low thing, but a God-like thing, though we are wronged by others, yet to be the first in seeking after peace. Such actings will speak out much of God with a man's spirit, &c.

Christians, it is not matter of liberty whether you will or you will not pursue after peace, but it is matter of duty that lies upon you ; you are bound by express precept to follow after peace ; and though it may seem to fly from you, yet you must pursue after it : 'Follow peace with all men, and holiness, without which no man can see the Lord,' Heb. xii. 14.[3] Peace and holiness are to be pursued after with the greatest eagerness that can be imagined. So the psalmist : 'Depart from evil, and do good ; seek peace and pursue it,' Ps. xxxiv. 14. The Hebrew word that is here rendered *seek*, is in *Piel*, and it signifies to seek earnestly, vehemently, affectionately, studiously, industriously. 'And pursue it.' That Hebrew word signifies earnestly to pursue, being a metaphor taken from the eagerness of wild beasts or ravenous fowls, which will run or fly both fast and far rather than be disappointed of their prey. So the apostle presses the same duty upon the Romans : 'Let us follow after the things that make for peace, and things wherein one may edify another,' Rom. xiv. 19. Ah ! you froward, sour, dogged Christians, can you look upon these commands of God without tears and blushing?

I have read a remarkable story of Aristippus, though but a heathen, who went of his own accord to Æschines his enemy, and said, 'Shall we never be reconciled till we become a table-talk to all the country?' and when Æschines answered he would most gladly be at peace with him, 'Remember, then, said Aristippus, that though I were the elder and better man, yet I sought first unto thee.' Thou art indeed, said Æschines, a far better man than I, for I began the quarrel, but thou the reconcilement.[4] My prayer

[1] They shall both have the name and the note, the comfort and the credit, of being most like unto God, who first begin to pursue after peace.

[2] Behold me! behold me! It is geminated [doubled] to shew God's exceeding forwardness to shew favour and mercy to them.

[3] Διώκετε, It signifies to follow after peace, as the persecutor doth him whom he persecuteth.

[4] Plutarch. [Cf. Diogenes Laërtius, ii. 65 ; also Horace, Ep. i. l. 18, and i. 17, 28.—G.]

shall be that this heathen may not rise in judgment against the flourishing professors of our times: 'Who whet their tongues like a sword, and bend their bows to shoot their arrows, even bitter words,' Ps. lxiv. 3.

Remedy (10). The tenth remedy against this device of Satan is, *For saints to join together and walk together in the ways of grace and holiness so far as they do agree, making the word their only touchstone and judge of their actions.* That is sweet advice that the apostle gives: 'I press toward the mark for the prize of the high calling of God in Christ Jesus,' Philip. iii. 14–16. 'Let us therefore, as many as be perfect,— comparatively or conceitedly[1] so,—be thus minded. And if in anything ye be otherwise minded, God shall reveal even this unto you. Nevertheless, whereto we have already attained, let us walk by the same rule, let us mind the same thing.' Ah! Christians, God loses much, and you lose much, and Satan gains much by this, that you do not, that you will not, walk lovingly together so far as your ways lie together. It is your sin and shame that you do not, that you will not, pray together, and hear together, and confer together, and mourn together, &c., because that in some far lesser things you are not agreed together. What folly and madness is it in those whose way of a hundred miles lies fourscore and nineteen together, yet will not walk so far together, because that they cannot go the other mile together; yet such is the folly and madness of many Christians in these days, who will not do many things they may do, because they cannot do everything they should do.[2] I fear God will whip them into a better temper before he hath done with them. He will break their bones, and pierce their hearts, but he will cure them of this malady, &c.

And be sure you make the word the only touchstone and judge of all persons and actions: 'To the law and to the testimony, if they speak not according to this word, it is because there is no light in them,' Isa. viii. 20. It is best and safest to make that to be the judge of all men and things now that all shall be judged by in the latter day: 'The word, saith Christ, that I have spoken, the same shall judge him in the last day,' John xii. 48. Make not your dim light, your notions, your fancies, your opinions, the judge of men's action, but still judge by rule, and plead, 'It is written.'

When a vain importunate soul cried out in contest with a holy man, 'Hear me, hear me,' the holy man answered, 'Neither hear me, nor I thee, but let us both hear the apostle.'[3]

Constantine, in all the disputes before him with the Arians, would still call for the word of God as the only way, if not to convert, yet to stop their mouths, &c.

Remedy (11). The eleventh remedy against this device of Satan is, *To be much in self-judging*: 'Judge yourselves, and you shall not be judged of the Lord,' 1 Cor. xi. 31. Ah! were Christians' hearts more taken up in judging themselves and condemning themselves, they would not be so apt to judge and censure others, and to carry it sourly and

[1] Those who have reason to *conceive* themselves 'perfect.'—G.

[2] Great is the power of joint prayer. Mary Queen of Scots, that was mother of king James, was wont to say that she feared Master Knox's prayer more than an army of ten thousand men. [Already used in this treatise: cf. page 125.—G.]

[3] *Nec ego te, nec tu me, sed ambo audiamus Apostolum.*

bitterly towards others that differ from them.[1] There are no souls in the world that are so fearful to judge others as those that do most judge themselves, nor so careful to make a righteous judgment of men or things as those that are most careful to judge themselves. There are none in the world that tremble to think evil of others, to speak evil of others, or to do evil to others, as those that make it their business to judge themselves. There are none that make such sweet constructions and charitable interpretations of men and things, as those that are best and most in judging themselves.[2] One request I have to you that are much in judging others and little in judging yourselves, to you that are so apt and prone to judge rashly, falsely, and unrighteously, and that is, that you will every morning dwell a little upon these scriptures: 'Judge not, that ye be not judged; for with what judgment ye judge, ye shall be judged; and with what measure ye mete, it shall be measured to you again,' Mat. vii. 1, 2. 'Judge not according to appearance, but judge righteous judgment,' John vii. 24. 'Let not him that eateth not judge him that eateth, for God hath received him. Why dost thou judge thy brother? or why dost thou set at nought thy brother?' Rom. xiv. 3, 10, 13. 'We shall all stand before the judgment-seat of Christ. Let us not judge one another any more, but judge this rather, that no man put a stumbling-block or an occasion to fall in his brother's way.' 'Judge nothing before the time, until the Lord come, who both will bring to light the hidden things of darkness, and will manifest the counsels of the heart, and then shall every man have praise of God,' 1 Cor. iv. 5. 'Speak not evil one of another, brethren: he that speaketh evil of his brother, and judgeth his brother, speaketh evil of the law, and judgeth the law; but if thou judgest the law, thou art not a doer of the law, but a judge. There is one lawgiver, who is able to save and to destroy,' James iv. 11, 12. 'Who art thou that judgest another man's servant? to his own master he standeth or falleth; yea, he shall be holden up, for God is able to make him stand,' Rom. xiv. 4.

One Delphidius accusing another before Julian about that which he could not prove, the party denying the fact, Delphidius answers, If it be sufficient to deny what is laid to one's charge, who shall be found guilty? Julian answers, And if it be sufficient to be accused, who can be innocent? You are wise, and know how to apply it.

Remedy (12). The twelfth remedy against this device of Satan is this, above all, *Labour to be clothed with humility.* Humility makes a man peaceable among brethren, fruitful in well-doing, cheerful in suffering, and constant in holy walking, 1 Pet. v. 5. Humility fits for the highest services we owe to Christ, and yet will not neglect the lowest service to the meanest saint, John xiii. 5. Humility can feed upon the meanest dish, and yet it is maintained by the choicest delicates, as God, Christ, and glory. Humility will make a man bless him that curses him, and pray for those that persecute him. An humble heart is an habitation for God, a scholar for Christ, a companion of angels, a preserver of grace, and a fitter for glory. Humility is the nurse of our graces, the preserver of our mercies, and the great pro-

[1] It is storied of Nero, himself being unchaste, he did think there was no man chaste.

[2] In the Olympic games, the wrestlers did not put their crowns upon their own heads, but upon the heads of others. It is just so with souls that are good at self-judging.

moter of holy duties. Humility cannot find three things on this side heaven: it cannot find fulness in the creature, nor sweetness in sin, nor life in an ordinance without Christ. An humble soul always finds three things on this side heaven: the soul to be empty, Christ to be full, and every mercy and duty to be sweet wherein God is enjoyed.[1] Humility can weep over other men's weaknesses, and joy and rejoice over their graces. Humility will make a man quiet and contented in the meanest condition, and it will preserve a man from envying other men's prosperous condition, 1 Thes. i. 2, 3. Humility honours those that are strong in grace, and puts two hands under those that are weak in grace, Eph. iii. 8. Humility makes a man richer than other men, and it makes a man judge himself the poorest among men. Humility will see much good abroad, when it can see but little at home. Ah, Christian! though faith be the champion of grace, and love the nurse of grace, yet humility is the beautifier of grace; it casts a general glory upon all the graces in the soul. Ah! did Christians more abound in humility, they would be less bitter, froward, and sour, and they would be more gentle, meek, and sweet in their spirits and practices. Humility will make a man have high thoughts of others and low thoughts of a man's self; it will make a man see much glory and excellency in others, and much baseness and sinfulness in a man's self; it will make a man see others rich, and himself poor; others strong, and himself weak; others wise, and himself foolish.[2] Humility will make a man excellent at covering others' infirmities, and at recording their gracious services, and at delighting in their graces; it makes a man joy in every light that outshines his own, and every wind that blows others good. Humility is better at believing than it is at questioning other men's happiness. I judge, saith an humble soul, it is well with these Christians now, but it will be far better with them hereafter. They are now upon the borders of the New Jerusalem, and it will be but as a day before they slide into Jerusalem. An humble soul is willinger to say, Heaven is that man's, than mine; and Christ is that Christian's, than mine; and God is their God in covenant, than mine. Ah! were Christians more humble, there would be less fire and more love among them than now is, &c.

Fourthly, As Satan hath his device to destroy gracious souls, so he hath his devices to destroy *poor ignorant souls*, and that sometimes,

By drawing them to affect ignorance, and to neglect, slight, and despise the means of knowledge. Ignorance is the mother of mistake, the cause of trouble, error, and of terror; it is the highway to hell, and it makes a man both a prisoner and a slave to the devil at once.[3] Ignorance unmans a man; it makes a man a beast, yea, makes him more miserable than the beast that perisheth.[4] There are none so easily nor so frequently taken in Satan's snares as ignorant souls. They are easily drawn to dance with the devil all day, and to dream of supping with Christ at night, &c.

[1] Humility is *conservatrix virtutum*, said Bernard, that which keeps all graces together.

[2] The humble soul is like the violet, which grows low, hangs the head downwards, and hides itself with its own leaves; and were it not that the fragrant smell of his many virtues discovered him to the world, he would choose to live and die in his self-contenting secrecy.

[3] Hosea iv. 6, Mat. xxii. 29.

[4] Ignorants have this advantage, *ut mitius ardeant*, they have a cooler hell.

Now the remedies against this device are these:

Remedy (1). The first remedy against this device of Satan is, seriously to consider, *That an ignorant heart is an evil heart.* 'Without knowledge the mind is not good,' Prov. xix. 2. As an ignorant heart is a naughty heart, it is a heart in the dark; and no good can come into a dark heart, but it must pass through the understanding: 'And if the eye be dark, all the body is dark,' Mat. vi. 22. A leprous head and a leprous heart are inseparable companions. Ignorant hearts are so evil that they let fly on all hands, and spare not to spit their venom in the very face of God, as Pharaoh did when thick darkness was upon him.[1]

Remedy (2). The second remedy against this device of Satan is, to consider, *That ignorance is the deformity of the soul.* As blindness is the deformity of the face, so is ignorance the deformity of the soul. As the want of fleshly eyes spoils the beauty of the face, so the want of spiritual eyes spoils the beauty of the soul. A man without knowledge is as a workman without his hands, as a painter without his eyes, as a traveller without his legs, or as a ship without sails, or a bird without wings, or like a body without a soul.

Remedy (3). The third remedy against this device of Satan is, solemnly to consider, *That ignorance makes men the objects of God's hatred and wrath.* 'It is a people that do err in their hearts, and have not known my ways. Wherefore I sware in my wrath, they should never enter into my rest,' Heb. iii. 10, 11. 'My people are a people of no understanding, therefore he that made them will have no mercy on them,' Isa. xxvii. 11. Christ hath said, 'That he will come in flaming fire, to render vengeance on them that know not God,' 2 Thes. i. 8. Ignorance will end in vengeance. When you see a poor blind man here, you do not loathe him, nor hate him, but you pity him. Oh! but soul-blindness makes you abominable in the sight of God. God hath sworn that ignorant persons shall never come into heaven. Heaven itself would be a hell to ignorant souls.[2]

'My people are destroyed for want of knowledge; because thou hast rejected knowledge, I will reject thee,' Hosea, iv. 6; [אמאסאך, cut off].

Chilo, one of the seven sages, being asked what God had done, answered, 'He exalted humble men, and suppressed proud ignorant fools.[3]

Remedy (4). The fourth remedy against this device of Satan is, to consider, *That ignorance is a sin that leads to all sins.* All sins are seminally in ignorance. 'You do err, not knowing the Scriptures,' Mat. xxii. 29. It puts men upon hating and persecuting the saints. 'They shall hate you, and put you out of the synagogues: yea, the time cometh, that whosoever killeth you will think that he doth God service. And these things will they do unto you, because they have not known the Father, nor me,' John xvi. 2, 3. Paul thanks his ignorance for all his cruelties to Christians. 'I was a blasphemer, and a persecutor, and injurious: but I obtained mercy, because I did it

[1] *Ignorat sane improbus omnis*, saith Aristotle.

[2] They must needs err that know not God's ways, yet cannot they wander so wide as to miss of hell.

[3] Rome saith, ignorance is the mother of devotion, but the Scripture saith, it is the mother of destruction.

ignorantly,' 1 Tim. i. 13.[1] It was ignorance that put the Jews upon crucifying Christ: 'Father, forgive them,' saith Christ of his murderers, 'for they know not what they do,' Luke xxiii. 34: 'for if the princes of this world had known, they would not have crucified the Lord of glory,' 1 Cor. ii. 8.[2] Sin at first was the cause of ignorance, but now ignorance is the cause of all sin. 'Swearing, and lying, and killing, and stealing, and whoring abound,' saith the prophet, 'because there is no knowledge of God in the land.' There are none so frequent, and so impudent in the ways of sin, as ignorant souls; they care not, nor mind not what they do, nor what they say against God, Christ, heaven, holiness, and their own souls. 'Our tongues are our own, who shall control us? They are corrupt, and speak wickedly concerning oppression: they speak loftily. They set their mouth against the heavens; and their tongue walketh through the earth. Have all the workers of iniquity no knowledge? who eat up my people as they eat bread, and call not upon the Lord?'[3] [4]

[1] It seems right to note that the apostle does not allege his ignorance, for which he was responsible, as the ground of the 'mercy' shewn him, but only as the source and explanation of his sin and violence. The clause, 'but I obtained mercy,' is parenthetic, and it is of importance to note this.—G.

[2] Aristotle makes ignorance the mother of all the misrule in the world.

[3] Ps. xiv. 4; lxxiii. 8, 9.

[4] They did like Œdipus, who killed his father Laius, king of Thebes, and thought he killed his enemy. [Euripides, *Phoen.* 39.—G.]

AN APPENDIX

TOUCHING FIVE MORE OF SATAN'S DEVICES,

Whereby he keepeth poor souls from believing in Christ, from receiving of Christ, from embracing of Christ, from resting, leaning, or relying upon Christ, for everlasting happiness and blessedness, according to the gospel; and remedies against these devices.

His first device to keep the soul from believing in Christ is,

Device (1). *By suggesting to the soul the greatness and vileness of his sins.* What! saith Satan, dost thou think that thou shalt ever obtain mercy by Christ, that hast sinned with so high a hand against Christ? that hast slighted the tenders[1] of grace? that hast grieved the Spirit of grace? that hast despised the word of grace? that hast trampled under feet the blood of the covenant, by which thou mightest have been pardoned, purged, justified, and saved? that hast spoken and done all the evil that thou couldest? No! no! saith Satan, he hath mercy for others, but not for thee; pardon for others, but not for thee; righteousness for others, but not for thee, &c., therefore it is in vain for thee to think of believing in Christ, or resting and leaning thy guilty soul upon Christ, Jer. iii. 5.

Now the remedies against this device are these:—

Remedy (1). The first remedy against this device of Satan is, to consider, *That the greater your sins are, the more you stand in need of a Saviour.* The greater your burden is, the more you stand in need of one to help to bear it. The deeper the wound is, the more need there is of the chirurgeon; the more dangerous the disease is, the more need there is of the physician. Who but madmen will argue thus: My burden is great, therefore I will not call out for help; my wound is deep, therefore I will not call out for balm; my disease is dangerous, therefore I will not go to the physician. Ah! it is spiritual madness, it is the devil's logic to argue thus: My sins are great, therefore I will not go to Christ, I dare not rest nor lean on Christ, &c.; whereas the soul should reason thus: The greater my sins are, the more I stand in need of mercy, of pardon, and therefore I will go to Christ, who delights in mercy,

1 'Offers.'—G.

who pardons sin for his own name's sake, who is as able and as willing to forgive pounds as pence, thousands as hundreds, Micah vii. 18, Isa. xliii. 25.

Remedy (2). The second remedy against this device of Satan is, solemnly to consider, *That the promise of grace and mercy is to returning souls.* And, therefore, though thou art never so wicked, yet if thou wilt return, God will be thine, and mercy shall be thine, and pardon shall be thine: 2 Chron. xxx. 9, 'For if you turn again unto the Lord, your brethren and your children shall find compassion before them that lead them captive, so that they shall come again into this land: for the Lord our God is gracious and merciful, and will not turn away his face from you, if ye return unto him.' So Jer. iii. 12, 'Go and proclaim these words towards the north, and say, Return, thou backsliding Israel, saith the Lord, and I will not cause my anger to fall upon you: for I am merciful, saith the Lord, and I will not keep anger for ever.' So Joel ii. 13, 'And rend your hearts, and not your garments, and turn unto the Lord your God: for he is gracious and merciful, slow to anger, and of great kindness, and repenteth him of the evil.' So Isa. lv. 7, 'Let the wicked forsake his ways, and the unrighteous man his thoughts: and let him return unto the Lord, and he will have mercy upon him; and to our God, for he will abundantly pardon,' or, as the Hebrew reads it, 'He will multiply pardon:' so Ezek. xviii.

Ah! sinner, it is not thy great transgressions that shall exclude thee from mercy, if thou wilt break off thy sins by repentance and return to the fountain of mercy. Christ's heart, Christ's arms, are wide open to embrace the returning prodigal. It is not simply the greatest[1] of thy sins, but thy peremptory persisting in sin, that will be thy eternal overthrow.

Remedy (3). The third remedy against this device of Satan is, solemnly to consider, *That the greatest sinners have obtained mercy, and therefore all the angels in heaven, all the men on earth, and all the devils in hell cannot tell to the contrary, but that thou mayest obtain mercy.* Manasseh was a notorious sinner; he erected altars for Baal, he worshipped and served all the host of heaven; he caused his sons to pass through the fire; he gave himself to witchcraft and sorcery; he made Judah to sin more wickedly than the heathen did, whom the Lord destroyed before the children of Israel; he caused the streets of Jerusalem to run down with innocent blood, 2 Kings xxi. Ah! what a devil incarnate was he in his actings! Yet when he humbled himself, and sought the Lord, the Lord was entreated of him and heard his supplication, and brought him to Jerusalem, and made himself known unto him, and crowned him with mercy and loving-kindness, as you may see in 2 Chron. xxxiii.[2] So Paul was once a blasphemer, a persecutor and injurious, yet he obtained mercy, 1 Tim. i. 13. So Mary Magdalene was a notorious strumpet, a common whore, out of whom Christ cast seven devils, yet she is pardoned by Christ, and dearly beloved of Christ, Luke vii. 37, 38. So Mark xvi. 9, 'Now, when Jesus was risen early the first day of the week, he appeared first to Mary Magdalene, out of whom he had cast seven devils.'[3]

[1] Qu. 'greatness'?—G.
[2] The Hebrew doctors writ that he slew Isaiah the prophet, who was his father-in-law.
[3] See footnote on page 100.—G.

Jansenius on the place saith, it is very observable that our Saviour after his resurrection first appeared to Mary Magdalene and Peter, that had been grievous sinners; that even the worst of sinners may be comforted and encouraged to come to Christ, to believe in Christ, to rest and stay their souls upon Christ, for mercy here and glory hereafter. That is a very precious word for the worst of sinners to hang upon, Ps. lxviii. 18. The psalmist speaking of Christ saith, 'Thou hast ascended on high, thou hast led captivity captive; thou hast received gifts for men; yea, for the rebellious also, that the Lord might dwell amongst them.'

What though thou art a rebellious child, or a rebellious servant! What though thou art a rebellious swearer, a rebellious drunkard, a rebellious Sabbath breaker! Yet Christ hath received gifts for thee, 'even for the rebellious also.' He hath received the gift of pardon, the gift of righteousness, yea, all the gifts of the Spirit for thee, that thy heart may be made a delightful house for God to dwell in.

Bodin[1] hath a story concerning a great rebel that had made a strong party against a Roman emperor. The emperor makes proclamation, that whoever could bring the rebel dead or alive, he should have such a great sum of money. The rebel hearing of this, comes and presents himself before the emperor, and demands the sum of money. Now, saith the emperor, if I should put him to death, the world would say I did it to save my money. And so he pardons the rebel, and gives him the money.

Ah, sinners! Shall a heathen do this, that had but a drop of mercy and compassion in him: and will not Christ do much more, that hath all fulness of grace, mercy, and glory in himself? Surely his bowels do yearn towards the worst of rebels. Ah! if you still but come in, you will find him ready to pardon, yea, one made up of pardoning mercy. Oh! the readiness and willingness of Jesus Christ to receive to favour the greatest rebels! The father of mercies did meet, embrace, and kiss that prodigal mouth which came from feeding with swine and kissing of harlots, Col. i. 19, ii 3, 4.[2]

Ephraim had committed idolatry, and was backslidden from God; he was guilty of lukewarmness and unbelief, &c., yet saith God, 'Ephraim is my dear son, he is a pleasant child, my bowels are troubled for him, I will have mercy,' or rather as it is in the original, 'I will have mercy, mercy upon him, saith the Lord,'[3]

Well! saith God, though Ephraim be guilty of crimson sins, yet he is a son, a dear son, a precious son, a pleasant child; though he be black with filth, and red with guilt, yet my bowels are troubled for him; I will have mercy, mercy upon him. Ah sinners, if these bowels of mercy do not melt, win, and draw you, justice will be a swift witness against you, and make you lie down in eternal misery for kicking against the bowels of mercy.

Christ hangs out still, as once that warlike Scythian did, a white flag of grace and mercy to returning sinners that humble themselves at his feet for favour; but if sinners stand out, Christ will put forth his red

[1] John Bodin died 1596: for above see *Universæ Naturæ Theatrum*, &c., &c., 1579; and Les six Livres de la Republique, &c., 1593.—G.

[2] Neh. ix. 15, Hebrew, But thou a God of pardons.

[3] Hosea iv. 17; v. 3; vi. 8, 11; xii. 12, 14; xiii. 12. *Vide* Jer. xxxi. 20.

flag, his bloody flag, and they shall die for ever by a hand of justice. Sinners! there is no way to avoid perishing by Christ's iron rod, but by kissing his golden sceptre.

Remedy (4). The fourth remedy against this device of Satan is, to consider, *That Jesus Christ hath nowhere in all the Scripture excepted against the worst of sinners that are willing to receive him, to believe in him, to rest upon him for happiness and blessedness.* Ah! sinners, why should you be more cruel and unmerciful to your own souls than Christ is? Christ hath not excluded you from mercy, why should you exclude your own souls from mercy? Oh that you would dwell often upon that choice Scripture, John vi. 37, 'All that the Father giveth me, shall come to me; and him that cometh to me I will in no wise cast out,' or as the original hath it, 'I will not not cast out.' Well! saith Christ, if any man will come, or is coming to me, let him be more sinful or less; more unworthy or less; let him be never so guilty, never so filthy, never so rebellious, never so leprous, &c., yet if he will but come, I will not not cast him off. So much is held forth in 1 Cor. vi. 9–11, 'Know ye not that the unrighteous shall not inherit the kingdom of God? Be not deceived: neither fornicators, nor idolaters, nor adulterers, nor effeminate, nor abusers of themselves with mankind, nor thieves, nor covetous, nor drunkards, nor revilers, nor extortioners, shall inherit the kingdom of God. And such were some of you: but ye are washed, but ye are sanctified, but ye are justified in the name of the Lord Jesus, and by the Spirit of our God.'

Ah! sinners, do not think that he that hath received such notorious sinners to mercy will reject you. 'He is yesterday, and to-day, and the same for ever,' Heb. xiii. 8. Christ was born in an inn, to shew that he receives all comers; his garments were divided into four parts, to shew that out of what part of the world soever we come, we shall be received. If we be naked, Christ hath robes to clothe us; if we be harbourless, Christ hath room to lodge us. That is a choice scripture, Acts x. 34, 35, 'Then Peter opened his mouth and said, Of a truth I perceive that God is no respecter of persons. But in every nation, he that feareth him, and worketh righteousness, is accepted with him.'

The three tongues that were written upon the cross, Greek, Latin, and Hebrew, John xix. 19, 20, to witness Christ to be the king of the Jews, do each of them in their several idiom avouch this singular axiom, that Christ is an all-sufficient Saviour; and 'a threefold cord is not easily broken.' The apostle puts this out of doubt: Heb. vii. 25, 'Wherefore he is able also to save them to the uttermost that come unto God by him, seeing he ever liveth to make intercession for them.' Now, he were not an all-sufficient Saviour if he were not able to save the greatest, as [well as] the least of sinners. Ah! sinners, tell Jesus Christ that he hath not excluded you from mercy, and therefore you are resolved that you will sit, wait, weep, and knock at the door of mercy, till he shall say, Souls, be of good cheer, your sins are forgiven, your persons are justified, and your souls shall be saved.

Remedy (5). The fifth remedy against this device of Satan is, to consider, *That the greater sinner thou art, the dearer thou wilt be to Christ, when he shall behold thee as the travail of his soul:* Isa. liii. 11, 'He shall see of the travail of his soul, and be satisfied.' The dearer we pay for anything, the dearer that thing is to us. Christ hath paid most, and prayed most, and sighed most, and wept most, and bled most for the greatest sinners, and therefore they are dearer to Christ than others that are less sinful. Rachel was dearer to Jacob than Leah, because she cost him more; he obeyed, endured, and suffered more by day and night for her than for Leah. Ah! sinners, the greatness of your sins does but set off the freeness and riches of Christ's grace, and the freeness of his love. This maketh heaven and earth to ring of his praise, that he loves those that are most unlovely, that he shews most favour to them that have sinned most highly against him, as might be shewed by several instances in Scripture, as Paul, Mary Magdalene, and others. Who sinned more against Christ than these? And who had sweeter and choicer manifestations of divine love and favour than these?

Remedy (6). The sixth remedy against this device of Satan is, seriously to consider, *That the longer you keep off from Christ, the greater and stronger your sins will grow.* All divine power and strength against sin flows from the soul's union and communion with Christ, Rom. viii. 10, 1 John i. 6, 7. While you keep off from Christ, you keep off from that strength and power which is only able to make you trample down strength, lead captivity captive, and slay the Goliaths that bid defiance to Christ. It is only faith in Christ that makes a man triumph over sin, Satan, hell, and the world, 1 John v. 4. It is only faith in Christ that binds the strong man's hand and foot, that stops the issue of blood, that makes a man strong in resisting, and happy in conquering, Mat. v. 15 to 35. Sin always dies most where faith lives most. The most believing soul is the most mortified soul. Ah! sinner, remember this, there is no way on earth effectually to be rid of the guilt, filth, and power of sin, but by believing in a Saviour. It is not resolving, it is not complaining, it is not mourning, but believing, that will make thee divinely victorious over that body of sin that to this day is too strong for thee, and that will certainly be thy ruin, if it be not ruined by a hand of faith.

Remedy (7). The seventh remedy against this device of Satan is, wisely to consider, *That as there is nothing in Christ to discourage the greatest sinners from believing in him, so there is everything in Christ that may encourage the greatest sinners to believe on him, to rest and lean upon him for all happiness and blessedness,* Cant. i. 3. If you look upon his nature, his disposition, his names, his titles, his offices as king, priest, and prophet, you will find nothing to discourage the greatest sinners from believing in him, but many things to encourage the greatest sinners to receive him, to believe on him.[1] Christ is the greatest good, the choicest good, the chiefest good, the most suitable good, the most necessary good. He is a pure good, a real good, a total good, an eternal good, and a soul-satisfying good, Rev. iii. 17, 18. Sinners, are you poor? Christ hath gold to enrich you. Are you naked? Christ hath royal robes, he hath white raiment to clothe you. Are you blind? Christ hath eye-salve to enlighten you. Are you hungry? Christ will be manna to feed you. Are you thirsty? He will be a well of living water to refresh you. Are you wounded? He hath a balm under his wings to heal you. Are you sick? He is a physician

[1] Col. i. 19, ii. 3, Cant. v. 10.

to cure you. Are you prisoners? He hath laid down a ransom for you. Ah, sinners! tell me, tell me, is there anything in Christ to keep you off from believing? No. Is there not everything in Christ that may encourage you to believe in him? Yes. Oh, then, believe in him, and then, 'Though your sins be as scarlet, they shall be as white as snow, though they be red like crimson, they shall be as wool,' Isa. i. 18. Nay, then, your iniquities shall be forgotten as well as forgiven, they shall be remembered no more. God will cast them behind his back, he will throw them into the bottom of the sea, Isa. xliii. 25, xxxviii. 17, Micah vii. 19.

Remedy (8). The eighth remedy against this device of Satan is, seriously to consider, *The absolute necessity of believing in Christ.* Heaven is too holy and too hot to hold unbelievers; their lodging is prepared in hell: Rev. xxi. 8, 'But the fearful and unbelieving, &c., shall have their part in the lake which burneth with fire and brimstone, which is the second death.' 'If ye believe not that I am he,' saith Christ, 'you shall die in your sins,' John viii. 24. And he that dies in his sins must to judgment and to hell in his sins. Every unbeliever is a condemned man: 'He that believeth not,' saith John, 'is condemned already, because he hath not believed in the name of the only begotten Son of God. And he that believeth not the Son, shall not see life, but the wrath of God abideth on him,' John iii. 18, 36. Ah, sinners! the law, the gospel, and your own consciences, have passed the sentence of condemnation upon you, and there is no way to reverse the sentence but by believing in Christ. And therefore my counsel is this, Stir up yourselves to lay hold on the Lord Jesus, and look up to him, and wait on him, from whom every good and perfect gift comes, and give him no rest till he hath given thee that jewel faith, that is more worth than heaven and earth, and that will make thee happy in life, joyful in death, and glorious in the day of Christ, Isa. lxiv. 7, James i. 17, Isa. lxii. 7.

And thus much for the remedies against this first device of Satan, whereby he keeps off thousands from believing in Christ.

The second device that Satan hath to keep poor sinners from believing, from closing with a Saviour, is,

Device (2). *By suggesting to them their unworthiness.* Ah! saith Satan, as thou art worthy of the greatest misery, so thou art unworthy of the least crumb of mercy. What! dost thou think, saith Satan, that ever Christ will own, receive, or embrace such an unworthy wretch as thou art? No, no; if there were any worthiness in thee, then, indeed, Christ might be willing to be entertained by thee. Thou art unworthy to entertain Christ into thy house, how much more unworthy art thou to entertain Christ into thy heart, &c.

Now the remedies against this device are these.

Remedy (1). The first remedy against this device of Satan is, seriously to consider, *That God hath nowhere in the Scripture required any worthiness in the creature before believing in Christ.* If you make a diligent search through all the scripture, you shall not find, from the first line in Genesis to the last line in the Revelations, one word that speaks out God's requiring any worthiness in the creature before the soul's believing in Christ, before the soul's leaning and resting upon Christ for happiness and blessedness; and why, then, should that be a bar and hindrance to thy faith, which God doth nowhere require of thee before thou comest to Christ, that thou mayest have life? Mat. xix. 8, John v. 29. Ah, sinners! remember Satan objects your unworthiness against you only out of a design to keep Christ and your souls asunder for ever; and therefore, in the face of all your unworthiness, rest upon Christ, come to Christ, believe in Christ, and you are happy for ever, John vi. 40, 47.

Remedy (2). The second remedy against this device of Satan is, wisely to consider, *That none ever received Christ, embraced Christ, and obtained mercy and pardon from Christ, but unworthy souls.* Pray, what worthiness was in Matthew, Zaccheus, Mary Magdalene, Manasseh, Paul, and Lydia, before their coming to Christ, before their faith in Christ? Surely none. Ah, sinners! you should reason thus: Christ hath bestowed the choicest mercies, the greatest favours, the highest dignities, the sweetest privileges, upon unworthy sinners, and therefore, O our souls, do not you faint, do not you despair, but patiently and quietly wait for the salvation of the Lord. Who can tell but that free grace and mercy may shine forth upon us, though we are unworthy, and give us a portion among those worthies that are now triumphing in heaven.

Remedy (3). The third remedy against this device of Satan is, *That if the soul will keep off from Christ till it be worthy, it will never close with Christ,* it will never embrace Christ. It will never be one with Christ, it must lie down in everlasting sorrow, Isa. l. 11. God hath laid up all worthiness in Christ, that the creature may know where to find it, and may make out after it. There is no way on earth to make unworthy souls worthy, but by believing in Christ, James ii. 23. Believing in Christ, of slaves, it will make you worthy sons; of enemies, it will make you worthy friends. God will count none worthy, nor call none worthy, nor carry it towards none as worthy, but believers, who are made worthy by the worthiness of Christ's person, righteousness, satisfaction, and intercession, &c., Rev. iii. 4.

Remedy (4). The fourth remedy against this device of Satan is solemnly to consider, *That if you make a diligent search into your own hearts, you shall find that it is the pride and folly of your own hearts that puts you upon bringing of a worthiness to Christ.* Oh! you would fain bring something to Christ that might render you acceptable to him; you are loath to come empty-handed. The Lord cries out, 'Ho, every one that thirsteth, come ye to the waters, and he that hath no money: come ye, buy and eat; yea, come, buy wine and milk without money, and without price. Wherefore do ye spend your money upon that which is not bread, and your labour for that which satisfieth not?' Isa. lv. 1, 2. Here the Lord calls upon moneyless, upon penniless souls, upon unworthy souls, to come and partake of his precious favours freely. But sinners are proud and foolish, and because they have no money, no worthiness to bring, they will not come, though he sweetly invites them. Ah, sinners! what is more just than that you should perish for ever, that prefer husks among swine before the milk and wine, the sweet and precious things of the gospel, that are freely and sweetly offered to you, &c. Well, sinners! remember this, it is not so much the sense of your unworthiness, as your pride, that keeps you off from a blessed closing with the Lord Jesus.

The third device that Satan hath to keep poor sinners from believing, from closing with a Saviour, is,

Device (3). *By suggesting to them the want of such and such preparations and qualifications.* Saith Satan, Thou art not prepared to entertain Christ; thou art not thus and thus humbled and justified; thou art not heart-sick of sin; thou hast not been under horrors and terrors as such and such; thou must stay till thou art prepared and qualified to receive the Lord Jesus, &c.

Now, the remedies against this device are these:

Remedy (1). The first remedy against this device of Satan is, solemnly to consider, *That such as have not been so and so prepared and qualified as Satan suggests, have received Christ, believed in Christ, and been saved by Christ.* Matthew was called, sitting at the receipt of custom, and there was such power went along with Christ's call, that made him to follow him, Mat. ix. 9. We read not of any horrors or terrors, &c., that he was under before his being called by Christ. Pray, what preparations and qualifications were found in Zaccheus, Paul, the jailor, and Lydia, before their conversion, Luke xix. 9, Acts xvi. 14, *seq.* God brings in some by the sweet and still voice of the gospel, and usually such that are thus brought into Christ are the sweetest, humblest, choicest, and fruitfullest Christians. God is a free agent to work by law or gospel, by smiles or frowns, by presenting hell or heaven to sinners' souls. God thunders from mount Sinai upon some souls, and conquers them by thundering. God speaks to others in a still voice, and by that conquers them. You that are brought to Christ by the law, do not you judge and condemn them that are brought to Christ by the gospel; and you that are brought to Christ by the gospel, do not you despise those that are brought to Christ by the law. Some are brought to Christ by fire, storms, and tempests, others by more easy and gentle gales of the Spirit. The Spirit is free in the works of conversion, and, as the wind, it blows when, where, and how it pleases, John iii. 8. Thrice happy are those souls that are brought to Christ, whether it be in a winter's night or in a summer's day.

Remedy (2). The second remedy against this device of Satan is, solemnly *To dwell upon these following scriptures, which do clearly evidence that poor sinners which are not so and so prepared and qualified to meet with Christ, to receive and embrace the Lord Jesus Christ, may, notwithstanding that, believe in Christ; and rest and lean upon him for happiness and blessedness, according to the gospel.* Read Prov. i. 20–33, and chap. viii. 1–11, and chap. ix. 1–6; Ezek. xvi. 1–14; John iii. 14–18, 36; Rev. iii. 15–20. Here the Lord Jesus Christ stands knocking at the Laodiceans' door; he would fain have them to sup with him, and that he might sup with them; that is, that they might have intimate communion and fellowship one with another.

Now, pray tell me, what preparations or qualifications had these Laodiceans to entertain Christ? Surely none; for they were lukewarm, they were 'neither hot nor cold,' they were 'wretched, and miserable, and poor, and blind, and naked;' and yet Christ, to shew his free grace and his condescending love, invites the very worst of sinners to open to him, though they were no ways so and so prepared or qualified to entertain him.

Remedy (3). The third remedy against this device of Satan is, seriously to consider, *That the Lord does not in all the Scripture require such and such preparations and qualifications before men come to Christ, before they believe in Christ, or entertain, or embrace the Lord Jesus.* Believing in Christ is the great thing that God presses upon sinners throughout the Scripture, as all know that know anything of Scripture.

Obj. But does not Christ say, 'Come unto me all ye that labour and are heavy laden, and I will give you rest'? Mat. xi. 28.

To this I shall give these three answers:

(1.) That though the invitation be to such that 'labour and are heavy laden,' yet the promise of giving rest, it is made over to 'coming,' to 'believing.'

(2.) I answer, that all this scripture proves and shews is, that such as labour under sin as under a heavy burden, and that are laden with the guilt of sin and sense of God's displeasure, ought to come to Christ for rest; but it doth not prove that only such must come to Christ, nor that all men must be thus burdened and laden with the sense of their sins and the wrath of God, before they come to Christ.

Poor sinners, when they are under the sense of sin and wrath of God, they are prone to run from creature to creature, and from duty to duty, and from ordinance to ordinance, to find rest; and if they could find it in any thing or creature, Christ should never hear of them; but here the Lord sweetly invites them: and to encourage them, he engages himself to give them rest: 'Come,' saith Christ, 'and I will give you rest.' I will not *shew* you rest, nor barely *tell* you of rest, but 'I will *give* you rest.' I am faithfulness itself, and cannot lie, 'I *will* give you rest.' I that have the greatest power to give it, the greatest will to give it, the greatest right to give it, 'Come, *laden sinners*, and I will give you rest.' Rest is the most desirable good, the most suitable good, and to you the greatest good. 'Come,' saith Christ, that is, 'believe in me, and I will give you rest;' I will give you peace with God, and peace with conscience; I will turn your storm into an everlasting calm; I will give you such rest, that the world can neither give to you nor take from you.

(3.) I answer, No one scripture speaks out the whole mind of God; therefore do but compare this one scripture with those several scriptures that are laid down in the second remedy last mentioned, and it will clearly appear, that though men are thus and thus burdened and laden with their sins and filled with horror and terror, if they may come to Christ, they may receive and embrace the Lord Jesus Christ.

Remedy (4). The fourth remedy against this device of Satan is, to consider, *That all that trouble for sin, all that sorrow, shame, and mourning which is acceptable to God, and delightful to God, and prevalent with God, flows from faith in Christ, as the stream doth from the fountain, as the branch doth from the root, as the effect doth from the cause.* Zech. xii. 10, 'They shall look on him whom they have pierced, and they shall mourn for him.' All gospel mourning flows from believing; they shall first look, and then mourn. All that know anything know this, that 'whatever is not of faith is sin,' Rom. xiv 33. Till men have faith in Christ, their best services are but glorious sins.

The fourth device that Satan hath to keep poor sinners from believing, from closing with a Saviour, is,

Device (4). *By suggesting to a sinner Christ's unwillingness to save.* It is true, saith Satan, Christ is able to save thee, but is he willing? Surely, though he is able, yet he is not willing to save such a wretch as thou art, that has trampled his blood under thy feet, and that has been in open rebellion against him all thy days, &c.

The remedy against this device of Satan is, briefly to consider these few things.

Remedy (1). *First, The great journey that he hath taken, from heaven to earth, on purpose to save sinners, doth strongly demonstrate his willingness to save them.* Mat. ix. 13, 'I came not to call the righteous, but sinners to repentance.' 1 Tim. i. 15, 'This is a faithful saying, and worthy of all acceptation, that Jesus Christ came into the world to save sinners, of whom I am chief.'

Secondly, His divesting himself of his glory in order to sinners' salvation, speaks out his willingness to save them. He leaves his Father's bosom, he puts off his glorious robes, and lays aside his glorious crown, and bids adieu to his glistering courtiers the angels; and all this he doth, that he may accomplish sinners' salvation.[1]

Thirdly, That sea of sin, that sea of wrath, that sea of trouble, that sea of blood that Jesus Christ waded through, that sinners might be pardoned, justified, reconciled, and saved, doth strongly evidence his willingness to save sinners, 1 Cor. v. 19, 20.

Fourthly, His sending his ambassadors, early and late, to woo and entreat sinners to be reconciled to him, doth with open mouth shew his readiness and willingness to save sinners.

Fifthly, His complaints against such as refuse him, and that turn their backs upon him, and that will not be saved by him, doth strongly declare his willingness to save them: John i. 11, 'He came to his own, and his own received him not.' So in John v. 40, 'But ye will not come to me, that ye may have life.'

Sixthly, The joy and delight that he takes at the conversion of sinners, doth demonstrate his willingness that they should be saved: Luke xv. 7, 'I say unto you, That likewise joy shall be in heaven over one sinner that repenteth, more than over ninety and nine just persons that need no repentance.' God the Father rejoiceth at the return of his prodigal son; Christ rejoices to see the travail of his soul; the Spirit rejoices that he hath another temple to dwell in; and the angels rejoice that they have another brother to delight in, &c., Isa. liii. 11.

The fifth device that Satan hath to keep poor sinners from believing, from closing with a Saviour, is,

Device (5). *By working a sinner to mind more the secret decrees and counsels of God, than his own duty.* What needest thou to busy thyself about receiving, embracing, and entertaining of Christ? saith

[1] From the cradle to the cross, his whole life was a life of sufferings.

Satan; if thou art elected, thou shalt be saved; if not, all that thou canst do will do thee no good. Nay, he will work the soul not only to doubt of its election, but to conclude that he is not elected, and therefore let him do what he can, he shall never be saved.

Now the remedies against this device are these:

Remedy (1). The first remedy against this device of Satan is, seriously to consider, *That all the angels in heaven, nor all the men on earth, nor all the devils in hell, cannot tell to the contrary, but that thou mayest be an elect person, a chosen vessel.* Thou mayest be confident of this, that God never made Satan one of his privy council, God never acquainted him with the names or persons of such that he hath set his love upon to eternity, &c.

Remedy (2). The second remedy against this device of Satan is, *To meddle with that which thou hast to do.* 'Secret things belong to the Lord, but revealed things belong to thee,' Deut. xxix. 29. Thy work, sinner, is, to be peremptory in believing, and in returning to the Lord; thy work is to cast thyself upon Christ, lie at his feet, to wait on him in his ways, and to give him no rest till he shall say, Sinner, I am thy portion, I am thy salvation, and nothing shall separate between thee and me.

Here followeth seven characters of false teachers, which let me add for a close, viz.:—

That Satan labours might and main, by false teachers, which are his messengers and ambassadors, to deceive, delude, and for ever undo the precious souls of men:[1] Jer. xxiii. 13, 'I have seen folly in the prophets of Samaria; they prophesied in Baal, and caused my people Israel to err;' Micah iii. 5, 'The prophets make my people to err.' They seduce them, and carry them out of the right way into by-paths and blind thickets of error, blasphemy, and wickedness, where they are lost for ever. 'Beware of false prophets, for they come to you in sheep's clothing, but inwardly they are ravening wolves,' Mat. vii. 15. These lick and suck the blood of souls: Philip. iii. 2, 'Beware of dogs, beware of evil workers, beware of the concision.' These kiss and kill; these cry, Peace, peace, till souls fall into everlasting flames, &c., Prov. vii.

Now, the best way to deliver poor souls from being deluded and destroyed by these messengers of Satan is, to discover them in their colours, that so, being known, poor souls may shun them, and fly from them as from hell itself.

Now you may know them by these characters following:

[1.] *The first character.* False teachers *are men-pleasers.*[2] They preach more to please the ear than to profit the heart: Isa. xxx. 10, 'Which say to the seers, See not; and to the prophets, Prophesy not unto us right things: speak to us smooth things; prophesy deceits.' Jer. v. 30, 31, 'A wonderful and horrible thing is committed in the land: the prophets prophesy falsely, and the priests bear rule by their means, and my people love to have it so. And what will you do in the end thereof?' They handle holy things rather with wit and dalliance than with fear and reverence. False teachers are soul-undoers. They

[1] Acts xx. 28–30, 2 Cor. xi. 13–15, Eph. iv. 14, 2 Tim. iii. 4–6, Titus i. 11, 12, 2 Peter ii. 18, 19.
[2] But so are not true teachers, Gal. i. 10, 1 Thes. ii. 1–4.

are like evil chirurgeons, that skin over the wound, but never heal it. Flattery undid Ahab and Herod, Nero and Alexander. False teachers are hell's greatest enrichers. *Non acerba, sed blanda,* Not bitter, but flattering words do all the mischief, said Valerian, the Roman emperor. Such smooth teachers are sweet soul-poisoners, &c., Jer. xxiii. 16, 17.[1]

[2.] *The second character.* False teachers *are notable in casting dirt, scorn, and reproach upon the persons, names, and credits of Christ's most faithful ambassadors.* Thus Korah, Dathan, and Abiram charged Moses and Aaron that they took too much upon them, seeing all the congregation was holy, Num. xvi. 3. You take too much state, too much power, too much honour, too much holiness upon you; for what are you more than others, that you take so much upon you? And so Ahab's false prophets fell foul on good Micaiah, paying of him with blows for want of better reasons, 1 Kings xxii. 10–26. Yea, Paul, that great apostle of the Gentiles, had his ministry undermined and his reputation blasted by false teachers: 'For his letters,' say they, 'are weighty and powerful, but his bodily presence is weak and contemptible,' 2 Cor. x. 10. They rather contemn him than admire him; they look upon him as a dunce rather than a doctor. And the same hard measure had our Lord Jesus from the Scribes and Pharisees, who laboured as for life to build their own credit upon the ruins of his reputation.[2] And never did the devil drive a more full trade this way than he does in these days, Mat. xxvii. 63. Oh! the dirt, the filth, the scorn that is thrown upon those of whom the world is not worthy. I suppose false teachers mind not that saying of Austin, *Quisquis volens detrahit famæ, nolens addit mercedi meæ,* He that willingly takes from my good name, unwillingly adds to my reward.

[3.] *The third character.* False teachers are *venters of the devices and visions of their own heads and hearts.*[3] Jer. xiv. 14, 'Then the Lord said unto me, The prophets prophesy lies in my name: I sent them not, neither have I commanded them, neither spake unto them: they prophesy unto you a false vision and divination, and a thing of nought, and the deceit of their heart;' chap. xxiii. 16, 'Thus saith the Lord of hosts, Hearken not unto the words of the prophets that prophesy unto you; they make you vain: they speak a vision of their own heart, and not out of the mouth of the Lord.' Are there not multitudes in this nation whose visions are but golden delusions, lying vanities, brain-sick phantasies? These are Satan's great benefactors, and such as divine jüstice will hang up in hell as the greatest malefactors, if the physician of souls do not prevent it, &c.

[4.] *The fourth character.* False teachers *easily pass over the great and weighty things both of law and gospel, and stand most upon those things that are of the least moment and concernment to the souls of men.*[4] 1 Tim. i. 5–7, 'Now the end of the commandment is charity

[1] Whilst an ass is stroked under the belly, you may lay on his back what burden you please.

[2] The proverb is, *Oculus et fama non patiuntur jocos,* a man's eye and his good name can bear no jests. Yea, and Lucian, that blasphemous atheist, termeth him the crucified cozener.

[3] Mat. xxiv. 4, 5, xi. 14, Titus i. 10, Rom. xvi. 18.

[4] Luther complained of such in his time as would strain at a gnat, and swallow a camel. This age is full of such teachers, such monsters. The high priest's spirit, Mat. xxiii. 24, lives and thrives in these days.

out of a pure heart, and of a good conscience, and of faith unfeigned; from which some having swerved, have turned aside unto vain jangling, desiring to be teachers of the law, and understand neither what they say nor whereof they affirm.' Mat. xxiii. 2, 3, 'Woe unto you, scribes and Pharisees, hypocrites! for ye pay tithe of mint, and anise and cummin, and have omitted the weightier matters of the law, judgment, mercy, and faith; these ought ye to have done, and not to leave the other undone.' False teachers are nice in the lesser things of the law, and as negligent in the greater. 1 Tim. vi. 3–5, 'If any man teach otherwise, and consent not to wholesome words, even the words of our Lord Jesus Christ, and to the doctrine which is according to godliness, he is proud, knowing nothing, but doting about questions and strife of words, whereof cometh envy, strife, railings, evil surmisings, perverse disputings of men of corrupt minds, and destitute of the truth, supposing that gain is godliness: from such withdraw thyself.' If such teachers are not hypocrites in grain, I know nothing, Rom. ii. 22. The earth groans to bear them, and hell is fitted for them, Mat. xxiv. 32.

[5.] *The fifth character.* False teachers *cover and colour their dangerous principles and soul-impostures with very fair speeches and plausible pretences, with high notions and golden expressions.* Many in these days are bewitched and deceived by the magnificent words, lofty strains, and stately terms of deceivers, viz. illumination, revelation, deification, fiery triplicity, &c. As strumpets paint their faces, and deck and perfume their beds, the better to allure and deceive simple souls,[1] so false teachers will put a great deal of paint and garnish upon their most dangerous principles and blasphemies, that they may the better deceive and delude poor ignorant souls. They know sugared poison goes down sweetly; they wrap up their pernicious, soul-killing pills in gold. Weigh the scriptures in the margin.[2]

In the days of Hadrian the emperor, there was one Ben-Cosbi gathered a multitude of Jews together, and called himself *Ben-cocuba*, the son of a star, applying that promise to himself, Num. xxiv. 17; but he proved *Bar-chosaba*, the son of a lie. And so will all false teachers, for all their flourishes prove at the last the sons of lies.

[6.] *The sixth character.* False teachers *strive more to win over men to their opinions, than to better them in their conversations.* Mat. xxiv. 17, 'Woe unto you, scribes and Pharisees, hypocrites! for ye compass sea and land to make one proselyte, and when he is made, ye make him twofold more the child of hell than yourselves.' They busy themselves most about men's heads. Their work is not to better men's hearts, and mend their lives; and in this they are very much like their father the devil, who will spare no pains to gain proselytes.[3]

[7]. *The seventh character.* False teachers *make merchandise of their followers:* 2 Peter ii. 1–3, 'But there were false prophets also among the people, even as there shall be false teachers among you, who privily shall bring in damnable heresies, even denying the Lord that bought them, and bring upon themselves swift destruction. And many shall

[1] Gal. vi. 12; 2 Cor. xi. 13–15; Rom. xvi. 17, 18; Mat. xvi. 6, 11, 12; vii. 15.

[2] See footnote *supra*.—G.

[3] For shame, says Epictetus to his Stoics; either live as Stoics, or leave off the name of Stoics. The application is easy.

follow their pernicious ways; by reason of whom the way of truth shall be evil spoken of. And through covetousness shall they with feigned words make merchandise of you: whose judgment now of a long time lingereth not, and their damnation slumbereth not.' They eye your goods more than your good; and mind more the serving of themselves, than the saving of your souls. So they may have your substance, they care not though Satan has your souls, Rev. xviii. 11–13. That they may the better pick your purse, they will hold forth such principles as are very indulgent to the flesh. False teachers are the great worshippers of the golden calf, Jer. vi. 13.[1]

Now, by these characters you may know them, and so shun them, and deliver your souls out of their dangerous snares; which that you may, my prayers shall meet yours at the throne of grace.

And now, to prevent objections, I shall lay down some propositions or conclusions concerning Satan and his devices, and then give you the reasons of the point, and so come to make some use and application of the whole to ourselves.

Propositions concerning Satan and his devices:

Proposition (1). The first proposition is this, *That though Satan hath his devices to draw souls to sin, yet we must be careful that we do not lay all our temptations upon Satan, that we do not wrong the devil, and father that upon him that is to be fathered upon our own base hearts.* I think that oftentimes men charge that upon the devil that is to be charged upon their own hearts. 'And the Lord said unto the woman, What is this that thou hast done? And the woman said, The serpent beguiled me, and I did eat,' Gen. iii. 13. Sin and shifting came into the world together.[2] This is no small baseness of our hearts, that they will be naught, ay, very naught, and yet will father that naughtiness upon Satan. Man hath an evil root within him; that were there no devil to tempt him, nor no wicked men in the world to entice him, yet that root of bitterness, that cursed sinful nature that is in him, would draw him to sin, though he knows beforehand that 'the wages of sin is eternal death,' Rom. vi. 23 'For out of the heart proceed evil thoughts, murders, adulteries, fornication, thefts, false witnesses, blasphemies,' Mat. xv. 19. The whole frame of man is out of frame. The understanding is dark, the will cross, the memory slippery, the affections crooked, the conscience corrupted, the tongue poisoned, and the heart wholly evil, only evil, and continually evil. Should God chain up Satan, and give him no liberty to tempt or entice the sons of men to vanity or folly, yet they would not, yet they could not but sin against him, by reason of that cursed nature that is in them, that will still be a-provoking them to those sins that will provoke and stir up the anger of God against them, Jude 15, 16. Satan hath only a persuading sleight, not an enforcing might. He may tempt us, but without ourselves he cannot conquer us; he may entice us, but without ourselves

[1] Crates threw his money into the sea, resolving to drown it, lest it should drown him. But false teachers care not who they drown, so they may have their money. [It may be well to distinguish above among the different persons of the name, as Crates of Thebes, son of Ascondus. Diog. Laërtius, vi. 85, 93, 96–98.—G.]

[2] *Cum primum nascimur in omni continuo pravitate versamur*, We are no sooner born, than buried in a bog of wickedness.—*Tully.*

he cannot hurt us. Our hearts carry the greatest stroke in every sin. Satan can never undo a man without himself; but a man may easily undo himself without Satan. Satan can only present the golden cup, but he hath no power to force us to drink the poison that is in the cup; he can only present to us the glory of the world, he cannot force us to fall down and worship him, to enjoy the world; he can only spread his snares, he hath no power to force us to walk in the midst of his snares. Therefore do the devil so much right, as not to excuse yourselves, by your accusing him, and laying the load upon him, that you should lay upon your own hearts.[1]

Prop. (2). The second proposition is, *That Satan hath a great hand and stroke in most sins.* It was Satan that tempted our first parents to rebellion; it was Satan that provoked David to number the people; it was Satan that put Peter upon rebuking Christ; therefore saith Christ, 'Get thee behind me, Satan;' it was Satan that put Cain upon murdering of righteous Abel, therefore it is that he is called 'a murderer from the beginning;' it was Satan that put treason into the heart of Judas against Christ, 'And supper being ended, the devil having put into the heart of Judas Iscariot, Simon's son, to betray him;' it was Satan that put Ananias upon lying, Peter said, 'Ananias, why hath Satan filled thine heart to lie to the Holy Ghost?'[2] As the hand of Joab was in the tale of the woman of Tekoah, so Satan's hand is usually in all the sins that men commit. Such is Satan's malice against God, and his envy against man, that he will have a hand one way or other in all the sins, though he knows that all the sins he provokes others to shall be charged upon him to his greater woe, and eternal torment.[3]

Ambrose brings in the devil boasting against Christ and challenging Judas as his own: 'He is not thine, Lord Jesus, he is mine; his thoughts beat for me; he eats with thee, but is fed by me; he takes bread from thee, but money from me; he drinks wine with thee, and sells thy blood to me.' Such is his malice against Christ, and his wrath and rage against man, that he will take all advantages to draw men to that, that may give him advantage to triumph over Christ and men's souls for ever.

Prop. (3). The third proposition is, *That Satan must have a double leave before he can do anything against us.* He must have leave from God, and leave from ourselves, before he can act anything against our happiness. He must have his commission from God, as you may see in the example of Job, Job i. 11, 12, ii. 3–5. Though the devil had malice enough to destroy him, yet he had not so much as power to touch him, till God gave him a commission.

They could not so much as enter into the swine without leave from Christ, Luke viii. 32. Satan would fain have combated with Peter, but this he could not do without leave. 'Satan hath desired to have you, to winnow you,' Luke xxii. 31. So Satan could never have overthrown Ahab and Saul, but by a commission from God, 1 Kings xxii. Ah! what a cordial, what a comfort should this be to the saints, that their

[1] Τὸ πυρ παρ' ἡμῶν δε φλοξ διαβολου σπομασα, the fire is our wood, though it be the devil's flame.—*Nazianzen.*

[2] Gen. iii. 1–5; 1 Chron. xxi. 1; Mat. xvi. 22, 23; John viii. 44, xiii. 2; Acts v. 3.—G.

[3] *Diabolus tentat, Deus probat.*—Tertullian.

greatest, subtlest, and watchfullest enemy cannot hurt nor harm them, without leave from him who is their sweetest Saviour, their dearest husband, and their choicest friend.

And as Satan must have leave from God, so he must have leave of us. When he tempts, we must assent; when he makes offers, we must hearken; when he commands, we must obey, or else all his labour and temptations will be frustrate, and the evil that he tempts us to shall be put down only to his account.[1] That is a remarkable passage in Acts v. 3, 'Why hath Satan filled thy heart to lie to the Holy Ghost?' He doth not expostulate the matter with Satan; he doth not say, Satan, 'Why hast thou filled Ananias's heart to make him lie to the Holy Ghost?' but he expostulates the case with Ananias; Peter said, 'Ananias, why hath Satan filled *thine* heart to lie to the Holy Ghost?' Why hast thou given him an advantage to fill thy heart with infidelity, hypocrisy, and obstinate audacity, to lie to the Holy Ghost? As if he had said, Satan could never have done this in thee, which will now for ever undo thee, unless thou hadst given him leave. If, when a temptation comes, a man cries out, and saith, Ah, Lord! here is a temptation that would force me, that would deflower my soul, and I have no strength to withstand it; oh! help! help! for thy honour's sake, for thy Son's sake, for thy promise' sake; it is a sign that Satan hath not gained your consent, but committed a rape upon your souls, which he shall dearly pay for.[2]

Prop. (4). The fourth proposition is, *That no weapons but spiritual weapons will be useful and serviceable to the soul in fighting and combating with the devil.* This the apostle shews: 'Wherefore take unto you,' saith he, 'the whole armour of God, that ye may be able to stand in the evil day, and having done all, to stand,' Eph. vi. 13. So the same apostle tells you, 'That the weapons of your warfare are not carnal, but mighty through God, to the casting down of strongholds,' 2 Cor. x. 4. You have not to do with a weak, but with a mighty enemy, and therefore you had need to look to it, that your weapons are mighty, and that they cannot be, unless they are spiritual. Carnal weapons have no might nor spirit in them towards the making of a conquest upon Satan.[3] It was not David's sling nor stone that gave him the honour and advantage of setting his feet upon Goliah, but his faith in the name of the Lord of hosts. 'Thou comest to me with a sword, with a spear, and with a shield, but I am come to thee in the name of the Lord of hosts, the God of the armies of Israel, whom thou hast defied,' 1 Sam. xvii. 45. He that fights against Satan, in the strength of his own resolutions, constitution or education, will certainly fly and fall before him. Satan will be too hard for such a soul, and lead him captive at his pleasure. The only way to stand, conquer, and triumph, is still to plead, 'It is written,' as Christ did, Mat. iv. 10. There is no sword but the two-edged sword of the Spirit, that will be

[1] *Adversaria potestas non habet vim cogendi sed persuadendi.*—Isidore.

[2] They are the worst and greatest liars who pretend religion, and the Spirit, and yet are acted only by carnal principles to carnal ends.

[3] We read of many that, out of greatness of spirit, could offer violence to nature, but were at a loss when they came to deal with a corruption or a temptation. Heraclitus [Heraclius] his motto was, *A Deo victoria*, It is God that gives victory; and that should be every Christian's motto.

found to be metal of proof when a soul comes to engage against Satan; therefore, when you are tempted to uncleanness, plead, 'It is written, be ye holy, as I am holy,' 1 Peter i. 16; and, 'Let us cleanse ourselves from all filthiness of the flesh and spirit, perfecting holiness in the fear of the Lord,' 2 Cor. vii. 1. If he tempts you to distrust God's providence and fatherly care of you, plead, 'It is written,' 'They that fear the Lord shall want nothing that is good,' Ps. xxxiv. 9.

It is written, 'The Lord will give grace and glory, and no good thing will he withhold from them that purely live,' Ps. lxxxiv. 11. If he tempt you to fear, that you shall faint, and fall, and never be able to run to the end of the race that is set before you, plead, It is written, 'The righteous shall hold on his way, and he that hath clean hands shall be stronger and stronger,' Job xvii. 9.

It is written, 'I will make an everlasting covenant with them, that I will not turn away from them, to do them good, but I will put my fear in their hearts, that they may not depart from me,' Jer. xxxii. 40.

It is written, 'They that wait upon the Lord, they shall renew their strength; they shall mount up with wings as eagles; they shall run, and not be weary; and they shall walk, and not faint,' Isa. xl. 31. If Satan tempt you to think that because your sun for the present is set in a cloud, that therefore it will rise no more, and that the face of God will shine no more upon you; that your best days are now at an end, and that you must spend all your time in sorrow and sighing; plead, It is written, 'He will turn again, he will have compassion upon us, and cast all our sins into the depth of the sea,' Micah vii. 19.

It is written, 'For a small moment have I forsaken thee, but with great mercies will I gather thee. In a little wrath I hid my face from thee for a moment, but with everlasting kindness will I have mercy on thee, saith the Lord, thy Redeemer,' Isa. liv. 7, 8, 10.

It is written, 'The mountains shall depart, and the hills be removed, but my kindness shall not depart from thee, neither shall the covenant of my peace be removed, saith the Lord that hath mercy on thee.'

It is written, 'Can a woman forget her sucking child, that she should not have compassion on the son of her womb? Yea, they may forget, yet will not I forget thee. Behold, I have graven thee upon the palms of my hands, thy walls are continually before me,' Isa. xlix. 15, 16.

If ever you would be too hard for Satan, and after all your assaults, have your bow abide in strength, then take to you the word of God, which is 'the two-edged sword of the Spirit, and the shield of faith, whereby you shall be able to quench the fiery darts of the devil,' Eph. vi. 17. It is not spitting at Satan's name, nor crossing yourselves, nor leaning to your own resolutions, that will get you the victory.

Luther reports of Staupitius, a German minister, that he acknowledged himself, that before he came to understand aright the free and powerful grace of God, that he vowed and resolved an hundred times against some particular sin, and never could get power over it. At last he saw the reason to be his trusting to his own resolution. Therefore be skilful in the word of righteousness, and in the actings of faith upon Christ and his victory, and that crown of glory that is set before you, and Satan will certainly fly from you, &c., James iv. 7.

Prop. (5). The fifth proposition is, *That we may read much of Satan's nature and disposition by the divers names and epithets that are given him in the Scripture.* Sometimes he is called Behemoth, which is *Bruta*, whereby the greatness and brutishness of the devil is figured, Job xl. 15. Those evil spirits are sometimes called Διαβολοι, *accusers*, for their calumnies and slanders; and πονηροι, *evil ones*, for their malice. Satan is *Adversarius*, an adversary, that troubleth and molesteth, 1 Pet. v. 8. *Abaddon* is a destroyer. They are *tempters*, for their suggestion; *lions*, for their devouring; *dragons*, for their cruelty; and *serpents*, for their subtilty, &c. As his names are, so is he; as face answers to face, so do Satan's names answer to his nature. He hath the worst names and the worst nature of all created creatures, &c.

Prop. (6). The sixth proposition is, *That God will shortly tread down Satan under the saints' feet.* Christ, our champion, hath already won the field, and will shortly set our feet upon the necks of our spiritual enemies. Satan is a foiled adversary. Christ hath led him captive, and triumphed over him upon the cross. Christ hath already overcome him, and put weapons into your hands, that you may overcome him also, and set your feet upon his neck. Though Satan be a roaring lion, yet Christ, who is the lion of the tribe of Judah, will make Satan fly and fall before you. Let Satan do his worst, yet you shall have the honour and the happiness to triumph over him.[1] Cheer up, you precious sons of Sion, for the certainty and sweetness of victory will abundantly recompense you for all the pains you have taken in making resistance against Satan's temptations. The broken horns of Satan shall be trumpets of our triumph and the cornets of our joy, &c.

Now I shall come to the reasons of the point, and so draw to a close, &c.

Reason (1). The first reason is, *That their hearts may be kept in an humble, praying, watching frame.* Oh! hath Satan so many devices to ensnare and undo the souls of men? How should this awaken dull, drowsy souls, and make them stand upon their watch! A saint should be like a seraphim, beset all over with eyes and lights, that he may avoid Satan's snares, and stand fast in the hour of temptation.

The Lord hath in the Scripture discovered the several snares, plots, and devices that the devil hath to undo the souls of men, that so, being forewarned, they may be forearmed; that they may be always upon their watch-tower, and hold their weapons in their hands, as the Jews did in Nehemiah's time.[2]

Reason (2). The second reason is, *From that malice, envy, and enmity that is in Satan against the souls of men.* Satan is full of envy and enmity, and that makes him very studious to suit his snares and plots to the tempers, constitutions, fancies, and callings of men, that so he may make them as miserable as himself.[3]

The Russians are so malicious, that you shall have a man hide some of

[1] Rom. xvi. 20, συντρίψει, from συντρίβω. The Greek word signifies to break or crush a thing to pieces. Being applied to the feet, it noteth that breaking or crushing which is by stamping upon a thing.

[2] The philosopher had a ball of brass in his hand, which, if he chanced to sleep with, the fall into a basin awaked him to his studies. You are wise, and know how to apply it.

[3] Malice cares not what it saith or doth, so it may kill or gall.

his own goods in the house of him whom he hateth, and then accuse him for the stealth of them.[1] So doth Satan, out of malice to the souls of men, hide his goods, his wares, as I may say, in the souls of men, and then go and accuse them before the Lord; and a thousand, thousand other ways Satan's malice, envy, and enmity puts him upon, eternally to undo the precious souls of men, &c.

Reason (3). The third reason is drawn from *that long experience that Satan hath had.* He is a spirit of mighty abilities; and his abilities to lay snares before us are mightily increased by that long standing of his. He is a spirit of above five thousand years' standing. He hath had time enough to study all those ways and methods which tend most to ensnare and undo the souls of men. And as he hath time enough, so he hath made it his whole study, his only study, his constant study, to find out snares, depths, and stratagems, to entangle and overthrow the souls of men. When he was but a young serpent, he did easily deceive and outwit our first parents, Gen. iii.; but now he is grown that 'old serpent,' as John speaks, Rev. xii. 9, he is as old as the world, and is grown very cunning by experience.

Reason (4). The fourth reason is, *In judgment to the men of the world, that they may stumble and fall, and be ensnared for ever.* Wicked men that withstand the offers of mercy, and despise the Spirit of grace, that will not open, though God knocks never so hard by his word and rod, by his Spirit and conscience, are given up by a hand of justice, to be hardened, deceived, and ensnared by Satan, to their everlasting ruin, 1 Kings xxii. 23. And what can be more just than that they should be taken and charmed with Satan's wiles, who have frequently refused to be charmed by the Spirit of grace, though he hath charmed never so wisely, and never so sweetly, &c.?

Reason (5). The fifth reason is, *That the excellency and power of God's grace may be more illustrated and manifested, by making men able to grapple with this mighty adversary, and that notwithstanding all the plots, devices, and stratagems of Satan, yet he will make them victorious here, and crown them with glory hereafter.* The greater and the subtler the enemies of the children of Israel were, the more did divine power, wisdom, and goodness, sparkle and shine; and that, notwithstanding all their power, plots, and stratagems, &c., yet to Canaan he would bring them at last. When Paul had weighed this, he sits down and glories in his infirmities and distresses and Satan's buffetings, that the power of Christ might rest upon him, 2 Cor. xii. 7–9.

The use of the point.

If Satan hath such a world of devices and stratagems to ensnare and undo the souls of men, then, instead of wondering that so few are saved, sit down and wonder that any are saved, that any escape the snares of this cunning fowler, who spreads his nets and casts forth his baits in all places, in all cases and companies.

But this is not the main thing that I intend to speak to; my main business shall be, to set before you some special rules and helps against all his devices.

[1] An envious heart and plotting head are inseparable companions.

The first help. If you would not be taken by any of Satan's devices, then *walk by rule.*[1] He that walks by rule, walks most safely; he that walks by rule, walks most honourably; he that walks by rule, walks most sweetly. When men throw off the word, then God throws off them, and then Satan takes them by the hand, and leads them into snares at his pleasure. He that thinks himself too good to be ruled by the word, will be found too bad to be owned by God; and if God do not, or will not own him, Satan will by his stratagems overthrow him. Them that keep to the rule, they shall be kept in the hour of temptation. 'Because thou hast kept the word of my patience, I also will keep thee from the hour of temptation, which shall come upon all the world, to try them that dwell upon the earth,' Rev. iii. 10.

The second help. As you would not be taken with any of Satan's devices, *take heed of vexing and grieving the Holy Spirit of God.*[2] It is the Spirit of the Lord Jesus Christ that is best able to discover Satan's snares against us; it is only he that can point out all his plots, and discover all his methods, and enable men to escape those pits that he hath digged for their precious souls. Ah! if you set that sweet and blessed Spirit a-mourning, that alone can secure you from Satan's depths, by whom will you be secured? Man is a weak creature, and no way able to discover Satan's snares, nor to avoid them, unless the Spirit of the Lord gives skill and power; therefore, whoever be grieved, be sure the Spirit be not grieved by your enormities, nor by your refusing the cordials and comforts that he sets before you, nor by slighting and despising his gracious actings in others, nor by calling sincerity hypocrisy, faith fancy, &c., nor by fathering those things upon the Spirit, that are the brats and fruits of your own hearts.[3] The Spirit of the Lord is your counsellor, your comforter, your upholder, your strengthener. It is only the Spirit that makes a man too great for Satan to conquer. 'Greater is he that is in you, than he that is in the world,' 1 John iv. 4.

The third help. If you would not be taken with any of Satan's devices, then *labour for more heavenly wisdom.*[4] Ah, souls! you are much in the dark, you have but a little to that others have, and to that you might have had, had you not been wanting to yourselves. There are many knowing souls, but there are but a few wise souls. There is oftentimes a great deal of knowledge, where there is but a little wisdom to improve that knowledge. Knowledge without wisdom is like mettle in a blind horse, which often is an occasion of the rider's fall, and of his bones being jostled against the walls.[5] It is not the most knowing Christian, but the most wise Christian, that sees, avoids, and escapes Satan's snares. 'The way of life is above to the wise,' saith Solomon, 'that he may depart from hell beneath,' Prov. xv. 24. Heavenly wisdom makes a man delight to fly high; and the higher any man flies, the more he is out of the reach of Satan's snares.[6] Ah, souls! you

[1] Prov. xii. 24; Gal. vi. 16.

[2] *Spiritus sanctus est res delicata*, the Divine Spirit is a very tender thing: if you grieve him, he will certainly grieve and vex your precious souls, Lam. i. 16.

[3] Isa. lxiii. 10; Ps. lxxiii. 28; 1 Thes. v. 19; Acts ii. 18.

[4] If men could but see the fair face of wisdom with mortal eyes, they would be in love with her, saith Plato.

[5] *Sine prudentia simplicitas stultitia est.*—Drusius.

[6] *Malim prudentiæ guttam quam fœcundioris fortunæ pelagus*, said Nazianzen. A serpent's eye is a singular ornament in a dove's head.

had need of a great deal of heavenly wisdom, to see where and how Satan lays his baits and snares; and wisdom to find out proper remedies against his devices, and wisdom to apply those remedies seasonably, inwardly, and effectually to your own hearts, that so you may avoid the snares which that evil one hath laid for your precious souls.

The fourth help. If you would not be taken with any of Satan's devices, then *make present resistance against Satan's first motions.* It is safe to resist, it is dangerous to dispute. Eve disputes, and falls in paradise, Gen. iii.; Job resists, and conquers upon the dunghill. He that will play with Satan's bait, will quickly be taken with Satan's hook. The promise of conquest is made over to resisting, not to disputing: 'Resist the devil, and he will fly from you,' James iv. 7. Ah, souls! were you better at resisting than at disputing, though happily you were not very expert at either, your temptations would be fewer, and your strength to stand would be greater than now it is, &c.

The fifth help. If you would not be taken with any of Satan's devices, then *labour to be filled with the Spirit.* The Spirit of the Lord is a Spirit of light and power; and what can a soul do without light and power 'against spiritual wickedness in high places'? Eph. vi. 12. It is not enough that you have the Spirit, but you must be filled with the Spirit, or else Satan, that evil spirit, will be too hard for you, and his plots will prosper against you. That is a sweet word of the apostle, 'Be filled with the Spirit, Eph. v. 18;[1] *i.e.* labour for abundance of the Spirit. He that thinks he hath enough of the Holy Spirit, will quickly find himself vanquished by the evil spirit. Satan hath his snares to take you in prosperity and adversity, in health and sickness, in strength and weakness, when you are alone and when you are in company, when you come on to spiritual duties and when you come off from spiritual duties, and if you are not filled with the Spirit, Satan will be too hard and too crafty for you, and will easily and frequently take you in his snares, and make a prey of you in spite of your souls. Therefore labour more to have your hearts filled with the Spirit than to have your heads filled with notions, your shops with wares, your chests with silver, or your bags with gold; so shall you escape the snares of this fowler, and triumph over all his plots, &c.[2]

The sixth help. If you would not be taken in any of Satan's snares, then *keep humble.* An humble heart will rather lie in the dust than rise by wickedness, and sooner part with all than the peace of a good conscience. Humility keeps the soul free from many darts of Satan's casting, and snares of his spreading; as the low shrubs are free from many violent gusts and blasts of wind, which shake and rend the taller trees. The devil hath least power to fasten a temptation on him that is most humble. He that hath a gracious measure of humility, is neither affected with Satan's proffers nor terrified with his threatenings.[3] I

[1] πληροῦσθε. To be filled with the Spirit, as the sails of a ship is filled with wind.

[2] Luther saith, a holy gluttony is to lay on, to feed hard, and to fetch hearty draughts, till they be even drunk with loves, and with the abundance of the Spirit. Oh that there were more such holy gluttony in the world!

[3] It is reported of Satan that he should say thus of a learned man, *Tu me semper vincis*, thou dost always overcome me; when I would exalt and promote thee, thou keepest thyself in humility; and when I would throw thee down, thou liftest up thyself in assurance of faith.

have read of one who, seeing in a vision many snares of the devil spread upon the earth, he sat down, and mourned, and said in himself, *Quis pertransiet ista?* who shall pass through these? whereunto he heard a voice answering, *Humilitas pertransiet*, humility shall. God hath said, that 'he will teach the humble,' and that 'he will dwell with the humble,' and that 'he will fill and satisfy the humble.'[1] And if the teachings of God, the indwellings of God, if the pourings in of God, will not keep the soul from falling into Satan's snares, I do not know what will. And therefore as you would be happy in resisting Satan, and blessed in triumphing over Satan and all his snares, keep humble; I say again, keep humble, &c.

The seventh help. If you would not be taken in any of Satan's snares, then *keep a strong, close, and constant watch*, 1 Thes. v. 6.[2] A secure soul is already an ensnared soul. That soul that will not watch against temptations, will certainly fall before the power of temptations. Satan works most strongly on the fancy when the soul is drowsy. The soul's security is Satan's opportunity to fall upon the soul and to spoil the soul, as Joshua did the men of Ai. The best way to be safe and secure from all Satan's assaults is, with Nehemiah and the Jews, to watch and pray, and pray and watch. By this means they became too hard for their enemies, and the work of the Lord did prosper sweetly in their hands. Remember how Christ chid his sluggish disciples, 'What! could you not watch with me one hour?' what, cannot you watch with me? how will you then die with me? if you cannot endure words, how will you endure wounds? &c. Satan always keeps a crafty and malicious watch, 'seeking whom he may devour (καταπίῃ), or whom he may drink or sip up, as the apostle speaks in that 1 Peter v. 8. Satan is very envious at our condition, that we should enjoy that paradise out of which he is cast, and out of which he shall be for ever kept.

Shall Satan keep a crafty watch, and shall not Christians keep a holy spiritual watch?[3] Our whole life is beset with temptations. Satan watches all opportunities to break our peace, to wound our consciences, to lessen our comforts, to impair our graces, to slur our evidences, and to damp our assurances, &c. Oh! what need then have we to be always upon our watch-tower, lest we be surprised by this subtle serpent. Watchfulness includes a waking, a rousing up of the soul. It is a continual, careful observing of our hearts and ways, in all the turnings of our lives, that we still keep close to God and his word.

Watchfulness is nothing else but the soul running up and down, to and fro, busy everywhere; it is the heart busied and employed with diligent observation of *quid inde*, what comes from within us, and of *quid inde*, what comes from without us and into us. Ah, souls! you are no longer safe and secure than when you are upon your watch. While Antipater kept the watch, Alexander was safe; and while we

[1] Ps. xxv. 9; Isa. lvii. 15; James iv. 6.

[2] We must not be like Agrippa's dormouse, that would not awake till cast into boiling lead, but effectually mind these following scriptures, wherein this duty of watchfulness is so strictly enjoined:—Mat. xxvi. 40; Mark xiii. 33, 34, 35, 37; 1 Cor. xvi. 13; Col. iv. 2; 1 Peter iv. 7; Rev. ii. 3.

[3] Hannibal never rested, whether he did conquer or was conquered. It is so with Satan. Learn, for shame of the devil, said blessed Latimer, to watch, seeing the devil is so watchful.

keep a strict watch, we are safe. A watchful soul is a soul upon the wing, a soul out of gun-shot, a soul upon a rock, a soul in a castle, a soul above the clouds, a soul held fast in everlasting arms.

I shall conclude this seventh head with this advice, Remember the dragon is subtle, and bites the elephant's ear, and then sucks his blood, because he knows that to be the only place which the elephant cannot reach with his trunk to defend; so our enemies are so subtle, that they will bite us, and strike us where they may most mischief us, and therefore it doth very much concern us to stand always upon our guard.

The eighth help. If you would not be taken with any of Satan's snares and devices, then *keep up your communion with God.*[1] Your strength to stand and withstand Satan's fiery darts is from your communion with God. A soul high in communion with God may be tempted, but will not easily be conquered. Such a soul will fight it out to the death. Communion with God furnisheth the soul with the greatest and the choicest arguments to withstand Satan's temptations. Communion is the result of union. Communion is a reciprocal exchange between Christ and a gracious soul. Communion is Jacob's ladder, where you have Christ sweetly coming down into the soul, and the soul, by divine influences, sweetly ascending up to Christ. Communion with Christ is very inflaming, raising and strengthening. While Samson kept up his communion with God, no enemy could stand before him, but he goes on conquering and to conquer; but when he was fallen in his communion with God, he quickly falls before the plots of his enemies. It will be so with your souls. So long as your communion with God is kept up, you will be too hard for 'spiritual wickedness in high places;' but if you fall from your communion with God, you will fall, as others, before the face of every temptation.[2] David, so long as he kept up his communion with God, he stands, and triumphs over all his enemies; but when he was fallen in his communion with God, then he falls before the enemies that were in his own bosom, and flies before those that pursued after his life. It will be so with your souls, if you do not keep up your communion with God. Job keeps up his communion with God, and conquers Satan upon the dunghill; Adam loses his communion with God, and is conquered by Satan in paradise. Communion with God is a shield upon land, as well as an anchor at sea; it is a sword to defend you, as well as a staff to support you; therefore keep up your communion.

The ninth help. If you would not be taken in any of Satan's snares, then *engage not against Satan in your own strength, but be every day drawing new virtue and strength from the Lord Jesus.*[3] Certainly that soul that engages against any old or new temptation without

[1] 1 Cor. vi. 19. The words are very significant in the original. There are two *ins*, as though God could never have near enough communion with them.

[2] The sea ebbs and flows, the moon increases and decreases; so it is with saints in their communion with God. Plutarch tells of Eudoxus, that he would be willing to be burnt up presently by the sun, so he might be admitted to come so near it as to learn the nature of it. What! should not we be content to suffer for the keeping up communion with Christ?—[Eudoxus: Delambre, *Hist. Astron. Anc.*, I. 107.—G.]

[3] There is a remarkable saying of Moses, Exod. xv., God is *fortitudo mea, et laus mea, et salus mea*, my strength, and my praise, and my salvation, all in the abstract. It is but look up and live; look unto me, and be saved, from the ends of the earth, Isa. xlv. 22.

new strength, new influences from on high, will fall before the power of the temptation. You may see this in Peter; he rested upon some old received strength—'Though all men should deny thee, yet will not I,' Mat. xxvi. 35—and therefore he falls sadly before a new temptation. He curses and swears, and denies him thrice, that had thrice appeared gloriously to him. Ah, souls! when the snare is spread, look up to Jesus Christ, who is lifted up in the gospel, as the brazen serpent was in the wilderness, and say to him, Dear Lord! here is a new snare laid to catch my soul, and grace formerly received, without fresh supplies from thy blessed bosom, will not deliver me from this snare. Oh! give me new strength, new power, new influences, new measures of grace, that so I may escape the snares. Ah, souls! remember this, that your strength to stand and overcome must not be expected from graces received, but from the fresh and renewed influences of heaven.[1] You must lean more upon Christ than upon your duties; you must lean more upon Christ than upon spiritual tastes and discoveries; you must lean more upon Christ than upon your graces, or else Satan will lead you into captivity, &c.

The tenth help. If you would not be taken in any of Satan's snares, then *be much in prayer.* Prayer is a shelter to the soul; a sacrifice to God and a scourge to the devil. David's heart was oft more out of tune than his harp. He prays, and then, in spite of the devil, cries, 'Return unto thy rest, O my soul.' Prayer is *porta cœli, clavis paradisi,* the gate of heaven, a key to let us into paradise. There is nothing that renders plots fruitless like prayer; therefore saith Christ, 'Watch and pray that ye enter not into temptation,' Mat. xxvi. 41. You must watch and pray, and pray and watch, if you would not enter into temptation.[2] When Sennacherib and Haman had laid plots and snares to have destroyed the Jews, they prayed, and their souls were delivered, and Sennacherib and Haman destroyed. David had many snares laid for him, and this puts him upon prayer. 'Keep me,' saith he, 'from the snares which they have laid for me, and the gins of the workers of iniquity.' 'Let the wicked fall into their own nets, whilst that I escape,' Ps. cxli. 9, 10. 'The proud,' saith he, 'have hid a snare for me, and cords: they have spread a net by the wayside; they have set gins for me. Selah. I said unto the Lord, Thou art my God: hear the voice of my supplication, O Lord!' Ps. cxl. 5, 6. Saul and many others had laid snares for David, and this puts him upon prayer, and so the snares are broken and he is delivered.[3] Ah, souls! take words to yourselves, and tell God that Satan hath spread his snares in all places and in all companies; tell God that he digs deep, and that he hath plot upon plot, and device upon device, and all to undo you; tell God that you have neither skill nor power to escape his snares; tell God that it is a work too high and too hard for any created creature to work your

[1] John xv. 5, χωρὶς ἐμοῦ, is *seorsim a me*, separate from me, or apart from me, ye can do nothing.

[2] Of Carolus Magnus it was spoken, *Carolus plus cum Deo quam cum hominibus loquitur*, that he spake more with God than with men. Ah! that I could say so of the Christians in our days.

[3] *Nunquam abs te, absque te recedo.*—Bernard. O Lord! saith he, I never go away from thee, without thee. Let us, saith Basil, with a holy impudence, make God ashamed, that he cannot look us in the face, if he do deny our importunity: Jacob-like, 'I will not let thee go, unless thou bless me.'

deliverance, unless he put under his own everlasting arms; tell God how his honour is engaged to stand by you, and to bring you off, that you be not ruined by his plots; tell God how the wicked would triumph, if you should fall into Satan's snares; tell God of the love of Christ, of the blood of Christ, and of the intercession of Christ for you, that a way may be found for your escape; tell God if he will make it his honour to save you from falling into Satan's snares, you will make it your glory to speak of his goodness and to live out his kindness. Christians must do as Dædalus, that when he could not escape by a way upon earth, went by a way of heaven,[1] and that is, the way of prayer, which is the only way left to escape Satan's snares, &c.

Use. The next use is a use *of thankfulness to those that escape Satan's snares, that are not taken by him at his will.* Ah! Christians, it stands upon you with that princely prophet David, to call upon your souls, and say, 'Bless the Lord, O our souls; and all that is within us, bless his holy name! Bless the Lord, O our souls, and forget not all his benefits!' Ps. ciii. 1, 2; who hath not given us to be a prey to Satan, and to be ensnared by those snares that he hath laid for our souls. The sense of this great favour did work up David's heart to praises: 'Blessed be the Lord,' saith he, 'who hath not given us a prey to their teeth. Our soul is escaped as a bird out of the snares of the fowlers: the snare is broken, and we are escaped,' Ps. cxxiv. 7. Ah! Christians, remember that the greatest part of the world, yea, the greatest part of professors, are taken in Satan's snares. Can you think seriously of this, and not blush to be unthankful? What are you better than others? and what have ye deserved of God, or done for God more than others, that you should by the help of a divine hand escape the snares, when others are taken and held in the snares of the devil to their eternal overthrow? &c.

Will you be thankful for the escaping the snares that men spread for your lives or estates, &c., and will you not be much more thankful for escaping those snares that Satan hath laid for your precious souls? Ps. lxxi. 14.[2]

Remember this, that deliverance from Satan's snares doth carry with it the clearest and the greatest evidence of the soul and heart of God to be towards us. Many a man by a common hand of providence escapes many a snare that man hath laid for him, but yet escapes not the snares that Satan hath laid for him. Saul, and Judas, and Demas, doubtless escaped many snares that men had laid for them, but none of them escaped the snares that the devil had laid for them. Many men are lifted up above the snares of men by a common hand of providence, that are left to fall into the snares of the devil by a hand of justice; your deliverance from Satan's snares is a fruit of special love. Can you thus look upon it and not be thankful, O precious soul? I judge not.

Use. The last use of this point is, *To bespeak Christians to long to be at home.*[3] Oh! long to be in the bosom of Christ! long to be in the

[1] The well-known legend of the 'wax-fixed wings' of Dædalus and Icarus.—G.

[2] The ancients use to say, *Ingratum dixeris, omnia dixeris*, say a man is unthankful, and say he is anything. Ps. lxxi. 14, 'I will yet praise thee more and more.' In the original it is, I will add to thy praise. The stork is said to leave one of her young ones where she hatcheth them; and the elephant to turn up the first sprig toward heaven, when he cometh to feed, out of some instinct of gratitude. Ah! souls, that these may not bear witness against you in the day of Christ.

[3] Austin wished that he might have seen three things: Rome flourishing, Paul preach-

land of Canaan! for this world, this wilderness, is full of snares, and all employments are full of snares, and all enjoyments are full of snares. In civil things, Satan hath his snares to entrap us; and in all spiritual things, Satan hath his snares to catch us. All places are full of snares, city and country, shop and closet, sea and land; and all our mercies are surrounded with snares. There are snares about our tables and snares about our beds, &c.; yea, Satan is so powerful and subtle that he will oftentimes make our greatest, nearest, and dearest mercies to become our greatest snares. Sometimes he will make the wife that lies in the bosom to be a snare to a man, as Samson's was, and as Job's was. Sometimes he will make the child to be a snare, as Absalom was and Eli's sons were; and sometimes he will make the servant to be a snare, as Joseph was to his mistress. Ah! souls, Satan is so cunning and artificial[1] that he can turn your cups into snares, and your clothes into snares, and your houses into snares, and your gardens into snares, and all your recreations into snares, &c. And oh! how should the consideration of these things work all your souls to say with the church, 'Make haste, my beloved, and be like a roe, or a young hart upon the mountain of spices,' and to love, and look, and long for the coming of Christ, Cant. viii. 14.[2] Shall the espoused maid long for the marriage day? the servant for his freedom? the captive for his ransom? the traveller for his inn? and the mariner for his harbour? and shall not the people of the Lord long much more to be in the bosom of Christ? there being nothing below the bosom of Christ that is not surrounded with Satan's snares, Philip. i. 23, and 2 Cor. v. 2, 4.

What Paul once spake of bonds and afflictions, that they attended him in every place, Acts xx. 23, that may all the saints say of Satan's snares, that they attend them in every place, which should cause them to cry out, *Migremus hinc, migremus hinc*, let us go hence, let us go hence; and to say with Monica, Austin's mother, What do we here? why depart we not hence? why fly we no swifter?[3] Ah! souls, till you are taken up into the bosom of Christ, your comforts will not be full, pure, and constant; till then, Satan will still be thumping of you, and spreading snares to entangle you; therefore you should always be crying out with the church, 'Come, Lord Jesus!' Rev. xxii. 20. Is not Christ the star of Jacob, that 'giveth light to them that are in darkness?' that Prince of peace who brings the olive branch to souls that are perplexed? Is not the greatest worth and wealth in him? Is not the petty excellencies and perfections of all created creatures epitomized in him? Is not he the crown of crowns, the glory of glories, and the heaven of heavens? Oh then, be still a-longing after a full, clear, and constant enjoyment of Christ in heaven; for till then, Satan will still have plots and designs upon you. He acts by an united[4] power, and will never let you rest till you are taken up to an everlasting rest in the bosom of Christ.[5]

ing, and Christ conversing with men upon the earth. Bede comes after, and, correcting this last wish, saith, Yea, but let me see the King in his beauty, Christ in his heavenly kingdom.

[1] 'Artful.'—G. [2] ברח דודי, *berach dodi*; flee away speedily, my beloved.

[3] Quid hic faciamus? cur non ocius migramus? cur non hinc avolamus?

[4] Qu. 'untired'?—G.

[5] It is as easy to compass the heavens with a span, and contain the sea in a nutshell, as to relate fully Christ's excellencies, or heaven's happiness.

THE STATIONER TO THE READER.

CHRISTIAN READER,—I thought good to present to thy view this letter following, which came to my hands, being sent from one in Devonshire to his brother in London, returning him much thanks for this book, and declaring the great benefit he received by it, and the comfortable effects it wrought upon him,—and I may say, not upon him only, for I have heard of several others that have reaped much profit and comfort from it and the other works of this author's lately published,—through the Lord's blessing, to whom be ascribed all the glory. I was induced to publish it, that so others may be encouraged to a more serious perusal of this and other solid practical divinity books, which may tend to their eternal welfare.

For as there are good and bad men in the world, so there are many good and bad books, and our time is a precious thing. Therefore we ought to 'redeem it,' Eph. v. 15, 16, and improve it to our best advantage.[1] I deny not but there are many moral historical books extant of very good use, yet it is too apparent that there are divers vain, idle, amorous romances, lascivious and vicious poetry, and profane playbooks, which chiefly tend to the corruption of youth, the mis-spending their precious time, and undoing their immortal souls. As I have known some foolish, ignorant people that have made earnest inquiry for merry books to pass away the time, Honest Reader, let me advise thee, next to the Bible, let it be thy chief care, as thou art curious and careful for wholesome food, for the health and preservation of thy body, so be no less careful to make sound and solid divinity books thy chiefest study and delight; which will be most for thy profit and edification, especially if thou readest them not for notion-sake, only to know, but to practise; then, as in this following young man's example, thou mayest have cause to bless God, and to be thankful to the author or instrument of thy good. *Vale,*

J. H.[2]

A TRUE COPY OF THE LETTER ABOVE MENTIONED.

BROTHER!—I thank you most kindly for that book of Mr Brooks's 'Precious Remedies'—you sent me; and I think I can never recompense you in a better manner than to acquaint you with what benefit I have received by it; for it was a great awaking of me, to see in what a lost condition I was without Christ, and how many ways Satan hath deceived me, in making me delay my careful providing for eternity. Brother! I was made within these few weeks so sensible of my condition, that for a week's space I was almost ready to despair of God's mercy; I was sore troubled that I had sinned so much against the mercy of the Lord, who had afforded me so much means of grace, and followed me

[1] See Mr Brooks's 'Apples of Gold.' Eccles. i. 2, 'Remember now thy Creator in the days of thy youth,' &c. See Mr Philip Goodwin in his 'Mystery of Dreams,' p. 50. Satan sends out his books as baits, by which many are cunningly caught, with the venom of which so many are poisoned.

[2] John Hancock. See title-page in note prefixed to the book, 'Precious Remedies,' &c.—G.

with convictions, wooing and entreating me by his messengers for many years, which made me think that my day of grace was past. But since, 'praised be the Lord, who hath comforted me,' and now I see that there is yet a door of hope open for me, which hath brought me to such a great change in the very thoughts of my heart, that I would not exchange for the whole world. Brother! let your prayers and the prayers of God's people be, that the Lord would increase and strengthen his grace in me, for I am as a new-born babe, 'desiring the sincere milk of the word, that I may grow thereby,' 1 Peter ii. 2. And I would gladly have more acquaintance with the Lord's people. Brother! my prayer shall be to the Lord for you, that you may grow more and more in grace, and in the knowledge of our Lord and Saviour Jesus Christ; and so I rest, yours in all brotherly love and affections till death,

W. L.

TIVERTON, *March* 1655.

APPLES OF GOLD.

NOTE.

'Apples of Gold' was originally preached as a 'funeral sermon,' and published in 1657. See Appendix to our reprint, where will be found, (1.) Copy of the first title-page, as it states the circumstances; (2.) The original 'Epistle Dedicatory,' afterwards withdrawn and another substituted; but reprinted thus as being very characteristic and pungent.

Our text is taken from the 'third edition, *corrected*.' Its title-page will be found below.* The '17th' edition appeared in 1693, and 'Apples of Gold' has always ranked with 'Precious Remedies' and the 'Mute Christian,' in acceptance.—G.

* APPLES OF GOLD
FOR
Young Men and Women,
AND,
A CROWN of GLORY for
Old Men and Women.
OR,
The Happiness of being Good betimes,
And the Honour of being an Old Disciple.
Clearly and fully discovered, and closely
and faithfully applied.
ALSO,
The Young Mans Objections answered.
And the Old Mans Doubts resolved.

By *THOMAS BROOKS* Preacher of the Gospel
at *Margarets* New *Fishstreet-hill.*

The Third Edition corrected.

But I thy Servant fear the Lord from my youth, 1 Kings 18. 12.
The hoary head is a Crown of Glory, if it bee found in a way of Righteousness, Prov. 16. 31.

London, Printed by *R. I.* for *John Hancock*, to be sold at the first Shop in *Popes-head-Alley*, next to *Corn-hill*, near the *Exchange*. 1660.

THE EPISTLE DEDICATORY.

TO ALL YOUNG PERSONS THROUGHOUT THE NATIONS,
especially those, of both sexes, who begin to turn their faces towards Zion.

DEAR HEARTS,—'A word spoken in due season, how good is it!'[1] Prov. xv. 23. 'It is' often 'like apples of gold in pictures of silver,' Prov. xxv. 11. Many times such a word is sweet, precious, pleasing, delectable, and strong in its operation. A company of near friends dining together one Sabbath day, one that was at table, to prevent impertinent[2] discourse, said 'that it was a question whether they should all go to heaven or no,' which struck them all into a dump, and caused every one to enter into a serious consideration with themselves. One thought, if any of this company go to hell, it must be I; and so thought another and another, and indeed so thought almost every one then present, as well servants that waited as those that sat at table, as it was afterwards acknowledged; and through the mercy and blessing of God this speech so wrought upon the spirits of most of them, that it proved the first instrumental means of their conversion.

I have my hopes, through grace, that this treatise, though it be sown in weakness, yet by the blessing of the Most High upon it, it may rise in power, and be an instrumental means of the winning of souls to Christ, which is my highest ambition in this world; and therefore I have broke through all difficulties and carnal reasonings that might otherwise have stifled this babe in the womb, and kept it from ever seeing of the light.

I have read of an emperor that delighted in no undertakings so much as those which in the esteem of his counsellors and captains were deemed most difficult and impossible. If they said such or such an enterprise would never be accomplished, it was argument enough to him to make the adventure; and he usually prospered, he seldom miscarried.

I have never found greater and choicer blessings to attend any of my poor weak labours than those that have been brought forth into the world through the greatest straits and difficulties.

[1] 'A word spoken (*gnal ophnah*) upon his wheels,' that is, with a due concurrence and observation of all circumstances of time, place, person, all which are as the wheels upon which our words and speeches should run, such a word is like apples of gold in pictures of silver.

[2] 'Not pertinent,' = irrelevant or frivolous.—G.

Valerius Maximus reports,[1] that one telling a soldier going to war against the Persians, that they would hide the sun with their arrows, he answered, We shall fight best in the shade. Nothing should discourage nor dishearten a soldier of Christ, 2 Tim. ii. 3, 4. Christ saith to all his soldiers (as the Black Prince his father said to him, fighting as it were in blood to the knees, and in great distress), Either vanquish or die.[2] Men of no resolution, or of weak resolution, will be but little serviceable to the good of souls. Such watchmen as will be free from the blood of souls, and be serviceable to the interest of Christ in turning sinners from darkness to light, must be men of spirit and resolution.

I remember Austin beginneth one of his sermons thus: *Ad vos mihi sermo, O juvenes flos ætatis, periculum mentis,* To you is my speech, O young men, the flower of age, the danger of the mind.'[3]

So say I, To you, O young men! do I dedicate the ensuing treatise, and that, first, Because the matter contained therein doth primarily and eminently concern you.

And secondly, Because of an earnest desire that I have of your internal and eternal welfare.

And thirdly, Because of some late impulses that have been upon my spirit to leave this treatise in your hands as a legacy of my love, and as a testimony and witness of my great ambition to help forward your everlasting salvation.

And fourthly, Because there is most hope of doing good amongst you, as I evidence more at large in the following treatise.

And fifthly, To countermine the great underminer of your souls, whose great design is to poison you, and to possess you, in the morning of your days.

Sixthly, To provoke others that are more able and worthy to be more serviceable to you in declaring themselves fully on this very subject, which none yet have done that I know of, though it be a point of as great concernment to young persons especially, as any I know in all the Scriptures, Eph. iv. 14.

Seventhly, and lastly, Because there are very many that do lie in wait to deceive, corrupt, and poison your persons with God-dishonouring, Christ-denying, conscience-wasting, and soul-damning opinions, principles, and blasphemies.[4]

I have read of one who boasted and gloried in this, that he had spent thirty years in corrupting and poisoning of youth. Doubtless, many wretches, many monsters there be among us, who make it their business, their glory, their all, to delude and draw young persons to those dangerous errors and blasphemies that lead to destruction. Error and folly, saith one very well, be the knots of Satan wherewith he ties children to the stake to be burned in hell.

There is a truth in what the tragedian [Terence?] said long since, '*Venenum in auro bibitur,*' poison is commonly drunk out of a cup of gold. So is an error or by-notion soonest taken into the judgment and conscience from persons of the fairest carriage and smoothest conversations.

[1] Valerius Maximus, lib. 3. c. *de Fiducia.* [2] Hist. of France, p. 196.
[3] Augustine, *de tempore*, serm. 256.
[4] A blind eye is worse than a lame foot. He that had the leprosy in his head, was to be pronounced utterly unclean.

Error is so foul an hag, that if it should come in its own shape, a man would loathe it, and fly from it as from hell.[1]

If Jezebel had not painted her face, she had not gotten so many young doating adulterers to have followed her to their own ruin.

Ah! young men, young men, the blessing of the Lord upon your serious and diligent perusal of this treatise may be a happy means to preserve you from being ensnared and deluded by those monsters 'who compass sea and land to make proselytes for hell,' Mat. xxiii. 15.

And thus I have given you the reasons of my dedicating this treatise to the service of your souls. I would willingly presume that it will be as kindly taken as it is cordially tendered. I hope none of you into whose hands it may fall, will say as one Antipater, king of Macedonia, did; when one presented him with a book treating of happiness, his answer was, Ου σχολάζω,[2] I have no leisure.

Ah! Young men and women, young men and virgins, as you tender[3] the everlasting welfare of your souls; as you would escape hell and come to heaven; as you would have an interest in Christ, a pardon in your bosoms; as you would be blessed here and glorious hereafter; find time, find leisure, to read over and over the following treatise, which is purposely calculated for your eternal good.

But before I go further, I think it needful, in some respects, to give the world some further account of other reasons or motives that hath prevailed with me to appear once more in print; and they are these:

First, Having preached a sermon occasionally[4] upon these words, on which this following discourse is built, I was earnestly importuned to print the sermon by some worthy friends. I did as long as in modesty I could, withstand their desires, judging it not worthy of them; but being at last overcome, and setting about the work, the breathings and comings in of God were such as hath occasioned that one sermon to multiply into many. Luther tells us, that when he first began to turn his back upon popery, he intended no more but to withstand popish pardons and selling indulgences; yet neither would God or his enemies let him alone till he resolved with Moses not to leave a hoof of popery unopposed, Exod. x. 26, &c. God many times in the things of the gospel carries forth his servants beyond their intentions, beyond their resolutions. But,

Secondly, The kind acceptance and good quarter that my other pieces have found in the world, and those signal and multiplied blessings that have followed them, to the winning of many over to Christ, and to the building up of others in Christ, hath encouraged me to present this treatise to the world, hoping that the Lord hath a blessing in store for this also. Gracious experiences are beyond notions and impressions; they are very quickening and encouraging.

[1] This anticipates by nearly a century Pope's famous couplet:—

> 'Vice is a monster of so frightful mien,
> As, to be hated, needs but to be seen.'

It may be well to add what follows:—

> 'Yet seen too oft familiar with her face,
> We first endure, then pity, then embrace.'

Epistle ii. lines 217-220.—G.

[2] Cf. Sibbes's Works, vol. ii. p. 440.—G.

[3] 'Care for.'—G.

[4] 'On a particular occasion.'—G.

Thirdly, That I might in some measure make up other neglects, whose age, whose parts, whose experiences, whose graces hath long called upon them to do something considerable in this way, and that they may be provoked by my weak assay[1] to do better, and to make up what is wanting through my invincible infirmities and spiritual wants and weaknesses, which are so many as may well make a sufficient apology for all the defects and weaknesses that in this treatise shall appear to a serious judicious eye. But,

Fourthly, The love of Christ and souls hath constrained me to it. As there is an attractive, so there is a compulsive, virtue in divine love. Love to Christ and souls will make a man willing to spend and be spent.[2] He that prays himself to death, that preaches himself to death, that studies himself to death, that sweats himself to death, for the honour of Christ and good of souls, shall be no loser in the end. Divine love is like a rod of myrtle, which, as Pliny reports, makes the traveller that carries it in his hand that he shall never be faint or weary.[3] Divine love is very operative; *si non operatur, non est*, if it do not work, it is an argument it is not at all. Divine love, like fire, is not idle, but active. He that loves cannot be barren. Love will make the soul constant and abundant in well-doing. God admits none to heaven, saith Justin Martyr, but such as can persuade him by their works that they love him. The very heathen Seneca hath observed, that God doth not love his children with a weak, womanish affection, but with a strong, masculine love; and certainly, they that love the Lord strongly, that love him with a masculine love, they cannot but lay out their little all for him and his glory. But,

Fifthly, I observe that Satan and his instruments are exceeding busy and unwearied in their designs, attempts, and endeavours in these days to corrupt and poison, to defile and destroy the young, the tender, the most hopeful, and most flourishing plants among us.

Latimer told the clergy in his time, that if they would not learn diligence and vigilance of the prophets and apostles, they should learn it of the devil,[4] who goes up and down his dioceses, and acts by an untired power, seeking whom he may destroy. When the wolves are abroad, the shepherd should not sleep, but watch; yea, double his watch, remembering that he were better have all the blood of all the men in the world upon him than the blood of one soul upon him by his negligence, or otherwise.

Satan is a lion, not a lamb; a roaring lion, not a sleepy lion; not a lion standing still, but a lion going up and down. As not being contented with the prey, the many millions of souls he hath got, 'he seeks whom he may sip up at a draught,' as that word, καταπίῃ, in the 1 Peter v. 8 imports; his greatest design is to fill hell with souls; which should awaken every one to be active, and to do all that may be done to prevent his design, and to help forward the salvation of souls.

Chrysostom compares good pastors to fountains that ever send forth

[1] 'Essay, or attempt.'—G.

[2] 2 Cor. v. 14, 2 Cor. xii. 15, *Solus amor nescit difficultates*, love knows no difficulties.

[3] Myrtle: lib. xv. 35–38.—G.

[4] It is said of Marcellus the Roman general, that he could not be quiet, *Nec victor, nec victus*, neither conquered nor conqueror; such a one is Satan. [Plutarch, *Marcellus*.—G.]

waters, or conduits that are always running, though no pail be put under.[1] But,

Sixthly and lastly, I know the whole life of man is but an hour to work in; and the more work any man doth for Christ on earth, the better pay he shall have when he comes to heaven. Every man shall at last 'reap as he sows.' Opportunities of doing service for Christ, and souls, are more worth than a world; therefore I was willing to take hold on this, not knowing how soon 'I may put off this earthly tabernacle;' and remembering, that as there is no believing nor repenting in the grave, so there is no praying, preaching, writing, nor printing in the grave; we had need to be up and doing, to put both hands to it, and to do all we do with all our might, knowing that 'the night draws on upon us, wherein no man can work.'[2] A Christian's dying day is the Lord's pay-day; that is, a time to receive wages, not to do work.

And thus I have given the world a true account of the reasons that moved me to print the following discourse. Before I close up, I desire to speak a word to young persons, and another to aged persons, and then I shall take leave of both.

My request to you who are in the primrose[3] of your days is this, If ever the Lord shall be pleased so to own and crown, so to bless and follow this following discourse, as to make it an effectual means of turning you to the Lord, of winning you to Christ, of changing your natures, and converting your souls—for such a thing as that I pray, hope, and believe—that then you would do two things for me.

First, That you would never cease bearing of me upon your hearts when you are in the mount, that I may be very much under the pourings out of the Spirit, that I may be clear, high, and full in my communion with God, and that I may be always close, holy, humble, harmless, and blameless in my walkings with God, and that his work may more and more prosper in my hand.

Secondly, That you would by word of mouth, letter, or some other way, acquaint me with what the Lord hath done for your souls, if he shall make me a spiritual father to you.[4] Do not hide his grace from me, but acquaint me how he hath made the seed that was sown in weakness to rise in power upon you, and that

(*First*) That I may do what I can to help on that work begun upon you; that your penny may become a pound, your mite a million, your drop an ocean.

(*Secondly*) That I may the better English some impressions that have been upon my own spirit since I began this work.

(*Thirdly*), That my joy and thankfulness may be increased, and my soul more abundantly engaged to that God, who hath blessed the day of small things to you, 1 Thes. ii. 19, 20; 2 Cor. ix. 2. Ponder these scriptures—2 Cor. vii. 3, 4, 13; Philip. ii. 2; iv. 1; Philem. 7; 2 John 3, 4—and then be ashamed to declare what the Lord hath done for you, if you can.

(*Fourthly*) It is better to convert one, than to civilise a thousand;

[1] Chrys. *in Mat. Ho.* 15.

[2] 1 Cor. xv. 58; 2 Cor. ix. 6; 2 Peter i. 13, 14: Eccles. ix. 10; John ix. 4.—G.

[3] That is, 'in the early spring of life.' A frequent word in the Elizabethan writers. 'The primrose path of dalliance,' Hamlet, i. 3.—G.

[4] Ps. lxvi. 16, and 1 Peter iii. 15.—G.

and will turn more at last to a minister's account in that day, wherein he shall say, 'Lo, here am I, and the children that thou hast given me,' Isa. viii. 18.[1] Such a man, with his spiritual children about him, shall look on God with more comfort and boldness, than those that are only able to say, 'Lo, here am I, and the many benefices;' 'Here am I, and the many ecclesiastical dignities and glories;' 'Here am I, and the many hundreds a year that man had given, and I have gotten.' But,

(*Fifthly and lastly*) The conversion of others is a secondary and more remote evidence of a man's own renovation and conversion. Paul was converted himself before God made him instrumental for others' conversion. God's usual method is, to convert by them who are converted.[2]

I do not remember any one instance in all the Scripture of God's converting any by such who have not been converted first themselves; yet I know his grace is free, and the wind blows where it lists, when it lists, and as it lists.

To aged persons I have a word, and then I have done.

First, To grey-headed saints. Ah, friends! ah, fathers! would you see your honour, your happiness, your blessedness? Then look into this treatise, and there you will find what an unspeakable honour it is to be an old disciple, what a glory it is to be good betimes, and to continue so to old age.

Secondly, To white-headed sinners whose spring is past, whose summer is overpast, and who are arrived at the fall of the leaf, and yet have a hell to escape, a Christ to believe in, sins to pardon, hearts to change, souls to save, and heaven to make sure; would such be encouraged from Scripture grounds to repent, believe, and hope, that yet there is mercy for such, let them seriously peruse this treatise, especially the latter part of it, and there they may find enough to keep them from despairing, and to encourage them to adventure their souls upon him that is mighty to save.

There are many things in this treatise that are of use to all, and several things of moment, that are not every day preached nor read. I have made it as pleasurable as time would permit, that so it might be the more profitable to the reader, and that I might the better take the young man by a holy craft; which is a high point of heavenly wisdom, there being no wisdom to that of winning of souls, 2 Cor. xii. 16; Prov. xi. 13. I shall now follow this poor piece with my weak prayers, that it may be so blest from heaven, as that it may bring in some, and build up others, and do good to all. And so rest,

Your friend and servant in the Gospel of Christ,

THOMAS BROOKS.

[1] Mat. xxv. 23; Dan. xii. 3; Prov. xi. 30.
[2] Acts ix. 3; Isa. vi. 5; Mal. ii. 5–7, &c.

THE YOUNG MAN'S DUTY AND EXCELLENCY.

And all Israel shall mourn for him, and bury him; for he only of Jeroboam shall come to the grave, because in him there is found some good thing toward the Lord God of Israel, in the house of Jeroboam.'—1 KINGS XIV. 13.

I SHALL only stand upon the latter part of this verse, because that affords me matter most suitable to my design.

'Because in him there is found some good thing toward the Lord God of Israel, in the house of Jeroboam.'

These words are a commendation of Abijah's life, 'in him was found some good thing toward the Lord,' &c. When Abijah was a child, vers. 3, 12, when he was in his young and tender years, he had the seeds of grace in him, he had the image of God upon him, he could discern between good and evil, and he did that which pleased the Lord.

The Hebrew word [*Nagnar*] translated child, ver. 3, is very often applied to such as we call youth, or young men; Exod. xxiv. 5; Num. xi. 28; 1 Sam. ii. 17, &c.[1]

Of such age and prudence was Abijah, as that he could choose good and refuse evil. He was a Lot in Sodom, he was good among the bad. The bent and frame of his heart was towards that which was good, when the heart both of his father and mother was set upon evil. Abijah began to be good betimes. He crossed that pestilent proverb, 'a young saint and an old devil.' It is the glory and goodness of God that he will take notice of the least good that is in any of his. There was but one good word in Sarah's speech to Abraham, and that was this, she called him Lord; and this God mentions for her honour and commendation, 'She called him lord,' 1 Peter iii. 6. God looks more upon one grain of wheat, than upon a heap of chaff, upon one shining pearl than upon a heap of rubbish. God finds a pearl in Abijah, and he puts it into his crown, to his eternal commendation, 'There was found in him some good thing toward the Lord,' &c. For the words, 'There was found in him,' the Hebrew word *Matsa*, sometimes signifies

[1] נער, is used for a young man, or stripling, Gen. xxii. 5, and often for a servant, though he be a man of ripe years, Esther ii. 2. Such as one evangelist calleth young men, Luke xii. 45, another calleth fellow-servants, Mat. xxiv. 49.

finding without seeking: Isa. lxv. 1, 'I am found of them that sought me not;' so Ps. cxvi. 3, 'The sorrows of death compassed me, and the pains of hell got hold upon me, I found trouble and sorrow.' I found trouble which I looked not for; I was not searching after sorrow, but I found it. There is an elegancy in the original; 'The pains of hell gat hold upon me,' so we read, but the Hebrew is, 'The pains of hell found me.' One word signifies both. They found me, I did not find them. 'There was *found* in Abijah some good thing towards the Lord,' *i. e.* there was found in him, without searching or seeking, some good thing towards the Lord. It was plain and visible enough. Men might see and observe it without inquiring or seeking. They might run and read some good thing in him towards the Lord.

Secondly, The word sometimes signifies finding by seeking or inquiry: Isa. lv. 6, 'Seek ye the Lord while he may be found,' &c. So upon search and inquiry there was found in Abijah, though young, 'some good thing toward the Lord.'

Thirdly, Sometimes the word notes the obtaining of that which is sufficient: Joshua xvii. 16; Num. xi. 22; Judges xxi. 14. In Abijah there was that good in him towards the Lord that was sufficient to evidence the work of grace upon him, sufficient to satisfy himself and others of the goodness and happiness of his condition, though he died in the prime and flower of his days, &c.

'And in him was found some good thing.' The Hebrew word *Tob*, that is here rendered good, signifies,

First, That which is right and just: 2 Sam. xv. 3, 'See thy matters are good and right,' *i. e.* just and right.

Secondly, That which is profitable: Deut. vi. 11, 'Houses full of all good things,' *i. e.* houses full of all profitable things.

Thirdly, That which is pleasing: 2 Sam. xix. 27, 'Do what is good in thine eyes,' *i. e.* do what is pleasing in thine eyes.

Fourthly, That which is full and complete: Gen. xv. 15, 'Thou shalt be buried in a good old age,' *i. e.* thou shalt be buried when thine age is full and complete.

Fifthly, That which is joyful and delightful: 1 Sam. xxv. 8, 'We come in a good day,' *i. e.* we come in a joyful and delightful day.

Now put all together, and you may see that there was found in Abijah, when he was young, that which was right and just, that which was pleasing and profitable, and that which was matter of joy and delight.

In the words you have two things that are most considerable.

First, *That this young man's goodness was towards the Lord God of Israel.* Many there are that are good, nay, very good towards men, who yet are bad, yea, very bad towards God.[1] Some there are who are very kind to the creature, and yet very unkind to their Creator. Many men's goodness towards the creature is like the rising sun, but their goodness towards the Lord is like a morning cloud, or as the early dew, which is soon dried up by the sunbeams, Hosea vi. 4; but Abijah's goodness was towards the Lord, his goodness faced the Lord, it looked towards the glory of God. Two things makes a good Christian, good actions and good aims; and though a good aim doth not make a bad

[1] This age affords many such hypocrites, such monsters, &c.

action good, as in Uzzah, yet a bad aim makes a good action bad, as in Jehu, whose justice was approved, but his policy punished, the first chapter of Hosea, and the fourth verse. Doubtless Abijah's actions were good, and his aims good, and this was indeed his glory, that his goodness was 'towards the Lord.'[1]

It is recorded of the Catanenses, that the made a stately monument, of kingly magnificence, in remembrance of two sons, who took their aged parents upon their backs, and carried them through the fire, when their father's house was all in a flame.[2] These young men were good towards their parents; but what is this to Abijah's goodness 'towards the Lord'? &c. A man cannot be good towards the Lord but he will be good towards others; but a man may be good towards others, that is not good towards the Lord. Oh that men's practices did not give too loud a testimony every day to this assertion! &c.[3]

Secondly, *He was good among the bad.* He was good 'in the house of Jeroboam.' It is in fashion to seem at least to be good among the good; but to be really good among those that are bad, that are eminently bad, argues not only a truth of goodness, but a great degree of goodness. This young man was good 'in the house of Jeroboam, who made all Israel to sin; who was naught, who was very naught, who was stark naught; and yet Abijah, as the fishes which live in the salt sea are fresh, so though he lived in a sink, a sea, of wickedness, yet he retained his 'goodness towards the Lord.'

They say roses grow the sweeter when they are planted by garlic. They are sweet and rare Christians indeed who hold their goodness, and grow in goodness, where wickedness sits on the throne; and such a one the young man in the text was.

To be wheat among tares, corn among chaff, pearls among cockles, and roses among thorns, is excellent.

To be a Jonathan in Saul's court, to be an Obadiah in Ahab's court, to be an Ebed-melech in Zedekiah's court, and to be an Abijah in Jeroboam's court, is a wonder, a miracle.

To be a Lot in Sodom, to be an Abraham in Chaldea, to be a Daniel in Babylon, to be a Nehemiah in Damascus, and to be a Job in the land of Husse,[4] is to be a saint among devils; and such a one the young man in the text was.

The poets affirm that Venus never appeared so beauteous as when she sat by black Vulcan's side. Gracious souls shine most clear when they be set by black-conditioned persons. Stephen's face never shined so angelically, so gloriously, in the church where all were virtuous, as before the council where all were vicious and malicious. So Abijah was a bright star, a shining sun, in Jeroboam's court, which for profaneness and wickedness was a very hell.

[1] There may be *malum opus in bona materia*, as in Jehu's zeal.

[2] The allusion is to the imperishable legend of the 'Pii Fratres,' Amphinomus and Anapias, who, on an eruption of Ætna, acted as above. The place of their burial was known as 'Campus Piorum.'—G.

[3] Happy are those souls that, with the sturgeon or crab-fish, can swim against the stream of custom and example; and with Atticus, can cleave to the right, though losing, side. [Atticus, bishop of Constantinople, who sided with Chrysostom.—G.]

[4] 'Uz.'—G.

The words that I have chosen to insist upon will afford us several observations, but I shall only name one, which I intend to prosecute at this time, and that is this, viz.:

CHAPTER I.

Doct. That it is a very desirable and commendable thing for young men to be really good betimes.

Other scriptures speak out this to be a truth, besides what you have in the text to confirm it; as that of the second of Chronicles, chap. xxxiv. 1–3, 'Josiah was eight years old when he began to reign, and he reigned in Jerusalem one and thirty years. And he did that which was right in the sight of the Lord, and walked in the ways of David his father, and declined neither to the right hand nor to the left; for in the eighth year of his reign, while he was yet young, he began to seek after the God of David his father; and in the twelfth year he began to purge Judah and Jerusalem, from the high places, and the groves, and the carved images, and the molten images.' It was Obadiah's honour that he feared the Lord from his youth, 1 Kings xviii. 3; and Timothy's crown that he knew the Scripture from a child, 2 Tim. vi. 1, 5, 15; and John's joy that he found children walking in the truth, 2 John 4, 5; this revived his good old heart, and made it dance for joy in his bosom. To spend further time in the proving of this truth, would be but to light candles to see the sun at noon.

The grounds and reasons of this point, viz.:

That it is a very desirable and commendable thing for young men to be really good betimes, are these that follow:[1]

Reason 1. *First*, Because *the Lord commands it; and divine commands are not to be disputed, but obeyed.* In the 12th chapter of Ecclesiastes, and the first verse, 'Remember now thy Creator in the days of thy youth, while the evil days come not, nor the years draw nigh, when thou shalt say, I have no pleasure in them.' Remember now; I say, now. Now is an atom; it will puzzle the wisdom of a philosopher, the skill of an angel, to divide. Now is a monosyllable in all learned languages: 'Remember *now* thy Creator.' Remember him presently, instantly, for thou dost not know what a day, what an hour, may bring forth; thou canst not tell what deadly sin, what deadly temptation, what deadly judgment, may overtake thee, if thou dost not now, even now, 'remember thy Creator.'

'*Remember* now thy Creator.' Remember to know him, remember to love him, remember to desire him, remember to delight in him, remember to depend upon him, remember to get an interest in him, remember to live to him, and remember to walk with him. 'Remember now thy Creator;' the Hebrew is Creators, Father, Son, and Spirit. To the making of man, a council was called in heaven, in the first of Genesis, and 26th verse. 'Remember thy Creators:' Remember the Father, so as to know him, so as to be inwardly acquainted with him. Remember the

[1] Deut. vi. 5, xi. 18. Augustine beginneth one of his sermons thus: 'Ad vos mihi sermo, O juvenes, flos ætatis, periculum mentis.'—*August. de Tempore. serm.* 246. To you is my speech, O young men, the flower of age, the danger of the mind.

Son, so as to believe in him, so as to rest upon him, so as to embrace him, and so as to make a complete resignation of thyself to him. Remember the Spirit, so as to hear his voice, so as to obey his voice, so as to feel his presence, and so as to experience his influence, &c.

'Remember now thy Creator *in the days of thy youth.*' He doth not say in the time of thy youth, but 'in the days of thy youth,' to note, that our life is but as a few days. It is but as a vapour, a span, a flower, a shadow, a dream; and therefore Seneca saith well, that 'though death be before the old man's face, yet he may be as near the young man's back,' &c.

Man's life is the shadow of smoke, the dream of a shadow. One doubteth whether to call it a dying life, or a living death.[1]

Ah! young men, God commands you to be good betimes. Remember, young men, that it is a dangerous thing to neglect any of his commands, who by another is able to command you into nothing, or into hell. To act or run cross to God's command, though under pretence of revelation from God, is as much as a man's life is worth, as you may see in that sad story, 1 Kings, xiii. 24, &c.

Let young men put all their carnal reasons, though never so many and weighty, into one scale, and God's absolute command in the other, and then write Tekel upon all their reasons, they are 'weighed in the balance and found too light.'

Ah, sirs! what God commands must be put in speedy execution, without denying or delaying, or disputing the difficulties that attend it.[2] Most young men in these days do as the heathens: when their gods called for a man, they offered a candle; or, as Hercules, offered up a painted man instead of a living. When God calls upon young men to serve him with the primrose of their youth, they usually put him off till they are overtaken with trembling joints, dazzled eyes, fainting hearts, failing hands, and feeble knees; but this will be bitterness in the end, &c.

Reason (2). *Because they have means and opportunities of being good betimes.*

Never had men better means and greater opportunities of being good, of doing good, and of receiving good, than now. Ah, Lord! how knowing, how believing, how holy, how heavenly, how humble, might young men be, were they not wanting to their own souls. Young men might be good, very good, yea, eminently good, would they but improve the means of grace, the tenders of mercy, and the knockings of Christ, by his word, works, and Spirit.

The ancients painted opportunity with a hairy forehead, but bald behind, to signify, that while a man hath opportunity before him, he may lay hold on it, but if he suffer it to slip away, he cannot pull it back again.[3]

How many young men are now in everlasting chains, who would give ten thousand worlds, had they so many in their hands to give, to enjoy but an opportunity to hear one sermon more, to make one prayer more, to keep one Sabbath more, but cannot! This is their hell, their torment; this is the scorpion that is still biting, this is the worm that is

[1] Aug. Confess. lib. i. [2] *Obedientia non discutit Dei mandata sed facit.*—Prosper.
[3] Erasmus [and 'The Emblems'].—G.

always gnawing. Woe! woe! to us, that we have neglected and trifled away those golden opportunities that once we had to get our sins pardoned, our natures changed, our hearts bettered, our consciences purged, and our souls saved, &c. I have read of a king,[1] who having no issue to succeed him, espying one day a well-favoured youth, took him to court, and committed him to tutors to instruct him, providing by his will, that if he proved fit for government, he should be crowned king; if not, he should be bound in chains and made a galley-slave. Now when he grew to years, the king's executors, perceiving that he had sadly neglected those means and opportunities, whereby he might have been fit for state-government, called him before them, and declared the king's will and pleasure concerning him, which was accordingly performed, for they caused him to be fettered, and committed to the galleys. Now what tongue can express how much he was affected and afflicted, with his sad and miserable state, especially when he considered with himself, that now he is chained, who might have walked at liberty; now he is a slave, who might have been a king; now he is overruled by Turks, who might once have ruled over Christians. The application is easy.

Ah! young men! young men! shall Satan take all opportunities to tempt you? shall the world take all opportunities to allure you? shall wicked men take all opportunities to ensnare you, and to undo you? and shall Christian friends take all opportunities to better you? and shall God's faithful messengers take all opportunities to save you? and will you, will you 'neglect so great salvation'? Heb. ii. 3. Plutarch writes of Hannibal, that when he could have taken Rome he would not, and when he would have taken Rome he could not.[2] Many, in their youthful days, when they might have mercy, Christ, pardon, heaven, they will not; and in old age, when they would have Christ, pardon, peace, heaven, they cannot, they may not. God seems to say, as Theseus said once, Go, says he, and tell Creon, Theseus offers thee a gracious offer. Yet I am pleased to be friends, if thou wilt submit; this is my first message; but if this offer prevail not, look for me to be up in arms.

Reason (3). *Because, when they have fewer and lesser sins to answer for and repent of, multitudes of sins and sorrows are prevented by being good betimes.*

The more we number our days, the fewer sins we shall have to number.[3] As a copy is then safest from blotting when dust is put upon it, so are we from sinning when, in the time of our youth, we remember that we are but dust. The tears of young penitents do more scorch the devils than all the flames of hell; for hereby all their hopes are blasted, and the great underminer countermined and blown up. *Mane* is the devil's verb; he bids tarry, time enough to repent; but *mane* is God's adverb; he bids repent early, in the morning of thy youth, for then thy

[1] Bellarm[ine]. *In conscione de cruciatibus Gehennæ.*

[2] It is storied of Charles, king of Sicily and Jerusalem, that he was called *Carolus Cunctator*, Charles the lingerer. This age affords many such lingerers, &c. [The agnomen *above* is very much earlier, having been applied to and accepted by the *Dictator* Q. Fabius Maximus. Cf. Livy, 30, 26; Quint., 8, 2, 11.—G.]

[3] Lord, saith Austin, I have loved thee late. The greater was his sins, and the more were his sorrows.—[Confessions, Book x. (xxvii.) 38. —G.

sins will be fewer and lesser. Well! young men, remember this: he that will not at the first-hand buy good counsel cheap, shall at the second-hand buy repentance over dear.

Ah! young men! young men! if you do not begin to be good betimes, those sins that are now as jewels sparkling in your eyes, will at last be millstones about your necks, to sink you for ever.[1] Among many things that Beza, in his last will and testament, gave God thanks for, this was the first and chief, that he, at the age of sixteen years, had called him to the knowledge of the truth, and so prevented many sins and sorrows that otherwise would have overtaken him, and have made his life less happy and more miserable. Young saints often prove old angels, but old sinners seldom prove good saints, &c.[2]

Reason 4. Because time is a precious talent, that young men must be countable for. The sooner they begin to be good, the more easy will be their accounts, especially as to that great talent of time. Cato and other heathens held that account must be given, not only of our labour, but also of our leisure. At the great day, it will appear that they that have spent their time in mourning have done better than they that have spent their time in dancing; and they that have spent many days in humiliation, than they that have spent many days in idle recreations.

I have read of a devout man who, when he heard a clock strike, he would say, Here is one hour more past that I have to answer for. Ah! young men, as time is very precious, so it is very short. Time is very swift; it is suddenly gone. In the 9th of Job, and the 25th verse, 'My days are swifter than a post, they flee away, they see no good.' The Hebrew word (*kalal*) translated 'swifter than a post,' signifies anything that is light, because light things are quick in motion.

The ancients emblemed time with wings, as it were, not running, but flying.[3] Time is like the sun, that never stands still, but is still a-running his race. The sun did once stand still, yea, went back, but so did never time. Time is still running and flying. It is a bubble, a shadow, a dream. Can you seriously consider of this, young men, and not begin to be good betimes? Surely you cannot. Sirs! if the whole earth whereupon we tread were turned into a lump of gold, it were not able to purchase one minute of time. Oh! the regrettings of the damned for misspending precious time![4] Oh! what would they not give to be free, and to enjoy the means of grace one hour! Ah! with what attention, with what intention,[5] with what trembling and melting of heart, with what hungering and thirsting, would they hear the word! Time, saith Bernard, were a good commodity in hell, and the traffic of it most gainful, where for one day a man would give ten thousand worlds, if he had them. Young men, can you in good earnest believe this, and not begin to be good betimes?

Ah! young men and women, as you love your precious immortal

[1] Ps. xxv. 7, Job xiii. 26.

[2] There is nothing puts a more serious frame into a man's spirit, than to know the worth of his time.

[3] Sophocles, *Phocilides*. [Query, 'Philoctetes'?—G.]

[4] Who is there among us that knows how to value time, and prize a day at a due rate? [Senec., Epist. i.—G.]

[5] Intentness, earnestness.—G.

souls, as you would escape hell, and come to heaven, as you would be happy in life, and blessed in death, and glorious after death, don't spend any more of your precious time in drinking and drabbing,[1] in carding, dicing, and dancing; don't trifle away your time, don't swear away your time, don't whore away your time, do not lie away your time, but begin to be good betimes, because time is a talent that God will reckon with you for.[2] Ah! young men and women, you may reckon upon years, many years yet to come, when possibly you have not so many hours to make ready your accounts. It may be this night you may have a summons, and then, if your time be done, and your work to be begun, in what a sad case will you be. Will you not wish that you had never been born?

Seneca was wont to jeer the Jews for their ill husbandry, in that they lost one day in seven, meaning their Sabbath.[3] Oh that it were not too true of the most of professors, both young and old, that they lose not only one day in seven, but several days in seven.

Sirs! Time let slip cannot be recalled. The foolish virgins found it so, and Saul found it so, and Herod found it so, and Nero found it so. The Israelites found it so; yea, and Jacob, and Josiah, and David, though good men, yet they found it so to their cost.[4]

The Egyptians draw the picture of time with three heads: the first of a greedy wolf, gaping, for time past, because it hath ravenously devoured the memory of so many things past recalling; the second of a crowned lion, roaring, for time present, because it hath the principality of all actions, for which it calls loud; the third of a deceitful dog, fawning, for time to come, because it feeds some men with many flattering hopes to their eternal undoing. Ah! young men and women, as you would give up your accounts at last with joy, concerning this talent of time, with which God hath trusted you, begin to be good betimes, &c.

Reason (5). *Because they will have the greater comfort and joy when they come to be old.*[5]

The 71st psalm, 5, 17, 18, compared, 'Thou art my hope, O Lord God: thou art my trust from my youth. O God, thou hast taught me from my youth: and hitherto I have declared thy wondrous works. Now also, when I am old and grey-headed, O God, forsake me not, until I have shewed thy strength unto this generation, and thy power unto every one that is to come.'

Polycarpus could say, when old, 'Thus many years have I served my Master Christ, and hitherto hath he dealt well with me.'[6] If early converts live to be old, no joy to their joy. Their joy will be the greatest joy, a joy like to the joy of harvest, a joy like to their joy that divide the spoil. Their joy will be soundest joy, the weightiest joy, the holiest joy, the purest joy, the strongest joy, and the most lasting joy,' Isa. ix. 3. The carnal joy of the wicked, the glistering golden joy of the

[1] 'Licentiousness.' See Halliwell, *sub voce*.—G.

[2] A heathen said he lived no day without a line; that is, he did something remarkable every day.—[Zeuxis, the Painter.—G.]

[3] Query, 'Tacitus,' not Seneca? Cf. Annals, ii. 85; xii. 3; xv. 44; Hist. i. 10; ii. 4; ii. 79; v. 1, 2, *et alibi*.—G.

[4] Mat. xxv. 5; Heb. iii. 17-19.

[5] Seneca, though a heathen, could say, Believe me, true joy is no light thing. [*Epist.* xxiii.—G.]

[6] *Martyrium S. Polycarpi.* Hefele, as before.—G.

worldling, and the flashing joy of the hypocrite, is but as the crackling of thorns under a pot, to the joy and comfort of such, who, when old, can say with good Obadiah, that they 'feared the Lord from their youth.' If, when you are young, your eyes shall be full of tears for sin, when you are old, your heart shall be full of joys. Such shall have the best wine at last.

Oh! that young men would begin to be good betimes, that so they may have the greater harvest of joy when they come to be old, &c. It is sad to be sowing your seed when you should be reaping your harvest; it is best to gather in the summer of youth against the winter of old age.

Reason 6. *Because an eternity of felicity and glory hangs upon those few moments that are allotted to them.*

It was a good question the young man proposed, 'What shall I do to inherit eternal life?' Luke x. 25. I know I shall be eternally happy or eternally miserable, eternally blessed or eternally cursed, eternally saved or eternally damned, &c.

'Oh! what shall I do to inherit eternal life!' My cares, my fears, my troubles are all about eternity! No time can reach eternity, no age can extend to eternity, no tongue can express eternity. Eternity is that *unum perpetuum hodie*, one perpetual day which shall never have end; what shall I do, what shall I not do, that I may be happy to all eternity?[1]

I am now young, and in the flower of my days; but who knows what a day may bring forth? The greatest weight hangs upon the smallest wires,[2] an eternity depends upon those few hours I am to breathe in this world. Oh! what cause have I therefore to be good betimes, to know God betimes, to believe betimes, to repent betimes, to get my peace made and my pardon sealed betimes, to get my nature changed, my conscience purged, and my interest in Christ cleared betimes, before eternity overtakes me, before my glass be out, my sun set, my race run, lest the dark night of eternity should overtake me, and I made miserable for ever.

I have read of one Myrogenes, who, when great gifts were sent unto him, he sent them all back again, saying, I only desire this one thing at your master's hand: to pray for me that I may be saved for eternity. Oh! that all young men and women, who make earth their heaven, pleasures their paradise, that eat the fat and drink the sweet, that clothe themselves richly, and crown their heads with rose-buds, that they would seriously consider of eternity, so as to hear as for eternity, and pray as for eternity, and live as for eternity, and provide as for eternity! Luke xv. 12–20. That they might say with that famous painter Zeuxis, *Æternitati pingo*, I paint for eternity.[3] We do all for eternity, we believe for eternity, we repent for eternity, we obey for eternity, &c.

[1] *Æternitas est semper et immutabile esse.* The old Romans were out, that thought eternity dwelt in statues and in marble monuments.

[2] This is a favourite 'Emblem' of the Puritans, and is prefixed to several of their books, *e. g.* John Goodwin's.—G.

[3] The proverb is more accurately *Pingo in æternitatem*, from the great artist's reply to Agatharcus, preserved by Plutarch (*De Amic. Mult.* v. p. 94 f.), 'I confess that I take a long time to paint; for I paint works to last a long time.'—G.

Oh! that you would not make those things eternal for punishment that cannot be eternal for use.[1]

Ah! young men and women, God calls, and the blood of Jesus Christ calls, and the Spirit of Christ in the gospel calls, and the rage of Satan calls, and your sad state and condition calls, and the happiness and blessedness of glorified saints calls; these all call aloud upon you to make sure a glorious eternity, before you fall out into that dreadful ocean. All your eternal good depends upon the short and uncertain moments of your lives; and if the thread of your lives should be cut before a happy eternity is made sure, woe to you that ever you were born! Do not say, O young man, that thou art young, and hereafter will be time enough to provide for eternity, for eternity may be at the door, ready to carry thee away for ever. Every day's experience speaks out eternity to be as near the young man's back as it is before the old man's face.

Oh grasp to-day the diadem of a blessed eternity, lest thou art cut off before the morning comes! Though there is but one way to come into this world, yet there is a thousand thousand ways to be sent out of this world. Well! young men and women, remember this, as the motions of the soul are quick, so are the motions of divine justice quick also; and if you will not hear the voice of God to-day, if you will not provide for eternity to-day, God may swear to-morrow that you shall never enter into his rest, Heb. iii. 7, 8, 15, 16, 18, 19. It is a very sad and dangerous thing to trifle and dally with God, his word, his offers, our own souls, and eternity. Therefore, let all young people labour to be good betimes, and not to let him that is goodness itself alone till he hath made them good, till he hath given them those hopes of eternity that will both make them good and keep them good; that will make them happy, and keep them happy, and that for ever. If all this will not do, then know that ere long those fears of eternity, of misery, that beget that monster Despair, which, like Medusa's head, astonisheth with its very aspect, and strangles hope, which is the breath of the soul, will certainly overtake you; as it is said, *Dum Spiro, Spero,* so it may be inverted *Dum Spero, Spiro;* other miseries may wound the spirit, but despair kills it dead. My prayer shall be, that none of you may ever experience this sad truth, but that you may all be good in good earnest, betimes, which will yield you two heavens, a heaven on earth, and a heaven after death.

Reason 8. *Because they do not begin to live till they begin to be really good.*

Till they begin to be good, they are dead God-wards, and Christ-wards, and heaven-wards, and holiness-wards. Till a man begins to be really good, he is really dead, and that first in respect of working; his works are called dead works, Heb. ix. 14. The most glistering services of unregenerate persons are but dead works, because they proceed not from a principle of life, and they lead to death, Rom. vi. 23, and leave a sentence of death upon the soul, till it be washed off by the blood of the Lamb. Secondly, he is dead in respect of honour; he is dead to all privileges, he is not fit to inherit mercy. Who will set the crown of

[1] *Cur ea quæ ad usum diuturna esse non possunt, ad supplicium diuturna deposcet?*—Ambrose in Luke iv. 5.

life upon a dead man? The crown of life is only for living Christians, Rev. ii. 10. The young prodigal was dead till he begun to be good, till he begun to remember his father's house, and to resolve to return home: 'My son was dead, but is alive,' Luke xv. 24; and the widow that 'liveth in pleasure is dead while she liveth,' 1 Tim. v. 6.

When Joshaphat asked Barlaam how old he was, he answered, Five and forty years old; to whom Joshaphat replied, Thou seemest to be seventy. True, saith he, if you reckon ever since I was born; but I count not those years which were spent in vanity.[1]

Ah, sirs! you never begin to live till you begin to be good, in good earnest. There is the life of vegetation, and that is the life of plants; secondly, there is the life of sense, and that is the life of beasts; thirdly, there is the life of reason, and that is the life of man; fourthly, there is the life of grace, and that is the life of saints; and this life you do not begin to live till you begin to be good. If 'a living dog is better than a dead lion,' as the wise man speaks, Eccles. ix. 4, and if a fly is more excellent than the heavens, because the fly hath life, which the heavens have not, as the philosopher saith, what a sad, dead, poor nothing is that person that is a stranger to the life of grace and goodness, that is dead even whilst he is alive!

Most men will bleed, sweat, vomit, purge, part with an estate, yea, with a limb, ay, limbs, yea, and many a better thing, viz., the honour of God and a good conscience, to preserve their natural lives; as he cries out, Give me any deformity, any torment, any misery, so you spare my life; and yet how few, how very few, are to be found who make it their work, their business, to attain to a life of goodness, or to begin to be good betimes, or to be dead to the world and alive to God, rather than to be dead to God and alive to the world. This is for a lamentation, and shall be for a lamentation, that natural life is so highly prized, and spiritual life so little regarded, &c.[2]

Reason 9. *Because the promise of finding God, of enjoying God, is made over to an early seeking of God.*

Prov. viii. 17, 'I love them that love me, and they that seek me early shall find me;' or, as the Hebrew hath it, they that 'seek me in the morning shall find me.' By the benefit of the morning light we come to find the things we seek. *Shahhar* [שׁחר] signifies to seek inquisitively, to seek diligently, to seek timely in the morning. As the Israelites went early in the morning to seek for manna, Exod. xvi. 21, and as students rise early in the morning and sit close to it to get knowledge, so saith wisdom, they that 'seek me in the spring and morning of their youth, shall find me.'[3]

Now, to seek the Lord early is to seek the Lord *firstly*. God hath in himself all the good of angels, of men, and universal nature; he hath all glories, all dignities, all riches, all treasures, all pleasures, all comforts, all delights, all joys, all beatitudes. God is that one infinite

[1] As it is a reproach to an old man to be in coats, so it is a disgrace to be an old babe, *i. e.* to be but a babe in grace when old in years, Heb. v. 12–14.

[2] Mæcenas in Seneca had rather live in many diseases than die. [Epist. CI.—G.] And Homer reporteth of his Achilles, that he had rather be a servant to a poor country clown here than to be a king to all the souls departed. [Odyssey, xi. 488.—G.]

[3] Scipio went first to the capitol and then to the senate. Tully, an heathen, frequently called God *Optimum maximum*, the best and greatest. God is *omnis super omnia*.

perfection in himself, which is eminently and virtually all perfections of the creatures, and therefore he is firstly to be sought. Abstracts do better express him than concretes and adjectives; he is being, bonity, power, wisdom, justice, mercy, goodness, and love itself, and therefore worthy to be sought before all other things. Seek ye first the good things of the mind, saith philosophy, and doth not divinity say as much?

Again, To seek early is to seek *opportunely*, to seek while the opportunity does present: Judges ix. 33, 'Thou shalt rise early, and set upon the city,' that is, thou shall opportunely set upon the city.[1]

Such there have been who, by having a glass of water opportunely, have obtained a kingdom, as you may see in the story of Thaumastus and king Agrippa.

Ah! young men and women, you do not know but that by an early, by an opportune, seeking of God, you may obtain a kingdom that shakes not, and glory that passeth not away, Heb. xii. 28.

There is a season wherein God may be found: 'Seek ye the Lord while he may be found, call ye upon him while he is near,' Isa. lv. 6; and if you slip this season, you may seek him and miss him: 'Though they cry unto me, I will not hearken unto them; 'When ye make many prayers, I will not hear;' 'Then shall they cry unto the Lord, but he will not hear;' 'Then shall they call upon me, but I will not answer; they shall seek me early, but shall not find me.'[2] This was Saul's misery: 'The Philistines are upon me, and God will not answer me,' 1 Sam. xxviii. 15. It is justice that they should seek and not find at at last, who might have found had they but sought seasonably and opportunely, &c.

Again, To seek early is to seek *earnestly, affectionately*: 'With my soul have I desired thee in the night; yea, with my spirit within me will I seek thee early,' Isa. xxvi. 9. The Hebrew word signifies both an earnest and an early seeking. In the morning the spirits are up, and men are earnest, lively, and affectionate.

Ah! such a seeking shall certainly be crowned with finding: 'My voice shalt thou hear in the morning, O Lord! in the morning will I direct [Heb. *marshal*] my prayer unto thee, and will look up' [Hebrew, *look out like a watchman*]. 'Let all those that put their trust in thee rejoice, let them ever shout for joy; because thou defendest them' [Hebrew, '*thou coverest over*, or *protectest them*']. 'Let them also that love thy name be joyful in thee: for thou, Lord, wilt bless the righteous; with favour wilt thou compass him [Hebrew, '*crown him*'] as with a shield.'[3] None have ever thus sought the Lord, but they have, or certainly shall find him: 'Seek and ye shall find,' Mat. vii. 7; 'your hearts shall live that seek God,' Ps. lxix. 32; 'The effectual fervent prayer of a righteous man availeth much,' Jas. v. 16, or, as the Greek hath it, 'The working prayer of a righteous man availeth much.'[4] That prayer that sets the whole man a-work will work wonders in heaven, in the heart, and in the earth. Earnest prayer, like Saul's sword and Jonathan's bow, never returns empty.

[1] Days of grace have their dates; therefore take heed of saying *cras, cras*, to-morrow, to-morrow.

[2] Jer. xi. 11, Isa. i. 15, Micah iii. 4, Prov. i. 28.

[3] Ps. v. 3, xi. 12. אערך ואצפה.

[4] ἐνεργουμένη, it signifies such a working as notes the liveliest activity that can be.

One speaking of Luther, who was a man very earnest in prayer, said, *Hic homo potuit apud Deum quod voluit*, this man could have what he would of God, &c.

Again, to seek early is to seek *chiefly, primarily*, after this or that thing. What we first seek, we seek as chief.[1] Now, to seek the Lord early is to seek him primarily, chiefly; in the 63d psalm, and the 1st verse, 'Thou art my God, early will I seek thee,' that is, I will seek thee as my choicest and my chiefest good. God is *Alpha*, the fountain from whence all grace springs, and *Omega*, the sea to which all glory runs, and therefore early and primarily to be sought. God is a perfect good, a solid good, *Id bonum perfectum dicitur, cui nil accedere, solidum, cui nil decedere potest* (Lactantius), That is a perfect good, to which nothing can be added; that a solid, from which nothing can be spared. Such a good God is, and therefore early and chiefly to be sought. God is a pure and simple good; he is a light in whom there is no darkness, a good in whom there is no evil, 1 John i. 5. The goodness of the creature is mixed, yea, that little goodness that is in the creature is mixed with much evil; but God is an unmixed good; he is good, he is pure good, he is all over good, he is nothing but good.[2] God is an all-sufficient good: 'Walk before me, and be upright: I am God all-sufficient,' in the 17th of Genesis and the first verse. *Habet omnia, qui habet habentem omnia*, (Augustine), He hath all that hath the haver of all. God hath in himself all power to defend you, all wisdom to direct you, all mercy to pardon you, all grace to enrich you, all righteousness to clothe you, all goodness to supply you, and all happiness to crown you. God is a satisfying good, a good that fills the heart and quiets the soul, Cant. ii. 3. In the 33d of Genesis, and the 11th verse, 'I have enough,' saith good Jacob; 'I have all,' saith Jacob, for so the Hebrew hath it (*Cholli*), I have all, I have all comforts, all delights, all contents, &c. In having nothing, I have all things, because I have Christ; having therefore all things in him, 'I seek no other reward, for he is the universal reward,' saith one. As the worth and value of many pieces of silver is to be found in one piece of gold, so all the petty excellencies that are scattered abroad in the creatures are to be found in God, yea, all the whole volume of perfections, which is spread through heaven and earth, is epitomised in him. No good below him that is the greatest good, can satisfy the soul. A good wife, a good child, a good name, a good estate, a good friend, cannot satisfy the soul. These may please, but they cannot satisfy. 'All abundance, if it be not my God, is to me nothing but poverty and want,' said one.

Ah! that young men and women would but in the morning of their youth seek, yea, seek early, seek earnestly, seek affectionately, seek diligently, seek primarily, and seek unweariedly this God, who is the greatest good, the best good, the most desirable good; who is a suitable good, a pure good, a satisfying good, a total good, and an eternal good.[3]

Reason 10. *Because the time of youth is the choicest and fittest time for service.*

Now your parts are lively, senses fresh, memory strong, and nature vigorous. The days of your youth are the spring and morning of your

[1] *Omne bonum in summo bono.* [2] *Quicquid est in Deo, est ipse Deus.*
[3] *Omnis copia quæ non est Deus meus, mihi egestas est.*—Aug[ustine] Soliloq. c. 13.

time, they are the first-born of your strength; therefore God requires your non-age, as well as your dotage, the wine of your times as well as the lees, as you may see typified to you in the first-fruits, which were dedicated to the Lord, and the first-born, Exod. xxiii. 16, Num. iii. 13. The time of youth is the time of salvation, it is the acceptable time; it is thy summer, thy harvest-time.[1] O young man! therefore do not sleep, but up and be doing; awaken thy heart, rouse up thy soul, and improve all thou hast; put out thy reason, thy strength, thy all, to the treasuring up of heavenly graces, precious promises, divine experiences, and spiritual comforts, against the winter of old age; and then old age will not be to thee an evil age, but as it was to Abraham, 'a good old age,' Gen. xv. 15; do not put off God with fair promises, and large pretences, till your last sands are running, and the days of dotage have overtaken you. That is a sad word of the prophet, 'Cursed be the deceiver, which hath in his flock a male, and yet offereth to the Lord a corrupt thing,' Mal. i. 14.

Ah! young men and women, who are like the almond tree;[2] you have many males in the flock, your strength is a male in your flock, your time is a male in the flock, your reason is a male in the flock, your parts are a male in the flock, and your gifts are a male in the flock. Now, if he be cursed that hath but one male in his flock, and shall offer to God a corrupt thing, a thing of no worth, of no value, how will you be cursed, and cursed, cursed at home, and cursed abroad, cursed temporally, cursed spiritually, and cursed eternally, who have many males in your flock, and yet deal so unworthily, so fraudulently, and false-heartedly with God, as to put him off with the dregs of your time and strength, while you spend the primrose of your youth in the service of the world, the flesh, and the devil, Mat. xxi. 20.

The fig-tree in the Gospel, that did not bring forth fruit timely and seasonably, was cursed to admiration.[3] The time of youth is the time and season for bringing forth the fruits of righteousness and holiness, and if these fruits be not brought forth in their season, you may justly fear, that the curses of heaven will secretly and insensibly soak and sink into your souls, and then woe! woe! to you that ever you were born. The best way to prevent this hell of hells, is to give God the cream and flower of your youth, your strength, your time, your talents. Vessels that are betimes seasoned with the savour of life never lose it, Prov. xxii. 6.

Reason 11. *Because death may suddenly and unexpectedly seize upon you; you have no lease of your lives.*

Youth is as fickle as old age. The young man may find graves enough of his length in burial places. As green wood and old logs meet in one fire, so young sinners and old sinners meet in one hell and burn together. When the young man is in his spring and prime, then he is cut off and dies; 'One dying in his full strength (or in the strength of his perfection, as the Hebrew hath it) being wholly at ease and quiet, his breasts are full of milk, and his bones are moistened with marrow,'

[1] The days of youth are called *ætas bona*, in Cicero, and *ætas optima*, in Seneca. [Epist. xlix.—G.]

[2] Jer. i. 11, the almond tree blossoms in January, while it is yet winter, and the fruit is ripe in March.

[3] 'Amazement.'—G.

Job xxi. 23, 24. David's children die when young, so did Job's and Jeroboam's, &c. Every day's experience tells us, that the young man's life is as much a vapour as the old man's is.[1]

I have read of an Italian poet, who brings in a proper young man, rich and potent, discoursing with death in the habit of a mower, with his scythe in his hand, cutting down the life of man, 'For all flesh is grass,' Isa. xl. 6. And wilt thou not spare any man's person, saith the young man? I spare none, saith death; man's life is but a day, a short day, a winter's day. Ofttimes the sun goes down upon a man before it be well up. Your day is short, your work is great, your journey long, and therefore you should rise early, and set forward towards heaven betimes, as that man doth that hath a long journey to go in a winter's day.[2]

The life of man is absolutely short: 'Behold, thou hast made my days as an hand's-breadth,' Ps. xxxix. 5. The life of man is comparatively short, and that if you compare man's life now to what he might have reached had he continued in innocency. Sin brought in death; death is a fall, that came in by a fall. Or if you compare man's life now to what they did reach to before the flood: then several lived six, seven, eight, nine hundred years, Gen. i. 9; or if you compare men's days with the days of God, 'Mine age is as nothing before thee,' Ps. xxxix. 5; or if you compare the days of man to the days of eternity.[3]

Ah! young men, young men! can you seriously consider of the brevity of man's life, and trifle away your time, the offers of grace, your precious souls, and eternity? &c. Surely you cannot, surely you dare not, if you do but in good earnest ponder upon the shortness of man's life. It is recorded of Philip, king of Macedon, that he gave a pension to one to come to him every day at dinner, and to cry to him, *Memento te esse mortalem*, Remember thou art but mortal.[4]

Ah! young men and old had need be often put in mind of their mortality; they are too apt to forget that day, yea, to put far from them the thoughts of that day. I have read of three that could not endure to hear that bitter word death mentioned in their ears; and surely this age is full of such monsters.

And as the life of man is very short, so it is very uncertain: now well, now sick; alive this hour, and dead the next. Death doth not always give warning beforehand; sometimes he gives the mortal blow suddenly; he comes behind with his dart, and strikes a man at the heart, before he saith, 'Have I found thee, O mine enemy?' 1 Kings xxi. 30. Eutychus fell down dead suddenly, Acts xx. 9;[5] death suddenly arrested David's sons and Job's sons; Augustus died in a compliment, Galba with a sentence, Vespasian with a jest;[6] Zeuxis died

[1] *Pares nascuntur, pares moriuntur*, in the womb and in the tomb they are all alike, Job xxi. 23, 24. It is an allegorical description of the highest prosperity.

[2] Death's motto is, *Nulli cedo*, I yield to none.

[3] The heathen could say that the whole life of man should be nothing else but *meditatio mortis*, a meditation of death. [That rare little Puritan book by the Earl of Manchester, 'Almondo, or Contemplatio Mortis et Immortalitatis' (5th edition, 1642), illustrates and unfolds *above* very suggestively.—G.]

[4] Cf. Sibbes's Works, vol. ii. pp. 433, 435.—G.

[5] Petrarch telleth of one who, being invited to dinner the next day, answered, *Ego à multis annis crastinum non habui*, I have not had a morrow for this many years.

[6] See Bacon's Essays. On Death.—G.

laughing at the picture of an old woman which he drew with his own hand; Sophocles was choked with the stone in a grape; Diodorus the logician died for shame that he could not answer a joculary question propounded at the table by Stilpo; Joannes Measius, preaching upon the raising of the woman of Nain's son from the dead, within three hours after died himself.

Ah! young men and women, have you not cause, great cause, to be good betimes? for death is sudden in his approaches. Nothing more sure than death, and nothing more uncertain than life. Therefore know the Lord betimes, turn from your sins betimes; lay hold on the Lord, and make peace with him betimes, that you may never say, as Cæsar Borgias said when he was sick to death, 'When I lived,' said he, 'I provided for everything but death; now I must die, and am unprovided to die,' &c.[1]

Reason (12). *Because it is ten to one, nay, a hundred to ten, if ever they are converted, if they are not converted when they are young.*

God usually begins with such betimes that he hath had thoughts of love and mercy towards them from everlasting.[2] The instances cited to prove the doctrine confirms this argument; and if you look abroad in the world, you shall hardly find one saint among a thousand but dates his conversion from the time of his youth. It was the young ones that got through the wilderness into Canaan, Num. xxvi.[3] If the tree do not bud and blossom, and bring forth fruit in the spring, it is commonly dead all the year after. If, in the spring and morning of your days, you do not bring forth fruit to God, it is an hundred to one that ever you bring forth fruit to him when the evil days of old age shall 'overtake you, wherein you shall say you have no pleasure,' Eccles. xii. 1. For, as the son of Sirach observes, if thou hast gathered nothing in thy youth, what canst thou find in thy age?[4] It is rare, very rare, that God sows and reaps in old age. Usually God sows the seed of grace in youth, that yields the harvest of joy in age.

Though true repentance be never too late, yet late repentance is seldom true. Millions are now in hell, who have pleased themselves with the thoughts of after-repentance. The Lord hath made a promise *to* late repentance, but where hath he made a promise *of* late repentance? Yea, what can be more just and equal, that such should seek and not find, who might have found but would not seek; and that he should shut his ears against their late prayers, who have stopped their ears against his early calls? Prov. i. 24–32. The ancient warriors would not accept an old man into their army, as being unfit for service; and dost thou think that God will accept of thy dry bones, when Satan hath sucked out all the marrow? What lord, what master, will take such into their service, who have all their days served their enemies? and will God? will God? The Circassians, a kind of mongrel Christians, are said to divide their life betwixt sin and devotion, dedicating their

[1] Much earlier than Borgia, being recorded of the dying emperor Septimus Severus as follows: 'Omnia fui, nihil expedit.'—G.

[2] Hosea xi. 1, 'When Israel was a child, then I loved him,' &c.

[3] An Hebrew doctor observes, that of those six hundred thousand that went out of Egypt, there were but two persons that entered Canaan.

[4] Ecclesiasticus xxv. 3; the first quotation by Brooks thus far from the Apocrypha.—G.

youth to rapine, and their old age to repentance.[1] If this be thy case, I would not be in thy case for ten thousand worlds.

I have read of a certain great man that was admonished in his sickness to repent, who answered, that he would not repent yet, for if he should recover, his companions would laugh at him; but growing sicker and sicker, his friends pressed him again to repent, but then he told them that it was too late, *Quia jam judicatus sum, et condemnatus*, for now, said he, I am judged and condemned.[2]

CHAPTER II.

Reason 13. *Because else they will never attain to the honour of being old disciples.*

It is a very great honour to be an old disciple.

Now this honour none reach to, but such as are converted betimes, but such as turn to the Lord in the spring and morning of their youth. It is no honour for an old man to be in coats, nor for an old man to be a babe in grace. An A B C old man is a sad and shameful sight. Oh! but it is a mighty honour to be a man, when he is old, that he can date his conversion from the morning of his youth. Now that it is an honour to be an old disciple, I shall prove by an induction of particulars.[3] As,

Particular 1. *All men will honour an old disciple:* Prov. xvi. 31, 'The hoary head is a crown of glory, if it be found in the way of righteousness.'[4] God requires that the aged should be honoured: Lev. xix. 32, 'Thou shalt rise up before the hoary head, and honour the face of the old man' (the old man here is by some expounded the wise man), 'and fear thy God, I am the Lord.' Hoariness is only honourable when found in a way of righteousness. A white head, accompanied with a holy heart, makes a man truly honourable. There are two glorious sights in the world: the one is, a young man walking in his uprightness; and the other is, an old man walking in ways of righteousness. It was Abraham's honour that he went to his grave in a good old age, or rather, as the Hebrew hath it, with a good grey head, Gen. xxv. 8. Many there be that go to their graves with a grey head, but this was Abraham's crown, that he went to his grave with a good grey head. Had Abraham's head been never so grey, if it had not been good, it would have been no honour to him. A hoary head, when coupled with an unsanctified heart, is rather a curse than a blessing. When the head is as white as snow, and the soul as black as hell, God usually gives up such to the greatest scorn and contempt. 'Princes are hanged up by their hands, the faces of elders were not honoured,' Lam. v. 12, and this God had threatened long before. 'The Lord shall bring against thee a nation from far, a nation of fierce countenance, which shall not regard the person of the old, nor shew favour to the young,' Deut. xxviii. 49, 50.

[1] Breerw. *Enqui.* [This is Edward Brerewood's 'Enquiries touching the diversity of languages,' &c 1614.—G.]

[2] Bede hath this story.

[3] What more ridiculous than *puer centum annorum*, a child of an hundred years old?

[4] A crown is a very glorious thing, but there are but few of them.

I have read of Cleanthes, who was wont sometimes to chide himself. Ariston wondering thereat, asked him, Whom chidest thou? Cleanthes laughed, and answered, I chide an old fellow, *Qui canos quidem habet, sed mentem non habet*, who hath grey hairs indeed, but wants understanding, and prudence worthy of them.[1] The application I will leave to the grey heads and grey beards of our time, who have little else to commend them to the world but their hoary heads and snowy beards.

Particular 2. *God usually reveals himself most to old disciples, to old saints:* Job xii. 12, 'With the ancient is wisdom; and in length of days understanding.'[2] God usually manifests most of himself to aged saints. They usually pray most and pay most, they labour most and long most after the choicest manifestations of himself and of his grace; and therefore he opens his bosom most to them, and makes them of his cabinet council. Gen. xviii. 17–19, 'And the Lord said, Shall I hide from Abraham that thing which I do; for I know him, that he will command his children, and his household after him, and they shall keep the way of the Lord, to do justice and judgment; that the Lord may bring upon Abraham that which he hath spoken of him.' Abraham was an old friend, and therefore God makes him both of his court and council. We usually open our hearts most freely, fully, and familiarly, to old friends. So doth God to his ancient friends. Ah, what a blessed sight and enjoyment of Christ had old Simeon, that made his very heart to dance in him! 'Now, Lord, lettest thou thy servant depart in peace, according to thy word, for mine eyes have seen thy salvation,' &c., Luke ii. 25–28. I have seen him, who is my light, my life, my love, my joy, my crown, my heaven, my all; therefore now 'Let thy servant depart in peace,' verses 36–38. So Anna, when she was fourscore and four years old, was so filled with the discoveries and enjoyments of Christ, that she could not but declare what she had tasted, felt, seen, heard, and received from the Lord. She was ripe and ready to discover the fulness, sweetness, goodness, excellency, and glory of that Christ whom she had long loved, feared, and served. So Paul lived in the light, sight, and sweet enjoyments of Christ, when he was aged in years and in grace, Philip. iv. 5, 7, 9. So, when had John that glorious vision of Christ among the golden candlesticks, and those discoveries and manifestations of the ruin of Rome, the fall of antichrist, the casting the beast and false prophet into a lake of fire, the conquest of the kingdoms of the world by Christ's bow and sword, the binding up of Satan, and the new Jerusalem coming down from God out of heaven, Rev. i. 7, *seq.*, but when he was old, when he was aged in years and in grace? The Lord speaks many a secret in the ears of saints, of old Christians, which young Christians are not acquainted with, as that phrase imports, 2 Sam. vii. 27, 'Thou, O Lord God of hosts, hast revealed to thy servant;' so you read it in your books, but in the Hebrew it is, 'Lord, thou hast revealed this to the ear of thy servant.'[3] Some wonder how that word 'to the ear' comes to be left out in your books, in which indeed the emphasis lies. We will tell many things in an old friend's

[1] The 'quaint penitence' of above saying, as it has been described, belongs to the Stoic of the name. Cf. Bp. Cotton's Memoirs in Smith's 'Dictionary of Greek and Roman Biography and Mythology.'—G.

[2] בישישים In the ancient is wisdom. Valentianius the emperor's motto was, *Amicus veterimus optimus*, an old friend is best.

[3] גליתה את־אזן, *Galitha ethozen.*

ear, which we will not acquaint young ones with. So doth God many times whisper an old disciple in the ear, and acquaints him with such things that he hides from those that are of younger years. And by this you may see what an honour it is to be an old disciple.

Particular 3. An old disciple, an old Christian, *he hath got the art of serving God, the art of religion; got the art of hearing, the art of praying, the art of meditating, the art of repenting, the art of believing, the art of denying his natural self, his sinful self, his religious self.*[1]

All trades have their mystery and difficulty, so hath the trade of Christianity. Young Christians usually bungle in religious works, but old Christians acquit themselves like workmen that 'need not be ashamed.' A young carpenter gives more blows and makes more chips, but an old artist doth the most and best work. A young Christian may make most noise in religious duties, but an old Christian makes the best work. A young musician may play more quick and nimble upon an instrument than an old, but an old musician hath more skill and judgment than a young. The application is easy, and by this you may also see what an honour it is to be an old Christian, &c.

Particular 4. An old disciple, an old Christian, *is rich in spiritual experiences.* Oh! the experiences that he hath of the ways of God, of the workings of God, of the word of God, of the love of God! 1 John ii. 1. Oh! the divine stories that old Christians can tell of the power of the word, of the sweetness of the word, of the usefulness of the word! Ps. cxix. 49, 50, as a light to lead the soul, as a staff to support the soul, as a spur to quicken the soul, as an anchor to stay the soul, and as a cordial to comfort and strengthen the soul![2] Oh! the stories that he can tell you concerning the love of Christ, the blood of Christ, the offices of Christ, the merits of Christ, the righteousness of Christ, the graces of Christ, and the influence of Christ! Oh! the stories that an old disciple can tell you of the indwellings of the Spirit, of the operations of the Spirit, of the teachings of the Spirit, of the leadings of the Spirit, of the sealings of the Spirit, of the witnessings of the Spirit, and of the comforts and joys of the Spirit! Oh! the stories that an old Christian can tell you of the evil of sin, the bitterness of sin, the deceitfulness of sin, the prevalency of sin, and the happiness of conquest over sin! Oh! the stories that he can tell you of the snares of Satan, the devices of Satan, the temptations of Satan, the rage of Satan, the malice of Satan, the watchfulness of Satan, and the ways of triumphing over Satan! As an old soldier can tell you of many battles, many scars, many wounds, many losses, and many victories, even to admiration;[3] so an old saint is able to tell you many divine stories even to admiration.

Pliny writes of the crocodile, that she grows to her last day, Hosea xiv. 5–7.[4] So aged saints, they grow rich in spiritual experiences to the last. An old Christian being once asked if he grew in goodness,

[1] Heb. v. 11–14. Yet as Solon was not ashamed to say that in his old age he was a learner, so those that are the greatest artists in Christianity will confess, that they are still but learners. [Plutarch's *Solon*.—G.]

[2] Old men love to speak of ancient things.

[3] 'Wonder.'—G.

[4] The following are references in Pliny to the crocodile: lib. viii. c. 37, 38, 40, 72; xxviii. 29. Probably Brooks's is a vague recollection of the first.—G.

answered, Yea, doubtless I do; for God hath said, 'The righteous shall flourish like the palm tree,' Ps. xcii. 12–14, (now the palm tree never loseth his leaf or fruit, saith Pliny); 'he shall grow like a cedar in Lebanon. Those that be planted in the house of the Lord shall flourish in the courts of our God. They shall still bring forth fruit in old age; they shall be fat and flourishing.' A fellow to this promise Isaiah mentions, Isa. xlvi. 3, 4, 'Hearken unto me, O house of Jacob, and all the remnant of the house of Israel, which are borne by me from the belly, which are carried from the womb: and even to your old age I am he; and even to hoary hairs will I carry you: I have made, and I will bear; even I will carry, and will deliver you.'

There is nothing more commendable in fulness of age than fulness of knowledge and experience, nor nothing more honourable than to see ancient Christians very much acquainted with the Ancient of days, Dan. vii. 9, 13–22.

It is a brave sight to see ancient Christians like the almond tree. Now the almond tree doth flourish and is full of blossoms in the winter of old age; for as Pliny tells us, the almond tree doth blossom in the month of January. Experiments[1] in religion are beyond notions and impressions. A sanctified heart is better than a silver tongue. No man so rich, so honourable, so happy as the old disciple, that is rich in spiritual experiences; and yet there is no Christian so rich in his experiences but he would be richer.

As Julianus said, that when he had one foot in the grave, he would have the other in the school; so, though an old disciple hath one foot in the grave, yet he will have the other in Christ's school, that he may still be treasuring up more and more divine experiments. And by this also you see what an honour it is to be an old disciple, &c.

Particular 5. An old disciple *is very stout, courageous, firm, and fixed in his resolution.* An old Christian is like a pillar, a rock; nothing can move him, nothing can shake him, Ps. xliv. 9, 26. What is sucked in in youth will abide in old age. Old soldiers are stout and courageous; nothing can daunt nor discourage them. When Joshua was an hundred and ten years old, oh how courageous and resolute was he! Joshua xxiv. 15, 29, 'And if it seem evil unto you to serve the Lord, choose you this day whom you will serve: whether the gods that your fathers served, that were on the other side of the flood; or the gods of the Amorites, in whose land ye dwell; but as for me and my house, we will serve the Lord. And it came to pass, after these things, that Joshua the son of Nun, the servant of the Lord, died, being an hundred and ten years old.'

[Q.] Considius, a senator of Rome, told Cæsar boldly that the senators durst not come to council for fear of his soldiers. He replied, Why then dost thou go to the senate? He answered, Because my age takes away my fear.[2]

Ah! none so courageous, none so divinely fearless, none so careless in evil days, as ancient Christians. An old Christian knows that that good will do him no good which is not made good by perseverance; his resolution is like that of Gonsalvo, who protested to his soldiers, shewing them Naples, that he had rather die one foot forwards, than to have

[1] 'Experiences.'—G. [2] Plutarch, *Cæsar*, 14; Cicero, *ad Att.*, ii. 24.—G.

his life secured for long by one foot of retreat. Shall such a man as I am flee? said undaunted Nehemiah, chap. vi. 11. He will courageously venture life and limb rather than by one foot of retreat discredit profession with the reproach of fearfulness. It was a brave, magnanimous speech of Luther, when dangers from opposers did threaten him and his associates, Come, saith he, let us sing the forty-sixth psalm, and then let them do their worst.

When Polycarpus was fourscore and six years old, he suffered martyrdom courageously, resolutely, and undauntedly.[1]

When one of the ancient martyrs was very much threatened by his persecutors, he replied, There is nothing of things visible, nothing of things invisible, that I fear. I will stand to my profession of the name of Christ, and 'contend earnestly for the faith once delivered to the saints,' Jude 3, come on it what will.[2]

Old disciples, old soldiers of Christ, that have the heart and courage of Shammah, one of David's worthies, who stood and defended the field when all the rest fled, 2 Sam. xxiii. 11, 12. The Hebrews call a young man *Nagnar*, which springs from a root that signifies to *shake off*, or to *be tossed to and fro*, to note how fickle and how constant in inconstancy young men are, Mat. xix. 20-22. They usually are persons either of no resolution for good, or of weak resolution; they are too often won with a nut, and lost with an apple. But now, aged Christians in all earthquakes they stand fast, 'like mount Sion, that cannot be removed.' And by this also you may see what an honour it is to be an old disciple, an old Christian.

Particular 6. An old disciple, an old Christian, *is prepared for death; he hath been long a-dying to sin, to the world, to friends, to self, to relations, to all, and no man so prepared to die as he that thus daily dies.*[3]

An old disciple hath lived sincerely to Christ, he hath lived eminently to Christ, he hath lived in all conditions,[4] and under all changes, to Christ; he hath lived exemplarily to Christ, he hath lived long to Christ, and therefore the more prepared to die and be with Christ. An old disciple hath a crown in his eye, a pardon in his bosom, and a Christ in his arms, and therefore may sweetly sing it out with old Simeon, 'Lord, now let thy servant depart in peace,' Luke ii. 29. As Hilary said to his soul, Soul, thou hast served Christ this seventy years, and art thou afraid of death? Go out, soul, go out.[5]

'Many a day,' said old Cowper, 'have I sought death with tears, not out of impatience, distrust, or perturbation, but because I am weary of sin, and fearful to fall into it.' Nazianzen calls upon the king of terrors, Devour me, devour me. And Austin, when old, could say, Shall I die ever? yes, or shall I die at all? yes. Why, then, Lord, if ever, why not now?[6] So when Modestus, the emperor's lieutenant, threatened to kill Basil, he answered, If that be all, I fear not; yea, your master cannot

[1] As before.—G.

[2] Aristotle, though heathen, could say that in some cases a man had better lose his life than be cowardly.—*Arist.*, *Ethic.* 3, *cap.* 1.

[3] Rom. vi. 6, Gal. v. 24, vi. 14.

[4] Rom. xiv. 7, 8; Philip. ii. 21-23.

[5] The correspondent of Augustine.—G.

[6] Zeno, a wise heathen, said, I have no fear but of old age. Cyprian could receive the cruellest sentence of death with a *Deo gratias*, God, I thank thee.

more pleasure me than in sending me unto my heavenly Father, to whom I now live, and to whom I desire to hasten.

I cannot say as he, said old Mr Stephen Martial[1] a little before his death. I have not so lived that I should now[2] be afraid to die; but this I can say, I have so learned Christ that I am not afraid to die. Old Christians have made no more to die than to dine. It is nothing to die when the Comforter stands by, Isa. lvii. 1, 2. Old disciples know that to die is but to lie down in their beds; they know that their dying day is better than their birthday; and this made Solomon to prefer his coffin before his crown, the day of his dissolution before the day of his coronation, Eccles. vii. 1.

The ancients were wont to call the days of their death *Natalia*, not dying days, but birthdays.

The Jews to this day stick not to call their Golgothas *Batte Caiim*, the houses or places of the living. Old Christians know that death is but an entrance into life; it is but a passover, a jubilee; it is but the Lord's gentleman-usher to conduct them to heaven; and this prepares them to die, and makes death more desirable than life; and by this you may see that it is an honour to be an old disciple.

Particular 7. An old disciple, an old Christian, *shall have a great reward in heaven.*

Old Christians have done much and suffered much for Christ; and the more any man doth or suffers for Christ here, the more glory he shall have hereafter.[3] It was the saying of an old disciple upon his dying bed, 'He is come, he is come'—meaning the Lord—'with a great reward for a little work.' Agrippa having suffered imprisonment for wishing Caius emperor, the first thing Caius did when he came to the empire, was to prefer Agrippa to a kingdom; he gave him also a chain of gold, as heavy as the chain of iron that was upon him in prison. And will not Christ richly reward all his suffering saints? Surely he will. Christ will at last pay a Christian for every prayer he hath made, for every sermon he hath heard, for every tear he hath shed, for every morsel he hath given, for every burden he hath borne, for every battle he hath fought, for every enemy he hath slain, and for every temptation that he hath overcome.

Cyrus, in a great expedition against his enemies, the better to encourage his soldiers to fight, in an oration that he made at the head of his army, promised upon the victory, to make every foot-soldier an horseman, and every horseman a commander, and that no officer that did valiantly should be unrewarded; but what are Cyrus his rewards to the rewards that Christ our general promises to his?[4] Rev. iii. 21, 'To him that overcometh, will I grant to sit with me in my throne, even as I also overcame, and am set down with my Father in his throne.' As there is no lord to Christ, so there is no rewards to Christ's. His rewards are the greatest rewards. He gives kingdoms, crowns, thrones; he gives grace and glory, Ps. xlviii. 11.

[1] Misprint undoubtedly for 'Marshall,' not at all uncommon. Marshall was one of the holiest, as he was one of the most venerable and revered, of the Westminster Assembly of Divines. His life was published in 1680, 4to.—G. [2] Qu. 'not'?—ED.

[3] 1 Cor. xv. 58; 2 Cor. ix. 6; Mat. v. 10–12. God will reward his servants *secundum laborem*, according to their labour, though not *secundum proventum*, according to the success of their labour. [4] Mat. xix. 28; Luke xxii. 30; Mat. v. 12.

It is said of Araunah, that noble Jebusite, renowned for his bounty, that he had but a subject's purse, but a king's heart; but Jesus Christ hath a king's purse as well as a king's heart, and accordingly he gives.

And as Christ's rewards are the greatest rewards, so his rewards are the surest rewards: 'He is faithful that hath promised,' 1 Thes. v. 24.[1]

Antiochus promised often but seldom gave, upon which he was called, in way of derision, a great promiser; but Jesus Christ never made any promise, but he hath or will perform it, 2 Cor. i. 20, nay, he is often better than his word, 1 Cor. ii. 9, he gives many times more than we ask. The sick man of the palsy asked but health, and Christ gave him health and a pardon to boot, Mat. ix. 2. Solomon desired but wisdom, and the Lord gave him wisdom, and honour, and riches, and the favour of creatures, as paper and pack-thread into the bargain, 2 Chron. i. 10–15. Jacob asked him but clothes to wear, and bread to eat, and the Lord gave him these things, and riches, and other mercies into the bargain.[2]

Christ doth not measure his gifts by our petitions, but by his own riches and mercies. Gracious souls many times receive many gifts and favours from God that they never dreamt of, nor durst presume to beg, which others extremely strive after and go without.

Archelaus being much importuned by a covetous courtier for a cup of gold wherein he drank, gave it unto Euripides that stood by, saying, Thou art worthy to ask, and be denied, but Euripides is worthy of gifts, although he ask not.

The prodigal craves no more but the place of a hired servant, but he is entertained as a son, he is clad with the best robe, and fed with the fatted calf, he hath a ring for his hand, and shoes for his feet, rich supplies more than he deserved, Luke xv. 19–25. Jacob's sons, in a time of famine, desired only corn, and they return with corn and money in their sacks, and with good news too—Joseph is alive, and governor of all Egypt, Gen. xlii.

And as his rewards are greater and surer than other rewards, so they are more durable and lasting than other rewards. The kingdom that he gives is a kingdom that shakes not; the treasures that he gives are treasures that corrupt not; and the glory that he gives is glory that fadeth not away; but the rewards that men give are like themselves, fickle and unconstant, they are withering and fading.[3]

Xerxes crowned his steersman in the morning, and beheaded him in the evening of the same day.

And Andronicus, the Greek emperor, crowned his admiral in the morning, and then took off his head in the afternoon.

Rossensis[4] had a cardinal's hat sent him, but his head was cut off before it came to him. Most may say of their crowns as that king said of his, O crown! more noble than happy. It was a just complaint which long ago was made against the heathen gods, *O faciles dare summa deos, eademque tueri difficiles*, they could give their favourites great gifts, but they could not maintain them in the possession of them.

[1] As the King in Plutarch said of a groat, it is no kingly gift, and of a talent, it is no base bribe.

[2] Gen. xxviii. 20 compared with Gen. xxxii. 10.

[3] Heb. xii. 28; Mat. vi. 19, 20; 1 Peter i. 4.

[4] Qu. 'Roffensis'?—ED.

The world may give you great things, but the world cannot maintain you in the possession of them; but the great things, the great rewards that Christ gives his, he will for ever maintain them in the possession of them, otherwise heaven would not be heaven, glory would not be glory. Now by all these things you see that it is a very great honour to be an old disciple, an old Christian; and this honour you will never attain to, except you begin to be really good betimes, except in the morning of your youth you return to the Lord, and get an interest in him.

I shall now come to make some use and application of this weighty truth to ourselves.

You see, beloved, that it is the great duty and concernment of young men to be really good betimes. If this be so, then,

Use 1. First, *This truth looks sourly and sadly upon such young men that are only seemingly good, that make some shows of goodness, but are not right towards God at the root.*

As Joash, when he was young, he seemed to have good things in him towards the Lord, whilst good Jehoiada lived; but when Jehoiada was dead, Joash his goodness was buried with him, 2 Chron. xxiv. 1–6, 13–16.

Ah! how many in these days, that have been seemingly good, have turned to be naught, very naught, yea, stark naught!

It is said of Tiberius, that whilst Augustus ruled, he was no ways tainted in his reputation; and that, whilst Drusus and Germanicus were alive, he feigned those virtues which he had not, to maintain a good opinion of himself in the hearts of the people; but after he had got himself out of the reach of contradiction and controlment, there was no fact in which he was not faulty, no crime to which he was not accessory.[1]

Oh! that this were not applicable to many young persons in these days, who have made great shows and taken upon them a great name, who have begun to outshine the stars, but are now gone out like so many snuffs, to the dishonour of God, the reproach of the gospel, the grief of others, and the hazard of their own souls.

It was a custom of old, when any was baptized, the minister delivered a white garment to be put on, saying, Take thou this white vestment, and see thou bring it forth without spot at the judgment-seat of Jesus Christ; whereupon one Maritta baptizing one Elpidophorus, who, when he was grown up, proved a profane wretch, he brings forth the white garment, and holding it up, shakes it against him, saying, This linen garment, Elpidophorus, shall accuse thee at the coming of Christ, which I have kept by me as a witness of thy apostasy.[2]

Ah! young men and women, your former professions will be a sad witness against you in the great day of our Lord Jesus, except you repent and return in good earnest to the Lord, Prov. xiv. 14.

Oh! it had been better that you had never made profession, that you

[1] Nero's first five years are famous, but afterwards who more cruel? There are some that write that, after Demas had forsaken Paul, he became a priest in an idol-temple. [The one authority for such apostasy is an over-pressing of the following in Epiphanius: . . . . Καὶ Δημᾶν, καὶ Ἑρμογένην, τοὺς ἀγαπήσαντας τὸν ἐνταῦθα αἰῶνα, καὶ καταλείψαντας τὴν ὁδὸν τῆς ἀληθείας.—*Haeres.* xli. 6.—G.]

[2] Crabs that go backwards are reckoned among the unclean creatures, Lev. xi. 10.

had never set your faces towards heaven, that you had never pretended to God and Christ, that you had never known the way of righteousness, than, after you have known it, to turn from the holy commandment.

Cyprian, in his sermon *de lapsis*, reporteth of divers who, forsaking the faith, were given over to evil spirits and died fearfully.

Oh! the delusions and the Christ-dethroning, conscience-wasting, and soul-undoing opinions and principles that many young ones, who once were hopeful ones, are given up to! That dreadful scripture seems to be made good in power upon them: 'All you that forsake the Lord shall come to be ashamed, and they that depart from him shall be written upon the dust,' Jer. xvii. 13. To begin well and not to proceed, is but to aspire to a higher pitch, that the fall may be the more desperate. Backsliding is a wounding sin, Hos. iv. 14. You read of no arms for the back, though you do for the breast, Eph. vi. 11–18. He that is but seemingly good will prove at last exceeding bad: 2 Tim. iii. 13, 'They wax worse and worse, deceiving, and being deceived.'

The wolf, though he often dissembles and closely hides his nature, yet he will one time or other shew himself to be a wolf.

In the days of Hadrian the emperor, there was one *Ben-cosbi*, who, gathering a multitude of Jews together, called himself *Ben-cocuba*, the son of a star, applying that prophecy to himself, Num. xxiii. 17; but his mask was taken off, his hypocrisy discovered, and he found to be *Bar-chosaba*, the son of a lie.[1] [2] This age hath afforded many such monsters, but their folly is discovered, and their practices abhorred. This was the young man's commendation in the text, 'That there was found in him some real good towards the Lord.'

Use 2. This truth looks sourly and sadly upon such young men who are so far from having good things in them towards the Lord, *that they give themselves up to those youthful lusts and vanities that are dishonouring, provoking, and displeasing to the Lord, who roar and revel, and gad,*[3] *and game, and dice, and drink, and drab,*[4] *and what not.* These make work with a witness for repentance, or hell, or the physician of souls.

I shall but touch upon the evils of youth, and then come to that which is mostly intended.

CHAPTER III.

The first evil that most properly attends youth is pride.

Evil 1. Pride of heart, pride of apparel, pride of parts, 1 Tim. iii. 6. Young men are apt to be proud of health, strength, friends, relations, wit, wealth, wisdom. Two things are very rare: the one is, to see a young man humble and watchful; and the other is, to see an old man contented and cheerful.

Bernard saith, that pride is the rich man's cozen, and experience every day speaks out pride to be the young man's cozen.[5] God, said

[1] For vivid account of the different 'False Christs,' see Hepworth Dixon's 'Holy Land.' 2 vols. 8vo. 1865.—G.
[2] Comets make a greater blaze than fixed stars.
[3] 'To go about giddily.'—G.
[4] Are 'licentious.'—G.
[5] 'Cheat.'—G.

one, had three sons, Lucifer, Adam, and Christ; the first aspired to be like God in power, and was therefore thrown down from heaven; the second to be like him in knowledge, and was therefore deservedly driven out of Eden when young; the third did altogether imitate and follow Him in his goodness, mercy, and humility, and by so doing obtained everlasting inheritance.[1]

Remember this, young men, and as you would get a paradise, and keep a paradise, get humble, and keep humble. Pride is an evil that puts men upon all manner of evil. Accius the poet, though he were a dwarf, yet would be pictured tall of stature.[2]

Psaphon, a proud Lybian, would needs be a god, and having caught some birds, he taught them to speak and prattle: the great god Psaphon.[3]

Menecrates, a proud physician, wrote thus to king Philip: Menecrates a god, to Philip a king.[4]

Proud Simon in Lucian, having got a little wealth, changed his name from Simon to Simonides, for that there were so many beggars of his kin; and set the house on fire wherein he was born, because nobody should point at it.[5]

What sad evils Pharaoh's pride, and Haman's pride, and Herod's pride, and Belshazzar's pride, put them upon, I shall not now mention.[6]

Ah! young men, young men, had others a window to look into your breasts, or did your hearts stand where your faces do, you would even be afraid of yourselves, you would loathe and abhor yourselves.

Ah! young men, young men, as you would have God to keep house with you, as you would have his mind and secrets made known to you, as you would have Christ to delight in you, and the Spirit to dwell in you, as you would be honoured among saints, and attended and guarded by angels, get humble, and keep humble.

Tertullian's counsel to the young gallants of those times was excellent: 'Clothe yourselves,' said he, 'with the silk of piety, with the satin of sanctity, and with the purple of modesty; so shall you have God himself to be your suitor.'[7]

Evil 2. The second evil that youth is subject to is, *sensual pleasures and delights.*[8] 'Rejoice, O young man, in thy youth, and let thy heart cheer thee in the days of thy youth, and walk in the ways of thy heart, and in the sight of thine eyes,' Eccles. xi. 9. The wise man, by an ironical concession, bids him rejoice, &c., sin, &c. Thou art wilful, and resolved upon taking thy pleasure; go on, take thy course. This he speaks by way of mockage and bitter scoff, &c.; but know thou, that for all these things God will bring thee into judgment. So Samson 'made a feast; for so used the young men to do,' Judges xiv. 10. The hearts of young men usually are much given up to pleasure. I have read of a young man, who was very much given up to pleasures; he

[1] Pride cannot climb so high, but justice will sit above.

[2] Mentioned by Cicero. *Brutus*, 28.—G.

[3] Qu. 'Psaon'?—G.

[4] The letter to Philip beginning, Μενεκράτης Ζεὺς Φιλίππῳ, χαίρειν, received this answer, Φίλιππος Μενεκράτει ὑγιαίνειν. Cf. Athenæus, vii. p. 289; Aelian, *Var. Hist.*, xii. 51, and Suidas, *s. v.* Μενεκράτης.—G.

[5] Cf. Suidas, *sub nomine.*—G.

[6] Acce, an old woman, seeing her deformity in a glass, went mad, &c. [Qu. '*Acca* Laurentia'?—G.]

[7] Tertullian de Cult. fœm, cap. 13.

[8] 2 Sam. xiii. 23–29. ἡδονὴ δέλεαρ κακῶν, Pleasure is the bait of sin, saith Plato.

standing by St Ambrose, and seeing his excellent death, turned to other young men by him, and said, 'Oh, that I might live with you, and die with him.'

Sensual pleasures are like to those locusts, Rev. ix. 7, the crowns upon whose heads are said to be only as it were such, or such in appearance, and like gold; but verse 10, it is said there were—not as it were, but—stings in their tails.

Sensual pleasures are but seeming and appearing pleasures,[1] but the pains that attend them are true and real. He that delights in sensual pleasures, shall find his greatest pleasures become his bitterest pains.

The heathens looked upon the back parts of pleasure, and saw it going away from them, and leaving a sting behind.

Pleasures pass away as soon as they have wearied out the body, and leave it as a bunch of grapes whose juice has been pressed out; which made one to say, *Nulla major voluptas, quam voluptatis fastidium*, I see no greater pleasure in this world than the contempt of pleasure.

Julian, though an apostate, yet professed that the pleasures of the body were far below a great spirit; and Tully saith, he is not worthy of the name of man, *qui unum diem velit esse in voluptate*, that would entirely spend one whole day in pleasures. It is better not to desire pleasures, than to enjoy them. 'I said of laughter, it is mad; and of mirth, What dost thou?' Eccles. ii. 2. The interrogation bids a challenge to all the masters of mirth, to produce any one satisfactory fruit which it affordeth, if they could.

Xerxes, being weary of all pleasures, promised rewards to the inventors of new pleasures, which being invented, he nevertheless remained unsatisfied. As a bee flieth from flower to flower and is not satisfied, and as a sick man removes from one bed to another, from one seat to another, from one chamber to another for ease, and finds none; so men given up to sensual pleasures go from one pleasure to another, but can find no content, no satisfaction in their pleasures: 'The eye is not satisfied with seeing, nor the ear filled with hearing,' Eccles. i. 8. There is a curse of unsatisfiableness lies upon the creature. Honours cannot satisfy the ambitious man, nor riches the covetous man, nor pleasures the voluptuous man. Man cannot take off the weariness of one pleasure by another, for after a few evaporated minutes are spent in pleasures, the body presently fails the mind, and the mind the desire, and the desire the satisfaction, and all the man.

Pleasures are Junos in the pursuit, and but clouds in the enjoyment. Pleasure is a beautiful harlot sitting in her chariot, whose four wheels are pride, gluttony, lust, and idleness. The two horses are prosperity and abundance, the two drivers are idleness and security, her attendants and followers are guilt, grief, late repentance, if any, and oft death and ruin. Many great men, and many strong men, and many rich men, and many hopeful men, and many young men, have come to their ends by her; but never any enjoyed full satisfaction and content in her.[2]

Ah! young men, young men, avoid this harlot, and come not near the door of her house. And as for lawful pleasures, let me only say this,

[1] They were much out that held pleasure to be man's *summum bonum*.

[2] Becanus saith, that the fruit of the tree of knowledge is sweet, but in the end it breeds *choler*; so do worldly pleasures.

it is your wisdom only to touch them, to taste them, and to use them, as Mithridates used poison, to fortify yourselves against casual extremities and maladies. When Mr Roger Ascham asked the Lady Jane Grey how she could lose such pastime, her father with the duchess being a-hunting in the park, smilingly answered, All the sport in the park is but a shadow of that pleasure I find in this book,—having a good book in her hand.[1]

Augustine, before his conversion, could not tell how to live without those pleasures which he delighted much in, but when his nature was changed, and his heart graciously turned to the Lord, Oh! how sweet, saith he, is it to be without those sweet delights.

Ah! young men, when once you come to experience the goodness and sweetness that is in the Lord, and in his word and ways, you will then sit down and grieve that you have spent more wine in the cup than oil in the lamp.

There are no pleasures so delighting, so satisfying, so ravishing, so engaging, and so abiding as those that spring from union and communion with God, as those that flow from a sense of interest in God, and from an humble and holy walking with God.

Evil 3. The third sin of youth is *rashness.*

They many times know little and fear less, and so are apt rashly to run on, and run out often to their hurt, but more often to their hazard.[2] 'Exhort young men to be sober-minded or discreet,' Titus ii. 6. They are apt to be rash, to be Hotspurs. As you may see in Rehoboam's young counsellors, who counselled him to tell the people, 1 Kings xii. 8–11, that groaned under their burdens, that 'his little finger should be thicker than his father's loins, and that he would add to their yoke; and that whereas his father had chastised them with whips, he would chastise them with scorpions.' This rash counsel proved Rehoboam's ruin; yea, David himself, though a good man, yet being in his warm blood and young, how sadly was he overtaken with rashness! 'As the Lord God of Israel liveth,' saith he, 'except thou hadst hastened and come to meet me, surely there had not been left unto Nabal, by to-morrow light, any that pisseth against the wall,' 1 Sam. xxv. 34, 35. And this he binds with an oath. Because the master was foolishly wilful, the innocent servants must all be woful; and because Nabal had been niggardly of his bread, David would be prodigal of his blood.[3]

Ah! how unlike a Christian, yea, how below a man doth David carry it when his blood is up, and he is a captive to rashness and passion! Rashness will admit of nought for reason, but what unreasonable self shall dictate for reason. As sloth seldom bringeth actions to good birth, so rashness makes them always abortive ere well formed. A rash spirit is an ungodlike spirit; a rash spirit is a weak spirit, it is an effeminate spirit. 'A man of understanding is of an excellent spirit,' or as the Hebrew will bear, is of a cool spirit, not rash and hot, ready at every turn to put out his soul in wrath, Prov. xvii. 27. Rashness unmans a man, it will put a man upon things below manhood. Ero-

[1] The memorable scene when Lady Jane was reading Plato, as quaintly told by the old 'Schoolmaster.'—G.

[2] Arist. Polit.

[3] *Diis proximus ille est, quem ratio, non ira, movet,* He is next to God, whom reason, not anger, moveth.—Seneca. [*De Ira*, very often.—G.]

stratus, a hotspur, an obscure base fellow, did in one night by fire destroy the temple of Diana at Ephesus, which was two hundred and twenty years in building, of all Asia, at the cost of so many princes, and beautified with the labours and cunning of so many excellent workmen. The truth is, there would be no end were I to discover the many sad and great evils that are ushered into the world by that one evil, rashness, which usually attends youth, &c.; and therefore, young men, decline it, and arm yourselves against it, &c.

Evil 4. The fourth sin that ordinarily attends on youth is, *Mocking and scoffing at religious men and religious things.*

They were young ones that scoffingly and scornfully said to the prophet, 'Go up, thou bald-head; go up, thou bald-head,' 2 Kings ii. 23, 24. And the young men derided and mocked Job: 'But now they that are younger than I have me in derision, whose fathers I would have disdained to have set with the dogs of my flock. Upon my right hand rise the youth; they push away my feet, and they raise up against me the ways of their destruction,' &c., Job. xxx. 1, 12–15. And oh! that this age did not afford many such monsters, who are notable, who are infamous in this black art of scoffing and deriding the people of God, and the ways of God!

The Athenians once scoffed at Sylla's [Sulla] wife, and it had well nigh cost the razing of their city, he was so provoked with the indignity;[1] and will you think it safe to scoff at the people of God, who are the spouse of Christ, who are as the apple of his eye, who are the signet on his right hand, his portion, his pleasant portion, his inheritance, his jewels, his royal diadem?[2] Ah! young men, young men! will you seriously consider how sadly and sorely he hath punished other scoffers and mockers, and by his judgments on them, be warned never to scoff at the people of God or his ways more? Julian the emperor was a great scoffer of Christians; but at last he was struck with an arrow from heaven, that made him cry out, *Vicisti, Galilæe,* thou Galilean—meaning our Saviour Christ—hast overcome me.[3] Felix, for one malicious scoff, did nothing day and night but vomit blood, till his unhappy soul was separated from his wretched body. Pherecydes was consumed by worms alive, for giving religion but a nickname. Lucian, for barking against religion like a dog, was, by the just judgment of God, devoured of dogs.[4] Remember these dreadful judgments of God on scoffers, and if you like them, then mock on, scoff on; but know, that justice will at last be even with you, nay, above you.

Evil 5. The fifth and last evil that I shall mention that attends and waits on youth is, *lustfulness and wantonness.*

Which occasioned aged Paul to caution his young Timothy to 'flee youthful lusts,' 2 Tim. ii. 22. Timothy was a chaste and chastened piece; he was much sanctified and mortified; his graces were high, and corruptions low; he walked up and down this world with dying thoughts, and with a weak, distempered, declining, dying body; his heart was in heaven, and his foot in the grave; and yet youth is such

[1] Plutarch, *Sulla.*—G.

[2] Cant. v. 1; Zech. ii. 8; Deut. xxxii. 9; Isa. xix. 25; Joel ii. 17; Ps. xxxiii. 12; Isa. lxii. 3.

[3] A commonplace of quotation ascribed to Julian.—G.

[4] Very doubtful.—G.

a slippery age, that Paul commands him to flee, to post from, youthful lusts. Though Timothy was a good man, a weak, sickly man, a marvellous temperate man, drinking water rather than wine, yet he was but a man, yea, a young man; and therefore Paul's counsel and command is, that he 'flee youthful lusts.' And Solomon, who had sadly experienced the slipperiness of youth, gives this counsel: 'Put away the evils of thy flesh: for childhood and youth are vanity,' Eccles. xi. 10. He was a young man that followed the harlot to her house; he was young in years, and young in knowledge, Prov. vii. 7–11, &c. Salazer upon the words saith: That was a happy age that afforded but one simple young man among many, whereas late times afford greater store. Ah! too many of the youths of this age, instead of flying from youthful lusts, they post and pursue after youthful lusts.

Chrysostom, speaking of youth, saith, it is *difficilem, jactabilem, fallibilem, vehementissimisque egentem frœnis*,[1] hard to be ruled, easy to be drawn away, apt to be deceived, and standing in need of very violent reins.

The ancients did picture youth like a young man naked, with a veil over his face; his right hand bound behind him, his left hand loose, and Time behind him pulling one thread out of his veil every day; intimating that young men are void of knowledge, and blind, unfit to do good, ready to do evil; till time, by little and little, make them wiser.[2] Well! young man, remember this, that the least sparklings and kindlings of lusts will, first or last, cost thee groans and griefs, tears and terrors enough.

These five are the sins that usually are waiting and attending on youth; but from these the young man in the text was by grace preserved and secured, which is more than I dare affirm of all into whose hand this treatise shall fall. But though these five are the sins of youth, yet they are not all the sins of youth; for youth is capable of and subject to all other sins whatsoever; but these are the special sins that most usually wait and attend on young men when they are in the spring and morning of their youth.

CHAPTER IV.

I shall now hasten to the main *use* that I intend to stand upon, and that is an use of *exhortation to all young persons*.

Ah, sirs! as you tender[3] the glory of God, the good of your bodies, the joy of your Christian friends, and the salvation of your own souls, be exhorted and persuaded to be really good betimes. It was the praise and honour of Abijah, that 'there was found in him some good thing towards the Lord' in the primrose of his childhood.[4]

Oh! that it might be your honour and happiness to be really good betimes, that it might be to you a praise and a name, that in the morning of your youth you have begun to seek the Lord, and to know and

[1] Chrysost. Homil. i. *Ad populum.* [2] A Lapide. [3] 'Regard.'—G.

[4] Other sins attend youth, as (1.) Ignorance, 1 Cor. xiv. 20; (2.) Falsehood, Ps. lviii. 3; (3.) Excessive love of liberty; (4.) Impatience of counsels and reproofs, Jer. xxxi. 18, 19; (5.) Impudence [insolence], Isa. iii. 5; (6.) A trifling spirit, Eccles. xi. 10; (7.) Prodigality.

love the Lord, and to get an interest and propriety[1] in the Lord. Now that this exhortation may stick and take, I beseech you seriously to weigh and ponder these following motives or considerations:

Motive (1). First consider, *It is an honour to be good betimes.* A young saint is like the morning star; he is like a pearl in a gold ring. It is mentioned as a singular honour to the believing Jews, that they first trusted in Christ; 'that we should be to the praise of his glory, who first trusted in Christ,' Eph. i. 12. This was their praise, their crown, that they were first converted and turned to Christ and Christianity. So Paul, mentioning Andronicus and Junia, doth not omit this circumstance of praise and honour, that they were in Christ 'before him,' Rom. xvi. 7. 'Salute Andronicus and Junia, my kinsmen and my fellow-prisoners, who are of note among the apostles, who also were in Christ before me.'

And so it was the honour of the house of Stephanas, that they were the first-fruits of Achaia, 1 Cor. xvi. 15. It was their glory that they were the first that received and welcomed the gospel in Achaia. It is a greater honour for a young man to outwrestle sin, Satan, temptation, the world, and lust, than ever Alexander the Great could attain unto. It was Judah his praise and honour, that they were first in fetching home David their king, 2 Sam. xix. 15.

Ah, young men and women! it will be your eternal praise and honour if you shall be before others, if you shall be the first among many, who shall know the Lord and seek the Lord; who shall receive the Lord, and embrace him; who shall cleave to the Lord, and serve him; who shall honour the Lord, and obey him; who shall delight in the Lord, and walk with him. The Romans built Virtue's and Honour's temple close together, to shew that the way to honour was by virtue; and, indeed, there is no crown to that which goodness sets upon a man's head: all other honour is fading and withering. Adoni-bezek, a mighty prince, is suddenly made fellow-commoner with the dogs, Judges i. 7; and Nebuchadnezzar, a mighty conqueror, turned a-grazing among the oxen, Dan. iv. 28; and Herod, reduced from a conceited god to be the most loathsome of men, living carrion, arrested by the vilest of creatures, upon the suit of his affronted Creator, Acts xii. 23; and Haman, feasted with the king one day, and made a feast for crows the next, Esth. vii. 10. I might tell you of Bajazet and Belisarius, two of the greatest commanders in the world, and many others, who have suddenly fallen from the top of worldly honour and felicity, into the greatest contempt and misery, but I shall not at this time. But that honour that arises from men's being gracious betimes, is such honour that the world can neither give nor take; it is honour, it is a crown that will still be green and flourishing; it is honour that will bed and board with a man, that will abide with a man under all trials and changes, that will to the grave, that will to heaven with a man.

Ah, sirs! it is no small honour to you, who are in the spring and morning of your days, that the Lord hath left upon record several instances of his love and delight in young men. He chose David, a younger brother, and passes by his elder brothers, 1 Sam. xvi. 11–13; he frowns upon Esau, and passes by his door, and sets his love and de-

[1] 'Property.'—G.

light upon Jacob the younger brother, Rom. ix. 12, 13; he kindly and lovingly accepts of Abel's person and sacrifice, and rejects both Cain's person and sacrifice, though he was the elder brother, Gen. iv. 3–6. Among all the disciples, John was the youngest and the most and best beloved, John xiii. 23. There was but one 'young man' that came to Christ, and he came not aright, Mark x. 19–21; and all the good that was in him was but some moral good, and yet Christ loved him with a love of pity and compassion. The Greek word (ἀγαπᾶν) signifies, to speak friendly and deal gently with one; and so did Christ with him, all which should exceedingly encourage young men to be good betimes, to be gracious in the morning of their youth. No way to true honour like this, but,

Motive (2). Secondly, consider, *Christ loved poor sinners and gave himself for them, when he was in the prime of his age* (being supposed to be about thirty and three), *and will you put him off with the worst of your time?*

Ah! young men, young men, Christ gave himself up to death, he made himself an offering for your sins, for your sakes, when he was in the prime and flower of his age;[1] and why then should you put off Christ to an old age? Did he die for sin in the prime of his age? and will not you die to sin in the prime of your age? Did he offer himself for you in the spring and morning of his years? and will not you offer up yourselves to him in the spring and morning of your years? Rom. xii. 1, 2. Oh give not Christ cause to say, I died for you betimes, but you have not lived to me betimes; I was early in my suffering for you, but you have not been early in your returning to me; I made haste to complete your redemption, but you have made no haste to make sure your vocation and election, 2 Pet. i. 10; I stayed not, I lingered not, but soon suffered what I was to suffer, and quickly did what was to be done for your eternal welfare; but you have stayed and lingered, like Lot in Sodom, Gen. xix. 16, and have not done what you might have done in order to your everlasting good. In the primrose of my days, I sweat for you, I wept for you, I bled for you, I hung on the cross for you, I bore the wrath of my Father for you; but you have not in the primrose of your days sweat under the sense of divine displeasure, nor wept over your sins, nor mourned over me, whom you have so often grieved and pierced, Zech. xii. 10. I could not be quiet nor satisfied till I had put you into a capacity, into a possibility of salvation, and yet you are well enough quieted and satisfied, though you do not know whether ever you shall be saved.

Ah, sirs! how sad would it be with you, if Jesus Christ should secretly thus expostulate with your consciences in this your day.

Oh! how terrible would it be with you, if Christ should thus visibly plead against you in his great day. Ah! young men, young men and women, who but souls much left of God, blinded by Satan, and hardened in sin, 2 Cor. 3, 4, can hear Jesus Christ speaking thus to them: I suffered for sinners betimes, I laid down a ransom for souls betimes, I pacified my Father's wrath betimes, I satisfied my Father's justice betimes, I merited grace and mercy for sinners betimes, I brought in

[1] The sacrifices in the law were young lambs and young kids, to shew that Christ our sacrifice should die and suffer for our sins, in the flower of his age.

an everlasting righteousness upon the world betimes, &c.; I say, who can hear Jesus Christ speaking thus, and his heart not fall in love and league with Christ, and his soul not unite to Christ and resign to Christ, and cleave to Christ, and for ever be one with Christ, except it be such that are for ever left by Christ? Well, remember this, *Quanto pro nobis vilior, tanto nobis charior*, the more vile Christ made himself for us, the more dear he ought to be unto us.

Ah! young men, remember this, when Christ was young, he was tempted and tried; when he was in the morning of his days, his wounds were deep, his burden weighty, his cup bitter, his sweat painful, his agony and torment above conception, beyond expression; when he was young, that blessed head of his was crowned with thorns; and those eyes of his, that were purer than the sun, were put out by the darkness of death;[1] and those ears of his which now hear nothing but hallelujahs of saints and angels, were filled with the blasphemies of the multitude; and that blessed beautiful face of his, which was fairer than the sons of men, was spit on by beastly filthy wretches; and that gracious mouth and tongue, that spake as never man spake, was slandered and accused of blasphemy; and those hands of his, which healed the sick, which gave out pardons, which swayed a sceptre in heaven and another on earth, were nailed to the cross; and those feet, that were beautiful upon the mountains, that brought the glad tidings of peace and salvation into the world, and that were like unto fine brass, were also nailed to the cross: all these great and sad things did Jesus Christ suffer for you in the prime and flower of his days, and oh! what an unspeakable provocation[2] should this be to all young ones, to give up themselves betimes to Christ, to serve, love, honour, and obey him betimes, even in the spring and morning of their youth.

Let the thoughts of a crucified Christ, saith one, be never out of your mind, let them be meat and drink unto you, let them be your sweetness and consolation, your honey and your desire, your reading and your meditation, your life, death, and resurrection.

Motive (3). The third motive or consideration to provoke you to begin to be good betimes, is this, viz., *That it is the best and choicest way in the world, to be rich in gracious experiences betimes*,[3] which are the best riches in all the world. As he that sets up for himself betimes is in the most hopeful way to be rich betimes, so he that is good in good earnest betimes, he is in the ready way, the highway of being rich in grace and rich in goodness. They usually prove men of great observation and great experience. God loves to shew these his 'beauty and his glory in his sanctuary.'[4] He delights to cause 'his glory and his goodness to pass before' such. These shall find all his 'paths drop marrow and fatness.' For these 'the Lord of hosts will make a feast of fat things, a feast of wines on the lees, of fat things full of marrow, of wines on the lees well refined.' These shall have all man-

[1] *Nolo vivere sine vulnere, cum te video vulneratum.*—Bonaventura. O my God, as long as I see thy wounds, I will never live without wounds. *Aut Deus naturæ patitur, aut mundi machina dissolvitur*, said Dionysius Alexandrinus; either the God of nature suffered, or the frame of the world will be dissolved. [Epist. *ad Polycarp.*: ascribed also to the astronomer Ptolemy.—G.]

[2] 'Stirring up.'—G.

[3] The philosopher once said, *solus sapiens dives*, only the wise man is the rich man.

[4] Ps. lxiii. 1, 2; Exod. iii. 3, xix. 22, &c.; Ps. lxv. 11, 12; Isa. xxv. 6; Cant. vii. 13.

ner of 'pleasant fruits' laid up 'at their gates for their well-beloved.' None have so many choice pledges of Christ's love, nor so many sweet kisses of Christ's mouth, nor so many embraces in Christ's arms, as those souls that are good betimes. Oh the grace, the goodness, the sweetness, the fatness that Christ is still a-dropping into their hearts! Christ will make their hearts his largest treasury, he will lay up most of his heavenly treasure in their souls. There he will store up mercies new and old; there he will treasure up all plenty, rarity, and variety; there he will lay up all that heart can wish or need require. Oh the many drops of myrrh that falls from Christ's fingers upon their hearts! Oh the many secrets that Christ reveals in their ears! Oh the many love-letters that Christ sends to these! Oh the many visits that he gives to these! Oh the turns, the walks, that he hath in paradise with these! There are none in the world for experience and intelligence to these. Ah! young men, young men, as you would be rich in the best riches, begin to be good betimes;[1] as there is no riches to spiritual riches, so there is no way to be rich in these riches, but by beginning to be good, in good earnest, betimes.

As for worldly riches, philosophers have contemned them, and preferred a contemplative life above them, and shall not Christians much more?[2] The prophet calls them 'thick clay,' which will sooner break the back than lighten the heart; they cannot better the soul, they cannot enrich the soul, Hab. ii. 6. Ah! how many threadbare souls are to be found under silken cloaks and gowns! How often are worldly riches like hangmen, they hide men's faces with a covering, that they may not see their own end, and then they hang them. And if they do not hang you, they will shortly leave you, they 'make themselves wings and fly away,' Prov. xxiii. 5. When one was a-commending the riches and wealth of merchants, I do not love that wealth, said a heathen, that hangs upon ropes; if they break, the ship miscarrieth, and all is lost. He is rich enough, saith Jerome, that lacketh not bread, and high enough in dignity that is not forced to serve.

> 'This world's wealth, that men so much desire,
> May well be likened to a burning fire,
> Whereof a little can do little harm,
> But profit much our bodies well to warm;
> But take too much, and surely thou shalt burn;
> So too much wealth to too much woe does turn.'

It was an excellent saying of Lewis of Bauyer,[3] emperor of Germany, *Hujusmodi comparandæ sunt opes quæ cum naufragio simul enatent*, such goods are worth getting and owning as will not sink or wash away if a shipwreck happen, but will wade and swim out with us. We see such are the spiritual riches that will attend those who, in the spring and morning of their youth, shall know the Lord and serve the Lord, and get an interest in the Lord; and thus much for the third motive.

Motive (4). The fourth motive to provoke young ones to be really good betimes is, to consider that *The present time, the present day, is the only season that you are sure of.*

[1] Earthly riches are full of poverty. *Divitiæ corporales paupertatis plenæ sunt.*

[2] If there were any happiness in riches, the gods would not want them, saith Seneca. [A frequent sentiment in his Letters.—G.]

[3] Bavaria?—G.

Time past cannot be recalled, and time to come cannot be ascertained: 'To-day, if you hear his voice, harden not your hearts,' Heb. iii. 15; 'Behold, now is the acceptable time, now is the day of salvation,' 2 Cor. vi. 2. Some there be that trifle away their time, and fool away their souls and their salvation.[1] To prevent this, the apostle beats upon the τό νῦν, the present opportunity, because if that be once past, there is no recovering of it. Therefore, as the mariner takes the first fair wind to sail, and as the merchant takes his first opportunity of buying and selling, and as the husbandman takes the first opportunity of sowing and reaping, so should young men take the present season, the present day, which is their day, to be good towards the Lord, to seek him and serve him, and not to post off the present season, for they know not what another day, another hour, another moment, may bring forth. That door of grace that is open to-day may be shut to-morrow; that golden sceptre of mercy that is held forth in the gospel this day may be taken in the next day; hat love that this hour is upon the bare knee entreating and beseeching young men to break off their sins by repentance, 'to return to the Lord, to lay hold on his strength, and be at peace with him,' may the next hour be turned into wrath, Isa. xxvii. 4, 5.

Ah! the noble motions that have been lost, the good purposes that have withered, the immortal souls that have miscarried, by putting off the present season, the present day. Paul discoursing before Felix of righteousness and temperance and judgment to come, Acts xxiv. 25, and in this discourse striking at two special vices that Felix was particularly guilty of, he falls a-trembling, and being upon the rack to hear such doctrine, he bids Paul 'depart for that time, and he would call for him at a convenient season.' Here Felix neglects his present season, and we never read that ever after this he found a convenient time or season to hear Paul make an end of the subject he had begun. So Christ made a very fair offer to the young man in the Gospel, 'Go and sell that thou hast, and give to the poor, and thou shalt have treasure in heaven,' Mat. xix. 21–24. Here Christ offers heavenly treasures for earthly treasures, unmixed treasures for mixed treasures, perfect treasures for imperfect treasures, satisfying treasures for unsatisfying treasures, lasting treasures for fading treasures; but the young man slips his opportunity, his season, and goes away sorrowful, and we never read more of him.

Ah! young men, young men, do not put off the present season, do not neglect the present day. There is no time yours but the present time, no day yours but the present day; and therefore do not please yourselves and feed yourselves with hopes of time to come, and that you will repent, but not yet, and lay hold on mercy, but not yet, and give up yourselves to the Lord next week, next month, or next year, for that God that hath promised you mercy and favour upon the day of your return, he hath not promised to prolong your lives till that day comes.[2] When a soldier was brought before Lamacus,[3] a commander, for a misbehaviour, and pleaded he would do so no more, Lamacus answered, *Non licet in*

[1] The whole earth hangs on a point; so doth heaven and eternity on an inch of opportunity.

[2] Often consider what the damned would give, were it in their hands, for one season of grace, for one opportunity of mercy.

[3] Lamachus. Plutarch, *Pericles*.—G.

bello bis peccare, no man must offend twice in war; so God, especially in these gospel days, wherein the motions of divine justice are more smart and quick than in former days, happily will not suffer men twice to neglect the day of grace, and let slip the season of mercy, Heb. iii. 2.

Ah! young men, young men, you say you will be good towards the Lord before you die, but if you are not good towards the Lord to-day, you may die to-morrow, nay, justice may leave him to be his own executioner to-morrow, who will not repent, nor seek the Lord to-day. I have read of a certain young man, who, being admonished of the evil of his way and course, and pressed to leave his wickedness by the consideration of death, judgment, and eternity that was a-coming, he answered, What do you tell me of these things? I will do well enough; for when death comes, I will speak but three words, and will help all; and so still he went on in his sinful ways, but in the end, coming to a bridge on horseback, to go over a deep water, the horse stumbling, and he labouring to recover his horse, but could not; at last, he let go the bridle, and gave up himself and horse to the waters, and was heard to say these three words, Devil take all, *Diabolus capiat omnia!* Here was three dreadful words indeed, and an example, with a witness, for all young men to beware who think to repent with a three-word repentance at last.

Otho, the emperor, slew himself with his own hands, but slept so soundly the night before, that the grooms of his chamber heard him snort.[1] [2]

Young men, I will suppose you to be good accountants; now if you please to count the number and mark the age of the sacrifices in the Old Testament, you shall find more kids and lambs offered than goats and old sheep. You have no lease of your lives, you are not sure that you shall live to Isaac's age, to live till your eyes wax dim, Gen. xxvii. 1; you are not sure that you shall live to Jacob's years, and die leaning upon the top of a staff, Heb. xi. 21. You read of them who 'die in their youth, and whose lives are among the unclean,' Job xxxvi. 14. Slip not the present season, neglect not this day of grace, let not Satan keep your souls and Christ any longer asunder, by telling of you that you are too young, that hereafter will be time enough.[3] Austin tells us, that by this very temptation the devil kept him off from receiving of Christ, from closing with Christ seven years together; he could no sooner think of inquiring after Christ, of getting an interest in Christ, of leaving off his sinful courses, &c., but Satan would be still a-suggesting, Thou art too young to leave thy drunkenness, thou art too young to leave thy Delilahs, to leave thy harlots; till at last he cried out, How long shall I say it is too soon? why may I not repent to-day? and lay hold on Jesus Christ to-day? &c. Ah! young men, this is your day, this is your season; if you will not now hearken and obey, you may perish for ever. Cæsar had a letter given him by Artemidorus that morning he went to the senate, wherein notice was given him of all the conspiracy of his murderers, so that with ease he might have prevented

[1] Suetonius and Plutarch, *Otho;* Dion Cassius, lxiv.—G.

[2] Plutarch reporteth the like of Cato. [*Sub nomine, i. e.* Cato the younger.—G.]

[3] As out of the boughs of a tree are taken wedges to cleave it in pieces, so out of our own lusts Satan works engines to destroy us.

his death, but neglecting the reading of it, was slain; he slipped his season, and dies for it.[1] Ah! how many for slipping gracious seasons and opportunities, have died for ever! Soul-opportunities are more worth than a thousand worlds; mercy is in them, grace and glory is in them, heaven and eternity is in them.

Motive (5). Fifthly, To provoke you to be good betimes, consider, *How just it is with God to reserve the dregs of his wrath for them who reserve the dregs of their days for him.*

How can a husband embrace that wife in her old age, who hath spent all the time of her youth in following after strangers? Will any man receive such into his service, who hath all their days served his enemies, and received such wounds, blows, and bruises, that renders them unfit for his service?

Ah! young men, young men, do not thus 'foolishly and unwisely requite the Lord,' Deut. xxxii. 6, for all his patient waiting, his gracious wooing, and his merciful dealing with you. Ah! do not put off God to old age; for old, lame, and sick sacrifices rarely reach as high as heaven. Is not old age very unteachable? in old age are not men very unapt to take in, and as unapt to give out? In old age, oftentimes, men are men, and no men; they have eyes, but see not, ears, but hear not, tongues, but speak not, feet, but walk not.[2] An aged man is but a moving anatomy, or a living mortuary. Now how unlovely, how uncomely, how unworthy, nay, how incensing, how provoking a thing must this needs be, when men will dally with God, and put him off till their doating days have overtaken them, till their spring is past, their summer overpast, and they arrived at the fall of the leaf, yea, till winter colours have stained their heads with gray and hoary hairs! How provoking this is, you may see in those sad words of Jeremiah: Jer. xxii. 21, 22, 'I spake unto thee in thy prosperity; but thou saidst, I will not hear: this hath been thy manner from thy youth, that thou obeyest not my voice.' But will God put up this at their hands? No. Therefore it follows in the next verse, 'Surely thou shalt be ashamed and confounded for all thy wickedness.'

Oh! that young men would let this scripture lie warm every morning upon their hearts, that so they may not dare to put off God and provoke him to their own commission.[3] Though you are young and in your strength, yet are you stronger than God, can you make your party good with him? If you will needs be a-provoking, provoke them that are your matches, and do not contend with him that is mightier than you, that can command you into nothing, or into hell at pleasure.

Motive (6). Sixthly, consider, *That the sooner you are good on earth, the greater will be your reward in heaven.*

The sooner you are gracious, the more at last you will be glorious. You read in the Scripture of a reward, of a great reward, and of a full

[1] Plutarch, *Cæs.* 65; Zonaras, vol. i. p. 491, ed. Paris.—G.

[2] *Multa senem circumveniunt incommoda, Horatius*, 'Many are the inconveniences that do encompass an old man.' [*Ars Poetica*, 169.—G.] The reproach of the evil of wickedness is not to be added to old age; *Solet enim senectus esse deformis, infirma, obliviosa, edentula, lucrosa, indocilis et molesta*, saith Plutarch, in *Apothegm. Rom.* For old age useth to be deformed, weak, forgetful, toothless, covetous, unteachable, unquiet. [Brooks seems, in the description of 'old age,' to remember Shakespeare's 'sans teeth, sans eyes, sans taste,' &c —*As you like it*, ii. 7. The careful reader will trace numerous tacit references of this kind in Brooks.—G.]

[3] Qu. 'confusion'?—ED.

reward. Now those that are good betimes, that know, seek, serve, and love the Lord in the spring and morning of their youth, they are in the fairest way of gaining the greatest and the fullest reward.[1]

And this I shall make clear by that which follows.

(1.) *First, The sooner any man begins to be really good, the more good he will do in this world.* Now, the more good any man doth on earth, the more glory he shall have in heaven. Therefore, my beloved brethren, 'Be ye stedfast, unmoveable, always abounding in the work of the Lord, forasmuch as you know that your labour is not in vain in the Lord,' 1 Cor. xv. 58.

Man's wages, man's reward, shall be according to his works. He that doth most work here shall have most reward hereafter. God will at last proportion the one to the other, the reward to the work: 'He which soweth sparingly shall reap sparingly; and he which soweth bountifully shall reap bountifully,' 2 Cor. ix. 6. Though no man shall be rewarded *for* his works, yet God will at last measure out happiness and blessedness to his people *according to* their service, faithfulness, diligence, and work in this world, Rom. ii. 5–7. Grace is glory in the bud, and glory is grace at the full; glory is nothing else but a bright constellation of graces; happiness nothing but the quintessence of holiness. Grace and glory differ *non specie, sed gradu,* in degree, not kind, as the learned speak. Grace and glory differ very little; the one is the seed, the other is the flower; grace is glory militant, and glory is grace triumphant; and a man may as well plead for equal degrees of grace in this world, as he may plead for equal degrees of glory in the other world. Surely the more grace here, the more glory hereafter; and the more work Christians do on earth, the more glory they shall have in heaven; and the sooner men begin to be good, the more good they will do in this world; and the more they do here, the more they shall have hereafter. Philosophers seem to weigh our virtues with our vices, and according to the preponderation of either, denominate us good or bad, and so deliver us up to reward or punishment.

No man can commend good works magnificently enough, saith Luther, for one work of a Christian is more precious than heaven and earth; and therefore all the world cannot sufficiently reward one good work. And in another place, saith the same author, 'If I might have my desire, I would rather choose the meanest work of a country Christian or poor maid, than all the victories and triumphs of Alexander the Great, and of Julius Cæsar.'

And, again, whatsoever the saints do, though never so small and mean, it is great and glorious; because they do all in faith and by the word, saith the same author. To prevent mistakes, you must remember, that the works that Jesus Christ will reward at last are supernatural works: they are, 1, works of God; 2, wrought from God; 3, for God; 4, in God; 5, according to God. They are works that flow from supernatural principles, and they are directed to supernatural ends, and performed in a supernatural way. Now the sooner a man begins to be good, the more he will abound in these good works; and the more doubtless any man abounds in such good works on earth, the greater reward he shall have in heaven. Yet it must not be forgotten

[1] Ps. lviii. 11; Gen. xv. 1; Ps. xix. 11; Mat. v. 12; Heb. x. 35; John ii. 8.

that the best actions, the best works of hypocrites, and all men out of Christ, are but *splendida peccata*, fair and shining sins, beautiful abominations. And as the phœnix in Arabia gathers sweet odoriferous sticks together, and then blows them with her wings, and burns herself with them, so many a carnal professor burns himself with his own good works, that is, by his expecting and trusting to receive that by his works that is only to be received and expected from Jesus Christ.[1] Though all that man can do towards the meriting of heaven is no more than the lifting up of a festraw[2] towards the meriting of a kingdom, yet such a proud piece man is, that he is ready enough to say with proud Vega, *Cœlum gratis non accipiam*, I will not have heaven of free cost.[3] A proud heart would fain have that of debt which is merely of grace, and desires that to be of purchase which God hath intended to be of free mercy; which made one to say, that he would swim through a sea of brimstone, that he might come to heaven at last; but he that swims not thither through the sea of Christ's blood, shall never come there. Man must swim thither, not through brimstone, but through blood, or he miscarries for ever.

(2.) Again, *the sooner a man begins to be good, the more serviceable he will be to others, and the more he will provoke others to good.* Now, all the good that you provoke others to by counsel or carriage,[4] shall be put down to your account, as all the sins that men provoke others to is put down to their accounts. David did but send a letter concerning the death of Uriah, and the charge cometh, 'Thou hast slain Uriah with the sword,' 2 Sam. xii. 8, 9. The more I stir up others to sow, the more at last I shall reap, Isa. xxxviii. 3, Neh. xiii. 14. The sooner a man begins to be good, the more good he will do, the more serviceable he will be in the town or city where he dwells, in the family where he lives, among his relations, wife, children, kindred, servants, &c., with whom he converses.[5]

The sooner a man begins to be gracious, the sooner and the more useful will his arts, his parts, his gifts, his graces, his mercies, his experiences, his life, his labours, his prayers, his counsels, his examples, be to all that are with him, to all that are about him.

Lilmod lelammed, we therefore learn that we may teach, is a proverb among the Rabbins. And I do therefore lay in and lay up, saith the heathen, that I may draw forth again, and lay out for the good of many.

Ah! young men, young men! as you would be useful and serviceable to many, begin to be good betimes, and to lay in and lay up and lay out betimes, for the profit and advantage of others. Augustine accounted nothing his own that he did not communicate to others. The bee doth store her hive out of all sorts of flowers for the common benefit. It is a base and unworthy spirit for a man to make himself the centre of all his actions. The very heathen man could say that a man's country, and his friends, and others, challenge a great part of him. And indeed

[1] David made use of his bow, but did not trust to his bow. The dove made use of her wings, but did not trust in her wings, but in the ark.

[2] That is, 'fescue.' Latin, *festuca*, a wire or *straw* used to teach the letters = a trifle. Cf. Wright, *sub voce*.—G.

[3] *Merces non est debita, sed gratuita.*

[4] 'Life or example.'—G.

[5] Synesius speaks of some who, having a treasure of rare abilities in them, would as soon part with their hearts as their conceptions; but such are rather monsters than men.

the best way to do ourselves good is to be a-doing good to others; the best way to gather is to scatter. Memorable is that story of Pyrrhias, a merchant of Ithaca, who at sea espying an aged man, a captive in a pirate's ship, took compassion of him, and redeemed him, and bought his commodities which the pirate had taken from him, which were certain barrels of pitch. The old man perceiving that not for any good service he could do him, nor for the gain of that commodity, but merely out of charity and pity he had done this, discovered a great mass of treasure hidden in the pitch, whereby the merchant in a very short time became very rich; at which very time God made that word good, 'He that soweth liberally shall reap liberally,' 2 Cor. ix. 6; and that word, 'The liberal soul shall be made fat,' Prov. xi. 25; and that word, 'The liberal deviseth liberal things, and by liberal things shall he stand,' Isa. xxxii. 8. It is fabled of Midas, that whatever he touched he turned it into gold. It is certain that a liberal hand, a liberal heart, turns all into gold, into gain, as Scripture and experience do abundantly evidence. Now, if you put all these things together, nothing is more evident than that those that begin to be good betimes are in the ready way, the high way, to be high in heaven when they shall cease from breathing on earth. And therefore, young men, as you would be high in heaven, as you would have a great reward, a full reward, a massy, weighty crown, oh labour to be good betimes; labour to get acquainted with the Lord, and an interest in the Lord, in the spring and morning of your days!

Motive (7). The seventh motive or consideration to provoke and incite you to be good betimes, is to consider, *That the Lord is very much affected and taken with your seeking of him, and following after him, in the spring and morning of your youth.*

Go and cry in the ears of Jerusalem, saying, 'I remember thee, the kindness of thy youth, the love of thine espousals, when thou wentest after me in the wilderness, in a land that was not sown,' Jer. ii. 2.

Ah! how kindly, how sweetly did the Lord take this at their hands, that they followed him in their youth, while their 'bones were full of marrow,' while they were strong and fit for service, while nature was fresh, lively, and vigorous. In the law, God called for the first of all things; he required not only the first-fruits, but the very first of the first: 'The first of the first fruits of thy land, thou shalt bring into the house of the Lord thy God,' Exod. xxiii. 19. God is the first being, the first good, and therefore deserves the first of the first, and the best of the best; the first and the best is not too good for him, who is goodness itself.[1] God, in that of Leviticus ii. 14, is so passionately set upon having the first of the first, that he will not stay till the green ears of corn be ripe, but will have the green ears of corn dried in the fire, lest he should lose his longing.

As many young women and sickly children cannot stay till the fruit be ripe, but must have it while it is green; even so, saith God, my heart, my desires, are so vehemently set upon the first-fruits, the first things, that I cannot stay, I cannot satisfy myself without them; and what would God teach us by all this, but to serve him with the first-fruits of our age, the primrose of our childhood, the morning of your youth. God hath given you of the best, do not put him off with the worst, with the

[1] It is truly said of God, that he is *Omnia super omnia.*

worst of your time, the worst of your days, the worst of your strength, lest he swear in his wrath that 'you shall never enter into his rest,' Heb. iii. 18.

Motive (8). The eighth motive or consideration to provoke you to be good betimes, to seek and serve the Lord in the morning of your youth, is to consider, that *This may be a special means to prevent many black temptations, and an encouragement to withstand all temptations that you may meet with from a tempting devil and a tempting world.*

An early turning to the Lord will prevent many temptations to despair, many temptations to neglect the means openly, to despise the means secretly; many temptations about the being of God, the goodness, faithfulness, truth and justice of God; temptations to despair, temptations to lay violent hands on a man's self. Temptations to question all that God hath said, and that Christ hath suffered, arises many times from men's delaying and putting off of God to the last; all which, with many others, are prevented by a man's seeking and serving of the Lord in the spring and morning of his youth.[1] It is reported of the harts of Scythia, that they teach their young ones to leap from bank to bank, from rock to rock, from one turf to another, by leaping before them, by which means, when they are hunted, no beast of prey can ever take them; so when persons exercise themselves in godliness when they are young, when they leap from one measure of holiness to another, when they are in the morning of their days, Satan, that mighty hunter after souls, may pursue them with his temptations, but he shall not overtake them, he shall not prevail over them. As you see in Moses, Joseph, Daniel, and the three children, these knew the Lord, and gave up themselves to the Lord in the prime and primrose of their youth, and these were all temptation-proof, Heb. xi., Gen. xxxix., Dan. iii. Satan and the world pursued them, but could not overtake them. When the devil and the world had done their worst, the young men's bows abode in strength, and their hands to resist were made strong by the hands of the mighty God of Jacob, Gen. xlix. 23, 24. *Ego non sum ego*, said that young convert when tempted, I am not the man that I was.

Luther tells of a young virgin that used to resist all temptations with this, *Christianus sum*, I am a Christian. Early converts may say, when tempted, as he, Tell me not, Satan, what I have been, but what I am and will be; or as he in the like case, Whatsoever I was, I am now in Christ a new creature, and that is it which troubleth thee; or as he, The more desperate my disease was, the more I admire the physician.[2] Yea, thou mayest yet strain it a peg higher, and say, The greater my sins were, the greater is my honour, as the devils which once Mary Magdalene had, are mentioned for her glory. When Pyrrhus tempted Fabricius the first day with an elephant, so huge and monstrous a beast, as before he had not seen, the next day with money and

[1] Early converts will never have cause to say, as that despairing pope said, the cross could do him no good, because he had so often sold it away.

[2] Bernard, Beza, Augustine. Such as thou art now, I was once, but such as I am now, thou wilt never be, said Diogenes to a base fellow that told him he had once been a forger of money.

promises of honour, he answered, I fear not thy force, I am too wise for thy fraud.

Ah! young men, young men, as you would be free from the saddest and darkest temptations, and as you would be armed against all temptations, oh labour as for life to be good betimes! seek and serve the Lord in the morning of your youth. No way like this for the preventing earthquakes, heartquakes, stormy days, and winter nights, &c.

Motive (9). The ninth motive or consideration to stir up young men to be good betimes, to seek and serve the Lord in the spring and morning of their youth, is, *To consider the worth and excellency of souls.*

A soul is a spiritual, immortal substance, it is capable of the knowledge of God, it is capable of union with God, of communion with God, and of a blessed and happy fruition of God, Mat. xix. 28; Acts vii. 59, 60; Philip. i. 23.

Christ left his Father's bosom for the good of souls; he assumed man's nature for the salvation of man's soul. Christ prayed for souls, he sweat for souls, he wept for souls, he bled for souls, he hung on the cross for souls, he trode the wine-press of his Father's wrath for souls, he died for souls, he rose again from death for souls, he ascended for souls, he intercedes for souls, and all the glorious preparations that he hath been a-making in heaven these sixteen hundred years is for souls, Heb. ii. 13–16; Isa. lxiii. 3; John xiv. 1–3.

Ah! young men, young men, do not play the courtier with your precious souls. The courtier doth all things late; he rises late, dines late, sups late, goes to bed late, repents late.

Ah! sirs, the good of your souls is before all, and above all other things in the world; to be first regarded and provided for, and that partly because it is the best and more noble part of man, and partly because therein mostly and properly is the image of God stamped, and partly because it is the first converted, and partly because it shall be the first and most glorified.[1]

Ah! young men, young men, if they be worse than infidels, that make no provision for their families, 1 Tim. v. 8; what monsters are they that make not provision for their own souls! This will be bitterness in the end.

Cæsar Borgias being sick to death, lamentably said, 'When I lived, I provided for everything but death; now I must die, and am unprovided to die.' This was a dart at his heart, and it will at last be a dagger at yours, who feast your bodies, but starve your souls; who make liberal provision for your ignoble part, but no provision for your more noble part.

If they deserve a hanging, who feast their slaves, and starve their wives; that make provision for their enemies, but none for their friend; how will you escape hanging in hell, who make provision for everything, yea, for your very lusts, but make no provision for your immortal souls? James iv. 2, 3; Hos. vii. 13, 14. We hate the Turks for selling Christians for slaves, and what shall we think then of those who sell themselves, their precious souls, for toys and trifles that cannot profit? who practically say, what once a profane nobleman of

[1] *O anima 'Dei insignita imagine, desponsata fide, donata spiritu.*—Bernard.

Naples verbally said, viz., that he had two souls in his body, one for God, and another for whosoever would buy it.[1]

Ah! young men, young men, do not pawn your souls, do not sell your souls, do not exchange away your souls, do not trifle and fool away your precious souls; they are jewels, more worth than a thousand worlds, yea, than heaven and earth. If they are safe, all is safe; but if they are lost, all is lost: God lost, and Christ lost, and the society of glorious angels and blessed saints lost, and heaven lost, and that for ever. Granetensis tells of a woman that was so affected with souls' miscarryings, that she besought God to stop up the passage into hell with her soul and body, that none might have entrance.

Ah! that all young persons were so affected with the worth and excellency of their souls, and so alarmed with the hazard and danger of losing their souls, as that they may in the spring and morning of their days inquire after the Lord, and seek him, and serve him with all their might, that so their precious and immortal souls may be safe and happy for ever. But if all this will not do, then in the last place,

Motive (10). Tenthly, Consider, young men, *That God will at last bring you to a reckoning.* He will at last bring you to judgment. 'Rejoice, O young man, in thy youth, and let thy heart cheer thee in the days of thy youth, and walk in the ways of thine heart, and in the sight of thine eyes; but know thou, that for all these things, God will bring thee unto judgment,' Eccles. xi. 9. In these words you have two things: (1.) An ironical concession; he bids him rejoice, &c.; he yields him what he would have, by an irony, by way of mockage and bitter scoff. Now thou art young and strong, lively and lusty, and thy bones are full of marrow; thou art resolved to be proud and scornful, to indulge the flesh, and to follow thy delights and pleasures. Well! take thy course if thou darest, or if thou hast a mind to it, if thy heart be so set upon it. 'Rejoice in thy youth,' &c. (2.) The second is a commination, or a sad and severe premonition:[2] 'But know thou, that for all these things, God will bring thee into judgment. 'Will bring thee;' these words import two things: first, the unwillingness of youth to come to judgment; secondly, the unavoidableness that youth must come to judgment; but how soon you shall be brought to judgment, is only known to God.

Augustine confesses in one of his books, that as long as his conscience was gnawed with the guilt of some youthful lust he was once ensnared with, the very hearing of a day of judgment, was even a hell to him.

Histories tell us of a young man, who being for some capital offence condemned to die, grew grey in one night's space, and was therefore pitied and spared.

Ah! young men, young men, that the serious thoughts of this great day, may put you upon breaking off the sins of your youth; and the dedicating of yourselves to the knowledge, love, and service of the Lord, in the spring and flower of your days. Ah! young men, consider the errors of your lives, the wickedness of your hearts, the sinfulness of

[1] *Callenuceus* relates this story.

[2] Jerome still thought that that noise was in his ears, *Surgite mortui, et venite ad judicium*, Arise, you dead, and come to judgment.

your ways, and that strict account that ere long you must be brought to before the judge of all the world.

The heathens themselves had some kind of dread and expectation of such a day; and therefore, when Paul spake of judgment to come, Felix trembled, though a heathen, Acts xxiv. 25.

The bringing into judgment is a thing which is known by reason, and is clear by the light of nature;[1] wherefore, in Austria, one of the nobles dying, who had lived fourscore and thirteen years, and had spent all his life in pleasures and delights, never being troubled with any infirmity, and this being told to Frederick the emperor, From hence, saith he, we may conclude the soul's immortality; for if there be a God that ruleth this world, as divines and philosophers do teach, and that he is just no one denieth, surely there are other places to which souls after death do go, and do receive for their deeds either reward or punishment, for here we see that neither rewards are given to the good, nor punishments to the evil.[2]

Ah, young men! 'knowing therefore the terror of the Lord,' 2 Cor. v. 9–11, and the terror of this day, oh! that you would be persuaded to flee from the wrath to come, to cast away the idols of your souls, to repent and be converted in the primrose of your youth, that your sins may be blotted out when 'the times of refreshing shall come from the presence of the Lord,' Acts iii. 19, or else woe! woe! to you that ever you were born! I have read a story of one who, being risen from the dead, and being asked in what condition he was, he made answer, No man doth believe, no man doth believe, no man doth believe. And being further asked what he meant by that repetition, he answered, No man doth believe how exactly God examineth, how strictly God judgeth, how severely he punisheth. Oh that the ways of most young persons did not declare to all the world that they do not, and that they will not believe the dread and terror of that day that will admit of no plea, nor place for apology or appeal! The highest and last tribunal can never be appealed from, or repealed.[3]

Now if, for all that hath been said, you are resolved to spend the flower of your days, and the prime of your strength, in the service of sin and the world, then know that no tongue can express, no heart can conceive that trouble of mind, that terror of soul, that horror of conscience, that fear and amazement, that weeping and wailing, that crying and roaring, that sighing and groaning, that cursing and banning, that stamping and tearing, that wringing of hands and gnashing of teeth, that shall certainly attend you, when God shall bring you into judgment for all your looseness and lightness, for all your wickedness and wantonness, for all your profaneness and baseness, for all your neglect of God, your grieving the Comforter, your trampling under foot the blood of a Saviour, for your despising of the means, for your prizing earth above heaven, and the pleasures of this world above the pleasures that be at God's right hand.[4]

[1] The philosophers had some dreams of a severe day of accounts, as appeareth by Plato's Georgi [Gorgias], and many passages in Tully, &c.

[2] Æneas Sylvius.

[3] The Turks have a tradition and frantic opinion, that wicked men shall at the great day carry their sins in latchets [Qu. 'satchels'?—G.] after their captain, Cain; but well would it be for them if this should be all their punishment in that great day.

[4] Chrysostom, speaking of this day, saith, For Christ at this day to say, Depart from me, is a thing more terrible than a thousand hells.—*Chrys. Hom. ad Pop. Antioch.*

Oh! how will you wish in that day when your sins shall be charged on you, when justice shall be armed against you, when conscience shall be gnawing within you, when the world shall be a flaming fire about you, when the gates of heaven shall be shut against you, and the flame of hell ready to take hold of you, when angels and saints shall sit in judgment upon you, and for ever turn their faces from you, when evil spirits shall be terrifying of you, and Jesus Christ for ever disowning of you; how will you, I say, wish in that day that you had never been born, or that you might now be unborn, or that your mothers' wombs had proved your tombs! Oh, how will you then wish to be turned into a bird, a beast, a stock, a stone, a toad, a tree! Oh that our immortal souls were mortal! Oh that we were nothing! Oh that we were anything but what we are!

I have read a remarkable story of a king[1] that was heavy and sad, and wept, which, when his brother saw, he asked him why he was so pensive? Because, saith he, I have judged others, and now I must be judged myself. And why, saith his brother, do you so take on for this? it will, happily, be a long time ere that day come, and besides that, it is but a slight matter. The king said little to it for the present. Now, it was a custom in that country, when any had committed treason, there was a trumpet sounded at his door in the night time, and he was next day brought out to be executed. Now, the king commanded a trumpet to be sounded at his brother's door in the night-time, who, awakening out of his sleep, when he heard it, arose, and came quaking and trembling to the king. How now? saith the king; what's the matter you are so affrighted? I am, saith he, attached of treason, and next morning I shall be executed. Why, saith the king to him again, are you so troubled at that, knowing that you shall be judged by your brother, and for a matter that your conscience tells you you are clear of? How much more, therefore, may I be afraid, seeing that God shall judge me, and not in a matter that my conscience frees me of, but of that whereof I am guilty? And beside this, if the worst come, it is but a temporary[2] death you shall die, but I am liable to death eternal, both of body and soul. I will leave the application to those young persons that put this day afar off, and whom no arguments will move to be good betimes, and to acquaint themselves with the Lord in the morning of their youth.

But now to those young men and women who begin to seek, serve, and love the Lord in the primrose of their days, the day of judgment will be to them *melodia in aure, jubilum in corde*, like music in the ear, and a jubilee in the heart. This day will be to them 'a day of refreshing,' a 'day of redemption,' a day of vindication, a day of coronation, a day of consolation, a day of salvation; it will be to them a marriage-day, a harvest-day, a pay-day.[3] Now the Lord will pay them for all the prayers they have made, for all the sermons they have heard, for all the tears they have shed. In this great day Christ will remember all the individual offices of love and friendship shewed to any of his. Now he will mention many things for their honour and comfort

[1] Joan. Damasc. et Author. Anonym. *De quat. Noviss. Impress. Daven.* Ann. 1494.
[2] 'Temporal.'—G.
[3] Acts iii. 19–22, Micah vii. 7–11, Rev. xix. 6–10, Mat. xxv. 34–41.

that they never minded, now the least and lowest acts of love and pity towards his shall be interpreted as a special kindness shewed to himself. Now the crown shall be set upon their heads, and the royal robes put upon their backs; now all the world shall see that they have not served the Lord for nought.[1] Now Christ will pass over all their weaknesses, and make honourable mention of all the services they have performed, of all the mercies they have improved, and of all the great things that for his name and glory they have suffered.

CHAPTER V.

Quest. But here an apt question may be moved, viz., *Whether at this great day, the sins of the saints shall be brought into the judgment of discussion and discovery, or no? Whether the Lord will in this day publicly manifest, proclaim, and make mention of the sins of his people, or no?*

I humbly judge, according to my present light, that he will not; and my reasons for it are these, viz.:

1. The first is drawn from Christ's judicial proceedings in the last day, set down largely and clearly in the 25th of Matthew, where he enumerateth only the good works they had done, but takes no notice of the spots and blots, of the stains and blemishes, of the infirmities and enormities, of the weaknesses and wickednesses of his people, Deut. xxxii. 4–6. My,

2. Second reason is taken from Christ's vehement protestations that they shall not come into judgment: John v. 24, 'Verily, verily, I say unto you, he that heareth my word, and believeth on him that sent me, hath everlasting life, and shall not come into condemnation, but is passed from death unto life.' Those words, 'shall not come into condemnation,' are not rightly translated; the original is, εἰς κρίσιν, shall not come into judgment, not into damnation, as you read it in all your English books. I will not say what should put men upon this exposition rather than a true translation of the original word.[2] Further, it is very observable, that no evangelist useth this double asseveration but John, and he never useth it but in matters of the greatest weight and importance, and to shew the earnestness of his spirit, and to stir us up to better attention, and to put the thing asserted out of all question, and beyond all contradiction;[3] as when we would put a thing for ever out of all question, we do it by a double asseveration, Verily, verily, it is so, &c.

3 Thirdly, Because his not bringing their sins into judgment doth most and best agree with many precious expressions that we find scattered, as so many shining, sparkling pearls, up and down in Scripture, as, *First,* (1.) With those of God's blotting out the sins of his people: 'I, even I, am he that blotteth out thy transgressions for my own sake, and will not remember thy sins.' 'I have blotted out as a thick cloud thy transgressions, and as a cloud thy sins,' Isa. xliii. 25, xliv. 22. Who is this that blots out transgressions? He that hath the keys of heaven

[1] 2 Tim. iv 8, Mal. iii, 17, 18.
[2] Vide Aquin. 87, Suppl. Estius. in l. iv. Sen. dist. 47.
[3] John i. 51; iii. 3, 11; vi. 26, 32, 47, 53, &c.

and hell at his girdle, that opens and no man shuts, that shuts and no man opens; he that hath the power of life and death, of condemning and absolving, of killing and making alive, he it is that blots out transgressions. If an under-officer should blot out an indictment, that perhaps might do a man no good, a man might for all that be at last cast by the judge; but when the judge or king shall blot out the indictment with their own hand, then the indictment cannot return. Now this is every believer's case and happiness. (2.) *Secondly,* To those glorious expressions of God's not remembering of their sins any more: Isa. xliii. 25, 'And I will not remember thy sins.' 'And they shall teach no more every man his neighbour, and every man his brother, saying, Know the Lord: for they shall all know me, from the least of them to the greatest of them, saith the Lord: for I will forgive their iniquity, and I will remember their sin no more,' Jer. xxxi. 34. So the apostle, 'For I will be merciful to their unrighteousness, and their sins and their iniquities will I remember no more,' Heb. viii. 12.

And again the same apostle saith, 'This is the covenant that I will make with them after those days, saith the Lord, I will put my laws into their hearts, and in their minds will I write them; and their sins and iniquities will I remember no more,' Heb. x. 17.

The meaning is, their iniquities shall quite be forgiven, I will never mention them more, I will never take notice of them more, they shall never hear more of them from me. Though God hath an iron memory to remember the sins of the wicked, yet he hath no memory to remember the sins of the righteous.[1] (3.) Thirdly, His not bringing their sins into judgment doth most and best agree with those blessed expressions of his casting their sins into the depth of the sea, and of his casting them behind his back: 'He will turn again, he will have compassion upon us, he will subdue our iniquities, and thou wilt cast all their sins into the depths of the sea,' Micah vii. 19. Where sin is once pardoned, the remission stands never to be repealed. Pardoned sins shall never come in account against the pardoned man before God any more, for so much doth this borrowed speech import. If a thing were cast into a river, it might be brought up again; or if it were cast upon the sea, it might be discerned and taken up again; but when it is cast into the depths, the bottom of the sea, it can never be buoyed up again.

By the metaphor in the text, the Lord would have us to know the sins pardoned shall rise no more, they shall never be seen more, they shall never come on the account more; he will so drown their sins, that they shall never come up before him the second time.

And so much that other scripture imports: 'Behold, for peace I had great bitterness, but thou hast in love to my soul delivered it from the pit of corruption; for thou hast cast all my sins behind thy back,' Isa. xxxviii. 17. These last words are a borrowed speech, taken from the manner of men, who are wont to cast behind their backs such things as they have no mind to see, regard, or remember. A gracious soul hath always his sins before his face: 'I acknowledge my transgressions, and my sin is ever before me;' and therefore no wonder if the Lord cast them behind his back. The father soon forgets and casts behind his back

[1] That which Cicero said flatteringly of Cæsar is truly affirmed of God, *Nihil oblivisci solet præter injurias,* he forgetteth nothing but the wrongs that daily are done him by his.

those faults that the child remembers and hath always in his eyes; so doth the Father of spirits. (4.) Fourthly, His not bringing their sins into judgment doth best agree with that sweet and choice expression of God's pardoning the sins of his people: 'And I will cleanse them from all their iniquity, whereby they have sinned against me; and I will pardon all their iniquities, whereby they have sinned, and whereby they have transgressed against me,' Jer. xxxiii. 8. So Micah: 'Who is a God like unto thee, that pardoneth iniquity, and passes by the transgressions of the remnant of his heritage (as though he would not see it, but wink at it), he retaineth not his anger for ever, because he delighteth in mercy,' Micah vii. 18. The Hebrew word *nose*, from *nasa*, that is here rendered *pardoneth*, signifies a taking away. When God pardons sin, he takes it sheer away: that it should be sought for, yet it could not be found, as the prophet speaks: 'In those days, and in that time, saith the Lord, the iniquity of Israel shall be sought for, and there shall be none; and the sins of Judah, and they shall not be found; for I will pardon them whom I reserve,' Jer. l. 20; and those words, 'and passeth by,' in the afore-cited 7th of Micah, and the 18th, according to the Hebrew *Vegnober Gnal*, is, and 'passeth over;'[1] God passeth over the transgression of his heritage, that is, he takes no notice of it As a man in a deep muse, or as one that hath haste of business, seeth not things before him, his mind being busied about other matters, he neglects all to mind his business; as David, when he saw in Mephibosheth the feature of his friend Jonathan, took no notice of his lameness, or any other defect or deformity; so God, beholding in his people the glorious image of his Son, winks at all their faults and deformities, which made Luther say, 'Do with me what thou wilt, since thou hast pardoned my sin;' and what is it to pardon sin but not to mention sin? Isa. xl. 1, 2. (5.) Fifthly, In his not bringing their sins into the judgment of discussion and discovery, doth best agree to those expressions of forgiving and covering: 'Blessed is he whose transgression is forgiven, whose sin is covered,' Ps. xxxii. 1. In the original it is in the plural, blessednesses. So here is a plurality of blessings, a chain of pearls.

The like expression you have in the 85th psalm, and the 2d verse: 'Thou hast forgiven the iniquity of thy people, thou hast covered all their sin. Selah.' For the understanding of these scriptures aright, take notice that to 'cover' is a metaphorical expression. Covering is such an action which is opposed to disclosure.[2] To be covered is to be so hid and closed as not to appear. Some make the metaphor from filthy, loathsome objects, which are covered from our eyes, as dead carcases are buried under the ground; some from garments, that are put upon us to cover our nakedness; others from the Egyptians, that were drowned in the Red Sea, and so covered with water; others from a great gulf in the earth, that is filled up and covered with earth injected into it; and others make it in the last place an allusive expression to the mercy-seat, over which was a covering. Now, all these metaphors in the general tend to shew this, that the Lord will not look, he will not see, he will not take notice of the sins he hath pardoned, to call them any more to a judicial account.

As when a prince reads over many treasons and rebellions, and meets with such and such which he hath pardoned, he reads on, he passeth

[1] עבר, Gnabar, he passed over.

[2] *Sic velantur, ut in judicio non revelentur.*

by, he takes no notice of them: the pardoned person shall never hear more of them, he will never call him to account for those sins more; so here, &c. When Cæsar was painted, he put his finger upon his scar, his wart. God puts his fingers upon all his people's scars and warts, upon all their weaknesses and infirmities, that nothing can be seen but what is fair and lovely: 'Thou art all fair, my love; and there is no spot in thee,' Cant. iv. 7. (6.) Sixthly, It best agrees to that expression of not imputing of sin: 'Blessed is the man to whom the Lord imputeth not iniquity, and in whose spirit there is no guile,' Ps. xxxii. 2. So the apostle in that Rom. iv. 6–8. Now, not to impute iniquity is not to charge iniquity, not to set iniquity upon his score, who is blessed and pardoned, &c. (7.) Seventhly and lastly, It best agrees with that expression that you have in the 103d Psalm, and the 11th and 12th verses: 'For as the heaven is high above the earth, so great is his mercy towards them that fear him. As far as the east is from the west, so far hath he removed our transgressions from us.' What a vast distance is there betwixt the east and the west! Of all visible latitudes, this is the greatest; and thus much for the third argument. The

4. Fourth argument that prevails with me, to judge that Jesus Christ will not bring the sins of the saints into the judgment of discussion and discovery in the great day, is because it seems unsuitable to three considerable things, for Jesus Christ to proclaim the infirmities and miscarriages of his people to all the world.

(1.) First, It seems to be unsuitable to the glory and solemnity of that day, which to the saints will be a day of refreshing, a day of restitution, a day of redemption, a day of coronation, as hath been already proved. Now how suitable to this great day of solemnity the proclamation of the saints' sins will be, I leave the reader to judge.

(2.) Secondly, It seems unsuitable to all those near and dear relations that Jesus Christ stands in towards his. He stands in the relation of a father, a brother, a head, a husband, a friend, an advocate. Now are not all these, by the law of relations, bound rather to hide and keep secret, at least from the world, the weaknesses and infirmities of their near and dear relations? and is not Christ? Is not Christ much more? By how much he is more a father, a brother, a head, a husband, &c., in a spiritual way, than any others can be in a natural way, &c.[1]

(3.) Thirdly, It seems very unsuitable to what the Lord Jesus requires of his in this world. The Lord requires that his people should cast a mantle of love, of wisdom, of silence, and secresy over one another's weaknesses and infirmities.

Hatred stirreth up strifes, but love covereth all sins, Prov. x. 12, 1 Pet. iv. 8. Love's mantle is very large; love will find a hand, a plaster to clap upon every sore. Flavius Vespasianus, the emperor, was very ready to conceal his friends' vices, and as ready to reveal their virtues. So is divine love in the hearts of the saints: 'If thy brother offend thee, go and tell him his fault between him and thee alone: if he shall hear thee, thou hast gained thy brother,' Mat. xviii. 15. As the pills of reprehension are to be gilded and sugared over with much gentleness and softness, so they are to be given in secret; tell him between him and thee alone. Tale-bearers and tale-hearers are alike abominable,

[1] Isa. ix. 6; Heb. ii. 11, 12; Ephes. i. 21, 22; Rev. xix. 7; John xv. 1; John ii. 1, 2.

heaven is too hot and too holy a place for them, Ps. xv. 3. Now will Jesus Christ have us carry it thus towards offending Christians, and will he himself act otherwise? Nay, is it an evil in us to lay open the weaknesses and infirmities of the saints to the world? and will it be an excellency, a glory, a virtue in Christ to do it in the great day? &c.

A fifth argument is this: It is the glory of a man to pass over a transgression: 'The discretion of a man deferreth his anger: and it is his glory to pass over a transgression,' Prov. xix. 11, or to pass by it, as we do by persons or things we know not, or would take no notice of. Now 'is it the glory of a man to pass over a transgression,' and will it not much more be the glory of Christ, silently to pass over the transgressions of his people in that great day?[1] The greater the treasons and rebellions are that a prince passes over and takes no notice of, the more is it his honour and glory; and so, doubtless, it will be Christ's in that great day, to pass over all the treasons and rebellions of his people, to take no notice of them, to forget them, as well as to forgive them.

The heathens have long since observed, that in nothing man came nearer to the glory and perfection of God himself, than in goodness and clemency. Surely if it be such an honour to man, 'to pass over a transgression,' it cannot be a dishonour to Christ to pass over the transgressions of his people, he having already buried them in the sea of his blood. Again, saith Solomon, 'It is the glory of God to conceal a thing,' Prov. xxv. 2. And why it should not make for the glory of divine love to conceal the sins of the saints in that great day, I know not; and whether the concealing the sins of the saints in that great day will not make most for their joy, and wicked men's sorrow, for their comfort and wicked men's terror and torment, I will leave you to judge, and time and experience to decide. And thus much for the resolution of that great question. Having done with the motives that may encourage and provoke young men to be good betimes, to know, love, seek, and serve the Lord, in the spring and morning of their days.

CHAPTER VI.

I shall now come to those directions and helps that must, by assistance from heaven, be put in practice, if ever you would be good betimes, and serve the Lord in the primrose of your days. Now all that I shall say will fall under these two heads.

First, Some things you must carefully and warily decline, and arm yourselves against; and

Secondly, There are other things that you must prosecute and follow. 1*st*, *There are some things that you must warily decline*, and they are these.

Direction (1). First, If ever you would be good betimes, if you would be gracious in the spring and morning of your youth, oh! then, *take heed of putting the day of death far from you*, Amos vi. 3.

Young men are very prone to look upon death afar off, to put it at a great distance from them. They are apt to say to death as Pharaoh said to Moses, 'Get thee from me, and let me see thy face no more,'

[1] *Non amo quemquam nisi offendam*, said a heathen.

Exod. x. 28. If old men discourse to them of death, they are ready to answer, as the high priest did Judas in a different case, Mat. xxvii. 4, 'What is that to us? look you unto it.' We know sickness will come, and death is a debt that we must all pay, but surely these guests are a great way from us; for doth not David say, 'The days of a man are threescore years and ten'? Ps. xc. 10. We have calculated our nativities, and we cannot abate a day, a minute, a moment, of 'threescore and ten;' and therefore it is even a death to think of death; there being so great a distance between our birth-day and our dying day, as we have cast up the account.

Ah! young men, it is sad, it is very sad, when you are so wittily wicked as to say with those in Ezekiel, 'Behold they of the house of Israel say, the vision that he seeth is for many days to come, and he prophesieth of the times that are afar off,' Ezek. xii. 27.

Ah! young men, young men, by putting far away this day you gratify Satan, you strengthen sin, you provoke the Lord, you make the work of faith and repentance more hard and difficult, you lay a sad foundation for the greatest fears and doubts.

Ah! how soon may that sad word be fulfilled upon you, 'The Lord of that servant (that saith his Lord delayeth his coming) shall come in a day when he looketh not for him, and in an hour that he is not aware of, and shall cut him asunder (or cut him off), and appoint him his portion with hypocrites; there shall be weeping and gnashing of teeth,' Mat. xxiv. 48–51. When Sodom, when Pharaoh, when Agag, when Amalek, when Haman, when Herod, when Nebuchadnezzar, when Belshazzar, when Dives, when the fool in the Gospel, were all in their prime, their pride, when they were all in a flourishing state, and upon the very top of their glory, how strangely, how suddenly, how sadly, how fearfully, how wonderfully, were they brought down to the grave, to hell!

Ah! young man, who art thou? and what is thy name or fame? what is thy power or place? what is thy dignity or glory? that thou darest promise thyself an exemption from sharing in as sad a portion as ever justice gave to those who were once very high, who were seated among the stars, but are now brought down to the sides of the pit, Isa. xiii. 10–17. I have read a story of one that gave a young prodigal a ring with a death's head, on this condition, that he should one hour daily, for seven days together, look and think upon it; which bred a great change in his life.

Ah! young men, the serious thoughts of death may do that for you that neither friends, counsel, examples, prayers, sermons, tears, have not done to this very day. Well! remember this; to labour not to die is labour in vain, and to put this day far from you, and to live without fear of death, is to die living. Death seizeth on old men, and lays wait for the youngest. Death is oftentimes as near to the young man's back as it is to the old man's face.[1]

It is storied of Charles the Fourth, king of France, that being one time affected with the sense of his many and great sins, he fetched a deep sigh, and said to his wife, By the help of God I will now so carry

[1] *Senibus mors in januis; adolescentibus in insidiis.*—Bernard. *De convers. ad Cler.*, c. 14.

myself all my life long, that I will never offend him more; which words he had no sooner uttered, but he fell down dead and died.[1]

Do not, young men, put this day far from you, lest you are suddenly surprised, and then you cry out, when too late, 'A kingdom for a Christ, a kingdom for a Christ; as once crooked-backed Richard the Third in his distress, 'A kingdom for a horse, a kingdom for a horse.'[2]

Ah! young men, did you never hear of a young man that cried out, 'Oh! I am so sick, that I cannot live, and yet, woful wretch that I am! so sinful, that I dare not die. Oh that I might live! oh that I might die! oh that I might do neither!' Well! young men, remember this, the frequent, the serious thoughts of death will prevent many a sin, it will arm you against many temptations, it will secure you from many afflictions, it will keep you from doating on the world, it will make you do much in a little time, it will make death easy when it comes, and it will make you look out betimes for a kingdom that shakes not, for riches that corrupt not, and for glory that fadeth not away. Therefore do not, Oh do not put the day of death far from you. Take heed of crying *Cras, cras*, to-morrow, to-morrow, saith Luther; for a man lives forty years before he knows himself to be a fool, and by that time he sees his folly his life is finished. So men die before they begin to live.

Direction (2). *Secondly*, If you would be good betimes, then take heed *of leaning to your own understanding.*

This counsel wise Solomon gives to his son (or the young men in his time): 'My son, forget not my law; but let thy heart keep my commandments. Trust in the Lord with all thy heart; and lean not to thy own understanding,' Prov. iii. 1, 5.

Youth is the age of folly, of vain hopes, and overgrown confidence. Ah! how wise might many have been, had they not been too early wise in their own opinion.

Rehoboam's young counsellors proved the overthrow of his kingdom. It is brave for youth at all times to be discreet and sober-minded. Three virtues, they say, are prime ornaments of youth, modesty, silence, and obedience.

Ah! young men, keep close in every action to this one principle, viz., in every action resolve to be discreet and wise, rather than affectionate[3] and singular.

I remember that a young gentleman of Athens, being to answer for his life, hired an orator to make his defence, and it pleased him well at his first reading; but when the young man by often reading it, that he might recite it publicly by heart, begun to grow weary and displeased with it, the orator bid him consider that the judges and the people were to hear it but once: and then it was likely that they at the first instant might be as well pleased as he.

Ah! young men, your leaning upon yourselves, or upon others, will in the end be bitterness and vexation of spirit. Young men are very apt to lean on their own wit, wisdom, arts, parts, as old men are to lean

[1] Doubtful.—G.

[2] Another tacit Shakesperian reminiscence probably. Cf. Richard III. v. 4. 'A horse! a horse! my kingdom for a horse!'—G.

[3] 'Affected.'—G.

on a staff to support them (as the Hebrew word [שען, *shagnan*] signifies, that is rendered *lean*, in that of Prov. iii. 5). This hath been the bane of many a choice wit, the loss of many a brave head, the ruin of many a subtle pate.

Ajax thought it was only for cowards and weaklings to lean upon the Lord for succour, not for him when he was foiled; lean not to great parts, lean not to natural or acquired accomplishments, lest you lose them and yourselves too. Leaning to natural or moral excellencies, is the ready way to be stripped of all. Babylon, that bore herself bold upon her high towers, thick walls, and twenty years' provision laid in for a siege, was surprised by Cyrus.[1]

It was said of Cæsar, that he received not his wounds from the swords of enemies, but from the hands of friends; that is, from trusting in them.

Ah! how many young men have been wounded, yea slain, by trusting to their own understandings, their own abilities!

It was an excellent saying of Austin, *In te stas, et non stas*, he that stands upon his own strength shall never stand. A creature is like a single drop left to itself, it spends and wastes itself presently, but if like a drop in the fountain and ocean of being, it hath abundance of security.

Ah! young men, young men, if you will needs be leaning, then lean upon precious promises, 2 Peter i. 4, Ps. xxvii. 1; lean upon the rock that is higher than yourselves, lean upon the Lord Jesus Christ, as John did, who was the youngest of all the disciples, and the most beloved of all the disciples, John xxi. 20, chap. xiii. 23. John leaned much, and Christ loved him much. Oh lean upon Christ's wisdom for direction, lean upon his power for protection, lean upon his purse, his fulness, for provision, Cant. viii. 5; lean upon his eye for approbation, lean upon his righteousness for justification, lean upon his blood for remission, lean upon his merits for salvation. As the young vine, without her wall to support her, will fall and sink, so will you, young men, without Christ puts under his everlasting arms to support you, and uphold you; therefore, above all leanings, lean upon him. By leaning on him, you will engage him; by leaning on him, you will gain more honour than you can give; by leaning on him, you may even command him, and make him eternally yours, &c.

Direction (3). Thirdly, If you would be good betimes, if you would seek and serve the Lord in the spring and morning of your days, then *take heed of flatterers and flattery*. Ah! how many young men might have been very good, who are now exceeding bad, by hearkening to flatterers, and affecting[2] flattery! Flattery undid young Rehoboam, Ahab, Herod, Nero, Alexander, &c. Flatterers are soul-murderers; they are soul-undoers; they are like evil chirurgeons, that skin over the wound, but never heal it.

Anastasius the emperor's motto was, *mellitum venenum blanda oratio*, smooth talk proves often sweet poison. Flattery is the very spring and mother of all impiety; it blows the trumpet, and draws poor souls into rebellion against God, as Sheba drew Israel to rebel against David. It put our first parents upon tasting the forbidden

[1] Cf. Sibbes's Works, Vol. II. pp. 217, 248.—G. [2] 'Courting.'—G.

fruit; it put Absalom upon dethroning of his father; it put Haman upon plotting the ruin of the Jews; it put Korah, Dathan, and Abiram upon rebelling against Moses; it makes men call evil good and good evil, darkness light and light darkness, &c.; it puts persons upon neglecting the means of grace, upon undervaluing the means of grace, and upon contemning the means of grace; it puts men upon abasing God, slighting Christ, and vexing the Spirit; it unmans a man; it makes him call black white and white black; it makes a man change pearls for pebbles, and gold for counters; it makes a man judge himself wise when he is foolish; knowing, when he is ignorant; holy, when he is profane; free, when he is a prisoner; rich, when he is poor: high, when he is low; full, when he is empty; happy, when he is miserable,[1] Rev. iii. 17, 18. Ah! young men, young men, take heed of flatterers; they are the very worst of sinners; they are left of God, blinded by Satan, hardened in sin, and ripened for hell. God declares sadly against them, and that in his word and in his works: in his word, as you may see by comparing these scriptures together, Deut. xxix. 18–20; Ps. lxxviii. 36, xxxvi. 1, 3; Job xvii. 5; Ezek. xii. 24; Dan. xi. 21, 32, 34. Ps. xii. 2, 3, 'They speak vanity every one with his neighbour: with flattering lips, and with a double heart, do they speak. The Lord shall cut off all flattering lips, and the tongue that speaketh proud things.'[2] And as God declares sadly against them in his word, so he hath declared terribly against them in his works, as you may run and read in his judgments executed upon Ahab's flattering prophets, and upon Haman, and upon Daniel's princely false accusers, &c. And why, then, will not you stop your ears against those wretches, that the hand and heart of God is so much against?

Again, as God declares against them, so good men detest them and declare against them, as you may see by comparing these scriptures together, Ps. v. 8–10; Prov. ii. 16, vii. 21, xxviii. 23; Job xxxii. 21, 22; 1 Thes. ii. 5, 10. Prov. xx. 19, 'Meddle not with him that flattereth with his lips.' Why so? Why! Because a man that flattereth his neighbour spreadeth a net for his feet, Prov. xxix. 5. The Hebrew word *Mahhalik*, from *hhalak*, that is here rendered flatterer, signifies a smooth-boots, a soft butter-spoken man, because flatterers use smooth, soft speeches. Also the word signifies 'to divide,' because a flatterer's tongue is divided from his heart. Flatterers have their nets, and those that give ear to them will be taken to their ruin.[3] A lying tongue hateth those that are afflicted by it, 'and a flattering mouth worketh ruin,' Prov. xxvi. 28. A flattering mouth ruins name, fame, estate, body, soul, life.[4]

Valerian, the Roman emperor, used to say, *Non acerba, sed blanda*, not bitter, but flattering words do all the mischief.

When Alexander the Great was hit with an arrow in the siege of an Indian city, which would not heal, he said to his parasites, You say that I am Jupiter's son, but this wound cries that I am but a man.

[1] The flatterers told Dionysius that his spittle was as sweet as honey.

[2] *Karah* signifies any cutting off, either by death or banishment, &c.

[3] A preacher in Constantine's time presumed to call the emperor saint to his face, but he went away with a check.—*Euseb. de vit. Const.* l. 44.

[4] The Hebrew word דחה, *Dahhah*, signifies such a violent forcing of one as he cannot stand it, signifies to throw down, to drive on forwards till a man fall into destruction.

Now shall good men detest them and abhor them, as they are the pest of pests, the plague of plagues, and will you own them, will you take pleasure in them, to your ruin here and hereafter? The Lord forbid! Oh say to all flatterers, as he to his idols, 'Get you hence, for what have I more to do with you?' Hosea xiv. 8.

Nay, once more consider, that not only the good, but the bad, not only the best, but some of the worst of men, have manifested their detestation of flatterers and flattery.

Leo the emperor used to say, *Occulti inimici pessimi*, a close enemy is far worse than an open. When a court parasite praised Sigismund the emperor above measure, the emperor gave him a sound box on the ear.

When Aristobulus the historian presented to Alexander, the great book that he had written of his glorious acts, wherein he had flatteringly made him greater than he was, Alexander, after he had read the book, threw it into the river Hydaspes, and said to the author, It were a good deed to throw thee after it.

When the flatterers flattered Antigonus, he cried out, *Mentiris, mentiris in gutture, hæ virtutes non latent in me*, thou liest, thou liest in thy throat; these virtues that thou speakest of I have not in me, but I am like a leopard, that have ten black spots to one white.

Augustus Cæsar and Tiberius Cæsar were deadly enemies to flatterers, insomuch that they would not be called lords by their own children.

A good symbol is attributed to Trebonianus Gallus,[1] viz. *Nemo amicus idem et adulator*, no flatterer can be a true friend.

Aristippus, the philosopher, seeing Diogenes washing of herbs for his dinner, said, If Diogenes knew how to make use of kings, he need not live upon raw herbs, as he doth; to which Diogenes replied, that if Aristippus could content himself with herbs, he need not to turn spaniel, or to flatter king Dionysius for a meal's meat.

Ah! young men, young men, shall God, shall good men, shall bad men, detest and declare against flatterers and flattery, and will not you turn a deaf ear upon them, yea, fly from them as from a serpent, and shun them as you would shun hell itself? If you do not, the very heathens but now cited will rise in judgment against you.

Flatterers are the very worst of sinners. The flatterers told Cæsar, that his freckles in his face were like the stars in the firmament; they bought and sold Aurelius the emperor at pleasure. And Augustus complained, when Varrus was dead, that he had none now left that would deal plainly and faithfully with him.

So men may gain by flattery; they will be like Harpalus, who said, *Quod regi placet, mihi placet*, that which pleaseth the king pleaseth me, when Astyages set his own son before him to feed upon him.

Oh! but let every young man say, into whose hands this treatise shall fall, *Quod Deo placet, mihi placet*, that which pleaseth God pleaseth me.

I have been the longer upon this, out of love to young men's souls, who are so apt to be ensnared in the flatterer's net. If ever you would be good in good earnest, you must abhor flatterers as the first-born of

[1] Roman emperor, A.D. 251–254.—G.

the devil, and as such as are most pernicious to men's happiness both here and hereafter.[1]

It is reported of one Oramazes, that he had an enchanted egg, in which, as he boasted himself, he had enclosed all the happiness of the world; but being broken, nothing was found in it but wind. Flatterers are the greatest cheaters, the greatest deceivers in the world.

They say of the crocodile, that when he hath killed a man, he will weep over him, as if he were sorry, and did repent for what he had done; the application is easy.

Direction (4). Fourthly, If you would be good betimes, if you would seek and serve the Lord in the spring and morning of your days, then *take heed of engaged affections to the things of the world.*

The young man in the Gospel took many a step towards heaven: 'All these things have I kept from my youth up: what lack I yet?' Mat. xix. 16–24. Christ makes a very fair offer to him in the next words: 'Jesus said unto him, If thou wilt be perfect, go and sell that thou hast, and give to the poor, and thou shalt have treasure in heaven; and come and follow me.' Thou shalt have heaven for earth, a sea for a drop, a treasure for a mite, a crown for a crumb. Ay, but the young man's affections were strongly engaged to the things of the world; and therefore he turns his back upon Christ, and goes away sorrowful, because he had great possessions.[2] Oh the madness, the folly of this young man, who, to enjoy a little temporal felicity, hath bid an everlasting farewell to Christ and glory! In that Gen. xiii. 2, it is said, that Abraham was very rich in cattle, in silver, and in gold; the Hebrew word *cabedh*, that is here rendered rich, signifies heavy; it signifies a burden, to shew us that riches are a heavy burden and an hindrance many times to heaven and happiness; and this young man in the Gospel found it so to his eternal undoing. Though the loadstone cannot draw the iron when the diamond is in presence, yet earthly possessions did draw this young man's soul away when Christ the pearl of price was present. The world is a silken net, and this young man found it so; the world is like golden fetters, and this young man found it so; the world is like sweet poison,[3] and this young man found it so; for he had drunk so large a draught of it, that there was no room in his soul for Christ or heaven, for grace or glory. Some say, that when the serpent Scytale cannot overtake the flying passenger, she doth with her beautiful colours so astonish and amaze them, that they have no power to pass away till she have stung them; such a serpent the world proved to the young man in the Gospel; it did so affect him and take him, so amaze him and amuse him, that he could not stir till it stung him to death.

When the moon is fullest, it is furthest from the sun; so the more men have of the world, the further commonly they are from God; and this the young man in the Gospel made good.

Many have ventured life and limb, and many a better thing, to gain the things of this world; and yet, after all, they have got nothing at

[1] Whilst an ass is stroked under the belly, you may lay on his back what burden you please.

[2] *Multi amando res noxias sunt miseri, habendo miseriores.*—August. in Ps. xxvi.

[3] They are *dulce venenum*, a sweet poison.—*Bernard.*

all. Achan's golden wedge proved a wedge to cleave him, and his garment a garment to shroud him.[1]

The whole world is circular, the heart of a man is triangular, and we know a circle cannot fill a triangle; yea, if it be not filled with the three persons in Trinity, it will be filled with the world, the flesh, and the devil. The world may be resembled to the fruit that undid us all, which was fair to the sight, smooth in handling, sweet in taste, but deadly in effect and operation.

Ah! young men, young men, have none of you found it so?

The world in all its bravery is no better than the cities which Solomon gave to Hiram, which he called *Cabul*, that is to say, displeasing or dirty, 1 Kings ix. 13; the world will afford nothing but trivial flowers, surrounded with many briers. Oh the vanity, the uncertainty, the imperfection of all things below! If a man should weigh his pay and his pains together, his miseries and his pleasures together, his joys and his sorrows together, his mercies and his crosses together, his good days and his bad days together, will he not conclude, Vanity of vanities, and all is vanity?

It was a wise and Christian speech of Charles the Fifth to the Duke of Venice, who, when he had shewed him the glory of his princely palace and earthly paradise, instead of admiring it, or him for it, only returned him this grave and serious *memento, Hæc sunt quæ faciunt invitos mori*, these are the things which make us unwilling to die. It was a good saying of one to a great lord, upon his shewing him his stately house and pleasant gardens, Sir, you had need make sure of heaven, or else when you die you will be a very great loser.[2]

Ah! young men, young men, it is only heaven that is above all winds, storms, and tempests; nor hath God cast man out of paradise for him to think to find out another paradise in this world. The main reason why many young men doat upon the world is, because they are not acquainted with a greater glory. Men ate acorns till they were acquainted with the use of wheat. The woman had the moon under her feet when she was clothed with the sun, and had a crown of twelve stars upon her head, Rev. xii. 1.

Ah! young men, were you but clothed with the Sun of righteousness, and had you a crown set upon your heads by the hand of faith, you would have all the things of this world which are as low, bespotted, and mutable as the moon, under your feet, Heb. xi. 24–27, 35, x. 34. Well! young men, as ever you would be good betimes, sit loose from the things of this world, be no longer worshippers of this golden calf, and never let the world, that shall be but your servant, become your Lord. Oh! let not the devil and the world have more service for an ounce of gold, than Christ shall have for the kingdom of heaven!

Ah, young men! the world and you must part, or Christ and you will never meet, 'you cannot serve God and mammon,' Mat. vi. 24. The two poles shall sooner meet, than the love of Christ and the love of the world.

[1] If money were thrown to the dogs, they would not so much as smell at it; the greater is their folly and madness that will go to hell-gates for it.

[2] In my other treatises, you may read more of the vanity, insufficiency, impotency, immutability, uncertainty, and inconstancy of the world; and to them I refer you.

Direction (5). Fifthly, If you would be good betimes, if you would know, seek, and serve the Lord in the spring and morning of your youth, then *take heed betimes of carnal reason, take heed of consulting with flesh and blood*, Gal. i. 15, 16.

Many a hopeful young man hath been undone temporally and undone eternally, by hearkening to those evil counsellors.

Carnal reason is an enemy, yea, an utter enemy, nay, it is not only an utter enemy, but it is enmity, yea, enmities, Rom. viii. 7.[1] An enemy may be reconciled, but enmity can never be reconciled. Carnal reason is not only averse, but it is utterly averse to all goodness; it builds strongholds and syllogisms against the most glorious gospel truths, and accounts the precious things of Christ as a strange thing. Carnal reason will make God and gospel do homage to it. When carnal reason is in the throne, Christ and his truths must all bow or be judged before its bar.

Ah! young men, young men, as ever you would be good betimes, stop your ears against all carnal reasonings within you. Carnal reason judges the choicest things of the gospel to be mere foolishness, 1 Cor. i. 23. It is purblind, and cannot see how to make a right judgment of Christ, his word, his ways, and yet will control all.

If you are resolved to be still scholars to this master, then you must resolve to be unhappy here and miserable hereafter. But it is safer and better for you to imitate those young men, who in the morning of their days have graciously, wisely, and resolutely withstood those evil counsellors, carnal reason, flesh and blood; Joseph and Moses, Daniel, Shadrach, Meshach, and Abednego, all these in the primrose of their youth were good at turning the deaf ear to carnal counsel and carnal counsellors, Gen. xxxix. 7–11, &c; Heb. xi. 24–26; Dan. i.

Cassianus reports of a young man that had given himself up to a Christian life, and his parents misliking that way, they wrote letters to him to persuade him from it; and when he knew there were letters come from them, he would not open them, but threw them into the fire. This example is worth a following.

Another famous example you have in the story of King Edward the Sixth, when Cranmer and Ridley came to him, and were very earnest to have him give way to his sister the Lady Mary to have mass. He stood out and pleaded the case with them, that it was a sin against God, and provoking to the eyes of his glory, &c., but they still continued to use many carnal arguments to persuade the king, who was but a child about fifteen years of age, but he withstood them a great while; but at length when he saw he could not prevail with all his pleading against those brave men, but that they still continued their suit, he burst out into bitter weeping and sobbing, desiring them to desist. The motioners seeing his zeal and constancy, went as fast as he, and being overcome, they went away and told one that the king had more divinity in his little finger, than they had in all their bodies.

Ah! young men, it will be your safety and your glory to write after this princely copy, when you are surrounded with carnal reason and carnal counsellors, &c.

[1] Cicero, a heathen, could say, that man would not be so wicked, and do so wickedly, were it not for his reason.

Direction (6). Sixthly and lastly, If you would be good betimes, then *take heed of comparing yourselves with those that are worse than yourselves.*

Young men are very apt to compare themselves with those that are worse than themselves, and this proves a snare unto them, yea, oftentimes their bane, their ruin, John ix. 39, 40, as it did the young pharisee in the Gospel, who pleaded his negative righteousness; he was not as other men are, 'extortioners, unjust, adulterers,' and stood on his comparative goodness, 'nor as this publican;' he stands not only upon his comparisons, but upon his disparisons, being blind at home, and too quick-sighted abroad; he contemneth and condemneth this poor publican, who was better than himself, Luke xviii. 11–14,[1] making good that saying of Seneca, 'The nature of man,' saith he, 'is very apt, *utimur perspicillis magis quam speculis*, to use spectacles to behold other men's faults, rather than looking-glasses to behold our own.' Such pharisees do justly incur the censure which that sour philosopher passed upon grammarians, that they were better acquainted with the evil of Ulysses than with their own.[2]

Ah! young man, young man, you know, he that drinks poison, though he drinks not so much as another, and he that commits treason, though not so great, so high treason as another, shall yet as certainly be poisoned, and hanged, as he that hath drunk a greater quantity of poison, and committed higher acts of treason.[3]

Sirs! do not delude and befool your own souls; if you are not as wicked as others, you shall not be as much tormented as others, but yet you shall be as certainly damned as others; you shall as certain to hell as others; you shall as sure be shut out for ever from God, Christ, saints, angels, and all the treasures, pleasures, and glories of heaven, as others, except it be prevented by timely repentance on your side, and pardoning mercy on God's. Wilt thou count it madness, O young man! in him that is sick, to reason thus?. I am not so sick as such and such, and therefore I will not send to the physician; and in the wounded man to say, I am not so desperately wounded as such and such, and therefore I will not send to the chirurgeon; and in the traitor to say, I am not guilty of so many foul and heinous treasons as such and such, and therefore I will not look after a pardon; and in the necessitous man to say, I am not so hard put to it as such and such, and therefore I will not welcome a hand of charity? And wilt thou not count it the greatest madness in the world for thee to put off thy repentance, and thy returning to the Lord in the spring and morning of thy youth, because that thou art not as sinful, as wicked as such and such. If to have a softer bed, a milder punishment in hell than others, will satisfy thee, then go on; but if thou art afraid of the worm that never dies, and of the fire that never goes out, being like that stone in Arcadia, which being once kindled could not be quenched, oh, then, begin to be good betimes! Oh seek and serve the Lord in the spring and morning of your days!

[1] Thales, one of the seven sages, being asked what was the easiest thing in the world to do? answered, to know other men's faults, and none of our own.

[2] Diogenes apud Laertium. lib. vi.

[3] Mat. xi. 22–25. As in heaven, one is more glorious than another, so in hell, one shall be more miserable than another.—*Aug*[*ustine*].

To think often of hell, is the way to be preserved from falling into hell.[1] Ah! young men, young men, that you would often consider of the bitterness of the damned's torments, and of the pitilessness of their torments, and of the diversity of their torments, and of the easelessness of their torments, and of the remedilessness of their torments. *Momentaneum est quod delectat, æternum quod cruciat,* The sinner's delight here is momentary, that which torments hereafter is perpetual. When a sinner is in hell, dost thou think, O young man! that another Christ shall be found to die for him, or that the same Christ will be crucified again for him, or that another gospel should be preached to him? Surely no. Ah! why then wilt thou not betimes return and seek out after the things that belong to thy everlasting peace? I have read of Pope Clement the Fifth, that when a young nephew of his died, he sent his chaplain to a necromancer, to know of him how it fared with him in the other world; the conjuror shewed him to the chaplain, lying in a fiery bed in hell, which, when the pope understood, he never joyed more, &c.[2]

Ah! young man, that these occasional hints of hell may be a means to preserve thee from lying in those everlasting flames.

Bellarmine tells us of a certain advocate of the court of Rome, that being at the point of death, was stirred up by them that stood by, to repent and call upon God for mercy; he, with a constant countenance, and without sign of fear, turned his speech to God, and said, Lord! I have a desire to speak unto thee, not for myself, but for my wife and children, for I am hastening to hell, neither is there anything that thou shouldst do for me; and this he spake, saith Bellarmine, who was present, and heard it, as if he had spoken of a journey to some village or town, and was no more affrighted.[3]

Sir Francis Bacon also, in his History of Henry the Seventh, relates how it was a common byword of the Lord Cordes, that he would be content to live seven years in hell, so he might win Calice [Calais] from the English;[4] but if thou, O young man, art given up to such desperate atheism, and carnal apprehensions of hell, I am afraid God will confute thee one day by fire and brimstone; but I would willingly hope better things of all those young persons, into whose hands this treatise shall fall; and thus you see what things must be declined and avoided, if ever you would be good betimes, if ever you would seek and serve the Lord in the spring and morning of your days.

CHAPTER VII.

But in the second place, *as those things must be declined, so other things must carefully and diligently be practised, if ever you would be good betimes.* I shall instance only in those that are most considerable and weighty; as,

First, If ever you would be good betimes, &c., then you must *labour to be acquainted with four things betimes.*

[1] Chrysostom. Hom. 44. in Mat.
[2] Jac. Rev. Hist Pont. Rom., 199.
[3] Bellar. *De arte Moriendi*, lib. ii. cap. 10.
[4] Works, by Spedding, Ellis, and Heath, vol. vi. p. 100.—G.

Duty (1). First, You must labour *to acquaint yourselves with the Scripture betimes.* You must study the word betimes. David studied the word in the morning of his days, in the primrose of his youth; and this made him wiser than his enemies, yea, than his teachers; this made him as much excel the ancients, as the sun excels the moon, or as the moon excels the twinkling stars, Ps. cxix. 97–103. Timothy was good betimes; and no wonder, for in the primrose of his days he was acquainted with the Scripture; he was inured to the word from his childhood, yea, from his infancy, as the word properly signifies.[1] So in that 119th Psalm, the 9th verse, 'Wherewithal shall a young man cleanse his way? By taking heed according to thy word.' There is no way to a holy heart and a clean life but by acquainting yourselves with the word betimes. One hath long since observed, that God hath bowed down the Scriptures to the capacity even of babes and sucklings, that all excuse may be taken away, and that young men may be encouraged to study the Scripture betimes.[2] Ah, young men! no histories are comparable to the histories of the Scriptures: 1, for antiquity; 2, rarity; 3, variety; 4, brevity; 5, perspicuity; 6, harmony; 7, verity. All other books cannot equal God's, either in age or authority, in dignity or excellency, in sufficiency or glory.[3]

Moses is found more ancient and more honourable than all those whom the Grecians make most ancient and honourable; as Homer, Hesiod, and Jupiter himself, whom the Greeks have seated in the top of their divinity.

The whole Scripture is but one entire love-letter, despatched from the Lord Christ to his beloved spouse; and who then but would still be a reading in this love-letter? Like Cæcilia, a Roman maiden of noble parentage, who carried always about her the New Testament, that she might still be a-reading in Christ's love-letter, and behold the sweet workings of his love and heart towards his dear and precious ones.[4]

Luther found so much sweetness in the word, in Christ's love-letter, that made him say he would not live in paradise, if he might, without the word; *at cum verbo etiam in inferno facile est vivere,* but with the word he could live in hell itself.

The word is like the stone garamantides, that hath drops of gold in itself, enriching of the believing soul. This the martyrs found, which made them willing to give a load of hay for a few leaves of the Bible in English.

Augustine professeth that the sacred Scriptures were his whole delight.

And Jerome tells us of one Nepotianus, who, by long and assiduous meditation on the holy Scriptures, had made his breasts the library of Jesus Christ.[5]

And *Rabbi Chiia,* in the *Jerusalem Talmud,* saith that in his account all the world is not of equal value with one word out of the law. That which a papist reports lyingly of their sacrament of the mass, viz.

[1] 2 Tim. iii. 15, ἀπὸ βρέφους, from a suckling.

[2] Augustine.—G.

[3] *Adoro plenitudinem Scripturarum.*—Tertullian. Gregory calls the Scripture *cor et animam Dei,* the heart and soul of God.

[4] Cf. Clarke's 'Martyrologie,' 3d edition, 1677, p. 35.—G.

[5] Hier. Epistola ad Heliod. in Epitaphium Nepotiani.

that there are as many mysteries in it as there be drops in the sea, dust on the earth, angels in heaven, stars in the sky, atoms in the sunbeams, or sands on the sea-shore, &c., may be truly asserted of the Holy Scriptures.

Oh! the mysteries, the excellencies, the glories that are in the word! Ah! no book to this book; none so useful, none so needful, none so delightful, none so necessary to make you happy and to keep you happy as this. It is said of Cæsar, *major fuit cura Cæsari libellorum, quam purpuræ*, that he had a greater care of his books than of his royal robes; for, swimming through the waters to escape his enemies, he carried his books in his hand above the waters, but lost his robe. Now, what are Cæsar's books to God's books?

Ah! young men, young men! the word of the Lord is a light to guide you, a counsellor to counsel you, a comforter to comfort you, a staff to support you, a sword to defend you, and a physician to cure you. The word is a mine to enrich you, a robe to clothe you, and a crown to crown you. It is bread to strengthen you, and wine to cheer you, and a honeycomb to feast you, and music to delight you, and a paradise to entertain you.[1]

Oh! therefore, before all and above all, search the Scripture, study the Scripture, dwell on the Scripture, delight in the Scripture, treasure up the Scripture; no wisdom to Scripture wisdom, no knowledge to Scripture knowledge, no experience to Scripture experience, no comforts to Scripture comforts, no delights to Scripture delights, no convictions to Scripture convictions, nor no conversion to Scripture conversion.

Augustine hearing a voice from heaven, that bade him take and read, *tolle et lege*, whereupon, turning open the New Testament, he fell upon that place, 'Let us walk honestly, as in the day; not in rioting and drunkenness, not in chambering and wantonness, not in strife and envying. But put ye on the Lord Jesus Christ, and make not provision for the flesh, to fulfil the lusts thereof,' Rom. xiii. 13, 14. This scripture so sunk into his heart, as that it proved the means of his conversion, as himself reports. This Augustine, as he was once preaching, his memory failing of him, contrary to his purpose, he fell upon reproving the Manicheans, and by a scripture or two, not before thought of, to confute their heresies, he converted Firmus, a Manichean, as he after acknowledged to Augustine, blessing God for that sermon.[2]

It is reported of one Adrianus, who seeing the martyrs suffer such grievous things in the cause of God, he asked what was that which caused them to suffer such things? and one of them named that text, 'Eye hath not seen, nor ear heard, neither hath it entered into the heart of man to conceive, the things which God hath prepared for them that love him,' 1 Cor. ii. 9. And this text was set home with such a power upon him, as that it converted him and made him to profess religion, and not only to profess it, but to die a martyr for it.

Cyprian was converted by reading the prophecy of Jonah. Junius was converted by reading the first chapter of John the evangelist.

I have read of a scandalous minister that was struck at the heart,

[1] The Jewish Rabbins were wont to say, that upon every letter of the law there hangs mountains of profitable matter.

[2] Lib. viii. Confes. cap. xi. *Possidon. de vita.*—Augustine.

and converted, in reading that scripture: 'Thou which teachest another, teachest thou not thyself?' &c., Rom. ii. 21.

We read that Paphnutius converted Thais and Ephron, two famous strumpets, from uncleanness, only with this scripture argument, 'That God seeth all things in the dark, when the doors are fast, the windows shut, the curtains drawn,' Heb. iv. 13.

I have read of a poor man who persuaded a young scholar to leave reading of poetry, &c., and fall upon reading of the Scripture, which accordingly he did; and it pleased the Lord, before he had read out Genesis, to change his heart and to turn him to the Lord in the primrose of his days, he being then but twenty years of age.

I have read of a young lady,[1] called Potamia, of a very illustrious family, who endured very much in her martyrdom, by the extreme cruelty of Basilides her executioner, yet, after her death, he bethinking himself of the holy words and scripture-expressions that were uttered by her, during her cruel torments, became a Christian, and within few days after was himself likewise crowned with martyrdom.

James Andreas, a godly minister, hearing of a Jew that for theft was hanged by the heels, with his head downward, having not seen that kind of punishment, he went to the place where he was hanging between two dogs that were always snatching at him to eat his flesh; the poor wretch repeated in Hebrew some verses of the Psalms, wherein he cried to God for mercy, whereupon Andreas went near to him and instructed him in the principles of Christian religion, about Christ the Messiah, &c., exhorting him to believe in him, and it pleased God so to bless his Scripture exhortations to him, that the dogs gave over tearing of his flesh, and the poor Jew desired him to procure that he might be taken down and baptized, and hung by the neck for the quicker despatch, which was done accordingly.

I might produce other instances, but let these suffice to provoke all young persons to a speedy, serious, diligent, and constant study of the Scripture.[2] Ah! sirs, you do not know how soon your blind minds may be enlightened, your hard hearts softened, your proud spirits humbled, your sinful natures changed, your defiled consciences purged, your distempered affections regulated, and your poor souls saved, by searching into the Scriptures, by reading the Scripture, and by pondering upon the Scripture. You should lay up the manna of God's word in your hearts, as Moses laid up the manna in the golden pot, Heb. ix. 4. And as Tamar did with the staff and signet that she received from Judah, she laid them up till she came to save her life, and did save her life by it, as you may see in holy story, Gen. xxxviii. 18–36. The laying up of the word now, may be the saving of your souls another day.

I have read of little bees, that when they go out in stormy weather, they will carry a little of their comb or gravel with them, that they may be balanced and not carried away with the wind.

Ah! young men, young men, you had need to have your thoughts and hearts balanced with the precious Word, that you may not be carried

[1] Origen was her schoolmaster. [Potamiena, *not* Potamia. See Clarke's 'Martyrologie,' as before, page 85, on Basilides.—G.]

[2] Much in the word is wrapped up in a little. It is more to be admired than to have Homer's Iliads comprised in a nutshell.

away with 'every wind of doctrine,' as many have been in these days, to their destruction and confusion.

Narcissus, a beautiful youth, though he would not love them that loved him, yet afterwards fell in love with his own shadow.[1] Ah, how many young men in these days, who were once lovely and hopeful, are now fallen in love with their own and others' shadows, with high, empty, airy notions, and with strange monstrous speculations to their own damnation! 2 Thess. ii. 10–12.

Holy Melancthon, being newly converted, thought it impossible for his hearers to withstand the evidence of the gospel, but soon after he complained that old Adam was too hard for young Melancthon.[2]

Ah! young men, young men, if you do not in good earnest give up yourselves to the reading, to the studying, to the pondering, to the believing, to the affecting, to the applying, and to the living up to the Scripture, Satan will be too hard for you, the world will be too hard for you, your lusts will be too hard for you, temptations will be too hard for you, and deceivers will be too hard for you, and in the end you will be miserable; and thus much for the first thing, &c.

Duty (2). Secondly, If you would be good betimes, then you must *acquaint yourselves with yourselves betimes.*

If you would be gracious in the spring and morning of your days, then you must see betimes how bad you are, how vile, how sinful, how wretched you are. No man begins to be good till he sees himself to be bad. The young prodigal never began to mend, he never thought of returning to his father, till he came to himself, till he began to return into his own soul, and saw himself in an undone condition, Luke xv. 12–22.

Ah! young men, young men, You must see yourselves to be children of wrath, to be enemies, to be strangers, to be afar off from God, from Christ, from the covenant, from heaven, to be sin's servants, and Satan's bond-slaves.[3] The ready way to be found, is to see yourselves lost; the first step to mercy, is to see your misery; the first step towards heaven is to see yourselves near to hell. You won't look after the physician of souls, you won't prize the physician of souls, you won't desire the physician of souls, you won't match with the physician of souls, you won't fall in love, in league with the physician of souls, you won't resign up yourselves to the physician of souls, till you come to see your wounds, till you come to feel your diseases, till you see the tokens, the plague-sores of divine wrath and displeasure upon you. As the whole do not need the physician, so they do not desire, they do not care for the physician.[4]

Ah! young men, as you would be good betimes, begin to acquaint yourselves with your sinful selves betimes, begin to acquaint yourselves betimes with your natural and undone condition.[5]

There is a threefold self.

(1.) There is a *natural self;* as a man's parts, wit, reason, will, affections, and inclinations, &c.

[1] Ovid. *Met.* iii. 341, *seq.*—G.

[2] Melch. Adam, *sub nomine.*—G.

[3] Eph. ii. 1–3, 12, 13; Rom. vi. 16; John viii. 44; 2 Tim. ii. 26.

[4] Austin saith, he would willingly go through hell to Christ, so will all that see their need of Christ.

[5] Zanchius writ a tractate, *Quod nihil scitur.*

(2.) A *religious self;* and so a man's duties, graces, obedience, righteousness, holiness, are called one's self.

(3.) There is a *sinful self;* and so a man's corruptions, lusts, sinful nature, and dispositions, are called one's self. Now, if ever you would be good betimes, you must acquaint yourselves with your sinful selves betimes.[1]

Demonicus being asked at what time he began to be a philosopher, answered, When I began to know myself. So a man never begins to be a Christian till he begins to know himself. And indeed, for a man to know himself, to acquaint himself with himself, is one of the hardest works in all the world. For as the eye can see all things but itself, so most can discern all faults but their own. Henry the Fourth, emperor of Germany, his usual speech was *Multi multa sciunt, se autem nemo,* many know much, but few know themselves.

The very heathens did admire that saying as an oracle, *nosce teipsum,* know and be acquainted with thy own self. The main exhortation of Chilo, one of the seven sages, was 'Know thyself.' And Plato recordeth that this saying of Chilo, 'Know thyself,' was written in letters of gold upon the portal of Apollo's temple.

Juvenal saith that this saying, 'Know thyself,' came from heaven. Macrobius saith that the oracle of Apollo, being demanded what course should be taken for attaining to felicity, answered, only teach a man to 'know himself.'[2]

Thus you see that both divinity and philosophy doth agree in this, that the best and surest way to true felicity is, to know ourselves, to acquaint ourselves with ourselves.

This duty the apostle charges upon the Ephesians, 'Remember that you, being in times past Gentiles in the flesh, that at that time you were without Christ, aliens from the commonwealth of Israel, and strangers from the covenant of promise, having no hope, and without God in the world,' Eph. ii. 11, 12.

Here are five *withouts:* without Christ, without the church, without the promise, without hope, and without God in the world.

Man in his natural state is afar off; he is without, three manner of ways:

(1.) In point of opinion and apprehension.

(2.) In point of fellowship and communion.

(3.) In point of grace and conversion.

As you would be good betimes, dwell much upon your corrupt nature betimes.[3] Ah! such is the corruption of our nature, that propound any divine good to it, it is entertained as fire by water, or wet wood with hissing; propound any evil, then it is like fire to straw; it is like the foolish satyr, that made haste to kiss the fire; it is like that unctuous matter which the naturalists say sucks and snatches the fire to it, with

[1] Luther said, that if a man could perfectly see his own faults, the sight thereof would be a very hell unto him.

[2] The precept, Γνῶθι σεαυτον, has gathered around it a little literature of its own. It has been assigned to Chilo, *as above*; but also to Pythagoras, Thales, Cleobulus, Bias, and Socrates, and to Phœmonoë, a Greek poetess of the pre-Homeric period. The reference to Juvenal is found in Sat. xi. 27, Ecœlo descendit γνῶθι σεαυτον.—G.

[3] Of dull and insensible men, one long since thus complained, *Patientius ferre Christi jacturam quam suam*, that they did more calmly pass by the injuries done to Christ than those that were done unto themselves Oh the plague of insensibleness!

which it is consumed. Till you come to be sensible of this, you will never begin to be good; you will never look to have your hearts changed, and your souls saved.

The Ethiopians paint angels black, and devils white, in favour of their own complexion; and they say that if the brute creatures could draw a picture of the divine nature, they would make their shape the copy, and thus they flatter and delude themselves. Take heed, young men, take heed that you do not put the like cheats upon your own souls; take heed that you be not like those limners who, so as they can make a man's picture gay and gaudy, care not to draw it so as to resemble him. It is safest and best, O young man! to know the worst of thyself, and to know thyself as thou art in thyself, and not as thy own flattering heart, or as other flatterers, may represent thee to thyself.

Duty (3). Thirdly, If you would be good betimes, then you must *acquaint yourselves with Jesus Christ betimes.*

You must know him betimes. A man never begins to be good till he begins to know him that is the fountain of all goodness: 'This is life eternal, to know thee, the only true God, and Jesus Christ, whom thou hast sent,' John xvii. 3.

The knowledge of Christ is the beginning of eternal life; it is the way to eternal life, it is a taste of eternal life, it is a sure pledge and pawn to the soul of eternal life.

The Spaniards say of Aquinas, that he that knows not him knows not anything, but he that knows him knows all things. He that knows Jesus Christ not notionally only, but practically, not apprehensively only, but affectively, he knows all things that may make him happy; but he that knows not Jesus Christ knows nothing that will stand him in stead, when he shall lie upon a dying bed, and stand before a judgment seat.

Justin Martyr relates that when, in his discourse with Trypho, he mentioned the knowledge of Christ as conducing to our happiness and perfection, Trypho's friends laughed at it; but I hope better things of all those into whose hands this treatise shall fall.

Sirs! the sun is not more necessary to the world, the eye to the body, the pilot to the ship, the general to the army, &c., than the knowledge of Christ betimes is necessary for all those that would be good betimes.

Dear hearts, as ever you would be good betimes, you must labour, even as for life, to know and be thoroughly acquainted with these six things concerning Jesus Christ betimes.

(1.) *First,* If you would be good betimes, then you must know betimes *that there is everything in Christ that may encourage you to seek him and serve him, to love him and obey him, to believe on him and to marry with him.*[1]

If you look upon his names, his natures, his offices, his graces, his dignities, his excellencies, his royalties, his glories, his fulnesses, they all speak out as much.

Are you poor? Why, Christ hath tried gold to enrich you, Rev. iii. 18. Are you naked? Christ hath white raiment to clothe you. Are you spiritually blind? Christ hath eye-salve to enlighten you. Are

[1] *Nec Christus, nec cœlum, patitur hyperbolem.*

you in straits? He hath wisdom to counsel you. Are you unrighteous? He will be righteousness to you? Are you unholy? He will be holiness and sanctification to you, 1 Cor. i. 30. Are you hungry? He is bread to feed you. Are you thirsty? He is wine and milk to satisfy you. Are you weary? He is a bed, a seat, to rest you. Are you sick? Why, he is a physician to cure you, &c. *Omne bonum in summo bono,* All good is in the chiefest good.[1]

The creatures have their particular goodness, health hath its particular goodness, and wealth hath its particular goodness, and learning hath its, and the favour of the creature hath its, &c., but now Jesus Christ he is an universal good.[2] All the petty excellencies that are scattered abroad in the creatures are united to Christ; yea, all the whole volume of perfections which is spread through heaven and earth is epitomised in him. *Ipse unus erit tibi omnia, quia in ipso uno bono, bona sunt omnia*—[*Augustine*], One Christ will be to thee instead of all things else, because in him are all good things to be found. Abraham's servant brought forth jewels of silver and jewels of gold, to win Rebekah's heart to Isaac; so should you, O young men! be often in presenting to your own view all those amiable and excellent things that be in Christ, to win your hearts over to Christ betimes.

Secondly, If you would be good betimes, then you must know betimes *that Jesus Christ is mighty to save.*

'He is able to save to the uttermost all them that come unto him, that believe in him, and that cast themselves upon him.'[3] The Lord hath laid help upon one that is mighty. Christ saves perfectly, thoroughly, perpetually, them that come unto him.

The three tongues that were written upon the cross, in Greek, Latin, and Hebrew, to witness Christ to be the king of the Jews, do each of them, in their several idioms, avouch this axiom, that Christ is an all-sufficient Saviour; and 'a threefold cord is not easily broken.' They say it is true of the oil at Rheims, that though it be continually spent in the [in]auguration of their kings of France, yet it never wasteth. Christ is that pot of manna, that cruse of oil, that bottomless ocean, that never fails his people. There is in Christ an all-sufficiency for all creatures at all times, in all places.[4]

The great Cham is said to have a tree full of pearls hanging by clusters; but what is the great Cham's tree to Christ, our tree of life, who hath all variety and plenty of fruit upon him.[5] The happinesses that come to believers by Christ are so many, that they cannot be numbered; so great, that they cannot be measured; so copious, that they cannot be defined; so precious, that they cannot be valued; all which speaks out the fulness and all-sufficiency of Christ.

There is in Christ *plenitudo abundantiæ*, and *plenitudo redundantiæ,* a fulness of abundance, and a fulness of redundancy, as well as a fulness of sufficiency.

[1] John vi. 48; Isa. lv. 1; Matt. xi. 28, ix. 12. [2] Christ is the *bonum in quo omnia bona.*

[3] Heb. vii. 25, εἰς τὸ παντελὲς, perpetually, constantly. Matt. ix. 28, Isa. lxiii. 1. Mighty to save.

[4] Christ is never *vacuis manibus*, empty-handed.

[5] Rev. xxii. 2. Christ is like the trees of the sanctuary, which were both for meat and for medicine, Ezek. xlvii. 12.

There is in Christ,

1. The fulness of the Spirit.
2. The fulness of grace.
3. The fulness of the image of God.
4. The fulness of the Godhead.
5. The fulness of glory.

But I must not now open nor dilate on these things, lest I should tire both myself and the reader.

Plutarch, in the life of Phocion, tells us of a certain gentlewoman of Ionia, who shewed the wife of Phocion all the rich jewels and precious stones she had. She answered her again, All my riches and jewels is my husband Phocion. So may a penitent sinner say of his blessed Saviour, Christ is all my jewels, my riches, my treasures, my pleasures, &c.; his sufficiency is all these, and more than these, to me.

The Spanish ambassador, coming to see the treasury of St Mark in Venice, which is cried up throughout the world, fell a-groping to find whether it had any bottom, and being asked why, answered, In this amongst other things, my great Master's treasure differs from yours, in that his hath no bottom, as I find yours to have,—alluding to the mines in Mexico and Potosi. But what are the Spaniard's treasures to Christ's treasures? A man may, without much groping, find the bottom of all earthly treasures, but who can find the bottom of Christ's treasures?[1] Should all created excellencies meet in one glorified breast, yet they could not enable that glorious God-like creature to sound the bottom of those riches and treasures which are in Christ, Ephes. iii. 8; all which speaks out Christ's all-sufficiency; and thus much for the second thing.

(3.) Thirdly, If you would be good betimes, then you must know betimes, *That there is a marvellous willingness and readiness in Christ to embrace, to entertain, to welcome returning sinners, and to shew mercy and favour to them.*

The young prodigal did but think of returning to his father, and he ran and met him, and instead of kicking or killing him, he kissed him and embraced him, his bowels rolled within him, and his compassions flowed out freely to him, Luke xv. 20–22. 'Ho every one that thirsteth, come ye to the waters, and he that hath no money; come ye, buy and eat, yea, come, buy wine and milk without money and without price,' Isa. lv. 1.[2] Nazianzen improveth this place thus: 'Oh, this easy way of contract, he giveth more willingly than others sell; if thou wilt but accept, that is all the price; though you have no merits, though you have nothing in yourselves to encourage you, yet will you accept? If you will, all is freely yours; the waters shall be yours to cleanse you, and the milk yours to nourish you, and the bread yours to strengthen you, and the wine yours to comfort you. Here poor sinners are called three times to come: Come, saith Christ, come, come, to shew how marvellous ready and willing he is that poor sinners should taste of gospel delicates.[3] So in that John vii. 37, 'Jesus stood and cried, If any man thirst, let him come to me and drink;' so in that Rev. xxii. 17, 'Let

[1] *Ipse Deus sufficit ad præmium.*—Bernard.

[2] The meaning is, sell thyself, thine own wit, reason, self-worth; and that is all Christ desires, saith Augustine upon the words.

[3] Cant. ii. 8, Christ comes leaping upon the mountains, and skipping upon the hills, to shew his readiness and willingness to do good to souls.

him that is athirst come, and whosoever will, let him take the water of life freely'; so in that Rev. iii. 20, 'Behold, I stand at the door and knock: if any man hear my voice, and open the door, I will come in to him, and will sup with him, and he with me;' and so in that Luke xiv. 21, 'The master of the house said to his servant, Go out quickly into the streets and lanes of the city, and bring in hither the poor, and the maimed, and the halt, and the blind.' Here is no man of quality, of dignity, of worldly pomp or glory, or of any self-sufficiency, that is invited to the feast, but a company of poor, ragged, deformed, slighted, neglected, impoverished, wounded sinners; these are invited to feast with Christ.

Concerning this willingness of Christ, I shall speak more when I come to deal with old sinners in the close of this discourse, and to that I refer you for further and fuller satisfaction concerning the great readiness and willingness of Jesus Christ to entertain returning sinners.

(4.) Fourthly, If you would be good betimes, then you must know betimes, *That Jesus Christ is designed, sealed, and appointed by the Father to the office of a Mediator.*[1]

'Labour not for the meat which perisheth, but for that meat which endureth to everlasting life, which the Son of man shall give unto you; for him hath God the Father sealed.' God the Father hath made Christ's commission authentical, as men do theirs by their seal. It is a metaphor, a simile taken from them who give commissions under hand and seal. God the Father hath given it under his hand and seal, that Jesus Christ is the only person that he hath appointed and sealed, allowed and confirmed, to the office of our redemption. If Jesus Christ were never so able to save, and never so willing and ready to save poor sinners, yet if he were not appointed, designed, and sealed, for that work, the awakened sinner would never look out after him, nor desire union with him, nor interest in him; and therefore it is of very great consequence to know that God the Father hath sent and sealed Christ to be a Saviour to his people: 'Him hath God the Father sealed.' Sealed by way of destination and sealed by way of qualification, sealed by his doctrine, sealed by his miracles, sealed by his baptism, sealed by his resurrection, but above all, sealed by his glorious unction. 'The Spirit of the Lord is upon me; because the Lord hath anointed me to preach good tidings unto the meek: he hath sent me to bind up the broken-hearted, to proclaim liberty to the captives, and the opening of the prison to them that are bound; to proclaim the acceptable year of the Lord, and the day of vengeance of our God; to comfort all that mourn; to appoint unto them that mourn in Zion, to give unto them beauty for ashes, the oil of joy for mourning, the garment of praise for the spirit of heaviness: that they might be called trees of righteousness, the planting of the Lord, that he might be glorified,' Isa. lxi. 1–3, Luke iv. 18.[2] Neither saints nor angels are sealed and anointed to the great work of redemption, but the Lord Jesus is. You should always look upon the Lord Jesus as sealed and anointed to the office of a Mediator, and accordingly plead with him.

[1] John vi. 27, The Father sealed, even God; so the Greek hath it.

[2] Christ was anointed of God, 1, by way of designation; 2, by way of qualification; 3, by way of inauguration. This anointing was ordinarily used in the installing men to offices of any eminence.

Ah, Lord! it is thy office, as thou art a sealed and an anointed Saviour and Redeemer, to subdue my sins, to change my nature, to sanctify my heart, to reform my life, and to save my soul; and therefore do it for thy name's sake, oh do it for thy office' sake, do it for thy glory's sake!

'Thou art anointed with the oil of gladness above thy fellows,' Ps. xlv. 8, Acts iv. 27. Thou hast a larger effusion of the Spirit upon thee than others; thou art anointed with the Holy Ghost and with power after an extraordinary measure and manner; thou art endued with all heroical gifts and excellencies, plentifully, abundantly, transcendently; thou art sealed and predestinated;[1] thou art invested into this office of Mediatorship under the Father's hand and seal: and therefore whither should I go for salvation, for remission, for redemption, for grace, for glory, but to thee?

(5.) Fifthly, If you would be good betimes, then you must know betimes, *that there is no way to salvation but by Jesus Christ.*

'Neither is there salvation in any other'[2] (speaking of Christ), 'for there is none other name under heaven, given among men, whereby we must be saved,' Acts iv. 12. If ever you are saved, you must be saved by him, and him only; you must not look for another saviour, nor you must not look for a co-saviour; you must be saved wholly by Christ and only by Christ, or you shall never be saved; you must cry out, as Lambert did when he was in the fire, and lifted up his hands, and fingers'-ends flaming, 'None but Christ, none but Christ'![3] When Augustus Cæsar desired the senate to join two consuls with him for the better government of the state, the senate answered, that they held it as a diminution of his dignity, and a disparagement of their own judgment, to join any with so incomparable a man as Augustus.[4]

Ah! friends, it is a diminution of Christ's dignity, sufficiency, and glory, in the business of your salvation, to join anything with the Lord Jesus; and it is the greatest disparagement in the world to your own judgments, knowledge, prudence, and wisdom, to yoke any with Christ in the work of redemption, in the business of salvation.

Augustine saith, that Marcellina hung Christ's picture and the picture of Pythagoras together; many there are, not only in Rome, but in England (yea, I am afraid in London), who join Christ and their works together, Christ and their prayers together, Christ and their teachers together, Christ and their mournings together, Christ and their hearings together, Christ and their alms together.

Ah, what a poor, what a weak, what an impotent, what an insufficient Saviour doth these men make Jesus Christ to be! Except these men come off from these things, and come up only to Jesus Christ, in the great business of salvation, they will as certainly and as eternally perish, notwithstanding their hearing, knowing, and talking much of Christ, as those that never heard of Jesus Christ.

In the Old Testament, God commands them not to wear a garment of divers sorts, as of woollen and linen together, 'neither shall a garment mingled of linen and woollen come upon thee,' Deut. xxii. 11.

This law was figurative, and shews us that in the case of our justification, acceptation, and salvation, we are not to join our works, our

[1] John i. 16. iii. 34.

[2] ἐν ἄλλῳ, that is, by or through the mediation of any other.

[3] Act. and Mon. [Foxe, *sub nomine.*—G.]

[4] Suetonius.

services, with the righteousness of Christ. God abhors a linsey-woolsey righteousness. And as by the letter of this law, in the Hebrews' account, one thread of wool in a linen garment, or one linen thread in a woollen garment, made it unlawful, so the least manner of mixture in the business of justification makes all null and void.[1] 'And if by grace, then it is no more of works, otherwise grace is no more grace. But if it be of works, then it is no more grace, otherwise work is no more work.'[2] He that shall mix his righteousness with Christ's, he that shall mix his puddle with Christ's purple blood, his rags with Christ's royal robes, his copper with Christ's gold, his water with Christ's wine, &c., is in the ready way to perish for ever.

On earth kings love no consorts; power is impatient of participation. Christ will be Alexander or *Nemo*, nobody; he will be all in all in the business of justification, or he will be nothing at all. We must say of Christ, as it was once said of Cæsar, *Socium habet neminem*, He may have a companion, &c., but he must not have a competitor, 1 Cor. i. 30, Rom. v. 19, 20.

Let us say of Christ, as the heathen once said of his petty gods, *Contemno minutulos istos deos, modo Jovem propitium habeam*, so long as he had his Jupiter to friend, he regarded them not. So, so long as we have our Jesus to friend, and his righteousness and blood to friend, we shall contemn all other things, and abhor the bringing of any thing into competition with him. A real Christian cares not for any thing that hath not *aliquid Christi*, something of Christ in it. He that holds not wholly with Christ, doth very shamefully neglect Christ, *Aut totum mecum tene, aut totum omitte*, saith Gregory Nazianzen. (Eph. iii. 9, 10, Ps. lxxi. 15, 16, 19, compared.)

There is no other name, no other nature, no other blood, no other merits, no other person to be justified and saved by, but Jesus Christ. You may run from creature to creature, and from duty to duty, and from ordinance to ordinance, and when you have wearied and tired out yourselves in seeking ease and rest, satisfaction and remission, justification and salvation, in one way and another, you will be forced after all to come to Christ, and to cry out, Ah! none but Christ, none but Christ! Isa. lv. 2, Rom. x. 3. Ah! none to Christ, none to Christ; no works to Christ; no duties, no services to Christ; no prayers, no tears to Christ; no righteousness, no holiness to Christ. Well! friends, remember this, that all the tears in the world cannot wipe off meritoriously one sin, nor all the grace and holiness that is in angels and men buy out the pardon of the least transgression. All remission is only by the blood of Christ.

(6.) Sixthly and lastly, If you would be good betimes, then you must know betimes, *that the heart of Jesus Christ is as much set upon sinners now he is in heaven, as ever it was when he was upon earth.*

Christ is no less loving, less mindful, less desirous of sinners' eternal welfare now he is heaven in a far country, than he was when he lived on earth. Witness his continuing the ministry of reconciliation among poor sinners in all ages; witness the constant treaties, that by his ambassadors and Spirit he still hath with poor sinners, about the things

[1] Philip. iii. 9, 10; Rev. xix. 8; Gal. iii. 28, ii. 16.
[2] Rom. xi. 6; Eph. ii. 5; Rom. v. 15–18.

of their peace, the things of eternity; witness his continual knockings, his continual callings upon poor sinners by his word, rod, Spirit, to open, to repent, to lay hold on mercy, and to be at peace with him; witness his continual wooing of poor sinners in the face of all neglects and put-offs, in the face of all delays and denials, in the face of all harsh entertainment and churlish answers, in the face of all gainsayings and carnal reasonings, in the face of all the scorn and contempt that wretched sinners put upon him,[1] and witness that plain word, 'Jesus Christ, the same yesterday, and to-day, and for ever,' Heb. xiii. 8. Christ is the same afore time, in time, and after time, he is unchangeable in his essence, in his promises, and in his affections: 'I am Alpha and Omega, the beginning and the ending, saith the Lord, which is, and which was, and which is to come,' Rev. i. 8, 11, xxi. 6, xxii. 13.[2]

The phrase is taken from the Greek letters, whereof Alpha is the first and Omega is the last. The first and last letter of the Greek alphabet is a description of me, saith Christ, who am before all and after all, who am above all and in all, who am unchangeable in myself, and in my thoughts and good will to poor sinners. Therefore do not, poor souls, entertain any hard thoughts concerning Jesus Christ, as if he was less mindful, less pitiful, and less merciful to poor souls now he is in heaven, than he was when his abode was in this world.

And thus I have gone over those six things that you must know concerning Christ betimes, if ever you be good betimes. When Pope Leo lay upon his death-bed, Cardinal Bembus citing a text of Scripture to comfort him, he replied, '*Apage has nugas de Christo*, away with these baubles concerning Christ!' But I hope better things of you, and do desire that you will say of all things below this knowledge of Christ that I have opened to you, as that devout pilgrim, who, travelling to Jerusalem, and by the way visiting many brave cities, with their rare monuments, and meeting with many friendly entertainments, would often say, I must not stay here, this is not Jerusalem. Ah! so do you, young men and women, in the midst of all your worldly delights and contents, cry out, Oh! we must not stay here, this is not Jerusalem, this is not that knowledge of Christ that I must have, if ever I am happy here and blessed hereafter.

Duty (4). Fourthly and lastly, If you would be good betimes, then you must *acquaint yourselves with those that are good betimes.*

Direction (1). *First,* If you would be gracious in the spring and morning of your youth, then you must begin betimes to be much in with them who are much in with Christ, who lie near his heart and know much of his mind. 'He that walketh with wise men shall be wise, but a companion of fools shall be destroyed,' or, as the Hebrew hath it, shall be broken in pieces, as when an army is broken and routed by an enemy.[3] *Holech* from *Halech,* walking with the wise, he shall be wise, for so the original hath it. It is not talking with the wise, but walking with the wise, that will make you wise; it is not your commending and praising of the wise, but your walking with the wise, that

[1] 2 Cor. v. 20; Rev. iii. 20; Isa. xxvii. 5, lvi. 4; Cant. v. 2; Prov. vi. 9; Matt. xxii. 4, 23, 27.

[2] It was a custom among the Turks, to cry out every morning from an high tower, God always was. and always will be, and so salute their Mahomet.

[3] Prov. xiii. 20, ירוע, shall be broken, or shall be worse, from רוע, to be naught.

will make you wise; it is not your taking a few turns with the wise that will make you wise, but your walking with the wise that will make you wise. There is no getting much good by them that are good, but by making them your ordinary and constant companions.[1]

Ah, friends! you should do as Joseph in Egypt, of whom the Scripture saith, Ps. cv. 22 (according to the Hebrew phrase), that he tied the princes of Pharaoh's court about his heart.

If ever you would gain by the saints, you must bind them upon your souls, you must labour to have very near, close, and intimate communion with them.

The Jews have a proverb, that two dry sticks put to a green one will kindle it. The best way to be in a flame God-ward, Christ-ward, heavenward, and holiness-ward, is to be among the dry sticks, the kindle-coals,[2] the saints; for as live coals kindle those that are dead, so lively Christians will heat and enliven those that are dead God-wards, Christ-wards, heaven-wards, and holiness-wards. 'As iron sharpeneth iron, so doth the face of a man his friend,' Prov. xxvii. 17.

Men's wits, parts, and gifts, and industry, commonly grow more strong, vigorous, and quick, by friendly conference and communion.

And as he that comes where sweet spices and ointments are stirring, carries away a sweet savour with him, so he that converseth with those that are good shall carry away that goodness and sweetness with him that shall render him sweet, desirable, and delectable to others. Polemon, that Augustine speaks of, who was all for wine and play, &c., became a brave man when he came acquainted with the philosopher's school.[3] So many young men, that have been all for wine and women, for playing and toying, for vanity and folly, have become brave men, precious men, by the company, counsel, and example of those who were gracious. Doctor Taylor, the martyr, rejoiced that ever he came into prison, because he came thither to have acquaintance with that angel of God John Bradford, as he calls him: so, doubtless, many young persons there be that have much cause to rejoice, and for ever to bless the Lord, that ever they came acquainted with such and such who fear the Lord, and who walk in his ways, for the good that they have received by them.

Algerius, an Italian martyr, said he had rather be in prison with Cato, than with Cæsar in the senate house.[4][5]

Ah! young men, young men, you were better be with the people of God, when they are in the lowest and most contemptible condition, than with the great wicked ones of the world, when they are in all their royalty and glory. In the day of account you will find that they have made the best market, who have rather chosen to keep company with Lazarus, though in his rags, than they would with others keep company with Dives, though in his purple robes.

Well! young men, remember this, clothes and company do oftentimes tell tales, in a mute but significant language.

[1] It was the saying of one, As oft as I have been among wicked men, I return home less a man than I was before. [Bernard.—G.]

[2] 'Kindling-coal,' or piece left over night in the fire-place.—G.

[3] Augustine, Ep. 130.

[4] See interesting account of Algerius in Clarke's 'Martyrologie,' as before, p. 187.—G.

[5] Moses was of the same mind and metal, Heb. xi. 24–27.

Tell me with whom thou goest, and I will tell thee what thou art, saith the Spanish proverb.[1] Cicero, though a heathen, had rather to have no companion, than a bad one. The Lord grant that this heathen, and others among them, that were of the same mind with him, may never rise up in judgment against any of you, into whose hands this treatise may fall.

And thus I have despatched those four things that you must be acquainted with betimes, viz., the Scripture, your own hearts and conditions, the Lord Jesus Christ, and those that fear him, if ever you would be good betimes.

Direction (2). *Secondly,* If you would be good betimes, if you would seek and serve the Lord in the spring and morning of your days, Then you must *shun the occasions of sin betimes.* A man will never begin to be good, till he begin to decline those occasions that have made him bad: 1 Thes. v. 22, 'Abstain from all appearances of evil.'[2]

You must shun and be shy of the very appearance of sin, of the very shows and shadows of sin. The word εἶδος, which is ordinarily rendered appearance, signifies kind, or sort; and so the meaning of the apostle seems to be this, 'Abstain from all sort, or the whole kind of evil;' from all that is truly so, be it never so small.

The least sin is dangerous. Cæsar was stabbed with bodkins, and many have been eaten up of mice and lice.

The least spark may consume the greatest house, the least leak may sink the greatest ship, the least sin is enough to undo thy soul; and therefore shun all the occasions that lead unto it.

Job made a covenant with his eyes, Job xxxi. 1; Joseph would not be in the room where his mistress was, Gen. xxxix. 10; and David, when himself, would not sit with vain persons, Ps. xxvi. 3–7. As long as there is fuel in our hearts for a temptation, we cannot be secure; he that hath gunpowder about him, had need keep far enough off from sparkles; he that is either tender of his credit abroad, or comfort at home, had need shun, and be shy of the very show and shadow of sin; he that would neither wound conscience nor credit, God nor gospel, had need hate 'the garment spotted with the flesh,' Jude 23.[3]

In the law, God commanded his people, not only that they should worship no idol, but that they should demolish all the monuments of them, and that they should make no covenant nor affinity with those who worshipped them, and all lest they should be drawn by those occasions to commit idolatry with them. He that would not taste of the forbidden fruit, must not so much as gaze on it; and he that would not be bit by the serpent, must not so much as parley with the serpent.

It is very observable, that in the law, the Nazarite was not only commanded to abstain from wine and strong drink, but also he might not eat grapes, whether moist or dry, or anything that is made of the vine

[1] Those that keep ill company, are like those that walk in the sun, who are tanned insensibly.

[2] We must shun, *quicquid fuerit male coloratum,* whatsoever looks but ill-favouredly, as Bernard hath it.

[3] The sin and the coat of the sin is to be hated, saith Ambrose. *Latet anguis inherba.* Snakes are found among roses, Num. vi. 3, 4. *Quid est vitare peccata, nisi vitare occasiones peccatorum?*—Melan[cthon]. What is it to avoid sin, but to avoid the occasions of sin?

tree, from the kernels even to the husk. But why not these small things, in which there could be no danger of drunkenness? Surely, lest by the contentment of these, he might be drawn to desire the wine, and so be brought on to sin, to break his vow, and so make work for hell, or for the physician of souls. God hereby forbidding the most remote occasions, shews how wary and exactly careful men should be to shun and avoid all occasions, provocations, and appearances of evil; and indeed we had need to keep off from slippery places who can hardly stand fast on dry ground; he that ventures upon the occasion of sin and then prays, 'Lord, lead me not into temptation,' is like him that thrusts his finger into the fire, and then prays that it may not be burnt; or like him that is resolved to quench the fire with oil, which, instead of quenching it, is as fuel to feed it and increase it. It was a notable saying of one, *Majus est miraculum inter vehementes occasiones non cadere, quam mortuos suscitare.*[1] It is a greater miracle not to fall, being among strong occasions, than it is to raise up the dead; he that would not be defiled, must not touch pitch; he that would not be burnt, must not carry fire in his bosom; he that would not eat the meat, must not meddle with the broth; he that would not fall into the pit, must not dance upon the brink; he that would not feel the blow, must keep off from the train:[2] 'Keep thee far from a false matter,' Exod. xxiii. 7. He that will not fly from the occasions and allurements of sin, though they may seem never so pleasant to the eye, or sweet to the taste, shall find them in the end more sharp than vinegar, more bitter than wormwood, more deadly than poison.

There is a great truth in that saying of the son of Sirach, 'He that loveth danger, shall perish therein; he that will not decline danger, shall not be able to decline destruction,' Ecclus. iii. 26, 27.[3]

Socrates speaks of two young men that flung away their belts when, being in an idol temple, the lustrating water fell upon them, detesting, saith the historian, 'the garment spotted by the flesh;' and will you, O young men, play and toy with the occasions of sin? The Lord forbid.

There are stories of several heathens that have shunned and avoided the occasions of sin, and will you dare to venture upon the occasions of sin?

Alexander would not see the woman after whom he might have lusted.

Scipio Africanus, warring in Spain, took New Carthage by storm, at which time a beautiful and noble virgin fled to him for succour to preserve her chastity. He being but four and twenty years old, and so in the heat of youth, hearing of it, would not suffer her to come into his sight for fear of temptation, but caused her to be restored in safety to her father.[4]

Livia counselled her husband Augustus, not only not to do wrong, but not to seem to do so, &c.

[1] Bernard in Cant. serm. 65.

[2] Prov. vi. 27–29. *Non diu tutus est, periculo proximus.*—Cyprian, He is not long safe that is near to danger.

[3] Brooks's second quotation from the Apocrypha thus far.—G.

[4] Aure: Victor. Dio. Laert. *in vita.*

Cæsar would not search Pompey's cabinet, lest he should find new matters of revenge.

Plato mounted upon his horse, and judging himself a little moved with pride, did presently light from his horse, lest he should be overtaken with loftiness in riding.

Theseus is said to cut off his golden locks, lest his enemies should take advantage by taking hold of them.

Ah! young men, young men, shall the very heathens thus shun and fly from the occasion of sin, and will not you? will not you who sit under the sunshine of the gospel? These will in the great day of account be sad and sore witnesses against those that dally and play with the occasions of sin.

To prevent carnal carefulness, Christ sends his disciples to school, to the irrational creatures (Matt. vi. 26–32). And to prevent your closing with the occasions of sin, let me send you to school to the like creatures, that you may learn by them to shun and avoid the occasions of sin.

The *Sepiæ*, a certain kind of fish, perceiving themselves in danger of taking, by an instinct which they have, they do darken the water, and so many times escape the net which is laid for them.

Geese, they say, when they fly over Taurus they keep stones in their mouths, lest by gaggling[1] they should discover themselves to the eagles, which are amongst the mountains waiting for them.[2] Now, if all these considerations put together will not work you to decline the occasions of sin, I know not what will. There is a truth in that old saying—

He that will no evil do,
Must do nothing belongs thereto.

The Israelites must have no leaven in their houses till the Passover be done, lest they should be tempted to eat of it, Exod. xiii.

Direction (3). *Thirdly*, If you would be good betimes, then you must *remember the eye of God betimes.*

If you would seek and serve the Lord in the spring and morning of your days, then you must study God's omnipresence betimes. 'Doth not he see my ways, and count all my steps?' 'For his eyes are upon the ways of man, and he seeth all his goings. There is no darkness, nor shadow of death, where the workers of iniquity may hide themselves,' Ps. cxxxix. 2–14; Job xxxi. 4, 21, 22.

I have read that Paphnutius converted two famous young strumpets, Thais and Ephron, from uncleanness only with this argument, that God seeth all things in the dark, when the doors are fast, the windows shut, and the curtains drawn.[3] By this very argument Solomon labours to take off his young men from carnal and sinful courses: 'And why wilt thou, my son, be ravished with a strange woman, and embrace the bosom of a stranger! For the ways of man are before the eyes of the Lord, and he pondereth all his goings,' Prov. v. 20, 21. Thou mayest deceive all the world, like that counterfeit Alexander in Josephus his

[1] 'Gabbling.'—G.

[2] Pliny has much curious lore on the 'goose' which Brooks here and elsewhere records. See *sub voce*.—G.

[3] *Non se putent adulteri noctis tenebris vel parietum obtegi.*—Bede.

story, but Augustus will not be deceived; he hath quicker and sharper eyes.[1]

Ah! young men, young men, you may deceive this man and that, and as easily deceive yourselves, but you cannot deceive him, who is *πανόφθαλμος*, *totus oculus*, all-eye. As the eyes of a well drawn picture are fastened upon thee which way soever thou turnest, so are the eyes of the Lord. I have read of one who, being tempted to adultery, said they could not be private enough, and being carried from room to room, answered, We are not yet private enough, God is here.

Ah, friends! His eyes, which are ten thousand times brighter than the sun, compasseth thy words, thy ways, thy works, thy thoughts, thy bed, thy board, thy bench. The Egyptian hieroglyphic for God was an eye on a sceptre, shewing that he sees and rules all things, Jer. xiii. 27, xxix. 23.

Ah, friends! All thoughts, words, hopes, and hearts, are naked, opened, dissected and quartered before that God with whom you have to do. God is very curious and exact in marking and observing what is done by men, that he may render to every man according to his works.[2]

Augustine speaks of an old comedian, when having no other spectators, went usually into the theatre, and acted before the statues of the gods.[3]

Ah! young men and women, the eye of God should be more to you than all the world besides. Oh that the Scripture might be written with the pen of a diamond upon your hearts. 'Hear ye not me,' saith the Lord, 'and will you not tremble at my presence?' Jer. v. 21, 22. There is a great truth in that saying of his, *Magna nobis ex hac indita est probitatis necessitas, quia omnia ante oculos judicis facimus cuncta cernentis.*[4] A great necessity of goodness is from hence put into us, because we do all things before the eyes of a judge that sees all things.

Direction (4). *Fourthly*, If you would be good betimes, then you must *hearken to the voice of conscience betimes*, 2 Tim. i. 3.

A man will never begin to be good till he begins to hearken to what conscience speaks. So long as a man turns a deaf ear to conscience, he is a safe prisoner to Satan, and a sure enemy to good, Ps. lviii. 4, John iii. 20, 21.

Ah! how good might many have been had they but begun betimes to hearken to conscience!

Ah! young men, do not dally with conscience, do not play, do not trifle with conscience, do not stop your ears against conscience. He that will not in his youth give conscience audience, shall at last be forced to hear such lectures from conscience, as shall make his life a very hell. A sleepy conscience is like a sleepy lion, when he awakes, he roars and tears; so will conscience, Mark ix. 22. Conscience is *mille testes*, a thousand witnesses for or against a man.[5] He that hath long turned the deaf ear to conscience, shall at last find his conscience like Prome-

[1] *Noli peccare; Deus videt, angeli astant, &c.* Take heed what thou doest, God beholds thee, angels observe thee.

[2] Heb. iv. 13, *τετραχηλισμένα.*

[3] Aug. *de civ. Dei.* l. vi. c. x.

[4] Bœtius *de consol.* l. v.

[5] Such shall find conscience to be *judex, index, vindex.*

theus's vulture, that lies ever a-gnawing. Judas found it so, and Spira found it so, and Blair, a great councillor of Scotland, found it so.

I have read of one *John Hofmeister*, that fell sick in his inn, as he was travelling towards Auspurge in Germany, and grew to that horror of conscience, that they were fain to bind him in his bed with chains, where he cried out, that he was for ever cast off by God, and that the promises that were set before him would do him no good, and all because he had wounded his conscience, and turned a deaf ear to conscience.[1]

Well! young men, if you will not betimes hearken to conscience, you shall at last hear conscience saying to you, as the probationer disciple said to Christ, 'Master, I will follow thee whithersoever thou goest,' Mat. viii. 19; so saith conscience, Sinner, I have called upon thee many a thousand times, and told thee, that I must by commission be thy best friend, or thy worst enemy, but thou wouldst not hear; and therefore now I will follow thee whither ever thou goest;[2] fast, and I will follow thee, and fill thee with horrors and terrors; feast, and I will follow thee, and shew thee such a handwriting upon the wall, as shall cause thy countenance to change, thy thoughts to be troubled, the joints of thy loins to be loosed, and thy knees dashed one against another, Dan. v. 5, 6; stay at home, and I will follow thee from bed to board; go abroad, and I will follow thee into all places and companies, and thou shalt know that it is an evil and a bitter thing, that thou hast so often and so long neglected my calls, and disobeyed my voice, and walked contrary to me; how thou shalt find a truth in that saying of Luther, *una guttula malæ conscientiæ totum mare*, &c., one drop of an evil conscience swallows up the whole sea of worldly joy.

Well! young men, there is a day coming wherein a good conscience will be better than a good purse, for then the Judge will not be put off with a suit of compliments or fair words, nor drawn aside with hope of reward; and therefore, as you would be able to hold up your heads in that day, make conscience of hearkening to the voice of conscience in this your day.

Direction (5). Fifthly, If you would be good betimes, then you must *know betimes wherein true happiness lies.*

For a man will never begin to be good till he begins to understand wherein his happiness consists.

The philosophers, speaking of happiness, were divided into two hundred and eighty-eight opinions, every one intending something, and yet resolving nothing.[3] Therefore the man in Plutarch, hearing them wrangle about man's *summum bonum*, chiefest good, one placing it in this, and another in that, he went to the market and bought up all that was good, hoping, among all, he should not miss of it, but he did. Many look for happiness in sin, others look for it in the creatures, but they must all say, It is not in us, Isa. lvi. 12, Job xxviii. 14: *Nil dat quod non habet*, nothing can give what it hath not. If the conduit pipe hath no water, it can give no water; if a man hath no money, he can give no money; if the creatures have no happiness, they can give

[1] Jo. Wolf. lect mem. To. II. *ad. an.* 1547. [Augsburg.—G.]

[2] *Tolle conscientiam, tolle omnia*, take away conscience, and take away all, said the heathen.

[3] *Quot homines, tot sententiæ*: so many men, so many minds.

no happiness. Now this jewel, this pearl, happiness, is not to be found in the breast, in the bosom of creatures. In a word, because I must hasten to a close, man's happiness lies,

First, In his communion with God, as experience and Scripture demonstrates. 'Happy is that people that is in such a case (but give me that word again), yea, happy is that people whose God is the Lord,' Ps. cxliv. 15. A man whose soul is in communion with God shall find more pleasure in a desert, in a dungeon, in a den, yea, in death, than in the palace of a prince, than in all worldly delights and contents, &c.

Secondly, In pardon of sin. 'Blessed is he whose transgression is forgiven, whose sin is covered: blessed is the man unto whom the Lord imputeth not iniquity, and in whose spirit there is no guile,' Ps. xxxii. 1, 2. It is not, blessed is the honourable man, but blessed is the pardoned man. It is not, blessed is the rich man, but blessed is the pardoned man. It is not, blessed is the learned man, but blessed is the pardoned man. It is not, blessed is the politic man, but blessed is the pardoned man. It is not, blessed is the victorious man, but blessed is the pardoned man. Do with me what thou wilt, since thou hast pardoned my sins, saith Luther.

Thirdly, In a complete fruition and enjoyment of God, when we shall be here no more. 'Blessed are the pure in heart, for they shall see God, Mat. v. 8; 'Now they see him but darkly, but in heaven they shall see him face to face; they shall know as they are known,' 1 Cor. xiii. 12. But of these things I have spoken largely elsewhere, and therefore shall satisfy myself with these hints.

Direction (6). *Lastly,* If you would be good betimes, then you must *break your covenant with sin betimes.*

You must fall out with your lusts betimes; you must arm and fence yourselves against sin betimes, Isa. xxviii. 15–18. A man never begins to fall in with Christ till he begins to fall out with his sins. Till sin and the soul be two, Christ and the soul cannot be one. Now, to work your hearts to this, you should always look upon sin under these notions:

Notion (1). *First,* If you would have the league dissolved betwixt sin and your souls betimes, then *look upon sin under the notion of an enemy betimes.*

'Dearly beloved, I beseech you as strangers and pilgrims, abstain from fleshly lusts, which war against the soul,' 1 Peter ii. 11. As the viper is killed by the young ones in her belly, so are poor sinners betrayed and killed by their own lusts, that are nourished in their bosoms.[1]

Pittacus, a philosopher, challenged Phlyon[2] the Athenian captain, in their wars against them, to single combat, carried a net privily, and so caught him, and overcame him; so doth sin with poor sinners, the dangerous, pernicious, malignant nature of sin. You may see in the story of the Italian, who first made his enemy deny God, and then

[1] Sins, especially against knowledge, are *peccata vulnerantia et devastantia*, wounding and wasting.

[2] Rather, Phrynon; the above feat is recorded by Diog. Laërtius, i. 75: Herodotus, v. 94, 95, &c., &c.—G.

stabbed him to the heart, and so at once murdered both body and soul. Sin betrays us into the hand of the devil, as Delilah did Samson into the hands of the Philistines.

Sugared poisons go down pleasantly. Oh! but when they are down, they gall and gnaw, and gripe the very heart-strings asunder; it is so with sin. Ah! souls, have not you often found it so?

When Phocas the murderer thought to secure himself by building high walls, he heard a voice from heaven telling him, that though he built his bulwarks never so high, yet sin within would soon undermine all.[1]

Ambrose reports of one Theotimus, that having a disease upon his body, the physician told him, that except he did abstain from intemperance, drunkenness, uncleanness, he would lose his eyes; his heart was so desperately set upon his sins, that he cries out, then, *Vale lumen amicum*, farewell, sweet light. Ah, how did his lusts war both against body and soul!

The '*old* man' is like a treacherous friend, and a friendly traitor. Though it be a harder thing to fight with a man's lusts, than it is to fight with the cross, yet you must fight or die; if you are not the death of your sins, they will prove the death of your souls.

The oracle told the Cyrrheans, *noctesque diesque belligerandum*, they could not be happy, unless they waged war night and day; no more can we, except we live and die fighting against our lusts.[2]

Ah! young men, can you look upon sin under the notion of an enemy, and not break with it, and not arm against it?

Well! remember this, the pleasure and sweetness that follows victory over sin, is a thousand times beyond that seeming sweetness that is in sin; and as victory over sin is the sweetest victory, so it is the greatest victory. There is no conquest to that which is gotten over a man's own corruptions. 'He that is slow to anger is better than the mighty: and he that ruleth his spirit than he that taketh a city,' Prov. xvi. 32.

It is noble to overcome an enemy without, but it is more noble to overcome an enemy within; it is honourable to overcome fiery flames, but it is far more honourable to overcome fiery lusts.

When Valentinian the emperor was upon his dying-bed, among all his victories only one comforted him, and that was victory over his worst enemy, viz., his own naughty heart.[3]

Ah! young men, young men, your worst enemies are within you, and all their plots, designs, and assaults are upon your souls, your most noble part. They know if that fort-royal be won, all is their own, and you are undone, and shall be their slaves for ever; and therefore it stands upon you to arm yourselves against these inbred enemies; and if you engage Christ in the quarrel, you will carry the day; and when you shall lie upon your dying-beds, you will then find that there is no comfort to that which ariseth from the conquests of your own hearts, your own lusts.

Notion (2). *Secondly*, If you would break covenant with sin, if you

[1] The 'monster' emperor of Constantinople, A.D. 602–610.—G.

[2] As one of the dukes of Venice died fighting against the Nauratines, with his weapons in his hand.

[3] Rom. vii. 22, 23; 2 Cor. x. 3–6; Gal. v. 17.

would arm and fence yourselves against sin betimes, then *look upon sin as the soul's bonds*, Gal. iii. 10, John viii. 34.

For as bonds tie things together, so doth sin tie the sinner and the curse together. It binds the sinner and wrath together, it links the sinner and hell together: 'I perceive that thou art in the gall of bitterness, and in the bond of iniquity,' Acts viii. 23. Iniquity is a chain, a bond. Now, bonds and chains gall the body, and so doth sin the soul; and as poor captives are held fast in their chains, so are sinners in their sins; they cannot redeem themselves by price, nor by power, 2 Tim. ii. 26.

Ah! young men, young men! no bondage to soul bondage, no slavery to soul slavery. The Israelites' bondage under Pharaoh, and the Christians' bondage under the Turks, is but the bondage of the body, of the baser and ignoble part of man; but yours is soul bondage, and soul slavery, which is the saddest and greatest of all.[1]

Ah, friends! you should never look upon your sins but you should look upon them as your bonds; yea, as the worst bonds that ever were. All other chains are golden chains, chains of pearl, compared to those chains of iron and brass, those chains of lust, with which you are bound. Ah! who can thus look upon his chains, his sins, and not loathe them, and not labour for freedom from them? Justinus the emperor's motto was *Libertas res inestimabilis*, liberty is invaluable. If civil liberty be, surely spiritual liberty is much more. If you ask souls that were once in a state of bondage, but are now Christ's free men, they will tell you so.

It was a good observation of Chrysostom, that Joseph was the free man and his mistress was the servant, when she was at the beck of her own lusts, when she tempted and he refused.[2] Such as live most above sin and temptation, are the greatest freemen; others, that live under the power of their lusts, are but slaves, and in bonds, though they dream and talk of freedom, Titus iii. 3.

Notion (3). *Thirdly*, If you would break league with sin, and arm and fence yourselves against it, then look always upon sin under the notion of fire.

'And others save with fear, pulling them out of the fire,' Jude 23.[3] Oh, snatch them out of their sins, as you would snatch a child, a friend, out of the fire, or as the angel snatched Lot out of Sodom, hastily, and with a holy violence. Natural fire may burn the house, the goods, the treasure, the servant, the child, the wife, the body; but this fire burns the soul, it destroys and consumes that noble part which is more worth than all the treasures of a thousand worlds. Every man hath a hand and a heart to quench the fire which burns his neighbour's house, but few men have either hands or hearts to quench the fire that burns their neighbour's souls; this is, and this shall be, for a lamentation.

I have read of one who, upon the violence of any temptation to sin, would lay his hand upon burning coals, and being not able to abide it, would say to himself, Oh, how unable shall I be to endure the pains of

[1] Augustine saith of Rome, that she was the great mistress of the world, and the great drudge of sin.

[2] Chrysost. Hom. xix. in prior. Epist. ad Corinth.

[3] ἁρπάζοντες signifies a violent snatching, as the tender-hearted mother, to save the life of her child, pulls it hastily, and with violence, out of the fire.

hell! and this restrained him from evil.[1] But what is the fire of hell to the fire of sin? Now, to provoke you to look upon sin under the notion of fire, consider with me the sundry resemblances between material and immaterial fire, between corporeal common fire and between this spiritual fire, sin. As,

[1.] *First, Fire is terrible and dreadful.* A ship on fire, an house on fire, oh how dreadful is it! So sin set home upon the conscience is exceeding terrible and dreadful. 'Mine iniquity,' so the Hebrew, 'is greater than I can bear.' Sin or iniquity is often put for the punishment of sin, by a metonymy of the efficient for the effect; for sin is the natural parent of punishment. 'Mine iniquity,' saith Cain, 'is so great, and lies so heavy, so terrible and dreadful upon my conscience, that it cannot be forgiven,' Gen. iv. 13, and thus, by his diffidence, he stabs two at once, the mercy of God, and his own soul.[2] So Judas, 'I have sinned, in that I have betrayed innocent blood; and he went and hanged himself,' Mat. xxvii. 3–5.

As there is no fighting with a mighty fire, so there is no bearing up when God sets home sin upon the conscience; a man will then choose strangling or hanging, rather than living under such wounds and lashes of conscience. Histories abound with instances of this nature; but I must hasten to a close.

[2.] *Secondly, Fire is most dangerous and pernicious* when it breaks forth of the chimney, or of the house; so it is with sin. Sin is bad in the eye, worse in the tongue, worser in the heart, but worst of all in the life. Fire, when out of its proper place, may do much hurt in the house, but when it flames abroad, then it doth most mischief to others, 2 Sam. xii. 9–15.

Sin in the heart may undo a man, but sin in the life may undo others as well as a man's self. Set a guard upon the eye, a greater upon thy heart, but the greatest of all upon thy life, Job xxxi. 1, Prov. iv. 23, Eph. v. 15.

Salvian relates how the heathen did reproach some Christians, who by their lewd lives made the gospel of Christ to be a reproach. 'Where,' said they, 'is that good law which they do believe? Where are those rules of godliness which they do learn? They read the holy Gospel, and yet are unclean; they hear the apostles' writings, and yet are drunk; they follow Christ, and yet disobey Christ; they profess a holy law, and yet do lead impure lives.[3]

But the lives of other Christians have been so holy, that the very heathens observing them, have said, Surely this is a good God, whose servants are so good.

It is brave[4] when the life of a Christian is a commentary upon Christ's life.

One speaking of the Scripture, saith [Augustine], *verba vivenda, non legenda,* they are words to be lived, and practised, not read only.

A heathen [Plutarch] adviseth us to demean ourselves so circumspectly, as if our enemies did always behold us. And said another [Epictetus], For shame, either live as Stoics, or leave off the name of Stoics; sirs, live as Christians, or lay down the name of Christians.

[1] Dr Denison's 'Threefold Resolution,' par. ii. sect. 2.
[2] *Mentiris, Cain,* Thou liest, Cain, saith one on the text.
[3] Salvianus, de G. D. l. 4.
[4] Noble, good.—G.

[3.] Thirdly, *Fire hardens*, it makes the weak and limber clay to become stiff and strong for the potter's use. So sin hardens: it hardens the heart against the commands of God, the calls of Christ, and the wrestlings of the Spirit. And as you see in Pharaoh, the Jews, and most that are under the sound of the gospel, Jer. v. 3, xix. 15; Isa. ix. 13.

Ah! how many hath this fire—sin—hardened in these days, by working them to slight soul-softening means, and by drawing them to entertain hardening thoughts of God, and to fall in with soul-hardening company, and soul-hardening principles, and soul-hardening examples of hardened and unsensible sinners, Jer. ii. 25, xviii. 12. One long since thus complained, that they did, *patientius ferre Christi jacturam, quam suam*, more calmly pass by the injuries done to Christ, than those which are done unto themselves. This age is full of such hardened unsensible souls.

[4.] Fourthly, *Fire is a lively active element*, so is sin.

Ah! how lively and active was this fire in Abraham, David, Job, Peter, Paul, and other saints! Though Christ by his death hath given it its mortal wound, yet it lives, and is and will be active in the dearest saints. Though sin and grace were not born together, neither shall they die together; yet while believers live in this world, they must live together. There is a history that speaks of a fig-tree that grew in a stone-wall, and all means was used to kill it. They cut off the branches and it grew again, they cut down the body and it grew again, they cut it up by the root and still it lived and grew, until they pulled down the stone-wall; till death shall pull down our stone-walls, sin will live, this fire will burn.[1]

We may say of sin as some say of cats, that they have many lives; kill them and they will live again, kill them again and they will live again; so kill sin once and it will live again, kill it again and it will live again, &c. Sin oftentimes is like that monster Hydra, cut off one head and many will rise up in its room.[2]

[5.] Fifthly, *Fire is of a penetrating nature*, it pierceth and windeth itself into every corner and chink, and so doth sin wind itself into our thoughts, words, and works. It will wind itself into our understandings to darken them, and into our judgments to pervert them, and into our wills to poison them, and into our affections to disorder them, and into our consciences to corrupt them, and into our carriages[3] to debase them. Sin will wind itself into every duty and every mercy, it will wind itself into every one of our enjoyments and concernments.

Hannibal having overcome the Romans, put on their armour on his soldiers, and so by that policy, they being taken for Romans, won a city; but what are Hannibal's wiles to sin's wiles or Satan's wiles? If you have a mind to be acquainted with their wiles, look over my treatise, called, 'Precious Remedies against Satan's Devices.'

[6.] Sixth and lastly, *Fire is a devouring, a consuming element*,

[1] Isidore the monk was very much out, who vaunted that he had felt in himself no motion to sin forty years together.

[2] Isa. i. 5, 6, Rom. vii. 13, 17. Sin is *malum catholicum*, a catholic evil. *Quodcunque in peccato, peccatum est*, whatsoever is in sin is sin.

[3] 'Walk and conversation' = conduct or actions.—G.

Ps. xxi. 9. It turns all fuel into ashes. It is a wolf that eats up all. So sin is a fire that devours and consumes all; it turned Sodom and Gomorrah into ashes; it hath destroyed the Chaldean, Persian, and Grecian kingdoms, and will at last destroy the Roman kingdom also. This wolf ate up Samson's strength, Absalom's beauty, Ahithophel's policy, and Herod's glory, &c. It hath drowned one world already, and will at last burn another, even this.[1] Oh the hopes, the hearts, the happiness, the joys, the comforts, the souls that this fire, sin, hath consumed and destroyed! &c.

Peter Camois, a bishop of Berry in France, in his Draught of Eternity, tells us, that some devout personages caused those words of the prophet Isaiah to be written in letters of gold upon their chimney-pieces: 'Who among us shall dwell with the devouring fire? who among us shall dwell with everlasting burnings?' Isa. xxxiii. 14.

Ah! young men, young men, I desire that you may always look upon sin under the notion of fire, yea, as such fire as lays the foundation for everlasting fire, for everlasting burnings; and this may work when other things will not.

I have read of a grave and chaste matron, who being moved to commit folly with a lewd Russian, after some discourse, she called for a pan of burning coals, requesting him for her sake to hold his finger in them but one hour; he answered, it is an unkind request; to whom she replied, that seeing he would not do so much as to put one finger upon the coals for one hour, she could not yield to do that for which she should be tormented, both body and soul, in hell-fire for ever. The application is easy, &c.

Notion (4). *Fourthly*, If you would break with sin betimes, if you would arm against sin in the spring and morning of your days, then you should *look upon sin under the notion of a thief.*

And, indeed, sin is the greatest thief, the greatest robber in the world. It robbed the angels of all their glory, 2 Pet. ii. 4; it robbed Adam of his paradise and felicity, Gen. iii., and it hath robbed all the sons of Adam of five precious jewels, the least of which was more worth than heaven and earth.

(1.) It hath robbed them of the *holy and glorious image of God*, which would have been fairly engraven upon them, had Adam stood, &c.

(2.) It hath robbed them of their *sonship;* and of sons hath made them slaves.

(3.) It hath robbed them of their *friendship*, and made them enemies.

(4.) It hath robbed them of their *communion and fellowship* with Father, Son, and Spirit, and made them strangers and aliens.

(5.) It hath robbed them of their *glory*, and made them vile and miserable. It hath robbed many a nation of the gospel, and many a parish of many a happy guide, and many a Christian of the favour of God, the joys of the Spirit, and the peace of conscience.[2]

Oh! the health, the wealth, the honour, the friends, the relations that sin hath robbed thousands of.

Nay, It hath robbed many of their gifts, their arts, their parts, their

[1] 2 Pet. ii. 5, 6; Prov. vi. 32; Eccl. ix. 18; Prov. xiii. 13, xi. 3, xv. 25, xxi. 7.

[2] Well did one of the fathers call pride and vain-glory, the sweet spoiler of spiritual excellencies, and a pleasant thief.

memory, their judgment, yea, their very reason, as you may see in Pharaoh, Nebuchadnezzar, Belshazzar, Ahithophel, Haman, Herod, and those Babylonish princes that accused Daniel.

And so in Menippus of Phœnicia, who, having lost his goods, strangled himself. And so Dinarcus Phidon, at a certain loss, cut his own throat to save the charge of a cord. And so Augustus Cæsar, in whose time Christ was born, was so troubled and astonished at the relation of an overthrow from Varus, that for certain months together, he let the hair of his head and beard grow still, and wore it long; yea, and other whiles would run his head against the doors, crying out, Quintilius Varus, deliver up my legions again;[1] by all which it is most apparent that sin is the greatest thief in all the world.

Oh! then, who would not break league and covenant with it, and be still in pressing of God to do justice upon it! &c.

Notion (5). *Fifthly,* If you would break with sin, and arm and fence yourselves against sin betimes, then you must *look upon sin under the notion of a burden betimes.*[2]

And indeed, sin of all burdens is the heaviest burden in all the world: 'Innumerable evils have compassed me about; mine iniquities have taken hold upon me, so that I am not able to look up: they are more than the hairs of my head; therefore my heart faileth me,' Ps. xl. 12.

And again, 'Mine iniquities are gone over my head,' saith the same person; 'as an heavy burden, they are too heavy for me to bear,' Ps. xxxviii. 4. Sin is a 'weight that easily besets,' Heb. xii. 1, poor souls; it is a burden that so troubles them and puzzles them, that so curbs them and girds them, that so presses and oppresses them, as that it wrings many bitter tears from their eyes, and many sad and grievous sighs and groans from their hearts, Rom. vii. 13.

Again, as sin is a burden to Christians, so it is a burden to heaven. It made heaven weary to bear the angels that fell; no sooner had they sinned but heaven groans to be eased of them, and it never left groaning till justice had turned them a-groaning to hell, Jude 6.

Again, as sin is a burden to heaven, so it is a burden to the earth. Witness her swallowing up Korah, Dathan, and Abiram, their wives, children, goods, servants, &c., Num. xvi. 26–35. Ah, sinners! your sins makes the very earth to groan, they make the earth weary of bearing you. Oh, how doth the earth groan and long to swallow up those earthly wretches, whose hopes, whose hearts, are buried in the earth! These shall have little of heaven, but enough of earth when they come to die.

Cornelius à Lapide tells a story, that he heard of a famous preacher, who, shewing the bondage of the creature, Rom. viii. 19–23, brings in the creature complaining thus: Oh, that we could serve such as are godly; oh, that our substance and our flesh might be incorporated into godly people, that so we might rise into glory with them; oh, that our flesh might not be incorporated into the flesh of sinners, for if it be, we shall go to hell, and would any creatures go to hell? oh, we are weary of bearing sinners! we are weary of serving of sinners! Thus the creatures groan, thus the creatures complain, the sinner's sins forcing them to it, &c.

[1] Suetonius.

[2] Nah. i. 1; Hab. i. 1; Mal. i. 1.

Again, sin is a burden to God: 'Behold, I am pressed under you, as a cart is pressed that is full of sheaves,' Amos ii. 13. By this plain, pithy, country comparison, God shews how sadly he is pressed and oppressed, how sorely he is wearied and tired with those people's sins. Divine patience is even worn out. Justice hath lift up her hand, and will bear with them no longer. God seems to groan under the pressure of their sins, as a cart seems to do under a heavy load. Of this God complains by the prophet Isaiah: 'Thou hast made me to serve with thy sins, thou hast wearied me with thine iniquities,' Isa. xliii. 24. I am as weary of your sins as a travailing woman is weary of her pains, saith God. Sin was such a burden to God, that he sweeps it off with a sweeping flood, Gen. vii., &c.

Again, sin is a burden to Christ: It made him sweat as never man sweat; it made him sweat great drops of clotted or congealed blood, Luke xxii. 44.[1] Sin put Christ's whole body into a bloody sweat; it made him groan piteously, when he bare our sins in his body on the tree. Sin made his soul heavy even to the death, and had he not been one that was mighty, yea, that was Almighty, he had fainted and failed under his burden, 1 Pet. ii. 24, Isa. ix. 6. And thus you see what a burden sin is to man, to the creatures, to heaven, to earth, to God, to Christ; and therefore, as you would break with sin betimes, look always upon it as a burden, yea, as the greatest and heaviest burden in all the world, &c.

Notion (6). *Sixthly* and lastly, If you would break covenant with sin, and arm and fence yourselves against it betimes, then you must *look upon it betimes under the notion of a tyrant.*

And indeed, sin is the worst and greatest tyrant in the world, Titus iii. 3. Other tyrants can but tyrannize over our bodies, but sin is a tyrant that tyrannizes over both body and soul, as you may see in the sixth and seventh of the Romans. Sin is a tyrant that hath a kind of jurisdiction in most men's hearts; it sets up the law of pride, the law of passion, the law of oppression, the law of formality, the law of hypocrisy, the law of carnality, the law of self-love, the law of carnal reason, the law of unbelief, and strictly commands subjection to them, and proclaims fire and sword to all that stand out. This saints and sinners, good men and bad, do sufficiently experience.

Sin is a tyrant of many thousand years' standing, and though it hath had many a wound, and many a foil, and received much opposition, yet still it plays the tyrant all the world over! Oh, the hearts that this tyrant makes to ache! the souls that this tyrant makes to bleed![2]

Pharaoh's tyranny was nothing to sin's tyranny. This tyrant will not so much as suffer his slaves to sleep. They sleep not, except they have done mischief, and their sleep is taken away unless they cause some to fall, Prov. iv. 16. 'The wicked are like the troubled sea, when it cannot rest, whose waters cast up mire and dirt. There is no peace to the wicked, saith my God,' Isa. lvii. 20, 21.

Other tyrants have been brought down and brought under by a human power, but this cannot but by a divine. The power of man

[1] A strange watering of a garden.—*Bernard.*

[2] Thales, one of the seven sages, used to say, that few tyrants lived to be old; but it is far otherwise with this tyrant sin.

hath brought down many of the tyrants of this world, but it is only the power of Christ that can bring down this tyrant, that can cast down his strongholds, 2 Cor. x. 3-6, &c. Therefore, engage Christ in the conflict, draw him into the battle, and in the end the conquest will be yours.

Vitellius, who had been emperor of all the world, yet was driven through the streets of Rome stark naked, and thrown into the river Tiber, &c.[1]

Andronicus the emperor, for his cruelty towards his people, was by them at last shamefully deposed, and, after many contumelies, hanged up by his heels.[2]

Ptolemy was put on a cross; Bajazet in an iron cage; Phocas broken on the wheel; Lycaon cast to the dogs, as well as Jezebel; Attalus thrust into a forge; King Gath into a beer barrel, &c. But none of these that have tamed these tyrants, that have brought down these mighty Nimrods, have been able to tame, to bring under the tyrants, the sins, the lusts, that have been in their own bosoms. Many a man hath had a hand in bringing down of worldly tyrants, who, notwithstanding, have died for ever by the hand of a tyrant within, &c.

CHAPTER VIII.

And thus much for the directions that young men must follow, if they would be good betimes, if they would seek and serve the Lord in the spring and morning of their days. I shall now give some brief answers to the young man's objections and the old man's scruples, and so close up this discourse.

Obj. 1. But some young men may object, and say, *You would have us to be good betimes, and to seek and serve the Lord in the primrose of our days. But it may be time enough hereafter to follow this counsel; we are young, and it may be time enough for us to mind these things hereafter, when we have satisfied the flesh so and so, or when we have got enough of the world, and laid up something that will stand us in stead, and that may oil our joints when we are old.* Now,

To this objection I answer,

1. First, *That it is the greatest folly and madness in the world to put off God and the great things of eternity with may-bes.* What tradesman, what merchant, what mariner, so mad, so foolish, so blockish, as to put off a present season, a present opportunity of profit and advantage, upon the account of a may-be? It may be I have as good a season, it may be I shall have as golden an opportunity to get, and to enrich myself as this is; and therefore farewell to this. No men that are in their right minds will argue thus; and why then should you, especially in the things that are of an everlasting concernment to you?

I have read of one monarch, a frantic Italian, who thought that all the kings of the earth were his vassals; and as frantic are they who wilfully neglect present seasons of grace, upon the account of a future may-be, &c.

[1] Previously dragged to the Gemoniæ Scalæ, where the body of Sabinus had been exposed. Cf. Tillemont, *Histoire des Empereurs*, i.—G.

[2] Doubtful.—G.

2. Secondly, I answer, *It may be if thou neglectest this present season and opportunity of grace, thou mayest never have another.*[1] It may be mercy may never knock more, if thou dost not open; it may be Christ shall never be offered to thee more, if now thou dost not close with him, and accept of him; it may be the Spirit will never strive more with thee, if now thou dost resist him and withstand him; it may be a pardon shall never be offered to thee more, if now thou wilt not take it; it may be the gospel shall never sound more in thy ears, if now thou wilt not hear it. Now set one may-be against another may-be, set God's may-be against thine own may-be; but,

3. Thirdly, *Doubtless there are many thousand thousands now in hell, who have pleased themselves and put off God and the seasons of grace with a may-be, hereafter may be time enough.* It may be when I have gratified such a lust, and when I have treasured so much of the world, I will return, and seek, and serve the Lord; but before ever this season or opportunity came, justice hath cut the thread of their lives, and they are now miserable for ever; and now they are still a-cursing themselves, because they have slipped their golden opportunities upon the account of a may-be,[2] &c. But,

4. Fourthly, and lastly, This putting off God and the present seasons of grace with a may-be, *is very provoking to God, as you may see, if you will but read from the 20th verse to the 33d of the first of Proverbs.* Nothing stirs and provokes a master more than his servants putting off his service or his commands with a may-be; it may be I will, it may be I may do this and that; nothing puts a master sooner into a heat, a flame, than this; nor nothing puts God more into a flame than this, as you may see by comparing Ps. xcv. ver. 6 to the end, with that 3d of the Hebrews, and the 7th, 8th, 9th, 10th, 11th, 15th, 16th, 17th, 18th, 19th. Read the words, and tremble at the thoughts of a may-be, at the thoughts of putting off of God and the seasons of grace.

I have read of two who cut off their right hand one for another, and then made it an excuse, a put off, they were lame, and so could not serve in the galleys of Francis the First, King of France; but this practice of theirs did so provoke the king that he sent them both to the gallows. I suppose the reader is not so young but knows how to apply it.

Object 2. If I should begin to be good betimes, and to seek and serve the Lord in the spring and morning of my days, I should lose my friends, I should lose their favours; for they are carnal and worldly, and had rather I should seek after gold than God, the creature than Christ, earth than heaven. &c.

Now to this I answer, Surely you are out, for

1. First, *This is the highway, the ready way, to gain the best, the surest, and the soundest friends.* 'When a man's ways please the Lord, he maketh even his enemies to be at peace with him,' Prov. xvi. 7. When a man falls in with God, God will work the creatures to fall in with him, Job lii. 23–28. Joseph found it so, and Jacob found it so,

[1] Young men, if you will but go into burial places, you shall find graves exactly of your length.

[2] It was an unspeakable vexation to King Lysimachus, that his staying to drink one draught of water lost him his kingdom. [As before.—G.]

and Job found it so, the three children found it so, and Daniel found it so, as you all know that have but read the Scripture. And many in this age, as bad as it is, have found, that the best way to make friends is, first to make God our friend. Ah! young men, young men, you shall not lose your friends by seeking and serving of the Lord in the spring and morning of your days, but only exchange bad ones for good ones, the worst for the best. He that gives up himself betimes to the Lord shall have God for his friend, and Christ for his friend, and the angels for his friends, and the saints for his friends. Christ will be to such, first, an omnipotent friend; secondly, an omniscient friend; thirdly, an omnipresent friend; fourthly, an indeficient friend; fifthly, an independent friend; sixthly, an immutable friend; seventhly, a watchful friend; eighthly, a loving friend; ninthly, a faithful friend; tenthly, a compassionate friend; eleventhly, a close friend, 'There is a friend that sticketh closer than a brother,' Prov. xviii. 24. Such a friend is Christ, and such a friend is as one's own soul, a rare happiness, hardly to be matched. Twelfthly, an universal friend; a friend in all cases and a friend in all places. Christ is so a friend to every one of his, as if he were a friend to none besides. Hence it is that they say, not only our Lord, our God, but my Lord, and my God. Christ is such an universal friend, as that he supplies the place, and acts the part of every friend, Thirteenthly, 'He is our first friend,' Ps. xc. 1; before we had a friend in all the world he was our friend, Prov. viii. 21. Lastly, he is a constant friend: 'Whom he loves, he loves to the end,' John xiii. 1.[1] [2]

Augustus Cæsar would not suddenly entertain a league of friendship with any, but was a constant friend to those he loved, *Amare nec cito desisto, nec temere incipio,* late ere I love, as long ere I leave. Where Christ begins to love, he always loves, Jer. xxxi. 3, 'I have loved thee with an everlasting love.' Now who would not venture the loss of all friends in the world to gain such a friend as this is?

Ah! young men and women, let me say to you what Seneca said to his friend Polibius, *Fas tibi non est de fortuna conqueri, salvo Cæsare,* never complain of thy hard fortune as long as Cæsar is thy friend. So say I; never complain of your loss of friends so long as by losing of them you gain Christ to be your friend.

2. Secondly, *Thou wert better be without their friendship and favour than to enjoy it upon any sinful aud unworthy accounts.* Thou wert better run the hazard of losing thy friends and their favour by seeking and serving the Lord in the primrose of thy days, than to run the hazard of losing God, Christ, heaven, eternity, and thy soul for ever by neglecting the things of thy peace, Matt. xvi. 26, Mark viii. 36.

It was a gallant return which the noble Rutilius made his friend, requesting of him an unlawful favour in such language as this: I had as good be without such a friend as with him who will not let me speed in what I ask; to whom he replied, I can want such a friend as you, if

[1] Luke xv. 7: Isa. vi. 7–9; Heb. iv. 13; Isa. lix. 16, 17, xliv. 24; Mal. iii. 6; Ps. cxxi. 4–6; 1 John iv. 16; Titus i. 2; Isa. lxiii. 9; Luke i. 45; John xx. 28; Philip. iv. 19.

[2] Alexander the Great cannot cut that knot of friendship that is tied betwixt Christ and his. [The allusion is to the sword-cut Gordian knot.—G.]

for your sake I must do that which is not honest. The application is easy.

Well! young men, remember this, the torments of a thousand hells, were there so many, comes far short of this one voice, to be turned out of God's presence with a *Non novi vos*, I know you not, Mat. vii. 23.

Ah, young man, young man! thou wert better ten thousand thousand times to be cast out of the thoughts and hearts of thy carnal friends and relations, than to be cast out of God's presence with cursed Cain, Gen. iv., for ever, than to be excommunicated out of 'the general assembly of the saints, and congregation of the first-born which are written in heaven,' Heb. xii. 23; and therefore away with this objection. But,

3. Thirdly, *The favour and friendship of such carnal persons is very fickle and inconstant; it is very fading and withering.* Now they stroke, and anon they strike; now they lift up, and anon they cast down; now they smile, and anon they frown; now they kiss, and anon they kill; now they cry, 'Hosannah! hosannah!' and anon they cry, 'Crucify him, crucify him!' Haman is one day feasted with the king, and the next day made a feast for crows, Esther vii. The princes of Babylon were highly in king Darius his favour one day, and cast into the lion's den the next, Dan. vi. The scribes and pharisees that cried up Judas one day, did in effect bid him go and hang himself the next day, Mat. xxvii. 3–5.

Such men's favour and friendship are as Venice glasses, quickly broken, and therefore not much to be prized or minded. Histories abound with instances of this nature.[1] But I must hasten: only remember this, that every day's experience tells us that wicked men can soon turn tables, and cross their books; their favour and friendship is usually like to a morning cloud, or like to Jonah's gourd: one hour flourishing and the next hour withering; and why then shouldest thou set thy heart upon that which is more changeable than the moon? But,

4. Fourthly and lastly, *Who but a bad man would adventure the loss of the king's favour to gain the favour of his page?* Who but a stark Bedlam would run the hazard of losing the judge's favour upon the bench, to purchase the good will of the prisoner at the bar?

Socrates preferred the king's countenance before his coin; and so must you prefer the favour of God, the countenance of Christ, Ps. iv. 6, 7, and the things of eternity, above all the favour and friendship of all the men in the world. When your nearest friends and dearest relations stands in competition with Christ, or the things above, you must shake them off, you must turn your backs upon them, and welcome Christ and the things of your peace. He that forsakes all relations for Christ, shall certainly find all relations in Christ;[2] he will be father, friend, husband, child; he will be everything to thee, who takest him for thy great all.

Object. 3. *Aye, but I shall meet with many reproaches from one and other, if I should labour to be good betimes, if I should seek and*

[1] Valerian, Valens, Belisarius, Bajazet, Pythias, Dionysius, Pompey, William the Conqueror, and many others, have found it so. Glaucus, who changed his armour of gold with Diomedes, for his armour of brass, stands upon record for a fool.

[2] Ps. xlv. 10; Mat. x. 37; Luke xiv. 26, 27.

serve the Lord in the spring and morning of my youth. Now, to this I answer,

1. First, *What are reproaches to the great things that others have suffered for Christ his gospel, and the maintaining of a good conscience?* What is a prick of a pin to a stab at the heart? what is a chiding to a hanging, a whipping to a burning? No more are all the reproaches thou canst meet with, to the great things that others have suffered for Christ's sake.[1]

Ah, young men! you should be like the Scythian that went naked in the snow, and when Alexander wondered how he could endure it, answered, I am not ashamed, for I am all forehead.

So should you in the cause and way of Christ; you should not be ashamed, you should be all forehead, you should be stout and bold.

Colonus, the Dutch martyr, under all his reproaches, called to the judge that had sentenced him to death, and desired him to lay his hand upon his heart, and then asked him, Whose heart did most beat, his or the judge's? All the reproaches in the world should not so much as make a Christian's heart beat; they should not in the least trouble him nor disturb him. But,

2. Secondly, I answer, *That all the reproaches thou meetest with in the way of Christ, and for the sake of Christ, they do but add pearls to thy crown; they are all additions to thy happiness and blessedness.* If ye be reproached for the name of Christ, happy are ye; for the Spirit of glory, and of God, resteth upon you; on their part he is evil spoken of, but on your part he is glorified, 1 Peter iv. 14. The more you are reproached for Christ's sake on earth, the greater shall be your reward in heaven; they that are most loaded with reproaches here, shall be most laden with glory hereafter, Mat. v. 11, 12. Christ hath written their names in golden letters in his book of life, that are written in black letters of reproach for his sake on earth. It was a good saying of one [Chrysostom]: A reproacher, saith he, is beneath a man, but the reproached that bear it well, are equal to angels; of all crowns, the reproached man's crown will weigh heaviest in heaven.[2] But,

3. Thirdly, I answer, *the best men have been mostly reproached.* David was, Ps. lxix. 7, lxxxix. 50, cxix. 22, xxxi. 11, cix. 25; and Job was, Job xix. 31, xx. 3,[3] xvi. 10; and Jeremiah was, Jer. xx. 7, 10. Yea, this hath been the common portion of the people of God in all ages of the world, In Nehemiah's time it was so: Neh. i. 3, 'And they said unto me, The remnant that are left of the captivity, are in great affliction and reproach.' In David's time it was so, Ps. lxxix. 4, and Ps. xliv. 13, 14; and in Jeremiah's time it was so: Lam. v. 1, 'Remember, O Lord, what is come upon us: consider, and behold our reproach.' And in Daniel's time it was so: Dan. ix. 16, 'Thy people are become a reproach to all that are about us;' and it was so in the apostle's time: Rom. iii. 8, 'And not rather, (as we be slanderously reported, as some affirm that we say,) Let us do evil, that good may come; whose damna-

[1] Hebrews xi. 33. Read of the ten persecutions. [See Sibbes's Works, vol. i. p. 384.—G.]

[2] So was Joseph, Mephibosheth, Naboth, and in latter times Luther, whom they said died despairing, when he was alive to confute it; and that Beza run away with another man's wife; and that Calvin was branded on the shoulder for a rogue: but there would be no end to this stuff, should I say all that might be said.

[3] The speaker here is Zophar, not Job.—G.

tion is just;' 2 Cor. vi. 8, 'By honour and dishonour, by evil report and good report: as deceivers and yet true;' so in that 1 Tim. iv. 10, 'For therefore we both labour and suffer reproach, because we trust in the living God,' &c. And it was so in the primitive times, for when the Christians met together before sun[rise] to pray, the heathens reported of them that they worshipped the sun, and aspired after monarchy, and committed adulteries and unnatural uncleannesses.[1] Now, who is troubled, who complains of that which is a common lot, as cold, winter, sickness, death? &c. No more should any complain of reproaches, it being the common lot of the people of God in all ages; yea, Christ himself was sadly reproached, falsely accused, and strangely traduced, disgraced, and scandalized. He was called a glutton, a drunkard, a friend of publicans and sinners, and judged to use the black art, casting out devils by Beelzebub the prince of devils, Mat. ix. 34, xii. 24. Christ hath suffered the greatest and the worst reproaches; why then should you be afraid to wear that crown of thorns that Christ hath worn before you? There is a great truth in what he said, *Non potest qui pati timet, ejus esse qui passus est*,[2] he that is afraid to suffer cannot be his disciple, who suffered so much. If the master hath been marked with a black coal, let not the servant think to go free. I am heartily angry, saith Luther, with those that speak of my sufferings, which, if compared with that which Christ suffered for me, are not once to be mentioned in the same day. But,

4. Fourthly, I answer, *That all reproachers shall at last be arraigned at the highest bar of justice, for all the reproaches that they have cast upon the people of God.*

They think it strange, for they think it a new world, that you 'run not with them to the same excess of riot, speaking evil of you, who shall give account to him that is ready to judge the quick and the dead,' 1 Pet. iv. 4.[3]

I am in ecstasy, saith Picus Mirandula, to think how profane men rail upon those now, whom one day they will wish they had imitated. It was excellent counsel that the heathen orator gave his hearers, *ita vivamus, ut rationem nobis reddendam arbitremur*, let us live as those that must give an account of all at last.[4]

Chrysostom brings in Christ comforting his disciples against reproaches, speaking thus unto them, What! is the wrong grievous to you that they now call you seducers and conjurors? It will not be long before they shall openly call you the saviours and blessings of the whole world; that time that shall declare all things that are now hid, shall rebuke them for their lying words against you, and shall kindle the splendour of your virtue; so they shall be found liars, evil speakers, false accusers of others; but you shall be more clear and illustrious than the sun, and you shall have all men witnesses of your glory. Such as wisely and humbly bear reproaches now, shall judge reproachers at last.[5] But,

5. Fifthly, I answer, *That God doth many times, even in this life, bear sad witness and testimony against the reproachers of his people.*

[1] Tertullian.
[2] Tertul. *de fuga in persecut.*
[3] ξενίζονται . . . . βλασφημοῦντες.
[4] Cicero iv. in Verr.
[5] Mal. iii. 17; Micah 7–11; 1 Cor. vi. 3, 4.

'I will bless them that bless thee, and I will curse them that curse thee,' Gen. xii. 3, and 2 Sam. xvi. 11–13. God will even in this life curse them with a witness, who curse them that he blesseth. Pharaoh found it so, and Saul found it so, and Jezebel found it so, and Haman found it so, and the princes of Babylon found it so, and the Jews find it so to this very day.[1]

And oh the dreadful judgments and curses that God hath poured out upon the reproachers of his name, of his Son, of his Spirit, of his word, of his ordinances, and of his people, in these days wherein we live! I might give you many sad instances of such in our days, whose feet justice hath taken in the snare, men of abstracted conceits and sublime speculations; and indeed such usually prove the great wise fools, who, like the lark, soareth higher and higher, peering and peering, till at length they fall into the net of the fowler; and no wonder, for such persons usually are as censorious as they are curious.

6. Sixthly, I answer, *Paul rejoiceth more in his suffering reproaches for Christ's sake, than he did in his being rapt up in the third heaven:* 2 Cor. xii. 10, 'Therefore I take pleasure in infirmities, in reproaches, in necessities, in persecutions, in distresses, for Christ's sake; for when I am weak, then am I strong.' And therefore you have him often a-singing this song, 'I Paul, a prisoner of Jesus Christ;' not I Paul, rapt up in the third heaven. He looked upon all his sufferings as God's love-tokens; he looked upon all reproaches as pledges and badges of his sonship; and therefore joys and glories under all. Christ shewed his glory to him in rapping him up in the third heaven, and he shewed his love to Christ, in his joyful bearing of reproaches for his sake. Paul rattles his chain, which he bears for the gospel, and was proud of it, as a woman of her ornaments, saith Chrysostom.[2]

Now why should that be matter of trouble and discouragement to you, that was matter of joy and rejoicing to him? Shall he look upon reproaches as a crown of honour, and will you look upon reproaches as a crown of thorns?

Oh! look upon reproach as a royal diadem, look upon it as Christ's livery, and count it your highest ambition in this world to wear this livery for his sake, who once wore a crown of thorns for your sakes. When Babylas was to die, he required this favour, to have his chains buried with him as the ensigns of his honour.[3] But,

7. Seventhly, I answer, *That by a wise and gracious behaviour under the reproaches thou meetest with for Christ's sake, thou mayest be instrumental to win others to Christ.*[4]

It was a noble saying of Luther, *Ecclesia totum mundum convertit sanguine et oratione,* the church converted the whole world by blood and prayer.

[1] Divine justice is like Vulcan's iron net that took the gods; it apprehends and condemns all that are reproachers and enemies to his people. [Vulcan, or rather Hephæstus: *Odyssey,* VIII. 266–358.—G.]

[2] *Crudelitas vestra gloria nostra,* your cruelty is our glory, said they in Tertullian; fire, sword, prison, famine, are all delightful to me, saith Basil.

[3] Sufferings are the ensigns of heavenly nobility, saith Calvin. [On Luke iv. 1–10.—G.]

[4] It was an observation of Mr John Lindsay, that the very smoke of Mr Hamilton converted as many as it blew upon. [That is, Patrick Hamilton, the proto-martyr of Scotland, 1527.—G.]

Divers have been won to Christ by beholding the gracious carriages of Christians under their sufferings and reproaches for Christ.

We read of Cecilia, a poor virgin, who, by her gracious behaviour under all her sufferings and reproaches for Christ, was the means of converting four hundred to Christ.[1]

Adrianus, beholding the gracious, cheerful carriages of the martyrs under all their sufferings and reproaches, was converted to Christ, and afterwards suffered martyrdom for Christ.

Justin Martyr was also converted by observing the holy and cheerful behaviour of the saints under all their sufferings and reproaches for Christ.[2] During the cruel persecutions of the heathen emperors, the Christian faith was spread through all places of the empire,[3] because the oftener they were mown down, saith Tertullian, the more they grew.

And Austin observed, that though there were many thousands put to death for professing Christ, yet they were never the fewer for being slain.

Ah! young men, you may, by a wise and gracious bearing of reproaches for Christ, be instrumental to win others to Christ; and therefore never plead there is a lion in the way. But I must hasten; and therefore,

8. In the eighth and last place, consider, *How bravely several of the very heathens have bore reproaches; and let that provoke you, in the face of all reproaches, to seek and serve the Lord in the morning of your youth*, &c.

When Demosthenes was reproached by one, I will not, saith he, strive with thee in this kind of fight, in which he that is overcome is the better man.

When one came and reproached Xenophon, says he, You have learned how to reproach, and I have learned how to bear reproach.

And Aristippus, the philosopher,[4] said, You are fit to cast reproaches, and I am fit to bear reproaches.

Demochares, an Athenian orator,[5] was sent to king Philip as ambassador. Philip asked him how he might pleasure the Athenians? Forsooth, said he, if you will hang yourself. The prince patiently sent him home again, and bid him ask, Whether were more noble, the patient hearer or venter of such unseemly language?

When one wondered at the patience of Socrates towards one who reviled and reproached him, If we should meet one, saith he, whose body were more unsound than ours, should we be angry with him, and not rather pity him? Why, then, should we not do the like to him whose soul is more diseased than ours?

Augustus Cæsar, in whose time Christ was born, bid Catullus the railing poet to supper, to shew that he had forgiven him.

It is a notable example that we find of one Pericles,[6] who, as he was

[1] Clarke's 'Martyrologie,' as before, pp. 35, 36.—G.

[2] His words are worth giving: 'I myself, when I took pleasure in the doctrines of Plato, and heard the Christians slandered, seeing them to be fearless of death, and of everything else that was thought dreadful, considered that it was impossible that they should live in wickedness,' &c., &c. (Apolog. ii. 12).—G.

[3] See also the History of the Council of Trent, 418, 2d edit.

[4] Founder of the Cyrenaic Philosophy.—G.

[5] The pupil of Demosthenes, and friend of Zeno.—Diog. Laërtius, iv. 41, vii. 14.—G.

[6] Plutarch *in vita* Pericles.

sitting with others in a great meeting, a foul-mouthed fellow bitterly reproached him, and railed all the day long upon him; and at night, when it was dark, and the meeting up, the fellow followed him, and railed at him even to his door, and he took no notice of him; but when he came at home, this is all he said, Friend, it is dark, I pray let my man light you home.[1]

Josephus reports of that Herod that is made mention of in Acts xii. 23, that when one Simon, a lawyer, had grievously reproached and scandalised him before the people, he sent for him, and caused him to sit down next to him, and in a kind manner he spake thus to him: Tell me, I pray thee, what thing thou seest fault-worthy or contrary to the law in me. Simon not having anything to answer, besought him to pardon him, which the king did, and was friends with him, and dismissed him, bestowing gifts on him.

Ah! young men, young men, shall the very heathen make nothing of reproaches? shall they bear up so prudently and bravely under the greatest loads of reproaches, and will not you? Will not you, who in your light, in your mercies, and in all gospel engagements, are so highly advanced above them? Oh! that none of them may be called to the bar in the great day to witness against any of you into whose hands this treatise shall fall. And so much by way of answer to the third objection. But,

Objection 4. *Fourthly*, The young man objects, and says, *You press us to be good betimes, and to seek and serve the Lord in the spring and morning of our days; but we observe that most men mind not these things, but rather give liberty to themselves to walk in ways that are most pleasing to the flesh; and why, then, should we be singular and nice? We were better do as the most do*, &c. Now to this I answer,

1. *That though bad examples are dangerous to all, yet usually they prove most dangerous and pernicious to young persons, who are more easily drawn to follow examples than precepts, especially those examples that tend most to undo them:* 2 Kings xv. 9, it is said of Zachariah, the king of Israel, that 'he did evil in the sight of the Lord, as his fathers had done; he departed not from the sins of Jeroboam;' he would be as his father was, and do as his father did, whatever came on it.[2]

So the Samaritans, of whom it is said, 2 Kings xvii. 41, 'These nations feared the Lord' (that is, they made some kind of profession of the true religion, as the ten tribes had done), 'and served their graven images (too); both their children and their children's children (did thus); as did their fathers, so do they unto this day.' By evil examples they were both drawn to idolatry, and rooted and confirmed in it. So the main reason why the kingdom and church of Judah were so settled in their idolatry, that there was no hope of reclaiming them, was this, that their children remembered their altars and their groves by the green trees upon the high hills, Jer. xvii. 1, 2. Tinder is not apter to

[1] Themistocles professed that if two ways were shewed him, one to hell, and the other to the Bar, he would choose that which went to hell, and forsake the other.

[2] *Præcepta docent, exempla movent*, Precepts may instruct, but examples do persuade. [As before.—G.]

take fire, nor wax the impression of the seal, nor paper the ink, than youth is to follow ill examples.

You may see in Radbad, king of Phrisia,[1] who coming to the font to be baptized, asked what was become of his ancestors? answer was made, that they died in a fearful state unbaptized; he replied that he would rather perish with the multitude than go to heaven with a few.

I remember the heathen brings in a young man who, hearing of the adulteries and wickednesses of the gods, said, What! do they so? and shall I stick at it? No, I will not. Sinful examples are very drawing and very encouraging; many have found it so to their eternal undoing. Those that have no ears to hear what you say, have many eyes to see what you do. Bad princes make bad subjects; bad masters make bad servants; bad parents make bad children; and bad husbands make bad wives. It is easier for the bad to corrupt the good, than for the good to convert the bad; it is easier to run down the hill with company, than to run up the hill alone.[2]

I would desire all young men often to remember that saying of Lactantius, *Qui malum imitatur, bonus esse non potest*, he who imitates the bad cannot be good. Young men, in these professing times, stand between good and bad examples, as Hercules in his dream stood between virtue and vice. Solicited by both, choose you must who to follow. Oh that you were all so wise as to follow the best; as a woman that hath many suitors is very careful to take the best, so should you. Life, heaven, happiness, eternity, hangs upon it.

But before I come to the second answer, let me leave this note or notion with those who make no conscience of undoing others by their examples,[3] viz.,

That a more grievous punishment is reserved for them who cause others to offend, than for them which sin by their occasion or example.

Thus the serpent was punished more than Eve, and Eve more than Adam.

So Jezebel felt a greater and sorer judgment than Ahab. To sin, saith one, hath not so much perdition in it as to cause others to sin. Friends, you have sins enough of your own to make you for ever miserable; why should you, by giving bad examples to others, make yourselves far more miserable? The lowest, the darkest, the hottest place in hell, will be for them that have drawn others thither by their example, Mat. xxiii. 15. Dives knew that if his brethren were damned, he should be double damned, because he had largely contributed to the bringing of them to hell by his wicked example; and therefore he desires that they might be kept out of hell, not out of any love or good will to them, but because their coming thither would have made his hell more hot, his torments more insufferable, Luke xvi. 28. But,

2. Secondly, I answer, *If you sin with others, you shall suffer with others;* if you will partake of other men's sins, you shall also partake

[1] Query—Frisia, *i. e.* the Frisii of North-western Germany?—G.

[2] Ethiopians lame themselves if their king be lame, saith Diodorus. Ælian reports that there was a whore that did boast that she could easily get scholars away from Socrates, but Socrates could get away no scholars from her.

[3] Sin is bad in the eye, worse in the tongue, worser in the heart, but worst of all in the life; and that because it then endangers other men's souls, as well as a man's own.

of other men's plagues, Rev. xviii. 4. They that have been, like Simeon and Levi, brethren in iniquity, they shall be brethren in misery; they that have sinned together impenitently shall be sent to hell jointly, they shall perish together eternally. If you will needs be companions with others in their sins, you shall be sure to be companions with them in their sorrows.[1] The old world sin together and are drowned together, Gen. vi.; the Sodomites, burning in lusts together, were burnt with fire and brimstone together, Gen. xix. Korah, Dathan, and Abiram, they sin together, they murmur and provoke the Lord together, and the earth opens her mouth and swallows them up together, Num. xvi. 26–34. Pharaoh and his hosts pursue Israel together, and they are drowned in the sea together, Exod. xiv. Zimri and Cosbi commit folly, uncleanness together, and Phinehas stabs them both together, Num. xxv. The Hebrew doctors have a very pretty parable to this purpose:—A man planted an orchard, and, going from home, was careful to leave such watchmen as might both keep it from strangers and not deceive him themselves; therefore he appointed one blind, but strong of his limbs, and the other seeing, but a cripple. These two, in their master's absence, conspired together, and the blind took the lame on his shoulders, and so gathered the fruit; their master returning and finding out their subtilty, punished them both together.

So will justice deal with you at last, who sin with others; therefore take heed, young men, of doing as others do. But,

3. Thirdly, I answer, *You must not live by examples, but by precepts.*[2] You are not to look so much at what others do, as at what God requires you to do: Exod. xxiii. 2, 'Thou shalt not follow a multitude to do evil, neither shalt thou speak in a cause to decline after many to wrest judgment;' Rom. xii. 2, 'Fashion not yourselves like unto this world;' that is, do not fashion and conform yourselves to the corrupt customs and courses of wretched worldlings, who have made gold their god, and gain their glory. The running cross to a divine command cost the young prophet his life, though he did it under pretence of revelation from God, as you may see in that sad story, 1 Kings xiii., &c., *Non parentum, aut majorum authoritas, sed Dei docentis imperium*, the command of God must outweigh all authority and example of men [Jerome].

And we must be as careful in the keeping of a light commandment as an heavy commandment. Saith a Rabbi, Divine commands must be obeyed against all contrary reasonings, wranglings, and examples. Austin brings in some excusing their compliance with the sinful customs and examples of those times in drinking healths thus: Great personages urged it, and it was at the king's banquet, where they judged of loyalty by luxury, and put us upon this election, drink or die. The not drinking of a health had been our death. He gives this answer, that God who sees that for love to him and his commands thou wouldst not conform to their drunken customs, will give thee favour in their eyes, who thus threatened thee to drink.[3]

Ah! young men, you that doat so much upon examples now, will find

[1] *Non minus ardebit, qui cum multis ardebit.*—Augustine, He burns no less that burns with company.

[2] *Obedientia non discutit Dei mandata, sed facit.*—Prosper.

[3] The complaint is ancient in Seneca, that commonly men live, not *ad rationem* but *ad similitudinem.*—Seneca, *de vita beata*, c. i.

that a stinging terrifying question, when put home by God or conscience, Who hath required those things at your hands? Isa. i. 12. But,

4. Fourthly, I answer, *Company and allurements to sin will be found no sufficient excuse for sin.*

If Eve lay her fault on the serpent, and Adam lay his on Eve, Gen. iii., God will take it off, and lay the curse on both. Saul's provocation by his people, and by Samuel's long stay to offer sacrifice, would not bear him out; but for his disobedience he must lose both his crown and life, 1 Sam. xv. 14, 15, 26, 27. The young man in the Proverbs, though tempted and solicited by the harlot, yet hath a dart struck through his heart, Prov. vii. 14, 15, 21. Though Jonah did plead God's gracious inclinations to shew mercy, and his fear of being disproved; yea, and though he might have pleaded his fear of cruel and savage usage from the Ninevites, whose hearts were desperately set upon wickedness, and his despair of ever doing good upon a people so blinded and hardened, and that they were Gentiles and he a Jew; and why should he then be sent with so strange, so terrible a message to such a people, nothing being more hateful and distasteful to a Jewish palate? But all these pleas and excuses will not bear off the blow. Jonah must into the sea for all this; yea, he must to 'the bottom of hell,' as himself phrases it. It is in vain for the bird to complain, that it saw the corn but not the pitfall; or for the fish to plead, it saw the bait but not the hook. So it will be in vain for sinners at last, when they are taken in an infernal pitfall, to plead company and allurements by which they have been enticed to undo their soul for ever.[1]

Dionysius, the Sicilian king, to excuse himself from the present delivery of the golden garment he took from his god Apollo, answered, that such a robe as that was could not be at any season of the year useful to his god, for it would not keep him warm in the winter, and it was too heavy for the summer, and so put off his idol god. But the God of spirits, the God of all flesh, will not be put off with any excuses or pretences, when he shall try and judge the children of men. But,

5. Fifthly and lastly, I answer, *That it is a very great judgment to be given up to follow evil examples*, Mat. xviii. 7. A man given up to evil examples is a man sadly left of God, wofully blinded by Satan, and desperately hardened in sin. It speaks a man ripe for wrath, for ruin, for hell: Jer. vi. 21, 'Behold,[2] I will lay stumbling-blocks before this people, and the fathers and the sons together shall fall upon them; the neighbour and his friend shall perish.' Oh! it is a dreadful thing when God shall make the sinful examples of others to be stumbling-blocks to a people, at which they shall stumble, and fall, and perish for ever; good had it been for such persons that they had never been born, as Christ once spake concerning Judas, Mat. xxvi. 24.

The Rhodians and Lydians enacted several laws, that those sons which followed not their fathers in their virtues, but followed vicious examples, should be disinherited, and their lands given to the most

[1] *Oculos quos peccatum claudit, pœna aperit.*—Gregory, The eyes that sin shuts, affliction opens; and Jonah found it so.

[2] This particle, Behold, is sometimes, (1.) a note of derision, Gen. iii. 22; (2.) a note of attention often, Isa. xxviii. 2; Mal. i. 13; Luke i. 20; (3.) a note of admiration often; (4.) a note of asseveration; (5.) a note of castigation; in all these senses we may take it here.—*Varro.*

virtuous of that race, not admitting any impious heir whatsoever to inherit; and do you think that God will not disinherit all those of heaven and happiness who follow vicious examples? Doubtless he will, 1 Cor. x. 5–12.

Objection (5). The fifth and last objection I shall mention is this, *God is a God of mercy; in him are bowels of mercy, yea, a sea, an ocean of mercy; he loves mercy, he delights in mercy, and he is ready to shew mercy to poor sinners, when they are even at the last cast, when there is but a short stride between them and the grave, between them and eternity; as we see in his extending mercy to the thief, and in his giving a pardon into his hand, and the assurance of paradise into his bosom, when he was ready to be turned off the ladder of life; and therefore I may spend the primrose of my days in following sin, and the delights, profits, vanities, and contents of this world, and at last cast I may have mercy as well as the thief. God is a God made up of mercy, and surely he will not deny some crumbs of mercy to a poor sinner in misery*, &c.

Now to this objection I shall give these following answers.

1. First, *God is as just as he is merciful;*[1] witness his casting the angels out of heaven, and Adam out of paradise; witness all the threatenings, the curses, the woes, that the Bible is filled with, from one end to the other; witness the hell, the horror, the terror and amazement that he raises in the consciences of sinners; witness the devastations that he hath made of the most stately and flourishing towns, cities, countries, and kingdoms, that have been in all the world; witness the variety of diseases, calamities, miseries, dangers, deaths, and hells, that always attend the inhabitants of the world; but above all, witness Christ's treading the wine-press of his Father's wrath; witness his hiding his face from him, and the pouring out of all his displeasure and vengeance upon him.

Zeleucus, the Locrensian lawgiver, thrust out one of his own son's eyes, for his transgressing of a wholesome law which he had enacted,[2] but God the Father thrust out both Christ's eyes for our transgressing of his royal law. Oh! the justice and severity of God. But,

2. Secondly, I answer, *That there is not a greater evidence of blindness, profaneness, hard-heartedness, spiritual madness, and hellish desperateness in all the world, than to make that an argument, an encouragement to sin, viz. the mercy of God, which should be the greatest argument under heaven to keep a man from sin:* as all know that have but read the Scripture; neither are there any sinners in the world that God delights to rain hell out of heaven upon, as upon such, who by their abuse of mercy, turn the God of mercy into a God of clouts,[3] and go on out-daring justice itself:[4] Deut. xxix. 19, 20, 'And it come to pass, when he heareth the words of this curse, that he bless himself in his heart, saying, I shall have peace (God is a God of mercy), though I walk in the imagination of my heart, to add drunkenness to thirst.' The Lord will not spare him, but then the anger of the Lord

[1] God is as well all hand to punish, as he is all grace to pardon.

[2] Valerius [Max.] lib. v. cap. 5 [§ 3]. [Rather Zaleucus. Besides Val. Max., see Aelian, V. H. xiii. 24.—G.]

[3] A mere scare-crow, to threaten without accomplishing.

[4] Read Isa. xxii. 12–15, and Ezek. xxiv. 11–14.

and his jealousy, shall smoke against that man, and all the curses that are written in this book shall lie upon him, and the Lord shall blot out his name from under heaven.' In these words you may observe, that God is absolute in his threatening, to shew that he will be resolute in punishing:[1] Ps. xi. 5, 6, 'The wicked, and him that loveth iniquity, doth his soul hate. Upon the wicked he shall rain snares, fire and brimstone, and an horrible tempest: this shall be the portion of their cup.'

Ah! that all poor sinners would make these two scriptures their companions, their constant bed-fellows, till they are got above that sad temptation of turning the mercy of God into an encouragement to sin.

Whilst Milo Crotoniates was tearing asunder the stock of an oak, his strength failing him,—the cleft suddenly closing,—was held so fast by the hands, that he became a prey to the beasts of the field.[2] All the abusers of mercy will certainly and suddenly become a prey to the justice of God, that will rend and tear them in pieces, as the Psalmist speaks: Ps. l. 22, 'Woe, woe, to that soul that fights against God with his own mercies;' that will be bad, because he is good; that will be sinful, because he is merciful; that will turn all the kindness of God, that should be as so many silver cords, to tie him to love and obedience, into arrows, and to shoot them back into the heart of God. Abused mercy will at last turn into a lion, a fierce lion; and then woe to the abusers and despisers of it! But,

3. Thirdly, In answer to that part of the objection concerning the thief on the cross, I offer these things briefly to your thoughts.

(1.) First, *That as one was saved to teach sinners not to despair, so another was damned to teach them not to presume.*[3]

A pardon is sometimes given to one upon the gallows, but whoso trusts to that, the rope may be his hire. It is not good, saith one, to put it upon the psalm of *miserere*, and the neck-verse,[4] for sometimes he proves no clerk, and so hangs for it.

(2.) Secondly, *It is an example without a promise.* Here is an example of late repentance, but where is there a promise of late repentance?

Oh! let not his late and sudden conversion be to thee a temptation, till thou hast found a promise for late and sudden conversion. It is not examples, but promises, that are foundations for faith to rest on, He that walks by an example of mercy without a precept to guide him, and a promise to support him, walks but by a dark lanthorn, that will deceive him. Well! young man, remember this, examples of mercy increase wrath, when the heart is not bettered by them. But,

(3). Thirdly, *This was a rare miracle of mercy, with the glory whereof Christ did honour the ignominy of his cross,* and therefore we may as well look for another crucifying of Christ as look for a sinner's conversion, when he hath scarce time enough to reckon up all those particular duties which make up the integrity of its constitution. But,

[1] A lover of iniquity is a liver in iniquity upon choice.

[2] For above incident see Diod. xii. 9; Paus. vi. 14, § 5–8, &c., &c.—G.

[3] *Exemplum latronis servati est admirandum, non imitandum.*

[4] On the 'neck-verse' see our Note in Sibbes's Works, vol. v. page 408.—G.

(4). Fourthly, I answer, *This thief knew not Christ before; he had not refused, neglected, nor slighted Christ before.* The sermon on the cross was the first sermon that ever he heard Christ preach, and Christ's prayer on the cross was the first prayer that ever he heard Christ make. He knew not Christ till he met him on the cross, which proved to him a happy meeting. His case was as if a Turk or a heathen should now be converted to the faith; and therefore thou hast little reason, O young man, to plead this example to keep Christ and thy soul asunder, who art every day under the call, the entreaties, and wooings of Christ. But,

(5). Fifthly, and lastly, I answer, *The circumstances of time and place are rightly to be considered.* Now when Christ was triumphing on the cross over sin, Satan, and the world; when he had made the devils a public spectacle of scorn and derision; when he was taking his leave of the world and entering into his glory; now he puts a pardon into the thief's hand, and crowds other favours and kindnesses upon him.

As in the Roman triumphs, the victor being ascended up to the capitol in a chariot of state, used to cast certain pieces of coin among the people for them to pick up, which he used not to do at other times; so our Lord Jesus Christ, in the day of his triumph and solemn inauguration into his heavenly kingdom, scatters some heavenly jewels that this thief might pick up, which he doth not, nor will not do every day. Or, as in these days it is usual with princes to save some notorious malefactors at their coronations when they enter upon their kingdoms in triumph, which they do not use to do afterwards, so did Jesus Christ carry it toward this thief. But this is not his ordinary way of saving and bringing souls to glory; and therefore do not, O young man! let not the thief's late conversion prove a temptation or an occasion of thy delaying thy repentance, and trifling away the primrose of thy days in vanity and folly. And this much may suffice to have spoken by way of answer to the young man's objections. I shall now speak a few words to old men, and so close up. Now,

CHAPTER IX.

Is it so commendable, so desirable, and so necessary for young men to be good betimes, to seek and serve the Lord in the spring and morning of their youth, as has been sufficiently demonstrated in this treatise? Oh, then, that I could so woo aged persons as to win them who yet have put off this great work to seek and serve the Lord before their glass be out, their sun set, and their souls lost for ever!

Oh, that that counsel of the prophet might take hold upon your hearts! 'Give glory to the Lord your God before he cause darkness, and before your feet stumble,' Jer. xiii. 16, through age 'upon the dark mountains, and while ye look for light, he turn it into the shadow of death, and make it gross darkness.'

Ay, but aged sinners may reply, *Is there any hope, any help for us?* Is there any probability, is there any possibility, that ever such as we are should return and find mercy and favour with the Lord? We who have lived so long without him! we that have sinned so much against him! we that to this day are strangers to him, yea, in arms against him!

Is there any hope that we white-headed sinners, who have withstood so many thousand offers of grace, and so many thousand motions of the the Spirit, and so many thousand checks of conscience, and so many thousand tenders[1] of Christ and heaven, that ever we should obtain mercy, that ever we should have our old hearts turned, our millions of sins pardoned, our vile natures changed, and poor souls saved, &c.

I answer, That there is hope even for such as you are. All the angels in heaven and all the men on earth cannot tell, but that you, even you, may obtain mercy and favour, that your souls die not. With the Lord nothing is impossible, and for the grace of the gospel nothing is too hard. Now this I shall make evident by an induction of particulars. Thus,

(1.) First, *All were not called nor sent to work in the vineyard at the first hour;* some were called at the third hour, others at the sixth, others at the ninth, and some at the eleventh. God hath his several times of calling souls to himself. The eleventh hour was about five in the afternoon, an hour before sunset; when it was even time to leave work; and yet at this hour some were called, employed, and rewarded with the rest.[2]

Some of the fathers, by the several hours mentioned in this parable, do understand the several ages of man, viz., childhood, youth, middle age, and old age, wherein poor souls are called and converted to Christ. The scope of the parable is to signify the free grace of God in the calling of some in the spring and morning of their days, and in the calling of others in their old age, in the evening of their days. But,

(2.) Secondly, *Abraham in the Old Testament, and Nicodemus in the New, were called and converted in their old age*, when there were but a few steps between them and the grave, between them and eternity.[3]

I have read of one Caius Marius Victorius, who was an old man, three hundred years after the apostles' time, and had been a pagan all his days, and in his old age he inquired and hearkened after Christ, and said he would be a Christian. Simplicianus hearing him say so, would not believe him, but when the church saw a work of grace indeed upon him, there was shouting and dancing for gladness, and psalms were sung in every church, Caius Marius Victorius is become a Christian. And this was written for a wonder, that he in his old age, and in his grey hairs, should become a gracious Christian.

Aretius also speaks of a certain man in his time. It is no feigned story, saith he, for I saw the man with my own eyes: he was one that had been a most vile and desperate sinner, a drunkard, a swearer, a wanton, a gamester, and so he continued to his grey hairs; but at last it pleased God to set his sins in order before him, and the man was so troubled in conscience that he threw himself down upon the ground, calling unto Satan to take him away, provoking Satan to take him away: Devil, take thy own; devil, take thy own; I am thy own, take thy own: whereupon, saith Aretius, prayer was made for him; Christians prayed, they fasted and prayed, they prayed night and day; and it pleased God at last that this poor aged sinner revived, converted to God, lived a godly life afterwards, and died comfortably.

[1] 'Offers.'—G. [2] Matt. xx. 1–17. The Roman penny was sevenpence halfpenny.
[3] Gen. xii. 4, John iii. 1–4, vii. 50.

Therefore, let not the grey-headed sinner despair, though his spring be past, his summer overpast, and he arrived at the fall of the leaf. But,

(3.) Thirdly, *Divine promises shall be made good to returning souls, to repenting souls, to believing souls, be they young or old.* 2 Chron. xxx. 9, 'The Lord your God is gracious and merciful, and will not turn away his face from you, if you return unto him.' Joel ii. 13, 'And rend your heart, and not your garments, and turn unto the Lord your God; for he is gracious and merciful, slow to anger, and of great kindness, and repenteth him of the evil.' Isa. lv. 7, 'Let the wicked forsake his way, and the unrighteous man his thoughts: and let him return unto the Lord, and he will have mercy upon him; and to our God, for he will abundantly pardon:' or he will multiply to pardon. More of this you may see by reading of the scriptures in the margin.[1] All sorts of sin shall be pardoned to all sorts of believing and repenting sinners.

The New Jerusalem hath twelve gates, to shew that there is every way access for all sorts and ranks of sinners to come to Christ. He was born in an inn, to shew that he receives all comers, young and old, poor and rich, &c. But,

(4.) Fourthly, *The Lord hath declared by oath a greater delight in the conversion and salvation of poor sinners, whether they are young or old, than in the destruction and damnation of such.* Ezek. xxxiii. 11, 'As I live, saith the Lord God, I have no pleasure in the death of the wicked; but that the wicked turn from his way and live: turn ye, turn ye from your evil ways; for why will ye die, O ye house of Israel?' Two things make a thing more credible.

[1.] The quality or dignity of the person speaking.

[2.] The manner of the speech. Now here you have the great God, not only speaking, promising, but solemnly swearing that he had rather poor sinners should live than die, be happy than miserable; therefore, despair not, O aged sinner! but return unto the Lord, and thou shalt be happy for ever. But,

(5.) Fifthly, *There is virtue enough in the precious blood of Jesus Christ, to wash and cleanse away all sin;*[2] not only to cleanse away the young man's sins, but also to cleanse away the old man's sins; not only to cleanse a sinner of twenty years, but to cleanse a sinner of fifty, sixty, yea, a hundred years old: 1 John i. 7, 'The blood of Jesus Christ his Son cleanseth us from all sin;' not simply from sin, but from all sin. There is such a power and efficacy in the blood of Christ, as is sufficient to cleanse all sorts of sinners from all sorts of sins. There is a virtue in the blood of the Lamb to wash out all the spots that are in the oldest sinners' hearts; and therefore let not old sinners despair, let them not say there is no hope, there is no help, as long as this fountain, the blood of Jesus Christ, is open for all sorts of sinners to wash in. But,

(6.) Sixthly, *The call and invitation of Christ in the gospel are general and indefinite, excluding no sort of sinners.* Rev. iii. 20, 'Behold, I stand at the door and knock, if any man' (mark the inde-

[1] Isa. i. 18; Jer. iii. 12; Isa. xliii. 22–25; lvii. 17, 18; Jer. li. 5; John iii. 16; Mark xvi. 16.

[2] *Una guttula plus valet, quam cœlum et terra.*—Luther, One little drop is more worth than heaven and earth.

finiteness of personal admittance) 'hear my voice, and open the door, I will come in to him, and will sup with him, and he with me.' Let the sinner be old or young, a green head, or a grey head, if he will but open the door, Christ will come in and have communion and fellowship with him. So in that Mat. xi. 28. Turn to these scriptures, Isa. lv. 1, John vii. 37, Rev. xxii. 17, and dwell upon them; they all clearly evidence the call and gracious invitations of Christ to be to all sinners, to every sinner; he excepts not a man, no, though never so old. Nothing shall hinder the sinner, any sinner, the worst and most aged sinner, from obtaining mercy, if he be willing to open to Christ, and to receive him as his Lord and king, John vi. 37. But,

(7.) Seventhly, *Christ's pathetical lamentation over all sorts and ranks of sinners, declares his willingness to shew mercy to them.* 'O Jerusalem, Jerusalem,' saith Christ, weeping over it, 'that thou hadst known in this thy day the things that belong to thy peace,' &c., Luke xix. 41, 42. 'Oh that my people had hearkened unto me!' Ps. lxxxi. 13. Christ weeps over Jerusalem; so did Titus, and so did Marcellus over Syracuse, and so did Scipio over Carthage; but they shed tears for them whose blood they were to shed; but Christ weeps over the necks of those young and old sinners who were to shed his blood. As a tender-hearted father weeps over his rebellious children, when neither smiles nor frowns, neither counsels nor entreaties, will win them, or turn them from their evil ways, so doth Jesus Christ over these rebellious Jews, upon whom nothing would work. But,

(8.) Eighthly, and lastly, *Though aged sinners have given Christ many thousand denials, yet he hath not taken them, but after all, and in the face of all denials, he still re-enforces his suit, and continues to beseech them by his Spirit, by his word, by his wounds, by his blood, by his messengers, and by his rebukes, to turn home to him, to embrace him, to believe in him, and to watch with him, that they may be saved eternally by him.* All which bespeaks grey-headed sinners not to despair, nor to dispute, but to repent, return, and believe, that it may go well with them for ever. Consider seriously what hath been spoken, and the Lord make you wise for eternity![1]

[1] Ps. lxv. 1, 2; Rom. x. 21, and 1 John v. 2, 3.

APPENDIX.

Agreeably to Note prefixed to 'Apples of Gold,' there is here added,

1. The title-page of the original edition.
2. The original 'Epistle Dedicatory.'—G.

APPLES OF GOLD
for Young Men,

AND

A Crown of Honour
for Old Men:

OR,

*The Young Mans Work, and
the Old Mans Reward.*

DISCOVERED

In a Sermon (with enlargements since)
Preached at *Clapham* at the interrment of
the Corps of Mr. *John Wood*, Mercer; and
Citizen of *London*, the 13. of *Novemb.* 1656.

By *THOMAS BROOKS*, Preacher of the
Gospel at *Margarets Fishstreet-hill.*

*But I thy Servant fear the Lord from my
Youth.* 1 King. 18. 12.

*The hoary head is a crown of Glory, if it bee
found in a way of righteousness,* Prov. 16. 31.

LONDON,
Printed by *R. I.* for *John Hancock*, to be sold
at the first Shop in *Popeshead-Alley* next
to *Corn-hill* neer the *Exchange.* 1657.

EPISTLE DEDICATORY.

To his honoured and worthily esteemed friends, Mrs Susan Wood (disconsolate widow to the late pious Mr John Wood, deceased), and Mr John Arthur (minister of the gospel at Clapham), and Mrs Dorothy, his wife; and to Mr John Wood, Esq. and Mrs Margaret, his wife (parents to the late deceased gentleman); and to Mr John Humfreys, Esq., and Mrs Elizabeth, his wife: all grace and peace, all consolation and supportation from God the Father, and the Lord Jesus Christ.

Honoured and beloved in our dearest Lord,

It was your earnest desires and serious importunity that midwifed this little treatise into the world. If it do not in all things answer expectation, you know who to thank. I look upon the following discourse as a comment upon his life and death, who is now entered upon a blessed state of eternity. I confess your loss is very very great; yet to prevent the breaking in of an irresistible torrent of sorrow and sadness upon your drooping spirits, be pleased to consider these four things:

1. Though your loss be great, yet there are six greater losses than yours.

(1.) First, *The loss of the soul* is a greater loss than the loss of a husband, a child, a kinsman, &c. The loss of the soul is an incomparable loss, it is an irreparable loss, it is an eternal loss. Francis Xaverius, counselled John the Third, King of Portugal, to meditate every day a quarter of an hour upon that text, What shall it profit a man to gain the world, and lose his soul? Mat. xvi. 26. Of the sadness and greatness of this loss, you may read more in the following discourse.

(2.) Secondly, *The loss of Christ* is a loss infinitely beyond the loss of the nearest and dearest relations. This made Luther say, that he had rather live in hell with Christ, than in heaven without him. He is the greatest good, and therefore the loss of him must needs be the greatest evil, *qui te non habet Domine Deus, totum perdidit* [Bernard] He that hath not thee, and thy Christ, he hath lost all; for Christ is all in all, Col. iii. 11. John Ardley professed to Bonner, when he told him of burning, that if he had as many lives as he had hairs on his head, he would lose them all in the fire, before he would lose his Christ.[1]

(3.) Thirdly, *The loss of the gospel* is a greater loss than all worldly comforts. Eli bore up sweetly till the ark was taken, and that news broke both his heart and neck.

Luther would not take all the world for one leaf of the Bible; nay, a gracious heart that hath experienced the sweetness of the word, will not take all the world for one line of the Bible.[2] The tabernacle was covered over with red,—and the purple-feathers tell us, they take that habit for the same intent,—to note that we must defend the truth even

[1] Clarke's 'Martyrologie,' as before, pages 452, 453.—G.

[2] *Si veritas est causa discordiæ, mori possum, tacere non possum*, said Jerome to Helvetius.

to the effusion of blood, and rather lose our lives than lose the truth. We must say, as the Spartan mother said to her son, either live in religion, or die for religion. When the gospel is lost, the glory of a nation is lost; yea, the glory of souls is lost.

(4.) Fourthly, *The loss of God's favour* is a greater loss than any worldly loss. If his loving-kindness be better than life, yea, than lives, as the Hebrew hath it,[1] then the loss of it is worse than death, yea, than deaths. Augustine, upon that answer of God to Moses, Thou canst not see my face and live, Exod. xxxiii. 20, makes this quick and sweet reply, 'Then, Lord! let me die, that I may see thy face.' It is divine favour that makes heaven to be heaven, and it is the want of that which makes hell to be hell. A Christian that hath been under the shinings of God's face, had rather suffer death, yea, any death, yea, all deaths, than to have the face of God clouded and covered.

(5.) Fifthly, *The loss of peace of conscience* is a greater loss than any worldly loss. If you ask souls that have experienced the sweetness of peace of conscience, but are now under terrors and horrors, what is the greatest loss? they will answer, loss of peace of conscience. If you ask them again what is the saddest loss? they will answer, loss of peace of conscience: no loss to this loss. *Una guttula malæ conscientiæ totum mare, mundum gaudii absorbet* (Luther), One drop of an evil conscience swallows up the whole sea of worldly joy.[2]

(6.) Sixthly, and lastly, *The loss of eternity* is a greater loss than any, than all worldly losses. No worldly loss is to be mentioned in the day wherein the loss of eternity is named. The loss of eternity compriseth all varieties of privative miseries, the loss of whatever we have enjoyed, and the loss of whatever we might have enjoyed; as God, Christ, the Comforter, the society of saints, angels, the treasures and pleasures that be at his right hand. It was a notable saying of Ambrose, *Cur ea quæ ad usum diuturna esse non possunt, ad supplicium diuturna deposces*, Why will you make that which cannot be eternal for use be eternal for punishment?[3] The loss of eternity is a comprehensive loss, a loss that takes in all losses; and therefore no loss to the loss of a happy eternity. And thus you see, beloved, that though your loss be very great, yet there be far greater losses than yours; and this should bear up your spirits from fainting and sinking under this sad dispensation. Though I have a will, yet I have not skill to express your loss and your sorrows to the life. Sorrows for near and dear relations are oftentimes so great, that they cannot be expressed.

Psammeticus, king of Egypt, being prisoner to Cambyses, king of Persia, seeing his own daughter passing before him in base array, being sent to draw water, at which sight his friends about him wept, but himself wept not; presently after his son was carried to execution before his face, neither did this move him to shew any passion; but afterwards, when a friend of his was to suffer, then he wept, and tare his hair, and shewed great sorrow. Being demanded the reason of this his carriage, he answered that the loss of a friend might be expressed, but not the grief for the loss of a child.

I have read of a certain painter, who being to express the sorrow of

[1] Ps. lxiii. 3, *Mehhaiim*.

[2] *Tolle conscientiam, tolle omnia*, said the heathen.

[3] Ambrose in Luc. iv. 5.

a weeping father, and having spent his skill before in setting forth of the passions and affections of his children, he thought it best to present him upon his table to the beholders' view with his face covered, that so he might have that grief to be imagined by them which he found himself unable to set out to the full.[1] I know I am not able to paint out your grief and sorrow for your sad loss, yet having proved that this your loss is no loss compared with the fore-mentioned sad losses, I cannot but hope that you will labour to bear up like those whose hopes, whose hearts, whose treasures are in heaven, &c.

2. Consider all outward losses may be made up; nay, God doth usually one way or another make up to his people all their outward losses. He did so to David, to Job, and many others; nay, they were great gainers by their losses. And so were the disciples, who, for the loss of Christ's personal presence, had abundance of the Spirit's influence. If he takes away a husband, and lies himself in his room, and fills up that relation, is not the loss made up? Will not the light and heat of the sun make up the loss of the light and heat of a twinkling star? If he take away a son, and give out more of himself, will you not say he is better than ten thousand sons? 1 Sam. i. 8. If he take away your only son, and give out to you more of his only Son, will you not say, that though your loss be very great, yet the great God hath made it up, by giving out more of the light, life, love, and glory of his only Son unto you? If, in the room of an only son, God shall give you a name that is better than sons and daughters, Isa. lvi. 5, will you not say, your loss is made up with advantage? *Hujusmodi lucri dulcis odor*, the smell of this gain is sweet to many. It was an apt saying of Tertullian,[2] *Negotiatio est aliquid amittere ut majora lucreris*, that is right and good merchandise, when something is parted with to gain more. He applies it to the martyrs' sufferings, wherein though the flesh lost something, yet the spirit got much more. Ah! dear friends, if your fleshly losses shall be made up in spiritual advantages, have you any cause to say, No loss to our loss, no sorrow to our sorrow? Surely no. When that noble Zedislaus had lost his hand in the wars of the King of Poland, the king sent him a golden hand for it.

Ah, friends! if God give you silver for brass, and gold for iron; if he give you spirituals for temporals, have you not more cause of rejoicing than of mourning?

When Paulinus Nolanus his city, was taken by the barbarians, he prayed thus to God: Lord! let me not be troubled at the loss of my gold, silver, honour, &c., for thou art all, and much more than all, these unto me. There is nothing beyond remedy but the tears of the damned. Those that are in the way to paradise should not place themselves in the condition of a little hell; and they that may or can hope for that great all, ought not to be dejected for any thing.

3. Thirdly, Consider that though your loss be great, yet his gain is greater: 'for him to live was Christ, and to die was gain,' Philip. i. 21. He hath exchanged mortality for immortality, the society of men for the society of angels, the sight of friends for the sight of God, a house made

[1] The allusion is to Agamemnon, on the sacrifice of Iphigenia.—G.
[2] Tertullian, in his book to the martyrs.
[3] The sooner I die, the sooner I shall be happy, said one.

with hands for one eternal in the heavens, the streams for the fountain, an earthly father for a heavenly Father; a careful, loving, sweet, suitable, tender-hearted, wise, yokefellow for to lie in the arms, the bosom, of a loving, gracious, tender-hearted Saviour. If you would but eye more his crown than your own cross, his gain than your own loss, you would divinely quench the burning flame of your passionate affections. It was a good saying of Francisco Soyit to his adversaries: You deprive me of this life, said he, and promote me to a better, which is as if you should rob me of counters, and furnish me with gold. Your deceased relation hath exchanged his counters for gold, his imperfection for perfection, and his earthly possession for a heavenly possession.

4. Fourthly and lastly, Consider how sweetly, how wisely, how bravely others have carried it, when the Lord hath passed the sentence of death upon their nearest and dearest relations; read the proofs in the margin,[1] and then never leave pressing those golden examples upon your own hearts, till they are brought over sweetly and quietly to lie down in the will of God, and to say amen to God's amen. When it was told Anaxagoras that both his sons, which was all he had, were dead, he being nothing terrified therewith, answered, *Sciebam me genuisse mortales*, I knew I begat mortal creatures.

Ah, friends! shall a heathen bear it out thus bravely, and shall not you much more? Pulvillus, another heathen [Pet. Mart.], when he was about to consecrate a temple to Jupiter, and news was brought to him of the death of his son, desisted not from his enterprise; but with a composed mind gave order for decent burial. Shall nature do this, and shall not grace do as much, nay, more? What a shame is it, saith Jerome, that faith should not be able to do that which infidelity hath done! What! not better fruit in the vineyard, in the garden of the Lord, than in the wilderness? What! not better fruit grown upon the tree of life than upon the root of nature?

Dear friends! since I yielded to your desires, and set about this work, I begun to consider that I had never heard nor read of any that had treated on this subject; also I seriously considered of the usefulness of it, especially in these times, wherein so many young persons have their faces towards Sion; which considerations, with the breaking in of God upon me beyond my expectation, has occasioned that sermon you heard to swell into a little treatise, which in all love I present unto you. The very same things that sounded in your ears I here present to your eyes, with enlargements and additions to what I first intended. The pains hath been mine; the profit that will redound to you and others, into whose hands it may fall, I hope will be such as will turn to all our accounts in the day of Christ.

I have read of an emperor's son who used to say, The longer the cooks are preparing the meat, the better will be the cheer; his meaning was, the longer he stayed for the empire, the greater it would be. The longer you have waited for this discourse, the better I desire it may prove. It had been in your hands long before this, if others that should have made more haste had not been more to blame than myself; yet I know it is not a child so late born that I need question your fathering of it. And

[1] Lev. x. 1-3; 1 Sam. iii. 11-19; 2 Sam. xii. 18-25; Job i., the whole chapter.

now I commend you all to God, and to the word of his grace, which is able to build you up, and to give you an inheritance among all them which are sanctified, Acts xx. 32.

Your servant in the work of Christ,

THOMAS BROOKS.

THE MUTE CHRISTIAN.

NOTE.

The 'Mute Christian' was originally published in 1659. A '2d' edition—though not so designated—was immediately called for, and appeared in 1660. Thereafter few books were more in demand, being next to the 'Precious Remedies.' The earlier portion of the title (as in above two editions) was 'The Silent Soul with Sovereign Antidotes,' &c. Our text is taken from 'the eighth edition, corrected,' collated with the original and subsequent intervening editions. Its title-page is given below.* G.

* THE

MUTE CHRISTIAN

UNDER THE

SMARTING ROD:

WITH

SOVEREIGN ANTIDOTES

Against the

Most Miserable Exigents:[1]

OR,

A Christian with an Olive-Leaf in his mouth, when he is under the greatest afflictions, the sharpest and sorest tryals and troubles, the saddest and darkest Providences and Changes, with Answers to divers Questions and Objections that are of greatest importance; all tending to win and work Souls to be still, quiet, calm and silent under all changes that have, or may pass upon them in this World, *&c.*

The *Eighth Edition*, Corrected.

By *THOMAS BROOKS*, late Preacher of the Word at St. *Margaret* New-Fish-Street, *London.*

The Lord is in his Holy Temple: Let all the Earth keep silence before him, Hab. 2. 20.

LONDON, Printed for *John Hancock*, and are to be sold at the *Three Bibles*, over against the *Royal Exchange* in *Cornhill.* 1684.

[1] This is one of the many Shakespearian words, referred to in our Preface, found in Brooks: 'Why do you cross me in this *exigent*?'—Julius Cæsar, v. 1. 'When the *exigent* should come.'—Antony and Cleopatra, iv. 12. Cf. also Sibbes's Works, vol. i. page 412.—G.

THE EPISTLE DEDICATORY.

To all afflicted and distressed, dissatisfied, disquieted, and discomposed Christians throughout the world.

DEAR HEARTS,—The choicest saints are 'born to troubles as the sparks fly upwards,' Job v. 7.[1] 'Many are the troubles of the righteous;' if they were many, and not troubles, then, as it is in the proverb, the more the merrier; or if they were troubles and not many, then the fewer the better cheer. But God, who is infinite in wisdom and matchless in goodness, hath ordered troubles, yea, many troubles to come trooping in upon us on every side. As our mercies, so our crosses seldom come single; they usually come treading one upon the heels of another; they are like April showers, no sooner is one over but another comes. And yet, Christians, it is mercy, it is rich mercy, that every affliction is not an execution, that every correction is not a damnation. The higher the waters rise, the nearer Noah's ark was lifted up to heaven; the more thy afflictions are increased, the more thy heart shall be raised heavenward.

Because I would not hold you too long in the porch, I shall only endeavour two things: first, to give you the reasons of my appearing once more in print; and secondly, a little counsel and direction that the following tract may turn to your soul's advantage, which is the white[2] that I have in my eye. The true reasons of my sending this piece into the world, such as it is, are these:

I. *First*, The afflicting hand of God hath been hard upon myself, and upon my dearest relations in this world, and upon many of my precious Christian friends, whom I much love and honour in the Lord, which put me upon studying of the mind of God in that scripture that I have made the subject-matter of this following discourse. Luther could not understand some Psalms till he was afflicted; the Christ-cross is no letter in the book, and yet, saith he, it hath taught me more than all the letters in the book. Afflictions are a golden key by which the Lord opens the rich treasure of his word to his people's souls; and this in some measure, through grace, my soul hath experienced. When Samson had found honey, he gave some to his father and mother to eat, Judges xiv, 9, 10; some honey I have found in my following text;

[1] Ps. xxxiv. 19 and lxxxviii. 3, 4. *Qui non est Crucianus non est Christianus.*—Luther.
[2] The 'mark.'—G.

and therefore I may not, I cannot be such a churl as not to give them some of my honey to taste, who have drunk deep of my gall and wormwood.[1] Austin observes on that, Ps. lxvi. 16, 'Come and hear, all ye that fear God, and I will declare what he hath done for my soul.' 'He doth not call them,' saith he, 'to acquaint them with speculations, how wide the earth is, how far the heavens are stretched out, what the number of the stars is, or what is the course of the sun; but come and I will tell you the wonders of his grace, the faithfulness of his promises, the riches of his mercy to my soul.' Gracious experiences are to be communicated. *Lilmod lelammed*, we therefore learn that we may teach, is a proverb among the Rabbins. And I do therefore 'lay in and lay up,' saith the heathen, that I may draw forth again and lay out for the good of many. When God hath dealt bountifully with us, others should reap some noble good by us. The family, the town, the city, the country, where a man lives, should fare the better for his faring well. Our mercies and experiences should be as a running spring at our doors, which is not only for our own use, but also for our neighbours', yea, and for strangers too.

Secondly, What is written is permanent; *litera scripta manet*, and spreads itself further by far, for time, place, and persons, than the voice can reach. The pen is an artificial tongue; it speaks as well to absent as to present friends; it speaks to them afar off as well as those that are near; it speaks to many thousands at once; it speaks not only to the present age but also to succeeding ages. The pen is a kind of image of eternity; it will make a man live when he is dead, Heb. xi. 4. Though 'the prophets do not live for ever,' yet their labours may, Zech. i. 6. A man's writings may preach when he cannot, when he may not, and when, by reason of bodily distempers, he dares not; yea, and that which is more, when he is not.[2]

Thirdly, Few men, if any, have iron memories. How soon is a sermon preached forgotten, when a sermon written remains! Augustine writing to Volusian, saith, 'That which is written is always at hand to be read, when the reader is at leisure.'[3] Men do not easily forget their own names, nor their father's house, nor the wives of their bosoms, nor the fruit of their loins, nor to eat their daily bread; and yet, ah! how easily do they forget that word of grace, that should be dearer to them than all! Most men's memories, especially in the great concernments of their souls, are like a sieve or boulter,[4] where the good corn and fine flour goes through, but the light chaff and coarse bran remain behind; or like a strainer, where the sweet liquor is strained out, but the dregs left behind; or like a grate[5] that lets the pure water run away, but if there be any straws, sticks, mud, or filth, that it holds, as it were, with iron hands. Most men's memories are very treacherous, especially in good things; few men's memories are a holy ark, a heavenly storehouse or magazine for their souls, and therefore they stand in the more need of a written word. But,

Fourthly, Its marvellous suitableness and usefulness under these

[1] Some have accounted nothing their own that they have not communicated to others.

[2] There are here, as elsewhere in Brooks, reminiscences of Thomas Adams, who was a prime favourite of our like-minded author. See Works, vol. i. page. xx—G.

[3] Aug. Ep. i. ad. Volus. [4] 'Sifter.'—G. [5] 'Grating.'—G.

great turns and changes that have passed upon us. As every wise husbandman observes the fittest seasons to sow his seed—some he sows in the autumn and fall of the leaf, some in the spring of the year, some in a dry season and some in a wet, some in a moist clay and some in a sandy dry ground, Isa. xxviii. 25,—so every spiritual husbandman must observe the fittest times to sow his spiritual seed in. He hath heavenly seed by him for all occasions and seasons, for spring and fall; for all grounds, heads, and hearts. Now whether the seed sown in the following treatise be not suitable to the times and seasons wherein we are cast, is left to the judgment of the prudent reader to determine; if the author had thought otherwise, this babe had been stifled in the womb.

Fifthly, The good acceptance that my other weak labours have found. God hath blessed them, not only to the conviction, the edification, confirmation, and consolation of many, but also to the conversion of many, Rom. xv. 21.[1] God is a free agent to work by what hand he pleases; and sometimes he takes pleasure to do great things by weak means, that 'no flesh may glory in his presence.' God will not 'despise the day of small things;' and who or what art thou, that darest despise that day? The Spirit breathes upon whose preaching and writing he pleases, and all prospers according as that wind blows, John iii. 8.

Sixthly, That all afflicted and distressed Christians may have a proper salve for every sore, a proper remedy against every disease, at hand. As every good man, so every good book is not fit to be the afflicted man's companion; but this is. Here he may see his face, his head, his hand, his heart, his ways, his works; here he may see all his diseases discovered, and proper remedies proposed and applied; here he may find arguments to silence him, and means to quiet him, when it is at worst with him; in every storm here he may find a tree to shelter him; and in every danger, here he may find a city of refuge to secure him; and in every difficulty, here he may have a light to guide him; and in every peril, here he may find a buckler to defend him; and in every distress, here he may find a cordial to strengthen him; and in every trouble, here he may find a staff to support him.[2]

Seventhly, To satisfy some bosom friends, some faithful friends. Man is made to be a friend, and apt for friendly offices. He that is not friendly is not worthy to have a friend, and he that hath a friend, and doth not shew himself friendly, is not worthy to be accounted a man. Friendship is a kind of life, without which there is no comfort of a man's life. Christian friendship ties such a knot that great Alexander cannot cut.[3] Summer friends I value not, but winter friends are worth their weight in gold; and who can deny such anything, especially in these days, wherein real, faithful, constant friends are so rare to be found? 1 Sam. xxii. 1–3. The friendship of most men in these days is like Jonah's gourd, now very promising and flourishing, and anon fading and withering; it is like some plants in the water, which have broad leaves on the surface of the water, but scarce any root at all; their friendship is like melons, cold within, hot without; their expressions are

[1] Philip. i. 15, xi.; 1 Cor. i. 17, ii. 9.
[2] Prov. xxv. 11. That remedy is no remedy that is not proper to the disease.
[3] The 'Gordian Knot' is alluded to.—G.

high, but their affections are low; they speak much, but do little.[1] As drums, and trumpets, and ensigns in a battle make a great noise and a fine show, but act nothing, so these counterfeit friends will compliment highly, bow handsomely, speak plausibly, and promise lustily, and yet have neither a hand nor heart to act anything cordially or faithfully. From such friends it is a mercy to be delivered, and therefore king Antigonus was wont to pray to God that he would protect him from his friends; and when one of his council asked him why he prayed so, he returned this answer, Every man will shun and defend himself against his professed enemies, but from our professed or pretended friends, of whom few are faithful, none can safe-guard himself, but hath need of protection from heaven. But for all this, there are some that are real friends, faithful friends, active friends, winter friends, bosom friends, fast friends; and for their sakes, especially those among them that have been long, very long, under the smarting rod, and in the fiery furnace, and that have been often poured from vessel to vessel, have I once more appeared in print to the world.

Eighthly and lastly, There hath not any authors or author come to my hand, that hath handled this subject as I have done; and therefore I do not know but it may be the more grateful and acceptable to the world; and if by this essay others that are more able shall be provoked to do more worthily upon this subject, I shall therein rejoice, 1 Thes. i. 7, 8, 1 Cor. ix. 1, 2. I shall only add, that though much of the following matter was preached upon the Lord's visitation of my dear yoke-fellow, myself, and some other friends, yet there are many things of special concernment in the following tract, that yet I have not upon any accounts communicated to the world. And thus I have given you a true and faithful account of the reasons that have prevailed with me to publish this treatise to the world, and to dedicate it to yourselves.

II. Secondly, The second thing promised was, the giving of you a little good counsel, that you may so read the following discourse, as that it may turn much to your soul's advantage; for, as many fish and catch nothing, Luke v. 5, so many read good books and get nothing, because they read them over cursorily, slightly, superficially; but he that would read to profit, must then,

First, Read and look up for a blessing: 'Paul may plant, and Apollos may water,' but all will be to no purpose, except 'the Lord give the increase,' 1 Cor. iii. 6, 7. God must do the deed, when all is done, or else all that is done will do you no good. If you would have this work successful and effectual, you must look off from man and look up to God, who alone can make it a blessing to you. As without a blessing from heaven, thy clothes cannot warm thee, nor thy food nourish thee, nor physic cure thee, nor friends comfort thee, Micah vi. 14; so without a blessing from heaven, without the precious breathings and influences of the Spirit, what here is done will do you no good, it will not turn to your account in the day of Christ; and therefore cast an eye heavenwards, Haggai i. 6. It is Seneca's observation, that the husbandmen in Egypt never look up to heaven for rain in the time of drought, but look after the overflowing of the banks of Nilus, as the

[1] O my friends, I have never a friend, said Socrates. A friend is a very mutable creature, saith Plato.

only cause of their plenty. Ah, how many are there in these days, who, when they go to read a book, never look up, never look after the rain of God's blessing, but only look to the river Nilus; they only look to the wit, the learning, the arts, the parts, the eloquence, &c., of the author, they never look so high as heaven; and hence it comes to pass, that though these read much, yet they profit little.

Secondly, He that would read to profit must read and meditate. Meditation is the food of your souls, it is the very stomach and natural heat whereby spiritual truths are digested. A man shall as soon live without his heart, as he shall be able to get good by what he reads, without meditation. Prayer, saith Bernard, without meditation, is dry and formal, and reading without meditation is useless and unprofitable.[1] He that would be a wise, a prudent, and an able experienced statesman, must not hastily ramble and run over many cities, countries, customs, laws, and manners of people, without serious musing and pondering upon such things as may make him an expert statesman; so he that would get good by reading, that would complete his knowledge, and perfect his experience in spiritual things, must not slightly and hastily ramble and run over this book or that, but ponder upon what he reads, as Mary pondered the saying of the angel in her heart. Lord! saith Austin, the more I meditate on thee, the sweeter thou art to me; so the more you shall meditate on the following matter, the sweeter it will be to you. They usually thrive best who meditate most. Meditation is a soul-fattening duty; it is a grace-strengthening duty, it is a duty-crowning duty. Gerson calls meditation the nurse of prayer; Jerome calls it his paradise; Basil calls it the treasury where all the graces are locked up; Theophylact calls it the very gate and portal by which we enter into glory; and Aristotle, though a heathen, placeth felicity in the contemplation of the mind. You may read much and hear much, yet without meditation you will never be excellent, you will never be eminent Christians.

Thirdly, Read, and try what thou readest; take nothing upon trust, but all upon trial, as those 'noble Bereans' did, Acts xvii. 10, 11. You will try and tell[2] and weigh gold, though it be handed to you by your fathers; and so should you all those heavenly truths that are handed to you by your spiritual fathers. I hope upon trial you will find nothing but what will hold weight in the balance of the sanctuary; and though all be not gold that glisters, yet I judge that you will find nothing here to glister, that will not be found upon trial to be true gold.

Fourthly, Read and do, read and practise what you read, or else all your reading will do you no good. He that hath a good book in his hand, but not a lesson of it in his heart or life, is like that ass that carrieth burdens, and feeds upon thistles.[3] In divine account, a man knows no more than he doth. Profession without practice will but make a man twice told a child of darkness; to speak well is to sound like a cymbal, but to do well is to act like an angel [Isidore]. He

[1] Animæ viaticum est meditatio.—*Bernard*. Lectio sine meditatione arida est, meditatio sine lectione erronea est; oratio sine meditatione livida est.—*Augustine*.

[2] 'Count.'—G.

[3] Augustine, speaking of the Scripture, saith, *Verba vivenda, non loquenda*.

that practiseth what he reads and understands, God will help him to understand what he understands not. There is no fear of knowing too much, though there is much fear in practising too little; the most doing man shall be the most knowing man; the mightiest man in practice will in the end prove the mightiest man in Scripture, John vii. 16, 17, Ps. cxix. 98–100. Theory is the guide of practice, and practice is the life of theory. Salvian relates how the heathen did reproach some Christians, who by their lewd lives made the gospel of Christ to be a reproach. 'Where,' said they, 'is that good law which they do believe? Where are those rules of godliness which they do learn? They read the holy gospel, and yet are unclean; they read the apostles' writings, and yet live in drunkenness; they follow Christ, and yet disobey Christ; they profess a holy law, and yet do lead impure lives.'[1] Ah! how may many preachers take up sad complaints against many readers in these days! They read our works, and yet in their lives they deny our works; they praise our works, and yet in their conversations they reproach our works; they cry up our labours in their discourses, and yet they cry them down in their practices: yet I hope better things of you into whose hands this treatise shall fall.[2] The Samaritan woman did not fill her pitcher with water, that she might talk of it, but that she might use it, John iv. 7; and Rachel did not desire the mandrakes to hold in her hand, but that she might thereby be the more apt to bring forth, Gen. xxx. 15. The application is easy. But,

Fifthly, Read and apply. Reading is but the drawing of the bow, application is the hitting of the white.[3] The choicest truths will no further profit you than they are applied by you; you were as good not to read, as not to apply what you read.[4] No man attains to health by reading of Galen, or knowing Hippocrates, his aphorisms, but by the practical application of them; all the reading in the world will never make for the health of your souls except you apply what you read. The true reason why many read so much and profit so little is, because they do not apply and bring home what they read to their own souls. But,

Sixthly, and lastly, Read and pray. He that makes not conscience of praying over what he reads, will find little sweetness or profit in his reading. No man makes such earnings of his reading, as he that prays over what he reads. Luther professeth that he profited more in the knowledge of the Scriptures by prayer, in a short space, than by study in a longer. As John by weeping got the sealed book open, so certainly men would gain much more than they do by reading good men's works, if they would but pray more over what they read.[5] Ah, Christians! pray before you read, and pray after you read, that all may be blessed and sanctified to you; when you have done reading, usually close up thus:—

So let me live, so let me die,
That I may live eternally.

[1] Salvianus de G. D. l. iv.
[2] Seneca had rather be sick, than idle and do nothing. [Epist. lvi.—G.]
[3] The 'centre-mark.'—G.
[4] The plaster will not heal if it be not applied.
[5] Prayer is *porta cœli, clavis paradisi.*

And when you are in the mount for yourselves, bear him upon your hearts, who is willing to 'spend and be spent' for your sakes, for your souls, 2 Cor. xii. 15. Oh! pray for me, that I may more and more be under the rich influences and glorious pourings out of the Spirit; that I may 'be an able minister of the New Testament, not of the letter, but of the Spirit,' 2 Cor. iii 6; that I may always find an everlasting spring and an overflowing fountain within me, which may alway make me faithful, constant, and abundant in the work of the Lord; and that I may live daily under those inward teachings of the Spirit, that may enable me to speak from the heart to the heart, from the conscience to the conscience, and from experience to experience; that I may be a 'burning and a shining light,' that everlasting arms may be still under me; that whilst I live, I may be serviceable to his glory and his people's good; that no discouragements may discourage me in my work; and that when my work is done, I may give up my account with joy and not with grief. I shall follow these poor labours with my weak prayers, that they may contribute much to your internal and eternal welfare, and so rest,

Your soul's servant in our dearest Lord,

THOMAS BROOKS.

THE MUTE CHRISTIAN UNDER THE SMARTING ROD.

I was dumb, I opened not my mouth; because thou didst it.—
Ps. XXXIX. 9.

Not to trouble you with a tedious preface, wherein usually is a flood of words, and but a drop of matter,

This psalm consists of two parts, the first exegetical or narrative, the second eutical[1] or precative.[2] 1. Narration and prayer take up the whole. In the former, you have the prophet's disease discovered; and in the latter, the remedy applied. My text falls in the latter part, where you have the way of David's cure, or the means by which his soul was reduced to a still and quiet temper. I shall give a little light into the words, and then come to the point that I intend to stand upon.

'I was dumb.' The Hebrew word נאלמתי from אלם signifies to be mute, tongue-tied, or dumb. The Hebrew word signifies also to bind, as well as to be mute and dumb, because they that are dumb are as it were tongue-tied; they have their lips stitched and bound up. Ah! the sight of God's hand in the afflictions that was upon him, makes him lay a law of silence upon his heart and tongue.[3]

'I opened not my mouth, because thou didst it.' He looks through all secondary causes to the first cause, and is silent: he sees a hand of God in all, and so sits mute and quiet. The sight of God in an affliction is of an irresistible efficacy to silence the heart, and to stop the mouth of a gracious man. In the words you may observe three things:

1. *The person speaking*, and that is, David; David a king, David a saint, David 'a man after God's own heart,' David a Christian; and here we are to look upon David, not as a king, but as a Christian, as a man whose heart was right with God.

2. *The action and carriage of David under the hand of God*, in these words, 'I was dumb, and opened not my mouth.'

3. *The reason of this humble and sweet carriage of his*, in these words, 'because thou didst it.' The proposition is this:

[1] *Sic;* and have collated all the editions. Qu.—from the old theological term *ethos* (ἦθος), by which the writer reveals his own disposition?—G. [Or, Qu. 'Euchical'?—Ed.]

[2] Supplicatory.—G.

[3] Some read it thus: 'I should have been dumb, and not have opened my mouth,' according to my first resolution, ver. 1, 2.

Doct. That it is the great duty and concernment of gracious souls to be mute and silent under the greatest afflictions, the saddest providences, and sharpest trials that they meet with in this world.

For the opening and clearing up of this great and useful truth, I shall inquire,

First, What this silence is that is here pointed at in the proposition.

Secondly, What a gracious, a holy, silence doth include.

Thirdly, What this holy silence doth not include.

Fourthly, The reasons of the point; and then bring home all by way of application to our own souls.

I. For the first, *What is the silence here meant?* I answer, There is a sevenfold silence.

First, There is a stoical silence. The stoics of old thought it altogether below a man that hath reason or understanding either to rejoice in any good, or to mourn for any evil; but this stoical silence is such a sinful insensibleness as is very provoking to a holy God, Isa. xxvi. 10, 11. God will make the most insensible sinner sensible either of his hand here, or of his wrath in hell. It is a heathenish and a horrid sin to be without natural affections, Rom. i. 31. And of this sin Quintus Fabius Maximus seems to be foully guilty, who, when he heard that his mother and wife, whom he dearly loved, were slain by the fall of an house, and that his younger son, a brave, hopeful young man, died at the same time in Umbria, he never changed his countenance, but went on with the affairs of the commonwealth as if no such calamity had befallen him. This carriage of his spoke out more stupidity than patience, Job xxxvi. 13.

And so Harpalus was not at all appalled when he saw two of his sons laid ready dressed in a charger, when Astyages had bid him to supper. This was a sottish insensibleness. Certainly if the loss of a child in the house be no more to thee than the loss of a chick in the yard, thy heart is base and sordid, and thou mayest well expect some sore awakening judgment.[1] This age is full of such monsters, who think it below the greatness and magnanimity of their spirits to be moved, affected, or afflicted with any afflictions that befall them. I know none so ripe and ready for hell as these.

Aristotle speaks of fishes, that though they have spears thrust into their sides, yet they awake not. God thrusts many a sharp spear through many a sinner's heart, and yet he feels nothing, he complains of nothing. These men's souls will bleed to death. Seneca, Epist. x., reports of Senecio Cornelius, who minded his body more than his soul, and his money more than heaven; when he had all the day long waited on his dying friend, and his friend was dead, he returns to his house, sups merrily, comforts himself quickly, goes to bed cheerfully. His sorrows were ended, and the time of his mourning expired before his deceased friend was interred. Such stupidity is a curse that many a man lies under. But this stoical silence, which is but a sinful sullenness, is not the silence here meant.

Secondly, There is a politic silence. Many are silent out of policy. Should they not be silent, they should lay themselves more open either

[1] Hosea vii. 9. Balaam's ass reproves this dumbness.

to the rage and fury of men, or else to the plots and designs of men to prevent which they are silent, and will lay their hands upon their mouths, that others might not lay their hands upon their estates, lives, or liberties: 'And Saul also went home to Gibeah, and there went with him a band of men, whose hearts God had touched. But the children of Belial said, How shall this man save us? and they despised him, and brought him no presents; but he held his peace,' or was as though he had been deaf, 1 Sam. x. 26, 27. This new king being but newly entered upon his kingly government, and observing his condition to be but mean and low, his friends but few, and his enemies many and potent, sons of Belial, *i.e.* men without yoke, as the word signifies, men that were desperately wicked, that were marked out for hell, that were even incarnate devils, who would neither submit to reason nor religion, nor be governed by the laws of nature nor of nations, nor yet by the laws of God: now this young prince, to prevent sedition and rebellion, blood and destruction, prudently and politicly chooses rather to lay his hand upon his mouth than to take a wolf by the ear or a lion by the beard; wanted neither wit nor will to be mute; he turns a deaf ear to all they say, his unsettled condition requiring silence.[1]

Henry the Sixth, emperor of Germany, used to say, *Qui nescit tacere, nescit loqui,* He that knows not how to be silent, knows not how to speak. Saul knew this was a time for silence; he knew his work was rather to be an auditor than an orator. But this is not the silence the proposition speaks of.

Thirdly, There is a foolish silence. Some fools there be that can neither do well nor speak well, and because they cannot word it neither as they would nor as they should, they are so wise as to be mute: Prov. xvii. 28, 'Even a fool, when he holds his peace, is counted wise, and he that shutteth his lips is esteemed a man of understanding.' As he cannot be wise that speaks much, so he cannot be known for a fool that says nothing. There are many wise fools in the world; there are many silly fools, who, by holding their tongues, gain the credit and honour of being discreet men. He that doth not discover his want of wisdom by foolish babbling, is accounted wise, though he may be otherwise. Silence is so rare a virtue, where wisdom doth regulate it, that it is accounted a virtue where folly doth impose it. Silence was so highly honoured among the old Romans, that they erected altars to it. That man shall pass for a man of understanding, who so far understands himself as to hold his tongue. For though it be a great misery to be a fool, yet it is a greater that a man cannot be a fool but he must needs shew it. But this foolish silence is not the silence here meant.

Fourthly, There is a sullen silence. Many, to gratify an humour, a lust, are sullenly silent; these are troubled with a dumb devil, which was the worst devil of all the devils you read of in the Scripture, Mark ix. 17–28. Pliny, in his Natural History, maketh mention of a certain people in the Indies, upon the river Ganges, called *Astomy,* that have no mouth, but do only feed upon the smell of herbs and flowers.[2] Cer-

[1] Hear, see, and be silent, if thou wilt live in peace, is a French proverb.

[2] Lib. vii. c. 2. The 'Astomi' are referred to, and the chief 'smell' supposed to be their 'food' is that of 'apples.' Cf. also Lib. vi. c. 20. Both references contain the oddest observations.—G.

tainly there is a generation amongst us, who, when they are under the afflicting hand of God, have no mouths to plead with God, no lips to praise God, nor no tongues to justify God. These are possessed with a dumb devil; and this dumb devil had possessed Ahab for a time: 1 Kings xxi. 4, 'And Ahab came into his house, heavy and displeased, and laid him down upon his bed, and turned away his face, and would eat no bread.' Ahab's ambitious humour, his covetous humour, being crossed, he is resolved to starve himself, and to die of the sullens. A sullen silence is both a sin and a punishment. No devil frets and vexes, wears and wastes the spirits of a man, like this dumb devil, like this sullen silence.

Some write of a certain devil, whom they call *Hudgin*, who will not, they say, hurt anybody, except he be wronged. I cannot speak so favourably of a sullen silence, for that wrongs many at once, God and Christ, bodies and soul. But this is not the silence here meant.

Fifthly, There is a forced silence. Many are silent per force. He that is under the power of his enemy, though he suffer many hard things, yet he is silent under his sufferings, because he knows he is liable to worse; he that hath taken away his liberty, may take away his life; he that hath taken away his money, may take off his head; he that hath let him blood in the foot, may let him blood in the throat if he will not be still and quiet: and this works silence per force. So, when many are under the afflicting hand of God, conscience tells them that now they are under the hand of an enemy, and the power of that God whom they have dishonoured, whose Son they have crucified, whose Spirit they have grieved, whose righteous laws they have transgressed, whose ordinances they have despised, and whose people they have abused and opposed; and that he that hath taken away one child, may take away every child; and he that hath taken away the wife, might have taken away the husband; and he that hath taken away some part of the estate, might have taken away all the estate; and that he who hath inflicted some distempers upon the body, might have cast both body and soul into hell-fire for ever; and he that hath shut him up in his chamber, may shut him out of heaven at pleasure. The thoughts and sense of these things makes many a sinner silent under the hand of God; but this is but a forced silence.[1] And such was the silence of Philip the Second, king of Spain, who, when his invincible Armada, that had been three years a-fitting, was lost, he gave command that all over Spain they should give thanks to God and the saints that it was no more grievous. As the cudgel forces the dog to be quiet and still, and the rod forces the child to be silent and mute, so the apprehensions of what God hath done, and of what God may do, forces many a soul to be silent, Jer. iii. 10, 1 Kings xiv. 5–18. But this is not the silence here meant: a forced silence is no silence in the eye of God.

Sixthly, There is a despairing silence. A despairing soul is *Magor-missabib*, a terror to himself; he hath a hell in his heart, and horror in his conscience. He looks upwards, and there he beholds God frowning, and Christ bleeding; he looks inwards, and there he finds conscience accusing and condemning of him;[2] he looks on the one side of him, and

[1] *Oculos quos peccatum claudit, pœna aperit.*—Gregory. The eye that sin shuts, affliction opens.

[2] Psalm xciv. 7; xxviii. 1.

there he hears all his sins crying out, We are thine, and we will follow thee; we will to the grave with thee, we will to judgment with thee, and from judgment we will to hell with thee; he looks on the other side of him, and there he sees infernal fiends in fearful shapes, amazing and terrifying of him, and waiting to receive his despairing soul as soon as she shall take her leave of his wretched body; he looks above him, and there he sees the gates of heaven shut against him; he looks beneath him, and there he sees hell gaping for him; and under these sad sights, he is full of secret conclusions against his own soul. There is mercy for others, saith the despairing soul, but none for me; grace and favour for others, but none for me; pardon and peace for others, but none for me; blessedness and happiness for others, but none for me: there is no help, there is no help, no, Jer. ii. 25, xviii. 12. This seems to be his case who died with this desperate saying in his mouth, *Spes et fortuna valete*, farewell, life and hope together.[1] Now, under these dismal apprehensions and sad conclusions about its present and future condition, the despairing soul sits silent, being filled with amazement and astonishment: Ps. lxxvii. 4, 'I am so troubled that I cannot speak.' But this is not the silence here meant. But,

Seventhly and lastly, There is a prudent silence, a holy, a gracious silence; a silence that springs from prudent principles, from holy principles, and from gracious causes and considerations; and this is the silence here meant. And this I shall fully discover in my answers to the second question, which is this:

II. *Quest.* 2. *What doth a prudent, a gracious, a holy silence include?*

Ans. 2. It includes and takes in these eight things:

First, It includes *a sight of God, and an acknowledgment of God as the author of all the afflictions that come upon us.* And this you have plain in the text: 'I was dumb, I opened not my mouth; because thou didst it.' The psalmist looks through secondary causes to the first cause, and so sits mute before the Lord. There is no sickness so little, but God hath a finger in it, though it be but the aching of the little finger. As the scribe is more eyed and properly said to write, than the pen; and he that maketh and keepeth the clock, is more properly said to make it go and strike, than the wheels and weights that hang upon it; and as every workman is more eyed and properly said to effect his works, rather than the tools which he useth as his instruments. So the Lord, who is the chief agent and mover in all actions, and who hath the greatest hand in all our afflictions, is more to be eyed and owned than any inferior or subordinate causes whatsoever;[2] so Job, he beheld God in all: Job i. 21, 'The Lord gave, and the Lord hath taken away.' Had he not seen God in the affliction, he would have cried out: Oh these wretched Chaldeans, they have plundered and spoiled me; these wicked Sabeans, they have robbed and wronged me! Job discerns God's commission in the Chaldeans' and the Sabeans' hands, and then

[1] As that despairing pope said, the cross could do him no good, because he had so often sold it.

[2] In second causes, many times a Christian may see much envy, hatred, malice, pride, &c. But in the first cause he can see nothing but grace and mercy, sweetness and goodness.

lays his own hand upon his mouth. So Aaron, beholding the hand of God in the untimely death of his two sons, holds his peace, Lev. x. 3. The sight of God in this sad stroke is a bridle both to his mind and mouth, he neither mutters nor murmurs. So Joseph saw the hand of God in his brethren's selling of him into Egypt, Gen. xlv. 8, and that silences him.

Men that see not God in an affliction, are easily cast into a feverish fit, they will quickly be in a flame, and when their passions are up, and their hearts on fire, they will begin to be saucy, and make no bones of telling God to his teeth, that they do well to be angry, Jonah iv. 8, 9. Such as will not acknowledge God to be the author of all their afflictions, will be ready enough to fall in with that mad principle of the Manichees, who maintained the devil to be the author of all calamities; as if there could be any evil of affliction in the city, and the Lord have no hand in it, Amos iii. 6. Such as can see the ordering hand of God in all their afflictions, will, with David, lay their hands upon their mouths, when the rod of God is upon their backs, 2 Sam. xvi. 11, 12. If God's hand be not seen in the affliction, the heart will do nothing but fret and rage under affliction.

Secondly, It includes and takes in *some holy, gracious apprehensions of the majesty, sovereignty, dignity, authority, and presence of that God under whose afflicting hand we are:* Hab. ii. 20, 'But the Lord is in his holy temple: let all the earth be silent,' or as the Hebrew reads it, 'Be silent, all the earth, before his face.' When God would have all the people of the earth to be hushed, quiet, and silent before him, he would have them to behold him in his temple, where he sits in state, in majesty, and glory: Zeph. i. 'Hold thy peace at the presence of the Lord God.' Chat not, murmur not, repine not, quarrel not; whist, stand mute, be silent, lay thy hand on thy mouth, when his hand is upon thy back, who is *totus oculus*, all eye to see, as well as all hand to punish. As the eyes of a well-drawn picture are fastened on thee which way soever thou turnest, so are the eyes of the Lord; and therefore thou hast cause to stand mute before him.

Thus Aaron had an eye to the sovereignty of God, and that silences him. And Job had an eye upon the majesty of God, and that stills him. And Eli had an eye upon the authority and presence of God, and that quiets him.[1] A man never comes to humble himself, nor to be silent under the hand of God, until he comes to see the hand of God to be a mighty hand: 1 Pet. v. 6, 'Humble yourselves therefore under the mighty hand of God.' When men look upon the hand of God as a weak hand, a feeble hand, a low hand, a mean hand, their hearts rise against his hand. 'Who is the Lord,' saith Pharaoh, 'that I should obey his voice?' Exod. v. 2. And until Pharaoh came to see the hand of God, as a mighty hand, and to feel it as a mighty hand, he would not let Israel go. When Tiribazus, a noble Persian,[2] was arrested, at first he drew out his sword and defended himself; but when they charged him in the king's name, and informed him that they came from the king, and were commanded to bring him to the king, he yielded willingly. So when afflictions arrest us, we shall murmur and grumble,

[1] Lev. x. 3; Job xxxvii. 13, 14; 1 Sam. iii. 11, 19.
[2] The favourite of Artaxerxes II.—G.

and struggle, and strive even to the death, before we shall yield to that God that strikes, until we come to see his majesty and authority, until we come to see him as the King of kings, and Lord of lords, Isa. xxvi. 11, 12. It is such a sight of God as this, that makes the heart to stoop under his almighty hand, Rev. i. 5. The Thracians being ignorant of the dignity and majesty of God; when it thundered and lightened, used to express their madness and folly in shooting their arrows against heaven threatening-wise.[1] As a sight of his grace cheers the soul, so a sight of his greatness and glory silences the soul.[2] But,

Thirdly, A gracious, a prudent silence, takes in *a holy quietness and calmness of mind and spirit, under the afflicting hand of God.* A gracious silence shuts out all inward heats, murmurings, frettings, quarrelings, wranglings, and boilings of heart: Ps. lxii. 1, 'Truly my soul keepeth silence unto God, or is silent or still;' that is, my soul is quiet and submissive to God; all murmurings and repinings, passions and turbulent affections, being allayed, tamed, and subdued. This also is clear in the text; and in the former instances of Aaron, Eli, and Job. They saw that it was a Father that put those bitter cups in their hands, and love that laid those heavy crosses upon their shoulders, and grace that put those yokes about their necks; and this caused much quietness and calmness in their spirits. Marius bit in his pain when the chirurgeon cut off his leg.[3] Some men, when God cuts off this mercy and that mercy from them, they bite in their pain, they hide and conceal their grief and trouble; but could you but look into their hearts, you will find all in an uproar, all out of order, all in a flame; and however they may seem to be cold without, yet they are all in a hot burning fever within. Such a feverish fit David was once in, Ps. xxxix. 3. But certainly a holy silence allays all tumults in the mind, and makes a man 'in patience to possess his own soul,' which, next to his possession of God, is the choicest and sweetest possession in all the world, Luke xxi. 19. The law of silence is as well upon that man's heart and mind, as it is upon his tongue, who is truly and divinely silent under the rebuking hand of God. As tongue-service abstracted from heart-service is no service in the account of God; so tongue-silence abstracted from heart-silence is no silence in the esteem of God. A man is then graciously silent when all is quiet within and without, Isa. xxix. 13, Mat. xv. 8, 9.

Terpander,[4] a harper and a poet, was one that, by the sweetness of his verse and music, could allay the tumultuous motions of men's minds, as David by his harp did Saul's. When God's people are under the rod, he makes by his Spirit and word such sweet music in their souls, as allays all tumultuous motions, passions, and perturbations, Ps. xciv. 17–19, Ps. cxix. 49, 50, so that they sit, Noah-like, quiet and still; and in peace possess their own souls.

Fourthly, A prudent, a holy silence, takes in *an humble, justifying, clearing and acquitting of God of all blame, rigour and injustice, in all the afflictions he brings upon us;* Ps. li. 4, 'That thou mayest be justified when thou speakest, and be clear when thou judgest,' that is,

[1] Herodotus. [2] *Animus cujusque est quisque*, the mind is the man.
[3] Query, M. Marius, the friend of Cicero?—G.
[4] Of Lesbos, the father of Greek music.—G.

when thou correctest.[1] God's judging his people is God's correcting or chastening of his people: 1 Cor. xi. 32, 'When we are judged, we are chastened of the Lord.' David's great care, when he was under the afflicting hand of God, was to clear the Lord of injustice. Ah! Lord, saith he, there is not the least show, spot, stain, blemish, or mixture of injustice, in all the afflictions thou hast brought upon me; I desire to take shame to myself, and to set to my seal, that the Lord is righteous, and that there is no injustice, no cruelty, nor no extremity in all that the Lord hath brought upon me.' And so in that Psalm cxix. 75, 137, he sweetly and readily subscribes unto the righteousness of God in those sharp and smart afflictions that God exercised him with. 'I know, O Lord, that thy judgments are right, and that thou in faithfulness hast afflicted me. Righteous art thou, O Lord, and righteous are thy judgments.' God's judgments are always just; he never afflicts but in faithfulness. His will is the rule of justice; and therefore a gracious soul dares not cavil nor question his proceedings. The afflicted soul knows that a righteous God can do nothing but that which is righteous; it knows that God is incontrollable, and therefore the afflicted man puts his mouth in the dust, and keeps silence before him. Who dare say, 'Wherefore hast thou done so?' 2 Sam. xvi. 10.

The Turks, when they are cruelly lashed, are compelled to return to the judge that commanded it, to kiss his hand, give him thanks, and pay the officer that whipped them, and so clear the judge and officer of injustice. Silently to kiss the rod, and the hand that whips with it, is the noblest way of clearing the Lord of all injustice.

The Babylonish captivity was the sorest, the heaviest affliction that ever God inflicted upon any people under heaven; witness that 1 Sam. xii., and Dan. ix. 12, &c. Yet under those smart afflictions, wisdom is justified of her children: Neh. ix. 33, 'Thou art just in all that is brought upon us, for thou hast done right, but we have done wickedly;' Lam. i. 18, 'The Lord is righteous, for I have rebelled against him.' A holy silence shines in nothing more than in an humble justifying and clearing of God from all that which a corrupt heart is apt enough to charge God with in the day of affliction. God, in that he is good, can give nothing, nor do nothing, but that which is good; others do frequently, he cannot possibly, saith Luther, on Ps. 120th.

Fifthly, A holy silence takes in *gracious, blessed, soul-quieting conclusions about the issue and event of those afflictions that are upon us,* Lam. iii. 27–34. In this choice scripture you may observe these five soul-stilling conclusions.

(1.) First, and that more generally, *That they shall work for their good:* ver. 27, 'It is good for a man that he bear the yoke in his youth.' A gracious soul secretly concludes, as stars shine brightest in the night, so God will make my soul shine and glister like gold, whilst I am in this furnace, and when I come out of the furnace of affliction: Job xxiii. 10, 'He knoweth the way that I take; and when he hath tried me, I shall come forth as gold.'

Surely, as the tasting of honey did open Jonathan's eyes, so this cross, this affliction, shall open mine eyes; by this stroke I shall come

[1] Plato calls God the horn of plenty, the ocean of beauty, without the least spot of injustice.

to have a clearer sight of my sins and of myself, and a fuller sight of my God, Job xxxiii. 27, 28; xl. 4, 5; xlii. 1–7.

Surely this affliction shall issue in the purging away of my dross, Isa. i. 25.

Surely as ploughing of the ground killeth the weeds, and harrowing breaketh hard clods, so these afflictions shall kill my sins, and soften my heart, Hosea v. 15, vi. 1–3.

Surely as the plaster draws out the core, so the afflictions that are upon me shall draw out the core of pride, the core of self-love, the core of envy, the core of earthliness, the core of formality, the core of hypocrisy, Ps. cxix. 67, 71.

Surely by these the Lord will crucify my heart more and more to the world, and the world to my heart, Gal. vi. 14; Ps. cxxxi. 1–3.

Surely by these afflictions the Lord will hide pride from my soul, Job xxxiii, 14–21.

Surely these afflictions are but the Lord's pruning-knives, by which he will bleed my sins, and prune my heart, and make it more fertile and fruitful; they are but the Lord's portion, by which he will clear me, and rid me of those spiritual diseases and maladies, which are most deadly and dangerous to my soul.

Affliction is such a potion, as will carry away all ill humours, better than all the *benedicta medicamenta*, as physicians call them, Zech. xiii. 8, 9.

Surely these shall increase my spiritual experiences, Rom. v. 3, 4.

Surely by these I shall be made more partaker of God's holiness, Heb. xii. 10. As black soap makes white clothes, so doth sharp afflictions make holy hearts.

Surely by these God will communicate more of himself unto me, Hosea ii. 14.

Surely by these afflictions the Lord will draw out my heart more and more to seek him, Isa. xxvi. 16. Tatianus told the heathen Greeks, that when they were sick, then they would send for their gods to be with them,[1] as Agamemnon did at the siege of Troy, send for his ten councillors. Hosea v. 15, 'In their afflictions they will seek me early,' or as the Hebrew hath it, 'they will morning me;' in times of affliction, Christians will industriously, speedily, early seek unto the Lord.

Surely by these trials and troubles the Lord will fix my soul more than ever upon the great concernments of another world, John xiv. 1–3; Rom. viii. 17, 18; 2 Cor. iv. 16–18.

Surely by these afflictions the Lord will work in me more tenderness and compassion towards those that are afflicted, Heb. x. 34, xiii. 3. As that Tyrian queen[2] said,

> Evils have taught me to bemoan,
> All that afflictions make to groan.

The Romans punished one that was seen looking out at his window with a crown of roses on his head, in a time of public calamity. Bishop Bonner was full of guts, but empty of bowels; I am afraid this age is full of such Bonners.

Surely these are but God's love-tokens: Rev. iii. 19, 'As many as I

[1] In his Πρὸς Ἕλληνας, *Oratio adversus Græcos.*—G.

[2] Dido in Virgil, *Nec ignara mali, miseris succurrere disco.*—Ed.

love, I rebuke and chasten.' Seneca persuaded his friend Polybius to bear his affliction quietly, because he was the emperor's favourite, telling him, that it was not lawful for him to complain whilst Cæsar was his friend. So saith the holy Christian, O my soul! be quiet, be still; all is in love, all is a fruit of divine favour. I see honey upon the top of every twig, I see the rod is but a rosemary branch, I have sugar with my gall, and wine with my wormwood; therefore be silent, O my soul! and this general conclusion, that all should be for good, had this blessed effect upon the church: Lam. iii. 28, 'He sitteth alone, and keepeth silence, because he hath borne it upon him.'[1]

Afflictions abase the loveliness of the world without, that might entice us; it abates the lustiness of the flesh within, which might else ensnare us! and it abates[2] the spirit in its quarrel against the flesh and the world; by all which it proves a mighty advantage unto us.

(2.) Secondly, *They shall keep them humble and low:* Lam. iii. 29, 'He putteth his mouth in the dust, if so be there may be hope.' Some say, that these words are an allusion to the manner of those that, having been conquered and subdued, lay their necks down at the conqueror's feet to be trampled upon, and so lick up the dust that is under the conqueror's feet. Others of the learned looked upon the words as an allusion to poor petitioners, who cast themselves down at princes' feet, that they may draw forth their pity and compassion towards them. As I have read of Aristippus, who fell on the ground before Dionysius, and kissed his feet, when he presented a petition to him; and being asked the reason, answered, *Aures habet in pedibus*, he hath his ears in his feet. Take it which way you will, it holds forth this to us, That holy hearts will be humble under the afflicting hand of God. When God's rod is upon their backs, their mouths shall be in the dust. A good heart will lie lowest, when the hand of God is lifted highest, Job xlii. 1-7; Acts ix. 1-8.

(3.) Thirdly, The third soul-quieting conclusion you have in Lam. iii. 31, 'For the Lord will not cast off for ever;' the rod shall not always lie upon the back of the righteous. 'At even-tide, lo there is trouble. but afore morning it is gone,' Isa. xvii. 13. As Athanasius said to his friends, when they came to bewail his misery and banishment, *Nubecula est, citò transibit;* it is but a little cloud, said he, and it will quickly be gone. There are none of God's afflicted ones, that have not their *lucida intervalla*, their intermissions, respites, breathing-whiles; yea, so small a while doth the hand of the Lord rest upon his people, that Luther cannot get diminutives enough to extenuate it; for he calls it a very little little cross that we bear: Isa. xxvi. 20, 'Come, my people, enter thou into thy chambers, and shut thy doors about thee: hide thyself as it were for a little moment (or for a little space, a little while), until the indignation be overpast.' The indignation doth not *transire*, but *pertransire*, pass, but over-pass. The sharpness, shortness, and suddenness of the saints' afflictions, is set forth by the travail of a woman, John xvi. 21, which is sharp, short, and sudden.[3]

[1] Some say, if a knife or needle be touched with a loadstone of an iron colour, it will cut or enter into a man's body, without any sense of pain at all; so will afflictions when touched with the loadstone of divine love.

[2] Qu. 'abets'?—Ed.

[3] A little storm, as he said of Julian's persecution, and an eternal calm follows.

(4.) Fourthly, The fourth soul-silencing conclusion you have in Lamentations iii. 32, 'But though he cause grief, yet will he have compassion, according to the multitude of his mercies.' 'In wrath God remembers mercy,' Hab. iii. 2. 'Weeping may endure for a night, but joy cometh in the morning,' Ps. xxx. 5. Their mourning shall last but till morning. God will turn their winter's night into a summer's day, their sighing into singing, their grief into gladness, their mourning into music, their bitter into sweet, their wilderness into a paradise. The life of a Christian is filled up with interchanges of sickness and health, weakness and strength, want and wealth, disgrace and honour, crosses and comforts, miseries and mercies, joys and sorrows, mirth and mourning; all honey would harm us, all wormwood would undo us; a composition of both is the best way in the world to keep our souls in a healthy constitution. It is best and most for the health of the soul that the south wind of mercy, and the north wind of adversity, do both blow upon it; and though every wind that blows shall blow good to the saints, yet certainly their sins die most, and their graces thrive best, when they are under the drying, nipping north wind of calamity, as well as under the warm, cherishing south wind of mercy and prosperity.

(5.) Fifthly, The fifth soul-quieting conclusion you have in Lament. iii. 33, 'For he doth not afflict willingly (or as the Hebrew hath it, 'from his heart'), 'nor grieve the children of men.' The church concludes, that God's heart was not in their afflictions, though his hand was. He takes no delight to afflict his children; it goes against the hair and the heart; it is a grief to him to be grievous to them, a pain to him to be punishing of them, a death to him to be striking of them; he hath no will, no motion, no inclination, no disposition, to that work of afflicting of his people; and therefore he calls it his 'work, his strange work,' Isa. xxviii. 21. Mercy and punishment, they flow from God, as the honey and the sting from the bee. The bee yieldeth honey of her own nature, but she doth not sting but when she is provoked. He takes delight in shewing of mercy, Micah vii. 18; he takes no pleasure in giving his people up to adversity, Hosea xi. 8. Mercy and kindness floweth from him freely, naturally; he is never severe, never harsh; he never stings, he never terrifies us, but when he is sadly provoked by us. God's hand sometimes may lie very hard upon his people, when his heart, his bowels, at those very times may be yearning towards his people, Jer. xxxi. 18–20. No man can tell how the heart of God stands by his hand; his hand of mercy may be open to those against whom his heart is set, as you see in the rich poor fool, and Dives, in the Gospel; and his hand of severity may lie hard upon those on whom he hath set his heart, as you may see in Job and Lazarus. And thus you see those gracious, blessed, soul-quieting conclusions about the issue and event of afflictions, that a holy, a prudent silence doth include.

Sixthly, A holy, a prudent silence includes and takes in *a strict charge, a solemn command, that conscience lays upon the soul to be quiet and still.*[1] Ps. xxxvii. 7, 'Rest in the Lord' (or as the Hebrew hath it, 'be silent to the Lord'), 'and wait patiently for him.' I charge

[1] The heathen could say, *A recta conscientia ne latum quidem unguem discedendum,* Man may not depart an hair's-breadth all his life long from the dictates of a good conscience. [Seneca in Epist. and *De Vita Beata.*—G.]

thee, O my soul, not to mutter, nor to murmur; I command thee, O my soul, to be dumb and silent under the afflicting hand of God. As Christ laid a charge, a command, upon the boisterous winds and the roaring raging seas,—Mat. viii. 26, 'Be still; and there was a great calm,'—so conscience lays a charge upon the soul to be quiet and still: Ps. xxvii. 14, 'Wait on the Lord; be of good courage, and he shall strengthen thy heart: wait, I say, on the Lord.' Peace, O my soul! be still, leave your muttering, leave your murmuring, leave your complaining, leave your chafing and vexing, and lay your hand upon your mouth, and be silent. Conscience allays and stills all the tumults and uproars that be in the soul, by such like reasonings as the clerk of Ephesus stilled that uproar: Acts xix. 40, 'For we are in danger to be called in question for this day's uproar, there being no cause whereby we may give an account of this concourse.' O my soul! be quiet, be silent, else thou wilt one day be called in question for all those inward mutterings, uproars, and passions that are in thee, seeing no sufficient cause can be produced why you should murmur, quarrel, or wrangle, under the righteous hand of God.

Seventhly, A holy, a prudent silence includes *a surrendering, a resigning up of ourselves to God, whilst we are under his afflicting hand.* The silent soul gives himself up to God.[1] The secret language of the soul is this: 'Lord, here am I; do with me what thou pleasest, write upon me as thou pleasest: I give up myself to be at thy dispose.'

There was a good woman, who, when she was sick, being asked whether she were willing to live or die, answered, 'Which God pleaseth.' But, said one that stood by, 'If God should refer it to you, which should you choose?' 'Truly,' said she, 'if God should refer it to me, I would even refer it to him again.' This was a soul worth gold. Well! saith a gracious soul, the ambitious man giveth himself up to his honours, but I give up myself unto thee; the voluptuous man gives himself up to his pleasures, but I give up myself to thee; the covetous man gives himself up to his bags, but I give up myself to thee; the wanton gives himself up to his minion, but I give up myself to thee; the drunkard gives himself up to his cups, but I give up myself to thee; the papist gives up himself to his idols, but I give myself to thee; the Turk gives up himself to his Mahomet, but I give up myself to thee; the heretic gives up himself to his heretical opinions, but I give up myself to thee. Lord! lay what burden thou wilt upon me, only let thy everlasting arms be under me [Luther]. Strike, Lord, strike, and spare not, for I am lain down in thy will, I have learned to say amen to thy amen; thou hast a greater interest in me than I have in myself, and therefore I give up myself unto thee, and am willing to be at thy dispose, and am ready to receive what impression thou shalt stamp upon me. O blessed Lord! hast thou not again and again said unto me, as once the king of Israel said to the king of Syria, 'I am thine, and all that I have,' 1 Kings xx. 4. I am thine, O soul! to save thee; my mercy is thine to pardon thee; my blood is thine to cleanse thee; my merits are thine to justify thee; my righteousness is thine to clothe thee; my Spirit is thine to lead thee; my grace is thine to enrich thee; and my glory is thine to reward thee; and therefore, saith a gracious soul, I cannot but

[1] Ps. xxvii. 8; James iv. 7; 1 Sam. iii. 18, xv. 25, 26; Acts xi. 13, 14, &c.

make a resignation of myself unto thee. 'Lord! here I am, do with me as seemeth good in thine own eyes.' I know the best way to have my own will, is to resign up myself to thy will, and to say amen to thy amen.

I have read of a gentleman, who, meeting with a shepherd in a misty morning, asked him what weather it would be? It will be, saith the shepherd, what weather pleaseth me; and being courteously requested to express his meaning, Sir, saith he, it shall be what weather pleaseth God, and what weather pleaseth God pleaseth me. When a Christian's will is moulded into the will of God, he is sure to have his will. But,

Eighthly and lastly, A holy, a prudent silence, takes in *a patient waiting upon the Lord under our afflictions until deliverance comes:* Ps. xl. 1–3; Ps. lxii. 5, 'My soul, wait thou only upon God, for my expectation is from him;' Lam. iii. 26, 'It is good that a man should both hope, and quietly (or as the Hebrew hath it, silently) wait for the salvation of the Lord.' The husbandman patiently waiteth for the precious fruits of the earth, the mariner patiently waiteth for wind and tide, and so doth the watchman for the dawning of the day; and so doth the silent soul in the night of adversity, patiently wait for the dawning of the day of mercy, James v. 7, 8. The mercies of God are not styled the swift, but the sure mercies of David, and therefore a gracious soul waits patiently for them. And thus you see what a gracious, a prudent silence doth include.

III. The third thing is, to discover *what a holy, a prudent silence under affliction doth not exclude.* Now there are eight things that a holy patience doth not exclude.

1. First, A holy, a prudent silence under affliction doth not exclude and shut out *a sense and feeling of our afflictions.* Ps. xxxix. 9, though he 'was dumb, and laid his hand upon his mouth,' yet he was very sensible of his affliction: verses 10, 11, 'Remove thy stroke away from me, I am consumed by the blow of thine hand. When thou with rebukes dost correct man for iniquity, thou makest his beauty to consume away like a moth: surely every man is vanity.' He is sensible of his pain as well as of his sin; and having prayed off his sin in the former verses, he labours here to pray off his pain. Diseases, aches, sicknesses, pains, they are all the daughters of sin, and he that is not sensible of them as the births and products of sin, doth but add to his sin and provoke the Lord to add to his sufferings, Isa. xxvi. 9–11. No man shall ever be charged by God for feeling his burden, if he neither fret nor faint under it. Grace doth not destroy nature, but rather perfect it. Grace is of a noble offspring; it neither turneth men into stocks nor to stoics. The more grace, the more sensible of the tokens, frowns, blows, and lashes of a displeased Father. Though Calvin, under his greatest pains, was never heard to mutter nor murmur, yet he was heard often to say, 'How long, Lord, how long?' A religious commander being shot in battle, when the wound was searched, and the bullet cut out, some standing by, pitying his pain, he replied, Though I groan, yet I bless God I do not grumble.[1] God allows his people to groan, though not to grumble. It is a God-provoking sin to be stupid and senseless under the afflicting hand of God. God will heat that man's furnace of afflic-

[1] Sir Philip Sydney?—G.

tion sevenfold hotter, who is in the furnace but feels it not:[1] Isa. xlii. 24, 25, 'Who gave Jacob for a spoil, and Israel to the robbers? did not the Lord, he against whom we have sinned? for they would not walk in his ways, neither were they obedient unto his law. Therefore he hath poured upon him the fury of his anger, and the strength of battle: and he hath set him on fire round about, yet he knew not; and it burned him, yet he laid it not to heart.' Stupidity lays a man open to the greatest fury and severity.

The physician, when he findeth that the potion which he hath given his patient will not work, he seconds it with one more violent; and if that will not work, he gives another yet more violent. If a gentle plaster will not serve, then the chirurgeon applies that which is more corroding; and if that will not do, then he makes use of his cauterizing knife. So when the Lord afflicts, and men feel it not; when he strikes, and they grieve not; when he wounds them, and they awake not: then the furnace is made hotter than ever; then his fury burns, then he lays on irons upon irons, bolt upon bolt, and chain upon chain, until he hath made their lives a hell. Afflictions are the saints' diet-drink; and where do you read in all the Scripture that ever any of the saints drunk of this diet-drink, and were not sensible of it.

2. Secondly, A holy, a prudent, silence doth not shut out *prayer for deliverance out of our afflictions.* Though the psalmist lays his hand upon his mouth in the text, yet he prays for deliverance: ver. 10, 'Remove thy stroke away from me;' and ver. 11, 12, 'Hear my prayer, O Lord! and give ear unto my cry; hold not thy peace at my tears; for I am a stranger with thee, and a sojourner, as all my fathers were. Oh spare me, that I may recover strength, before I go hence and be no more;' James v. 13, 'Is any among you afflicted? let him pray;' Ps. l. 15, 'Call upon me in the day of trouble: I will deliver thee, and thou shalt glorify me.' Times of affliction, by God's own injunction, are special times of supplication.[2] David's heart was more often out of tune than his harp; but then he prays and presently cries, 'Return to thy rest, O my soul.' Jonah prays in the whale's belly, and Daniel prays when among the lions, and Job prays when on the dunghill, and Jeremiah prays when in the dungeon, &c.; yea, the heathen mariners, as stout as they were, when in a storm, they cry every man to his god, Jonah i. 5, 6. To call upon God, especially in times of distress and trouble, is a lesson that the very light and law of nature teaches. The Persian messenger, though an heathen, as Æschylus observeth, saith thus: 'When the Grecian forces hotly pursued our host, and we must needs venture over the great water Strymon, frozen then, but beginning to thaw, when a hundred to one we had all died for it, with mine eyes I saw, saith he, many of those gallants whom I had heard before so boldly maintain there was no God, every one upon his knees, and devoutly praying that the ice might hold till they got over.'[3] And shall blind nature do more than grace? If the time of affliction be not a time of supplication, I know not what is.

As there are two kinds of antidotes against poison, viz. hot and cold,

[1] No judgment to a stupid spirit, a hardened heart, and a brazen brow.

[2] It is an old saying, *Qui nescit orare, discat navigare,* he that would learn to pray, let him go to sea.

[3] Cf. Æschylus, *Suppl.* 258; *Agam.* 192.—G.

so there are two kinds of antidotes against all the troubles and afflictions of this life, viz. prayer and patience: the one hot, the other cold; the one quenching, the other quickening. Chrysostom understood this well enough when he cried out: Oh! saith he, it is more bitter than death to be spoiled of prayer; and thereupon observes that Daniel chose rather to run the hazard of his life than to lose his prayer. Well! this is the second thing. A holy silence doth not exclude prayer; but,

3. Thirdly, A holy, a prudent silence doth not exclude *men's being kindly affected and afflicted with their sins as the meritorious cause of all their sorrows and sufferings.*[1] Lam. iii. 39, 40, 'Wherefore doth a living man complain, a man for the punishment of his sin? Let us search and try our ways, and turn again to the Lord;' Job xl. 4, 5, 'Behold, I am vile, what shall I answer thee? I will lay my hand upon my mouth. Once have I spoken, but I will not answer; yea, twice, but I proceed no further;' Micah vii. 9, 'I will bear the indignation of the Lord, because I have sinned.' In all our sorrows we should read our sins; and when God's hand is upon our backs, our hands should be upon our sins.

It was a good saying of one, 'I hide not my sins, but I shew them; I wipe them not away, but I sprinkle them; I do not excuse them, but accuse them. The beginning of my salvation is the knowledge of my transgression.'[2] When some told Prince Henry,[3] that *deliciæ generis humani*, that darling of mankind, that the sins of the people brought that affliction on him, Oh no! said he, I have sins enough of my own to cause that. 'I have sinned, saith David, but what have these poor sheep done?' 2 Sam. xxiv. 17. When a Christian is under the afflicting hand of God, he may well say, I may thank this proud heart of mine, this worldly heart, this froward heart, this formal heart, this dull heart, this backsliding heart, this self-seeking heart of mine; for that this cup is so bitter, this pain so grievous, this loss so great, this disease so desperate, this wound so incurable; it is mine own self, mine own sin, that hath caused these floods of sorrows to break in upon me. But,

4. Fourthly, A holy, a prudent silence doth not exclude *the teaching and instructing of others when we are afflicted.* The words of the afflicted stick close; they many times work strongly, powerfully, strangely, savingly, upon the souls and consciences of others. Many of Paul's epistles were written to the churches when he was in bonds, viz., Galatians, Ephesians, Philippians, Colossians, Philemon; he begot Onesimus in his bonds, Philem. 10. And many of the brethren in the Lord waxed bold and confident by his bonds, and were confirmed, and made partakers of grace by his ministry, when he was in bonds, Philip. i. 7, 13, 14. As the words of dying persons do many times stick and work gloriously, so many times do the words of afflicted persons work very nobly and efficaciously. I have read of one Adrianus, who, seeing the martyrs suffer such grievous things for the cause of Christ, he asked what that was which enabled them to suffer such things? and one of them named that 1 Cor. ii. 9, 'Eye hath not seen, nor ear heard,

[1] Read Ezra ix.; Neh ix; Dan. ix. 5, 15, with Job vii. [2] [Joh. Lud.] Vivaldus.
[3] Son of James I., whose death was 'married to immortal verse' by George Chapman.—G.

neither have entered into the heart of man, the things which God hath prepared for them that love him.' This word was like apples of gold in pictures of silver, Prov. xxv. 11, for it made him not only a convert, but a martyr too. And this was the means of Justin Martyr's conversion, as himself confesseth. Doubtless, many have been made happy by the words of the afflicted. The tongue of the afflicted hath been to many as choice silver. The words of the afflicted many times are both pleasing and profitable; they tickle the ear and they win upon the heart; they slide insensibly into the hearers' souls, and work efficaciously upon the hearers' hearts: Eccles. x. 12, 'The words of a wise man's mouth are gracious,' or grace, as the Hebrew hath it; and so Jerome reads it, *Verba oris sapientis gratia*, the words of the mouth of a wise man are grace. They minister grace to others, and they win grace and favour from others. Gracious lips make gracious hearts; gracious words are a grace, an ornament to the speaker, and they are a comfort, a delight, and an advantage to the hearer.

Now, the words of a wise man's mouth are never more gracious than when he is most afflicted and distressed. Now, you shall find most worth and weight in his words; now his lips, like the spouse's, are like a thread of scarlet; they are red with talking much of a crucified Christ, and they are thin like a thread, not swelled with vain and unprofitable discourses. Now his mouth speaketh of wisdom, and his tongue talketh judgment, for the law of the Lord is in his heart, Ps. xxxvii. 30; now his lips drop as honey-combs, Cant. iv. 11; now his tongue is a tree of life, whose leaves are medicinable, Prov. xii. 18. As the silver trumpets sounded most joy to the Jews in the day of their gladness, so the mouth of a wise man, like a silver trumpet, sounds most joy and advantage to others in the days of his sadness, Num. x. 10.

The heathen man could say, *Quando sapiens loquitur, aulea animi aperit*, when a wise man speaketh, he openeth the rich treasure and wardrobe of his mind; so may I say, when an afflicted saint speaks, Oh the pearl, the treasures that he scatters! But,

5. Fifthly, A holy, a prudent silence doth not exclude *moderate mourning or weeping under the afflicting hand of God.* Isa. xxxviii. 3, 'And Hezekiah wept sore,' or, as the Hebrew hath it, 'wept with great weeping.[1] But was not the Lord displeased with him for his great weeping? No; ver. 5, 'I have heard thy prayers, I have seen thy tears: behold, I will add unto thy days fifteen years.' God had as well a bottle for his tears, as a bag for his sins, Ps. lvi. 8. There is no water so sweet as the saints' tears, when they do not overflow the banks of moderation. Tears are not mutes; they have a voice, and their oratory is of great prevalency with the almighty God. And therefore the weeping prophet calleth out for tears: Lam. ii. 18, 'Their heart crieth unto the Lord, O wall of the daughter of Zion, let tears run down like a river day and night: give thyself no rest; let not the apple of thine eye cease;' or, as the Hebrew hath it, 'let not the daughters of thine eye be silent.'[2] That which we call the ball or apple of the eye, the Hebrews call the daughter of the eye, because it is as dear and

[1] Ps. vi. 6; xxxix. 1; Jer. ix. 1, 2; Lam. i.; ii. 11, 18.

[2] And the Greeks call the apple of the eye, the damsel of the eye, the girl of the eye; and the Latins call it the babe of the eye.

tender to a man as an only daughter; and because therein appears the likeness of a little daughter. Upon which words, saith Bellarmine, *Clames assiduè ad Deum, non lingua, sed oculis, non verbis sed lachrymis, ista enim est oratio, quæ pacare solet:* cry aloud, not with thy tongue, but with thine eyes; not with thy words, but with thy tears; for that is the prayer that maketh the most forcible entry into the ears of the great God of heaven. When God strikes, he looks that we should tremble; when his hand is lifted high, he looks that our hearts should stoop low; when he hath the rod in his hand, he looks that we should have tears in our eyes, as you may see by comparing of these scriptures together, Ps. lv. 2, xxxviii. 6, Job xxx. 26–32. Good men weep easily, saith the Greek poet;[1] and the better any are, are more inclining to weeping, especially under affliction: as you may see in David, whose tears, instead of gems, were the common ornaments of his bed, Jonathan, Job, Ezra, Daniel, &c. How, saith one, shall God wipe away my tears in heaven, if I shed none on earth? And how shall I reap in joy, if I sow not in tears? I was born with tears, and I shall die with tears; and why then should I live without them in this valley of tears?

There is as well a time to weep, as there is a time to laugh; and a time to mourn, as well as a time to dance, Eccles. iii. 4. The mourning garment among the Jews was the black garment, and the black garment was the mourning garment: Ps. xliii. 2, 'Why go ye mourning?' The Hebrew word *Kedar* signifies black. Why go ye in black? Sometimes Christians must put off their gay ornaments, and put on their black, their mourning garments, Exod. xxxiii. 3–6. But,

6. Sixthly, A gracious, a prudent silence doth not exclude *sighing, groaning, or roaring under afflictions.*[2] A man may sigh, and groan, and roar under the hand of God, and yet be silent. It is not sighing, but muttering; it is not groaning, but grumbling; it is not roaring, but murmuring, that is opposite to a holy silence: Exod. ii. 23, 'And the children of Israel sighed by reason of the bondage.' Job iii. 24, 'For my sighing cometh before I eat,' (or, as the Hebrew hath it) 'before my meat;' his sighing, like bad weather, came unsent for and unsought: so Ps. xxxviii. 9, 'Lord, all my desire is before thee; and my groaning is not hid from thee.' Ps. cii. 5, 'By reason of the voice of my groaning, my bones cleave to my skin.' Job iii. 24, 'And my roarings are poured out like the waters.' Ps. xxxviii. 8, 'I am feeble and sore broken; I have roared by reason of the disquietness of my heart.' Ps. xxii. 1, 'My God! my God! why hast thou forsaken me? why art thou so far from helping me, from the words of my roaring?' Ps. xxxii. 3, 'When I kept silence, my bones waxed old, through my roarings all the day long.' He roars, but doth not rage; he roars, but doth not repine. When a man is in extremity, nature prompts him to roar, and the law of grace is not against it; and though sighing, roaring, groaning, cannot deliver a man out of his misery, yet they do give some ease to a man under his misery. When Solon wept for his son's death, one said to him, Weeping will not help. He answered, Alas!

[1] Cf. Seneca de Consolatione ad Polybium, iv. § 2, and Juvenal, xv. 133.—G.

[2] You may see much of this by comparing the following scriptures: Lam. iv. 4, 11, 21, 22; Ps. xxxi. 10; Jer. xlv. 3; Exod. ii. 24; Job xxiii. 8; Ps. vi. 6.

therefore do I weep, because weeping will not help. So a Christian many times sighs, because sighing will not help; and he groans, because groaning will not help; and he roars, because roaring will not help. Sometimes the sorrows of the saints are so great, that all tears are dried up, and they can get no ease by weeping; and therefore for a little ease they fall a-sighing and groaning; and this may be done, and yet the heart may be quiet and silent before the Lord. Peter wept and sobbed, and yet was silent. Sometimes the sighs and groans of a saint do in some sort tell that which his tongue can in no sort utter. But,

7. Seventhly, A holy, a prudent silence, doth not exclude nor shut out *the use of any just or lawful means, whereby persons may be delivered out of their afflictions.*[1] God would not have his people so in love with their afflictions, as not to use such righteous means as may deliver them out of their afflictions: Mat. x. 23, 'But when they persecute you in this city, flee you into another;' Acts xii. 5, When Peter was in prison, the saints thronged together to pray, as the original hath it, ver. 12; and they were so instant and earnest with God in prayer, they did so beseech and besiege the Lord, they did so beg and bounce at heaven-gate, ver. 5, that God could have no rest, till, by many miracles of power and mercy, he had returned Peter as a bosom-favour to them: Acts ix. 23–25, 'And after that many days were fulfilled, the Jews took counsel to kill him: but their laying await was known of Saul: and they watched the gates day and night to kill him. Then the disciples took him by night, and let him down by the wall in a basket.' The blood of the saints is precious in God's eye, and it should not be vile in their own eyes. When providence opens a door of escape there is no reason why the saints should set themselves as marks and butts for their enemies to shoot at: 2 Thes. iii. 1, 2, the apostles desire the brethren 'to pray for them, that they may be delivered from unreasonable (ἄτοποι, absurd) and wicked (πονηρῶν, villainous) men; for all men have not faith.' It is a mercy worth a seeking, to be delivered out of the hands of absurd, villainous, and troublesome men.

Afflictions are evil in themselves, and we may desire and endeavour to be delivered from them, James v. 14, 15, Isa. xxxviii. 18–21; both inward and outward means are to be used for our own preservation. Had not Noah built an ark, he had been swept away with the flood, though he had been with Nimrod and his crew on the tower of Babel, which was raised to the height of one thousand five hundred forty-six paces, as Heylin reports.[2] Though we may not trust in means, yet we may and ought to use the means; in the use of them, eye that God that can only bless them, and you do your work. As the pilot that guides the ship hath his hand upon the rudder, and his eye on the star that directs him at the same time; so when your hand is upon the means, let your eye be upon your God, and deliverance will come. We may neglect God as well by neglecting of means as by trusting in means; it is best to use them, and in the use of them, to live above them. Augustine tells of a man, that being fallen into a pit, one passing by falls a-questioning of him, what he made there, and how he came in? Oh! said the poor

[1] 2 Kings v. 14, 15; Mat. iv. 6, 7; xxii. 4, 5, 8; Luke xiv. 16–24; Acts xxvii. 24, 25, 31.

[2] Heylin Cosm. l. iii.

man, ask me not how I came in, but help me and tell me how I may come out. The application is easy. But,

8. Eighthly, and lastly, A holy, a prudent silence, doth not exclude *a just and sober complaining against the authors, contrivers, abettors, or instruments of our afflictions:* 2 Tim. iv. 14, 'Alexander the coppersmith did me much evil; the Lord reward him according to his works.' This Alexander is conceived by some to be that Alexander that is mentioned, Acts xix. 33, who stood so close to Paul at Ephesus, that he run the hazard of losing his life by appearing on his side;[1] yet if glorious professors come to be furious persecutors, Christians may complain: 2 Cor. xi. 24, 'Of the Jews five times received I forty stripes, save one.' They inflict, saith Maimonides, no more than forty stripes, though he be as strong as Samson, but if he be weak, they abate of that number. They scourged Paul with the greatest severity, in making him suffer so oft the utmost extremity of the Jewish law, whenas they that were weak had their punishment mitigated: ver. 25, 'Thrice was I beaten with rods,' that is, by the Romans, whose custom it was to beat the guilty with rods.

If Pharaoh make Israel groan, Israel may make his complaint against Pharaoh to the Keeper of Israel, Exod. ii.; if the proud and blasphemous king of Assyria shall come with his mighty army to destroy the people of the Lord, Hezekiah may spread his letter of blasphemy before the Lord, Isa. xxxvii. 14-21.

It was the saying of Socrates, that every man in this life had need of a faithful friend and a bitter enemy; the one to advise him, and the other to make him look about him; and this Hezekiah found by experience.

Though Joseph's bow abode in strength, and the arm of his hands were made strong by the hands of the mighty God of Jacob, yet Joseph may say, that the archers, or the arrow-masters, as the Hebrew hath it, have sorely grieved him, and shot at him, and hated him, Gen. xlix. 23, 24. And so David sadly complained of Doeg, Ps. cix. 1, 21; yea, Christ himself, who was the most perfect pattern for dumbness and silence under sorest trials, complains against Judas, Pilate, and the rest of his persecutors, Ps. lxix. 20, 30, &c.; yea, though God will make his people's enemies to be the workmen that shall fit them and square them for his building, to be goldsmiths to add pearls to their crown, to be rods to beat off their dust, scullions to scour off their rust, fire to purge away their dross, and water to cleanse away their filthiness, fleshliness, and earthliness, yet may they point at them, and pour out their complaints to God against them, Ps. cxxxii. 2-18. This truth I might make good by above a hundred texts of Scripture; but it is time to come to the reasons of the point.

IV. *Why must Christians be mute and silent under the greatest afflictions, the saddest providences, and sharpest trials that they meet with in this world?* I answer,

Reason 1. *That they may the better hear and understand the voice of the rod.* As the word hath a voice, the Spirit a voice, and conscience

[1] Calvin *in loc.* assumes this, designating him as one *martyris propinquus*; and Trapp adds, Brooks-like, 'A glorious professor may become a furious persecutor.'—G.

a voice, so the rod hath a voice.[1] Afflictions are the rod of God's anger, the rod of his displeasure, and his rod of revenge; he gives a commission to his rod, to awaken his people, to reform his people, or else to revenge the quarrel of his covenant upon them, if they will not bear the rod, and kiss the rod, and sit mute and silent under the rod: Micah vi. 9, 'The Lord's voice crieth unto the city, and the man of wisdom shall see thy name: hear ye the rod, and who hath appointed it.' God's rods are not mutes, they are all vocal, they are all speaking as well as smiting; every twig hath a voice. Ah! soul, saith one twig, thou sayest it smarts; well! tell me, is it good provoking of a jealous God? Jer. iv. 18. Ah! soul, saith another twig, thou sayest it is bitter, it reacheth to thy heart, but hath not thine own doings procured these things? Rom. vi. 20, 21. Ah! soul, saith another twig, where is the profit, the pleasure, the sweet that you have found in wandering from God? Hosea ii. 7. Ah! soul, saith another twig, was it not best with you, when you were high in your communion with God, and when you were humble and close in your walking with God? Micah vi. 8. Ah! Christian, saith another twig, wilt thou search thy heart, and try thy ways, and turn to the Lord thy God? Lam. iii. 40. Ah! soul, saith another twig, wilt thou die to sin more than ever, and to the world more than ever, and to relations more than ever, and to thyself more than ever? Rom. xiv. 6–8; Gal. vi. 18. Ah! soul, saith another twig, wilt thou live more to Christ than ever, and cleave closer to Christ than ever, and prize Christ more than ever, and venture further for Christ than ever? Ah! soul, saith another twig, wilt thou love Christ with a more inflamed love, and hope in Christ with a more raised hope, and depend upon Christ with a greater confidence, and wait upon Christ with more invincible patience, &c.? Now, if the soul be not mute and silent under the rod, how is it possible that it should ever hear the voice of the rod, or that it should ever hearken to the voice of every twig of the rod? The rod hath a voice that is in the hands of earthly fathers, but children hear it not, they understand it not, till they are hushed and quiet, and brought to kiss it, and sit silently under it; no more shall we hear or understand the voice of the rod that is in our heavenly Father's hand, till we come to kiss it, and sit silently under it. But,

Reason 2. Gracious souls should be mute and silent under their greatest afflictions and sharpest trials, *that they may difference and distinguish themselves from the men of the world, who usually fret and fling, mutter or murmur, curse and swagger, when they are under the afflicting hand of God:* Isa. viii. 21, 22, 'And they shall pass through it hardly bestead and hungry: and it shall come to pass, that, when they shall be hungry, they shall fret themselves, and curse their king, and their God, and look upward. And they shall look unto the earth; and behold trouble and darkness, dimness of anguish; and they shall be driven to darkness.' Ah! how fretful and froward, how disturbed and distracted, how mad and forlorn, are these poor wretches under the rebukes of God! They look upward and downward, this way and that way, on this side and on that, and finding no help, no succour, no support, no deliverance, like Bedlams, yea, like incarnate devils, they fall upon cursing of God, and their king: Isa. lix. 11, 'We

[1] *Schola crucis est schola lucis.*

roar all like bears, and mourn sore like doves: we look for judgment, but there is none; for salvation, but it is far from us.'[1] They express their inward vexation and indignation by roaring like bears. When bears are robbed of their whelps, or taken in a pit, oh how dreadfully will they roar, rage, tear, and tumble! So when wicked persons are fallen into the pit of affliction, oh how will they roar, rage, tear, and cry out! not of their sins, but of their punishments; as Cain, 'My punishment is greater than I am able to bear,' Gen. iv. 13; Isa. li. 20, 'Thy sons have fainted, they lie at the head of all the streets, as a wild bull in a net: they are full of the fury of the Lord, the rebuke of thy God.' When the huntsman hath taken the wild bull in his toil, and so entangled him, that he is not able to wind himself out, oh, how fierce and furious will he be! how will he spend himself in struggling to get out! Such wild bulls are wicked men, when they are taken in the net of affliction.

It is said of Marcellus the Roman general, that he could not be quiet, *nec victor, nec victus*, neither conquered nor conqueror! It is so with wicked men; they cannot be quiet, neither full nor fasting, neither sick nor well, neither in wealth nor want, neither in bonds nor at liberty, neither in prosperity nor in adversity: Jer. li. 37, 38, 'And Babylon shall become heaps, a dwelling-place for dragons, an astonishment, and an hissing, without an inhabitant. They shall roar together like lions: and they shall yell as lions' whelps.' When the lion roars, all the beasts of the field tremble, Amos iii. 8. When the lion roars, many creatures that could outrun him are so amazed and astonished at the terror of his roar, that they are not able to stir from the place.[2] Such roaring lions are wicked men, when they are under the smarting rod: Rev. xvi. 9–12, 'They gnaw their tongues for pain, and they blaspheme the God of heaven, because of those sores, pains, and plagues that are poured upon them; and they repented not of their deeds, to give him glory.' And therefore gracious souls have cause to be silent under their sorest trials, that they may difference and distinguish themselves from wicked men, who are 'like the troubled sea, when it cannot rest, whose waters cast up mire and dirt,' Isa. lvii. 20. The verb רשע, signifies to make a stir, to be exceeding busy, unquiet, or troublesome. Ah! what a stir do wicked men make, when they are under the afflicting hand of God! Ah! the sea is restless and unquiet when there is no storm; it cannot stand still, but hath his flux and reflux; so it is much more restless, when by tempest upon tempest it is made to roar and rage, to foam and cast up mire and dirt. The raging sea is a fit emblem of a wicked man that is under God's afflicting hand.

Reason 3. A third reason why gracious souls should be silent and mute under their sharpest trials is, *that they may be conformable to Christ their head, who was dumb and silent under his sorest trials:* Isa. liii. 7, 'He was oppressed, and he was afflicted; yet he opened not his mouth: he is brought as a lamb to the slaughter; and as a sheep before his shearers is dumb, so he opened not his mouth.' Christ was tongue-tied under all his sorrows and sufferings: 1 Peter ii. 21–23,

[1] The bear, as Aristotle observeth, licketh her whelps into form, and loveth them beyond measure, and is most fierce, roaring and raging when she is robbed of them. [Cf. Pliny, *sub voce*.—G.]

[2] Ambrose on Amos iii. 3.

'Christ also suffered for us, leaving us an example, that ye should follow his steps: who did no sin, neither was guile found in his mouth: who, when he was reviled, reviled not again; when he suffered, he threatened not; but committed himself to him that judgeth righteously.'[1] Christ upon the cross did not only read us a lecture of patience and silence, but he hath also set us ὑπογραμμὸν, a copy or pattern of both, to be transcribed and imitated by us when we are under the smarting rod. It will be our sin and shame if we do not bear up with patience and silence under all our sufferings, considering what an admirable copy Christ hath set before us. It is said of Antiochus, that being to fight with Judas, captain of the host of the Jews, he shewed unto his elephants the blood of the grapes and mulberries, to provoke them the better to fight.[2] So the Holy Ghost hath set before us the injuries and contumelies, the sorrows and sufferings, the pains and torments, the sweat and blood of our dearest Lord, and his invincible patience, and admirable silence under all, to provoke us and encourage us to imitate the Captain of our salvation, in patience and silence under all our sufferings.

Jerome having read the life and death of Hilarion,—one that lived graciously and died comfortably,—folded up the book, saying, Well! Hilarion shall be the champion that I will follow; his good life shall be my example, and his good death my precedent. Oh! how much more should we all say, We have read how Christ hath been afflicted, oppressed, distressed, despised, persecuted, &c.; and we have read how dumb, how tongue-tied, how patient, and how silent he hath been under all; oh! he shall be the copy which we shall write after, the pattern which we will walk by, the champion which we will follow. But, alas! alas! how rare is it to find a man that may be applauded with the eulogy of Salvian, *Singularis domini preclarus imitator*, an excellent disciple of a singular master. The heathens had this notion amongst them, as Lactantius reports, that the way to honour their gods was to be like them;[3] and therefore some would be wicked, counting it a dishonour to their gods to be unlike to them. I am sure the way to honour our Christ, is in patience and silence to be like to Christ, especially when a smarting rod is upon our backs, and a bitter cup put into our hands.

Reason 4. The fourth reason why the people of God should be mute and silent under their afflictions, is this, because *it is ten thousand times a greater judgment and affliction, to be given up to a fretful spirit, a froward spirit, a muttering or murmuring spirit under an affliction, than it is to be afflicted.* This is both the devil's sin, and the devil's punishment. God is still afflicting, crossing and vexing of him, and he is still a-fretting, repining, vexing, and rising up against God. No sin to the devil's sin, no punishment to the devil's punishment. A man were better to have all the afflictions of all the afflicted throughout the world at once upon him, than to be given up to a froward spirit, to a muttering, murmuring heart under the least affliction.

[1] Justin Martyr being asked which was the greatest miracle that our Saviour Christ wrought, answered, *Patientia ejus tanta in laboribus tantis*, his so great patience in so great trouble.

[2] 1 Macc. vi. 34. [Third quotation from Apocrypha thus far.—G.]

[3] The Arabians, if their king be sick or lame, they all feign themselves so.

When thou seest a soul fretting, vexing, and stamping under the mighty hand of God, thou seest one of Satan's first-born, one that resembles him to the life.[1] No child can be so much like the father, as this froward soul is like to the father of lies; though he hath been in chains almost this six thousand years, yet he hath never lain still one day, nor one night, no nor one hour in all this time, but is still a-fretting, vexing, tossing and tumbling in his chains, like a princely bedlam. He is a lion, not a lamb; a roaring lion, not a sleepy lion; not a lion standing still, but a lion going up and down; he is not satisfied with the prey he hath got, but is restless in his designs to fill hell with souls, 1 Pet. v. 8. He never wants an apple for an Eve, nor a grape for a Noah, nor a change of raiment for a Gehazi, nor a wedge of gold for an Achan, nor a crown for an Absalom, nor a bag for a Judas, nor a world for a Demas. If you look into one company, there you shall find Satan a-dishing out his meat to every palate; if you look into another company, there you shall find him fitting a last to every shoe; if you look into a third company, there you shall find him suiting a garment to every back. He is under wrath, and cannot but be restless. Here, with Jael, he allures poor souls in with milk, and murders them with a nail; there, with Joab, he embraces with one hand, and stabs with another. Here with Judas, he kisses and betrays; and there, with the whore of Babylon, he presents a golden cup with poison in it. He cannot be quiet, though his bolts be always on; and the more unquiet any are under the rebukes of God, the more such resemble Satan to the life, whose whole life is filled up with vexing and fretting against the Lord. Let not any think, saith Luther, that the devil is now dead, nor yet asleep, for as he that keepeth Israel, so he that hateth Israel, neither slumbereth nor sleepeth. But in the next place,

Reason 5. A fifth reason why gracious souls should be mute and silent under the greatest afflictions and sharpest trials that do befall them is this, because *a holy, a prudent silence under afflictions, under miseries, doth best capacitate and fit the afflicted for the receipt of miseries.*[2] When the rolling bottle lies still, you may pour into it your sweetest or your strongest waters; when the rolling, tumbling soul lies still, then God can best pour into it the sweet waters of mercy, and the strong waters of divine consolation. You read of the 'peaceable fruits of righteousness': Heb. xii. 11, 'Now no chastening for the present seemeth to be joyous, but grievous; nevertheless, afterwards it yieldeth the peaceable fruits of righteousness unto them which are exercised thereby;' James iii. 18, 'And the fruit of righteousness is sown in peace, of them that make peace.' The still and quiet soul is like a ship that lies still and quiet in the harbour; you may take in what goods, what commodities you please, whilst the ship lies quiet and still: so when the soul is quiet and still under the hand of God, it is most fitted and advantaged to take in much of God, of Christ, of heaven, of the promises, of ordinances, and of the love of God, the smiles of God, the communications of God, and the counsel of God; but when souls are unquiet, they are like a ship in a storm, they can take in nothing.[3]

Luther, speaking of God, saith, God doth not dwell in Babylon, but

[1] Irenæus calleth such *ora diaboli*, the devil's mouth. [2] Qu. 'mercies'?—Ed.
[3] The angels are most quiet and still, and they take in most of God, of Christ, of heaven.

in Salem. Babylon signifies confusion, and Salem signifies peace. Now God dwells not in spirits that are unquiet and in confusion, but he dwells in peaceable and quiet spirits. Unquiet spirits can take in neither counsel nor comfort, grace nor peace, &c.: Ps. lxxvii. 2, 'My soul refused to be comforted.' The impatient patient will take down no cordials; he hath no eye to see, nor hand to take, nor palate to relish, nor stomach to digest anything that makes for his health and welfare. When the man is sick and froward, nothing will down; the sweetest music will make no melody in his ears: Exod. vi. 6–9, 'Wherefore, say unto the children of Israel, I am the Lord, and I will bring you out from under the burdens of the Egyptians, and I will rid you out of their bondage, and I will redeem you with a stretched-out arm, and with great judgment. And I will take you to me for a people, and I will be to you a God, and ye shall know that I am the Lord your God, which bringeth you out from under the burdens of the Egyptians. And I will bring you in unto the land concerning the which I did sware to give it to Abraham, to Isaac, and to Jacob, and I will give it to you for a heritage; I am the Lord.' The choicest cordials and comforts that heaven or earth could afford are here held forth to them, but they have no hand to receive them. Here Moses his lips drops honey-combs, but they can taste no sweetness in them. Here the best of earth and the best of heaven is set before them, but their souls are shut up, and nothing will down. Here is such ravishing music of paradise as might abundantly delight their hearts and please their ears, but they cannot hear. Here are soul-enlivening, soul-supporting, soul-strengthening, soul-comforting, soul-raising, and soul-refreshing words, but they cannot hearken to them: ver. 9, 'And Moses spake so unto the children of Israel, but they hearkened not unto Moses, for anguish of spirit, and for cruel bondage.' They were under their anguish[1] feverish fits, and so could neither hear nor see, taste nor take in, anything that might be a mercy or a comfort to them.[2] They were sick of impatiency and discontent: and these humours being grown strong, nothing would take with them, nothing would agree with them. When persons are under strong pangs of passion, they have no ears neither for reason nor religion.

Reason 6. A sixth reason why gracious souls should be silent under the smarting rod, is this, viz., because *it is fruitless, it is bootless to strive, to contest or contend with God.* No man hath ever got anything by muttering or murmuring under the hand of God, except it hath been more frowns, blows, and wounds. Such as will not lie quiet and still, when mercy hath tied them with silken cords, justice will put them in iron chains; if golden fetters will not hold you, iron shall.[3] If Jonah will vex and fret and fling, justice will fling him overboard, to cool him, and quell him, and keep him prisoner in the whale's belly, till his stomach be brought down, and his spirit be made quiet before the Lord. What you get by struggling and grumbling, you may put in your eye, and weep it out when you have done: Jer. vii. 19, 'Do they provoke me to anger, saith the Lord? Do they not provoke them-

[1] Qu. 'aguish'?—Ed. [2] No air agrees well with weak, peevish, sickly bodies.

[3] If bedlams will not lie quiet, they are put into darker rooms, and heavier chains are put upon them.

selves to the confusion of their own faces?' By provoking of me, they do but provoke themselves; by angering of me, they do but anger themselves; by vexing of me, they do but fret and vex themselves: 1 Cor. x. 22, 'Do we provoke the Lord to jealousy? Are we stronger than he?' Zanchy[1] observes these two things from these words:

1. That it is ill provoking God to wrath, because he is stronger than we.

2. That though God be stronger than we, yet there are those who provoke him to wrath; and certainly there are none that do more provoke him than those who fume and fret when his hand is upon them. Though the cup be bitter, yet it is put into your hand by your Father; though the cross be heavy, yet he that hath laid it on your shoulders will bear the heaviest end of it himself; and why, then, should you mutter? Shall bears and lions take blows and knocks from their keepers, and wilt thou not take a few blows and knocks from the keeper of Israel? Why should the clay contend with the potter, or the creature with his creator, or the servant with his lord, or weakness with strength, or a poor nothing creature with an omnipotent God? Can stubble stand before the fire? Can chaff abide before the whirlwind? or can a worm ward off the blow of the Almighty? A froward and impatient spirit under the hand of God will but add chain to chain, cross to cross, yoke to yoke, and burden to burden. The more men tumble and toss in their feverish fits, the more they strengthen the distemper, and the longer it will be before the cure be effected. The easiest and the surest way of cure is to lie still and quiet till the poison of the distemper be sweat out. Where patience hath its perfect work, there the cure will be certain and easy. When a man hath his broken leg set, he lies still and quiet, and so his cure is easily and speedily wrought; but when a horse's leg is set, he frets and flings, he flounces and flies out, unjointing it again and again, and so his cure is the more difficult and tedious. Such Christians that under the hand of God are like the horse or mule, fretting and flinging, will but add to their own sorrows and sufferings, and put the day of their deliverance further off.

Reason 7. A seventh reason why Christians should be mute and silent under their afflictions is, because hereby they *shall cross and frustrate Satan's great design and expectation.* In all the afflictions he brought upon Job, his design was not so much to make Job a beggar as it was to make him a blasphemer; it was not so much to make Job outwardly miserable, as it was to make Job inwardly miserable, by occasioning him to mutter and murmur against the righteous hand of God, that so he might have had some matter of accusation against him to the Lord. He is the unwearied accuser of the brethren: Rev. xii. 10, 'The accuser of the brethren is cast down, which accuseth them before our God day and night.' Satan is the great make-bait between God and his children. He hath a mint constantly going in hell, where, as an untired mint-master, he is still a-coining and hammering out of accusations against the saints. First, he tempts and allures souls to sin, and then accuses them of those very sins he hath tempted them to, that so he may disgrace them before God, and bring them, if it were possible, out of favour with God; and though he knows beforehand

[1] Jerome Zanchius, not to be confounded with his contemporary Basil Zanchius.—G.

that God and his people are, by the bond of the covenant, and by the blood of the Redeemer, so closely united that they can never be severed, yet such is his rage and wrath, envy and malice, that he will endeavour that which he knows he shall never effect. Could he but have made Job froward or fretful under the rod, he would have quickly carried the tidings to heaven, and have been so bold as to have asked God whether this was a carriage becoming such a person, of whom himself had given so glorious a character.[1] Satan knows that there is more evil in the least sin, than there is in all the afflictions that can be inflicted upon a person; and if he could but have made a breach upon Job's patience, ah, how would he have insulted over God himself! could he but have made Job a mutineer, he would quickly have pleaded for martial law to have been executed upon him; but Job, by remaining mute and silent under all his trials, puts Satan to a blush, and spoils all his projects at once. The best way to outwit the devil, is to be silent under the hand of God; he that mutters is foiled by him, but he that is mute overcomes him, and to conquer a devil is more than to conquer a world.

Reason 8. The eighth and last reason why Christians should be silent and mute under their sorest trials, is this, *that they may be conformable to those noble patterns that are set before them by other saints, who have been patient and silent under the smarting rod.*[2] As Aaron, Lev. x. 3; so Eli, 1 Sam. iii. 18; so David, 2 Sam. xvi. 7–13; so Job, chap. i. 21, 22; so Eliakim, Shebnah, and Joab, Isa. xxxvi. 11, 12. So those saints in that Acts xxi. 12–15; and that cloud of witnesses, pointed at in Heb. xii. 1. Gracious examples are more awakening, more convincing, more quickening, more provoking, and more encouraging than precepts, because in them we see that the exercise of grace and godliness is possible, though it be difficult. When we see Christians, that are subject to like infirmities with ourselves, mute and silent under the afflicting hand of God, we see that it is possible that we may attain to the same noble temper of being tongue-tied under a smarting rod. Certainly it is our greatest honour and glory, in this world, to be eyeing and imitating the highest and worthiest examples. What Plutarch said of Demosthenes, that he was excellent at praising the worthy acts of his ancestors, but not so at imitating them, may be said of many in these days. Oh! they are very forward and excellent at praising the patience of Job, but not at imitating it; at praising the silence of Aaron, but not at imitating it; at praising David's dumbness, but not at imitating it; at praising Eli's muteness, but not at imitating it. It was the height of Cæsar's glory to walk in the steps of Alexander, and of Selymus,[3] a Turkish emperor, to walk in Cæsar's steps, and of Themistocles to walk in Miltiades's steps. Oh! how much more should we account it our highest glory to imitate the worthy examples of those worthies, of whom this world is not worthy! It speaks out much of God within, when men are striving to write after the fairest copies. And thus much for the reasons of the point. I come now to the application.

[1] That devil that accused God to man (Gen. iii.), and Christ to be an impostor, will make no bones to accuse the saints, when they miscarry under the rod.

[2] *Præcepta docent, exempla movent*, Precepts may instruct, but examples do persuade. before.—G.] [3] Solyman?—G.

V. You see, beloved, by what hath been said, that it is the greatest duty and concernment of Christians to be mute and silent under the greatest afflictions, the saddest providences, and the sharpest trials that they meet with in this world. If this be so, then this truth looks sourly and wistly[1] upon several sorts of persons. As,

1. *First*, This looks sourly and sadly *upon murmurers, upon such as do nothing but mutter and murmur under the afflicting hand of God.* This was Israel's sin of old,[2] and this is England's sin this day. Ah! what murmuring is there against God, what murmuring against instruments, and what murmuring against providences, is to be found amongst us! Some murmur at what they have lost, others murmur at what they fear they shall lose; some murmur that they are no higher, others murmur because they are so low; some murmur because such a party rules, and others mutter because themselves are not in the saddle; some murmur because their mercies are not so great as others' are; some murmur because their mercies are not so many as others' are; some murmur because they are afflicted, and others murmur because such and such are not afflicted as well as they. Ah, England, England! hadst thou no more sins upon thee, thy murmuring were enough to undo thee, did not God exercise much pity and compassion towards thee. But more of this hereafter, and therefore let this touch for the present suffice.

2. *Secondly*, This truth looks sourly upon those that *fret, chafe, and vex, when they are under the afflicting hand of God.* Many when they feel the rod to smart, ah, how they do fret and fume! Isa. viii. 21, 'When they were hardly bestead and hungry, they fret themselves, and curse their king and their God;' Prov. xix. 3, 'The foolishness of man perverteth his way, and his heart fretteth against the Lord.' The heart may be fretful and froward when the tongue doth not blaspheme. Folly brings man into misery, and misery makes man to fret; man in misery is more apt to fret and chafe against the Lord, than to fret and chafe against his sin that hath brought him into sufferings, 2 Kings vi. 33, Ps. xxxvii. 1, 7, 8. A fretful soul dares let fly at God himself. When Pharaoh is troubled with the frets, he dare spit in the very face of God himself: 'Who is the Lord, that I should obey him?' Exod. v. 2. And when Jonah is in a fretting humour, he dares tell God to his face, 'that he doth well to be angry,' Jonah iv. 8. Jonah had done well if he had been angry with his sin, but he did very ill to be angry with his God. God will vex every vein in that man's heart, before he hath done with him, who fumes and frets, because he cannot snap in sunder the cords with which he is bound, Ezek. xvi. 43. Sometimes good men are sick of the frets, but when they are, it costs them dear, as Job and Jonah found by experience. No man hath ever got anything by his fretting and flinging, except it hath been harder blows or heavier chains; therefore fret not when God strikes.

3. *Thirdly*, This truth looks sourly upon those who *charge God foolishly in the day of their adversity.* Lam. iii. 39, 'Why doth a living man complain?' He that hath deserved a hanging hath no reason to charge the judge with cruelty if he escape with a whipping;

[1] 'Wistfully,' earnestly.—G.

[2] Exod. xvi. 7–9; Numb. xii. 14, xvii. 5, 10; Exod. xv. 24; Deut. i. 27; Ps. cvi. 25.

and we that have deserved a damning have no reason to charge God for being too severe, if we escape with a fatherly lashing.[1] Rather than a man will take the blame, and quietly bear the shame of his own folly, he will put it off upon God himself, Gen. iii. 12. It is a very evil thing, when we shall go to accuse God, that we may excuse ourselves, and unblame ourselves, that we may blame our God, and lay the fault anywhere rather than upon our own hearts and ways. Job was a man of a more noble spirit: Job i. 22, 'In all this Job sinned not, nor charged God foolishly.' When God charges many men home, then they presently charge God foolishly; they put him to bear the brunt and blame of all; but this will be bitterness in the end. When thou art under affliction, thou mayest humbly tell God that thou feelest his hand heavy; but thou must not blame him because his hand is heavy. No man hath ever yet been able to make good a charge against God; and wilt thou be able? Surely no. By charging God foolishly in the day of thy calamity, thou dost but provoke the Lord to charge thee through and through, more fiercely and furiously, with his most deadly darts of renewed misery. It is thy greatest wisdom to blame thy sins, and lay thy hand upon thy mouth; for why should folly charge innocency? That man is far enough off from being mute and silent under the hand of God, who dares charge God himself for laying his hand upon him. But,

4. *Fourthly,* This truth looks sourly and sadly upon such *as will not be silent nor satisfied under the afflicting hand of God,*[2] *except the Lord will give them the particular reasons why he lays his hand upon them.* Good men sometimes dash their feet against this stumbling stone: Jer. xv. 18, 'Why is my pain perpetual, and my wound incurable?' &c. Though God hath always reason for what he doth, yet he is not bound to shew us the reasons of his doings. Jeremiah's passion was up, his blood was hot; and now nothing will silence nor satisfy him but the reasons why his pain was perpetual, and his wound incurable. So Job, chap. vii. 20, 'Why hast thou set me as a mark against thee, so that I am a burden to myself?' It is an evil and a dangerous thing to cavil at or to question his proceedings, who is the chief Lord of all, and who may do with his own what he pleaseth, Rom. ix. 20, Dan. iv. 3, 36. He is unaccountable and uncontrollable; and therefore who shall say, What doest thou? As no man may question his right to afflict him, nor his righteousness in afflicting of him, so no man may question the reasons why he afflicts him. As no man can compel him to give a reason of his doings, so no man may dare to ask him the particular reasons of his doings. Kings think themselves are not bound to give their subjects a reason of their doings; and shall we bind God to give us a reason of his doings, who is the King of kings and Lord of lords, and whose will is the true reason and only rule of justice? Eccles. viii. 4, Rev. i. 5. The general grounds and reasons that God hath laid down in his word why he afflicts his people, as, viz., for their profit, Heb. xii. 10; for the purging away of their sins, Isa. i. 25;

[1] Lam. i. 12; Ps. lxxvii. 7, i. 2; Ezek. xviii. 25; xix. 33; xvii. 20, 29. Some of the heathens, as Homer observes, would lay the evils that they did incur by their own folly upon their gods: so do many upon the true God.

[2] Exod. xxxii. 1; Ps. xxii. 1, 2; Job iii. 11, 12; xix. 11, 13, 14.

for the reforming of their lives, Ps. cxix. 67, 71; and for the saving of their souls, 1 Cor. xi. 32,—should work them to be silent and satisfied under all their afflictions, though God should never satisfy their curiosity in giving them an account of some more hidden causes which may lie secret in the abysses of his eternal knowledge and infallible will. Curiosity is the spiritual drunkenness of the soul; and look, as the drunkard will never be satisfied, be the cup never so deep, unless he see the bottom of it, so some curious Christians, whose souls are overspread with the leprosy of curiosity, will never be satisfied till they come to see the bottom and the most secret reasons of all God's dealings towards them; but they are fools in folio, who affect to know more than God would have them. Did not Adam's curiosity render him and his posterity fools in folio? And what pleasure can we take to see ourselves every day fools in print? As a man by gazing and prying into the body of the sun may grow dark and dim, and see less than otherwise he might, so many, by a curious prying into the secret reasons of God's dealings with them, come to grow so dark and dim, that they cannot see those plain reasons that God hath laid down in his word why he afflicts and tries the children of men.

I have read of one Sir William Champney, in the reign of King Henry the Third, once living in Tower Street, London, who was the first man that ever built a turret on the top of his house, that he might the better overlook all his neighbours, but so it fell out, that not long after he was struck blind; so that he that could not be satisfied to see as others did see, but would needs see more than others, saw just nothing at all, through the just judgment of God upon him.[1] And so it is a just and righteous thing with God to strike such with spiritual blindness, who will not be satisfied with seeing the reasons laid down in the word why he afflicts them, but they must be curiously prying and searching into the hidden and more secret reasons of his severity towards them. Ah, Christian! it is your wisdom and duty to sit silent and mute under the afflicting hand of God upon the account of revealed reasons, without making any curious inquiry into those more secret reasons that are locked up in the golden cabinet of God's own breast, Deut. xxix. 29.

5. *Fifthly,* This truth looks sourly and sadly upon those who, instead of being silent and mute under their afflictions, *use all sinful shifts and ways to shift themselves out of their troubles; who care not though they break with God, and break with men, and break with their own consciences, so they may but break off the chains that are upon them; who care not by what means the prison door is opened, so they may but escape; nor by what hands their bolts are knocked off, so they may be at liberty.* Job xxxvi. 21, 'Take heed, regard not iniquity, for this hast thou chosen rather than affliction.' He makes but an ill choice, who chooses sin rather than suffering; and yet such an ill choice good men have sometimes made, as you may see by the proofs in the margin,[2] when troubles have compassed them round about. Though no lion roars like that in a man's own bosom,—conscience,—yet some, to deliver themselves from troubles without, have set that lion a-roaring

[1] John Stow's 'Survey of London.' [*Sub nomine.*—G.]

[2] 1 Sam. xxi. 12–15; Gen. xii. 12, 15; xx. 18, 20; xxvi. 7–9; Jonah i. 1, *seq.*; 1 Sam. xxviii. throughout.

within. Some, to deliver themselves from outward tortures, have put themselves under inward torments. He purchases his freedom from affliction at too dear a rate, who buys it with the loss of a good name or a good conscience.

Now, because there is even in good men sometimes too great an aptness and proneness to sin and shift themselves out of afflictions, when they should rather be mute and silent under them, give me leave to lay down these six considerations to prevent it.

(1.) First Consider, *that there is infinitely more evil in the least sin than there is in the greatest miseries and afflictions that can possibly come upon you; yea, there is more evil in the least sin than there is in all the troubles that ever come upon the world, yea, than there is in all the miseries and torments of hell.* The least sin is an offence to the great God, it is a wrong to the immortal soul, it is a breach of a righteous law; it cannot be washed away but by the blood of Jesus; it can shut the soul out of heaven, and shut the soul up a close prisoner in hell for ever and ever.[1] The least sin is rather to be avoided and prevented than the greatest sufferings; if this cockatrice be not crushed in the egg, it will soon become a serpent; the very thought of sin, if but thought on, will break out into action, action into custom, custom into habit, and then both body and soul are lost irrecoverably to all eternity. The least sin is very dangerous. Cæsar was stabbed with bodkins; Herod was eaten up of lice; Pope Adrian was choked with a gnat; a mouse is but little, yet killeth an elephant if he gets up into his trunk; a scorpion is little, yet able to sting a lion to death; though the leopard be great, yet he is poisoned with a head of garlic; the least spark may consume the greatest house, and the least leak sink the greatest ship; a whole arm hath been impostumated with the prick of a little finger; a little postern opened may betray the greatest city; a dram of poison diffuseth itself to all parts, till it strangle the vital spirits, and turn out the soul from the body. If the serpent can but wriggle in his tail by an evil thought, he will soon make a surprisal of the soul, as you see in that great instance of Adam and Eve. The trees of the forest, saith one in a parable, held a solemn parliament, wherein they consulted of the innumerable wrongs which the axe had done them, therefore made an act, that no tree should hereafter lend the axe an helve, on pain of being cut down. The axe travels up and down the forest, begs wood of the cedar, oak, ash, elm, even of the poplar; not one would lend him a chip. At last he desired so much as would serve him to cut down the briars and bushes, alleging, that such shrubs as they did but suck away the juice of the ground, and hinder the growth, and obscure the glory of the fair and goodly trees; hereupon they were all content to afford him so much: he pretends a thorough reformation, but behold a sad deformation, for when he had got his helve, down went both cedar, oak, ash, elm, and all that stood in his way.[2] Such are the subtle reaches of sin; it will promise to remove the briars, and business of afflictions

[1] James iii. 5, 11; Prov. viii. 35; 1 John iii. 4; i. 7; Rev. xxi. 8. If you consider sin strictly, there cannot be any little sin, no more than there can be a little God, a little hell, or a little damnation; yet comparatively some sins may be said to be little.

[2] Thomas Adams. See Works, vol. ii. page 359, Sermon, 'The Bad Leaven.' Brooks amplifies the fable.—G.

and troubles, that hinder the soul of that juice, sweetness, comfort, delight, and content that otherwise it might enjoy. Oh! do but now yield a little to it, and instead of removing your troubles, it will cut down your peace, your hopes, your comforts, yea, it will cut down your precious soul. What is the breathing of a vein to the being let blood in the throat, or the scratch on the hand to a stab at the heart? No more are the greatest afflictions to the least sins; and therefore, Christians, never use sinful shifts to shift yourselves out of troubles, but rather be mute and silent under them, till the Lord shall work out your deliverance from them. But,

(2.) Secondly, Consider *it is an impossible thing for any to sin themselves out of their troubles.* Abraham, Job, and Jonah attempted it, but could not effect it. The devils have experienced this near this six thousand years; they had not been now in chains, could they but have sinned themselves out of their chains. Could the damned sin themselves out of everlasting burning, there would have been none now a-roaring in that devouring unquenchable fire, Isa. xxxiii. 14. Hell would have no inhabitants, could they but sin themselves out of it. Ah! Christians, devils and damned spirits shall as soon sin themselves out of hell, as you shall be able to sin yourselves out of your afflictions. Christians! you shall as soon stop the sun from running her course, contract the sea in a nut-shell, compass the earth with a span, and raise the dead at your pleasure, as ever you shall be able to sin yourselves out of your sufferings; and therefore it is better to be silent and quiet under them, than to attempt that which is impossible to accomplish. This second consideration will receive further confirmation by the next particular;—

(3.) Thirdly, *As it is an impossible thing, so it is a very prejudicial, a very dangerous thing, to attempt to sin yourselves out of your troubles;* for by attempting to sin yourselves out of your trouble, you will sin yourselves into many troubles, as Jonah and Jacob did; and by labouring to sin yourselves out of less troubles, you will sin yourselves into greater troubles, as Saul did; and by endeavouring to sin yourselves from under outward troubles, you will sin yourselves under inward troubles and distresses, which are the sorest and saddest of all troubles; thus did Spira, Jerome of Prague, Bilney, and others. Some there have been, who, by labouring to sin themselves out of their present sufferings, have sinned themselves under such horrors and terrors of conscience, that they could neither eat, nor drink, nor sleep, but have been ready to lay violent hands upon themselves.

And Cyprian, in his sermon *de lapsis*, speaks of divers who, forsaking the faith to avoid sufferings, were given over to be possessed of evil spirits, and died fearfully. O man! thou doest not know what deadly sin, what deadly temptation, what deadly judgment, what deadly stroke, thou mayest fall under, who attempts to sin thyself out of troubles. What is it to take Venice, and to be hanged at the gates thereof? It is better to be silent and mute under thy afflictions, than by using sinful shifts to sin thyself under greater afflictions.

(4.) Fourthly, Consider *it is a very ignoble and unworthy thing to go to sin yourselves out of your troubles and straits.* It argues a poor, a low, a weak, a dastardly, and an effeminate spirit, to use base shifts to shuffle yourselves out of your troubles. Men of noble, courageous, and magnanimous spirits will disdain and scorn it, Dan. iii. 8, vi., Heb. xi. 24. As you may see in the three children, David, and those worthies, in that 11th of the Hebrews, of whom 'this world was not worthy.' Jerome writes of a brave woman, who, being upon the rack, bade her persecutors do their worst, for she was resolved to die rather than lie. And the prince of Conde, being taken prisoner by Charles the Ninth, king of France, and put to his choice whether he would go to mass or be put to death, or suffer perpetual imprisonment, his noble answer was, that by God's help he would never choose the first, and for either of the latter, he left to the king's pleasure and God's providence.[1]

A soul truly noble will sooner part with all than the peace of a good conscience. Thus blessed Hooper desired rather to be discharged of his bishopric than yield to certain ceremonies.

I have read of Marcus Arethusus, an eminent servant of the Lord in gospel-work, who, in the time of Constantine, had been the cause of overthrowing an idol temple;[2] but Julian, coming to be emperor, commanded the people of that place to build it up again. All were ready so to do, only he refused it; whereupon his own people, to whom he had preached, fell upon him, stripped off all his clothes, then abused his naked body, and gave it up to children and school-boys to be lanched[3] with their penknives; but when all this would not do, they caused him to be set in the sun, having his naked body anointed all over with honey, that so he might be bitten and stung to death by flies and wasps; and all this cruelty they exercised upon him, because he would not do anything towards the rebuilding of that idol temple; nay, they came so far, that if he would but give one halfpenny towards the charge, they would release him, but he refused it with a noble Christian disdain, though the advancing of an halfpenny might have saved his life. And in so doing, he did but live up to that noble principle that most commend, but few practise, viz., that Christians must choose rather to suffer the worst of torments, than commit the least of sins, whereby God should be dishonoured, his name blasphemed, religion reproached, profession scorned, weak saints discouraged, and men's consciences wounded and their souls endangered. Now tell me, Christians, is it not better to be silent and mute under your sorest trials and troubles, than to labour to sin, and shift yourselves out of them, and so proclaim to all the world, that you are persons of very low, poor, and ignoble spirits? But,

(5.) Fifthly, Consider, *sinful shifts and means God hath always cursed and blasted.*[4] Achan's golden wedge was but a wedge to cleave him, and his garments a shroud to shroud him. Ahab purchases a vineyard with the blood of the owner, but presently it was watered with his own blood, according to the word of the Lord. Gehazi must needs have a talent of silver and two changes of raiment, and that with a lie, I say with a lie; well! he hath them, and he hath with them a leprosy that cleaved to him and his seed for ever, 2 Kings v. 22–27. With those

[1] Lactantius speaks of many such brave spirits. I might produce a cloud of witnesses from among the primitive Christians, who have been noble and gallant this way.

[2] A favourite example of Brooks. See Index, *sub nomine.*—G. [3] 'Lanced.'—G.

[4] Jer. v. 5, 6, 11; Ezek. vii. 13; 1 Sam. xxviii. 5–8, &c.; 1 Kings xxi. 18, 19, compared with chap. xxii. 23.

very hands that Judas took money to betray his master, with those very hands he fitted a halter to hang himself. The rich and wretched glutton fared delicately, and went bravely every day, but the next news you hear of him, is of his being in hell, crying out for a drop, who, when he was on earth, would not give a crumb. The coal that the eagle carried from the altar to her nest, set all on fire.

Crassus did not long enjoy the fruit of his covetousness, for the Parthians taking of him, poured melted gold down his throat.[1]

Dionysius[2] did not long enjoy the fruit of his sacrilege and tyranny, for he was glad to change his sceptre into a ferule, and turn schoolmaster for his maintenance. Ah! Christians, Christians, is it not far better to sit quiet and silent under your afflictions, than to use such sinful shifts and means which God will certainly blast and curse? But

(6.) Sixthly and lastly, Consider this, *that your very attempting to sin and shift yourselves out of troubles and afflictions, will cost you dear.* It will cost you many prayers and tears, many sighs, many groans, many gripes, many terrors, and many horrors. Peter, by attempting to sin himself out of trouble, sins himself into a sea of sorrows: Mat. xxvi. 75, 'He went forth and wept bitterly.'[3]

Clement observes, That every night when he heard the cock crow, he would fall upon his knees and weep bitterly; others say, that his face was furrowed with continual tears. Were Abraham, David, Jacob, and Jonah now alive, they would tell you, that they have found this to be a truth in their own experience. Ah! Christians, it is far better to be quiet and silent under your sufferings, than to pay so dear for attempting to sin and shift yourselves out of your sufferings. A man will not buy gold too dear, and why then should he buy himself out of troubles at too dear a rate?

But now I shall come to that use that I intend to stand most upon, and that is, *an use of exhortation.* Seeing it is the great duty and concernment of Christians to be mute and silent under the greatest afflictions, the saddest providences, and sharpest trials that they meet with in this world: oh that I could prevail with you, Christians, to mind this great duty, and to live up and live out this necessary truth; which that I may, give me leave to propound some considerations, to engage your souls to be mute and silent under your greatest troubles and your saddest trials. To that purpose,

1. Consider first, *the greatness, sovereignty, majesty, and dignity of God, and let that move thee to silence,* Jer. x. 7; v. 22: Ps. xlvi. 8–10, 'Come, behold the works of the Lord, what desolations he hath made in the earth. He maketh wars to cease unto the end of the earth; he breaketh the bow, and cutteth the spear in sunder; he burneth the chariot in the fire. Be still, and know that I am God: I will be exalted among the heathens, I will be exalted in the earth.' Who can cast his eye upon the greatness of God, the majesty of God, and not sit still before him? Zeph. i. 7, 'Hold thy peace at the presence of the Lord God.' Oh, chat not, murmur not, fret not, but stand mute before him! Shall the child be hushed before his father, the servant before

[1] See Index, *sub nomine*, for a former annotated mention of this in 'Precious Remedies.' —G.

[2] The 'Tyrant' of Sicily.—G.

[3] A man may buy anything too dear but Christ, grace, his own soul, and the gospel.

the master, the subject before his prince, and the guilty person before the judge, when he majestically rises off his judgment seat, and composes his countenance into an aspect of terror and severity, that his sentence may fall upon the offender with the greater dread? and shall not a Christian be quiet before that God that can bathe his sword in heaven, and burn the chariots on earth? Nay, shall the sheep be hushed before the wolf, birds before the hawk, and all the beasts of the field before the lion? and shall not we be hushed and quiet before him, who is the Lion of the tribe of Judah? Rev. v. 5. God is mighty in power, and mighty in counsel, and mighty in working, and mighty in punishing; and therefore be silent before him. It appears that God is a mighty God, by the epithet that is added unto *El*, which is *Gibbon*, importing that he is a God of prevailing might; in Daniel he is called *El Elim*, the mighty of mighties. Moses magnifying of his might, saith, 'Who is like unto thee among the gods?' Now certainly this epithet should be a mighty motive to work souls to that which Habakkuk persuaded to: Hab. ii. 20, 'The Lord is in his holy temple: let all the earth keep silence before him.' Upon this very consideration Moses commands Israel to hold their peace, Exod. xiv. 13, 14.

It is reported of Augustus the emperor, and likewise of Tamerlane that warlike Scythian, that in their eyes sat such a rare majesty, that many in talking with them, and often beholding of them, have become dumb.[1] O my brethren, shall not the brightness and splendour of the majesty of the great God, whose sparkling glory and majesty dazzles the eyes of angels, and makes those princes of glory stand mute before him, move you much more to silence, to hold your peace, and lay your hands upon your mouths. Surely yes. But,

2. Secondly, Consider, *That all your afflictions, troubles, and trials shall work for your good:* Rom. viii. 28, 'And we know that all things shall work together for good to them that love God.' Why then should you fret, fling, fume, seeing God designs you good in all? The bee sucks sweet honey out of the bitterest herbs; so God will by afflictions teach his children to suck sweet knowledge, sweet obedience, and sweet experiences, &c., out of all the bitter afflictions and trials he exercises them with.[2] That scouring and rubbing, which frets others, shall make them shine the brighter; and that weight which crushes and keeps others under, shall but make them, like the palm tree, grow better and higher; and that hammer which knocks others all in pieces, shall but knock them the nearer to Christ, the corner stone. Stars shine brightest in the darkest night; torches give the best light when beaten; grapes yield most wine when most pressed; spices smell sweetest when pounded; vines are the better for bleeding; gold looks the brighter for scouring; juniper smells sweetest in the fire; chamomile, the more you tread it the more you spread it; the salamander lives best in the fire; the Jews were best, when most afflicted; the Athenians would never mend, till they were in mourning; the Christ's cross, saith Luther, is no letter in the book, and yet, saith he, it hath taught me more than

[1] Turk. Hist., 236, 415.

[2] *Afflictiones benedictiones*, afflictions are blessings.—*Bernard.* Doubtless Manasseh would not exchange the good he got by his iron chains, for all the gold chains that be in the world.

all the letters in the book. Afflictions are the saints' best benefactors to heavenly affections; where afflictions hang heaviest, corruptions hang loosest. And grace that is hid in nature, as sweet water in rose leaves, is then most fragrant when the fire of affliction is put under to distil it out. Grace shines the brighter for scouring, and is most glorious when it is most clouded.

Pliny in his Natural History[1] writeth of certain trees growing in the Red Sea, which being beat upon by the waves, stand like a rock, immoveable, and that they are battered by the roughness of the waters. In the sea of afflictions, God will make his people stand like a rock; they shall be immoveable and invincible, and the more the waves of afflictions beat upon them, the better they shall be, the more they shall thrive in grace and godliness. Now how should this engage Christians to be mute and silent under all their troubles and trials in this world, considering that they shall all work for their good! God chastises our carcases to heal our consciences; he afflicts our bodies to save our souls; he gives us gall and wormwood here, that the pleasures that be at his right hand may be more sweet hereafter; here he lays us upon a bed of thorns, that we may look and long more for that easy bed of down,—his bosom in heaven.

As there is a curse wrapped up in the best things he gives the wicked, so there is a blessing wrapped up in the worst things he brings upon his own, Ps. xxv. 10, Deut. xxvi. 16. As there is a curse wrapped up in a wicked man's health, so there is a blessing wrapped up in a godly man's sickness; as there is a curse wrapped up in a wicked man's strength, so there is a blessing wrapped up in a godly man's weakness; as there is a curse wrapped up in a wicked man's wealth, so there is a blessing wrapped up in a godly man's wants; as there is a curse wrapped up in a wicked man's honour, so there is a blessing wrapped up in a godly man's reproach; as there is a curse wrapped up in all a wicked man's mercies, so there is a blessing wrapped up in all a godly man's crosses, losses, and changes: and why then should he not sit mute and silent before the Lord? But,

3. Thirdly, Consider, *That a holy silence is that excellent precious grace, that lends a hand of support to every grace*, Rom. xv. 4. Silence is *custos*, the keeper, of all other virtues; it lends a hand to faith, a hand to hope, a hand to love, a hand to humility, a hand to self-denial, &c. A holy silence hath its influences upon all other graces that be in the soul; it causes the rosebuds of grace to blossom and bud forth. Silence is *virtus versata circa adversa*, a grace that keeps a man gracious in all conditions. In every condition silence is a Christian's right hand; in prosperity, it bears the soul up under all the envy, hatred, malice, and censures of the world; in adversity, it bears the soul up under all the neglect, scorn, and contempt that a Christian meets with in the world. It makes every bitter sweet, every burden light, and every yoke easy. And this the very heathen seemed to intimate in placing the image of *Angeronia*[2] with the mouth bound, upon the altar of *Volupia*,[3] to shew that silence under sufferings was the ready way to attain true comfort, and make every bitter sweet. No man honours God, nor no man justifies God at so high a rate, as he who lays

[1] Lib. xii. 1, 9.

[2] More accurately *Angerona*, goddess of silence.—G.

[3] *Volupia*, goddess of pleasure.—G.

his hand upon his mouth, when the rod of God is upon his back. But,

4. Fourthly, To move you to silence under your sorest and your sharpest trials, consider, *That you have deserved greater and heavier afflictions than those you are under*, Lam. iii. 39; Micah vii. 7-9. Hath God taken away one mercy? Thou hast deserved to be stripped of all. Hath he taken away the delight of thine eyes? He might have taken away the delight of thy soul. Art thou under outward wants? Thou hast deserved to be under outward and inward together. Art thou cast upon a sick bed? Thou hast deserved a bed in hell. Art thou under that ache and that pain? Thou hast deserved to be under all aches and pains at once. Hath God chastised thee with whips? Thou hast deserved to be chastised with scorpions, 1 Kings xii. 14. Art thou fallen from the highest pinnacle of honour to be the scorn and contempt of men? Thou hast deserved to be scorned and contemned by God and angels. Art thou under a severe whipping? Thou hast deserved an utter damning. Ah Christian! let but your eyes be fixed upon your demerits, and your hands will be quickly upon your mouths; whatever is less than a final separation from God, whatever is less than hell, is mercy; and therefore you have cause to be silent under the smartest dealings of God with you. But,

5. Fifthly, Consider, *a quiet silent spirit is of great esteem with God.* God sets the greatest value upon persons of a quiet spirit: 1 Peter iii. 4. 'But let it be the hidden man of the heart, in that which is not corruptible, even the ornament of a meek and quiet spirit, which is in the sight of God of great price.' A quiet spirit is a spark of the divine nature, it is a ray, a beam of glory; it is a heaven-born spirit. No man is born with a holy silence in his heart, as he is born with a tongue in his mouth. This is a flower of paradise; it is a precious gem that God makes very great reckoning of. A quiet spirit speaks a man most like to God; it capacitates a man for communion with God; it renders a man most serviceable to God; and it obliges a man to most accurate walking with God. A meek and quiet spirit is an incorruptible ornament, much more valuable than gold.

(1.) First, There is a mutual[1] quietness, which proceeds from a good temper and constitution of body.

(2.) Secondly, There is a moral quietness, which proceeds from good education and breeding, which flows from good injunctions, instructions, and examples.

(3.) Thirdly, There is an artificial quietness; some have an art to imprison their passions, and to lay a law of restraint upon their anger and wrath, when they are all in a flame within: as you may see in Cain, Esau, Absalom, and Joab, who for a time cast a close cloak over their malice, when their hearts were set on fire of hell. So Domitian would seem to love them best, whom he willed least should live.

(4.) Fourthly, There is a gracious quietness, which is of the Spirit's infusion, Gal. v. 22-25. Now this quietness of spirit, this spiritual frame of heart, is of great price in the sight of God. God values it above the world, and therefore who would not covet it more than the world, yea, more than life itself? Certainly the great God sets a great price upon nothing but that which is of an invaluable price; what stretching,

[1] Qu. 'natural'?—Ed.

struggling, and striving is there for those things that the great ones of the earth do highly prize! Ah! what stretching of wits, interests, and consciences is there this day, to gain and hold up that which justice will cast down! how much better would it be, if all persons would in good earnest struggle and strive, even as for life, after a quiet and silent spirit, which the great and glorious God sets so great a price upon! This is a pearl of greatest price, and happy is he that purchases it, though it were with the loss of all. But,

6. Sixthly, Consider, *That if you sit not silent and quiet under your greatest troubles and your sorest trials, you will be found fighters against your own prayers.* How often have you prayed that the will of God may be done, yea, that it may be done on the earth, as the angels, those glistering courtiers, those princes of glory, do it now in heaven! Mat. vi. 10. When troubles and afflictions come upon you, the will of God is done, his will is accomplished; why then should you fret, fling, and fume, and not rather quietly lie down in his will, whose will is a perfect will, a just and righteous will, a wise will, an overruling will, an infinite will, a sovereign will, a holy will, an immutable will, an uncontrollable will, an omnipotent will, and an eternal will? Certainly you will but add affliction to affliction, by fighting against your own prayers, and by vexing and fretting yourselves when the will of God is done. It is sad to see a man to fight against his friends, it is sadder to see him fight against his relations, it is saddest of all to see him fight against his prayers; and yet this every Christian doth, who murmurs and mutters when the rod of God is upon him.[1] Some there be that pray against their prayers, as Augustine, who prayed for continency with a proviso, Lord! give me continency, but not yet; and some there be who fight against their prayers, as those who pray that the will of God may be done, and yet when his will is done upon them, they are like the troubled sea when it cannot rest, they are still fretting against the Lord. Ah, Christians! have you not sins to fight against, and temptations to fight against, and a devil to fight against, yea, a whole world to fight against? Why then should you be found fighting against your own prayers? But,

7. Seventhly, Consider, *A holy silence under the heaviest burdens, the greatest afflictions, the saddest providences and changes, will make all tolerable and easy to a Christian.* The silent soul can bear a burden without a burden. Those burdens and troubles that will break a froward man's back, will not so much as break a silent man's sleep; those afflictions that lie as heavy weights upon a murmurer, will lie as light as a feather upon a mute Christian, Micah vii. 7–10, Ps. xcii. 1, 6; that bed of sorrow, which is as a bed of thorns to a fretful soul, will be as a bed of down to a silent soul. A holy silence unstings every affliction, it takes off the weight of every burden, it adds sweet to every bitter, it changes dark nights into sunshiny days, and terrible storms into desirable calms. The smallest sufferings will easily vanquish an unquiet spirit, but a quiet spirit will as easily triumph over the greatest sufferings. As little mercies are great mercies, so great sufferings are but little sufferings, in the eye of a silent soul. The silent soul never

[1] *Voluntas Dei necessitas rei.* Every gracious soul should say Amen to God's Amen; he should put his *fiat*, his *placet* to God's, go it never so much against the hair with him.

complains that his affliction is too great, his burden too heavy, his cross too weighty, his sufferings too many; silence makes him victorious over all. And therefore, as ever you would have heavy afflictions light, and be able to bear a burden without a burden, labour as for life after this holy silence.

8. Eighthly, Consider *that a holy silence under afflictions will be your best armour of proof against those temptations that afflictions may expose you to.* Times of afflictions often prove times of great temptations, and therefore afflictions are called temptations:[1] James i. 12, 'Blessed is the man which endureth temptations, for when he is tried he shall receive the crown of life,' &c. The Greek word πειρασμὸν, is to be understood of temptations of probation, of afflicting temptations, and not of temptations of suggestion, of seduction; for they are not to be endured, but resisted and abhorred, James iv. 7, 1 Peter v. 9. Now, affliction is called temptation,

(1.) Because, as temptation tries what metal a Christian is made of, so do afflictions.

(2.) Because, as Satan usually hath a great hand in all the temptations that come upon us, so he hath a great hand in all the afflictions that befall us; as you see in that great instance of Job.

(3.) Because, as temptations drive men to God, 2 Cor. xii. 7, 8, so do afflictions, Isa. xxvi. 16, Hosea v. 15; but mainly because Satan chooses times of afflictions as the fittest seasons for his temptations. When Job was sorely afflicted in his estate, children, wife, life, then Satan lets fly, and makes his fiercest assaults upon him. Now, Satan tempts him to entertain hard thoughts of God; to distrust, to impatiency, to murmuring and muttering. As when Israel was feeble, faint, and weary, Amalek assaulted them, and smote the hindmost of them, Deut. xxv. 17, 18; so when Christians are most afflicted, then usually they are most tempted.[2]

Luther found this by experience when he said, I am without set upon by all the world, and within by the devil and all his angels. Satan is a coward, and loves to strike us and trample upon us when afflictions have cast us down. When besieged towns, cities, and castles are in greatest straits and troubles, then the besiegers make their fiercest assaults; so when Christians are under the greatest straits and trials, then Satan assaults them most, like a roaring lion. Now, silence under afflictions is the best antidote and preservative against all those temptations that afflictions lay us open to. Silence in afflictions is a Christian's armour of proof; it is that shield that no spear or dart of temptation can pierce. Whilst a Christian lies under the rod, he is safe. Satan may tempt him, but he will not conquer him; he may assault him, but he cannot vanquish him. Satan may entice him to use sinful shifts to shift himself out of trouble; but he will choose rather to lie, yea, die, in trouble, than get out upon Satan's terms. But,

9. Ninthly, Consider, *That holy silence under afflictions and trials will give a man a quiet and peaceable possession of his own soul:* 'In patience possess your souls,' Luke xxi. 19.[3] Now, next to the pos-

[1] Luke xxii. 31–34, Mat. iv. 1, 13.

[2] Many saints have experienced this truth, when they have been upon their sick and dying beds.

[3] Vide Greg. in Evang. Hom. 35.

session of God, the possession of a man's own soul is the greatest mercy in this world. A man may possess honours, and riches, and dear relations, and the favour and assistance of friends under his trials, but he will never come to a possession of his own soul under his troubles till he comes to be mute, and to lay his hand upon his mouth. Now what are all earthly possessions to the possession of a man's own soul? He that possesseth himself possesseth all; he that possesseth not himself possesses nothing at all. He possesses not the use, the sweet, the comfort, the good, the blessing of anything he enjoys, who enjoys not himself. That man that is not master of himself, he is a master of nothing. Holy silence gives a man the greatest mastery over his own spirit; and mastery over a man's own spirit is the greatest mastery in the world, Prov. xvi. 32. The Egyptian goddess they paint upon a rock standing in the sea, where the waves come roaring and dashing upon her, with this motto, *Semper eadem*, Storms shall not move me. A holy silence will give a man such a quiet possession of his own soul, that all the storms of afflictions shall not move him; it will make him stand like a rock in a sea of troubles. Let a man but quietly possess himself, and troubles will never trouble him. But,

10. Tenthly, Consider *the commands and instructions that God in his word hath laid upon you to be silent, to be mute and quiet, under all the troubles, trials, and changes that have or may pass upon you:*[1] Zech. ii. 13, 'Be silent, O all flesh, before the Lord, for he is raised up out of his holy habitation;' Isa. xli. 1, 'Keep silence before me, O islands;' Hab. ii. 20, 'The Lord is in his holy temple; let all the earth keep silence before him;' Amos v. 13, 'Therefore the prudent shall keep silence in that time, for it is an evil time;' Ps. xlvi. 10, 'Be still, and know that I am God;' Ps. iv. 4, 'Commune with your heart, and be still;' Exod. xiv. 13, 'Stand still, and see the salvation of God;' 2 Chron. xx. 17, 'Stand ye still, and see the salvation of the Lord, with you, O Judah, and Jerusalem;' Job xxxvii. 14, 'Hearken unto this, O Job; stand still, and consider the wondrous works of God.' It is a dangerous thing for us to neglect one of his commands, who by another is able to command us into nothing, or into hell at pleasure. To act or run cross to God's express command, though under pretence of revelation from God, is as much as a man's life is worth, as you may see in that sad story, 1 Kings xiii. 24, &c. Divine commands must be put in speedy execution, without denying or delaying, without debating or disputing the difficulties that may attend our subjection to them.[2] God's commands are spiritual, holy, just, and good; and therefore to be obeyed without muttering or murmurings. Divine commands are backed with the strongest reason, and attended with the highest encouragements. Shall the servant readily obey the commands of his master, the subject the commands of his prince, the soldier the commands of his general, the child the commands of his father, the wife the commands of her husband, and shall not a Christian as readily obey the commands of his Christ? Nay, shall vain men readily and willingly obey the sinful and senseless commands of men, and shall not we be willing to obey the commands of God? 2 Sam. xiii. 28, 29, 'Now Absalom had commanded

[1] God's commands are like those of the Medes, that cannot be changed.
[2] *Obedientia non discutit Dei mandata, sed facit.*—Prosper. Rom. vii.12–14.

his servant, saying, Mark ye now when Amnon's heart is merry with wine, and when I say unto you, Smite Amnon: then kill him, fear not: have not I commanded you? be courageous, and be valiant. And the servants of Absalom did unto Amnon as Absalom had commanded.' They made no bones of obeying the bloody commands of Absalom, against all law, reason, and religion.

I have read of one Johannes Abbas who willingly fetched water near two miles every day for a whole year together, to pour upon a dry stick, upon the bare command of his confessor.[1]

I have also read of the old kings of Peru, that they were wont to use a tassel or fringe made of red wool, which they wore upon their heads, and when they sent any governor to rule as viceroy in any part of their country, they delivered unto him one of the threads of the tassel, and for one of those simple threads he was as much obeyed as if he had been the king himself. Now, shall one single thread be more forcible to draw infidels to obedience, than all those golden commands, last cited, shall be of force to draw you to be quiet and silent under the troubles and changes you meet with in this world? The Lord forbid!

Shall carnal and wicked persons be so ready and willing to comply with the bloody, and senseless, and superstitious commands of their superiors? And shall not Christians be more ready and willing to comply with the commands of the great God, whose commands are all just and equal, and whose will is the perfect rule of righteousness. *Prior est authoritas imperantis, quam utilitas servientis* [Tertullian]. The chief reason of obedience is the authority of the Lord, not the utility of the servant.[2] Ah, Christians! when your hearts begin to fret and fume under the smarting rod, charge one of those commands last cited upon your hearts; and if they shall mutter, charge another of those commands upon your hearts; and if after this, they shall vex and murmur, charge another of those commands upon your hearts; and never leave charging and rubbing those commands one after another upon your hearts, till you are brought to lay your hands upon your mouths, and to sit silent before the Lord under your greatest straits and your sorest trials.

11. Eleventhly, Consider, *That mercy is nearest, deliverance and salvation is at hand, when a Christian stands still, when he sits quiet and silent under his greatest troubles and his sorest trials.*[3] Exod. xiv., they were in very great straits. Pharaoh with a mighty army was behind them, the Red Sea before them, mountains on each hand of them, and no visible means to deliver them. But now they stand still to see the salvation of the Lord, ver. 13, and within a few hours their enemies are destroyed, and they are gloriously delivered, ver. 24, *et seq.* Ps. xxxix. 9, David is dumb, he sits mute under his smart afflictions; but if you look to the second and third verses of the fortieth Psalm, you shall find mercy draw near to him and work salvation for him. 'He brought me up also out of an horrible pit, out of the mire and clay, and set my feet upon a rock, and established my goings. And he hath put

[1] Cassian. *de instit. renunciant.* l. iv. c. 14.

[2] *Non parentum aut majorum authoritas, sed Dei docentis imperium*, the commands of God must needs outweigh all authority and example of men.—*Jerome.*

[3] Acts xii. 7–11; Dan. ix 20, 24; Isa. xxxviii. 1; xxx. 19.

a new song into my mouth, even praise unto our God; many shall see it and fear, and shall trust in the Lord.' And so when Absalom had made a great conspiracy against him, and his subjects fell off from him, and he was forced to flee for his life, his spirit was quiet and calm. 2 Sam. xv. 25, 26, 'And the king said unto Zadok, Carry back the ark of God into the city: if I shall find favour in the eyes of the Lord, he will bring me again, and shew me both it and his habitation. But if he thus say, I have no delight in thee; behold, here am I, let him do to me as seemeth good unto him.' And the same calmness and quietness of spirit was upon him when Shimei bitterly cursed him, and railed upon him, chap. xvi. 5–14; and within a few days, as you may see in the two following chapters, the conspirators are destroyed, and David's throne more firmly established. Mercy is always nearest when a man can in quietness possess his own soul. Salvation is at hand when a Christian comes to lay his hand upon his mouth. Mercy will be upon the wing, loving-kindness will ride post to put a period to that man's troubles who sits silent in the day of his sorrows and sufferings. Ah, Christians! as you would have mercy near, as you would see to the end of your afflictions, as you would have deliverance come flying upon the wings of the wind, sit mute and silent under all your troubles. As wine was then nearest when the water-pots were filled with water, even to the brim; so when the heart is fullest of quietness and calmness, then is the wine of mercy, the wine of deliverance, nearest.

12. The twelfth and last motive to work you to silence under your greatest trials is this, seriously consider *the heinous and dangerous nature of murmuring.* Now that you may, let me propose these following particulars to your most sober consideration.

(1.) First, Consider that murmuring *speaks out many a root of bitterness to be strong in thy soul,* Heb. iii. 12. Murmuring speaks out sin in its power, corruption upon its throne, Heb. xii. 1. As holy silence argues true grace, much grace, yea, grace in its strength and in its lively vigour, so murmuring, muttering under the hand of God, argues much sin, yea, a heart full of sin; it speaks out a heart full of self-love, Exod. xv. 24; xvi. 7, 8; and full of slavish fears, Numb. xiii. 32, 33; xiv. 1–3; and full of ignorance, John vi. 41, 42; and full of pride and unbelief, Ps. cvi. 24, 25; 'yea, they despised the pleasant land,' or the land of desire, Ps. lxxvii. 19, 20: there is their pride; 'they believed not in his word': there is their unbelief;[1] what follows? They murmured in their tents, and hearkened not unto the voice of God. They were sick of the sullens, and preferred Egypt before Canaan, a wilderness before a paradise. As in the first chaos there were the seeds of all creatures, so in the murmurer's heart there is not only the seeds of all sin, but a lively operation of all sin. Sin is become mighty in the hearts of murmurers, and none but an almighty God can root it out. Those roots of bitterness have so spread and strengthened themselves in the hearts of murmurers, that everlasting strength must put in, or they will be undone for ever, Isa. xxvi. 4. But,

(2.) Secondly, consider, *That the Holy Ghost hath set a brand of infamy upon murmurers. He hath stigmatised them for ungodly persons:* Jude 15, 16, 'To execute judgment upon all, and to convince

[1] Unbelief is virtually all sin.

all that are ungodly among them of all their ungodly deeds which they have ungodly committed, and of all their hard speeches which ungodly sinners have spoken against him.' But who are these ungodly sinners? 'They are murmurers, complainers, walking after their own lusts,' &c., ver. 16. When Christ comes to execute judgment upon ungodly ones, murmurers shall be set in the front, they shall experience the fierceness of his wrath and the greatness of his wrath. The front, you know, is first assaulted, and most strongly assaulted. Christ will bend all his power and strength against murmurers; his little finger shall be heavier upon them, than his loins shall be upon others, 1 Kings xii. 11, 14; other sinners shall be chastised with whips, but ungodly murmurers shall be chastised with scorpions. If you can joy in that black character of ungodly sinners, be murmurers still; if not, cease from murmurings. Where murmuring is in its reign, in its dominion, there you may speak and write that person ungodly. Let murmurers make what profession they will of godliness, yet if murmuring keeps the throne in their hearts, Christ will deal with them at last as ungodly sinners. A man may be denominated ungodly, as well from his murmuring, if he lives under the dominion of it, as from his drunkenness, swearing, whoring, lying, stealing, &c. A murmurer is an ungodly man, he is an ungodlike man; no man on earth more unlike to God than the murmurer; and therefore no wonder if when Christ comes to execute judgment, he deals so severely and terribly with him. In the wars of Tamberlain,[1] one having found a great pot of gold, that was hid in the earth, he brought it to Tamberlain, who asked whether it had his father's stamp upon it? But when he saw that it had not his father's stamp, but the Roman stamp upon it, he would not own it, but cast it away. The Lord Jesus, when he shall come with all his saints to execute judgment, Oh! he will not own murmurers; nay, he will cast them away for ever, because they have not his Father's stamp upon them. Ah, souls! souls! as you would not go up and down this world with a badge of ungodliness upon you, take heed of murmuring.

(3). Thirdly, Consider *that murmuring is the mother-sin; it is the mother of harlots, the mother of all abominations; a sin that breeds many other sins*, viz., disobedience, contempt, ingratitude, impatience, distrust, rebellion, cursing, carnality; yea, it charges God with folly, yea, with blasphemy, Num. xvi. 41, xvii. 10, Judges xvii. 2. The language of a murmuring, a muttering soul is this, Surely God might have done this sooner, and that wiser, and the other thing better, &c. As the river Nilus bringeth forth many crocodiles, and the scorpion many serpents at one birth, so murmuring is a sin that breeds and brings forth many sins at once. Murmuring is like the monster hydra; cut off one head, and many will rise up in its room. Oh! therefore, bend all thy strength against this mother-sin. As the king of Syria said to his captains, 'Fight neither with small nor great, but with the king of Israel,' 1 Kings xxii. 31, so say I, Fight not so much against this sin or that, but fight against your murmuring, which is a mother-sin. Make use of all your Christian armour, make use of all the ammunition of heaven, to destroy the mother, and in destroying of her, you will destroy the daughters, Eph. vi. 10, 11. When Goliath was slain, the

[1] Tamerlane.—G.

Philistines fled. When a general in an army is cut off, the common soldiers are easily and quickly routed and destroyed. So, destroy but murmuring, and you will quickly destroy disobedience, ingratitude, impatience, distrust, &c. Oh! kill this mother-sin, that this may never kill thy soul. I have read of Sennacherib, that after his army was destroyed by an angel, Isa. xxxvii., and he returned home to his own country, he inquired of one about him, what he thought the reason might be why God so favoured the Jews? He answered that there was one Abraham, their father, that was willing to sacrifice his son to death at the command of God, and that ever since that time God favoured that people. Well! said Sennacherib, if that be so, I have two sons, and I will sacrifice them both to death, if that will procure their God to favour me; which, when his two sons heard, they, as the story goeth, slew their father, Isa. xxxvii. 38, choosing rather to kill than to be killed. So do thou choose rather to kill this mother-sin than to be killed by it, or by any of those vipers that are brought forth by it, Ps. cxxxvii. 8, 9.

(4.) Fourthly, Consider *that murmuring is a God-provoking sin; it is a sin that provokes God not only to afflict, but also to destroy a people:* Num. xiv. 27–29, 'How long shall I bear with this evil congregation which murmur against me? I have heard the murmuring of the children of Israel, which they murmur against me. Say unto them, As truly as I live, saith the Lord, as you have spoken in mine ears, so will I do to you. Your carcases shall fall in this wilderness, and all that were numbered of you, according to your whole number, from twenty years old and upward, which have murmured against me.' 1 Cor. x. 10, 'Neither murmur ye, as some of them also murmured, and were destroyed of the destroyer.' All our murmurings do but provoke the Lord to strike us and destroy us.

I have read of Cæsar, that, having prepared a great feast for his nobles and friends, it so fell out that the day appointed was extreme foul, that nothing could be done to the honour of their meeting; whereupon he was so displeased and enraged, that he commanded all them that had bows to shoot up their arrows at Jupiter, their chief god, as in defiance of him for that rainy weather; which, when they did, their arrows fell short of heaven, and fell upon their own heads, so that many of them were very sorely wounded. So all our mutterings and murmurings, which are as so many arrows shot at God himself, they will return upon our pates, hearts; they reach not him, but they will hit us; they hurt not him, but they will wound us: therefore it is better to be mute than to murmur; it is dangerous to provoke a consuming fire, Heb. xii. 29.

(5.) Fifthly, Consider, *That murmuring is the devil's image, sin and punishment.*[1] Satan is still a-murmuring; he murmurs at every mercy that God bestows, at every dram of grace he gives, Job i. 8, 9; he murmurs at every sin he pardons, and at every soul he saves. A soul cannot have a good look from heaven, nor hear a good word from heaven, nor receive a love-letter from heaven, but Satan murmurs at it; he murmurs and mutters at every act of pitying grace, and at every act of preventing grace, and at every act of supporting grace, and at every act

[1] Irenæus calleth murmurers *ora diaboli*, the devil's mouth.

of strengthening grace, and at every act of comforting grace that God exercises towards poor souls; he murmurs at every sip, at every drop, at every crumb of mercy that God bestows. Cyprian, Aquinas, and others conceive that the cause of Satan's banishment from heaven was his grieving and murmuring at the dignity of man, whom he beheld made after God's own image, insomuch that he would relinquish his own glory, to divest so noble a creature of perfection, and rather be in hell himself, than see Adam placed in paradise.[1] But certainly, after his fall, murmuring and envy at man's innocency and felicity put him upon attempting to plunge man into the bottomless gulf of sin and misery; he knowing himself to be damned, and lost for ever, would needs try all ways how to make happy man eternally unhappy, Mr Howell tells it as a strange thing, that a serpent was found in the heart of an Englishman when he was dead;[2] but, alas! this old serpent was by sad experience found to have too much power in the heart of Adam whilst alive, and whilst in the height of all his glory and excellency. Murmuring is the first-born of the devil; and nothing renders a man more like to him than murmuring. Constantine's sons did not more resemble their father, nor Aristotle's scholars their master, nor Alexander's soldiers their general, than murmurers do resemble Satan. And as murmuring is Satan's sin, so it is his punishment. God hath given him up to a murmuring spirit; nothing pleases him; all things go against him; he is perpetually a-muttering and murmuring at persons or things. Now, oh what a dreadful thing is it to bear Satan's image upon us, and to be given up to be the[3] devil's punishment! It were better not to be, than thus to be given up; and therefore cease from murmuring, and sit mute under your sorest trials. But,

(6.) Sixthly, Consider, *That murmuring is a mercy-embittering sin, a mercy-souring sin;* as put the sweetest things into a sour vessel, it sours them, or put them into a bitter vessel, and it embitters them. Murmuring puts gall and wormwood into every cup of mercy that God gives into our hands. As holy silence gives a sweet taste, a delightful relish, to all a man's mercies, so murmuring embitters all. The murmurer can taste no sweetness in his sweetest morsels; every mercy, every morsel, tastes like the white of an egg to him, Job vi. 6. This mercy, saith the murmurer, is not toothsome, nor that mercy is not wholesome; here is a mercy wants salt, and there is a mercy wants sauce. A murmurer can taste no sweet, can feel no comfort; he can take no delight in any mercy he enjoys. The murmurer writes *marah*, that is, bitterness, upon all his mercies, and he reads and tastes bitterness in all his mercies. All the murmurer's grapes are grapes of gall, and all their clusters are bitter, Deut. xxxii. 23. As to 'the hungry soul every bitter thing is sweet,' Prov. xxvii. 7, so to the murmuring soul every sweet thing is bitter. The mute Christian can suck sweetness from every breast of mercy, but the murmurer cries out, Oh it is bitter! Oh these breasts of mercy are dry!

(7.) Seventhly, Consider, *That murmuring is a mercy-destroying*

[1] Satan can never be quiet, *nec victor, nec victus*, neither conquered, nor conqueror. [Said of Marcellus, as before.—G.]

[2] In his *Epistolæ Ho-Elianæ;* or, Familiar Letters. 1650. 3 vols.—G.

[3] Qu. 'to the'?—Ed.

sin, a mercy-murdering sin. Murmuring cuts the throat of mercy; it stabs all our mercies at the heart; it sets all a man's mercies a-bleeding about him at once: Num. xiv. 30, 'Doubtless ye shall not come into the land concerning which I sware to make you dwell therein, save Caleb the son of Jephunneh, and Joshua the son of Nun.' God promises them that they should possess the holy land upon the condition of their obedience. This condition they brake; and therefore God was not foresworn though he cut them off in the wilderness, and kept them out of Canaan, Deut. xxxi. 16, 17. But what is the sin that provokes the Lord to bar them out of the land of promise, and to cut them off from all those mercies that they enjoyed which entered into the holy land? Why, it was their murmuring; as you may see in Numbers xiv. 1–3, 26–29. As you love your mercies, as you would have the sweet of your mercies, and as you would enjoy the life of your mercies, take heed of murmuring. Murmuring will bring a consumption upon your mercies; it is a worm that will make all your mercies to wither. As there be some that love their mercies into the grave, and others that plot their mercies into the grave, so there be some that murmur their mercies into the grave. As you would have your mercies always fresh and green, smiling and thriving, as you would have your mercies to bed and board with you, to rise up and lie down with you, and in all conditions to attend you, murmur not, murmur not. The mute Christian's mercies are most sweet and most long-lived; the murmurer's mercies, like Jonah's gourd, will quickly wither. Murmuring hath cut the throat of national mercies, of domestical mercies, and of personal mercies; and therefore, oh how should men fly from it as from a serpent! as from the avenger of blood! yea, as from hell itself!

(8.) Eighthly, Consider, *That murmuring unfits the soul for duty,* Exod. vi. 7–10. A murmurer can neither hear to profit, nor pray to profit, nor read to profit, nor meditate to profit. The murmurer is neither fit to do good, nor receive good. Murmuring unfits the soul for doings of duties; it unfits the soul for delighting in duties; it unfits the soul for communion with God in duties. Murmuring fills the soul with cares, fears, distractions, vexations; all which unfits a man for duty, 1 Cor. vii. 33–35. As a holy quietness and calmness of spirit prompts a man to duty, as it makes every duty easy and pleasant to the soul, Prov. iii. 17; so it is murmuring that unhinges the soul, and indisposes the soul, so that it takes off the chariot wheels of the soul, that the soul cannot look up to God, nor do for God, nor receive from God, nor wait on God, nor walk with God, nor act faith upon God, &c., Ps. xl. 12. Oh! therefore, as ever you would be in a blessed preparedness, and a blessed fittedness for duty, take heed of murmuring, and sit mute and silent under the afflicting hand of God, Isa. xxvi. 9–11.

(9.) Ninthly, Consider, *That murmuring unmans a man;* it strips him of his reason and understanding; it makes him call evil good, and good evil; it puts light for darkness and darkness for light, bitter for sweet and sweet for bitter; it calls saviours destroyers, and deliverers murderers, Isa. v. 18–20; as you see in the murmuring Israelites, Exod. xiv.–xvi. Murmuring uncrowns a man. The murmurer may say, 'My crown is fallen from my head,' Lam. v. 16. Murmuring strips a man of all his glory; it spoils all his excellency; it destroys the nobility of man; it speaks him out to be a base ignoble creature. Murmuring clouds a man's understanding; it perverts the judgment, it puts out the eye of reason, stupefies his conscience; it sours the heart, disorders the will, and distempers the affections; it be-beasts a man, yea, it sets him below the beasts that perish; for he were better be a beast, than be like a beast. The murmurer is the hieroglyphic of folly; he is a comprehensive vanity; he is a man and no man; he is sottish and senseless; he neither understands God nor himself nor anything as he should; he is the man that must be sent to school, to learn of the beasts of the field, and the birds of the air, and the creeping things of the earth, how to cease from murmuring, and how to be mute, Isa. iii. 8, Jer. vii. 6. Ah! sirs, as you would have the name, the honour, the reputation of being men, I say men, Take heed of murmuring, and sit silent before the Lord.

(10.) Tenthly, *Murmuring is a time-destroying sin.* Ah! the precious time that is buried in the grave of murmuring? When the murmurer should be a-praying, he is a-murmuring against the Lord; when he should be a-hearing, he is a-murmuring against the divine providences; when he should be a-reading, he is a-murmuring against instruments. The murmurer spends much precious time in musing; in musing how to get out of such a trouble, how to get off such a yoke, how to be rid of such a burden, how to revenge himself for such a wrong, how to supplant such a person, how to reproach those that are above him, and how to affront those that are below him; and a thousand other ways murmurers have to expend that precious time that some would redeem with a world; as Queen Elizabeth on her deathbed cried out, 'Time, time, a world of wealth for an inch of time.'[1] The murmurer lavishly and profusely trifles away that precious time, that is his greatest interest in this world to redeem, Eph. v. 16. Every day, every hour in the day, is a talent of time, and God expects the improvement of it, and will charge the non-improvement of it upon you at last, Rev. ii. 21, 25; 1 Peter iv. 2. Cæsar[2] observing some ladies in Rome to spend much of their time in making much of little dogs and monkeys, asked them, Whether the women in that country had no children to make much of? Ah! murmurers, murmurers, you who by your murmuring, trifle away so many godly hours and seasons of mercy, have you no God to honour? have you no Christ to believe in? have you no hearts to change, no sins to be pardoned, no souls to save, no hell to escape, no heaven to seek after? Oh! if you have, why do you spend so much of your precious time in murmuring against God, against men, against this or that thing? Eternity rides upon the back of time. *Hoc est momentum*, this is the moment: if it be well improved, you are made for ever; if not, you are undone for ever. *Aut malè, aut nihil, aut aliud agendo.*

I have read of Archias a Lacedæmonian [Plutarch], that whilst he was rioting and quaffing in the midst of his cups, one delivers him a letter, purposely to signify that there were some that lay in wait to take away his life, and withal desires him to read it presently, because it was a serious business and matter of high concernment to him. Oh, said he, *seria cras*, I will think of serious things to-morrow; but that night he

[1] *Sumptus preciosissimus tempus:* time is of precious cost, saith Theophrastus.
[2] Plutarch in the life of *Pericles*.

was slain. Ah! murmurer, cease from murmuring to-day, or else thou mayest be for ever undone by murmuring to-morrow. The old saying, *Nunc aut nunquam*, now or never; so say I, Now or never, now or never give over murmuring, and let it swallow up no more of your precious time. What would not many a murmurer give for one of those days, yea, for one of those hours which he hath trifled away in murmuring, when it is a day too late!

The Rabbins glory in this conceit, that a man hath so many bones as there be letters in the decalogue, and just so many joints and members as there be days in the year; to shew that all our strength and time should be expended in God's service. Ah, murmurers! you will gain more by one day's faithful serving of God, than ever you have gained by murmuring against God. But,

(11.) Eleventhly, Consider this, Christians, *that of all men in the world, you have least cause, yea, no cause, to be murmuring and muttering under any dispensation that you meet with in this world.* Is not God thy portion? Chrysostom propounds this question, Was Job miserable when he had lost all that God had given him? and gives this answer, No, he had still that God that gave him all.[1] Is not Christ thy treasurer? is not heaven thine inheritance? and wilt thou murmur? Hast thou not much in hand, and more in hope? Hast thou not much in possession, but much more in reversion; and wilt thou murmur? Hath not God given thee a changed heart, a renewed nature, and a sanctified soul; and wilt thou murmur? Hath he not given thee himself to satisfy thee,[2] his Son to save thee, his Spirit to lead thee, his grace to adorn thee, his covenant to assure thee, his mercy to pardon thee, his righteousness to clothe thee; and wilt thou murmur? Hath he not made thee a friend, a son, a brother, a bride, an heir; and wilt thou murmur? Hath not God often turned thy water into wine, thy brass into silver, and thy silver into gold; and wilt thou murmur? When thou wast dead, did not he quicken thee; and when thou wast lost, did not he seek thee; and when thou wast wounded, did not he heal thee; and when thou wert falling, did not he support thee; and when thou wert down, did not he raise thee; and when thou wert staggering, did not he establish thee; and when thou wert erring, did not he reduce thee; and when thou wert tempted, did not he succour thee; and when thou wert in dangers, did not he deliver thee; and wilt thou murmur? What! thou that art so highly advanced and exalted above many thousands in the world? Murmuring is a black garment, and it becomes none so ill as saints.

(12.) Twelfthly, and lastly, Consider *that murmuring makes the life of man invisibly miserable.* Every murmurer is his own executioner. Murmuring vexes the heart; it wears and tears the heart, it enrages and inflames the heart, it wounds and stabs the heart. Every murmurer is his own martyr, every murmurer is a murderer; he kills many at once, viz. his joy, his comfort, his peace, his rest, his soul. No man so inwardly miserable as the murmurer; no man hath such inward gripes and griefs as he, such inward bitterness and heaviness as he, such inward contentions and combustions as he. Every murmurer is his own tor-

[1] Lam. iii. 24; Eph. iii. 8; 1 Peter iii. 4. Chrysostom, hom. 4, *de Patientia Jobi.*
[2] *Omne bonum in summo bono*, God is all in all, and all without all.

mentor. Murmuring is a fire within that will burn up all, it is an earthquake within that will overturn all, it is a disease within that will infect all, it is a poison within that will prey upon all.

And thus I have done with those motives that may persuade us not to murmur nor mutter, but to be mute and silent under the greatest afflictions, the saddest providences and sharpest trials that we meet with in this world.

I shall now address myself to answer those objections, and to remove those impediments which hinder poor souls from being silent and mute under the afflicting hand of God, &c.

Obj. 1. Sir! did I but know that I were afflicted in love, I would hold my peace under my affliction, I would sit mute before the Lord; but oh! how shall I come to understand that these strokes are the strokes of love, that these wounds are the wounds of a friend? I answer:

1. *First, If thy heart be drawn more out to the Lord by thy afflictions, then the afflictions are in love.* If they are so sanctified as that they draw out thy soul to love the Lord more, and to fear the Lord more, and to please the Lord more, and to cleave to the Lord more, and to wait on the Lord more, and to walk with the Lord more, then they are in love. Oh, then they are the wounds of a friend indeed![1] It is reported of the lioness, that she leaves her young whelps till they have almost killed themselves with roaring and yelling, and then at the last gasp, when they have almost spent themselves, she relieves them, and by this means they become more courageous; and so if the afflictions that are upon us do increase our courage, strengthen our patience, raise our faith, inflame our love, and enliven our hopes, certainly they are in love, and all our wounds are the wounds of a friend. But,

2. Secondly, *If you are more careful and studious how to glorify God in the affliction, and how to be kept from sinning under the affliction, than how to get out of the affliction, then certainly your affliction is in love,* Dan. iii. and v. 16, 17, Heb. xi. Where God smites in love, there the soul makes it his study how to glorify God, and how to lift up God, and how to be a name and an honour to God. The daily language of such a soul under the rod is this: Lord! stand by me that I sin not, uphold me that I sin not, strengthen me that I sin not, John vii. 7–10. He that will not sin to repair and make up his losses, though he knew assuredly that the committing of such a sin would make up all again, he may conclude that his affliction is in love.

I have read of a nobleman whose son and heir was supposed to be bewitched, and being advised to go to some wizard or cunning man, as they are called, to have some help for his son, that he might be unwitched again, he answered, Oh, by no means, I had rather the witch should have my son than the devil. His son should suffer rather than he would sin him out of his sufferings. He that will not break the hedge of a fair command to avoid the foul way of some heavy affliction, may well conclude that his affliction is in love. Christians! what say you, when you are in the mount; do you thus bespeak the Lord? Lord! take care of thy glory, and let me rather sink in my affliction than sin under my affliction. If this be the bent and frame of thy heart, it is

[1] Ps. xviii. 1–8, cxvi. 1–5, cxix. 67, 69; Isa. xxxviii. 1, *seq.*

certain the affliction that is upon thee is in love. The primitive times afforded many such brave spirits, though this age affords but few.

3. Thirdly, *If you enjoy the special presence of God with your spirits in your affliction, then your affliction is in love*, Ps. xxiii. 4–6. Isa. xliii. 2, 'When thou passest through the waters, I will be with thee; and through the rivers, they shall not overflow thee: when thou walkest through the fire, thou shalt not be burnt, neither shall the flames kindle upon thee.'[1] Hast thou a special presence of God with thy spirit, strengthening of that, quieting of that, stilling of that, satisfying of that, cheering and comforting of that? Ps. xciv. 19, 'In the multitude of my thoughts,'—that is, of my troubled, intricate, ensnared, intertwined and perplexed thoughts, as the branches of a tree by some strong wind are twisted one within another, as the Hebrew word properly signifies,—'thy comforts delight my soul.' Here is a presence of God with his soul, here is comforts and delights that reach the soul, here is a cordial to strengthen the spirit. When all things went cross with Andronicus, the old emperor of Constantinople,[2] he took a psalter into his hand, and opening the same, he lighted upon Ps. lxviii. 14, 'When the Almighty scattered kings, they shall be white as snow in Salmon;' which scripture was a mighty comfort and refreshment to his spirit. Now you are to remember that Salmon signifies shady and dark; so was this mount, by the reason of many lofty fair-spread trees that were near it, but made lightsome by snow that covered it. So that to be white as snow in Salmon, is to have joy in affliction, light in darkness, mercy in misery, &c. And thus God was to the psalmist as snow in Salmon in the midst of his greatest afflictions. When Paul would wish his dear son Timothy the best mercy in all the world, the greatest mercy in all the world, the most comprehensive mercy in all the world, a mercy that carries the virtue, value, and sweetness of all mercies in it, he wishes the presence of God with his spirit: 2 Tim. iv. 22, 'The Lord Jesus Christ be with thy spirit,' in point of honour, in point of profit and pleasure, in point of safety and security, and in point of comfort and joy; it is the greatest blessing and happiness in this world to have the presence of God with our spirits, especially in times of trials: 2 Cor. iv. 16, 'For which cause we faint not; but though our outward man perish, yet the inward man is renewed day by day.' By the 'outward man,' you are to understand not merely our bodies, but our persons, estates, and outward condition in this world; and by the 'inward man,' you are to understand our souls, our persons considered according to our spiritual estate. Now when the inward man gains new strength by every new trouble, when as troubles, pressures, afflictions, and tribulations are increased, a Christian's inward strength is increased also, then his afflictions are in love. When the presence of God is with our inward man, cheering, comforting, encouraging, strengthening, and renewing of that, we may safely conclude that all these trials, though they are never so sharp and smart, yet they are in love.

I have read of a company of poor Christians that were banished into some remote parts, and one standing by, seeing them pass along, said

[1] The bush, which was a type of the church, consumed not all the while it burned with fire, because God was in the midst of it.

[2] [Richard] Knowlles's Turk. Hist. p. 164. [1610, folio; and 1638.—G.]

that it was a very sad condition those poor people were in, to be thus hurried from the society of men, and to be made companions with the beasts of the field. True, said another, it were a sad condition indeed if they were carried to a place where they should not find their God; but let them be of good cheer, God goes along with them, and will exhibit the comforts of his presence whithersoever they go. The presence of God with the spirits of his people, is a breast of comfort that can never be drawn dry; it is an everlasting spring that will never fail, Heb. xiii. 5, 6. Well! Christian, thou art under many great troubles, many sore trials: but tell me, doth God give unto thy soul such cordials, such supports, such comforts, and such refreshments, that the world knows not of? Oh! then, certainly thy affliction is in love.

4. Fourthly, *If by your affliction you are made more conformable to Christ in his virtues, then certainly your afflictions are in love.* Many are conformable to Christ in their sufferings, that are not made conformable to Christ in his virtues by their sufferings; many are in poverty, neglect, shame, contempt, reproach, &c., like to Christ, who yet by these are not made more like to Christ in his meekness, humbleness, heavenliness, holiness, righteousness, faithfulness, fruitfulness, goodness, contentedness, patience, submission, subjection.[1] Oh! but if in these things you are made more like to Christ, without all peradventure your afflictions are in love. If by afflictions the soul be led to shew forth, or to preach forth, the virtues of Christ, as that word imports in that 1 Peter ii. 9,[2] then certainly those afflictions are in love; for they never have such an operation but where they are set on by a hand of love. When God strikes as an enemy, then all those strokes do but make a man more an enemy to God, as you see in Pharaoh and others; but when the strokes of God are the strokes of love, oh! then they do but bring the soul nearer Christ, and transform the soul more and more into the likeness of Christ, Isa. xxvi. 8–10, Jer. vi. 3, Amos vi. 1. If by thy afflictions thou art made more holy, humble, heavenly, &c., they are in love. Every afflicted Christian should strive to be honoured with that eulogy of Salvian, *Singularis domini præclarus imitator*, an excellent disciple of a singular master. But,

5. Fifthly, *If by outward afflictions thy soul be brought more under the inward teachings of God, doubtless thy afflictions are in love,* Job xxxiv. 31, 32: Ps. xciv. 12, 'Blessed is the man whom thou chastenest, O Lord, and teachest him out of thy law.' All the chastening in the world, without divine teaching, will never make a man blessed; that man that finds correction attended with instruction, and lashing with lessoning, is a happy man. If God, by the affliction that is upon thee, shall teach thee how to loathe sin more, how to trample upon the world more, and how to walk with God more, thy afflictions are in love. If God shall teach thee by afflictions how to die to sin more, and how to die to thy relations more, and how to die to thy self-interest more, thy afflictions are in love. If God shall teach thee by afflictions how to live to Christ more, how to lift up Christ more, and how to long for Christ more, thy afflictions are in love. If God shall teach thee by afflictions to get assurance of a better life, and to be still in a gracious readiness

[1] Witness Judas, Demas, and those in the sixth of John, and many Quakers and other deluded people amongst us at this day.

[2] ἐξαγγείλητε, publicly to set forth.

and preparedness for the day of thy death, thy afflictions are in love. If God shall teach thee by afflictions how to mind heaven more, how to live in heaven more, and how to fit for heaven more, thy afflictions are in love. If God by afflictions shall teach thy proud heart how to lie more low, and thy hard heart how to grow more humble, and thy censorious heart how to grow more charitable, and thy carnal heart how to grow more spiritual, and thy froward heart how to grow more quiet, &c., thy afflictions are in love. When God teaches thy reins as well as thy brains, thy heart as well as thy head, these lessons, or any of these lessons, thy afflictions are in love. Pambo, an illiterate dunce, as the historian terms him, was a-learning that one lesson, 'I said I will take heed to my ways that I sin not with my tongue,' nineteen years, and yet had not learned it.[1] Ah! it is to be feared that there are many who have been in the school of affliction above this nineteen years, and yet have not learned any saving lesson all this while. Surely their afflictions are not in love, but in wrath. Where God loves, he afflicts in love, and wherever God afflicts in love, there he will, first or last, teach such souls such lessons as shall do them good to all eternity. But,

(6.) Sixthly, *If God suit your burdens to your backs, your trials to your strength, according to that golden promise,* 1 Cor. x. 13, *your afflictions are in love.* 'There hath no temptation taken you, but such as is common to man: but God is faithful, who will not suffer you to be tempted above what ye are able; but will with the temptation also make a way to escape, that ye may be able to bear it.' When God's strokes and a Christian's strength are suited one to another, all is in love, Isa. xxvii. 8, Jer. xxx. 11, xlvi. 28. Let the load be never so heavy that God lays on, if he put under his everlasting arms, all is in love, Gen. xlix. 23, 24. As Egypt had many venomous creatures, so it had many antidotes against them. When God shall lay antidotes into the soul against all the afflictions that befall a Christian, then they are all in love. It is no matter how heavy the burden is, if God gives a shoulder to bear it: all is in love; it is no matter how bitter the cup is, if God give courage to drink it off; it is no matter how hot the furnace is, if God gives power to walk in the midst of it: all is in love.

(7.) Seventhly, *If thou art willing to lie in the furnace till thy dross be consumed; if thou art willing that the plaster should lie on, though it smart, till the cure be wrought; if thou art willing that the physic should work, though it makes thee sick, till the humours be expelled; all is in love,* Job xxiii. 10, Micah vii. 9. Cain, and Saul, and Pharaoh, were all for the removing away of the stroke, the affliction; they cry not out, 'Our sins are greater than we are able to bear,' but they cry out, 'Our punishment is greater than we are able to bear;' they cry not out, 'Lord, take away our sins,' but 'Lord, remove the stroke of thy hand.'[2] Oh! but when an affliction comes in love upon a soul, the language of that soul is this: Lord, remove the cause rather than the effect, the sin rather than the punishment, my corruption rather than my affliction. Lord! what will it avail me to have the sore skinned over, if the corrupt matter still remain in? there is no evil, Lord, to the evil of sin; and therefore deliver me rather from the evil of sin than the evil of suffering. I know, Lord, that affliction cannot be so displeasing

[1] Socrates, l. ii. c. 18. [2] Gen. iv. 13; Isa. xxviii. 1, 6, lix. 9–17; Exod. vii.–x.

to me as sin is dishonourable and displeasing to thee; and therefore, Lord, let me see an end of my sin, though in this world I should never see an end of my sorrows; oh, let me see an end of my corruptions, though I should never see an end of my corrections; Lord, I had rather have a cure for my heart than a cure for my head, I had rather be made whole and sound within than without, I had rather have a healthy soul than a healthy body, a pure inside than a beautiful outside. If this be the settled frame and temper of thy spirit, certainly thy afflictions are in love.

There was one who, being under marvellous great pains and torments in his body, occasioned by many sore diseases that were upon him, cried out, Had I all the world I would give it for ease, and yet for all the world I would not have ease till the cure be wrought. Sure his afflictions were in love. The first request, the great request, and the last request of a soul afflicted in love, is, A cure, Lord! a cure, Lord! a cure, Lord! of this wretched heart, and this sinful life, and all will be well, all will be well.

(8.) Eighthly and lastly, *If you live a life of faith in your afflictions, then your afflictions are in love.* Now, what is it to live by faith in affliction, but to live in the exercising of faith upon those precious promises that are made over to an afflicted condition?[1] God hath promised to be with his people in their afflictions, Isa. xliii. 2, 3; he hath promised to support them under their affliction, Isa. xli. 10; he hath promised to deliver his people out of their afflictions, Ps. l. 15; he hath promised to purge away his people's sins by affliction, Isa. i. 25; he hath promised to make his people more partakers of his holiness by affliction, Heb. xii. 10; he hath promised to make affliction an inlet to a more full and sweet enjoyment of himself, Hos. ii. 14; he hath promised that he will never leave nor forsake his people in their afflictions, Heb. xiii. 5, 6; he hath promised that all their afflictions shall work for their good, Zech. xiii. 9, Rom. viii. 28. Now if thy faith be drawn forth to feed upon these promises, if these be heavenly manna to thy faith, and thy soul lives upon them, and sucks strength and sweetness from them, under all the trials and troubles that are upon thee, thy afflictions are in love.

A bee can suck honey out of a flower, which a fly cannot. If thy faith can extract comfort and sweetness in thy saddest distresses, out of the breasts of precious promises, and gather one contrary out of another, honey out of the rock, Deut. xxxii. 13, thy afflictions are in love. The promises are full breasts, and God delights that faith should draw them[2]; they are *pabulum fidei, et anima fidei*, the food of faith, and the very soul of faith; they are an everlasting spring that can never be drawn dry; they are an inexhaustible treasure that can never be exhausted; they are the garden of paradise, and full of such choice flowers that will never fade, but be always fresh, sweet, green, and flourishing; and if, in the day of affliction, they prove thus to thy soul, thy afflictions are in love. Sertorius[3] paid what he promised with fair

[1] These following promises have been choice cordials to many Christians under sore distresses. Isa. lvii. 15, xli. 10; 1 Tim. i. 15; John x. 27–29; Isa. xxvi. 3; Mat. xi. 28; 1 John iii. 14.

[2] As the mother delights that the child should draw hers.

[3] Plutarch, *Sertorius*.—G.

words, but so doth not God. Men many times eat their words, but God will never eat his; all his promises in Christ are yea and in him amen, 1 Cor. i. 20. Hath he spoken it, and shall it not come to pass? If in all thy troubles thy heart be drawn forth to act faith upon the promises, thy troubles are from love. And thus much by way of answer to the first objection.

Obj. 2. 'Oh, but, sir! the Lord hath smitten me in my nearest and dearest comforts and contentments, and how then can I hold my peace? God hath taken away a husband, a wife, a child, an only child, a bosom-friend, and how then can I be silent? &c.

Ans. To this I answer,

(1.) First, *If God did not strike thee in that mercy which was near and dear unto thee, it would not amount to an affliction.* That is not worthy the name of an affliction that does not strike at some bosom mercy; that trouble is no trouble that doth not touch some choice contentment; that storm is no storm that only blows off the leaves, but never hurts the fruit; that thrust is no thrust that only touches the clothes, but never reaches the skin; that cut is no cut that only cuts the hat, but never touches the head; neither is that affliction any affliction that only reaches some remote enjoyment, but never reaches a Joseph, a Benjamin, &c.

(2.) Secondly, *The best mercy is not too good for the best God.* The best of the best is not good enough for him who is goodness itself; the best child, the best yoke-fellow, the best friend, the best jewel in all thy crown must be readily resigned to thy best God. There is no mercy, no enjoyment, no contentment worthy of God, but the best. The milk of mercy is for others, the cream of mercy is due to God. The choicest, the fairest, and the sweetest flowers, are fittest for the bosom of God; if he will take the best flower in all the garden, and plant it in a better soil, hast thou any cause to murmur? Wilt thou not hold thy peace? Mal. i. 13, 14.

(3.) Thirdly, *Your near and dear mercies were first the Lord's before they were yours, and always the Lord's more than they were yours.* When God gives a mercy, he doth not relinquish his own right in that mercy: 1 Chron. xxix. 14, 'All things come of thee, and of thine own have we given thee.' The sweet of mercy is yours, but the sovereign right to dispose of your mercies is the Lord's. *Quicquid es, debes creanti; quicquid potes, debes redimenti* [Bernard], whatsoever thou art, thou owest to him that made thee; and whatsoever thou hast, thou owest to him that redeemed thee. You say it is but just and reasonable that men should do with their own as they please, and is it not just and reasonable that God, who is Lord paramount, should do with his own as he pleases? Dost thou believe that the great God may do in heaven what he pleases? and on the seas what he pleases? and in the nations and kingdoms of the world what he pleases? and in thy heart what he pleases? And dost thou not believe that God may do in thy house what he pleases, and do with thy mercies what he pleases? Job ix. 12, 'Behold, he taketh away,' or he snatcheth away, it may be a husband, a wife, a child, an estate, 'who can hinder him? Who will say unto him, what doest thou?'[1] Who dares cavil against God? Who

[1] Job plainly alludes to God's taking away his children, servants, and cattle.

dares question that God that is unquestionable, that chief Lord that is uncontrollable, and who may do with his own what he pleaseth? Dan. iv. 35, 'And all the inhabitants of the earth are reputed as nothing: and he doeth according to his will in the army of heaven, and among the inhabitants of the earth; and none can stay his hand, or say unto him, What doest thou?' Where is the prince, the peasant, the master, the servant, the husband, the wife, the father, the child, that dares say to God, What doest thou? Isa. xlv. 9. In matters of arithmetical accounts, set one against ten, ten against a hundred, a hundred against a thousand, a thousand against ten thousand, although there be great odds, yet there is some comparison; but if a man could set down an infinite number, then there could be no comparison at all, because the one is infinite, the other finite; so set all the princes and powers of the earth in opposition to God, they shall never be able to withstand him. It was once the saying of Pompey, that with one stamp of his foot he could raise all Italy in arms;[1] but let the great God but stamp with his foot, and he can raise all the world in arms, to own him, to contend for him, or to revenge any affronts that by any are put upon him, and therefore who shall say unto him, What doest thou? Water is stronger than earth, fire stronger than water, angels stronger than men, and God stronger than them all; and therefore who shall say unto God, What doest thou; when he takes their nearest and their dearest mercies from them? But,

(4.) Fourthly, *It may be thou hast not made a happy improvement of thy near and dear mercies whilst thou enjoyedst them.* Thou hast been taken with thy mercies, but thy heart hath not been taken up in the improvement of them. There are many who are very much taken with their mercies, who make no conscience of improving their mercies. Have thy near and dear mercies been a star to lead thee to Christ? Have they been a cloud by day, and a pillar of light by night, to lead thee towards the heavenly Canaan? Have they been a Jacob's ladder to thy soul? Hast thou by them been provoked to give up thyself to God as a living sacrifice? Rom. xii. 1. Hast thou improved thy near and dear mercies to the inflaming of thy love to God, to the strengthening of thy confidence in God, to the raising of thy communion with God, and to the engaging of thy heart to a more close and circumspect walking before God? &c. If thou hast not thus improved them, thou hast more cause to be mute than to murmur, to be silent than to be impatient, to fall out with thyself than to fall out with thy God. Children and fools are taken with many things, but improve nothing. Such children and fools are most men; they are much taken with their mercies, but they make no improvement of their mercies; and therefore no wonder if God strip them of their mercies. The candle of mercy is set up not to play by, but to work by.

Pliny speaks of one Cressinus,[2] who improved a little piece of ground to a far greater advantage than his neighbours could a greater quantity of land. Thereupon he was accused of witchcraft; but he, to defend himself, brought into the court his servants and their working tools, and said, *Veneficia mea, Quirites, hæc sunt,* these are my witchcrafts,

[1] Plutarch *in vita Pompeii.*

[2] Lib. xviii. c. 6. [The name is C. Furius Chresimus, *not* Cressinus, and the reference c. 8, *not* 6.—]

O ye Romans; these servants, and these working tools, are all the witchcraft that I know of. When the people heard this plea, with one consent they acquitted him, and declared him not guilty; and so his little piece of ground was secured to him. There is no way to secure your mercies but by improving of them; there is nothing that provokes God to strip you of your mercies like the non-improvement of them: Mat. xxv. 28–31, 'Take therefore the talent from him, and give it unto him which hath ten talents.' By some stroke or other God will take away the mercy that is not improved. If thy slothfulness hath put God upon passing a sentence of death upon the dearest mercy, thank thyself, and hold thy peace.

(5.) Fifthly, *If in this case God had made thee a precedent to others, thou must have held thy peace; how much more, then, shouldst thou be mute when God hath made many others precedents to thee!* Did not God smite Aaron in his dear and near enjoyments, Lev. x. 1, 2, and doth he not hold his peace? Did not God smite David in his Absalom, and Abraham in his Sarah, and Job in his sons, daughters, estate, and body, and Jonah in his gourd? Art thou more beloved than these? No. Hast thou more grace than these? No. Hast thou done more for divine glory than these? No. Art thou richer in spiritual experiences than these? No. Hast thou attained to higher enjoyments than these? No. Hast thou been more serviceable in thy generation than these? No. Hast thou been more exemplary in thy life and conversation than these? &c. No. Then why shouldst thou murmur and fret at that which hath been the common lot of the dearest saints?

Though God hath smitten thee in this or that near and dear enjoyment, it is thy wisdom to hold thy peace, for that God that hath taken away one, might have taken away all. Justice writes a sentence of death upon all Job's mercies at once, and yet he holds his peace, Job i.; and wilt not thou hold thine, though God hath cropped the fairest flower in all thy garden?

Anytus, a young spark of Athens,[1] came revelling into Alcibiades's house; and as he sat at supper with some strangers, he arose on a sudden, and took away one half of his place.[2] Thereupon the guests stormed, and took on at it. He bade them be quiet, and told them that he had dealt kindly with him, since that he had left the one half, whereas he might have taken all. So when our hearts begin to storm and take on when God smites us in this near mercy and in that dear enjoyment, oh let us lay the law of silence upon our hearts! let us charge our souls to be quiet! for that God that hath taken away one child, might have took away every child; and he that hath taken away one friend, might have taken away every friend; and he that hath taken away a part of thy estate, might have taken away thy whole estate: therefore hold thy peace; let who will murmur, yet be thou mute.

(6.) Sixthly, *It may be thy sins have been much about thy near and dear enjoyments.* It may be thou hast over-loved them, and over-prized them, and over-much delighted thyself in them; it may be they have often had thy heart, when they should have had but thy hand; it may be that care, that fear, that confidence, that joy that should have been

[1] The foremost of the accusers of Socrates, and the infamous friend of Alcibiades. Cf. Plato and Plutarch, *sub nomine*.—G. [2] Qu. 'plate'?—Ed.

expended upon more noble objects, hath been expended upon them. Thy heart, O Christian! is Christ's bed of spices, and it may be thou hast bedded thy mercies with thee, when Christ hath been put to lie in an outhouse, Luke ii. 7; thou hast had room for them, when thou hast had none for him; they have had the best, when the worst have been counted good enough for Christ. It is said of Reuben, that he went up to his father's bed, Gen. xlix. 4. Ah! how often hath one creature comfort and sometimes another put in between Christ and your souls! how often have your dear enjoyments gone up to Christ's bed! It is said of the Babylonians, that they came in to Aholah and Aholibah's bed of love, Ezek. xxiii. 17; may it not be said of your near and dear mercies, that they have come into Christ's bed of love, your hearts; they being that bed wherein Christ delights to rest and repose himself? Cant. iii. 7. Now, if a husband, a child, a friend shall take up that room in thy soul that is proper and peculiar to God, God will either embitter it, remove it, or be the death of it. If once the love of a wife runs out more to a servant than to her husband, the master will turn him out of doors, though otherwise he were a servant worth gold. The sweetest comforts of this life, they are but like treasures of snow; now do but take a handful of snow, and crush it in your hands, and it will melt away presently; but if you let it lie upon the ground, it will continue for some time. And so it is with the contentments of this world; if you grasp them in your hands and lay them too near your hearts, they will quickly melt and vanish away; but if you will not hold them too fast in your hands, nor lay them too close to your hearts, they will abide the longer with you. There are those that love their mercies into their graves, that hug their mercies to death, that kiss them till they kill them. Many a man hath slain his mercies, by setting too great a value upon them; many a man hath sunk his ship of mercy, by taking up in it; over-loved mercies are seldom long lived: Ezek. xxiv. 21, 'When I take from them the joy of their glory, the desire of their eyes, and that whereupon they set their minds, their sons and their daughters.' The way to lose your mercies is to indulge them; the way to destroy them is to fix your minds and hearts upon them. Thou mayest write bitterness and death upon that mercy first that hath first taken away thy heart from God. Now, if God hath stripped thee of that very mercy with which thou hast often committed spiritual adultery and idolatry, hast thou any cause to murmur? Hast thou not rather cause to hold thy peace, and to be mute before the Lord? Christians, your hearts are Christ's royal throne, and in this throne Christ will be chief, as Pharaoh said to Joseph, Gen. xli. 40; he will endure no competitor. If you shall attempt to throne the creature, be it never so near and dear unto you, Christ will dethrone it, he will destroy it; he will quickly lay them in a bed of dust who shall aspire to his royal throne. But,

(7.) Seventhly, *Thou hast no cause to murmur because of the loss of such near and dear enjoyments, considering those more noble and spiritual mercies and favours that thou still enjoyest.* Grant that Joseph is not, and Benjamin is not, Gen. xlii. 36, yet Jesus is; he is yesterday, and to-day, and the same for ever, Heb. xiii. 8; thy union and communion with Christ remains still; the immortal seed abides in thee still, 1 John iii. 9; the Sun of righteousness shines upon thee still; thou art in favour with God still, and thou art under the anointings of the Spirit still, and under the influences of heaven still, &c.; and why then shouldst thou mutter, and not rather hold thy peace? I have read of one Didymus, a godly preacher, who was blind; Alexander, a godly man, once asked him, whether he was not sore troubled and afflicted for want of his sight? Oh yes! said Didymus, it is a great affliction and grief unto me. Then Alexander chid him, saying, Hath God given you the excellency of an angel, of an apostle, and are you troubled for that which rats and mice and brute beasts have?[1] So say I. Ah, Christians! hath God blessed you with all spiritual blessings in heavenly places? Eph. i. 3, 4. Hath the Lord given you himself for a portion? Hath he given you his Son for your redemption, and his Spirit for your instruction; and will you murmur? Hath he given his grace to adorn you, his promises to comfort you, his ordinances to better you, and the hopes of heaven to encourage you; and will you mutter? Paulinus Nolanus,[2] when his city was taken from him, prayed thus: Lord! said he, let me not be troubled at the loss of my gold, silver, honour, &c., for thou art all, and much more than all, these unto me. In the want of all your sweetest enjoyments, Christ will be all in all unto you, Col. iii. 11. My jewels are my husband, said Phocion's wife;[3] my ornaments are my two sons, said the mother of the Gracchi; my treasures are my friends, said Constantius; and so may a Christian under his greatest losses say, Christ is my richest jewels, my chiefest treasures, my best ornaments, my sweetest delights. Look what all these things are to a carnal heart, a worldly heart, that and more is Christ to me.

(8.) Eighthly, *If God, by smiting thee in thy nearest and dearest enjoyments, shall put thee upon a more thorough smiting and mortifying of thy dearest sins, thou hast no cause to murmur.* God cures David of adultery by killing his endeared child. There is some Delilah, some darling, some beloved sin or other, that a Christian's calling, condition, constitution, or temptations leads him to play withal, and to hug in his own bosom, rather than some other, Ps. xviii. 23, Heb. xii 1. As in a ground that lieth untilled, amongst the great variety of weeds there is usually some master-weed that is rifer and ranker than all the rest; and as it is in the body of man, that although in some degree or other, more or less, there be a mixture of all the four elements, not any of them wholly wanting, yet there is some one of them predominant that gives the denomination, in which regard some are said to be of a sanguine, some of a phlegmatic, some of a choleric, and some of a melancholic constitution; so it is also in the souls of men: though there be a general mixture and medley of all evil and corrupt qualities, yet there is some one usually that is paramount, which, like the prince of devils, is most powerful and prevalent, that swayeth and sheweth forth itself more eminently and evidently than any other of them do. And as in every man's body there is a seed and principle of death, yet in some there is a proneness to one kind of disease more than other that may hasten death; so, though the root of sin and bitterness hath spread itself over all, yet every man hath his inclination to one kind of sin rather than another, and this may be called a man's proper sin, his bosom sin, his darling sin. Now, it is one of the hardest works in this world

[1] Jerome. [2] Paulinus of Nola.—G. [3] Plutarch *in vita* Phocion.

to subdue and bring under this bosom sin. Oh! the prayers, the tears, the sighs, the sobs, the groans, the gripes that it will cost a Christian before he brings under this darling sin!

Look upon a rabbit's skin, how well it comes off till it comes to the head, but then what hauling and pulling is there before it stirs! So it is in the mortifying, in the crucifying of sin; a man may easily subdue and mortify such and such sins, but when it comes to the head-sin, to the master-sin, to the bosom-sin, oh! what tugging and pulling is there! what striving and struggling is there to get off that sin, to get down that sin! Now, if the Lord, by smiting thee in some near and dear enjoyment, shall draw out thy heart to fall upon smiting of thy master-sin, and shall so sanctify the affliction, as to make it issue in the mortification of thy bosom corruption, what eminent cause wilt thou have rather to bless him, than to sit down and murmur against him! And doubtless if thou art dear to God, God will, by striking thy dearest mercy, put thee upon striking at thy darling sin; and therefore hold thy peace, even then when God touches the apple of thine eye.

(9.) Ninthly, consider *That the Lord hath many ways to make up the loss of a near and dear mercy to thee;* he can make up thy loss in something else that may be better for thee, and he will certainly make up thy loss, either in kind or in worth, Mat. xix. 27–30. He took from David an Absalom, and he gave him a Solomon; he took from him a Michal, and gave him a wise Abigail; he took from Job seven sons and three daughters, and afterwards he gives him seven sons and three daughters; he took from Job a fair estate, and at last doubled it to him; he removed the bodily presence of Christ from his disciples, but gave them more abundantly of his spiritual presence, which was far the greater and the sweeter mercy. If Moses be taken away, Joshua shall be raised in his room; if David be gathered to his fathers, a Solomon shall succeed him in his throne; if John be cast into prison, rather than the pulpit shall stand empty, a greater than John, even Christ himself, will begin to preach.[1] He that lives upon God in the loss of creature comforts, shall find all made up in the God of comforts; he shall be able to say, Though my child is not, my friend is not, my yoke-fellow is not, yet my God liveth, and 'blessed be my rock,' Ps. lxxxix. 26. Though this mercy is not, and that mercy is not, yet covenant-mercies, yet 'the sure mercies of David' continue, 2 Sam. xxiii. 5; these bed and board with me, these will to the grave and to glory with me. I have read of a godly man, who, living near a philosopher, did often persuade him to become a Christian. Oh! but, said the philosopher, I must, or may, lose all for Christ; to which the good man replied, if you lose anything for Christ, he will be sure to repay it a hundredfold. Ay, but, said the philosopher, will you be bound for Christ, that if he doth not pay me, you will? Yes, that I will, said the good man. So the philosopher became a Christian, and the good man entered into bond for performance of covenants. Some time after it happened that the philosopher fell sick on his deathbed, and, holding the bond in his hand, sent for the party engaged, to whom he gave up the bond, and said, Christ hath paid all, there is nothing for you to pay, take your bond, and cancel it. Christ will suffer none of his children to go by the loss; he hath all,

[1] The first and last chapters of Job, compared. John xvi. 7, 8, &c.; Acts ii.

and he will make up all to them. In the close, Christ will pay the reckoning. No man shall ever have cause to say that he hath been a loser by Christ. And, therefore, thou hast much cause to be mute, thou hast no cause to murmur, though God hath snatched the fairest and the sweetest flower out of thy bosom.

(10.) Tenthly, *How canst thou tell but that which thou callest a near and dear mercy, if it had been continued longer to thee, might have proved the greatest cross, the greatest calamity and misery that ever thou didst meet with in this world?*[1] Our mercies, like choice wines, many times turn into vinegar; our fairest hopes are often blasted; and that very mercy which we sometimes have said should be a staff to support us, hath proved a sword to pierce us. How often have our most flourishing mercies withered in our hands, and our bosom contentments been turned into gall and wormwood! If God had continued the life of David's child to him, it would have been but a living monument of his sin and shame; and all that knew the child would have pointed at him, Yonder goes David's bastard; and so have kept David's wound still a-bleeding, 2 Sam. xii. 16. Many parents who have sought the lives of their children with tears, have lived afterwards to see them take such courses and come to such dismal ends as have brought their grey head with sorrow to their graves.[2] It had been ten thousand times a greater mercy to many parents to have buried their children so soon as ever they had been born, than to see them come to such unhappy ends as they often do. Well! Christian, it may be the Lord hath taken from thee such a hopeful son, or such a dear daughter, and thou sayest, How can I hold my peace? but hark, Christian, hark, canst thou tell me how long thou must have travailed in birth with them again before they had been twice born? Would not every sin that they had committed against thy gracious God caused a new throe in thy soul? Would not every temptation that they had fallen before been as a dagger at thy heart? Would not every affliction that should have befallen them been as a knife at thy throat? What are those pains, and pangs, and throes of child-birth to those after pains, pangs, and throes that might have been brought upon thee by the sins and sufferings of thy children? Well! Christians, hold your peace, for you do not know what thorns in your eyes, what goads in your sides, nor what spears in your hearts, such near and dear mercies might have proved had they been longer continued.

(11.) Eleventhly, *Thou canst not tell how bad thy heart might have proved under the enjoyment of those near and dear mercies that now thou hast lost.*[3] Israel were very bad whilst they were in the wilderness, but they were much worse when they came to possess Canaan, that land of desires. Man's blood is apt to rise with the outward good. In the winter, men gird their clothes close about them, but in the summer they let them hang loose. In the winter of adversity, many a Christian girds his heart close to God, to Christ, to gospel, to godliness, to ordinances, to duties, &c., who in the summer of mercy hangs loose from all.

I have read of the pine tree, that, if the bark be pulled off, it will last

[1] The Lamentations of Jeremiah are a full proof of this.

[2] This age affords many sad instances of this nature. Who can think of Tyburn, and question it? and of killing and drowning, and say, How can this be?

[3] Deut. xxxii. 5, to the end. Jer. v. 7–9, ii. 31, and xxii. 21: Hosea iv. 7.

a long time; but if it continue long on, it rots the tree. Ah! how bad, how rotten, how base, would many have proved, had God not pulled off their bark of health, wealth, friendship! &c. Near and dear relations, they stick as close to us as the bark of a tree sticks to the tree, and if God should not pull off this bark, how apt should we be to rot and corrupt ourselves; therefore God is fain to bark us, and peel us, and strip us naked and bare of our dearest enjoyments and sweetest contentments, that so our souls, like the pine tree, may prosper and thrive the better. Who can seriously consider of this, and not hold his peace, even then when God takes a jewel out of his bosom? Heap all the sweetest contentments and most desirable enjoyments of this world upon a man, they will not make him a Christian; heap them upon a Christian, they will not make him a better Christian. Many a Christian hath been made worse by the good things of this world; but where is the Christian that hath been bettered by them? Therefore be quiet when God strips thee of them.

(12.) Twelfthly, and lastly, *Get thy heart more affected with spiritual losses, and then thy soul will be less afflicted with those temporal losses that thou mournest under.*[1] Hast thou lost nothing of that presence of God that once thou hadst with thy spirit? Hast thou lost none of those warnings, meltings, quickenings, and cheerings that once thou hadst? Hast thou lost nothing of thy communion with God, nor of the joys of the Spirit, nor of that peace of conscience that once thou enjoyedst? Hast thou lost none of that ground that once thou hadst got upon sin, Satan, and the world? Hast thou lost nothing of that holy vigour and heavenly heat that once thou hadst in thy heart? If thou hast not, which would be a miracle, a wonder; why dost thou complain of this or that temporal loss? For what is this but to complain of the loss of thy purse, when thy God[2] is safe? If thou art a loser in spirituals, why dost thou not rather complain that thou hast lost thy God than that thou hast lost thy gold; and that thou hast lost thy Christ than that thou hast lost thy husband; and that thou hast lost thy child, and that thou art damnified in spirituals than that thou art damnified in temporals? Dost thou mourn over the body the soul hath left? mourn rather over the soul that God hath forsaken, as Samuel did for Saul, saith one. 1 Sam. xv. 14, *seq.*

I have read of Honorius, a Roman emperor, who was simple and childish enough; when one told him Rome was lost, he was exceedingly grieved, and cried out, Alas! alas! for he supposed that it was his hen that was called Rome, which hen he exceedingly loved; but when it was told him it was his imperial city of Rome, that was besieged by Alaricus, and taken, and all the citizens rifled, and made a prey to the rude enraged soldiers, then his spirits were revived that his loss was not so great as he imagined.[3] Now, what is the loss of a husband, a wife,

[1] *Qui te non habet, Domine Deus, totum perditit.*—Bernard. [2] Qu. 'gold'?—Ed.

[3] Grotesque as this anecdote sounds, it is historical. When Rome was plundered by Alaric, a eunuch who had the care of the royal poultry, announced to Honorius that 'Rome was destroyed' (Ῥώμη ἀπόλωλε.) 'And yet,' was the reply, 'she just ate out of my hands,' referring to a favourite hen of great size which he called 'Rome.' 'I mean,' said the eunuch, 'that the city of Rome has been destroyed by Alaric.' 'But I,' said the emperor, 'thought that my hen "Rome" was dead.' So stupid, adds Procopius, do they say this emperor was.—G.

a child, a friend, to the loss of God, Christ, the Spirit, or the least measure of grace or communion with God? &c. I say, What are all such losses, but the loss of a hen to the loss of Rome? And yet so simple and childish are many Christians, that they are more affected and afflicted with the loss of this and that poor temporal enjoyment than they are with the loss of their most spiritual attaiments. Ah, Christians! be but more affected with spiritual losses, and you will be more quiet and silent under temporal losses. Let the loss of Rome trouble you more, and then the loss of your hen will not trouble you at all. Let these things suffice for answer to the second objection.

Obj. 3. Oh, but my afflictions, my troubles have been long upon me! and how then can I hold my peace? Were they but of yesterday, I would be quiet; but they are of a long continuance; and therefore how can I be silent, &c.?

To this I answer,

(1.) First, *Thou canst not date thy affliction from the first day of thy pollution.* Thou hast been polluted from the womb, but thou hast not been afflicted from the womb, Ps. li. 5; many have been the days, the years, since thou wast born in sin; few have been the days, the years, that thou hast experienced sorrow. Thou canst not easily number the days of thy sinning, thou canst easily number the days of thy sufferings; thou canst not number thy days of mercy, thou canst easily number thy days of calamity; thou canst not number thy days of health, but thou canst easily tell over thy days of sickness.

(2.) Secondly, *Thy afflictions are not so long as the afflictions of other saints.* Compare thy winter nights and other saints' winter nights together; thy storms and troubles and other saints' storms and troubles together; thy losses and other saints' losses together; thy miseries and other saints' miseries together; witness the proofs in the margin.[1] Thy afflictions are but as a moment, they are but as yesterday compared with the afflictions of other saints, whose whole lives have been made up of sorrows and sufferings, as the life of Christ was. Many a man's life hath been nothing but a lingering death: Job xxi. 25, 'And another dieth in the bitterness of his soul, and never eateth with pleasure.' There are those that have never a good day all their days, who have not a day of rest among all their days of trouble, nor a day of health among all their days of sickness, nor a day of gladness among all their days of sadness, nor a day of strength among all their days of weakness, nor a day of honour among all their days of reproach; whose whole life is one continued winter's night, who every day drink gall and wormwood, who lie down sighing, who rise groaning, and who spend their days in complaining, 'No sorrow to our sorrows, no sufferings to our sufferings!' Some there be who have always tears in their eyes, sorrows in their hearts, rods on their backs, and crosses in their hands: but it is not so with thee; therefore be silent.

(3.) Thirdly, *The longer thy affliction hath been, the sweeter will heaven be to thee at last;* the longer the Israelites had been in the wilderness, the sweeter was Canaan to them at last; the longer the storm, the sweeter the calm; the longer the winter nights, the sweeter

[1] Ps. lxxvii. and lxxxviii.; Gen. xv. 12, 13; Exod. xii. 40–42; Jer. xxv. 11, 12.

the summer days.[1] Long afflictions will much set off the glory of heaven. The harbour is most sweet and desirable to them that have been long tossed upon the seas; so will heaven be to those who have been long in a sea of trouble. The new wine of Christ's kingdom is most sweet to those that have been long a-drinking of gall and vinegar, Luke xxii. 18; the crown of glory will be most delightful to them who have been long in combating with the world, the flesh, and the devil. The longer our journey is, the sweeter will be our end, and the longer our passage is, the sweeter will our haven be. The higher the mountain, the gladder we shall be when we are got to the top of it; the longer the heir is kept from his inheritance, the more delight he will have when he comes to possess it.

(4.) Fourthly, *They are not long, but short, if compared to that eternity of glory that is reserved for the saints*, 2 Cor. iv. 16–18.[2] If you turn to the words, you shall find for affliction, glory; for light afflictions, a weight of glory; and for short momentany afflictions, eternal glory. There will quickly be an end of thy sadness, but there will never be an end of thy happiness; there will soon be an end of thy calamity and misery, there will never be an end of thy felicity and glory.[3] The kingdoms of this world are not lasting, much less are they everlasting; they have all their climacterical years, but the kingdom of heaven is an everlasting kingdom; of that there is no end. There are seven sorts of crowns that were in use among the Roman victors, but they were all fading and perishing; but the crown of glory that at last God will set upon the heads of his saints, shall continue as long as God himself continues. Who can look upon those eternal mansions that are above, and those everlasting pleasures that be at God's right hand, and say, that his affliction is long? Well! Christian, let thy affliction be never so long, yet one hour's being in the bosom of Christ will make thee forget both the length and strength of all thy afflictions.

(5.) Fifthly, *The longer you have been afflicted, the more in spiritual experiences you have been enriched:* 2 Cor. i. 5, 'For as the sufferings of Christ abound in us, so our consolation also aboundeth by Christ.' The lower the ebb the higher the tide, the more pain the more gain, the more afflicted the more comforted, the lower we are cast the higher we shall be raised. Of all Christians, none so rich in spiritual experiences, as those that have been long in the school of affliction.[4] Oh! the blessed stories that such can tell of the power of God supporting them, of the wisdom of God directing them, of the favour of God comforting them, of the presence of God assisting them. Oh! the love-tokens, the love-letters, the bracelets, the jewels that they are able to produce since they have been in the furnace of affliction. Oh! the sin that long afflictions have discovered and mortified. Oh! the temptations that long afflictions have prevented and vanquished. You shall as soon number the stars of heaven and the sands of the sea, as you shall number up the heavenly experiences of such Christians that have been long under afflictions. The afflicted Christian's heart is fullest of spiritual treasure.

[1] Ps. cxxvi. 1, 2, 5, 6, compared.
[2] See this largely opened in my 'String of Pearls.' [Included in the present volume.—G.]
[3] Ps. xlv., lxxii., and lxxxix.: Isa ix. 7; 1 Peter i 4, ii. 11.
[4] Heb. xii. 11; 2 Cor. i. 8, 9; Job xxxiii. 17–22.

Though he may be poor in the world, yet he is rich in faith and holy experiences, James ii. 5; and what are all the riches of this world to spiritual experiences? One spiritual experience is more worth than a world, and upon a dying bed and before a judgment-seat, every man will be of this opinion. The men of this world will with much quietness and calmness of spirit bear much, and suffer much, and suffer long, when they find their sufferings to add to their revenues; and shall nature do more than grace? It is the common voice of nature, 'Who will shew us any good?' Ps. iv. 6; how shall we come to be great, and high, and rich in the world? We care not what we suffer, nor how long we suffer, so we may but add house to house, heap to heap, bag to bag, and land to land, Isa. v. 8. Oh how much more then should Christians be quiet and calm under all their afflictions, though they are never so long, considering that they do but add jewels to a Christian's crown; they do but add to his spiritual experiences. The long afflicted Christian hath the fullest and the greatest trade; and in the day of account, will be found the richest man.

(6.) Sixthly, *Long afflictions sometimes are but preparatives to long-lived mercies.* Joseph's thirteen years' imprisonment was but a preparative to fourscore years' reigning like a king; David's seven years' banishment was but a preparative to forty years' reigning in much honour and glory; Job's long afflictions were but preparatives to more long-lived mercies, as you may see in that last of Job; and those sad and sore trials that the Jews have been under for above these sixteen hundred years, are to prepare them for those matchless mercies, and those endless glories, in some sense, that God in the latter days will crown them with:[1] Isa. liv. 11–14, 'O thou afflicted, tossed with tempests, and not comforted, behold, I will lay thy stones with fair colours, and lay thy foundation with sapphires. And I will make thy windows of agates, and thy gates of carbuncles, and all thy borders of pleasant stones. And all thy children shall be taught of the Lord, and great shall be the peace of thy children. In righteousness shalt thou be established: thou shalt be far from oppression, for thou shalt not fear; and from terror, for it shall not come near thee.' Though they have been long afflicted and tossed, yet they shall at last upon glorious foundations be established; God will not only raise them out of their distressed estate wherein now they are, but he will advance them to a most eminent and glorious condition in this world; they shall be very glorious, and outshine all the world in spiritual excellencies and outward dignities: Isa. lx. 14, 15, 'The sons also of them that afflicted thee shall come bending unto thee, and all they that despised thee shall bow themselves down at the soles of thy feet: and they shall call thee, the city of the Lord, the Zion of the Holy One of Israel. Whereas thou hast been forsaken and hated, so that no man went through thee, I will make thee an eternal excellency, a joy of many generations.' Ah, Christians! do not mutter nor murmur under your long afflictions, for you do not know but that by these long afflictions God may prepare and fit you for such favours and blessings that may never have end. By long afflictions God many times prepares his people for temporal, spiritual, and eternal mercies. If God by long afflictions makes more room

[1] Isa. lxii., lxiii., and lxvi.

in thy soul for himself, his Son, his Spirit, his word; if by long afflictions he shall crucify thy heart more to the world and to thy relations, and frame and fashion thy soul more for celestial enjoyments; hast thou any cause to murmur? Surely no. But,

(7.) Seventhly, *The longer a saint is afflicted on earth, the more glorious he shall shine in heaven; the more affliction here, the more glory hereafter.*[1] This truth may be thus made out:

[1.] *First, The more gracious souls are afflicted, the more their graces are exercised and increased*, Heb. xii. 10, Rom. v. 3-5. Now, the more grace here, the more glory hereafter; the higher in grace, the higher in glory. Grace differs nothing from glory but in name: grace is glory in the bud, and glory is grace at the full. Glory is nothing but the perfection of grace; happiness is nothing but the perfection of holiness. Grace is glory in the seed, and glory is grace in the flower; grace is glory militant, and glory is grace triumphant. Grace and glory differ *non specie sed gradu*, in degree, not kind, as the learned speak. Now, it is most certain that the more gracious souls are afflicted, the more their graces are exercised; and the more grace is exercised, the more it is increased, as I have sufficiently demonstrated in this treatise already. But,

[2.] *Secondly, The longer a gracious soul is afflicted, the more his religious duties will be multiplied.* Ps. cix. 4, 'For my love they are my adversaries; but I give myself unto prayer;' or as the Hebrew reads it, 'But I am prayer,' or 'a man of prayer.' In times of afflictions a Christian is all prayer; he is never so much a man of prayer, a man given up to prayer, as in times of affliction.[2] A Christian is never so frequent, so fervent, so abundant in the work of the Lord, as when he is afflicted: Isa. xxvi. 16, 'Lord! in trouble have they visited thee, they poured out a prayer when thy chastening was upon them.' Now, they do not only pray, but they pour out a prayer; they were freely, largely, and abundantly in prayer when the rod was upon them. Look! as men plentifully pour out water for the quenching of a fire, so did they plentifully pour out their prayers before the Lord; and as affliction puts a man upon being much in prayer, so it puts him upon other duties of religion answerably. Now, this is most certain, that though God will reward no man *for* his works, yet he will reward every man *according to* his works:[3] 1 Cor. xv. 58, 'Therefore, my beloved brethren, be ye stedfast, unmoveable, always abounding in the work of the Lord; forasmuch as ye know that your labour is not in vain in the Lord.' 2 Cor. ix. 6, 'But this I say, he which soweth sparingly shall reap sparingly; and he which soweth bountifully shall reap bountifully;' or he which soweth in benedictions or blessings shall reap in benedictions, as it runs in the original.

It is an excellent observation of Calvin upon God's rewarding the Rechabites' obedience, Jer. xxxv. 19; God, saith he, oft recompenseth the shadows and seeming-appearance of virtue, to shew what complacency he takes in the ample rewards he hath reserved for true and sincere piety. Now, if the longer a Christian is afflicted, the more his

[1] 2 Cor. iv. 16–18; Mat. v. 10–12; 1 Cor. iii. 21–23.
[2] Ps. xlii. 1–5, lxiii. 1, 2, 3, 8; Jer. xxxi. 18, 19; Hosea vi. 11 with 1. 2; Ps. cxvi. 3, 4 and cxlv. 6, 7.
[3] God will reward his people *secundum laborem.—Bernard.*

religious services will be multiplied, and the more they are multiplied, the more his glory at last will be increased, then the longer a saint is afflicted on earth, the more glory he shall have when he comes to heaven. But,

[3.] Thirdly, *The longer any saint is afflicted, the more into the image and likeness of Christ he will be transformed.*[1] It is one of God's great designs and ends in afflicting of his people, to make them more conformable to his Son; and God will not lose his end. Men often lose theirs, but God never hath nor will lose his; and experience tells us that God doth every day, by afflictions, accomplish his end upon his people. The longer they are afflicted, the more they are made conformable to Christ in meekness, lowliness, spiritualness, heavenliness, in faith, love, self-denial, pity, compassion, &c. Now certainly, the more like to Christ, the more beloved of Christ. The more a Christian is like to Christ, the more he is the delight of Christ; and the more like to Christ on earth, the nearer the soul shall sit to Christ in heaven. Nothing makes a man more conformable to Christ than afflictions. Justin Martyr, in his second Apology for the Christians, hath observed, that there is scarce any prediction or prophecy concerning our Saviour, Christ the Son of God, to be made man, but the heathen writers, who were all after Moses, did from thence invent some fable, and feign it to have been acted by some one or other of Jupiter's sons; only the prophecies about the cross of Christ they have taken for the ground of no fable. They have not, among all their fictions, told us of any one of Jupiter's sons that was crucified, that acted his part upon the cross.[2] Many would wear the crown with Christ, that do not care for bearing the cross with Christ. But,

(8.) Eighthly, *The longer they have been, the greater cause thou hast to be silent and patient, for impatience will but lengthen out the day of thy sorrows.* Every impatient act adds one link more to the chain; every act of frowardness adds one lash more to those that have already been laid out; every act of muttering will but add stroke to stroke, and sting to sting; every act of murmuring will but add burden to burden, and storm to storm. The most compendious way to lengthen out thy long afflictions is to fret, and vex, and murmur under them. As thou wouldst see a speedy issue of thy long afflictions, sit mute and silent under them.

(9.) Ninthly, *God's time is the best time; mercy is never nearer* Salvation is at hand, deliverance is at the door, when a man's heart is brought into such a frame as to be freely willing that God should time his mercy and time his deliverance for him, Acts xxvii. 13–44. The physician's time is the best time for the patient to have ease. The impatient patient cries out to his physician, Oh! sir, a little ease, a little refreshment! Oh the pains, the tortures, that I am under! Oh, sir, I think every hour two, and every two ten, till comfort comes, till refreshment comes! But the prudent physician hath turned the hour-glass, and is resolved that this physic shall work so long, though his patient frets, flings, roars, tears. So, when we are under afflictions, we are apt

[1] Rom. viii. 28, &c.; 2 Cor. i. 5–7; Philip. iii. 10; Heb. ii. 10; 2 Tim. ii. 12.

[2] Gale's 'Court of the Gentiles' is an elaborate demonstration of this remark of Brooks. For the non-imitation of the crucifixion, see Justin Martyr: Apol. § 72.—G.

to cry out, How long, Lord, shall it be before ease comes, before deliverance comes? Oh the tortures, oh the torments, that we are under! Lord, a little refreshment! Oh how long are these nights! oh how tedious are these days! But God hath turned our glass, and he will not hearken to our cry till our glass be out. After all our fretting and flinging, we must stay his time, who knows best when to deliver us, and how to deliver us, out of all our troubles, and who will not stay a moment when the glass is out that he hath turned.[1] But,

(10.) Tenthly, and lastly, *They shall last no longer than there is need, and then they shall work for thy good.* It is with souls as it is with bodies; some bodies are more easily and more suddenly cured than others are, and so are some souls. God will not suffer the plaster to lie one day, no, not one hour, no, not a moment, longer than there is need. Some flesh heals quickly; proud flesh is long a-healing. By affliction God quickly heals some, but others are long a-healing: 1 Pet. i. 6, 'If need be, ye are in heaviness, through manifold temptations,' or through various afflictions. The burden shall lie no longer upon thee than needs must; thy pain shall endure no longer than needs must; thy physic shall make thee no longer sick than needs must, &c. Thy heavenly Father is a physician as wise as he is loving. When thy heart begins to grow high, he sees there is need of some heavy affliction to bring it low; when thy heart grows cold, he sees there is need of some fiery affliction to heat it and warm it; when thy heart grows dull and dead, he sees there is need of some smart affliction to enliven and quicken it. And as thy afflictions shall continue no longer than there is need, so they shall last no longer than they shall work for thy good. If all along they shall work for thy good, thou hast no cause to complain that thy afflictions are long. That they shall thus work, I have fully proved in the former part of this book. And thus much for answer to the third objection.

Obj. 4. I would be mute and silent under my afflictions, but my afflictions daily multiply and increase upon me; like the waves of the sea, they come rolling over the neck of one another, &c.; and how then can I hold my peace? How can I lay my hand upon my mouth, when the sorrows of my heart are daily increased?

To this I answer thus:

(1.) First, *Thy afflictions are not so many as thy sins,* Ps. xl. 12. Thy sins are as the stars of heaven, and as the sand upon the sea, that cannot be numbered. There are three things that no Christian can number: 1, his sins; 2, divine favours; 3, the joys and pleasures that be at Christ's right hand; but there is no Christian so poor an accountant, but that he may quickly sum up the number of his troubles and afflictions in this world. Thy sins, O Christian, are like the Syrians that filled the country, but thy afflictions are like the two little flocks of kids that pitched before them, 1 Kings xx. 27; therefore hold thy peace.

(2.) Secondly, *If such should not be mute and silent under their afflictions, whose afflictions are increased and multiplied upon them, then there are none in the world who will be found mute and silent under their afflictions: for certainly there are none who do not find the waters of affliction to grow daily upon them.* If this be not so, what

[1] Ps. vi. 3; Ps. xiii. 1, 2; Ps. xciv. 9, 10; Rev. vi. 10.

means the bleating of the sheep, and the lowing of the oxen? 1 Sam. xv. 14. What means the daily sighs, groans, and complaints of Christians, if their troubles, like the waters in Ezekiel's sanctuary, be not still increasing upon them? Ezek. xlvii. 1, 20. Every day brings us tidings of new straits, new troubles, new crosses, new losses, new trials, &c.

(3.) Thirdly, *They are not so many as God might have exercised thee with.* God could as easily exercise thee with ten as with two, and with a hundred as with ten, and with a thousand as with a hundred. Let thy afflictions be never so many, yet they are not so many as they might have been, had God either consulted with thy sins, with thy deserts, or with his own justice. There is no comparison between those afflictions that God hath inflicted upon thee, and those that he might have inflicted. Thou hast not one burden of a thousand that God could have laid on, but he would not; therefore hold thy peace.[1]

(4.) Fourthly, *Thy afflictions are not so many as thy mercies, nay, they are not to be named in the day wherein thy mercies are spoken of.* What are thy crosses to thy comforts, thy miseries to thy mercies, thy days of sickness to thy days of health, thy days of weakness to thy days of strength, thy days of scarcity to thy days of plenty? And this is that the wise man would have us seriously to consider: Eccles. vii. 14, 'In the day of adversity consider,'—but what must we consider?—'that God hath set the one over against the other.' As God hath set winter and summer, night and day, fair weather and foul, one over against another, so let us set our present mercies over against our present troubles, and we shall presently find that our mercies exceed our trouble, that they mightily over-balance our present afflictions; therefore let us be silent, let us lay our hands upon our mouths.

(5.) Fifthly, *If you cast up a just and righteous account, you will find that they are not so many as the afflictions that have befallen other saints.* Have you reckoned up the affliction that befell Abraham, Jacob, Joseph, Job, Asaph, Haman, the prophets and apostles?[2] If you have, you will say that your afflictions are no afflictions to those that have befallen them; their lives were filled up with sorrows and sufferings, but so are not yours; therefore kiss the rod and be silent. It may be, if thou lookest upon thy relations, thy friends, thy neighbours, thou mayest find many whose afflictions for number and weight do much outweigh thine; therefore be silent, murmur not, hold thy peace.

(6.) Sixthly, ***Not so many as attended our Lord Jesus; whose whole life, from the cradle to the cross, was nothing but a life of sufferings.***[3] Osorius, writing of the sufferings of Christ, saith, That the crown of thorns bored his head with seventy-two wounds. Many seventy-two afflictions did Christ meet with whilst he was in this world. None can be ignorant of this who have but read the New Testament. He is called 'a man of sorrows;' his whole life was filled up with sorrows. When he was but a little past thirty years of age, sorrows, pains,

[1] Lam. iii. 39, Luke xxiii. 41. What are the number of princes to the subjects that are under them? or what are the number of generals to the number of soldiers that are commanded by them? No more are thy afflictions to thy mercies.

[2] Read but [of] the ten persecutions, and thou wilt be full of this opinion.

[3] Isa. 53d, read the whole chapter.

troubles, oppositions, persecutions, had so worn him, that the Jews judged him towards fifty, John viii. 57. A man were as good compare the number of his bosom friends with the stars of heaven, as compare his afflictions and the afflictions of Christ together.

(7.) Seventhly, *Muttering and murmuring will but add to the number.* When the child is under the rod, his crying and fretting doth but add lash to lash, blow to blow; but of this enough before.

(8.) Eighthly, and lastly, *Though they are many, yet they are not so many as the joys, the pleasures, the delights that be at Christ's right hand.* As the pleasures of heaven are matchless and endless, so they are numberless.[1] Augustine, speaking concerning what we can say of heaven, saith,[2] that it is but a little drop of the sea, and a little spark of the great furnace; those good things of eternal life are so many, that they exceed number; so great, that they exceed measure; so precious, that they are above all estimation. *Nec Christus, nec cœlum patitur hyperbolem,* neither Christ nor heaven can be hyperbolised; for every affliction many thousand joys and delights will attend the saints in a glorified estate. What will that life be, or rather what will not that life be, saith one, speaking of heaven, since all good either is not at all, or is in such a life; light which place cannot comprehend; voices and music which time cannot ravish away; odours which are never dissipated; a feast which is never consumed; a blessing which eternity bestoweth, but eternity shall never see at an end. And let this suffice for answer to this fourth objection.

Obj. 5. My afflictions are very great, how then can I hold my peace? Though they were many, yet if they were not great, I would be mute, but alas! they are very great. Oh! how can I be silent under them? How can I now lay my hand upon my mouth?

Ans. (1.) To this I answer, *Though they are great, yet they are not so great as thy sins, thyself being judge; therefore hold thy peace:*[3] Ezra ix. 13, 'And after all that is come upon us for our evil deeds, and for our great trespasses, seeing that thou our God hast punished us less than our iniquities deserve.' They that were under the sense and guilt of great sins, have cause to be silent under their greatest sufferings. Never complain that thy afflictions are great, till thou canst say that thy sins are not great. It is but justice that great afflictions should attend great sins; therefore be quiet. Thy sins are like great rocks and mighty mountains, but so are not thy afflictions; therefore lay thy hand upon thy mouth. The remembrance of great sins should cool and calm a man's spirit under his greatest troubles; and if the sense of thy great sins will not stop thy mouth and silence thy heart, I know not what will.

(2.) Secondly, *It may be they are not great, if you look upon them with Scripture spectacles,* 1 Peter v. 10. Flesh and blood many times looks upon molehills as mountains, and scratches upon the hand as stabs at the heart; we make elephants of flies, and of little pigmies we frame giants. Carnal reason often looks upon troubles through false glasses. As there are some glasses that will make great things seem little, so there are others that will make little things seem great, and

[1] Ps. xvi. 11; Isa. lxiv. 4; 1 Cor. ii. 9. [2] Aug *de Triplici habitu,* c. iv.
[3] Read Ps. cvi., Neh. ix.

it may be that thou lookest upon thy afflictions through one of them, Isa liv. 7, 8. Look upon thy afflictions in the glass of the word; look upon them in a Scripture dress, and then they will be found to be but little. He that shall look into a gospel glass, shall be able to say, heavy afflictions are light, long afflictions are short, bitter afflictions are sweet, and great afflictions are little, 2 Cor. iv. 16–18. It is good to make a judgment of your afflictions by a gospel light and by a gospel rule.

Artemon, an engineer, was afraid of his own shadow.[1] Men that look not upon their afflictions in a Scripture dress, will be afraid even of the shadow of trouble, they will cry out, No affliction to our affliction, no burden to our burden, no cross to our cross, no loss to our loss; but one look into a gospel glass would make them change their note. The lion is not always so great nor so terrible as he is painted; neither are our troubles always so great as we fancy them to be. When Hagar's bottle of water was spent, she sat down and fell a-weeping, as if she had been utterly undone, Gen. xxi. 17–19; her provision and her patience, her bottle and her hope were both out together; but her affliction was not so great as she imagined, for there was a well of water near, though for a time she saw it not. So many Christians, they eye the empty bottle, the cross, the burden that is at present upon them, and then they fall a-weeping, a-whining, a-complaining, a-repining, a-murmuring, as if they were utterly undone; and yet a well of water, a well of comfort, a well of refreshment, a well of deliverance is near, and their case is no way so sad, nor so bad as they imagine it to be.

(3.) Thirdly, *The greater thy afflictions are, the nearer is deliverance to thee.* When these waters rise high, then salvation comes upon the wings; when thy troubles are very great, then mercy will ride post to deliver thee:[2] Deut. xxxii. 36, 'For the Lord shall judge his people, and repent himself for his servants, when he seeth that their power (or hand) is gone, and there is none shut up, and left.' Israel of old, and England of late years, hath often experienced this truth. Wine was nearest, when the water-pots were filled with water up to the brim, John ii. 1–11; so oftentimes mercy is nearest, deliverance is nearest, when our afflictions are at the highest. When a Christian is brim-full of troubles, then the wine of consolation is at hand; therefore hold thy peace, murmur not, but sit silent before the Lord.

(4.) Fourthly, *They are not great, if compared to the glory that shall be revealed,* 2 Cor. iv. 16–18: Rom. viii. 18, 'For I reckon, that the sufferings of this present time are not worthy to be compared with the glory that shall be revealed in us, or upon us.' The apostle, upon casting up of his accounts, concludes that all the pains, chains, troubles, trials, and torments that they meet with in this world, was not to be put in the balance with the glory of heaven. As the globe of the earth, which after the mathematicians' account is many thousands of miles in compass, yet being compared unto the greatness of the starry sky's circumference, is but a centre, or a little prick; so the troubles, afflictions, and sorrows of this life, in respect of eternal happiness and blessedness, are to be reputed as nothing; they are but as the prick of a pin to the starry heavens. They that have heard most of the glory of heaven, have not

[1] Plutarch, *Pericles*, 27; Diod. xii. 28.—G.

[2] Scripture and history speaks fully to this head.

heard one quarter of that which the saints shall find there; that glory is unconceivable and unexpressible. Augustine in one of his epistles hath this relation: that the very same day wherein Jerome died, he was in his study, and had got pen, ink, and paper, to write something of the glory of heaven to Jerome, and suddenly he saw a light breaking into his study, and a sweet smell that came unto him, and this voice he thought he heard: O Augustine! what doest thou? Dost thou think to put the sea into a little vessel? When the heavens shall cease from their continual motion, then shalt thou be able to understand what the glory of heaven is, and not before, except you come to feel it as now I do.[1] Nicephorus speaks of one Agbarus, a great man, that hearing so much of Christ's fame, by reason of the miracles he wrought, sent a painter to take his picture, and that the painter when he came was not able to do it, because of that radiancy and divine splendour which sat on Christ's face.[2] Such is the splendour, the brightness, the glory, the happiness, and blessedness that is reserved for the saints in heaven, that had I all the tongues of men on earth, and all the excellencies of the angels in heaven, yet should I not be able to conceive, nor to express that vision of glory to you. It is best hastening thither, that we may feel and enjoy that which we shall never be able to declare.

(5.) Fifthly, *They are not great, if compared with the afflictions and torments of such of the damned, who when they were in this world, never sinned at so high a rate as thou hast done.*[3] Doubtless there are many now in hell, who never sinned against such clear light as thou hast done, nor against such special love as thou hast done, nor against such choice means as thou hast done, nor against such precious mercies as thou hast done, nor against such singular remedies as thou hast done.[4] Certainly there are many now a-roaring in everlasting burnings, who never sinned against such deep convictions of conscience as thou hast done, nor against such close and strong reasonings of the Spirit as thou hast done, nor against such free offers of mercy and rich tenders of grace as thou hast done, nor against such sweet wooings and multiplied entreaties of a bleeding dying Saviour as thou hast done; therefore hold thy peace. What are thy afflictions, thy torments, to the torments of the damned, whose torments are numberless, easeless, remediless, and endless; whose pains are without intermission or mitigation; who have weeping served in for the first course, and gnashing of teeth for the second, and the gnawing worm for the third, and intolerable pain for the fourth,—yet the pain of the body is but the body of pain, the very soul of sorrow and pain is the soul's sorrow and pain,—and an everlasting alienation and separation from God for the fifth? Ah, Christian! how canst thou seriously think on these things, and not lay thy hand upon thy mouth, when thou art under the greatest sufferings? Thy sins have been far greater than many of theirs, and thy great afflictions are but a flea-bite to theirs; therefore be silent before the Lord.

[1] One of the commonplaces in the biographies of Augustine and Jerome. See Ep. of the former, *sub nomine*.—G.

[2] *Eccles. Hist.* [A well-known myth.—G.]

[3] 1 Peter iii. 18–20; Jude 6, 7; Mat. x. 15, xi. 23, 24.

[4] Isa. xxxiii. 14. The fire in hell is like that stone in Arcadia, which being once kindled, could not be quenched. [Asbestos.—G.]

(6.) Sixthly and lastly, *If thy afflictions are so great; then what madness and folly will it be for thee to make them greater by murmuring!* Every act of murmuring will but add load unto load, and burden to burden. The Israelites under great afflictions fell a-murmuring, and their murmuring proved their utter ruin, as you may see in that Num. xiv. Murmuring will but put God upon heating the furnace seven times hotter; therefore hold thy peace, 1 Cor. x. 11. But of this I have spoken sufficiently already.

Object. 6. Oh! but my afflictions are greater than other men's afflictions are; and how then can I be silent? Oh! there is no affliction to my affliction; how can I hold my peace? I answer,

(1.) *First, It may be thy sins are greater than other men's sins*, Jer. iii. 6–12. If thou hast sinned against more light, more love, more mercies, more experiences, more promises than others, no wonder if thy afflictions are greater than others'. If this be thy case, thou hast more cause to be mute than to murmur; and certainly, if thou dost but seriously look into the black book of thy conscience, thou wilt find greater sins there than any thou canst charge upon any person or persons on earth. If thou shouldst not, I think thou wouldst justly incur the censure which that sour philosopher passed upon grammarians, viz., that they were better acquainted with the evils of Ulysses than with their own.[1] Never complain that thy afflictions are greater than others', except thou canst evidence that thy sins are lesser than others'.

(2.) Secondly, *It may be thou art under some present distemper, that disenables thee to make a right judgment of the different dealings of God with thyself and others.*[2] When the mind is distempered, and the brain troubled, many things seem to be that are not; and then little things seem very great. Oh! the strange passions, the strange imaginations, the strange conclusions, that attend a distempered judgment.

I have read of a foolish emperor, who, to shew the greatness of his city, made show of many spiders. When the mind is disturbed, men many times say they know not what, and do they know not what. It may be, when these clouds are blown over, and thy mind cleared, and thy judgment settled, thou wilt be of another opinion. The supplicant woman appealed from drunken king Philip to sober king Philip. It is good to appeal from a distempered mind to a clear composed mind, for that is the way to make a righteous judgment of all the righteous dispensations of God, both towards ourselves and towards others.

(3.) Thirdly, *It may be that the Lord sees that it is very needful that thy afflictions should be greater than others'.*[3] It may be thy heart is harder than other men's hearts, and prouder and stouter than other men's hearts; it may be thy heart is more impure than others, and more carnal than others, or else more passionate and more worldly than others, or else more deceitful and more hypocritical than others, or else more cold and careless than others, or else more secure than others, or more formal and lukewarm than others. Now, if this be thy case, certainly God sees it very necessary, for the breaking of thy hard heart,

[1] Diogenes *apud Laertium.*
[2] Deut. xxviii. 28. Good men are sometimes strangely besotted and infatuated.
[3] Nothing but strong vomits, strong purges, strong clysters, will cure some.

and the humbling of thy proud heart, and the cleansing of thy foul heart, and the spiritualising of thy carnal heart, &c., that thy afflictions should be greater than others; and therefore hold thy peace. Where the disease is strong, the physic must be strong, else the cure will never be wrought. God is a wise physician, and he would never give strong physic if weaker could effect the cure, Jer. xxx. 11, and xlvi. 28; Isa. xxvii. 8. The more rusty the iron is, the oftener we put it into the fire to purify it; and the more crooked it is, the more blows and the harder blows we give to straighten it. Thou hast been long a-gathering rust; and therefore, if God deal thus with thee, thou hast no cause to complain.

(4.) Fourthly, *Though thy afflictions are greater than this and that particular man's afflictions, yet doubtless there are many thousands in the world whose afflictions are greater than thine.* Canst thou seriously consider the sore calamities and miseries that the devouring sword hath brought upon many thousand Christians in foreign parts, and say that thy afflictions are greater than theirs? Surely no. Pliny, in his Natural History, writeth[1] that the nature of the basilisk is to kill all trees and shrubs it breathes upon, and to scorch and burn all herbs and grass it passeth over. Such are the dismal effects of war.[2] The sword knows no difference between Catholics and Lutherans, as once the duke of Medina Sidonia said, betwixt the innocent and the guilty, betwixt young and old, betwixt bond and free, betwixt male and female, betwixt the precious and the vile, the godly and the profane, betwixt the prince and the subject, betwixt the nobleman and the beggar. The sword eats the flesh and drinks the blood of all sorts and sexes, without putting any difference betwixt one or the other. The poor protestants under the Duke of Savoy, and those in Poland, Denmark, Germany, and several other parts, have found it so; many of their wounds are not healed to this day. Who can retain in his fresh and bleeding memory the dreadful work that the sword of war hath made in this nation, and not say, Surely many thousands have been greater sufferers than myself; they have resisted unto blood, but so have not I, Heb. xii. 4. But,

(5.) Fifthly, *As thy afflictions are greater than other men's, so it may be thy mercies are greater than other men's mercies; and if so, thou hast no cause but to hold thy peace.* As Job's afflictions were greater than other men's, so his mercies were greater than other men's, and Job wisely sets one against another, and then lays his hand upon his mouth, Job i. 21, 22. It may be thou hast had more health than others, and more strength than others, and more prosperity than others, and more smiling providences than others, and more good days than others, and more sweet and comfortable relations than others; and if this be thy case, thou hast much cause to be mute, thou hast no cause to murmur. If now thy winter nights be longer than others, remember thy summer days have formerly been longer than others; and therefore hold thy peace. But,

(6.) Sixthly and lastly, *By great afflictions the Lord may greaten thy graces, and greaten thy name and fame in the world,* James v.

[1] Lib. viii. c. 21. [2] Read Josephus, and the History of the Bohemian Persecution.

10, 11. By Job's great afflictions, God did greaten his faith, and greaten his patience, and greaten his integrity, and greaten his wisdom and knowledge, and greaten his experience, and greaten his name and fame in the world, as you all know that have but read his book. Bonds and afflictions waited on Paul in every city, Acts xx. 23, 2 Cor. xi.; his afflictions and sufferings were very great, but by them the Lord greatened his spirit, his zeal, his courage, his confidence, his resolution, and his name and fame, both among sinners and saints. Certainly, if thou art dear to Christ, he will greaten thee in spirituals, by all the great afflictions that are upon thee; he will raise thy faith, and inflame thy love, and quicken thy hope, and brighten thy zeal, and perfect thy patience, and perfume thy name, and make it like a precious ointment, 'like a precious ointment poured forth,' Prov. xxii. 1, Eccles. vii. 1; so that good men shall say, and bad men shall say, Lo, here is a Christian indeed, here is a man more worth than the gold of Ophir; therefore, hold thy peace, though thy afflictions are greater than others.

Object. 7. I would be silent, but my outward affliction is attended with sore temptations; God hath not only outwardly afflicted me, but Satan is let loose to buffet me; and therefore how can I be silent? how can I hold my peace, now I am fallen under manifold temptations? To this I answer:

(1.) First, *No man is the less beloved because he is tempted; nay, those that God loves best are usually tempted most,* Eph. vi. 12. Witness David, Job, Joshua, Peter, Paul, yea, Christ himself, Mat. iv., who, as he was beloved above all others, so he was tempted above all others; he was tempted to question his Sonship; he was tempted to the worst idolatry, even to worship the devil himself; to the greatest infidelity, to distrust his Father's providence, and to use unlawful means for necessary supplies; and to self-murder, 'Cast thyself down,' &c. Those that were once glorious on earth, and are now triumphing in heaven, have been sorely tempted and assaulted. It is as natural and common for the choicest saints to be tempted, as it is for the sun to shine, the bird to fly, the fire to burn. The eagle complains not of her wings, nor the peacock of his train, nor the nightingale of her voice, because these are natural to them; no more should saints of their temptations, because they are natural to them. Our whole life, saith Austin, is nothing but a tentation; the best men have been worst tempted; therefore, hold thy peace.[1]

(2.) Secondly, *Temptation resisted and bewailed, will never hurt you, nor harm you.* Distasted temptations seldom or never prevail. So long as the soul distastes them and the will remains firmly averse against them, they can do no hurt; so long as the language of the soul is, 'Get thee behind me, Satan,' Mat. xvi. 23, the soul is safe. It is not Satan tempting but my assenting, it is not his enticing but my yielding, that mischiefs me. Temptations may be troubles to my mind, but they are not sins upon my soul whilst I am in arms against them. If thy heart trembles and thy flesh quakes when Satan tempts, thy condition is good enough; if Satan's temptations be thy greatest afflictions,

[1] I am without, set upon by all the world, and within, by the devil and all his angels, saith Luther.

his temptations shall never worst thee nor harm thee; and therefore, if this be thy case, hold thy peace.[1]

(3.) Thirdly, *Temptations are rather hopeful evidences that thy estate is good, that thou art dear to God, and that it shall go well with thee for ever, than otherwise.* God had but one Son without corruption, but he had none without temptation, Heb. ii. 17, 18. Pirates make the fiercest assaults upon those vessels that are most richly laden; so doth Satan upon those souls that are most richly laden with the treasures of grace, with the riches of glory. Pirates let empty vessels pass and repass, without assaulting them; so doth Satan let souls that are empty of God, of Christ, of the Spirit, of grace, pass and repass without tempting or assaulting of them. When nothing will satisfy the soul, but a full departure out of Egypt, from the bondage and slavery of sin, and that the soul is firmly resolved upon a march for Canaan, then Satan, Pharaoh-like, will furiously pursue after the soul with horses and chariots, that is, with a whole army of temptations, Exod. xiv. 9.[2] Well! a tempted soul, when it is worst with him, may safely argue thus: If God were not my friend, Satan would not be so much my enemy; if there were not something of God within me, Satan would never make such attempts to storm me; if the love of God were not set upon me, Satan would never shoot so many fiery darts to wound me; if the heart of God were not towards me, the hand of Satan would not be so strong against me. When Beza was tempted, he made this answer, Whatsoever I was, Satan, I am now 'in Christ a new creature,' and that is it which troubles thee; I might have so continued long enough ere thou wouldst have vexed at it, but now I see thou dost envy me the grace of my Saviour. Satan's malice to tempt is no sufficient ground for a Christian to dispute God's love upon; if it were, there is no saint on earth that should quietly possess divine favour a week, a day, an hour. The jailor is quiet, when his prisoner is in bolts, but if he be escaped, then he pursues him with hue and cry; you know how to apply it. Men hate not the picture of a toad, the wolf flies not upon a painted sheep; no more doth Satan upon those he hath in chains; therefore hold thy peace, though thou art inwardly tempted, as well as outwardly afflicted.

(4.) Fourthly, *Whilst Satan is tempting of thee, Christ in the court of glory is interceding for thee*:[3] Luke xxii. 31, 32, 'And the Lord said, Simon, Simon, behold, Satan hath desired to have you, that he may sift you as wheat: but I have prayed for thee, that thy faith fail not.' Satan would fain have been shaking of him up and down, as wheat is shaken in a fan; but Christ's intercession frustrates Satan's designed temptations. Whenever Satan stands at our elbow to tempt us, Christ stands at his Father's to intercede for us: Heb. vii. 25, 'He ever lives to make intercession.' Some of the learned think, that Christ intercedes only by virtue of his merits; others think that it is done only with his mouth; probably it may be done both ways, the rather because he hath a tongue, as also a whole glorified body in heaven; and is it likely, that

[1] He that can say when he is tempted, as that young convert, *Ego non sum ego*, is happy enough under all his temptations.

[2] Israel going into Egypt had no opposition, but travelling into Canaan, they were never free.

[3] Rom. viii. 34; 1 John ii. 1; Zech. iii. 1–3.

that mouth which pleaded so much for us on earth, John xvii. should be altogether silent for us in heaven? Christ is a person of highest honour; he is the greatest favourite in the court of heaven; he always stands between us and danger. If there be any evil plotted or designed against us by Satan, the great accuser of the brethren, he foresees it, and by his intercession prevents it. When Satan puts in his pleas and commences suit upon suit against us, Christ still undertakes our cause; he answers all his pleas, and non-suits Satan at every turn, and in despite of hell he keeps us up in divine favour. When Satan pleads, Lord! here are such and such sins that thy children have committed! and here are such and such duties that they have omitted! and here are such and such mercies that they have not improved! and here are such and such ordinances that they have slighted! and here are such and such motions of the Spirit which they have quenched! divine justice answers, All this is true, but Christ hath appeared on their behalf; he hath pleaded their cause; he hath fully and fairly answered whatever hath been objected and given complete satisfaction to the utmost farthing; so that here is no accusation nor condemnation that can stand in force against them; upon which account the apostle triumphs in that Rom. viii. 34, 'Who is he that condemneth? It is Christ that died, yea rather, that is risen again, who is even at the right hand of God, who also maketh intercession for us.' Christ's intercession should be the soul's anchor-hold in time of temptation. In the day of thy temptation thou needest not be disturbed nor disquieted, but in peace and patience possess thine own soul, considering what a friend thou hast in the court of glory, and how he is most active for thee, when Satan is most busy in tempting of thee.[1]

(5.) Fifthly and lastly, *All temptations that the saints meet with, shall work much for their good; they shall be much for their gain.* The profit and advantage that will redound to tempted souls by all their temptations is very great, Rom. viii. 28, Lam. i. 12. Now this will appear to be a most certain truth by an induction of particulars thus:

[1.] First, *By temptations God multiplies and increases his children's spiritual experiences, the increase of which is better than the increase of gold.*[2] In the school of temptation, God gives his children the greatest experience of his power supporting them, of his word comforting of them, of his mercy warming of them, of his wisdom counselling of them, of his faithfulness joying of them, and of his grace strengthening of them: 2 Cor. xii. 9, 'My grace shall be sufficient for thee.' Paul never experienced so deeply what almighty power was, what the everlasting arms of mercy were, and what infinite grace and goodness was, as when he was under the buffetings of Satan.

[2.] Secondly, *All their temptations shall be physical; their temptations shall be happy preventions of great abominations*: 2 Cor. xii. 7, 'Lest I should be exalted, lest I should be exalted.' It is twice in that one verse; he begins with it, and he ends with it. If he had not been buffeted, he might have been more highly exalted in his own conceit

[1] Saith Christ, Lord! here is wisdom for their folly, humility for their pride, heavenliness, holiness, for their earthliness, for their wickedness, &c.

[2] Rom. v. 3, 4, Frequent engagements add to the soldier's skill, and much increase his experiences.

than he was before in his ecstasy. Ah, tempted souls! you say you are naught, very naught, but had it not been for the school of temptation, you might have been stark naught before this time. You say you are sick, you are even sick to death. Why, your sickness had before this time killed you, had not temptations been physical[1] to you. You are bad under temptations; but doubtless you would have been much worse had not God made temptation a diet-drink to you.[2]

[3.] Thirdly, *Temptation shall much promote the exercise of grace.* As the spring in the watch sets all the wheels agoing, and as Solomon's virtuous woman set all her maidens to work, so temptation sets faith on work, and love on work, and repentance on work, and hope on work, and holy fear on work, and godly sorrow on work,[3] Prov. xxx. 10–33; 1 Peter i. 6. As the wind sets the mill at work, so the wind of temptations sets the graces of the saints agoing. Now faith runs to Christ, now it hugs a promise, now it pleads the blood of Christ, now it looks to the recompence of reward, now it takes the sword of the Spirit, &c.; now love cleaves to Christ, now love hangs upon Christ, now love will fight it out to the death for Christ; now hope flies to the horns of the sanctuary, now hope puts on her helmet, now hope casts her anchor upon that within the veil,[4] &c. Grace is never more acted than when a Christian is most tempted. Satan made a bow of Job's wife; of his rib, as Chrysostom speaks, and shot a temptation by her at Job, thinking to have shot him to the heart: 'Curse God, and die;' but the activity of Job's graces was a breastplate that made him temptation-proof. The devil, tempting Bonaventure, told him he was a reprobate, and therefore persuaded him to drink in the present pleasures of this life; for, said he, thou art excluded from the future joys with God in heaven. Bonaventure's graces being active, he answered, No; not so, Satan: if I must not enjoy God after this life, let me enjoy him as much as I can in this life.

[4.] Fourthly, *By temptations the Lord will make you the more serviceable and useful to others.*[5] None so fit and able to relieve tempted souls, to sympathise with tempted souls, to succour tempted souls, to counsel tempted souls, to pity tempted souls, to support tempted souls, to bear with tempted souls, and to comfort tempted souls, as those who have been in the school of temptations: 2 Cor. i. 3, 4, 'Blessed be God, even the Father of our Lord Jesus Christ, the Father of mercies, and the God of all comfort; who comforteth us in all our tribulation, that we may be able to comfort them which are in any trouble, by the comfort wherewith we ourselves are comforted of God.' By temptations God trains up his servants, and fits and capacitates them to succour and shelter their fellow-brethren. One tempted Christian, saith Luther, is more profitable and useful to other Christians than a hundred, I may add, than a thousand, that have not known the depths of Satan, that have not been in the school of temptation.[6] He that is master of arts in the school of temptation hath learned an art to comfort, to succour, and gently to handle tempted and distressed souls, infinitely beyond what all human arts can reach unto.

[1] = as 'physic,' medicine.—G.

[2] Those soldiers that are most in fighting, are least in sinning, and most free from diseases. [3] Tapers burn clearest in the dark. [4] Cant. iii. 6, 7; Heb. vi. 19.

[5] The skilfullest commanders and leaders are of the greatest service and use to the soldiers. [6] Luther in Gen. xxvii.; Rev. ii. 24.

No doctor to him that hath been a doctor in the school of temptation; all other doctors are but illiterate dunces to him.

[5.] Fifthly, *It is an honour to the saints to be tempted, and in the issue to have an honourable conquest over the tempter.* It was a great honour to David that he should be put to fight hand to hand with Goliath, and in the issue to overcome him, 1 Sam. xvii.; but it was far greater honour to Job and Paul, that they should be put to combat in the open field with Satan himself, and in the close to gain a famous conquest over him, as they did, Job i.; 2 Cor. xii. 7–10. It was a very great honour to David's three mighty men, that in jeopardy of their lives they brake through the host of the Philistines, to bring water to David out of the well of Bethlehem, and did effect it in spite of all the strength and power of their enemies, though it were to the extremest hazard of their blood and lives, 2 Sam. xxiii. 13–18; but it is a far greater honour to the saints to be furnished with a spirit of strength, courage, and valour, to break through an army of temptations, and in the close to triumph over them, Rom. viii. 15–28; and yet this honour have all the saints: 1 Cor. x. 13, 'But God is faithful, who will not suffer you to be tempted above that ye are able; but will with the temptation also make a way to escape, that ye may be able to bear it;' Rom. xvi. 20, 'And the God of peace shall tread Satan under your feet shortly;' 1 John ii. 13, 14, 'I write unto you, fathers, because ye have known him that is from the beginning. I write unto you, young men, because ye have overcome the wicked one. I write unto you, children, because ye have known the Father. I have written unto you, fathers, because ye have known him that is from the beginning. I have written unto you, young men, because ye are strong, and the word of God abideth in you, and ye have overcome the wicked one.' 1 John v. 18, 'We know that whosoever is born of God sinneth not,' that is, 'that sin that is unto death,' ver. 16; nor he sinneth not as other men do, delightfully,[1] greedily, customarily, resolvedly, impenitently, &c. 'But he that is begotten of God keepeth himself, and that wicked one toucheth him not.' The glorious victory that the people of God had over Pharaoh and his great host, Exod. xiv., was a figure of the glorious victory that the saints shall obtain over Satan and his instruments, which is clear from that Rev. xv. 3, where we have the song of Moses and of the Lamb. But why the song of Moses and of the Lamb, but to hint this to us, that the overthrow of Pharaoh was a figure of the overthrow of Satan? and the triumphal song of Moses was a figure of that song which the saints shall sing for their overthrow of Satan. As certainly as Israel overcame Pharaoh, so certainly shall every true Israelite overcome Satan. The Romans were worsted in many fights, but never were overcome in a set war; at the long run they overcame all their enemies. Though a Christian may be worsted by Satan in some particular skirmishes, yet at the long run he is sure of an honourable conquest. God puts a great deal of honour upon a poor soul when he brings him into the open field to fight it out with Satan. By fighting he overcomes, he gains the victory, he triumphs over Satan, and leads captivity captive. Augustine gives this reason why God permitted Adam at first to be tempted, viz. That he might have had the

[1] 'Delightedly.'—G.

more glory in resisting and withstanding Satan's temptation. It is the glory of a Christian to be made strong to resist, and to have his resistance crowned with a happy conquest.

[6.] Sixthly, *By temptations the Lord will make his people more frequent and more abundant in the work of prayer.* Every temptation proves a strong alarm to prayer. When Paul was in the school of temptation, he prayed thrice, that is, often, 1 Cor. xii. 8, 9. Days of temptation are days of great supplication; Christians usually pray most when they are tempted most. They are most busy with God when Satan is most busy with them. A Christian is most upon his knees when Satan stands most at his elbow.

Augustine was a man much tempted, and a man much in prayer. Holy prayer, saith he, is a shelter to the soul, a sacrifice to God, and a scourge to the devil.

Luther was a man under manifold temptations, and a man much in prayer. He is said to have spent three hours every day in prayer. He used to say that prayer was the best book in his study.

Chrysostom was much in the school of temptation, and delighted much in prayer. Oh! saith he, it is more bitter than death to be spoiled of prayer, and hereupon, as he observes, Daniel chose rather to run the hazard of his life than to lose his prayer.[1] But,

[7.] Seventhly, *By temptations the Lord will make his people more and more conformable to the image of his Son.* Christ was much tempted, he was often in the school of temptation; and the more a Christian is tempted, the more into the likeness of Christ he will be transformed. Of all men in the world, tempted souls do most resemble Christ to the life, in meekness, lowliness, holiness, heavenliness, &c. The image of Christ is most fairly stamped upon tempted souls. Tempted souls are much in looking up to Jesus, and every gracious look upon Christ changes the soul more and more into the image of Christ. Tempted souls experience much of the succourings of Christ, and the more they experience the sweet of the succourings of Christ, the more they grow up into the likeness of Christ. Temptations are the tools by which the Father of spirits doth more and more carve, form, and fashion his precious saints into the similitude and likeness of his dearest Son.[2]

[8.] Eighthly and lastly, take many things in one; *God by temptations makes sin more hateful, and the world less delightful, and relations less hurtful.* By temptations God discovers to us our own weakness and the creature's insufficiency in the hour of temptation to help us or succour us. By temptations, God will brighten our Christian armour, and make us stand more upon our Christian watch, and keep us closer to a succouring Christ. By temptations, the Lord will make his ordinances to be more highly prized, and heaven to be more earnestly desired. Now seeing that temptations shall work so eminently for the saints' good, why should not Christians be mute and silent? why should they not hold their peace, and lay their hands upon their mouths, though their afflictions are attended with great temptations?[3]

[1] So Bernard, Basil, Gorgonia [Gorgonius?]. Trucilla; James, Jacob, Daniel.

[2] Heb. xii. 1, 2; 2 Cor. ii. 28; Heb. ii. 17, 18

[3] 1 Pet. v. 8; Eph. vi. 10, 18; 2 Cor. v. 1-3.

Obj. 8. Oh! but God hath deserted me! he hath forsaken me! and 'he that should comfort my soul stands afar off!' how can I be silent? The Lord hath hid his face from me; clouds are gathered about me; God hath turned his back upon me; how can I hold my peace?

Supposing that the desertion is real, and not in appearance only, as sometimes it falls out: I answer,

(1.) First, *It hath been the common lot, portion, and condition of the choicest saints in this world, to be deserted and forsaken of God,* Ps. xxx. 6, 7; Ps. lxxvii. 6, and lxxxviii. 6; Job xxiii. 8, 9; Cant. iii. 1–4, v. 6, 7; Isa. viii. 17; Micah vii. 7-9. If God deals no worse with thee than he hath dealt with his most bosom friends, with his choicest jewels, thou hast no reason to complain. But,

(2.) Secondly, *God's forsaking of thee is only partial, it is not total,* Psa. ix. 4; Gen. xlix. 23, 24. God may forsake his people in part, but he never wholly forsakes them; he may forsake them in respect of his quickening presence, and in respect of his comforting presence, but he never forsakes them in respect of his supporting presence; 2 Cor. xii. 9, 'My grace is sufficient for thee; for my strength is made perfect in weakness;' Ps. xxxvii. 23, 24, 'The steps of a good man are ordered by the Lord; and he delighteth in his way. Though he fall, he shall not be utterly cast down: for the Lord upholdeth him with his hand.'[1] God's supporting hand of grace is still under his people: Ps. lxiii. 8, 'My soul followeth hard after thee: thy right hand upholdeth me.' Christ hath always one hand to uphold his people, and another hand to embrace them, Cant. ii. 16. The everlasting arms of God are always underneath his people, Deut. xxxiii. 27. And this the saints have always found; witness David, Heman, Asaph, Job, &c.

Geographers write that the city of Syracuse, in Sicily, is so curiously situated that the sun is never out of sight. Though the children of God sometimes are under some clouds of afflictions, yet the Sun of mercy, the Sun of righteousness, is never quite out of sight. But,

(3.) Thirdly, *Though God hath forsaken thee, yet his love abides and continues constant to thee; he loves thee with an everlasting love:* Jer. xxxi. 3, 'Where he loves, he loves to the end;' John xiii. 1; Isa. xlix. 14–16, 'But Zion said, The Lord hath forsaken me, and my Lord hath forgotten me.' But was not Zion mistaken? yes, 'Can a woman forget her sucking child, that she should not have compassion on the son of her womb? yea, they may forget, yet will not I forget thee. Behold, I have graven thee upon the palms of my hands; thy walls are continually before me.'[2] Look! as persons engrave the mark, name, or picture of those whom they dearly love and entirely affect, upon some stone that they wear at their breasts, or upon some ring that they wear on their finger, so hath God engraven Zion upon the palms of his hands; she was still in his eye, and always dear to his heart, though she thought not so. As Joseph's heart was full of love to his brethren, Gen xlii. and xliii., even then when he spake roughly to them, and withdrew himself from them, for he was fain to go aside and ease his heart by weeping; so the heart of God is full of love to his people, even then when he

[1] As the nurse upholds the little child, &c.

[2] The very heathen hath observed that God doth not love his children with a weak affection, but with a strong masculine love.—*Seneca.*

seems to be most displeased with them, and to turn his back upon them. Though God's dispensations may be changeable towards his people, yet his gracious disposition is unchangeable towards them, Mal. iii. 6. When God puts the blackest veil of all upon his face, yet then his heart is full of love to his people, then his bowels are yearning towards them: Jer. xxxi. 18–20, 'Is Ephraim my dear son? is he a pleasant child? for since I spake against him, I do earnestly remember him still; therefore my bowels are troubled for him: I will surely have mercy upon him, saith the Lord.' The mother's bowels cannot more yearn after the tender babe than God doth after his distressed ones. As Moses his mother, when she had put him into the ark of bulrushes, Exod. ii., wept to see the babe weep, and when she was turned from him, she could not but cast a weeping eye of love towards him; so when God turns aside from his people, yet he cannot but cast an eye of love towards them: Hos. xi. 1, 'How shall I give thee up, O Ephraim!' &c. Here are four several 'hows' in the text, the like not to be found in the whole book of God. I am even at a stand, justice calls for vengeance, but mercy interposeth; my bowels yearn, my heart melts, oh, how shall I give thee up! oh, I cannot give thee up! I will not give thee up! God's love is always like himself, unchângeable; his love is everlasting; it is a love that never decays nor waxes cold; it is like the stone albestos,[1] of which Solinus[2] writes, that being once hot, it can never be cooled again.

(4.) Fourthly, *Though the Lord hath hid his face from thee, yet certainly thou hast his secret presence with thee.* God is present when he is seemingly absent: 'The Lord was in this place, and I knew it not,' saith Jacob, Gen. xxviii. 16. The sun many times shines when we do not see it, and the husband is many times in the house when the wife doth not know it. God [is] in thy house, he is in thy heart, though thou seest him not, thou feelest him not, though thou hearest him not: Heb. xiii. 5, 'I will never leave thee, nor forsake thee;' or, as it may be rendered according to the Greek, 'I will not leave thee, neither will I not forsake thee.' Art thou not now drawn out to prize God and Christ, and his love above all the world? Yes. Art thou not now drawn out to give the Lord many a secret visit, in a corner, behind the door, Cant. ii. 14, in some dark hole where none can see thee nor hear thee but the Lord? Ps. xlii. 1–3, lxiii. 1–3. Yes. Are there not strong breathings, pantings, and longings after a clearer vision of God, and after a fuller fruition of God? Yes. Art thou not more affected and afflicted with the withdrawings of Christ than thou art with the greatest afflictions that ever befell thee? Cant. v. 6. Yes. Austin, upon that answer of God to Moses, 'Thou canst not see my face and live,' Exod. xxxiii. 20, makes this quick and sweet reply, 'Then, Lord! let me die, that I may see thy face.' Dost thou not often tell God that there is no punishment to the punishment of loss, and no hell to that of being forsaken of God? Ps. xxx. 6, 7. Yes. Dost thou not find a secret power in thy soul, drawing thee forth to struggle with God, to lay hold on God, and patiently to wait on God, till he shall return unto thee, and lift up the

[1] 'Asbestos.'—G.

[2] The 'ape' of Pliny, whose grotesque 'Worke,' quaintly rendered by Golding (1587), was a favourite with the Puritans.—G.

light of his countenance upon thee? Yes. Well, then, thou mayest be confident that thou hast a secret and blessed presence of God with thee, though God, in regard of his comfortable presence, may be departed from thee. Nothing below a secret presence of God with a man's spirit will keep him waiting and working till the Sun of righteousness shines upon him, Mal. iv. 2. If any vain persons should put that deriding question to thee, Where is thy God? thou mayest safely and boldly answer them, 'My God is here; he is nigh me, he is round about me, yea, he is in the midst of me: Zeph. iii. 17, 'The Lord thy God in the midst of thee is mighty, he will save, he will rejoice over thee with joy, he will rest in his love, he will joy over thee with singing.' The bush, which was a type of the church, consumed not all the while it burned with fire, because God was in the midst of it. It is no argument that Christ is not in the ship, because tempests and storms arise.

(5.) Fifthly, *Though God be gone, yet he will return again.* Though your sun be now set in a cloud, yet it will rise again; though sorrow may abide for a night, yet joy comes in the morning.[1] A Christian's mourning shall last but till morning: Micah vii. 19, 'He will turn again, he will have compassion upon us;' Cant. iii. 4, 'It was but a little that I passed from them, but I found him whom my soul loveth; I held him, and I would not let him go,' &c.; Ps. xciv. 19, 'In the multitude of my thoughts within me, thy comforts delight my soul;' Isa. liv. 7, 8, 10, 'For a moment have I forsaken thee, but with great mercies will I gather thee. In a little wrath I hid my face from thee for a moment, but with everlasting kindness will I have mercy on thee, saith the Lord thy Redeemer; for the mountains shall depart, and the hills be removed, but my kindness shall not depart from thee; neither shall the covenant of my peace be removed, saith the Lord, that hath mercy on thee.' God will not suffer his whole displeasure to rise upon his people, neither will he forsake them totally or finally. The saints shall taste but some sips of the cup of God's wrath, sinners shall drink the dregs; their storm shall end in a calm, and their winter night shall be turned into a summer day. There was a woman who was thirteen years under desertion, which was so vehement, that for the most part of her time she was fain to keep her bed through weakness. A godly minister, who was affected with her condition, went to comfort her, and to pray with her; but when he came and offered to do it, she shrieked out, utterly refusing and forbidding him to pray with her, for, said she, I have too many abused mercies to answer for already. Yet he would not be put off, but prayed by her, and so prevailed with God on her behalf, that the next morning she was delivered from all her fears, and had such exceeding joy, that the like hath rarely been heard of. The Lord, that had been long withdrawn from her, returned at length in a way of singular mercy to her.[2] There was another precious woman who was several years deserted, and hearing a precious godly minister preach, she of a sudden fell down, overwhelmed with joy, crying out, Oh! he is come whom my soul loveth! and for divers days after she was filled

[1] Isa. xvii. 14; Ps. xxx. 5; xl. 1–3; v. 11; xlii. 5, 8, 9, 11.

[2] So Mrs Honeywood, Mrs Katherine Brettergh, and divers others. [See note *ante* on Mrs Brettergh, and our Index *sub nomine.*—G.]

with such exceeding joys, and had such gracious and singular ravishing expressions so fluently coming from her, that many came to hear the rare manifestations of God's grace in her. The lowest of her pious expressions did exceed the highest that ever the minister had read in the book of martyrs. But,

(6.) Sixthly and lastly, *God's deserting, God's forsaking of his people, shall many ways work for their good.* As,

[1.] First, *God by withdrawing from his people, will prepare and fit them for greater refreshings, manifestations, and consolations:* Ps. lxxi. 11, 20, 21, 'Saying, God hath forsaken him: persecute and take him; for there is none to deliver him.' But shall this forlorn condition work for his good? Yes, 'Thou, which hast shewed me great and sore troubles, shall quicken me again, and shalt bring me up again from the depths of the earth. Thou shalt increase my greatness, and comfort me on every side.' When Joseph's brethren were in their greatest distress, then Joseph makes known himself most fully to them, Gen. xlv. 2–4; so doth Christ, our spiritual Joseph, to his people. Hudson the martyr, deserted at the stake, went from under his chain, and having prayed earnestly, was comforted immediately, and suffered valiantly.[1]

[2.] *By God's withdrawing from his people, he prevents his people's withdrawing from him; and so by an affliction he prevents sin.*[2] For God to withdraw from me is but my affliction, but for me to withdraw from God, that is my sin, Heb. x. 38, 39; and therefore it were better for me that God should withdraw a thousand times from me, than that I should once withdraw from God. God therefore forsakes us, that we may not forsake our God. God sometimes hides himself that we may cleave the closer to him, and hang the faster upon him; as the mother hides herself from the child for a time, that the child may cleave the closer and hang the faster upon her all the day long. God sometimes hid himself from David: Ps. xxx. 7, 'Thou didst hide thy face, and I was troubled,' I was all amort.[3] Well! and is that all? No; ver. 8, 'I cried to thee, O Lord, and unto the Lord I made my supplication.' Now he cries louder, and cleaves closer to God than ever; so in that Ps. lxiii. 1, 2, 'O God, thou art my God; early will I seek thee: my soul thirsteth for thee, my flesh longeth for thee in a dry and thirsty land, where no water is; to see thy power and thy glory, so as I have seen thee in thy sanctuary.' Well! and how do those withdrawings of God work? Why! this you may see in ver. 8, 'My soul followeth hard after thee,' or as the Hebrew reads it, 'My soul cleaveth after thee.' Look! as the husband cleaves to his wife, so doth my soul cleave to the Lord. The psalmist now follows God even hard at heels, as we say. But,

[3.] Thirdly, *The Lord, by withdrawing from his people, will enhance and raise the price, and commend the worth, excellency, sweetness, and usefulness of several precious promises, which otherwise would be but as dry breasts, and as useless weapons to the soul,* 2 Peter i. 4. As that Micah vii. 18, 19, 'He will turn again, he will have compassion

[1] Clark's 'Martyrologie,' as before, page 499.—G.
[2] Christ, the captain of our salvation, will execute martial law upon them that withdraw from their colours, &c. [3] 'Dejected.'—G.

upon us,' &c.; and that Isa. liv. 7, 8, but now opened; and that Heb. xiii. 5, 6; and that Heb. ii. 3; and that Ps. v. 12, 'For thou, Lord, wilt bless the righteous; with favour thou wilt compass him,' or crown him, 'as with a shield.' The Lord will compass the righteous about with his favour, as the crown compasses about the head, as the Hebrew imports; and that Ps. cxii. 4, 'Unto the upright there ariseth light in darkness: he is gracious, and full of compassion, and righteous.' And that Jer. xxxi. 37, 'Thus saith the Lord, If heaven above can be measured, and the foundations of the earth searched out beneath, I will also cast off all the seed of Israel, for all that they have done, saith the Lord.'[1] As sure as heaven cannot be measured, nor the foundations of the earth searched by the skill or power of any mortal man, so sure and certain it is, that God will not utterly cast off his people, no, not for all the evil that they have done. Now at what a rate doth a deserted soul value these precious promises? Well! saith he, these promises are sweeter than the honey or the honey-comb; they are more precious than gold, than fine gold, than much gold, than all the gold in the world; I prefer them before my food, before my delightful food, yea, before my necessary food, before my appointed portion.[2] As Alexander laid up Homer's Iliad in a cabinet embroidered with gold and pearls; so deserted souls will lay up these precious promises in the cabinet of their hearts, as the choicest treasure the world affords. Dolphins, they say, love music, so do deserted souls the music of the promises. That promise, 1 Tim. i. 15, was music to Bilney the martyr; and that promise, John x. 29, was music to Ursinus; and that promise, Isa lvii. 15, was music to another; and that promise, Isa. xxvi. 3, was music to another; and that to another, Mat. xi. 28, &c. Promises that are suited to a deserted man's condition, make the sweetest music in his ear, and are the most sovereign cordials to bear up the spirits that God can give, or heaven afford, or the soul desire: Deut. xxxii. 13, 'He made him to ride on the high places of the earth, that he might eat the fruits of the field; and he made him to suck honey out of the rock, and oil out of the flinty rock.' Ah! the honey, the oil that deserted souls suck of such promises that speak home and close to their conditions!

[4.] Fourthly, *By God's hiding his face and withdrawing himself from thee, thou wilt be enabled more feelingly, and more experimentally to sympathise with others, and to have compassion on others that are or may be in the dark and forsaken of God, as now thou art*, Heb. v. 2. Heb. xiii. 2, 'Remember them that are in bonds, as bound with them; and them which suffer adversity, as being yourselves also in the body.' It is observed of the bees, that when one is sick they all mourn;[3] and of the sheep, that if one of them be faint, the rest of the flock will stand betwixt it and the sun until it be revived. In the natural body, if one member grieve and is in pain, all suffer with it. When a thorn is got into the foot, how doth the back bow, and the eyes pry, and the hands go to pluck the thorn out! None so compassionate towards deserted souls as those who have been deserted and for-

[1] And that John xiv. 21–23; and that Sam. xii. 20; Isa. lx. 19–22.

[2] Ps. cxix. 72, 103, xix. 10; Prov. viii. 11; Job xxiii. 12.

[3] Pliny in Nat. Hist. l. xi. c. 17. [The remark is made concerning the 'king' (queen) bee.—G.]

saken of God themselves. Oh! they know what an evil and a bitter thing it is to be left and forsaken of God, and therefore their bowels, their compassions run out much to such, yea, most to such. They know that there is no affliction, no misery, no hell, to that of being forsaken of God.

Anaxagoras, seeing himself old and forsaken of the world, laid himself down, and covered his head close, determining to starve himself to death with hunger [Plutarch]. But, alas! what is it to be forsaken of the world, to a man's being forsaken of God? Were there as many worlds as there be men in the world, a man were better be forsaken by them all than to be forsaken of God. There is a great truth in that saying of Chrysostom, viz., That the torments of a thousand hells, if there were so many, come far short of this one, to wit, to be turned out of God's presence with a *Non novi vos*, I know you not, Mat. vii. 23.[1] The schools have long since concluded, that *pœna sensus*, the pain of sense, is far greater than *pœna damni*, the pain of loss. What a grief was it to Absalom to see the king's face clouded; and how sadly was Eli and his daughter affected with the loss of the ark, which was but a testimony of God's presence! but oh! how much more is a Christian affected and afflicted with the loss of the face and favour of God, the remembrance of which makes his heart to melt and his bowels to yearn towards those whose sun is set in a cloud?

[5.] Fifthly, *Hereby the Lord will teach his people to set a higher price upon his face and favour when they come to enjoy it.*[2] Cant. iii. 4, 'It was but a little that I passed from them, but I found him whom my soul loveth; I held him, and I would not let him go,' &c. No man sets so high a price upon Christ, as he that hath lost him and found him again. Jesus in the China tongue signifies the rising sun, and so he is, Mal. iv. 2, especially to souls that have been long clouded. The poor northern nations of Strabo, who want the light of the sun for some months together, when the term of his return approaches, they climb up into the highest mountains to spy it, and he that spies it first was accounted the best and most beloved of God, and usually they did choose him king; at such a rate did they prize the return of the sun. Ah! so it is with a poor soul, that for some months, years, hath been deserted; oh, how highly doth he prize and value the Sun of righteousness his returning to him, and shining upon him! Ps. lxiii. 3, 'Thy loving-kindness is better than life,' or, 'better than lives,' as the Hebrew hath it [*Chaiim*]. Divine favour is better than life; it is better than life with all its revenues, with all its appurtenances, as honours, riches, pleasures, applause, &c., yea, it is better than many lives put together. Now you know at what a high rate men value their lives; they will bleed, sweat, vomit, purge, part with an estate, yea, with a limb, yea, limbs, to preserve their lives. As he cried out, Give me any deformity, any torment, any misery, so you spare my life. Now, though life be so dear and precious to a man, yet a deserted soul prizes the returnings of divine favour upon him above life, yea, above many lives. Many men have been weary of their lives, as is evident in

[1] Chrysostom, ad Pop. Antioch. Hom. 47, and in Mat. Hom. 24.

[2] Austin saith, Lord, I am content to suffer any pains and torments in this world, if I might see thy face one day; at such a rate did he prize the face of God.

Scripture and history; but no man was ever yet found that was weary of the love and favour of God. No man sets so high a price upon the sun as he that hath laid long in a dark dungeon, &c. But,

[6.] Sixthly, *Hereby the Lord will train up his servants in that precious life of faith, which is the most honourable and the most happy life in all the world:* 2 Cor. v. 7, 'For we walk by faith, and not by sight.' The life of sense, the life of reason, is a low life, a mean life; the life of faith is a noble life, a blessed life. When Elisha demanded of the Shunamite what he should do for her, whether he should speak for her to the king or the captain of the host, she answered, 'I dwell among my people,' 2 Kings iv. 13; that is, I dwell nobly and happily among my people; I have no need to make any suit to king or captain; and this she accounts her great happiness, and indeed it is the greatest happiness in this world to live much in the exercise of faith. No man lives so free a life, so holy a life, so heavenly a life, so happy a life, as he that lives a life of faith. By divine withdrawings the soul is put upon hanging upon a naked God, a naked Christ, a naked promise, Isa. l. 10; lxiii. 15, 16. Now the soul is put upon the highest and the purest acts of faith, viz., to cleave to God, to hang upon God, and to carry it sweetly and obediently towards God, though he frowns, though he chides, though he strikes, yea, though he kills, Job xiii. 15.[1] Those are the most excellent and heroic acts of faith that are most abstracted from sense and reason; he that suffers his reason to usurp upon his faith, will never be an excellent Christian. He that goes to school to his own reason, hath a fool to his schoolmaster; and he that suffers his faith to be overruled by his reason, shall never want woe. Where reason is strongest, faith usually is weakest. But now the Lord, by forsaking of his people for a time, he makes them skilful in the life of faith, which is the choicest and the sweetest life in this world. But,

[7.] Seventhly, *By divine withdrawings, you are made more conformable to Christ your head and husband, who was under spiritual desertion as well as you:* Mat. xxvii. 46, 'My God, my God, why hast thou forsaken me?' Ps. xxii. 1, 2. There is an hidden emphasis in the Hebrew word: *El* signifies a strong God; *Eli, Eli,* My strong God, my strong God. The unity of Christ's person was never dissolved, nor his graces were never diminished.[2] In the midst of this terrible storm, his faith fortifieth and strengtheneth itself upon the strength of God, *My* God, *my* God; yet in respect of divine protection and divine solace, he was for some time forsaken of his Father. And if this be thy case, thou art herein but made conformable to thy Lord and master; nay, thou dost but sip of that bitter cup of which Christ drank deep; thy cloud is no cloud to that which Christ was under. But,

[8.] Eighthly and lastly, *By these transient and partial forsakings, the Lord will exceedingly sweeten the clear, full, constant, and uninterrupted enjoyments of himself in heaven to all his people,* Ps. lxxi. 10, 21. Ah! how sweet and precious was the face and favour of the king to Absalom, after he had for a time been banished, and at length restored to his royal favour again! Onesimus departed from Philemon

[1] Faith acts in the most kingly way when it hangs upon a killing God.

[2] Christ was only forsaken in regard of his human nature, not in respect of his Godhead.

for a season, that he might receive him for ever. So the Lord departs from his people for a time, that they may receive him for ever; he hides himself for a season, that his constant presence amongst his children in glory may be the more sweet and delightful to them, &c.

Object. 9. Oh! but I am falsely accused and sadly reproached, and my good name, which should be as dear or dearer to me than my life, is defamed and fly-blown, and things are laid to my charge that I never did, that I never knew, &c.; and how then can I be silent? how can I hold my peace? I cannot forget the proverb, *Oculus et fama non patiuntur jocos*, a man's eye and his good name can bear no jests; and how then can I be mute to see men make jests upon my good name? and every day to see men lade it with all the scorn and contempt imaginable, that they may utterly blast it? &c. To this I say,

(1.) First, *That it must be granted that a good name is one of the choicest jewels in a Christian's crown.* Though a great name many times is little worth, yet a good name is rather to be chosen than great riches. It is better to have a good name abroad, than silver or gold laid up in a chest at home. 'A good name is better than precious ointment,' Eccles. vii. 1. Precious ointments were greatly in use and highly esteemed of amongst the Israelites in those eastern parts; they were laid up amongst the most precious things even in the king's treasury, Isa. xxxix. 2. Sweet ointments can but affect the smell, and comfort the brain, and delight the outward man; they reach not the best part, the noble part, viz., the soul, the conscience of a Christian; but a good name doth both. What is the perfume of the nostrils to the perfume of the heart?[1]

I have read that in some countries they have a certain art of drawing of pigeons to their dove-houses in those countries, by anointing the wings of one of them with sweet ointment, and that pigeon being sent abroad, doth, by the fragrancy of that ointment, decoy, invite, and allure others to that house, where itself is a domestic. Such is the fragrancy of a good name, that it draws other men after the savour thereof. Among all sorts and ranks of men in the world, a good name hath an attractive faculty; it is a precious ointment that draws hearers to attend good preachers, patients to attend physicians, clients to attend lawyers, scholars to attend schoolmasters, and customers to attend shopkeepers, who, with Demetrius, hath a good report of all good men, 3d epistle of John 12. Let a man's good name be but up, and he cannot easily want anything that men or money can help him to. A good name will bring a man into favour, and keep a man in favour with all that are good; therefore, say the moralists:

> Omnia si perdas, famam servare memento,
> Qua semel amissa, postea nullus eris.[2]

Whatsoever commodity you lose, be sure yet to preserve that jewel of a good name. A Christian should be most chary of his good name, for a good name answers to all things, as Solomon spake of money. *Ergo si bonam famam servasso, sat dives ero,* If I may but keep a good name, I have wealth enough, said the heathen [Plautus]. A Christian should rather forego gold than let go a good name; and he that robs a Chris-

[1] A good renown is better than a golden girdle, saith the French proverb.
[2] Claudian, De Cons. Mall. Theod. v. 3.—G.

tian of his good name is a worse thief than he that robs him of his purse, and better deserves a hanging than he, &c.[1] But,

(2.) Secondly, *It must be granted, that a good name once lost, is very hardly recovered again.* A man may more easily recover a lost friend, a lost estate, than a lost name. A good name is like a princely structure, quickly ruined, but long a-rearing. The father of the prodigal could say of his lost son, 'This my son was lost, but is found; he was dead, but is alive,' Luke xv. 32; but how few Christians can say, This my good name was lost, but is found; it was dead, but now it lives. As when Orpah once left Naomi, she returned no more to her, Ruth i. 14; so when once a good name leaves a man, it hardly returns to him again. A cracked credit will hardly be sodered[2] anew; new wine is rarely put into old bottles. A man should stand upon nothing more than the credit of his conscience and the credit of his name.

In Japan, the very children are so zealous of their reputation, that in case you lose a trifle, and say to one of them, Sirrah, I believe you have stolen it, without any pause, the boy will immediately cut off a joint from one of his fingers, and say, Sir, if you say true, I wish my finger may never heal again. Three things a Christian should stiffly labour to maintain: 1, the honour of God; 2, the honour of the gospel; 3, the honour of his own name. If once a Christian's good name sets in a cloud, it will be long before it rises again.

(3.) Thirdly, *Though all this be true, yet it hath been the portion of God's dearest saints and servants to be slandered, reproached, vilified, and falsely accused:*[3] Ps. xxxi. 18, 'Let the lying lips be put to silence, which speak grievous things, proudly, and contemptuously against the righteous.' How sadly and falsely was Joseph accused by his wanton mistress; David by Doeg and Shimei; Job of hypocrisy, impiety, inhumanity, cruelty, partiality, pride, and irreligion! Was not Naboth accused of speaking blasphemy against God and the king? Did not Haman present the Jews to the king as refractories and rebels? Esther iii. Was not Elias accused to be the troubler of Israel, and Jeremiah the trumpet of rebellion; the Baptist a stirrer up of sedition, and Paul a pestilent incendiary?[4] Were not the apostles generally accounted deceivers and deluders of the people, and the offscouring of the world? &c. Athanasius and Eustathius were falsely accused of adultery.[5] Heresy and treason were charged upon Cranmer, parricide upon Philpot, sedition upon Latimer. As the primitive persecutors usually put Christians into bears' skins and dogs' skins, and then baited them;[6] so they usually loaded their names and persons with all the reproach, scorn, contempt, and false reports imaginable, and then baited them, and then acted all their malice and cruelty upon them. I think there is no Christian, but sooner or later, first or last, will have cause to say with David, Ps. xxxv. 11, 'False witnesses did rise up; they laid to my charge

[1] Another reminiscence by our Puritan of Shakespeare's, 'Who steals my purse steals trash,' &c.—Othello III. 3.—G.

[2] 'Soldered.—G.

[3] Mat. v. 10–12; 1 Peter iii. 14; Ps. lxix. 7; Gen. xxxix. 13, 14; Ps. lii. 1, 2; 2 Sam. iii. 11, 12; vi. 13–16; Jer. li. 51.

[4] Jer. xx. 7–9; Rom. iii. 8; 2 Cor. vi. 8; 1 Cor. iv. 12, 13.

[5] Act. and Mon. [Foxe.—G.]

[6] As Tertullian, Minutius Felix, and others declare. [Cf. Clarke's 'Martyrologie,' as before, with quaint illustrations to as quaint a text.—G.]

things that I knew not;' they charged me with such things whereof I was both innocent and ignorant. It was the saying of one [Hippias], that there was nothing so intolerable as accusation, because there was no punishment ordained by law for accusers, as there was for thieves, although they stole friendship from men, which is the goodliest riches men can have. Well! Christians, seeing it hath been the lot of the dearest saints to be falsely accused, and to have their names and reputes in the world reproached and fly-blown, do you hold your peace, seeing it is no worse with you than it was with them, 'of whom this world was not worthy.' The Rabbins say [Kimchi], that the world cannot subsist without patient bearing of reproaches. But,

(4.) Fourthly, *Our Lord Jesus Christ was sadly reproached and falsely accused.* His precious name, that deserves to be always writ in characters of gold, as the Persians usually writ their king's, was often eclipsed before the sun was eclipsed at his death. His sweet name, that was sweeter than all sweets, was often crucified before his body. Oh, the stones of reproach that were frequently rolled upon that name by which we must be saved, if ever we are saved! Oh, the jeers, the scoffs, the scorns that were cast upon that name that can only bless us! The name of Jesus, saith Chrysostom, hath a thousand treasures of joy and comfort in it. The name of a Saviour, saith Bernard, is honey in the mouth, and music in the ear, and a jubilee in the heart; and yet where is the heart that can conceive, or the tongue that can express, how much dung and filth hath been cast upon Christ's name; and how many sharp arrows of reproach and scorn hath been, and daily, yea, hourly, are, shot by the world at Christ's name and honour? Such ignominious reproaches were cast upon Christ and his name in the time of his life and at his death, that the sun did blush, and masked himself with a cloud, that he might no longer behold them.[1] Mat. xi. 19, 'The Son of man came eating and drinking, and they say, Behold a man gluttonous, and a winebibber, a friend of publicans and sinners.' But was he such an one? No: 'Wisdom is justified of her children.' Wisdom's children will stand up and justify her before all the world. Mat. xxvii. 63, 'Sir, we remember that that deceiver said, while he was yet alive, After three days, I will rise again.' But was he a deceiver of the people?[2] No, he was the faithful and true witness, Rev. i. 5, chap. iii. 14. John vii. 20, 'The people answered and said, Thou hast a devil; who goeth about to kill thee?' chap. viii. 48, 'Then answered the Jews, and said unto him, Say we not well, that thou art a Samaritan, and hast a devil?' chap. x. 20, 'And many of them said, He hath a devil, and is mad; why hear ye him?' It was a wonder of wonders that the earth did not open and swallow up these monsters, and that God did not rain hell out of heaven upon these horrid blasphemers; but their blasphemous assertions were denied and disproved by some of wisdom's children: ver. 21, 'Others said, These are not the words of him that hath a devil: can a devil open the eyes of the blind?' The devil hath no such power, nor any such goodness, as to create eyes to him that was born blind.

[1] It is a foolish thing, saith Cato, to hope for life by another's death. The world practically speaks as much every day.

[2] The Greek word signifies one who doth profess an art of cozening people to their faces.

Will you yet see more scorn, dirt, and contempt cast upon the Lord of glory? Why, then, cast your eyes upon that: Luke xvi. 14, 'And the pharisees also, who were covetous, heard all these things, and they derided him;' or as the Greek reads it, 'They blew their noses at him in scorn and derision.'[1] The pharisees did not only laugh, fleer, and jeer at Christ, but they have also external signs of scorn and derision in their countenance and gestures; they blew their noses at him, they contemned him as a thing of nought. And in chap. xxv. 35, both people and rulers blew their noses at him; for the original word is the same with that in the fore-mentioned chapter. John xix. 12, he is accused for being an enemy to Cæsar. Now, who can seriously consider of the scorn, reproach, and contempt that hath been cast upon the name and honour of our Lord Jesus, and not sit silent and mute under all the scorn and contempt that hath been cast upon his name or person in this world?

(5.) Fifthly, *To be well spoken of by them that are ill spoken of by God, to be in favour with them who are out of favour with God, is rather a reproach than an honour to a man.* Our Saviour himself testifieth that in the church and nation of the Jews, they that had the most general approbation and applause, they who were most admired and cried up, were the worst, not the best, men; they were the false, not the true, prophets: Luke vi. 26, 'Woe unto you when all men shall speak well of you, for so did their fathers to the false prophets.'[2] Austin feared the praises of good men, and detested the praises of evil men. I would not, saith Luther, have the glory and fame of Erasmus; my greatest fear is the praises of men. Phocion had not suspected his speech had not the common people applauded it. Antisthenes mistrusted some ill in himself for the vulgar commendations. Socrates ever suspected that which passed with the most general commendations. To be praised of evil men, said Bion, is to be praised for evil doing; for the better they speak of a man the worse, and the worse the better. The Lacedæmonians would not have a good saying sullied with a wicked mouth. A wicked tongue soils all the good that drops into it. It is a mercy to be delivered from the praises of wicked men; wicked men's applauses oftentimes become the saints' reproaches. The heathen [Socrates] could say, *Quid mali feci?* what evil have I done, that this bad man commends me. There is a truth in that saying of Seneca, *Recti argumentum est, pessimis displicere,* the worst men are commonly most displeased with that which is best. Who can seriously dwell on these things, and not be mute and silent under all the reproaches and scorn that is cast upon his name and credit in this world?

(6.) Sixthly, *There will come a day when the Lord will wipe off all the dust and filth that wicked men have cast upon the good names of his people.*[3] There shall be a resurrection of names as well as of bodies; their names that are now buried in the open sepulchres of evil throats

[1] Read this, Mark xv. 19; Isa. lvii. 4; Mat. xxvii. 2, 29. [The word is ἐξεμυκτήριζον, *sneered* with outward marks of derision; *μυκτήρ*, *nasus*, as in Horace, S. i. 6. 5, 'Naso suspendere adunco,' which Brooks probably had in mind.—G.]

[2] The tongues of wicked men are like the Duke of Medina Sidonia's sword, that knew no difference between a catholic and an heretic. The lashes of lewd tongues is as impossible to avoid as necessary to contemn.

[3] Isa. lxv. 15, lxi. 7; Ps. lxviii. 13; Mal. iii. 17, 18.

shall surely rise again.[1] 'Their innocency shall shine forth as the light, and their righteousness as the noon-day,' Ps. xxxvii. 6. Though the clouds may for a time obscure the shining forth of the sun, yet the sun will shine forth again as bright and glorious as ever: 'The righteous shall be had in everlasting remembrance,' Ps. cxii. 6. Though the malicious slanders and false accusations of wicked men may for a time cloud the names of the saints, yet those clouds shall vanish, and their names shall appear transparent and glorious. God will take that care of his people's good name, that the infamy, calumnies, and contumelies that are cast upon it shall not long stick. The Jews rolled a stone upon Christ to keep him down, that he might not rise again, but an angel quickly rolls away the stone, and in despite of his keepers, he rises in a glorious triumphant manner, Mat. xxviii. 2. So though the world may roll this stone and that of reproach and contempt upon the saints' good names, yet God will roll away all those stones; and their names shall have a glorious resurrection in despite of men and devils. That God that hath always one hand to wipe away his children's tears from their eyes, that God hath always another hand to wipe off the dust that lies upon his children's names. Wronged innocency shall not long lie under a cloud. Dirt will not stick long upon marble nor statues of gold. Well! Christians, remember this, the slanders and reproaches that are cast upon you, they are but badges of your innocency and glory: Job xxxi. 35, 36, 'If mine adversary should write a book against me: surely I would take it upon my shoulder, and bind it as a crown to me.' All reproaches are pearls added to a Christian's crown. Hence Austin, *Quisquis volens detrahit famæ meæ, nolens addit mercedi meæ*, he that willingly takes from me my good name, unwillingly adds to my reward; and this Moses knew well enough, which made him prefer Christ's reproach before Pharaoh's crown, Heb. xi. 25, 26. That God that knows all his children by name will not suffer their names to be long buried under the ashes of reproach and scorn; and therefore hold thy peace. The more the foot of pride and scorn tramples upon thy name for the present, the more splendent and radiant it will be, as the more men trample upon a figure graven in gold, the more lustrous they make it. Therefore lay thy hand upon thy mouth. But,

(7.) Seventhly, *The Lord hath been a swift and a terrible witness against such that have falsely accused his children, and that have laded their names with scorn, reproach, and contempt*, Isa. xli. 2; Jude 15. Ahab and Jezebel, that suborned false witness against Naboth, had their bloods licked up by dogs, 1 Kings xxii. 21, 22; 2 Kings ix. 30. Amaziah, who falsely accused the prophet Amos to the king, met with this message from the Lord: 'Thy wife shall be an harlot in the city, thy sons and daughters shall fall by the sword, and thy land shall be divided by line; thou shalt die in a polluted land,' Amos vii. 17. Haman, who falsely accused the Jews, was one day feasted with the king, and the next day made a feast for crows, Esth. vii. 10, ix. 10. The envious courtiers, who falsely accused Daniel, were devoured of lions, Dan. vi. 24. Let me give you a taste of the judgments of God upon such persons out of histories.

Caiaphas the high-priest, who gathered the council and suborned false

[1] A reminiscence of Sibbes. Cf. Memoir, vol. i. pp. xxii, xxiii, and 30, 31.—G.

witnesses against the Lord Jesus, was shortly after put out of office, and one Jonathan substituted in his room, whereupon he killed himself. John Cooper, a godly man, being falsely accused in Queen Mary's days, by one Grimwood, shortly after the said Grimwood, being in perfect health, his bowels suddenly fell out of his body, and so he died miserably.[1]

Narcissus, a godly bishop of Jerusalem, was falsely accused by three men of many foul matters, who sealed up with oaths and imprecations their false testimonies; but shortly after that, one of them, with his whole family and substance, was burnt with fire; another of them was stricken with a grievous disease, such as in his imprecation he had wished to himself; the third, terrified with the sight of God's judgment upon the former, became very penitent, and poured out the grief of his heart in such abundance of tears, that thereby he became blind.[2]

A wicked wretch [Nicephorus], under Commodus the emperor, accused Apollonius, a godly Christian, to the judges for certain grievous crimes, which, when he could not prove, he was adjudged to have his legs broken, according to an ancient law of the Romans.

Gregory Bradway falsely accused one Brook; but shortly after, through terrors of conscience, he sought to cut his own throat, but being prevented, he fell mad.

I have read of Socrates's two false accusers, how that the one was trodden to death by the multitude, and the other was forced to avoid the like by a voluntary banishment. I might produce a multitude of other instances, but let these suffice, to evidence how swift and terrible a witness God hath been against those that have been false accusers of his people, and that have laded their precious names with scorn and reproach, the serious consideration of which should make the accused and reproached Christian to sit dumb and silent before the Lord.[3]

(8.) Eighthly, and lastly, *God himself is daily reproached.* Men tremble not to cast scorn and contempt upon God himself. Sometimes they charge the Lord that his ways are not equal, that it is a wrong way he goeth in, Ezek. xviii. 25, Jer. ii. 5, 6; sometimes they charge God with cruelty, 'My punishment is greater than I am able to bear,' Gen. iv. 13; sometimes they charge God with partiality and respect of persons, because here he strokes, and there he strikes; here he lifts up, and there he casts down; here he smiles, and there he frowns; here he gives much, and there he gives nothing; here he loves, and there he hates; here he prospers one, and there he blasts another: Mal. ii. 17, 'Where is the God of judgment?' *i.e.* nowhere; either there is no God of judgment, or at least not a God of exact, precise, and impartial judgment, &c.[4] Sometimes they charge God with unbountifulness; that he is a God that will set his people too hard work, too much work, but will pay them no wages, nor give them no reward: Mal. iii. 14, 'Ye have said, it is in vain to serve God, and what profit is it that we have kept his ordinances, and that we have walked mournfully before the Lord of hosts?' Sometimes they charge God that he is a hard master, and that he reaps where he hath not sown, and gathers where he hath

[1] [Foxe] Acts and Monuments. [2] Eusebius.
[3] For these references see Beard's Theatre of Judgment.
[4] Ps. l. 21. It were very strange that I should please a world of men, when God himself doth not give every man content.—*Salv*[*ian*].

not strewed, Mat. xxv. 24, &c. Oh! the infinite reproach and scorn that is every day, that is every hour in the day, cast upon the Lord, his name, his truth, his ways, his ordinances, his glory! Alas! all the scorn and contempt that is cast upon all the saints all the world over, is nothing to that which is cast upon the great God every hour; and yet he is patient. Ah! how hardly do most men think of God, and how hardly do they speak of God, and how unhandsomely do they carry it towards God; and yet he bears. They that will not spare God himself, his name, his truth, his honour; shall we think it much that they spare not us or our names? &c. Surely no. Why should we look that those should give us good words that cannot afford God a good word from one week's end to another? yea, from one year's end to another? Why should we look that they should cry out 'Hosanna, hosanna!' to us, whenas every day they cry out of Christ, 'Crucify him, crucify him!' Mat. x. 25, 'It is enough for the disciple that he be as his master, and the servant as his lord; if they have called the master of the house Beelzebub' (or a master-fly, or a dunghill god, or the chief devil), 'how much more shall they call them of his household!' It is preferment enough for the servant to be as his Lord; and if they make no bones of staining and blaspheming the name of the Lord, never wonder if they fly-blow thy name. And let this suffice to quiet and silence your hearts, Christians, under all that scorn and contempt that is cast upon your names and reputations in this world.

The tenth and last objection is this,

Obj. 10. Sir, In this my affliction I have sought to the Lord for this and that mercy, and still God delays me, and puts me off; I have several times thought that mercy had been near, that deliverance had been at the door, but now I see it is afar off; how can I then hold my peace? How can I be silent under such delays and disappointments? To this objection, I shall give you these answers.

(1.) First, *The Lord doth not always time his answers to the swiftness of his people's expectations.*[1] He that is the God of our mercies, is the Lord of our times. God hath delayed long his dearest saints, times belonging to him, as well as issue: Hab. i. 2, 'O Lord, how long shall I cry, and thou wilt not hear! even cry out unto thee for violence, and thou wilt not help!' Job xix. 7, 'Behold, I cry out of violence, but I have no answer; I cry, but there is no judgment.' Ps. lxix. 3, 'I am weary of crying, my throat is dry, mine eyes fail while I wait for my God.' Ps. xl. 17, 'Make no tarrying, O my God.' Though God had promised him a crown, a kingdom, yet he puts him off from day to day, and for all his haste he must stay for it till the set time is come. Paul was delayed so long, till he even despaired of life, and had the sentence of death in himself, 2 Cor. i. 8, 9. And Joseph was delayed so long, till the irons entered into his soul, Ps. cv. 17–19. So he delayed long the giving in of comfort to Mr Glover, though he had sought him frequently, earnestly, and denied himself to the death for Christ.[2] Augustine being under convictions, a shower of tears came from him, and casting himself on the ground under a fig tree, he cries out, 'O Lord,

[1] Ps. lxx. 5; xciv. 3, 4; xiii. 1, 2; Zech. i. 12.

[2] Clarke's 'Martyrologie,' as before, pp, 463, 464.—G.

how long?' How long shall I say, To-morrow, to-morrow? why not to-day, Lord, why not to-day? Though Abigail made haste to prevent David's fury, and Rahab made haste to hang out her scarlet thread; yet God doth not always make haste to hear and save his dearest children. And therefore hold thy peace. He deals no worse with thee than he hath done by his dearest jewels.

(2.) Secondly, *Though the Lord doth defer and delay you for a time, yet he will come, and mercy and deliverance shall certainly come.*[1] He will not always forget the cry of the poor: Heb. x. 37, 'For yet a little, little while, and he that shall come will come, and will not tarry.' Hab. ii. 3, 'The vision is yet for an appointed time, but at the end it shall speak, and not lie: though it tarry, wait for it.' God will come, and mercy will come; though for the present thy sun be set, and thy God seems to neglect thee, yet thy sun will rise again, and thy God will answer all thy prayers, and supply all thy necessities: Ps. lxxi. 20, 21, 'Thou which hast shewed me great and sore troubles, shalt quicken me again, and shalt bring me up again from the depths of the earth. Thou shalt increase my greatness, and comfort me on every side.' Three martyrs being brought to the stake, and all bound, one of them slips from under his chain, to admiration, and falls down upon the ground, and wrestled earnestly with God for the sense of his love, and God gave it in to him then, and so he came and embraced the stake, and died cheerfully a glorious martyr. God delays him till he was at the stake, and till he was bound, and then sweetly lets out himself to him.

(3.) Thirdly, *Though God do delay thee, yet he doth not forget thee.* He remembers thee still; thou art still in his eye, Isa. xlix. 14–16, and always upon his heart, Jer. xxxi. 20. He can as soon forget himself, as forget his people, Ps. lxxvii. 9, 10. The bride shall sooner forget her ornaments, and the mother shall sooner forget her sucking child, Isa. liv. 7–10, and the wife shall sooner forget her husband, Isa. lxii. 3–5, than the Lord shall forget his people. Though Sabinus in Seneca could never in all his life-time remember those three names of Homer, Ulysses, and Achilles, yet God always knows and remembers his people by name, Gen. viii. 1; xix. 29–31; 1 Sam. i. 9; Jonah iv. 9–11, &c. Therefore be silent, hold thy peace; thy God hath not forgotten thee, though for the present he hath delayed thee.

(4.) Fourthly, *God's time is always the best time: God always takes the best and fittest seasons to do us good.* Isa. xlix. 8, 'Thus saith the Lord, In an acceptable time have I heard thee, and in a day of salvation have I helped thee.' I could have heard thee before, and have helped thee before, but I have taken the most acceptable time to do both. To set God his time is to limit him, Ps. lxxviii. 41; it is to exalt ourselves above him, as if we were wiser than God. Though we are not wise enough to improve the times and seasons which God hath set us, to serve and honour him in, yet we are apt to think that we are wise enough to set God his time, when to hear, and when to save, and when to deliver. To circumscribe God to our time, and to make ourselves lords of time; what is this but to divest God of his royalty and sove-

[1] Deut. xxxii. 36; ὅσον ὅσον, Heb. x. 37; Exod. xii. 17, 41, 42, 51.

reignty of appointing times? Acts i. 7, xvii. 26. It is but just and equal, that that God that hath made time, and that hath the sole power to appoint and dispose of time, that he should take his own time to do his people good. We are many times humorous,[1] preposterous, and hasty, and now we must have mercy or we die, deliverance or we are undone; but our impatience will never help us to a mercy, one hour, one moment, before the time that God hath set. The best God will always take the best time to hand out mercies to his people. There is no mercy so fair, so ripe, so lovely, so beautiful, as that which God gives out in his own time. Therefore hold thy peace; though God delays thee, yet be silent, for there is no possibility of wringing a mercy out of God's hand, till the mercy be ripe for us, and we ripe for the mercy, Eccles. iii. 11.

[5.] Fifthly, *The Lord in this life will certainly recompense, and make his children amends for all the delays and put-offs that he exercises them with in this world,*[2] as he did Abraham in giving him such a son as Isaac was, and Hannah in giving her a Samuel. He delayed Joseph long, but at length he changes his iron fetters into chains of gold, his rags into royal robes, his stocks into a chariot, his prison into a palace, his bed of thorns into a bed of down, his reproach into honour, and his thirty years of suffering into eighty years reigning in much grandeur and glory. So God delayed David long, but when his suffering hours were out, he is anointed, and the crown of Israel is set upon his head, and he is made very victorious, very famous and glorious for forty years together, 2 Sam. i. Well! Christians, God will certainly pay you interest upon interest for all the delays that you meet with; and therefore hold your peace. But,

[6.] Sixthly and lastly, *The Lord never delays the giving in of this mercy, or that deliverance, or the other favour, but upon great and weighty reason;* and therefore hold thy peace.

Quest. But what are the reasons that God doth so delay and put off his people from time to time, as we see he doth?

Ans. [1.] First, *for the trial of his people, and for the differencing and distinguishing of them from others.*[3] As the furnace tries gold, so delays will try what metal a Christian is made of. Delays will try both the truth and the strength of a Christian's graces. Delays are a Christian touchstone, a *lapis Lydius,* that will try what metal men are made of, whether they be gold or dross, silver or tin, whether they be sincere or unsound, whether they be real or rotten Christians. As a father, by crossing and delaying his children, tries their dispositions, and makes a full discovery of them, so that he can say, that child is of a muttering and grumbling disposition, and that it is of an humorous and wayward disposition, but the rest are of a meek, sweet, humble, and gentle disposition: so the Lord, by the delaying and crossing of his children, discovers their different dispositions. The manner of the Psylli, which are a kind of people of that temper and constitution that no venom will hurt them, is, that if they suspect any child to be none of their own, they set an adder upon it to sting it, and if it cry, and the

[1] Given to 'humours,' or capricious.—G.
[2] Ps. xc. 15, and the first and last chapters of Job compared.
[3] Mat. xv. 21–29; 1 Peter i. 7; Job xxiii. 8–10; Deut. viii. 2

flesh swell, they cast it away as a spurious issue, but if it do not cry, if it do not so much as quatch,[1] nor do not grow the worse for it, then they account it for their own, and make very much of it;[2] so the Lord by delays, which are as the stinging of the adder, tries his children; if they patiently, quietly, and sweetly can bear them, then the Lord will own them, and make much of them, as those that are near and dear unto him; but if under delays they fall a-crying, roaring, storming, vexing, and fretting, the Lord will not own them, but reckon them as bastards, and no sons, Heb. xii. 8.

[2.] Secondly, *That they may have the greater experience of his power, grace, love, and mercy in the close.* Christ loved Martha, and her sister, and Lazarus, yet he defers his coming for several days, and Lazarus must die, be put in the grave, and lie there till he stinks. And why so, but that they might have the greater experience of his power, grace, and love towards them? John xi. 3, 5, 6, 17.

[3.] Thirdly, *To sharpen his children's appetite, and to put a greater edge upon their desires;* to make them cry out as a woman in travail, or as a man that is in danger of drowning, Cant. iii. 1–4; Isa. xxvi. 8, 9, 16. God delays, that his people may set upon him with greater strength and importunity; he puts them off, that they may put on with more life and vigour; God seems to be cold, that he may make us the more hot; he seems to be slack, that he may make us the more earnest; he seems to be backward, that he may make us the more forward in pressing upon him. The father delays the child, that he may make him the more eager, and so doth God his, that he may make them the more divinely violent. When Balaam had once put off Balak, 'he sent again,' saith the text, 'certain princes more, and more honourable than they,' Num. xxii. 15. Balaam's put-offs did but make Balak the more importunate, it did but increase and whet his desires. This is that that God aims at by all his put-offs, to make his children more earnest, to whet up their spirits, and that they may send up more and yet more honourable prayers after him, that they may cry more earnestly, strive more mightily, and wrestle more importunately with God, and that they may take heaven with a more sacred violence. Anglers draw back the hook, that the fish may be the more forward to bite; and God sometimes seems to draw back, but it is only that we may press the more on. And therefore, as anglers, when they have long waited, and perceive that the fish do not so much as nibble at the bait, yet do they not impatiently throw away the rod, or break the hook and line, but pull up, and look upon the bait and mend it, and so throw it in again, and then the fish bites: so when a Christian prays, and prays, and yet catches nothing, God seems to be silent, and heaven seems to be shut against him; yet let him not cast off prayer, but mend his prayer; pray more believingly, pray more affectionately, and pray more fervently, and then the fish will bite, then mercy will come, and comfort will come, and deliverance will come. But,

[4.] Fourthly, *God delays and puts off his people many times, that he may make a fuller discovery of themselves to themselves.* Few

[1] 'Betray,' viz. the pain suffered.—G.

[2] Pliny, lib. vii. 2. Cf. also Lucan, *Pharsalia*, lib. ix. l. 890, *et seq.*; and Œlian, *Hist. Anim*, lib. i. c. 57, and lib. xvi. c. 27, 28.—G.

Christians see themselves and understand themselves. By delays God discovers much of a man's sinful self to his religious self; much of his worser part to his better part, of his ignoble part to his most noble part. When the fire is put under the pot, then the scum appears; so when God delays a poor soul, Oh! how doth the scum of pride, the scum of murmuring, the scum of quarrelling, the scum of distrust, the scum of impatience, the scum of despair, discover itself in the heart of a poor creature? Ezek. xxiv. 6. I have read of a fool, who being left in a chamber, and the door locked when he was asleep; after he awakes, and finds the door fast and all the people gone, he cries out at the window, O myself, myself, O myself! So when God shuts the door upon his people, when he delays them, and puts them off, Ah! what cause have they to cry out of themselves, to cry out of proud self, and worldly self, and carnal self, and foolish self, and froward self, &c.? We are very apt, saith Seneca, *utimur perspicillis magis quam speculis,* to use spectacles to behold other men's faults, rather than looking-glasses to behold our own; but now God's delays are as a looking-glass, in which God gives his people to see their own faults, Ps. lxxiii. 11, 12. Oh! that baseness, that vileness, that wretchedness, that sink of filthiness, that gulf of wickedness, that God by delays discovers to be in the hearts of men! But,

[5.] Fifthly, *God delays and puts off his people to enhance, to raise the price of mercy, the price of deliverance.* We usually set the highest price, the greatest esteem upon such things that we obtain with greatest difficulty. What we dearly buy, that we highly prize, Acts xxi. 8, Cant. iii. 4. The more sighs, tears, weepings, waitings, watchings, strivings, and earnest longings, this mercy and that deliverance, and the other favour costs us, the more highly we shall value them. When a delayed mercy comes, it tastes more like a mercy, it sticks more like a mercy, it warms more like a mercy, works more like a mercy, and it endears the heart to God more like a mercy than any other mercy that a man enjoys.

This is the child, said Hannah,—after God had long delayed her,—for which I prayed, and the Lord hath given me my petition which I asked of him, 1 Sam. i. 27. Delayed mercy is the cream of mercy; no mercy so sweet, so dear, so precious to a man, as that which a man hath gained after many put-offs. Mr Glover, the martyr, sought the Lord earnestly and frequently for some special mercies, and the Lord delayed him long; but when he was even at the stake, then the Lord gave in the mercies to him; and then, as a man overjoyed, he cries out to his friend, 'He is come, he is come.'[1] But,

[6] Sixthly, *The Lord delays his people, that he may pay them home in his own coin.* God sometimes loves to retaliate, Prov. i. 23, 33. The spouse puts off Christ: Cant. v. 3, 'I have put off my coat, how can I put it on?' &c.; and Christ puts her off, ver. 5–8. Thou hast put off God from day to day, from month to month, yea, from year to year; and therefore, if God put thee off from day to day, or from year to year, hast thou any cause to complain? Surely no. Thou hast often and long put off the motions of his Spirit, the directions of his word, the offers of his grace, the entreaties of his Son; and therefore what can be

[1] See *ante.*—G.

more just than that God should delay thee for a time, and put thee off for a season, who hast delayed him, and put off him days without number? If God serves thee as thou hast often served him, thou hast no reason to complain. But,

[7.] Seventhly, and lastly, *The Lord delays his people, that heaven may be the more sweet to them at last.* Here they meet with many delays and with many put-offs; but in heaven they shall never meet with one put-off, with one delay; here many times they call and cry, and can get no answer; here they knock and bounce,[1] and yet the door of grace and mercy opens not to them; but in heaven they shall have mercy at the first word, at the first knock. There, whatever heart can wish shall without delay be enjoined.[2] Here God seems to say sometimes, Souls! you have mistaken the door, or I am not at leisure, or others must be served before you, or come some other time, &c. But in heaven God is always at leisure, and all the sweetness and blessedness and happiness of that state presents itself every hour to the soul there. God hath never, God will never, say to any of his saints in heaven, Come to-morrow. Such language the saints sometimes hear here, but such language is noway suitable to a glorified condition; and therefore, seeing that the Lord never delays his people, but upon great and weighty accounts, let his people be silent before him, let them not mutter nor murmur, but be mute. And so I have done with the objections.

I shall come now in the last place to propound some helps and directions that may contribute to the silencing and stilling of your souls under the greatest afflictions, the sharpest trials, and the saddest providences that you meet with in this world; and so close up this discourse.

(1.) First, *All the afflictions that come upon the saints, they are the fruits of divine love.*[3] Rev. iii. 19, 'As many as I love, I rebuke and chasten: be zealous therefore, and repent;' Heb. xii. 6, 'For whom the Lord loveth he chasteneth, and scourgeth every son whom he receiveth;' Job v. 17, 'Behold! happy is the man whom God correcteth; therefore despise not thou the chastening of the Almighty;' chap. vii. 17, 18, 'What is man, that thou shouldest magnify him? and that thou shouldest set thine heart upon him? And that thou shouldest visit him every morning, and try him every moment?' Isa. xlviii. 10, 'Behold, I have refined thee, but not with silver; I have chosen thee in the furnace of affliction.' When Munster lay sick, and his friends asked him how he did, and how he felt himself, he pointed to his sores and ulcers, whereof he was full, and said, These are God's gems and jewels wherewith he decketh his best friends, and to me they are more precious than all the gold and silver in the world. A gentleman highly prizes his hawk, he feeds her with his own hand, he carries her upon his fist, he takes a great deal of delight and pleasure in her; and therefore he puts vervels upon her legs, and a hood upon her head; he hoodwinks her, and fetters her, because he loves her, and takes delight in her; so the Lord by afflictions hoodwinks and fetters his children, but all is because he loves them, and takes delight and pleasure in them. There cannot be a greater evidence of God's hatred and wrath, than his refusing

[1] 'Swell,' boast.—G. [2] Qu. 'enjoyed'?—Ed. [3] Prov. ii. 12, Jer. x. 7.

to correct men for their sinful courses and vanities. 'Why should you be smitten any more? you will revolt more and more,' Isa. i. 5. Where God refuses to correct, there God resolves to destroy; there is no man so near the axe, so near the flames, so near hell, as he whom God will not so much as spend a rod upon. God is most angry where he shews no anger. Jerome, writing to a sick friend, hath this expression, I account it a part of unhappinesss not to know adversity; I judge you to be miserable, because you have not been miserable. Nothing, saith another [Demetrius], seems more unhappy to me, than he to whom no adversity hath happened.[1] God afflicts thee, O Christian, in love; and therefore Luther cries out, Strike, Lord; strike, Lord, and spare not. Who can seriously muse upon this, and not hold his peace, and not be silent under the most smarting rod?

(2.) Secondly, *Consider, that the trials and troubles, the calamities and miseries, the crosses and losses that you meet with in this world, is all the hell that ever you shall have.* Here you have your hell; hereafter you shall have your heaven. This is the worst of your condition, the best is to come. Lazarus had his hell first, his heaven last; but Dives had his heaven first, and his hell at last, Luke xvi. 24–31. Thou hast all thy pangs, and pains, and throes here that ever thou shalt have; thy ease, and rest, and pleasure is to come. Here you have all your bitter, your sweet is to come; here you have your sorrows, your joys are to come; here you have all your winter nights, your summer days are to come; here you have your passion-week, your ascension-day is to come; here you have your evil things, your good things are to come. Death will put a period to all thy sins, and to all thy sufferings; and it will be an inlet to those joys, delights, and contents that shall never have end; and therefore hold thy peace, and be silent before the Lord.[2]

(3.) Thirdly, *Get an assurance that Christ is yours, and pardon of sin yours, and divine favour yours, and heaven yours; and the sense of this will exceedingly quiet and silence the soul under the sorest and sharpest trials a Christian can meet with in this world.* He that is assured that God is his portion, will never mutter nor murmur under his greatest burden; he that can groundedly say, 'Nothing shall separate me from the love of God in Christ,' he will be able to triumph in the midst of the greatest tribulations, Rom. viii. 33–39; he that with the spouse can say, 'My beloved is mine, and I am his,' Cant. ii. 16, will bear up quietly and sweetly under the heaviest afflictions. In the time of the Marian persecution there was a gracious woman, who being convened before bloody Bonner, then bishop of London, upon the trial of religion, he threatened her that he would take away her husband from her. Saith she, Christ is my husband. I will take away thy child. Christ, saith she, is better to me than ten sons. I will strip thee, saith he, of all thy outward comforts. Yea, but Christ is mine, saith she, and you cannot strip me of him. Oh! the assurance that Christ was hers bore up her heart, and quieted her spirit under all.[3]

[1] *Nihil est infelicius eo cui nil unquam contigit adversi.*—Seneca. [De Providentia.—G.]

[2] See my treatise called 'Heaven on Earth.' [In Vol. II. of these Works.—G.]

[3] [Foxe] Act. and Mon. So John Noyes, Alice Driver, Mr Bradford, Mr Taylor, and Justin Martyr, with many more.

You may take away my life, saith Basil, but you cannot take away my comfort; my head, but not my crown. Yea, quoth he, had I a thousand lives, I would lay them all down for my Saviour's sake, who hath done abundantly more for me. John Ardley professed to Bonner, when he told him of burning, and how ill he could endure it, that if he had as many lives as he had hairs on his head, he would lose them all in the fire before he would lose his Christ.[1] Assurance will keep a man from muttering and murmuring under the sorest afflictions. Henry and John, two Augustine monks, being the first that were burnt in Germany, and Mr Rogers, the first that was burnt in Queen Mary's days, did all sing in the flame. A soul that lives in the assurance of divine favour, and in its title to glory, cannot but bear up patiently and quietly under the greatest sufferings that possibly can befall it in this world. That scripture is worth its weight in gold, 'The inhabitants of Sion shall not say, I am sick; the people that dwell therein shall be forgiven their iniquity,' Isa. xxxiii. 24. He doth not say they were not sick. No. But though they were sick, yet they should not say they were sick. But why should they forget their sorrows, and not remember their pains, nor be sensible of their sickness? Why! the reason is, because the Lord had forgiven them their iniquities. The sense of pardon took away the sense of pain; the sense of forgiveness took away the sense of sickness. Assurance of pardon will take away the pain, the sting, the trouble of every trouble and affliction that a Christian meets with. No affliction will daunt, startle, or stagger an assured Christian. An assured Christian will be patient and silent under all, Ps. xxiii. 1, 4–7. Melancthon makes mention of a godly woman, who, having upon her deathbed been in much conflict, and afterward much comforted, brake out into these words: Now, and not till now, I understand the meaning of these words, 'Thy sins are forgiven;' the sense of which did mightily cheer and quiet her. He that hath got this jewel of assurance in his bosom, will be far enough off from vexing or fretting under the saddest dispensations that he meets with in this world.

(4.) Fourthly, If you would be quiet and silent under your present troubles and trials, *then dwell much upon the benefit, the profit, the advantage that hath redounded to your souls by former troubles and afflictions that have been upon you.*[2] Eccles. vii. 14, 'In the day of adversity consider.' Oh! now consider, how by former afflictions the Lord hath discovered sin, prevented sin, and mortified sin: consider how the Lord by former afflictions hath discovered to thee the impotency, the mutability, the insufficiency, and the vanity of the world, and all worldly concernments: consider how the Lord by former afflictions hath melted thy heart, and broken thy heart, and humbled thy heart, and prepared thy heart for clearer, fuller, and sweeter enjoyments of himself: consider what pity, what compassion, what bowels, what tenderness, and what sweetness former afflictions have wrought in thee towards others in misery: consider what room former afflictions have made in thy soul for God, for his word, for good counsel, and for divine

[1] Clarke's 'Martyrologie,' as before, pp. 452, 453.—G.

[2] There was a good man that had got so much good by his afflictions, that he counted it his greatest affliction to want an affliction; and therefore he would sometimes cry out, O my friends, I have lost an affliction, I have lost an affliction!

comfort: consider how by former afflictions the Lord hath made thee more partaker of his Christ, his Spirit, his holiness, his goodness, &c.: consider how by former afflictions the Lord hath made thee to look towards heaven more, to mind heaven more, to prize heaven more, and to long for heaven more, &c. Now, who can seriously consider of all that good that he hath got by former afflictions, and not be silent under present afflictions? Who can remember those choice, those great, and those precious earnings that his soul hath made of former afflictions, and not reason himself into a holy silence under present afflictions thus: O my soul! hath not God done thee much good, great good, special good, by former afflictions? Yes. O my soul! hath not God done that for thee by former afflictions, that thou wouldst not have to do for ten thousand worlds? Yes. And is not God, O my soul! as powerful as ever, as faithful as ever, as gracious as ever, and as ready and willing as ever to do thee good by present afflictions, as he hath been to do thee good by former afflictions? Yes, yes. Why, why then dost thou not sit silent and mute before him under thy present troubles? O my soul! It was the saying of one, that an excellent memory was needful for three sorts of men: First, for tradesmen; for they, having many businesses to do, many reckonings to make up, many irons in the fire, had need of a good memory. Secondly, great talkers; for they, being full of words, had need to have a good storehouse in their heads to feed their tongues. Thirdly, for liars; for they telling many untruths, had need of a good memory, lest they should be taken in their lying contradictions: and I may add for a fourth, viz., those that are afflicted, that they may remember the great good that they have gained by former afflictions, that so they may be the more silent and quiet under present troubles.

(5.) Fifthly, To quiet and silence your souls under the sorest afflictions and sharpest trials, consider, *that your choicest, your chiefest treasure is safe;* your God is safe, your Christ is safe, your portion is safe, your crown is safe, your inheritance is safe, your royal palace is safe, and your jewels, your graces are safe; therefore hold your peace, 2 Tim. i. 12; iv. 8.

I have read a story of a man that had a suit, and when his cause was to be heard, he applied himself to three friends, to see what they could do for him: one answered, he would bring him as far on his journey as he could; the second promised him that he would go with him to his journey's end; the third engaged himself to go with him before the judge, and to speak for him, and not to leave him till his cause was heard and determined. These three are a man's riches, his friends, and his graces. His riches will help him to comfortable accommodations while they stay with him, but they often take leave of a man before his soul takes leave of his body. His friends will go with him to his grave, and then leave him; but his graces will accompany him before God, they will not leave him nor forsake him; they will go to the grave, to glory, with him, 1 Tim. vi. 18, 19.

In that famous battle at Leuctrum,[1] where the Thebans got a signal victory, but their captain, Epaminondas, a little before his death, demanded whether his buckler were taken by the enemy, and when he

[1] Rather Leuctra, and to be distinguished from Leuctrum.—G.

understood that it was safe, and that they had not so much as laid their hands on it, he died most willingly, cheerfully, and quietly. Well! Christians, your shield of faith is safe, your portion is safe, your royal robe is safe, your kingdom is safe, your heaven is safe, your happiness and blessedness is safe; and therefore under all your afflictions and troubles, in patience possess your own souls. But,

(6.) Sixthly, If you would be silent and quiet under your sorest troubles and trials, then *set yourselves in good earnest upon the mortification of your lusts.*[1] It is unmortified lust which is the sting of every trouble, and which makes every sweet bitter, and every bitter more bitter. Sin unmortified adds weight to every burden, it puts gall to our wormwood, it adds chain to chain; it makes the bed uneasy, the chamber a prison, relaxations troublesome, and everything vexatious to the soul. James iv. 1, 'From whence come wars and fightings amongst you? come they not hence, even of your lusts, that war in your members?' So say I, from whence comes all this muttering, murmuring, fretting, and vexing, &c., come they not hence, even from your unmortified lusts? Come they not from your unmortified pride, and unmortified self-love, and unmortified unbelief, and unmortified passion, &c.? Surely they do. Oh, therefore, as ever you would be silent under the afflicting hand of God, labour for more and more of the grace of the Spirit, by which you may mortify the lusts of the flesh, Rom. viii. 13. It is not your strongest resolutions or purposes, without the grace of the Spirit, that can overmaster a lust. A soul-sore, till it be indeed healed, will run, though we resolve and say it shall not be. It was the blood of the sacrifice, and the oil, that cleansed the leper in the law; and that by them was meant the boood of Christ and the grace of his Spirit, is agreed on all hands, Lev. xiv. 14–16. It was a touch of Christ's garment that cured the woman of her bloody issue, Mark v. 25, *et seq.* Philosophy, saith Lactantius, may hide a sin, but it cannot quench it; it may cover a sin, but it cannot cut off a sin. Like a black patch instead of a plaster, it may cover some deformities in nature, but it cures them not; neither is it the papists' purgatories, watchings, whippings, &c., nor St Francis his kissing or licking of lepers' sores, which will cleanse the fretting leprosy of sin. In the strength of Christ, and in the power of the Spirit, set roundly upon the mortifying of every lust. Oh, hug none, indulge none, but resolvedly set upon the ruin of all! One leak in a ship will sink it; one wound strikes Goliah dead as well as three-and-twenty did Cæsar; one Delilah may do Samson as much spite and mischief as all the Philistines; one broken wheel spoils all the whole clock; one vein bleeding will let out all the vitals as well as more; one fly will spoil a whole box of ointment; one bitter herb all the pottage. By eating one apple Adam lost paradise, one lick of honey endangered Jonathan's life, one Achan was a trouble to all Israel, one Jonah raises a storm and becomes lading too heavy for a whole ship; so one unmortified lust will be able to raise very strange and strong storms and tempests in the soul in the days of affliction. And therefore, as you would have a blessed calm and quietness in your own spirits under your sharpest trials, set thoroughly upon the work of mortification. Gideon had

[1] Austin saith, If thou kill not sin till it die of itself, sin hath killed thee, and not thou thy sin.

seventy sons, and but one bastard, and yet that bastard destroyed all his seventy sons, Judges viii. 30, 31, chap. ix. 1, 2. Ah, Christian! dost thou not know what a world of mischief one unmortified lust may do? and therefore let nothing satisfy thee but the blood of all thy lusts.

(7.) Seventhly, If you would be silent under your greatest afflictions, your sharpest trials, then make this consideration your daily companion, viz., *That all the afflictions that come upon you, come upon you by and through that covenant of grace that God hath made with you.* In the covenant of grace, God hath engaged himself to keep you from the evils, snares, and temptations of the world; in the covenant of grace, God hath engaged himself to purge away your sins, to brighten and increase your graces, to crucify your hearts to the world, and to prepare you and preserve you to his heavenly kingdom; and by afflictions he effects all this, and that according to his covenant too: Ps. lxxxix. 30–34, 'If his children forsake my law, and walk not in my commandments; if they break my statutes, and keep not my commandments.' In these words you have a supposition that the saints may both fall into sins of commission and sins of omission; in the following words you have God's gracious promise: 'Then will I visit their transgressions with the rod, and their iniquities with stripes.' God engages himself by promise and covenant, not only to chide and check, but also to correct his people for their sins: 'Nevertheless, my loving-kindness will I not utterly take from him, nor suffer my faithfulness to fail.' Afflictions are fruits of God's faithfulness, to which the covenant binds him. God would be unfaithful, if first or last, more or less, he did not afflict his people. Afflictions are part of that gracious covenant which God hath made with his people; afflictions are mercies, yea, covenant mercies, Ps. cxix. 75. Hence it is that God is called the terrible God, keeping covenant and mercy, Neh. i. 5; because, by his covenant of mercy, he is bound to afflict and chastise his people. God by covenant is bound to preserve his people, and not to suffer them to perish; and happy are they that are preserved, whether in salt and vinegar, or in wine and sugar. All the afflictions that come upon a wicked man come upon him by virtue of a covenant of works, and so are cursed unto him; but all the afflictions that come upon a gracious man, they come upon him by virtue of a covenant of grace, and so they are blessed unto him; and therefore he hath eminent cause to hold his peace, to lay his hand upon his mouth.

(8.) Eighthly, If you would be silent and quiet under afflictions, then dwell much upon this, viz., *That all your afflictions do but reach the worser, the baser, and the ignobler part of a Christian, viz., his body, his outward man:* 'Though our outward man decay, yet our inward man is renewed day by day,' 2 Cor. iv. 16. As Aristarchus the heathen said, when he was beaten by the tyrants: Beat on; it is not Aristarchus you beat, it is only his shell. Timothy had a very healthful soul in a crazy body, 1 Tim. v. 23; and Gaius had a very prosperous soul in a weak distempered body, 3 Ep. of John 2. Epictetus and many of the more refined heathens, have long since concluded that the body was the organ or vessel, the soul was the man and merchandise. Now, all the troubles and afflictions that a Christian meets with, they do not reach his soul, they touch not his conscience, they make no breach upon his noble part; and therefore he hath cause to hold his peace, and to lay his hand upon his mouth. The soul is the breath of God, Heb. xii. 9, Zech. xii. 1, the beauty of man, the wonder of angels, and the envy of devils; it is a celestial plant, and of a divine offspring; it is an immortal spirit. Souls are of an angelic nature; a man is an angel clothed in clay; the soul is a greater miracle in man than all the miracles wrought amongst men; the soul is a demi-semi-God dwelling in a house of clay Now it is not in the power of any outward troubles and afflictions that a Christian meets with to reach his soul; and therefore he may well sit mute under the smarting rod.

(9.) Ninthly, If thou wouldst be silent and quiet under the saddest providences and sorest trials, then *keep up faith in continual exercise.* Now faith, in the exercise of it, will quiet and silence the soul, thus,

[1.] By bringing the soul to sit down satisfied in the naked enjoyments of God, John xiv. 8, Ps. xvii. 15.

[2.] By drying up the springs of pride, self-love, impatience, murmuring, unbelief, and the carnal delights of this world.

[3.] By presenting to the soul greater, sweeter, and better things in Christ, than any this world doth afford, Heb. xi. 3, Philip. iii. 7, 8.

[4.] By lessening the soul's esteem of all outward vanities. Do but keep up the exercise of faith, and thou wilt keep silent before the Lord. No man so mute, as he whose faith is still busy about invisible objects.

(10.) Tenthly, If you would keep silent, then *keep humble before the Lord.* Oh! labour every day to be more humble and more low and little in your own eyes. Who am I, saith the humble soul, but that God should cross me in this mercy, and take away that mercy, and pass a sentence of death upon every mercy? I am not worthy of the least mercy, I deserve not a crumb of mercy, I have forfeited every mercy, I have improved never a mercy. Only by pride comes contention. It is only pride that puts men upon contending with God and men; an humble soul will lie quiet at the foot of God, it will be contented with bare commons, Prov. xiii. 16. As you see sheep can live upon the bare commons, which a fat ox cannot. A dinner of green herbs relisheth well with the humble man's palate, whereas a stalled ox is but a coarse dish to a proud man's stomach. An humble heart thinks none less than himself, nor none worse than himself; an humble heart looks upon small mercies as great mercies, and great afflictions as small afflictions, and small afflictions as no afflictions; and therefore sits mute and quiet under all. Do but keep humble, and you will keep silent before the Lord. Pride kicks, and flings, and frets, but an humble man hath still his hand upon his mouth. Every thing on this side hell is mercy, much mercy, rich mercy to an humble soul; and therefore he holds his peace.[1]

(11.) Eleventhly, If you would keep silence under the afflicting hand of God, then *keep close, hold fast these soul-silencing and soul-quieting maxims or principles.* As,

[1.] First, *That the worst that God doth to his people in this world, is in order to the making of them a heaven on earth.* He brings them into a wilderness, but it is, that he may speak comfortably to

[1] Austin being asked, What was the first grace? he answered, humility; what the second? humility; what the third? humility.

them, Hosea ii. 14; he casts them into the fiery furnace, but it is, that they may have more of his company; do the stones come thick and threefold about Stephen's ears, it is but to knock him the nearer to Christ, the corner-stone, &c., Acts vii.

[2.] Secondly, If you would be silent, then hold fast this principle, viz. *That what God wills is best*, Heb. xii. 10. When he wills sickness, sickness is better than health; when he wills weakness, weakness is better than strength; when he wills want, want is better than wealth; when he wills reproach, reproach is better than honour; when he wills death, death is better than life. As God is wisdom itself, and so knows that which is best, so he is goodness itself, and therefore cannot do anything but that which is best: therefore hold thy peace.

[3.] Thirdly, If thou wouldst be silent under thy greatest afflictions, then hold fast to this principle, viz. *That the Lord will bear thee company in all thy afflictions*, Isa. xli. 10; chap. xliii. 2; Ps. xxiii. 4; Ps. xc. 15; Dan. iii. 25; Gen. xxxix. 20, 21; 2 Tim. iv. 16, 17. These scriptures are breasts full of divine consolation, these wells of salvation are full; will you turn to them and draw out, that your souls may be satisfied and quieted?

[4.] Fourthly, If you would be silent under your afflictions, then hold fast this principle, *That the Lord hath more high, more noble, and more blessed ends in the afflicting of you than he hath in the afflicting of the men of the world.* The stalk and the ear of corn fall upon the threshing floor, under one and the same flail, but the one is shattered in pieces, the other is preserved; from one and the same olive, and from under one and the same press is crushed out both oil and dregs; but the one is turned up for use, the other thrown out as unserviceable; and by one and the same breath the fields are perfumed with sweetness, and annoyed with unpleasant savours: so, though afflictions do befall good and bad alike, as the Scripture speaks, Eccles. ix. 2, yet the Lord will effect more glorious ends by those afflictions that befall his people, than he will effect by those that befall wicked men; and therefore the Lord puts his people into the furnace for their trial, but the wicked for their ruin: the one is bettered by affliction, the other is made worse; the one is made soft and tender by afflictions, the other is more hard and obdurate; the one is drawn nearer to God by afflictions, the other is driven further from God, &c.

[5.] Fifthly, If you would be silent under your afflictions, then you must hold fast this principle, viz. *That the best way in this world to have thine own will, is to lie down in the will of God, and quietly to resign up thyself to the good will and pleasure of God*, Mat. xv. 21, 29. Luther was a man that could have anything of God, and why? Why! because he submitted his will to the will of God; he lost his will in the will of God. O soul! it shall be even as thou wilt, if thy will be swallowed up in the will of God.

[6.] Sixthly and lastly, If thou wouldst be silent under the afflicting hand of God, then thou must hold fast to this principle, viz. *That God will make times of afflictions to be times of special manifestations of divine love and favour to thee.* Tiburtius saw a paradise when he walked upon hot burning coals. I could affirm this by a cloud of witnesses, but that I am upon a close.[1] Ah, Christians! as ever you would be quiet and silent under the smarting rod, hold fast to these principles, and keep them as your lives. But,

(12.) Twelfthly and lastly, To silence and quiet your soul under the afflicting hand of God, *dwell much upon the brevity or shortness of man's life.* This present life is not *vita, sed via ad vitam,* life, but a motion, a journey towards life. Man's life, saith one, is the shadow of smoke, yea, the dream of a shadow: saith another, man's life is so short, that Austin doubted whether to call it a dying life or a living death.[2] Thou hast but a day to live, and perhaps thou mayest be now in the twelfth hour of that day; therefore hold out faith and patience. Thy troubles and thy life shall shortly end together; therefore hold thy peace. Thy grave is going to be made; thy sun is near setting; death begins to call thee off the stage of this world; death stands at thy back; thou must shortly sail forth upon the ocean of eternity; though thou hast a great deal of work to do, a God to honour, a Christ to close with, a soul to save, a race to run, a crown to win, a hell to escape, a pardon to beg, a heaven to make sure, yet thou hast but a little time to do it in; thou hast one foot in the grave, thou art even going ashore on eternity, and wilt thou now cry out of thy affliction? Wilt thou now mutter and murmur when thou art entering upon an unchangeable condition? What extreme folly and madness is it for a man to mutter and murmur when he is just a-going out of prison, and his bolts and chains are just a-knocking off! Why, Christian, this is just thy case; therefore hold thy peace. Thy life is but short, therefore thy troubles cannot be long; hold up and hold out quietly and patiently a little longer, and heaven shall make amends for all, Rom. viii. 18.

[1] Ps. xciv. 19; Dan. ix. 19, 24; Acts xvi. and xxvii.; Hosea ii. 14.

[2] Augustine, *Confessions.*

A STRING OF PEARLS.

NOTE.

The 'String of Pearls' was first published in 1657, in a particularly pretty volume. The title supplied by the bookseller for this edition, intended for the back, was, 'Mr Brooks His Chain of Pearls.' Our text is taken from the 'second edition, *corrected*.' Its title-page is given below.* Though originally a private 'funeral sermon,' it was immediately equally popular with its author's other writings, having rapidly passed through numerous editions. The '14th' bears the date of 1703. Cf. Sibbes's Works, vol. i. pages 341, 350. G.

* A

STRING OF PEARLS:

OR,

The best things reserved till last.

Discovered in a *SERMON*

Preached in *London*, *June* 8. 1657.

AT

The Funeral of (that Triumphant Saint) Mris. *Mary Blake*, late Wife to (his Worthy Friend) Mr. *Nicholas Blake*, Merchant, with an Elegy on her Death.

By *Thomas Brooks* (her much endeared Friend, Spiritual Father, Pastor, and Brother, in the Fellowship of the Gospel, and) Preacher of the Word at *Margarets New-Fish-street.*

The Second Edition corrected.

The Righteous shall bee had in everlasting remembrance, Psal. 112. 6.

Precious in the sight of the Lord is the Death of his Saints, Psal. 116. 15.

London, Printed by *R. I.* for *John Hancock*, at the first shop in Popes-head-Alley, neer the Exchange. 1660.

THE EPISTLE DEDICATORY.

To his honoured and worthily-esteemed friends, Mr NICHOLAS BLAKE, merchant, husband to the late virtuous Mrs MARY BLAKE, deceased; and Mr THOMAS MATTHEWES, merchant, and Mrs MARTHA MATTHEWES his wife, parents to the late deceased gentlewoman; and to the rest of his and her relations.

All grace and peace, all consolation and supportation from God the Father, through our Lord Jesus Christ.

Dear Friends,—This little piece had been sooner in your hands, but that my being in the country, and some other important business that hath lain hard upon my hands, hath prevented it till now.

I have read of a certain painter, who, being to express the sorrow of a weeping father, and having spent his skill before in setting forth of the passions and affections of his children, he thought it best to present him upon his table to the beholders' view, with his face covered, that so he might have that grief to be imagined by them, which he found himself unable to set out to the full. I know I am not able to paint out your great grief and sorrow for the loss of such a wife, of such a child, of such a sister, &c., and I could wish that this piece, which is brought forth to satisfy your importunity, may not make the wound to bleed afresh. However, if it doth, thank yourselves, blame not me.[1]

I could heartily wish that you and all others concerned in this sad loss, were more taken up in minding the happy exchange that she hath made, than with your present loss. She hath exchanged earth for heaven, a wilderness for a paradise, a prison for a palace, a house made with hands for one eternal in the heavens, 2 Cor. v. 1, 2. She hath exchanged imperfection for perfection, sighing for singing, mourning for rejoicing, prayers for praises, the society of sinful mortals for the company of God, Christ, angels, and the spirits of just men made perfect, Heb. xii. 22–24; an imperfect transient enjoyment of God for a more clear, full, perfect, and permanent enjoyment of God. She hath exchanged pain for ease, sickness for health, a bed of weakness for a bed of spices, a complete blessedness. She hath exchanged her brass for silver, her counters for gold, and her earthly contentments for heavenly enjoyments.

[1] Many a man hath been drowned in his own tears, 2 Cor. vii. 10.

And as I desire that one of your eyes may be fixed upon her happiness, so I desire that the other of your eyes may be fixed upon Christ's fulness. Though your brook be dried up, yet Christ the fountain of light, life, love, grace, glory, comfort, joy, goodness, sweetness, and satisfaction is still at hand, and always full and flowing, yea, overflowing, John i. 16, Col. i. 19, ii. 3.[1] As the worth and value of many pieces of silver is contracted in one piece of gold, so all the sweetness, all the goodness, all the excellencies that are in husbands, wives, children, friends, &c., are contracted in Christ; yea, all the whole volume of perfections which is spread through heaven and earth, is epitomised in Christ; *Ipse unus erit tibi omnia, quia in ipso uno bono, bona sunt omnia*, saith Augustine, one Christ will be to thee instead of all things else, because in him are all good things to be found.

Dear friends! what wisdom, what knowledge, what love, what tenderness, what sweetness, what goodness did you observe and find in this deceased and now glorified saint, that is not eminently, that is not perfectly, to be enjoyed in Christ? and if so, why do not you bear up sweetly and cheerfully, and let the world know, and let friends see, that though you have lost her corporally, yet you enjoy her spiritually in Jesus? The apostle Paul was so much taken with Christ, that he was ever in his thoughts, always near his heart, and ever upon his tongue; he names him sixteen or seventeen times in one chapter,[2] 1 Cor. i. Now, oh that your hearts and thoughts were thus busied about Christ, and taken up with Christ, and with those treasures of wisdom, knowledge, grace, goodness, sweetness, &c., that is in him; this would very much allay your grief and sorrow, and keep your hearts quiet and silent before the Lord; this would be like that tree which made the bitter waters of Marah sweet, Exod. xv. 23–25.

Plutarch, in the life of Phocion, tells us of a certain gentlewoman of Ionia, who shewed the wife of Phocion all the rich jewels and precious stones she had; she answered her again, All my riches and jewels is my husband Phocion. So should Christians say, Christ is our riches, our jewels, our treasure, our heaven, our crown, our glory, our all. He is all comforts to us, and all contents to us, and all delights to us, and all relations to us. He is husband, wife, child, father, mother, brother, sister. He is all these; yea, he is more than all these to us, 2 Cor. vi. 10, Eph. iii. 8, Cant. v. 10.

I have read of one [St Martin], who, walking in the fields by himself, of a sudden fell into loud cries and weeping, and being asked by one that passed by and overheard him, the cause of that his lamentation, I weep, saith he, to think that the Lord Jesus should do so much for us men, and yet not one man of a thousand so much as minds him, or thinks of him. But I hope better things of you; yea, I hope and desire that this present counsel will take hold of your hearts, and work as counsel works, when it is set home by a hand of heaven.

Again, friends, it is your wisdom and your glory to mind more your present work, your present duty, than your loss, than your present calamity. David's passion was got above his wisdom, his discretion, when he said, 'O my son Absalom! my son, my son Absalom, would God I had died for thee, O Absalom, my son, my son!' 2 Sam. xviii. 33. Your

[1] *Omne bonum in summo bono.*

[2] Chrysostom.

present work is not to cry, O my dear wife! O my precious child! O my loving sister! but, O my soul, submit to God! justify God, lie down in the will of God; say amen to God's amen. O my soul! think well of God, and speak well of God, and carry it well towards God, &c. This is your present work; make it but your work, and then, though 'sorrow may abide for a night, yet joy will come in the morning,' Ps. xxx. 5.

Again, Observe how other saints have carried it under such a dispensation as you are under, and do you likewise.[1] To that purpose read and compare these scriptures together: Gen. xxiii. 1, 2, 3, 4, 8; Ezek. xxiv. 16–18; 2 Sam. xii. 17–22; 1 Sam. iii. 17–19; 2 Sam. xv. 25–27; Job i. 13–22. It is a more excellent, a more blessed thing to be good at imitating the pious examples of others, than to be good at praising of them. Stories speak of some that could not sleep when they thought of the trophies of other worthies that went before them.[2] The best and highest examples should be very quickening and provoking. Pious examples usually are more wakening than precepts; and they are more convincing and more encouraging; and the reason is, because we see in them, that the exercise of the most difficult points of godliness is yet possible. Other saints' pious examples should be looking-glasses for us to dress ourselves by; and happy are those that make such an improvement of them. Oh, happy husband! oh, happy parents! oh, happy brethren and sisters! if you write after that blessed copy, that this glorified saint, wife, child, sister, hath set before you; which that you may, I desire you seriously to dwell upon the following narrative.

One hint more, and then I have done. Augustine, in one of his epistles, hath this relation, that the very same day wherein Jerome died, he was in his study, and had got pen, ink, and paper, to write something of the glory of heaven to Jerome. Suddenly he saw a light breaking into his study, and a sweet smell that came unto him, and this voice he thought he heard, O Augustine! what dost thou? Dost think to put the sea into a little vessel? When the heavens shall cease from their continual motion, then shalt thou be able to understand what the glory of heaven is, and not before, except thou come to feel it, as I now do.

A little before this glorified saint's translation from earth to heaven, I had thoughts and resolutions to write to her about this blessed state to which she was hastening, but was prevented; however, in the following sermon you will find something of that glorious state glimpsed out unto you, which now she is in possession of. Now, dear friends, above all gettings, get an interest in that glory that she is filled with, and keep up the sense of that interest in your own souls and consciences; and then you will be happy in life, and blessed in death, and assuredly meet her and know her, and for ever enjoy her in perfect happiness and blessedness; which, that you may, is and shall be the constant desires and earnest prayers of

Your soul's servant,

THOMAS BROOKS.

[1] *Bonus dux, bonus comes*, a good leader makes a good follower, was Carus* the emperor's motto. *Præcepta docent, exempla movent*, precepts may instruct, but examples do persuade.—[* 'Carolus'?—G.]

[2] As Themistocles of Miltiades, and Cæsar of Alexander.—G.

A STRING OF PEARLS;

OR, THE BEST THINGS RESERVED TILL LAST.

Before I name my text, give me leave to speak a few words upon another text, viz., the glorified saint deceased, at whose funeral we are here met.

She was one of those dear spiritual children that the Lord had given me, Isa. viii. 18; she was a precious seal of my ministry, she was my living epistle, 2 Cor. iii. 1, 2; my walking certificate, my letter testimonial, Philip. iv. 1, 2. In life she was my joy, and in the day of Christ she will be my crown, as Paul speaks, 1 Thes. ii. 19, 20, 'For what is our hope, or joy, or crown of rejoicing? Are not even ye in the presence of our Lord Jesus Christ at his coming? For ye are our glory and joy.' Her application of those words of the apostle to me hath been often a very great refreshing and comfort to my soul: 'For though you have ten thousand instructors in Christ, yet have ye not many fathers; for in Christ Jesus I have begotten you through the gospel,' 1 Cor. iv. 15. The work of grace upon her heart was clear, powerful, and thorough, as all know that knew her inwardly. I should tire both myself and you, and frustrate the end of your meeting, which is to hear a sermon, should I give you an exact and particular account thereof: I shall therefore mention only a few things among many for your imitation, satisfaction, and supportation under this sad dispensation.

She was a knowing woman in the things of Christ; and her knowledge was inward, experimental, growing, humbling, transforming, and practical, Prov. iii. 18; she knew Christ in the mystery as well as in the history; in the spirit as well as in the letter; feelingly, as well as notionally; she did not only eat of the tree of knowledge, but also tasted of the tree of life.

She was as sincere and plain a hearted Christian, I think, as any lives out of heaven; for plain-heartedness she was a Jacob; for uprightness she was a Job. Sincerity is the shine, the lustre, the beauty, the glory of all a Christian's graces, and in this she did excel.[1] A sincere soul is like a crystal glass with a light in the midst of it, which gives light every way; and such a one was she. A sincere soul is like

[1] *Sinceritas serenitatis mater*, sincerity is the mother of serenity.

the violet, which grows low, and hides itself and its own sweetness, as much as may be, with its own leaves; and such a one was she. She had as many choice, visible characters of sincerity and uprightness upon her, as ever I read upon any Christian that I have had the happiness to be acquainted with. But I must not dwell on these things; I shall only say she was not like the actor in the comedy, who cried with his mouth, *O cœlum*, O heaven! but pointed with his finger to the earth. Such professors there be, but she was none of them.

She was as rich in spiritual experiences as most that I have been acquainted with. Ah! how often hath she warmed, gladded, and quickened my spirit, by acquainting me with what the Lord hath done for her precious soul. Experiments[1] in religion are beyond notions and impressions. A sanctified heart is better than a silver tongue; and she found it so. Oh! the stories that she was able to tell of the love of God, the presence of Christ, the breathings of the Spirit, the exercise of grace, the sweetness of the word, the deceitfulness of sin, and the devices and methods of Satan, &c. And though she made use of her experiences, as crutches to lean on, yet she only made use of the promises as a foundation to build on. As the star led the wise men to Christ, so her experiences led her to a higher and sweeter living upon Christ; her experiences were her sauce, but Christ was still her food.

She did drive a very great private trade towards heaven. She was much in secret duties, in closet communion with God, and this did very much enrich her and advance her in spiritual experiences, when she had once found the sweetness of enjoying Christ behind the door, Cant. ii. 14, Mat. vi. 5, 6. Oh, how inflamedly, how abundantly was her soul carried forth in secret duties! She knew that Peter went up upon the house-top to pray, and that Christ was oft alone, Acts x. 9. As secret meals make a fat body, so she found secret duties made a fat soul; and this made her much in that work. It was a witty and divine speech of Bernard, That Christ, the soul's spouse, is bashful, neither willingly cometh to his bride in the presence of a multitude; and is it not so with the bride in her actings towards her bridegroom, Christ?

She was many times in the school of temptation, which God made to her the school of instruction.[2] The Lord did usually so help her to handle the shield of faith and the sword of the Spirit, the word of God, that she commonly triumphed over Satan's temptations, and led captivity captive. Though that arrow-master, Satan, hath shot often at her, yet her 'bow still abode in strength, her hands and heart being made strong by the hands of the mighty God of Jacob.' Augustine gave thanks to God that the heart and the temptation did not meet together, and so hath she many a time. She was good at withstanding the beginnings of a temptation, knowing that after-remedies often come too late. She was a Christian all over.[3] She was a Christian in profession, and a Christian in practice; a Christian in lip, and a Christian in life; a Christian in word, and a Christian in work; a Christian in show, and a Christian in power and spirit. She was not only for the general duties of Christianity, as hearing, praying, &c., but also for the

[1] 'Experiences.'—G.

[2] 2 Cor. xii. 7–10; Eph. vi. 16, 17; 2 Cor. ii. 14; Gen. xlix. 23, 24.

[3] 1 Thes. v. 23; Acts xiii. 22, xxiv. 16; Luke i. 5, 6.

relative duties of religion, as to be a good wife, a good mother, a good child, a good sister, a good mistress, &c. Most sincerity and holy ingenuity shines in the relative duties of religion; and in those she was excellent. She was also very conscientious and constant, yea, abundant in the general duties of religion, as hearing, praying, &c. She did duties, but durst not for a world trust to her duties, but to her Jesus, as the dove made use of her wings to fly to the ark, but trusted not in her wings, but in the ark. In duty, she had learned the holy art of living above duty; in the business of acceptation with God, and justification before God, and reconciliation to God, and salvation by God, she knew no duty but Jesus.[1] She was as happy in denying religious self as she was resolute in denying of sinful self.

She was, for patience and cheerfulness under her long lingering weakness, as exemplary as any that ever I was acquainted with, James i. 2–4; v. 10, 11. If at any time she groaned, yet she blessed God, as she used to say, that she did not grumble. Oh how quiet, how like a lamb was she under all her trials! Oh how well would she speak of God! Oh how sweetly did she carry it towards God! Oh how much was she taken up in justifying of God throughout her pining, wasting sicknesses!

Time and strength would fail me should I but tell you what I could concerning her faith, her love to God, to Christ, to his ways, to his people, whether poor or rich, weak or strong; and of her humility, lowliness, meekness, wherein she hath left few fellows behind her. She was very high in spiritual worth, and as low in heart; she was clothed with humility as with a royal robe, and with 'the ornament of a meek and quiet spirit, which is in the sight of God of great price,' 1 Pet. v. 5, iii. 4. But I must hasten to my text, for I see time slides away.

If Ezekiel can commend Daniel, and match him with Noah and Job for his power in prayer, and Peter highly praise Paul, and if the ancient church had her diptychs or public tables, wherein the persons most noted for piety were recorded; nay, if Plato called Aristotle the intelligent reader, and Aristotle set up an altar in honour of Plato, then I hope you will not impute it to me as a transgression that I have presented to you the shining virtues of this glorified saint for your imitation.

What eyes thou read'st with, reader, know I wot,
Mine were not dry when I this story wrote.

AN ELEGY

Upon the death of the virtuous, his dear and never-to-be-forgotten friend, Mrs Mary Blake.

If that affection could but make a poet,
Could grief and sorrow help, sure I should do it;
Mary is dead, a woman whom truth and fame,
With virtue, ever shall embalm her name;
A Mary for love, a Mary for weeping,
A Mary for choice, a Mary for seeking.

[1] Duties trusted to will undo you; when trusted to, they prove but a smooth, a silken way to hell.

With Mary she had chosen the better part;
With Mary she did lay Christ near'st her heart.
Such were her parts, her piety,
Her youth it was a full maturity.
Grave although young; who in her heart did prize
Grace, truth, and Christ her only sacrifice;
Gracious, religious, and sincere was she,
Courteous, without all court-hypocrisy.

Christ was her study, his glory was her aim;
It was her heaven for to advance the same.
Within the holy treasury of her mind
Were the choice virtues of all womankind;
A knowing woman, and an humble too,
Which joyed all Christians who had with her to do.
A praying woman and believing too,
Which did the praises of other saints renew:
A holy woman, and a harmless too.
In saying this, I give her but her due.
A lively Christian and thriving in grace;
Few towards heaven did ever hold her pace.
The word and ways of God were her delight,
And in the same she had a great insight.
A fixed woman, when others staggering were,
Which was the fruit of holy pains and care;
A tried Christian, whose trials were not small,
Yet faith and patience overcame them all;
She lived the sermons which on earth she heard,
And now receives the crown which was for her prepared;
A woman which had more than common worth;
I want a tongue, enough to set it forth.

Her latest precious breathings had respect
To nothing more than divine dialect;
Which she committed to her mourning friends,
In exhortations to their better ends.
Could prayers, tears, and sighs have kept her here,
She had not died, you need it not to fear;
She lives, though dead, in th' memory of those,
Who knew her life, and saw its holy close.
No golden letters half so long as we,
Shall keep her precious worth in memory;
No costly marble need on her be spent,
Her deathless worth is her own monument.
Now, shall I let you know what you have lost?
She was a temple of the Holy Ghost.
This we'll apply, that though we lose her here,
Her soul doth shine in a celestial sphere.
Mary is to the celestial Canaan gone,
Where as a star she shines in perfection.
Mary hath chosen sure the better part,
Mary with angels sure doth now partake.

But stay, needs she encomiums? Reader, know,
She joys above, while we here wail below.
But now, dear friends, let's mourn in hope and weep,
Believing this blest saint in Christ doth sleep.
Hark, don't you hear her sweet delightful voice?
Saying, Friends, weep not, but see that ye rejoice
For me, for now I am perfectly free,
From sorrow, sin, death, and mortality;
Surely you cannot doubt my happiness,
Who have beheld my faith and stedfastness;
Oh then from sorrow see that now ye cease,
To interrupt my joy and your own peace;
Surely our loss to her was greatest gain,
For crowned in heaven she ever shall remain;

No sighs, no groans, now from her do come,
But everlasting joys are in their room.
She now without control, no question, sings
Eternal praises to the King of kings;
She now enjoys that ever blessed face,
In hopes whereof she run a happy race:
She now hath chang'd her crosses for a crown,
Her bed of weakness for a royal throne.

Farewell! blessed saint, farewell! to thee we'll haste,
For till we meet in heaven we cannot rest.

THOMAS BROOKS,
Of Margaret's, New-Fish-street.

A WORD TO THE READER.

Now, Reader, if you please to cast a look,
Or spend some spare-time on this little book,
And in it anything that's good do view,
Then challenge it, for it belongs to you;
What's weak or worthless in it, that decline
And pass it by, I challenge that for mine.

THE BEST THINGS RESERVED TILL LAST.

To an inheritance incorruptible, and undefiled, and that fadeth not away, reserved in heaven for you.—1 PETER I. 4.

BELOVED,—I have chosen this text upon a double ground.

1. To make a diversion of immoderate sorrow and grief from my own spirit and yours, who are most nearly concerned in this sad loss. And,

2. Because it will afford us matter most suitable to the blessed state and condition of this glorified saint, at whose funeral we are here met.

In the inscription, verses 1, 2, you have first a holy salutation, shewing first by whom this epistle was written, viz. Peter, an apostle of Jesus Christ; secondly, to whom it was written. Now they are described two ways: first, by their outward condition, 'strangers, scattered throughout Pontus, Galatia, Cappadocia, Asia, and Bithynia.' There are divers opinions about these strangers, but the most common and received opinion among the learned is, that Peter wrote this epistle to the converted Jews, scattered through the provinces in Asia, who met with much opposition and affliction for the gospel's sake.[1] Secondly, they are described by their spiritual and inward condition, which is set forth,

(1.) By the fundamental cause of it, to wit, election of God.

(2.) By the final cause, to wit, sanctification of the Spirit unto obedience.

(3.) By the subservient cause, to wit, reconciliation, conferred in obedience and sprinkling of the blood of Jesus Christ.

In the third verse you have, (1.) A very stately proem, and such as can hardly be matched again, 'Blessed be the God and Father of our Lord Jesus Christ.' (2.) You have regeneration or effectual calling described, and that

[1.] First, By the principal efficient cause thereof, which is, 'God the Father of our Lord Jesus Christ.'

[2.] By the impulsive cause thereof, the mercy of God, which is described by the quantity of it, 'abundant.'

[3.] By the immediate effect thereof, a 'lively hope,' the singular

[1] **Pareus. Compare the 2d of the Acts, the 8th of the Acts, and the 11th of the Acts, with the 1st and 2d verses of this chapter.**

cause whereof is shewed to be the resurrection of Jesus Christ from the dead, 1 John iii. 2, 3.[1] Now hope is called a lively hope,

[1.] Because it makes a man lively and active for God and goodness.

[2.] Because it cheers, comforts, and revives the soul. It brings, it breeds, it feeds, it preserves spiritual life in the soul. This lively hope is like Myrtilus his shield, which after the use he had of it in the field, having it with him at sea, and suffering shipwreck, it served him for a boat to waff[2] him to shore, and so preserved his life.[3] This lively hope is a shield ashore, and an anchor at sea.

[3.] It is called a lively hope, in opposition to the fading, withering, dying hopes of hypocrites, and profane persons, 'Whose hope is as a spider's web,' 'the crackling of thorns under a pot,' and 'the giving up of the ghost.'[4]

A Christian's hope is not like that of Pandora, which may fly out of the box, and bid the soul farewell; no, it is like the morning light: the least beam of it shall commence into a complete sunshine; it is *aurora gaudii*, and it shall shine forth brighter and brighter till perfect day; but the hypocrite's hope, the presumptuous sinner's hope is like a cloud, or the morning dew.

Now, in my text you have the object about which this 'lively hope' is exercised; and that is, 'an inheritance incorruptible, and undefiled, and that fadeth not away' [What these words import I shall shew you when I open that doctrine which I intend to stand upon at this time], 'reserved in heaven for you.'

There are three heavens: the first is *cœlum aërium*, the airy heaven, where the fowls of heaven do fly; the second is *cœlum astriferum*, where the stars of heaven are; the third is *cœlum beatorum*, the heaven of the blessed, where God appears in eminency, and where Christ shines in glory; and this is the heaven the text speaks of.

The text will afford several points, but I shall only name one, which I intend to stand on at this time, and that is this,

Doct. That God reserves the best and greatest favours and blessings for believers till they come to heaven.

Now, I shall prove this proposition by an induction of particulars; and then give you the reasons of it. I will begin with the inheritance spoken of in the text.

I. *The best inheritance is reserved for believers till they come to heaven.* This is clear and fair in the text,[5] yet I shall make this further out to you thus:

(1.) First, The inheritance reserved for believers till they come to heaven, *is a pure, undefiled, and incorruptible inheritance.* It is an inheritance that cannot be defiled nor blemished with abuse one way or another. Other inheritances may, and often are, with oaths, cruelty, blood, deceit, &c. The Greek word ἀμίαντος signifies a precious stone, which, though it be never so much soiled, yet it cannot be blemished nor defiled; yea, the oftener you cast it into the fire, and take it out, the more clear, bright, and shining it is.[6] All earthly inheritances are true

[1] *Corpus spirando, anima sperando vivit*, as the body lives by breathing, so the soul by hoping.

[2] The early form of 'waft'?—G.

[3] The giver of its name to the Myrtoan sea.—G.

[4] Job viii. 13, 14, xi. 20, xxvii. 8; Prov. xi. 7.

[5] *Vide Zanchium.*

[6] *Quam sordet mihi terra, cum cœlum intueor.*—Adrian.

gardens of Adonis, where we can gather nothing but trivial flowers, surrounded with many briers, thorns, and thistles, Gen. iii. 18, Isa. xxiii. 9. Oh the hands, the hearts, the thoughts, the lives that have been defiled, stained, and polluted with earthly inheritances! Oh the impure love, the carnal conscience, the vain boastings, the sensual joys, that earthly inheritances have filled and defiled poor souls with! All earthly inheritances, they are no better than the cities which Solomon gave to Hiram, which he called *Cabul*, 1 Kings ix. 13, that is to say, displeasing or dirty. The world doth but dirt and dust us. But,

(2.) Secondly, *It is a sure, a secure, inheritance:* 'To an inheritance reserved in heaven for you.' See the text. The Greek word that is here rendered 'reserved,' is from τηρέω, *tereo*, which signifies to keep solicitously, to keep as with watch and ward. This inheritance is kept and secured to us by promise, by power, by blood, by oath; and therefore must needs be sure.[1] It is neither sin, nor Satan, nor the world that can put a Christian by his inheritance. Christ hath already taken possession of it in their names and in their rooms; and so it is secure to them. If weakness can overcome strength, impotency omnipotency. then may a Christian be kept out of his inheritance, but not till then. But earthly inheritances they are not sure, they are not secure. How often doth might overcome right, and the weakest go to the wall! How many are kept out, and how many are cast out, of their inheritances, by power, policy, craft, cruelty. It was a complaint of old, our inheritance is turned to strangers, our houses to aliens, James v. 2.

(3.) Thirdly, *It is a permanent, a lasting, inheritance:*[2] 'To an inheritance incorruptible, undefiled, and that fadeth not away.' The Greek word ἀμάραντος is the proper name of a flower, which is still fresh and green after it hath a long time hung up in the house. It is an inheritance that shall continue as long as God himself continues. Of this inheritance there shall be no end. Though other inheritances may be lasting, yet they are not everlasting; though sometimes it be long before they have an end, yet they have an end. Where is the glory of the Chaldean, Persian, Grecian, and Roman kingdoms? *Sic transit gloria mundi;* but the glory of believers shall never fade nor wither; it shall never grow old nor rusty: 1 Pet. v. 4, 'And when the chief Shepherd shall appear, ye shall receive a crown of glory, which fadeth not away.' A believer's inheritance, his glory, his happiness, his blessedness, shall be as fresh and flourishing after he hath been many thousand thousands of years in heaven as it was at his first entrance into it. Earthly inheritances are like tennis-balls, which are bandied up and down from one to another, and in time wore out, 1 Tim. vi. 17. The creature is all shadow and vanity; it is *filia noctis*, like Jonah's gourd. Man can sit under its shadow but a little, little while; it soon decays and dies; it quickly fades and withers. There is a worm at the root of all earthly inheritances, that will consume them in time. All earthly comforts and contents are but like a fair picture that is drawn upon the ice, which continueth not; or like the morning cloud, that soon passeth away; but a believer's inheritance endureth for ever. When

[1] Heb. vi. 12–20; Rom. viii. 33, 39; Eph. ii. 6; John xiv. 1–3, x. 27–30. If this inheritance were not kept for us, it might haply go the same way paradise did.

[2] Daniel ii. 44, vii. 27; Heb. xii. 27, 28; 2 Peter i. 11.

this world shall be no more, when time shall be no more, the inheritance of the saints shall be fresh, flourishing, and continuing. *Nescio quid erit, quod ista vita non erit, ubi lucet, quod non capiat locus, ubi sonat, quod non rapit tempus, ubi olet, quod non spargit flatus, ubi sapit, quod non minuit edacitas, ubi hæret, quod non divellit æternitas*, said Augustine; what will that life be, or rather what will not that life be, since all good either is not at all, or is in such a life? Light, which place cannot comprehend; voices and music, which time cannot ravish away; odours, which are never dissipated; a feast, which is never consumed; a blessing, which eternity bestoweth, but eternity shall never see at an end. So this, all this, is the heritage of all God's Jacobs.

(4.) Fourthly, *It is the freest inheritance.* It is an inheritance that is free from all vexation and molestation. There shall be no sin to molest the soul, nor no devil to vex the soul. 'There shall be no pricking brier nor grieving thorn unto the house of Israel,' Ezek. xxviii. 24; there shall be no Jebusites to be 'as pricks in your eyes, and thorns in your sides,' Num. xxxiii. 55. There shall be no crying, Oh my bones! oh my bowels! oh the deceit of this man! oh the oppression of that man! &c. No; they shall have a crown without thorns, a rose without prickles, and an inheritance without the least encumbrance. This inheritance flows from free love, and is freely offered, though the soul hath neither money nor money-worth. There is nothing, there is not the least thing about this inheritance that is purchased or paid for by us, Isa. lv. 1, 2. It is all frank, it is all free, it is all of grace. Here is such an inheritance that no eye ever saw, that no mortal ever possessed; and that for nothing.[1] It is freely offered, and it is freely given: Acts xx. 32, 'And now, brethren, I commend you to God, and to the word of his grace, which is able to build you up, and to give you an inheritance among all them which are sanctified.' All is mercy, all is of free mercy, that God alone may have the glory. Other inheritances they have their encumbrances. Oh the vexations, the molestations that do attend them! Oh the debates, the disputes, the law-suits that are about earthly inheritances, such as have made many a man to go with a heavy heart, an empty purse, and a thread-bare coat; which made Themistocles profess, that if two ways were shewed him, one to hell, and the other to the bar, he would decline that which did lead to the bar, and choose that which went to hell.[2]

(5.) Fifthly, *It is an inheritance that is universally communicable*,[3] to Jews, to Gentiles; to bond, to free; to rich, to poor; to high, to low; to male, to female: Gal. iii. 28, 29, 'There is neither Jew nor Greek, there is neither bond nor free, there is neither male nor female, for ye are all one in Christ Jesus;' 'And if ye be Christ's, then are ye Abraham's seed, and heirs according to the promise,' Rom. viii. 17. Among men, all sons and daughters be not heirs, yet all God's children, be they sons, be they daughters, be they bond or free, &c., they are all heirs, without exception. Jehoshaphat gave his younger sons 'great gifts of

[1] Rom. vii. 25; Isa. lxiv. 4; 1 Cor. ii. 9.

[2] Plutarch, *Themistocles*.—G.

[3] Acts x. 35; 1 Cor. xii. 13. Oh that excellent inheritance, saith Bernard, *Non angustior multitudine hæredum*, whose portions are not scanted by reason of the number and multitude of co-heirs.

silver and gold, and of precious things, with fenced cities, but the kingdoms gave he to Jehoram, because he was the first-born,' 2 Chron. xxi. 3. And Abraham gave gifts to the rest of his sons, but Isaac only had the inheritance, Gen. xxv. 5, 6. In some countries all children be not heirs, but sons only; and in other countries not all sons, but the eldest son alone. Usually men divide their earthly inheritances. If all the sons be heirs, some inherit one place, others others; but here the whole inheritance is enjoyed by every child; here every child is an heir to all, and hath right to all. In earthly inheritances, the more you divide, the less is every one's part; but this inheritance is not diminished by the multitude of possessors, nor impaired by the number of co-heirs; it is as much to many as to a few, and as great to one as to all. Not a room, not a mansion, not a walk, not a flower, not a jewel, not a box of myrrh, but what is common to all; not a smile, not a good word, not a sweet look, not a robe, not a dish, not a delicate, not a pleasure, not a delight, but is universally communicable, and universally fit for all the thousands millions of thousands that are heirs of this inheritance. If there be a thousand together, every one sees as much of the sun, hears as much of the sound, smells as much of the sweet, as he should do if there were no more than himself alone; so here.

(6.) Sixthly, and lastly, *It is a soul-satisfying inheritance.* He that hath it shall sit down and say, I have enough, I have all.[1] As one master satisfies the servant, and as one father satisfies the child, and as one husband satisfies the wife, so one God, one Christ, one inheritance, satisfies the believing soul: Ps. xvi. 5, 6, 'The Lord is the portion of mine inheritance, and of my cup: thou maintainest my lot. The lines are fallen unto me in a pleasant place; yea, I have a goodly heritage.' Will an inheritance of glory satisfy them? Why! this they shall have, 1 John iii. 3, Col. iii. 4. Will an inheritance of power and dominion satisfy them? Why, this they shall have, 1 Cor. iii. 21, 'All things are yours,' &c. Mat. xix. 28, 1 Cor. vi. 2, 3, &c. Will Abraham's bosom satisfy you? Why! this you shall have, Luke xvi. 22.[2] The bosom is the place where love lodges all her children; the bosom is the place of delight and satisfaction, and this you shall have; nay, you shall have a better, a choicer, a sweeter bosom to solace your souls in than Abraham's, to wit, the bosom of Jesus Christ, which will be a paradise of pleasure and delight to you. Will Christ's best robe, will his own signet put upon you, satisfy you? Why! this you shall have. Will it satisfy you to be where Christ is, and to fare as Christ fares, and wear as Christ wears, and enjoy as Christ enjoys? Why! this you shall have: John xii. 26, 'Where I am, there shall also my servant be; if any man serve me, him will my Father honour.' If all these things will satisfy souls, then surely the inheritance reserved in heaven for them will satisfy them; for that inheritance takes in these things, and many more. The good things that this inheritance is made up of are so many, that they exceed number; so great, that they exceed measure; so precious, that they are above all estimation; and therefore it must

[1] *Habet omnia qui habet habentem omnia.*—Augustine. Gen. xxxiii. 11, I have enough, saith Jacob, לִי כֹל, *Li chol*, I have all.

[2] *Si aliud præter Deum habeo, nec aliud plene possideo nec Deum. Deus qui non deficit, solus mihi sufficit.*—Eusebius, Nuremb.

needs be a soul-satisfying inheritance.[1] But now all other inheritances they cannot satisfy the heart of man:[2] Eccles. v. 10, 'He that loveth silver, shall not be satisfied with silver; nor he that loveth abundance, with increase: this is also vanity.' If you please, you may read the words nearer the original thus: 'He that loveth silver, shall not be satisfied with silver; and he that loveth it, in the multitude of it, shall not have fruit.' It is the love of silver that is the mischief of it; it is the love of silver that makes men unsatisfied with silver. Such a man will still be adding house to house, land to land, bag to bag, and heap to heap, and yet after all be still unsatisfied. Bernard[3] compareth such a man to one that, being very hungry, gapeth continually for wind, with which he may be puffed, but cannot be filled and satisfied; and so the same author elsewhere saith well, *Anima rationalis cæteris omnibus occupari potest, impleri non potest,* the reasonable soul may be busied about other things, but it cannot be filled with them; they can no more fill up the soul than a drop of water can fill up the huge ocean; they can no more satisfy the desires of the soul than a few drops of water can the thirst of a man inflamed with a violent fever; nay, as oil increases the flame of the fire, so the more a man hath of the world, the more his heart is inflamed after it.[4] When Alexander had conquered the known part of the world, say some, he sat down and wished for another world to conquer. Charles the Fifth, emperor of Germany, whom of all men the world judged most happy, cried out with detestation to all his honours, pleasures, trophies, riches, *Abite hinc, abite longe;* get you hence, let me hear no more of you. They could not satisfy him, they could not quiet him. Such things that a fancy, a conceit, an ungrounded fear will rob a man of the comfort of, can never satisfy him; but such are all worldly enjoyments, 2 Kings vii. 6, 7. One man will not live because his Delilah will not love; another with Ahab will be sick, and die because he cannot get his neighbour's inheritance, 1 Kings xxi.; another wishes himself dead because his commodities lie dead on his hands; another with Haman can find no sweetness in all his enjoyments, because Mordecai sits at the king's gate, Esther v. 9–14; as those things which delude a man can never satisfy him. But the world deludes a man, and puts cheats upon him; it promises a man pleasure, and pays him with pain; it promises profit—'all this will I give thee' —and pays him with loss; loss of God, of Christ, of peace of conscience, of comfort, of heaven, of happiness, of all: it promises contentment, and fills him with torment;—and therefore can never satisfy the soul of man, &c.

But the inheritance reserved in heaven, that will satisfy; it will afford nothing that may offend the soul, it will yield everything that may delight the soul, that may quiet and satisfy the soul; by all which it is most evident, that the best inheritance is reserved for the saints till they come to heaven. But,

II. Secondly, As the best inheritance, so *the best is reserved for believers till they come to heaven.* This life is full of trials, full of troubles, and full of changes. Sin within, and Satan and the world without, will

[1] August. *de Triplici. habitu.* cap. iv.

[2] This the great caliph of Babylon, Charles the Fifth, and others, found by experience.

[3] Bernard, *Tract. de diligendo Deum*, cap. iii.

[4] Bernard, Hom. Mat. xix. 17.

keep a Christian from rest, till he comes to rest in the bosom of Christ. The life of a Christian is a race; and what rest have they that are still a-running their race? The life of a Christian is a warfare; and what rest have they that are still engaged in a constant warfare? The life of a Christian is the life of a pilgrim; and what rest hath a pilgrim, who is still a-travelling from place to place?[1] A pilgrim is like Noah's dove, that could find no rest for the sole of her foot. The fears, the snares, the cares, the changes, &c., that attends believers in this world, are such that will keep them from taking up their rest here. A Christian hears that word always sounding in his ears, 'Arise, for this is not thy resting-place,' Micah ii. 10. A man may as well expect to find heaven in hell, as expect to find rest in this world. It was the complaint of Ambrose, *Quid in hac vita non experimur adversi? Quas non procellas tempestatesque perpetimur? Quibus non exagitamur incommodis? Cujus parcitur meritis?*[2] What misery do we not undergo in this life? What storms and tempests do we not endure? with what troubles are we not tossed? whose worth is spared? Man's sorrows begin when his days begin, and his sorrows are multiplied as his days are multiplied; his whole life is but one continued grief; labour wears him, care tears him, fears toss him, losses vex him, dangers trouble him, crosses disquiet him, nothing pleases him; in the day he wishes, Would God it were night, and in the night, Would God it were day; before he rises he sighs; before he washes he weeps; before he feeds he fears; under all his abundance he is in wants, and 'in the midst of his sufficiency he is in straits,' Job xx. 22; his heart, as Gregory Nyssene speaks,[3] *Non tantum gaudet in iis quæ habet, quantum tristatur ob ea quæ desunt,* is not so much quieted in those things which it hath, as it is tormented for those things which it hath not. In a word, all the rest we have in this world, is but a very short nap, to that glorious rest that is reserved in heaven for us: Heb. iv. 9, 10, 'There remaineth therefore a rest to the people of God. For he that is entered into his rest, he also hath ceased from his own works, as God did from his.' There remains a rest to the people of God, or as the Greek hath it, a sabbatism, a celestial rest, an eternal rest, a Sabbath that shall never have end.[4] When God had made man, we read that the next day he rested; and why is this set down, saith Anselm, *Nisi per hoc vellet innuere, quod illum post cujus creationem requievit, ad requiem fecit?* but that the Spirit of God would shew unto us, that God made him for rest, after the making of whom God is said to have rested?[5] Rest is a jewel very desirable on earth, but we shall not wear it in our bosoms till we come to heaven. Ambrose well observes,[6] that *sex diebus mundus est factus, septimo requietum est die; ultra mundum ergo est quies, ultra mundum etiam fructus quietis,* in six days the world was made, on the seventh day there was rest; it is beyond this world, therefore, that rest is, and it is beyond this world that the fruit of rest is to be had.

[1] Heb. xii. 1; 2 Tim. iv. 7, 8; Isa. xl. 2; 2 Cor. x. 4; 1 Tim. i. 18; Ps. cxix. 54; Heb. xi. 13; 1 Peter ii. 11.

[2] Ambrose *de fide resurrectionis.*

[3] Gregor. Nyssen. *in Eccles. Hom.* 7.

[4] *σαββατισμὸς*, a sabbatizing.

[5] Estius—and others—understands this text of a celestial rest, &c.

[6] Ambrose *in Evangel. Lu.* c. ix.

I shall shew you, observing brevity, the excellency of that rest that is reserved for believers in heaven. As,

(1.) First, *It is a superlative rest;* a rest that infinitely exceeds all earthly rest. All other rest is not to be named in the day wherein this rest is spoken of. Some have purchased rest, for a time, with silver and gold, but this is a rest that all the gold and silver in the world can never purchase. Over this rest is written, not the price of gold, but the price of blood, yea, the price of the best and noblest blood that ever run in veins. That rest we have here must needs be a poor, low-priced rest, *ubi multa cautela custoditur salus corporis, custodita etiam amittitur, amissa cum gravi labore reparatur, et tamen reparata in dubio semper est,*[1] where the health of the body is preserved with much watchfulness, being preserved, is also lost; being lost, is recovered with much labour; and yet being recovered, is always in danger and doubtfulness, what will become of it. Our estate in this world is not a fixed estate; what then is our rest? Our very living is but a passing away; our lives are full of troubles, and they fill our souls full of unquietness. After the Trojans had been tossing and wandering in the Mediterranean Sea, as soon as they espied Italy, they cried out with exulting joy, 'Italy! Italy!' and so when saints, after all their tossings and restlessness in this world, shall come to heaven, then, and not till then, they will cry out, Rest, rest, no rest to this rest. But,

(2.) Secondly, The rest reserved in heaven for believers, *it is an universal rest,* Rev. xiv. 13, a rest from all sin and a rest from all sorrow; a rest from all afflictions and a rest from all temptations; a rest from all oppression and a rest from all vexations; a rest from all labour and pains, from all trouble and travail, from all aches, weaknesses, and diseases. There is no crying out, O my bones! O my back! O my bowels! O my sides! O my head! O my heart! Our rest here is only in part and imperfect; here we have rest in one part and pain in another, quiet in one part and torment in another. Sometimes when the head is well, the heart is sick; and sometimes when there is peace in the conscience, there is pain in the bones. Here many return us hatred for our love, and this hinders our rest;[2] here we are apt to create cares and fears to ourselves, rather than we will want them, and this hinders our rest; here we are very apt to give offence, and as apt to take offence, though none be given, and this hinders our rest, 1 Cor. x. 32. Sometimes we have rest abroad and none at home; sometimes rest at home and none abroad, Job vii. 13–16. Our rest here is imperfect and incomplete, but our rest in heaven shall be most perfect and complete; there the inward and the outward man shall be both at rest, &c. But,

(3.) Thirdly, *It is an uninterrupted rest;* it is a rest that none can interrupt.[3] Here sometimes sin interrupts our rest, sometimes temptations interrupts our rest, sometimes divine withdrawings interrupts our rest, sometimes the sudden changes and alterations that God makes in our conditions interrupts our rest; sometimes the power, and sometimes the policy, and sometimes the cruelty of wicked men interrupts our rest, sometimes the crossness of friends, sometimes the deceitfulness of friends,

[1] Greg. Mor. l. xi. c. 26.
[2] Ps. xxxviii. 20, cix. 4, Mat. vi. 25–34.
[3] Ps. xl. 12; 2 Cor. xii. 7–9; Ps. xxx. 6, 7; Cant. iii. 5; Job iii. 25, 26, &c.

sometimes the loss of friends, and sometimes the death of friends interrupts our rest; one thing or another is still interrupting our rest.[1] Oh! but in heaven there shall be no sin, no devil, no sinner, no false friends; there shall be nothing, there shall not be the least thing that may interrupt a saint's rest; indeed, heaven could not be heaven, did it admit of anything that might interrupt a saint's rest. Heaven is above all winds and weather, storms and tempests, earthquakes and heartquakes. There is only that which is amiable and desirable; there is nothing to cloud a Christian's joy, or to interrupt a Christian's rest. When once a soul is asleep in the bosom of Abraham, none can awake him, none can molest or disturb him. Here is joy without sorrow, blessedness without misery, health without sickness, light without darkness, abundance without want, beauty without deformity, honour without disgrace, ease without labour, and peace without interruption or perturbation. Here shall be eyes without tears, hearts without fears, and souls without sin. Here shall be no evil to molest the soul; here shall be all good to cheer the soul, and all happiness to satisfy the soul; and what then can possibly interrupt the rest of the soul? But,

(4.) Fourthly, As it is an uninterrupted rest, so *it is a peculiar rest;* it is a rest peculiar to sons, to saints, to heirs, to beloved ones: Ps. cxxvii. 2, 'So he gives his beloved rest,' or as the Hebrew hath it, dearling, or dear beloved, quiet rest, without care or sorrow.[2] The Hebrew word שנא, *Shena*, is written with א, a quiet dumb letter, which is not usual, to denote the more quietness and rest. This rest is a crown that God sets only upon the head of saints; it is a gold chain that he only puts about his children's necks; it is a jewel that he only hangs between his beloveds' breasts; it is a flower that he only sticks in his darlings' bosoms. This rest is a tree of life that is proper and peculiar to the inhabitants of that heavenly country; it is children's bread, and shall never be given to dogs. Here wicked men have their good things; their peace, their rest, their quiet, &c., their heaven, whilst the people of God are troubled and disquieted on every side;[3] but the day is a-coming wherein the saints shall have rest, and sinners shall never have a good day more, never have an hour's rest more; their torments shall be endless and ceaseless. The old world had their resting-time, but at last patience and justice, tired and abused, put a period to their rest, by washing and sweeping them to hell with a flood; and then Noah, and those righteous souls that were with him, had their time of rest and peace; and so shall it be with sinners and saints at last, &c. But,

(5.) Fifthly, The rest reserved for the saints in heaven, as it is a peculiar rest, so *it is a rest that is universally communicable to all the sons and daughters of God.* 'And to you who are troubled, rest with us,' saith the apostle Paul; 'rest with us,' with us apostles, with us saints, and with all the family of heaven together, 2 Thess. i. 6, 7. Here some saints are at liberty, when others are in prison; here some

[1] *Quid est aliud hic nasci, nisi ingredi laboriosam vitam?* What is it else to be born here, than to enter into a troublesome life?—*Augustine.*

[2] לידידו, it is an allusion to Solomon's name, Jedidiah, 2 Sam. xii. 25.

[3] Luke xvi. 25; Ps. lxxiii. 3–21; Job xxi. 7–14.

sit under their own vines and drink the blood of the grape, whilst others have their blood poured out as water upon the ground, &c.; but in heaven they shall all have rest together, the believing husband and the believing wife shall rest together, and believing parents and believing children shall rest together. Here one relation hath rest, when the other hath not, but there they shall all rest together. There the painful[1] preacher and the diligent hearer shall rest together; there the gracious master and the pious servant shall rest together, &c.: Isa. lvii. 2, 'He shall enter into peace, they shall rest in their beds, each one walking in his uprightness; they shall rest in their beds,' or as some read it, they shall rest in their bee-hives, expressing the Hebrew by the Latin; *cubile* signifies a bee-hive, as well as a couch or bed. Look, as the poor wearied bees do rest all together in their bee-hives, in their honey-houses, so all the saints shall rest together in heaven, which is their bee-hive, their honey-house; and oh what a happy rest will that be, when all the saints shall rest together! But,

(6.) Sixthly and lastly, *It is a permanent, a constant rest.* Of this rest there shall be no end. It is a rest that shall last as long as heaven lasts; yea, as long as God himself shall continue. Time shall be no more, and this world shall be no more, but this rest shall remain for ever, Rev. x. 6, 2 Pet. iii. 10, *et seq.* The rest of the people of God in this world is transient, it is inconstant. Now they have rest, and anon they have none; now a calm, presently a storm; now all is in quiet, anon all is in an uproar. Their rest in this world is like a morning cloud and the early dew, which is soon dried up by the beams of the sun, Hosea vi. 4. Since God hath cast man out of paradise, out of his first rest, he can find but little rest in this world; sometimes the unfitness of the creature troubles him, sometimes the fickleness of the creature vexes him, sometimes the treachery of the creature enrages him, and sometimes the want of the creature distracts him. When in his heart he saith, Now I shall have rest, now I shall be quiet, then troubles and changes come, so that his whole life is rather a dreaming of rest than an enjoying of rest. Oh! but in heaven the rest of the saints shall have no end; there shall be nothing that can put a period to their rest, there shall be everything that may conduce to the perpetuating of their rest. Heaven would be but a poor low thing, did it not afford a perpetual rest.

III. Thirdly, As the best rest, so *the best sight and knowledge of God is reserved for believers till they come to heaven.* I readily grant that even in this world the saints do know the Lord, inwardly, spiritually, powerfully, feelingly, experimentally, transformingly, practically; but yet, notwithstanding all this, the best knowledge of God is reserved for heaven, which I shall evidence by an induction of particulars, thus:

(1.) First, *They shall have the clearest knowledge and revelation of God in heaven.*[2] Here our visions of God are not clear; and this makes many a child of light to sit and sigh in darkness, Lam. iii. 44. God veils himself, he covers himself with a cloud. Man, when he is silent concerning God, seemeth to be something, but when he begins to speak of God, it plainly appears that he is nothing.

Simonides being asked by Hiero, the tyrant, what God was, craved

[1] 'Painstaking.'—G.

[2] *Nihil notum in terra, nihil ignotum in cœlo.*

a day for to deliberate about an answer; but the more he sought into the nature of God, the more difficult he found it to express; therefore, the next day after being questioned, he asked two days, the third day he craved four, and so from that time forth doubled the number; and being asked why he did so, he answered, that the more he studied, the less he was able to define what he was, so incomprehensible is his nature.[1]

Our visions of God here are dark and obscure. Augustine, asking the question, what God is? gives in this answer,[2] *Certe hic est, de quo et quum dicitur, non potest dici; quum æstimatur, non potest æstimari; quum comparatur, non potest comparari; quum definitur, ipse sua definitione crescit:* surely it is he, who when he is spoken of cannot be spoken of, who when he is considered of cannot be considered of, who when he is compared to any thing cannot be compared, and when he is defined, groweth greater by defining of him. It is observable, that it was not the Lord which the prophet Ezekiel saw, it was only a vision, Ezek. i. 28. In the vision it was not the glory of the Lord which he saw, but the likeness of it; nay, it was not the likeness of it, but the appearance of the likeness of the glory of the Lord, that made him to fall on his face, as not being able to behold it. Sin hath so weakened, dazzled, and darkened the eye of our souls, that we cannot bear the sight of the glory of the Lord, nor the likeness of it, no! nor the appearance of the likeness of it.

In the Psalms the Lord is said to ride upon a cherub, Ps. xviii. 10; upon which words one saith thus, *Cherub quippe plenitudo scientiæ dicitur, proinde super plenitudinem scientiæ ascendisse perhibetur, quia majestatis ejus plenitudinem scientia nulla comprehendit,* a cherub is so called, as being a fulness of knowledge; and therefore is God said to ascend above the fulness of knowledge, because no knowledge comprehendeth the fulness of his majesty.[3]

But when believers come to heaven, then they shall have a more clear vision and sight of God: 1 Cor. xiii. 12, 'For now we see through a glass, darkly; but then face to face: now I know in part; but then shall I know even as also I am known.'[4] Now we see him obscurely, as in a glass, but then we shall see him distinctly, clearly, immediately; we shall then apprehend him clearly, though, even then, we cannot comprehend him fully.[5] Some sense those words, I shall know even as I am known, thus: Look, as God knoweth me after a manner agreeable to his infinite excellency, so shall I know God according to my capacity, not obscurely, but perfectly, as it were, face to face; and this is the greatest height of blessedness and happiness. Now all veils shall be taken off, and we shall have a clear prospect of God's excellency and glory, of his blessedness and fulness, of his loveliness and sweetness.[6] Now all masks, clouds, and curtains, shall be drawn for ever, that saints may clearly see the breadth, length, depth, and height of divine love, and that they may clearly see into the mystery of the Trinity, the mystery of Christ's incarnation, the mystery of man's redemption, the mys-

[1] Cicero, *de natura deor.* l. i.

[2] Augustine *de fide cont. Arrian.* c. vi.

[3] Gregory *Mor.* l. vii. c. 15.

[4] ἐν αἰνίγματι, in a riddle.

[5] In this life, saith Bernard, *erit mira serenitas, plena securitas, æterna fœlicitas,* there will be wonderful serenity, full security, eternal felicity.

[6] *Visio clara non comprehensiva.*

tery of providences, the mystery of prophesies; and all those mysteries that relate to the nature, substances, offices, orders, and excellencies of the angels, those princes of glory, who still keep their standings in the court of heaven; and all those mysteries that concern the nature, original, immortality, spirituality, excellency, and activity of our own souls, beside a world of other mysteries that respect the decrees and counsels of God, the creation of the world, the fall of Adam, and the fall of angels. Now the most knowing men in the world are much in the dark about these things; but when we come to heaven, we shall have a close and a clear sight and knowledge of them. Now we shall know, as we are known; now we shall see God face to face. *O beata visio, videre Regem angelorum, sanctum sanctorum, Deum cœli, Rectorem terræ, patrem viventium!* Oh blessed sight! to behold the King of angels, the holy of holies, the God of heaven, the Ruler of the earth, the Father of the living![1] *O beata visio, videre Deum in seipso, videre in nobis, et nos in eo.* Oh blessed vision and contemplation, wherein we shall see God in himself, God in us, and ourselves in God![2] But,

(2.) Secondly, As in heaven they shall have the clearest knowledge of God, so in heaven *they shall have the fullest knowledge of God.* Here our knowledge of God is weak, as well as dark, but in heaven it shall be full and complete. 'Here we know but in part; but there we shall know as we are known,' 1 Cor. xiii. 12. As the apostle speaks, here we are able to take in but little of God, either sin or Satan, or else fears, doubts, and scruples, or else the pleasures or profits, the comforts or contents of this world doth so defile the soul, and so fill the soul, that it is able to take in but very little of God. 'How little a portion,' saith Job, 'is heard of him!' Job xxvi. 14. It is but a portion, a little portion, that we can conceive of him. The Hebrew is שמץ, *shemets, particulam,* a little bit, nay, it is said, שמץ דבר, *shemets dabar, particulam verbi,* a little piece of a word, or *particulam alicujus,* a little piece of something, that we do hear of him. 'I have many things to say unto you,' saith Christ, 'but ye cannot bear them now,' John xvi. 12.[3] Man is a poor, low, weak creature, and is not able to bear any great or full discoveries of God. As weak shoulders cannot bear heavy burdens, nor weak stomachs digest strong meats; no more were they able to bear the revelation of many high, spiritual, precious, and glorious truths, that Christ was willing to discover to them. Those that have weak eyes, or that have a blemish in their eyes, cannot discern things aright. Now we have all weak eyes, we have all one blemish or another in our eye, which hinders us from a full sight and knowledge of God, and of his excellency and glory. Oh! but now in heaven, we shall have a full and perfect knowledge of God; there shall be no sore eyes, no clouds, no mists to hinder us from a full sight of the Sun of righteousness.[4] Here our understandings shall be full of the knowledge of God, our minds full of the wisdom of God, our wills full of the righteousness and holiness of God, and our affections full of the love and delights of God.

[1] Augustine, *lib. de spir., &c.* c. lvii.

[2] Bernard, *Meditat.* c. iv.

[3] 1 Cor. iii. 1–3; Heb. v. 12–14.

[4] Our knowledge of God now is rather negative than positive; we know not so well what God is, as what he is not; as that he is not a man, as that he is not changeable, &c. Now it is observed to our hand, *ex puris negativis nihil concluditur,* that from pure negatives there can be no certain conclusion made.

Here we have but weak and shallow apprehensions of God, but there, as Bernard speaks sweetly, *Deus implebit animam rationalem sapientia, concupiscibilem justitia, irascibilem perfecta tranquillitate,* God will fill the soul with light of wisdom, the concupiscible faculty with righteousness, the irascible with perfect tranquillity.

If a man did dwell within the body of the sun, surely he would be full of light; if a man did dwell in the midst of a fountain, surely he would be filled with that fountain; so when the saints come to heaven, they shall dwell as it were in the body of the Sun of righteousness; and therefore they cannot be but full of light; they shall dwell in the midst of the fountain of life; and therefore they shall sure be full of the fountain. But,

(3.) Thirdly, The sight and knowledge that we shall have of God in heaven, *will be immediate,* 1 Cor. xiii. 12. Here our knowledge of God is mediate; here we see him, but it is either through the glass of his word, or the glass of his works.[1] Sometimes through the glass of his word God shews himself; sometimes through the glass of prayer God gives some representation of himself to his people; sometimes through the glass of the Lord's supper he discovers some rays and beams of his glory. All the sight and knowledge that we have of God in this world is through some glass or other. Now there is a vast difference between seeing an object directly, immediately, and in its own proper colours, and beholding it through a glass. The sight of an object through a glass is very weak and unsatisfying. One direct view of the Lord, one immediate sight of God, will infinitely transcend all those sights and views that we have had in this world, either through the glass of his word, or the glass of his works, either through the glass of ordinances, or the glass of the promises, or the glass of providences, Mat. v. 8. One real direct sight of a friend or relation, doth more cheer, quiet, and satisfy us, than a thousand representations of them in glasses, or by their pictures. In heaven we shall see God face to face, without the interposition of men or means; and this direct and immediate sight of God, is that which makes heaven to be heaven to the saints. All the glory of heaven would be but a poor low thing in the eye of a saint, had he not a direct and immediate sight of God there. In heaven all mediums shall be removed, all glasses shall be broken, and the glorified saint shall behold God with open face; all curtains being for ever withdrawn from between God and the soul. Good souls in heaven are like good angels, who are still beholding the face of God, Mat. xviii. 10. As God is still a-looking upon them as the jewels of his crown, so they are still crying and looking upon God as their heaven, yea, as their great all, and that by a direct and immediate act of their souls. But,

(4.) Fourthly and lastly, The sight and knowledge that they shall have of God in heaven, *shall be permanent and constant.* Now saints have a happy sight of God, and anon they have lost it; this hour they have a precious sight of God in the mount, and the next hour they have lost this sight. 'Behold, he that should comfort my soul stands afar off,' Lam. i. 16; and 'he hath covered himself with a cloud, that our prayers cannot pass through,' Lam. iii. 44. Our visions of God here are

[1] God is a supersubstantial substance, an understanding not to be understood, a word never to be spoken.—Dionys. Areop. *de divin. Nom c.* 1.

transient and vanishing. The visions, the glimpses of majesty and glory which Moses and Peter saw in the mount, were not permanent but transient; their sun was quickly clouded, and both of them soon after were found walking in the dark;[1] and therefore well saith Augustine, *Beatitudo hic parari potest, possideri non potest*,[2] happiness may be obtained here, but here we cannot have the plenary and take possession thereof. Oh but in heaven, our sight of God, our knowledge of God shall be permanent, it shall be lasting; there shall be no sin, no cloud, no mist, no curtain, to hinder us from a constant sight and vision of God; there we shall see God clearly, fully, eternally. The spouse's question, 'Did you see him whom my soul loves?' Cant. iii. 3, shall never be heard in heaven, because God shall be always in their eye, and still upon their hearts; nor Job's complaint, 'Behold, I go forward, but he is not there; and backward, but I cannot perceive him: on the left hand, where he doth work, but I cannot behold him: he hideth himself on the right hand, that I cannot see him,' Job xxiii. 8, 9. Heaven would not be heaven, were it not always day with the soul; did not the soul live in a constant sight and apprehension of God, all the glory of heaven could not make a heaven to a glorified soul. But,

IV. Fourthly, As the best sight and knowledge of God is reserved till last, *so the best and choicest presence of God and Christ is reserved till last;* and this I shall thus make good.

(1.) First, In heaven saints shall have *the greatest and the fullest presence of God.*[3] No man in this world hath so complete and full a presence of God but he may have a fuller; but in heaven the presence of God shall be so full and complete, as that nothing can be added to it to make it more complete. Sometimes sin, sometimes Satan, sometimes the world, sometimes resting in duties, sometimes the weakness of our graces, hinder us from enjoying a full presence of God here; but in heaven there shall be nothing to interpose between God and us; there shall be nothing to hinder us from enjoying a full and complete presence of God. It is this full presence of God that is the heaven of heaven, the glory of all our glory. An imperfect and incomplete presence of God in heaven would darken all the glory of that state. It is the full and perfect presence of God in heaven that is the most sparkling diamond in the ring of glory; and this you shall have. But,

(2.) Secondly, They shall have *a soul-satisfying presence of God in heaven.* They shall be so satisfied with the presence of God in heaven, that they shall say, We have enough, we have all, because we enjoy that presence that is virtually all, that is eminently all, that is all light, all life, all love, all heaven, all happiness, all comforts, all contents, &c:[4] Ps. xvii. 15, 'As for me, I will behold thy face in righteousness; I shall be satisfied, when I awake, with thy likeness.' Though the spiritual and gracious presence of God with the saints in this world doth much cheer and comfort them, yet it doth not satisfy them. They are still crying out, More of this blessed presence! oh more of this presence! Lord, less money will serve, so we may but have more of thy presence!

[1] Exod. xxxiii., Mat. xvii. 1–4.
[2] Serm. xlvi. *de sanctis*.
[3] Ps. xvi. 11. *Ipse unus erit tibi omnia, quia in ipso uno bono, bona sunt omnia.*—Augustine.
[4] *Omne bonum in summo bono*, all good is in the chiefest good.

less of the creature will serve, so we may have but more of thy presence! Ps. xlii. 1, 2, xxxvii. 1–3. As the king of Sodom said unto Abraham, 'Give me the persons, and take the goods to thyself,' Gen. xiv. 21, so say gracious souls, Give us more and more of the presence of God, and let the men of the world take the world and divide it amongst them selves. Divine presence is very inflaming; a soul that hath but tasted the sweetness of it cannot but long for more of it; as those that had tasted of the grapes of Canaan longed to be in Canaan, and as the Gauls, who, when they had tasted of the sweet wine that was made of the grapes that grew in Italy, they were very eager after Italy, crying out, 'O Italy! Italy!'[1] so precious souls that have experienced the sweetness of divine presence, they cannot be satisfied with a little of it, but in every prayer this is the language of their souls, Lord! more of thy presence! and in every sermon they hear, Lord! let us have more of thy presence! and in every sacrament they receive, Lord! vouchsafe to us more of thy presence!

Nay, this gracious presence of God that they enjoy here makes them very earnest in their desires and longings after a celestial, a glorious presence of God and Christ in heaven, which presence alone can satisfy their souls.[2] Look, as the espoused maid longs for the marriage day, the apprentice for his freedom, the captive for his ransom, the traveller for his inn, and the mariner for his haven, so do souls that are under the power and sweet of God's gracious presence long for to enjoy his glorious presence in heaven, which alone can fill and satisfy their immortal souls. As Monica, Austin's mother, a precious godly woman, who enjoyed much of the gracious presence of Christ, with her spirit she cried out, *Quid hic faciemus? cur non ocyus migramus? cur non hinc avolamus?* What do we here? why depart we not swifter? why fly we not hence?

So saith another [Bernard], As what I have, if offered to thee, pleaseth not thee without myself, so, O Lord! the good things we have from thee, though they refresh us, yet they satisfy us not without thyself. Lord! I am willing to die, to have a further discovery of thyself.

And so saith another [Augustine], Thou hast made us, O Lord, for thyself, and our hearts are unquiet till they come unto thee.

And so when Modestus, the emperor's lieutenant,[3] threatened to kill Basil, he answered, If that be all, I fear not; yea, your master cannot more pleasure me than in sending me unto my heavenly Father, to whom I now live, and to whom I desire to hasten.

And saith another [Augustine], Let all the devils in hell beset me round, let fasting macerate my body, let sorrows oppress my mind, let pains consume my flesh, let watchings dry me, or heat scorch me, or cold freeze me; let all these, and what can come more, happen unto me, so I may enjoy my Saviour.

Austin wishing that he might have seen three things, Rome flourishing, Paul preaching, and Christ conversing with men upon the earth, Bede comes after, and correcting this last wish, saith, Yea, but let me see the King in his beauty, Christ in his heavenly kingdom; by all which you see that it is not a spiritual presence, but the glorious presence of God and Christ in heaven, that can satisfy the souls of the

[1] Plutarch, *in vita Camilli.* [2] 2 Cor. v. 1–8; Philip. i. 23; Cant. viii. 14.
[3] Cf. Gell. iii. 9. Macrob. Saturn i. 4, 10, 16.—G.

saints. It was a great mercy for Christ to be with Paul on earth, but it was a greater mercy, and a more satisfying mercy, for Paul to be with Christ in heaven, Philip. i. 23. They enjoy much who enjoy the presence of God on earth, but they enjoy more who enjoy the presence of God in heaven; and no presence below this presence can satisfy a believing soul. But,

(3.) Thirdly, As they shall enjoy a satisfying presence of God in heaven, so they shall enjoy *a constant, a permanent presence of God in heaven.* Here God comes and goes, he is often a removing court, but in heaven the King of glory will be always present: 1 Thes. iv. 17, 18, 'Then we which are alive and remain shall be caught up together with them in the clouds, to meet the Lord in the air, and so shall we be ever with the Lord. Wherefore comfort one another with these words.' It is the constant presence of God in heaven, that makes a heaven of comfort to blessed souls. Should this sun ever set, should this presence ever fail, heaven would be as dark as hell, yea, heaven would be another hell. Here Jonah complains that he was cast out of God's presence, and the church complains, that he that should comfort her soul, stands afar off.[1] No saint enjoys the gracious presence of God at all times alike. They that enjoy most of this presence may say of it, as Jacob spake of Laban's countenance, I see, said he, your Father's countenance is not towards me as before, Gen. xxxi. 5; so may they say, Oh we see, Oh we feel, that the presence of God is not with us as before! Oh what a warming, what a cheering, what a quickening, what an enlivening, what a comforting, what a melting, what an encouraging, what an assisting presence of God had we once! Oh but it is not so now with us! we that used always to be upon Christ's knee, or in his arms, are now at a distance from him; he that used to lie day and night as a bundle of myrrh betwixt our breasts, hath now covered himself with a cloud, Cant. i. 13. Oh we cannot see his face, we cannot hear his voice, as in the days of old! &c. But now in heaven saints shall enjoy a constant presence of God; there shall not be one moment to all eternity, wherein they shall not enjoy the glorious presence of God; and, indeed, it is this constant presence of God in heaven, that puts a glory upon all the saints' glory. Heaven, without this constant presence of God, would be but as a court without a king, or as the firmament without the sun. And thus you see that the best and choicest presence of God and Christ is reserved for heaven. But,

V. Fifthly, *The perfection of grace is reserved for glory.*[2] Though our graces be our best jewels, yet they are imperfect, and do not give out their full lustre; they are like the moon, which when it shineth brightest, hath a dark spot: 1 Cor. xiii. 9, 10, 'For we know in part, and we prophesy in part. But when that which is perfect is come, then that which is in part shall be done away.' Here 'we are all as an unclean thing, and all our righteousnesses are as filthy rags,' Isa. lxiv. 6. Oh the stains, the spots, the blots, the blemishes that attend our choicest graces and services! Our best personal righteousness is stained with much unrighteousness, perfection of grace and holiness is

[1] Jonah ii. 4; Lam. i. 16; Ps. xxx. 6, 7; Isa. viii. 17; Micah vii. 7–9.
[2] *Perfectum id est cui nihil deest.*

reserved for heaven, Eph. v. 25–27; Jude 24; Eph. iv. 13. In the work of conversion, God lays the foundation of grace in the souls of his people, but the putting on the top-stone is reserved for heaven. Grace here is but a king in the cradle, but in heaven it will be a king upon its throne.

For the making this truth more fully out, I will only instance in the joy of the saints, and that thus:

[1.] First, *The joy of the saints in heaven shall be pure joy.* Here our joy is mixed with sorrow, our rejoicing with trembling, Ps. ii. 11: Mat. xxviii. 8, 'The women departed from the sepulchre with fear and great joy.' This composition of two contrary passions is frequently found in the best hearts. Here the best have sorrow with their joy, water with their wine, vinegar with their oil, pain with their ease, winter with their summer, and autumn with their spring, &c. But in heaven, Rev. vii. 17, they shall have joy without sorrow, light without darkness, sweetness without bitterness, summer without winter, health without sickness, honour without disgrace, glory without shame, and life without death: Rev. xxi. 4, 'And God shall wipe away all tears from their eyes; and there shall be no more death, neither sorrow, nor crying, neither shall there be any more pain: for the former things are passed away.' But,

[2.] Secondly, As they shall have in heaven pure joy, so they shall have in heaven *plenitudinem gaudii, fulness of joy.* Here all joy is at an ebb, but there is the flood of joy, there is fulness of joy: Ps. xvi. 11, 'In his presence is fulness of joy, and at his right hand are pleasures for evermore.' Here shall be *gaudium super gaudium*, joy above joy, joy surmounting all joy. Here shall be such great joys, as no geometrician can measure; so many joys, as no arithmetician can number; and so wonderful, as no rhetorician can utter, had he the tongue of men and angels.[1] Here shall be joy within thee, and joy without thee, and joy above thee, and joy beneath thee, and joy about thee. Joy shall spread itself over all the members of your bodies, and over all the faculties of your souls. In heaven, your knowledge shall be full, your love full, your visions of God full, your communion with God full, your fruition of God full, and your conformity to God full, and from thence will arise fulness of joy. If all the earth were paper, and all the plants of the earth were pens, and all the sea were ink, and if every man, woman, and child, had the pen of a ready writer, yet were they not able to express the thousandth part of those joys that saints shall have in heaven.[2] All the joy we have here in this world, is but pensiveness to that we shall have in heaven; all pleasure here to that but heaviness, all sweetness here to that but bitterness. But,

[3.] Thirdly, The joy of the saints in heaven shall be *a lasting joy, an uninterrupted joy.* Here their joy is quickly turned into sorrow, their singing into sighing, their dancing into mourning. Our joy here is like the husbandman's joy in harvest, which is soon over, and then we must sow again in tears, before we can reap in joy. David's joy was

[1] If one drop of the joys of heaven should fall into hell, it would swallow up all the bitterness of hell.—*Augustine.*

[2] A reminiscence of the old poem commencing 'Could we with ink the ocean fill,' on which see various curious articles in 'Notes and Queries,' First Series.—G.

soon interrupted: 'In my prosperity I said, I should never be removed; but thou didst hide thy face, and I was troubled,' Ps. xxx. 6, 7. Now David had the oil of joy and gladness, and by and by the spirit of heaviness and sadness: 'Restore to me the joy of thy salvation,' Ps. li. 12. Jacob had much joy at the return of his sons with corn from Egypt; but this joy was soon interrupted by his parting with his dear Benjamin.

I might shew you this truth in other instances, as in Abraham, Job, and other saints; but surely there is no believer but finds that sometimes sin interrupts his joy, and sometimes Satan disturbs his joy, and sometimes afflictions and sometimes desertions eclipse his joy; sometimes the cares of the world, and sometimes the snares of the world, and sometimes the fears of the world, mars our joy; sometimes great crosses, sometimes near losses, and sometimes unexpected changes, turns a Christian's harping into mourning, and his organ into the voice of them that weep.[1]

Some say of Rhodes, that there is not one day in the year in which the sun shines not clearly on them. Surely there is hardly one day in the year, yea, I had almost said one hour in the day, wherein something or other doth not fall in to interrupt a Christian's joy.

But now in heaven the joy of the saints shall be constant; there shall nothing fall in to disturb or to interrupt their joy: Ps. xvi. 11, 'In thy presence is fulness of joy, and at thy right hand is pleasures for ever more.' Mark, for quality, there are pleasures; for quantity, fulness; for dignity, at God's right hand; for eternity, for evermore. And millions of years multiplied by millions, make not up one minute to this eternity of joy that the saints shall have in heaven. In heaven there shall be no sin to take away your joy, nor no devil to take away your joy, nor no man to take away your joy: John xvi. 22, 'Your joy no man taketh from you.' The joy of the saints in heaven is never ebbing, but always flowing to all contentment. The joys of heaven never fade, never wither, never die, nor never are lessened nor interrupted. The joy of the saints in heaven is a constant joy, an everlasting joy, in the root and in the cause, and in the matter of it and in the objects of it. *Æterna erit exultatio, quæ bono lætatur æterno*, their joy lasts for ever whose objects remains for ever.[2] Isa. xxxv. 10, 'And the redeemed of the Lord shall return, and come to Zion with songs, and everlasting joys upon their heads; they shall obtain joy and gladness, and sorrow and sighing shall fly away.' In this world not only the joy of hypocrites and the joy of profane persons, but also the joy of the upright, is oftentimes 'as the crackling of thorns under a pot,' or as the blaze of a brush faggot, now all on a flame, and as suddenly out again; or as the beast *ephemeron*, that dieth on the day it is born;[3] but the joy of believers in heaven shall be like the fire on the altar, that never went out. When Cæsar was sad, he used to say to himself, *Cogitate Cæsarem esse*, think thou art Cæsar; so when your hearts are sad and sorrowful, oh! then think of these everlasting joys that you shall have in heaven. But I must hasten; and therefore in the

[1] Job xxx. 26–31. Some worm or other is still a-gnawing at the very root of our joy, like the worm that made Jonah his gourd to wither.

[2] *In quibus operamur, in illis et gaudemus*, saith Tertullian: in what things or persons we act, in those things we rejoice.

[3] ἐφήμερος, = living but a day, rather than *a* particular 'beast' as above; applied to men, ἐφήμεροι, creatures of a day.—G.

VI. Sixth place, As the best joys, so *the best society, the best company, is reserved till last.* It is reserved till believers come to heaven: Heb. xii. 22–24, 'But ye are come unto mount Sion, and unto the city of the living God, the heavenly Jerusalem, and to an innumerable company of angels,[1] to the general assembly and church of the first-born, which are written in heaven, and to God the Judge of all, and the spirits of just men made perfect, and to Jesus the Mediator of the new covenant, and to the blood of sprinkling, that speaketh better things than that of Abel.' Here *erimus cives cœli, socii angelorum, cohæredes Christi,* we shall be citizens of heaven, fellows of angels, co-heirs with Christ, citizens with saints, and of the household of God. *O beata visio, videre Regem angelorum, sanctum sanctorum, Deum cœli, Rectorem terræ, Patrem viventium!*[2] Oh blessed sight, to behold the King of angels, the holy of holies, the God of heaven, the Ruler of the earth, the Father of the living! Woe to me, saith one, which am not where the holy saints be; for their life is out of all gun-shot and danger of death, their knowledge without error, their love without offence, and their joy without any annoy. The dignity and diversity of the inhabitants of heaven doth much set forth the glory of heaven. This earth, this world, is full of sinners, but heaven is full of saints; this world is full of men, but heaven is full of angels; this world is full of friends and enemies, but in heaven there shall be only friends and sons. Here the nobility and majesty of the guest casts a great deal of honour and splendour upon the royal palace where they meet. No company so noble, so sweet, so desirable, so delightsome, so comfortable, so suitable as this.

[1.] First, *Here all shall be of one mind, of one judgment.* In heaven there shall be no discord, no wrangling, no quarrelling, no dividing. Here all shall think the same things, and speak the same things, and do the same things. Now, Turks and pagans can agree, and bears and lions, wolves and tigers, can agree; nay, a legion of devils can better agree in one body, than a handful of saints can agree in one city, in one nation, &c.[3] There was a temple of Concord among the heathen; and yet how rare is it to find a temple of concord among them that are the temple of the Holy Ghost? Whilst there was a contest among the birds about a rose found in the way, a mischievous owl came in the night and carried the flower away; you know how to apply it. But now in heaven there shall be no heats, no contests, no debates, no disputes, but as the curtains of the tabernacle were all looped together, so all the saints in heaven shall be all looped together in one mind, in one judgment, and in one way.

[2.] Secondly, All the saints in heaven shall be *of a sweet golden disposition.*[4] Here the different dispositions of saints doth much hinder that sweetness of communion which otherwise would be amongst them. Here some are of a sour disposition, and of a cross and rugged temper, but in heaven all saints shall be of a sweet, a soft, a silken dis-

[1] *μυριάσιν*, to the myriads, or many ten thousands, of angels.

[2] Aug. *Lib. de Spir.*, &c., cap. 57

[3] Strigelius desired to die, to be freed from the implacable strife of divines. [Victorinus Strigelius, one of The Reformers. Died, 1569. His Υπομνηματα, *in omnes libros Nov. Test.*, 1565, 2 vols., and other exegetical writings, were favourites with the Puritans. His 'Psalms' of David were early translated by Rich. Robinson. 1582–96.—G.]

[4] Grace in a cross unhewn nature is like a diamond set in iron.

position, which will exceedingly sweeten that royal communion. Here grace in a man of an untoward crooked disposition is like a brass ring upon a leprous finger; and grace in a man of a sweet disposition is like a gold ring upon an alabaster hand. Now in heaven all the saints shall be of a golden disposition, yea, of a God-like disposition, which is the sweetest, the noblest, the choicest. But,

[3.] Thirdly, In heaven the saints shall have *a constant enjoyment of one another.* As they shall ever be with the Lord, so they shall ever be one with another. Here they meet and part, but in heaven they shall meet and never part. Now it is their life to meet and their death to part; now it is their heaven to meet, and their hell to part; but in heaven they shall be always in one another's eye, in one another's arms, or upon one another's knees, 1 Thes. iv. 17, 18.

Themistocles,[1] having a piece of ground to sell, appointed the crier to proclaim, that whosoever would buy it, should have a good neighbour; the saints in heaven shall be always sure of good neighbourhood, they shall never want good company. In this world Abraham and Lot must live asunder, but there they shall always live together. The cynic [Diogenes] of old was fain to look for an honest man with a candle, because of the scarcity of them; but heaven shall be always full of such saints, as shall shine as so many stars, yea, as so many suns in glory.

[4.] Fourthly and lastly, The saints shall have *a real, a personal, a particular knowledge of one another in heaven.* Here we know but a few saints, but in heaven we shall know all; *in cœlo nullus erit alienus,* there shall be no stranger in heaven. Now this truth I shall make good by some arguments brought to hand, and by the addition of others. Take them thus:—

(1.) First, *Adam, when he was in his innocency, knew Eve to be bone of his bone, and flesh of his flesh, as soon as he saw her, though he had never seen her before,* Gen. ii. 23. Now certainly our knowledge in heaven shall be more ample, full, and perfect, than ever Adam's was in innocency. Therefore without all peradventure, the saints shall know one another in heaven. Luther, the night before he died, discoursing with his Christian friends, the question was put, Whether the saints should know one another in heaven? Luther held the affirmative, and this was one of the reasons he gave to prove it, that Adam knew Eve as soon as ever he saw her, and that not by discourse, but by divine revelation, and so shall all the saints know one another in heaven.[2] But,

(2.) Secondly, *The disciples, Peter, James, and John, being in the mount at Christ's transfiguration, though they had but a taste, a glimpse of the glory of heaven, yet they knew Moses and Elias, though they were dead many hundred years before,* Mat. xvii. 1–4. Now if the disciples, in an unglorified condition, knew Moses and Elias, then certainly when saints shall be in a full glorified condition, they shall know them and all the rest of that royal family. Here they knew Moses from Elias, and Elias from Moses, whom they never saw before, and both

[1] Plutarch in vita *Themistoclis.*

[2] Melch. Adam. [The great authority on Reformation biography. His 'Lives' have passed through many editions.—G.]

from Christ; and therefore we need not doubt but in that state of blessedness, wherein God shall be all in all, and wherein we shall know as we are known, we shall have a particular and personal knowledge of one another. Chrysostom saith, that in heaven we shall point out the saints, and say, Lo, yonder is Peter, and that is Paul; lo, yonder is Abraham, the great believer, and yonder is Jacob, who as a prince prevailed with God; lo, yonder is Moses, who was the meekest man in all the world, and there is Job, that was the patientest man in all the world; lo, there is Joshua and Caleb, that followed the Lord fully, and there is Jeremiah, that was once in the dungeon; lo, there is Jonah, that was once in the whale's belly, and there is Daniel, that was once in the lions' den; lo, yonder is John the beloved disciple, that used to lie in the bosom of Christ; and there is Mary that hath chosen the better part. But,

(3.) Thirdly, *The saints shall rise with the same bodies that now they lay down in the grave; and if so, then doubtless they shall know one another in heaven:* the husband the wife, the wife the husband; the father the child, and the child the father; the pastor his people, and the people their pastor; the master his servant, and the servant his master. Now that the saints shall rise with the very same individual body is clear: Job xix. 25, 26, 'For I know that my Redeemer liveth, and that he shall stand at the latter day upon the earth: and though after my skin worms destroy this body, yet in my flesh shall I see God: whom I shall see for myself, and mine eyes shall behold, and not another; though my reins be consumed within me.' In these words we see that Job useth the word my, 'and my eyes shall behold;' as it were pointing to it with his finger, adding not only positively, but exclusively, this and no other. Job did fully believe that the same numerical[2] body, at which he pointed, should rise again; and Paul saith, not a mortal, a corruptible body at large, but *hoc*, '*This* corruptible must put on incorruption, and this mortal must put on immortality,' 1 Cor. xv. 53. The apostle did, as it were, lay his hand upon his own body; and then saith he, this corruptible body, and not another, this mortal, and not another, shall be raised when the trumpet sounds. It cannot stand with the unspotted justice and holiness of God, that one body should sow, and another body should reap that never sowed; that one body should labour, toil, sweat, suffer, and another body that hath done none of this should carry the reward. Tertullian saith, that he will pray that the same body may rise again, for the resurrection is not of another body, but of the same that falleth; not a new creation, but a raising up; the self-same body shall certainly rise again, else were it a raising up of a new, rather than a raising again of the old. It cannot stand with equity and right, that one body should sin and another body should suffer. No righteous judge will suffer a victorious person to die, and another that never struck stroke to have the crown of his deservings. It is but justice that those very eyes that have dropped many a tear before God, should be wiped by God; I say those

[1] 1 Cor. xv. 42–45; Acts iv. 2, xvii. 18, xxiii. 6; Mat. xxii. 32; Ezek. xxxvii.

[2] Even down to South this term was in use; *e.g.*, 'We may contemplate upon his supernatural, astonishing works; particularly in the resurrection and reparation of the same *numerical* body, by a reunion of all the scattered parts.' Vol. I., Sermon 1st.—G.

very eyes, and not another pair of new-made eyes; it is but justice that that very tongue that hath blessed God, should be blessed by God; it is but justice that those very hands that have been much in doing for Christ, and those very lips that have been much in praising of Christ, and those very backs that have been laded with many heavy burdens for Christ, and those very feet that have been in the stocks for Christ, and that have run in the ways of Christ, should at last be raised and crowned by Christ. And this truth you may see clear in the glorious resurrection of Christ from the dead; that very same body that was wounded, crucified, and slain, that very same body did rise again. Christ could very easily, if he had pleased, in three days, nay, in three hours, ay, in three moments, have cured his wounds, but he would not; to confirm his disciples, and to shew that he had the very same body which was wounded and crucified for their sins, for their sakes; and therefore he bids Thomas to reach his finger, and behold his hands, and to reach his hand to thrust it into his side, John xx. 27; Luke xxiv. 36–47; whereby Christ made it evident, that that very same body of his which was wounded, crucified, and buried, was raised, and not another; and therefore as in the head the same body which died rose again, so shall it be with all his members in the great day of the resurrection. Now seeing that we shall rise again with the very same individual or numerical bodies that we lay down in the grave, we need not question but that we shall know one another in heaven. But,

(4.) Fourthly, *That knowledge which may most increase the joy and comfort of the saints, shall certainly be in heaven, but that is a perfect personal knowledge of each other; therefore there shall be a particular personal knowledge of one another in heaven;* the husband shall know the wife, the wife the husband, the father the child, and the child the father, &c.

I have read a story of Austin, how that a widow grieving for the loss of her husband, to comfort her, he told her that it was but a short time that they were parted, and that of all persons she should enjoy her husband most in heaven; nay, saith he, thou shalt not only know thy husband, but all the elect shall know thee, and thou shalt know all them. The personal knowledge of the saints on earth, doth exceedingly increase our joy and comfort; it makes this wilderness to be a paradise. 'They that fear thee will be glad when they see me,' saith the Psalmist, Ps. cxix. 74; yea Seneca, the heathen, saw so much excellency that morality put upon a man, that he saith, that *ipse aspectus boni viri delectat,* the very looks of a good man delight one. Ah! how often are the saints delighted, warmed, and gladded by hearing well of other saints, whose faces they have never seen! and when God gives them the honour to see their faces, and to enjoy their persons, their presence, oh how doth this advance their joy, and increase their comfort. What a heaven doth this make on this side heaven to their souls! Oh, then, what tongue can express, what heart can conceive, what pen can describe, the unspeakable joy and comfort that will be raised in the hearts of the saints, upon that perfect, particular, personal knowledge that the saints shall have one of another in heaven? Heaven would be but an uncomfortable place, if the saints there should be strangers one to another. The faces, the words, the ways, the works of strangers, are very little pleasing and delightful to us here; what would they then be in heaven? But,

(5.) Fifthly, *The saints, in the great day of account, shall know the persons of wicked men, who shall be indicted, arraigned, condemned, and judged by Jesus Christ, and all his saints about him.*[1] This great day will be a declaration of the just judgment of God. In this great day, every wicked work, and every wicked worker, shall be brought to light; and indeed it would be but in vain to bring evil works to light, if the evil worker be not also brought to the light. In this great day the saints shall see and know Cain in his person, they shall be able to point at him, and say, Yonder stands that bloody Cain who slew his brother Abel, because he was more righteous than he. And there stands Pharaoh, the great oppressor of God's Israel, and he that stood it out against heaven itself; and look, there stands bloody Saul, who lost his crown, his kingdom, his soul, his all, by disobedience; and there is Haman, who was feasted with the king one day, and made a feast for crows the next; lo, there stands Pilate, that condemned Christ, and there is Judas that betrayed Christ. In this great day that word shall be made good, every man shall appear to account for the works that he hath done in his body, 2 Cor. v. 10; so that both wicked works and wicked workers shall plainly appear before our Lord Jesus and all his saints, who with him shall judge the world. Now certainly, if the saints shall know the wicked in that great day, they shall then much more know one another; when they shall all sit as fellow-justices round about Jesus Christ the righteous judge, to pass a righteous sentence upon all unrighteous souls. But,

(6.) Sixthly, *Christ tells the Jews that they shall see Abraham, Isaac, and Jacob, and all the prophets in the kingdom of God.*[2] All the saints shall have communion with Abraham, Isaac, and Jacob, in the kingdom of God; they shall have communion with them, not only as godly men, but as Abraham, Isaac, and Jacob. The phrase of seeing Abraham, Isaac, and Jacob in the kingdom of heaven, doth doubtless import thus much, that they shall be known personally and distinctly from all other persons in the kingdom of heaven. Saints in heaven shall be able to point at Abraham, and say, There is Abraham, that was the great pattern for believing; and there is Isaac, that was a sweet pattern for meditating; and there is Jacob, who had the honour and happiness of prevailing with God.[3] The saints' happiness in heaven shall be greatly increased by mutual communion, and by their personal knowledge of one another in that blessed state. But,

(7.) Seventhly, and lastly, *In heaven the saints shall know as they are known*, 1 Cor. xiii. 12, Exod. xxxiii. 12. Now God knows all the saints, personally, particularly, corporally, yea, he knows them all by name; and so doubtless all the saints in heaven shall know one another personally, and by name, else how shall they know as they are known? Here in this world we know one another many times only by report, or by writing, or by face, but in heaven we shall know one another by name. So God knows us now, and so we shall know one another in

[1] 1 Cor. vi. 1–4; Rom. ii. 5; Eccles. xii. 14; 1 John iii. 12.

[2] Luke xiii. 28; Mat. viii. 11 See Beza and Piscator.

[3] Rom. iv. 16–23; Gen. xxiv. 63; xxxii. 22–30.

heaven; and this is none of the least parts of glory, that we shall know one another in glory; yea, that we shall know one another personally, and by name; the serious consideration of which may much support us, and comfort us under the sad losses of our friends and relations in the Lord. But in the,

VII. Seventh and last place, As the best society is reserved till last, so *the glorifying of our bodies is reserved till last.* I shall a little hint unto you the glory and blessedness of the bodies of the saints when they shall all meet in heaven. I shall not stand upon the privative blessedness of glorified bodies, which consists in their freedom from all defects, deformities, diseases, and distempers which here they are subject to. Here our bodies stand in need of clothes to cover them, food to feed them, sleep to refresh them, physic to ease them, air to breath them, and houses to shelter them, from all which glorified bodies shall be free, Rev. vii. 16, 17. But I shall only speak of the positive prerogatives and heavenly endowments that glorified bodies shall be invested with. As,

(1.) First, *They shall be like the glorious body of Christ.* Philip. iii. 21, 'Who shall change our vile body, that it may be fashioned like unto his glorious body, according unto the working whereby he is able even to subdue all things unto himself.' Our bodies shall be as lovely and comely, as bright and glorious, as the body of Christ is. Chrysostom saith, that the bodies of the saints shall be *septies clarioria sole,* seven times brighter than the sun. Certainly saints shall be as handsome-bodied and as comely-featured as Christ is. Though their bodies be sown in dishonour, yet they shall be raised in glory, 1 Cor xv. 43. If Stephen's face did shine as if it had been the face of an angel, that is, bright and glorious, Acts vi. 15; and if there were such a lustre and glory upon Moses his face, that the children of Israel were afraid to come near him, and he forced to put a veil upon it till he had done speaking with them, Exod. xxxiv. 29–36; I say, if there were such a glory upon the face of these two mortals, Oh then! how will the faces and bodies of the saints glitter and shine when their bodies shall be made conformable to the glorious body of Jesus Christ, Mat. xiii. 43.[1] Certainly, as the light and glory of the sun doth far exceed the light of the least twinkling star, so much and more shall the glory of the saint's bodies excel that glory and splendour that was upon the faces of Moses and Stephen. The bodies of the saints in heaven shall be surpassingly comely, well-favoured, beautiful, and amiable. Plutarch, in the life of Demetrius, saith, That he was so passing fair of face and countenance, as no painter was able to draw him. I am sure I am no ways able to paint out the beauty and glory that shall be upon the bodies of the saints in that day of glory, wherein the saints shall shine as so many suns. But,

(2.) Secondly, *Their bodies shall in a kind be spiritual:* 1 Cor. xv. 44, 'It is sown a natural body, it is raised a spiritual body. There is a natural body, and there is a spiritual body.' Their bodies shall be spiritual, *non substantiæ, sed qualitatum respectu,* not in regard of

[1] What is a spark in the chimney, to the sun in the firmament?

substance, but state and condition.[1] *Spiritual* in the text is not opposed to *visible*, but to *natural;* for their bodies, though in a sense they are spiritual, yet they shall be as visible as the glorious body of Christ. When I say their bodies shall be spiritual, you must not think that I mean that their bodies shall be turned into spirits. Oh no! for they shall keep their bodily dimensions, and be true bodies still. Look, as in change of old and broken vessels, the matter is the same, only the colour is fresher and brighter, and the fashion newer and better, so in the day of glory, our bodies shall be the same for substance that now they are; they shall retain the same flesh, blood, and bones, and the same figure and members, that now is, only they shall be overlaid or clothed with spiritual and heavenly qualities and prerogatives; their bodies shall be glorious, of a due and comely proportion, of an exquisite feature and stature, of a lively colour, of cheerful aspect, and full of beauty and glory, splendour and favour. Now the bodies of the saints shall be spiritual, *first, in respect of their full, perfect, and perpetual freedom from all heats, colds, hungerings, thirstings, sickness, weakness, wants.* Here one cries out, Oh my back, my back! another, Oh my belly, my belly! with the prophet, Hab. iii. 16; another, Oh my head, my head! with the Shunamite's son, 2 Kings iv. 19; another, Oh my son, my son! as David for Absalom, 2 Sam. xviii. 33; another, Oh my father, my father! with Elisha, 2 Kings ii. 12. Every one here hath some ailment or other, some want or other, some grief or other, which fills his eyes with tears and his heart with sorrow; but when these natural bodies, these animal or soully bodies, shall be made glorious, then they shall be fully and perpetually freed from all manner of miseries and calamities; they shall be as the angels, not subject to any sickness, weakness, or wants: Rev. vii. 16, 17, 'They shall hunger no more, neither thirst any more; neither shall the sun light on them, nor any heat. For the Lamb, which is in the midst of the throne, shall feed them, and shall lead them unto living fountains of water; and God shall wipe away all tears from their eyes.' Rev. xxi. 4, 'God shall wipe away all tears from their eyes; and there shall be no more death, neither sorrow, nor crying, neither shall there be any more pain: for the former things are passed away;' and in this respect their bodies may be said to be spiritual. But, *secondly,* they may be said to be spiritual *in respect of their spiritual agility and nimbleness.* Now, our bodies are gross, dull, and heavy in their motion: and by this the soul is many times hindered in its lively operations; for when the soul would mount up on high, and busy herself about eternal objects, the body, like a lump of lead, keeps it down; but now, in this glorious state, the body shall put off all grossness, dulness, and heaviness, and be exceeding agile, light, and apt to motion, far beyond the swiftest bird that flies, Isa. xl. 31; 1 Thes. iv. 17.

I know not by what to set forth the agility of glorified bodies; a post, a bird, a torrent, are too short to set forth their agility.

Luther saith, that a glorified body shall move up and down like a thought.

[1] σῶμα ψυχικόν, an animal or soully body, that is, actuated and animated by the soul after a natural way and manner, by the intervention of natural helps, such as eating, drinking, sleeping, and the like.

And Austin saith, The body will presently be here and there, where the soul would have it.[1] Certainly the speed and motion of glorified bodies will be extraordinary and incredible. A glorified saint desiring to be in such or such a place a thousand miles off or more, he will be there in such an incredible short time, that one calls it *imperceptible*, hardly to be discerned: in which respect their bodies may be said to be spiritual. But, *thirdly* and lastly, they may be said to be spiritual, *because of that perfect, full, absolute, and complete subjection that they shall delightfully and perpetually yield to the Spirit of God.* Now they often vex and grieve, affront and fight against the Spirit of God. The members of our bodies, as well as the faculties of our souls, do often make war upon the Spirit of grace, as the apostle fully shews in that Rom. vi. 'The spirit often lusts against the flesh, and the flesh against the spirit,' Gal. v. 17. Now the body says to the soul, 'Be not righteous over-much; neither make thyself over-wise: why shouldest thou destroy thyself?' Eccles. vii. 16. Cyprian readeth this verse thus, *Noli esse multum justus, et noli argumentari plus quam oportet*, be not just over-much, and do not argue and dispute more than is meet. The body is often apt to say to the soul, Thou art just over-much, O soul; and thou dost argue and dispute against this sin and that way, and this comfort and that enjoyment, more than is meet; and the soul seems to answer, ver. 17, 'Be not over-much wicked, neither be thou foolish: why shouldest thou die before thy time?'

But now in heaven the bodies of the saints shall be fully, perfectly, and delightfully, under the command, conduct, and guidance of the spirit; and therefore may truly be said to be spiritual. As the spirit serving the flesh may not unfitly be called carnal, saith one,[2] so the body obedient to the soul may rightly be termed spiritual. Glorified bodies are spiritual, not in their essence, but in condition and quality, as being fully and perpetually under the government of the Spirit. Now the tongue grieves the Spirit, and now the deaf ear is turned to the voice of the Spirit, and now the eye is rolling, when it should be reading the things of the Spirit; and now the feet are wandering when they should be walking in the ways of the Spirit; and now the hand is idle that should be diligent in the work of the Spirit, Eph. iv. 29–31, Isa. lxiii. 10. Oh! but now in heaven, the tongue, the eye, the ear, the hands, the feet, shall be all brought into an angelical, willing, and delightful obedience to the Spirit; upon which account glorified bodies may truly be termed spiritual. But,

(3.) Thirdly, and lastly, As their bodies shall be spiritual, *so they shall be immortal, they shall be incorruptible*, 1 Cor. xv. 42, 54. Here these elementary bodies of ours, by reason of their earthly and dreggish composition, are subject to mortality and corruption; and indeed man is so poor a piece, that he no sooner begins to live, but he begins to die; his whole life is but a lingering death. Death every hour lies at the door; this sergeant[3] constantly attends all men, in all places, companies, changes, and conditions. Petrarch telleth of one, who being invited to

[1] Aug. *de Civ. Dei.* l. xxii. c. 30. Wisdom, iii. 7, In the time of their visitation they shall shine, and run to and fro like sparks among the stubble. [Above is Brooks's fourth quotation from Apocrypha thus far.—G.] [2] Aug. *de civ. Dei.* l. xiii. c. xx.

[3] Another Shakesperian reminiscence: 'This fell sergeant Death is strict.'—Hamlet, V. 2.—G.

dinner the next day, answered, *Ego a multis annis crastinum non habui*, I have not had a morrow for this many years. Many dangers, many deaths, every hour surround these lives of ours. Here, saith one, *accedimus*, we enter into the world; *succedimus*, we succeed one another in the world; *decedimus*, we depart all out of the world. Oh! but in heaven we shall have immortal bodies! Luke xx. 36, 'Neither can they die any more, and are equal to the angels.' By the power, presence, and goodness of God, their bodies shall be so perfumed and embalmed, that they shall never corrupt, nor be subject to mortality. Manna, by a divine power, was kept many hundred years in the golden pot without putrefying or corrupting, and so shall the glorified bodies of the saints be preserved and kept pure and immortal. The immortality of glorified bodies shall far excel that of Adam's in paradise, for they shall be free from all possibility of dying; for they shall be perfectly and perpetually freed from all corruptible and corrupting elements. Glorified bodies shall have no seeds of corruption in them, nor any corruptive, harmful, malignant, or afflictive passion attending them.[1] Adam in his noble estate was in a possibility of dying, but the saints in their glorified condition are above all possibility of dying. This is a happiness that Adam could not reach to in his state of integrity; the greater obligation lies upon all that shall come to glory.

It is reported of the Duke of Bullone [Bouillon] and his company, that when they went to Jerusalem, as soon as they saw the high turrets they gave a mighty shout, that even made the earth ring, crying out, 'Jerusalem, Jerusalem![2] so when the saints shall all meet in the heavenly Jerusalem, oh how will they make even heaven to ring again, crying out, Immortality! immortality! immortality!

And thus, I suppose, I have clearly and fully made good that great truth, to wit, that the best and greatest things are reserved for believers till they come to heaven. I shall now give you a brief account of the reasons of this point; and then come to the application and bringing home of this precious truth to our own souls. Now the reasons of the point are these.

Reason 1. First, *Because it is his good will and pleasure to reserve the best things for his people till last:* Luke xii. 32, 'Fear not, little flock' (there are two diminutives in the Greek[3]), 'for it is your Father's good pleasure to give you the kingdom.' As it is God's good pleasure to give you a kingdom, so it is his good pleasure not to give you the kingdom till last, 2 Tim. iv. 7, 8. Edward the Sixth could not give his kingdom away; if he could, it had not come as it did to Queen Mary; but our heavenly Father doth now give a kingdom of grace, and will at last also give a kingdom of glory, to them that walk uprightly, Ps. lxxxiv. 11. But,

Reason 2. Secondly, *That he may keep the hearts of his people in a longing and in a waiting frame, for the enjoyment of those great and glorious things that he hath reserved for them till last:* Heb. xiii. 14, 'Here we have no continuing city, but we seek one to come.'[4] The greater and better the things are that are laid up for us, the more we

[1] Aug. *de civ. Dei.* l. xxii. c. xxx.

[2] Immortalised by Tasso.—G.

[3] *μικρὸν ποίμνιον*, Little, little in their own esteem, and in the world's account.

[4] Heb. xi. 14–16; Col. iii. 1–5.

should long and wait for the happy enjoyment of them. Abraham waited long for a son, and Hannah waited long for a child, and Joseph waited long for his advancement, and David waited long for the crown, the kingdom; and they had all a most happy issue. The longer we wait, the better we shall speed;[1] as that emperor's son said, the longer the cooks are preparing the meat, the better will be the cheer; meaning, the longer he stayed for the empire, the greater it would be. The longer we wait for happiness, the more at last we shall have of happiness. The great things of eternity are worth nothing, if they are not worth a longing and a waiting for. But,

Reason 3. Thirdly, God hath reserved the best and greatest things for his people till last, and that *because else they were above all men in the world the most miserable:* 1 Cor. xv. 19, 'If in this life only we have hope in Christ, we are of all men most miserable.' No men usually out of hell are so much afflicted, tempted, oppressed, scorned, despised, and neglected as they are. Here they have their hell, they had need of a heaven to come; here they are clothed with shame, they had need hereafter to be crowned with honour, or else they would be the unhappiest men in all the world; here the life of a believer is filled *multis et multiplicibus miseriis,* with many and multiplied miseries; with miseries of body, with miseries of mind. Multiplied miseries attend him, at bed and board, at home and abroad. Every condition is full, and every relation is full, of miseries and calamities; and therefore one saith well, *Quomodo potest amari hæc vita, tantas habens amaritudines? Quomodo etiam dicitur vita, tot generans mortes?*[2] How can this life be loved, which is so full of loathsome bitterness? Yea, how can it be called a life, which bringeth forth so many deaths? Yet he is a fool, saith one,[3] that looketh upon a godly man under trouble and sorrow, and thinketh him to be unhappy, because, as a fool, *attendit quid patitur, et non attendit quid illi servetur,* he attendeth what he suffereth, and doth not attend what is reserved for him. If the best things were not reserved for believers till last, they should have the saddest portion of all men, viz., a hell here, and a hell hereafter; and so sinners should have but one hell, and saints two, which would be blasphemy to affirm. But,

Reason 4. Fourthly, God reserves the best things for his people till last, *for the greater terror and horror, conviction and confusion of wicked and ungodly persons, who now revile them, and judge them to be the unhappiest men in all the world.* Oh! but when the Lord shall in the sight of all the world gloriously own them, and put royal robes upon their backs, and golden crowns upon their heads, then, Oh! what a shame, what covering of the face, what terror, what trembling, with Haman, will possess the hearts of wicked men.[4] The great honour and glory that God will put upon his people at last, will be to wicked men what the handwriting upon the wall was to Belshazzar, Dan. v. 1–8. Oh! it will make their countenance to change, their thoughts to be troubled, the joints of their loins to be loosed, and their knees dashed one against another. Now that word shall be eminently made

[1] Waiting is *bonum utile*, a profitable good.

[2] A-Kempis, *de Imitat. Christi*, l. 3, c. 20.

[3] Augustine in Ps. xci.

[4] Ps. lviii. 11; Lam. iv. 2; Esther vi. 6, *et seq.*

good: 'He setteth the poor on high from affliction, and maketh him families like a flock. The righteous shall see it and rejoice, and all iniquity shall stop her mouth,' Ps. cvii. 41, 42. Oh! what trouble of mind, what horror of conscience, what distraction and vexation, what terror and torment, what weeping and wailing, what crying and roaring, what wringing of hands, what tearing of hair, what dashing of knees, what gnashing of teeth, will there be among the wicked, when they shall see the saints in all their splendour, dignity, and glory! 'When they shall see Abraham, Isaac, and Jacob, and all the prophets in the kingdom of God, and themselves shut out for ever,' Luke xiii. 28. Now shall the wicked lamentingly say, Lo! these are the men that we counted fools, madmen, and miserable. Oh but now we see that we were deceived and deluded! Oh that we had never despised them! Oh that we had never reproached them! Oh that we had never trampled upon them! Oh that we had been one with them! Oh that we had imitated them! Oh that we had walked as they, and done as they, that so we might now have been as happy as they! Oh but this cannot be! Oh this may not be! Oh this shall never be! therefore Oh that we had never been born! Oh that now we might be unborn! Oh that we might be turned into a bird, a beast, a toad, a stone! Oh that we were anything but what we are! or, Oh that we were nothing! Oh that now our immortal souls were mortal! Oh that we might so die, that we may not eternally die! but it is now too late. Oh we see that there is a reward for the righteous! and we shall suddenly feel, that by all the contempt that we have cast upon these glorious shining saints, whose splendour and glory doth now darken the very glory of the sun, Dan. xii. 3; we have but treasured up wrath against the day of wrath, Rom. ii. 4–7; we have but added fuel to those burning coals, to those everlasting flames, in which we must now lie for ever, Ps. cxl. 10. But,

Reason 5. Fifthly, The Lord hath reserved the best things for his people till they come to heaven, *that so he may save his honour and secure his glory.* Would it make for the honour and glory of God, to put his children, his servants, upon doing hard things, and upon suffering great things, and at last to put them off with nothing? Surely it would not; and therefore the Lord, to save the honour of his great name, hath reserved the best wine till last, the best and choicest favours for his people till they come to heaven, John ii. 10. The sweetest honey lies at the bottom. I cannot see how God should save his glory, if he should put his children always upon sowing, and never suffer them to reap, 2 Cor. ix. 6, 7; that they should still be sowing in tears, if at last they should not reap in joy, Ps. cxxvi. 4–6. Men that love but their names and honour in the world, will not be served for nought, and will God? Will God, who is infinitely more tender of his name and honour, than any created being can be of theirs? Isa. xlii. 8, xlviii. 11.

I have read of Alphonsus, a king of Spain, who when a knight falling into want and being arrested for debt, there was a petition to the king to succour him, Ay, said the King, if he had spent his estate in mine, or in the commonwealth's service, it were reason he should be provided for by me, or the commonwealth. Men of honour will provide for them that spend themselves in their service; and will not God? Will not God do as much, yea more, for them that spend themselves in his service? Surely he will, Heb. xi. 16. 'But now they desire a better country, that is, an heavenly: wherefore God is not ashamed to be called their God; for he hath prepared for them a city.' As if he had said, Had not God prepared for them a city, had he not made some blessed provision for them, who left so much for him, who did so much for him, and who suffered such great and bitter things for him, they might well have complained that they had but a bad bargain of it, and that God was a hard master; and so God should have been ashamed. Had not God made such happy and blessed provision for them who had run through so many dangers and deaths for his sake, had he not provided and laid up for them, according to his promise, and suitable to his greatness and goodness, his dignity and glory, it would have put God to the blush, to speak after the manner of men. I have read concerning Dionysius of Sicily, that being extremely delighted with a minstrel that sung well, he promised to give him a great reward, and that raised the fancy of the man, and made him play better; but when the music was done, and the man waited for his reward, the king dismissed him empty, telling him that he should carry away as much of the promised reward as himself did of the music, and that he had paid him sufficiently with the pleasure of the promise for the pleasure of his song. But it will not stand with the honour of the King of kings to put off his servants so poorly, whose prayers, praises, and tears, have been most sweet and delightful music to him; no, he will do like himself at last, and that his children know. It troubled a martyr at the stake, that he was going to a place where he should ever be a-receiving wages, and do no more work. But,

Reason 6. Sixthly, *That he may make his children temptation-proof*, he hath reserved for them the best things till they come to heaven. The great things that God hath reserved for believers in heaven, was that which made those worthies, of whom this world was not worthy, temptation-proof; as you may see in that 10th of the Hebrews, 33d, 34th, 35th, verses, and throughout the 11th chapter of that Epistle. The pleasures, the treasures, the dignities and glories that are reserved for believers in heaven, make them bravely and nobly to resist all those temptations that they meet with from a tempting world or a tempting devil.

Austin blessed God, that his heart and the temptation did not meet together. By the precious things that are reserved for believers in heaven, God keeps their hearts and temptations asunder. When Basil was tempted with money and preferment, saith he, *Pecuniam da quæ permaneat ac continuo duret, gloriam quæ semper floreat*, give me money that may last for ever, and glory that may eternally flourish.[1] Satan made a bow of Job's wife, of his rib, as Chrysostom speaks, and shot a tentation by her at Job, thinking to have shot him to the heart, 'Curse God and die;' but Job's sincerity and integrity, and his hopes of immortality and glory, was a breastplate that made him temptation-proof. Ah Christians! do not you daily find, that the glorious things reserved for you in heaven, do mightily arm you against all the temptations that you meet with on earth? I know you do. But,

[1] Basil in xl. Martyrs.

Reason 7. Seventhly, God hath reserved the best things for his people, till they come to heaven, *because they are not in this mortal and frail condition able to bear, they are not able to take in the glory that is reserved for them*, 2 Cor. iv. 17.[1] Glory is such a great, such an exceeding, such an excessive, such an eternal weight, that no mortal is able to bear it. We must have better and larger hearts, and we must have stronger and broader backs, before we shall be capable of bearing that excellent, exceeding, and excelling weight of glory that is reserved in heaven for us. Nay, glory is such a weight, that when the saints shall enter into it, if then the Lord should not put under his everlasting arms and bear them up by his almighty power, it were impossible they should be able to bear it. In this our frail mortal state, we are not able to bear the appearance, the presence, the glory of one angel.

Ah! how much less then are we able to bear the weight of all that glory that is reserved for us, and of which I have given you some glimpses in what I have already said. But,

Reason 8. Eighthly and lastly, The Lord hath reserved the best things for his people till they come to heaven, *because while they are in this world they are under age. They are not come to full age.*[2] Here saints are in their non-age, but when they come to heaven, then they come to their full age, and then they shall have the inheritance by the Father of mercies freely and fully settled upon them. Children in their non-age are under tutors and governors, but when they come to age, then is the inheritance settled upon them: so here, it is not for us in our non-age, to mount into the clouds, to pierce this fulness of light, to break into this bottomless depth of glory, or to dwell in that unapproachable brightness.[3] This is reserved till we come to full age.

And thus I have given you the reasons why God hath reserved the best and greatest things for his people till they come to heaven. We shall now come to the use and application of this point to our own souls, remembering that close application is the very life and soul of teaching. And as a man doth not attain to health by reading of Galen, or knowing Hippocrates his aphorisms, but by the practical application of them to remove the disease; so no man will attain to true happiness by hearing, reading, or commending what I have spoke or writ, but by a close application and bringing home of all to his own soul. The opening of a point is the drawing of the bow; but the application of the point is the hitting of the mark, the white; and therefore,

(1.) First, If God hath reserved the best things for believers till last, then by the rule of contraries *the worst things are reserved for unbelievers till last.*[4] Here wicked men have their heaven, hereafter they shall have their hell. The time of this life is the day of their joy and triumph; and when this short day is ended, everlasting lamentations, mournings, and woes follow. Luke xvi. 22–25, 'The rich man also died, and was buried; and in hell he lift up his eyes, being in torments, and seeth Abraham afar off, and Lazarus in his bosom. And he cried, and said, Father Abraham, have mercy on me, and send Lazarus, that

[1] The apostle alludeth to the Hebrew and Chaldee words, *Chabodh* and *Jakar*, which signify both weight and glory.

[2] Gal. iv. 1–4; Ephes. iv. 10–14.

[3] Bernard, Cant. Serm. 38.

[4] Job xxi. 7–22; Ps. lxxiii. 3–12 compared with the 17th, 18th, 19th, 20th verses; Rev. xxi. 8.

he may dip the tip of his finger in water, and cool my tongue; for I am tormented in this flame. But Abraham said, Son, remember that thou in thy lifetime receivedst thy good things, and likewise Lazarus evil things: but now he is comforted, and thou art tormented.'

Ah sinners! sinners! that day is hastening upon you, wherein you shall have punishment without pity, misery without mercy, sorrow without succour, pain without pleasure, and torments without end: Ps. xi. 6, 'Upon the wicked he shall rain snares, fire and brimstone, and an horrible tempest: this shall be the portion of their cup.' Ps. cxl. 10, 'Let burning coals fall upon them: let them be cast into the fire; into deep pits, that they rise not up again.'

Chrysologus, upon that passage in the Gospel, that the angels carried away poor Lazarus into Abraham's bosom, and hell swallowed up the rich glutton, saith: *Ecce fratres, mors pauperis totam vitam divitis vicit, et elatio sola pauperis totam divitis pompam transcendit et gloriam.*[1] Behold! brethren, the very death of the poor man excelleth the whole life of the wicked, and the carrying away only of the poor man transcendeth all the pomp and glory of the rich man.

Charon, in Lucian, requesting Mercurius to shew him Jupiter's palace above, How! says Mercurius, that such a caitiff as thou, whose conversation hath been altogether with black shades and impure ghosts, shouldst set thy foot in that pure place of light? What a dishonour and derogation were that to the place!

Ah, sinners! sinners! what a dishonour would it be to God, to Christ, to angels, to saints, to heaven, if such wretches as you are should be admitted into that royal palace, that heavenly paradise, above.

Ah! your portion is below, and you are already adjudged to those torments that are endless, easeless, and remediless, where the worm never dies, and the fire never goes out, Rev. xiv. 11. The day is coming upon you, sinners, when all your sweet shall be turned into bitter; all your glory into shame; all your plenty into scarcity; all your joys into sorrows; all your recreations into vexations; and all your momentany comforts into everlasting torments.

Now you reign as kings, you look big, you speak proudly, you carry it highly, you walk contemptuously; but there is an after-reckoning a-coming that will appal you, and torture you for ever.

The time of this life is your summer; but there is a winter a-coming upon you that shall never have end. God could not be just if your worst were not yet to come; neither could he be just if the saints' best were not yet to come. The time of this life is the saints' hell, and the sinners' heaven; but the next life will be the saints' heaven, and the sinners' hell. But,

(2.) Secondly, *Then patiently wait for the enjoyment of those great things that are reserved for you in heaven.* Men will wait, and wait long, for some outward good; and will not you for the best and greatest good? Are there not many things that speak out the greatness of that glory that is reserved for you? as the price that Christ hath paid for it, and the great and glorious things by which it is shadowed out to us? as Canaan, Jerusalem, paradise; and the dignity of the inhabitants, there being none admitted under the degree of a king; and the great and glorious earnest of the Spirit; and the great care, cost, and charge that God hath

[1] Chrysologus, *Serm.* 121.

been at to prepare and fit souls for the enjoyment of it.[1] What do all these things speak out, but that the glory that is reserved for believers is great glory; and is it not then worth a waiting for? Let not Satan's slaves wait more patiently for a few ounces of gold, than you do for the kingdom of heaven.

Again, as the things reserved for you in heaven are great, and therefore wait, so *they are certain and sure*; and therefore wait, oh patiently wait for the enjoyment of them! Heb. vi. 16–19. When the beggar at the door is sure of speeding, he will wait patiently, he will wait unweariedly. The glorious things reserved in heaven for you, they are made sure and certain to you by word, by covenant, by oath, by blood, by the earnest, by the first-fruits, and by Christ's taking possession of them in your rooms, in your steads, Eph. ii. 6, John xiv. 1–4; therefore patiently wait for the enjoyment of them. O Christians! it is but a very short time that God hath proposed to be between grace and glory, between our title to the crown and our wearing the crown; between our right to the heavenly inheritance, and our possession of the heavenly inheritance. Ah, Christians! bear up bravely, bear up sweetly, bear up patiently, for it will be but a little, little, little while, before he that shall come will come, and will not tarry, Heb. x. 35–37, ἔτι γὰρ μικρὸν ὅσον ὅσον; and when he doth come, he will not come *vacuis manibus*, empty-handed; no, when he comes, he brings his reward with him, Rev. xxii. 12; when he comes, he will reward thee for every prayer that thou hast made, and for every sermon that thou hast heard, and for every tear that thou hast shed, and for every hour that thou hast patiently waited; and therefore wait patiently till the promised crown be set upon thy head. But,

(3.) Thirdly, If the best things are reserved for believers till they come to heaven, oh then, *let no believer envy nor be troubled at the outward prosperity and felicity of the men of the world.* What is darkness to light, chaff to wheat, dross to gold, gall to honey, pebbles to pearls, earth to heaven? No more is all the glory and felicity that wicked men have in possession to those great and glorious things that saints have in reversion; and therefore, O believer, let not wicked men's prosperity be thy calamity![2]

There is a truth in that saying of Chrysostom,[3] *præstat serpentem provolutum in visceribus habere, quam invidiam*, a man were better have a serpent tumbling in his bowels than envy; for if a serpent have food given it, it will not feed upon a man; but the more food is given to envy, the more it gnaweth him in whose bowels it is. It is the justice of envy to kill and torment the envious. Envy, it tortures the affections, it vexes the mind, it inflames the blood, it corrupts the heart, it wastes the spirits; and so it becomes man's tormentor and man's executioner at once. Take heed, Christians, take heed of an envious eye, for that usually looks upon other men's enjoyments through a multiplying glass, and so makes them appear greater and bigger than they are; and this increases torment, this often makes a hell.

It is reported of Panormitanus, that a question being asked before

[1] Rev. xxi.; i. 5, 6; Eph. i. 13, 14; Col. i. 12.
[2] Ps. xxxvii. 1; lxxiii. 3–7; Job xxi. 7-18; Jer. xii. 1, 2.
[3] Chrys. in ii. *ad Corin.* Homil. xix.

king Frederick, what was good for the eye-sight, and the physicians answering some one thing, some another, Sannizarius answered, that envy was very good ; at which the company smiling, he gave this reason for it, because that envy makes all things appear bigger than they are. Ah, Christians! envy is a serpent, a devil, that should be abhorred and shunned more than hell itself. O Christian! with what heart canst thou envy wicked men's prosperity and worldly felicity, if thou dost but look up to thine own glory, and seriously consider of their sad reckoning and future calamity? Dives was one day rustling in his purple robes, riches, and worldly glory, and the next day he was rolling and roaring in the flames of hellish misery; and how soon this may be the portion of those thou enviest, who can tell? and therefore rather pity them than envy them. None need more prayer and pity than those that want hearts, than those that have neither skill nor will to pity themselves, to pray for themselves; and such are wicked men under their outward prosperity and worldly glory, Job xxi. 7–20. But,

(4.) Fourthly, If the best things are reserved for believers till they come to heaven, oh then *let all believers be contented, though they have but short commons in this world!* He that is an heir to a great estate, though in his non-age he be kept short, yet this comforts and contents him, that though things are now short with him, it will be but a little while before the inheritance is settled upon him, and this makes him bear up sweetly and contentedly under all his wants and straits, Philip. iv. 12–14, 1 Tim. vi. 6–8. Ah, Christians! Christians! though for the present your wants may be many, and God may cut you short in many desirable enjoyments, yet it will not be long before the crown, the inheritance, be fully settled upon you, and then you shall never know what want means more, what short commons means more ; therefore be content with your present condition, with your present portion, though it be never so little, never so mean: Heb. xiii. 5, 'Let your conversation be without covetousness ; and be content with such things as you have' (or as the Greek hath it, τοῖς παροῦσιν, the things that are present[1]). At this time the Hebrews had been plundered of all their goods, and goodly things, chap. x. 34, and so had nothing, or that which is as good as nothing, left, yet they must be content with present things. When they had changed their raiment for rags, their silver for brass, their plenty for scarcity, their houses for holes and caves, and dens, yet then they must be contented with present things. When men cannot bring their means to their minds, then they must bring their minds to their means, and, when this is done, then a little will serve the turn.[2] A very little will serve to carry a man through his pilgrimage, and to bear his charges till he comes to his home, till he comes to heaven ; a little will serve nature, less will serve grace, though nothing will serve a man's lusts. I have read of one Didymus, a godly preacher, who was blind ; Alexander, a godly man, being with him, asked him whether he was not much troubled and afflicted for want of his sight? Oh yes! said Didymus, the want of my sight is a very great grief and affliction to me ; whereupon Alexander chid him, saying, Hath God given thee the

[1] *Contenti præsentibus.* So Beza.

[2] If thou live according to nature, thou wilt never be poor; if according to opinion, thou wilt never be rich, said the heathen.—*Jerome.*

excellency of an angel, of an apostle, and art thou troubled for the want of that which rats, and mice, and brute beasts have? And so Augustine, upon the 12th Psalm, brings in God rebuking a discontented Christian thus: What is thy faith? have I promised thee these things? what! wert thou made a Christian that thou shouldst flourish here in this world?[1] So may I say to Christians that are discontented, disquieted, and disturbed about the want of this or that worldly comfort: Why are you troubled about the want of this or that worldly enjoyment? you that have an interest in God, an interest in the covenant, a right to Christ, a title to heaven; you that have so much in hand and more in hope; you that have so much in expectation and so much in reversion; why do you sit sighing for the want of this outward comfort, and complaining for the want of that outward contentment, considering what great and glorious things are reserved in heaven for you? It was said of the great Duke of Guise, that though he was poor, as to his present possessions, yet he was the richest man in France in bills, bonds, and obligations; because he had engaged all the noblemen in France unto himself by advancing of them. A Christian, though a Lazarus at Dives's door; yet, in respect of his propriety[2] in God and his interest in the covenant, he is the richest and the happiest man in all the world; and why then should he not be content. Well! remember, Christian, that the shortest cut to riches and all worldly contentments is by their contempt. It is great riches, it is the best riches not to desire riches; and God usually gives him most that covets least. When two monks came to king William Rufus to buy an abbot's place, and endeavoured to outbid each other, a third monk that came to wait on them was asked what he would give, he answered, Not a penny; I came to wait on him that shall have the place; upon which the king gave the waiter the place. Just so doth God often carry it towards his people in this world; they that seek it least shall have most. Solomon begs a wise heart, and God gives him that, and abundance of gold and silver and honour, and what not, into the bargain. The best way to have much, is to be contented with a little.

I have read of Dionysius [Plutarch], how he took away from one of his nobles almost his whole estate, and seeing him nevertheless continue as cheerful and well contented as ever, he gave him that again, and as much more. This is a common thing with God, as Job and many thousands can witness;[3] the best way to have a pound is to be contented with a penny, the best way to have hundreds is to be contented with pounds, and the best way to have thousands is to be contented with hundreds. Ah! thou unquiet and discontented Christian, canst thou read over that saying of Cato, a heathen, and not blush? *Si quid est quo utar, utor: si non, scio quis sum; mihi vitio vertunt, quia multis egeo; et ego illis, quia nequeunt egere.*[4] I have neither house, nor plate, nor garments of price in my hands; what I have, I can use; if not, I can want it; some blame me, because I want many things, and I blame them, because they cannot want. How many thousand Christians in these knowing and professing days might

[1] If there were any happiness in riches, the gods would not want them, said Seneca. [See this quoted *before* in 'Mute Christian.'—G.]
[2] 'Property.'—G.
[3] Job i. and the last of Job compared.
[4] Aulus Gellius reports this of him.

this heathen put to the blush! O Christians! Christians! let the remembrance of the crown, the kingdom, the treasures, pleasures, and glories that are reserved in heaven for you, make you bear up sweetly and contentedly under all your outward wants in this world. But,

(5.) Fifthly, If the best and greatest things are reserved for believers till they come to heaven, then *make not a judgment of the saints' condition by their present state.*[1] If you do, you will 'condemn the generation of the just.' What though they are now in rags, it will not be long before they are clothed in their royal robes; what though they are now abased, it will not be long before they shall in the sight of all the world be highly advanced; what though they are now under many wants, it will not be long before they shall be filled with all fulness; what though they are now under many trials and afflictions, yet it will not be long before all tears shall be wiped away from their eyes, and their sighing turned into singing, 'and everlasting joys shall be upon their heads;' and therefore do not judge of their condition by their present state. If you will needs be judging, then look that you judge righteous judgment, John vii. 24; then look more at the latter end of a Christian than the beginning. Remember the patience of Job, James v. 11, and consider what end the Lord made with him. Look not upon Lazarus lying at Dives's door, but lying in Abraham's bosom; look not to the beginning of Joseph, who was so far from his dream, that the sun and moon should reverence him, that for two years he was cast where he could neither see sun nor moon; but behold him at last made ruler over all Egypt, and reigning fourscore years like a king, Gen. xxxvii. 9, xli. 40–46. Look not upon David, as there was but a step between him and death, nor as he was envied by Saul, and hated by his courtiers; but behold him seated in his royal throne, where he reigned forty years gloriously, and died in his bed of honour, and his son Solomon, and his nobles about him. When Israel was dismissed out of Egypt, it was with gold and ear-rings, Exod. xi.; and when the Jews were dismissed out of Babylon, it was with great gifts, jewels, and all necessary utensils, Ezra i. 'Mark the perfect man, and behold the upright; the end of that man is peace,' Ps. xxxvii. 37. Whatever the wants, the straits, the troubles, the trials of the saints are in this world, yet their end shall be peace, their end shall be glorious; the best things are reserved for them till last; and therefore do not, oh do not judge of their condition by their present state, but rather judge of them by their future condition, by that glory that is reserved for them in heaven. But,

(6.) Sixthly, If the greatest and choicest things are reserved for believers till they come to heaven, why, then, *let believers keep up in their own souls a lively, hopeful expectation of enjoying these great and glorious things that are laid up for them.* The keeping up of those hopes will be the keeping up of your hearts; the keeping up of these hopes will be the bettering of your hearts; the keeping up of these hopes will make every bitter sweet, and every sweet more sweet; the keeping up of these hopes will make you bear much for God, and do much for God.[2]

[1] Ps. lxxiii. 12–15; Mat. vii. 1, 2; 1 Cor. iv. 5.

[2] Rom. viii. 24, 25, ii. 5; Titus i. 2; Acts xxvi. 7; Titus iii. 7; Col. i. 5; 1 Thes. v 8; 1 Peter i. 3; 1 John iii. 2, 3.

When Alexander went upon a hopeful expedition, he gave away his gold; and when he was asked what he kept for himself, he answered, *Spem majorum et meliorum*, the hope of greater and better things.

Ah! Christians, there is no work so high and noble, there is no work so hard and difficult, there is no work so low and contemptible, but the hopes of the great things reserved in heaven for you will put you upon it.

Galen speaks of a fish called *uranoscopus*,[1] which hath but one eye, and that is so placed that it is always looking upwards towards heaven; and so should a Christian's eye of hope be always fixed on God, on promises, on heaven, on the inheritance of the saints in light, and on all those precious and glorious things that are laid up for them in that royal palace where Christ is all in all.

A devout pilgrim travelling to Jerusalem, and by the way visiting many brave cities, with their rare monuments, and meeting with many friendly entertainments, would often say, I must not stay here, this is not Jerusalem, this is not Jerusalem; so saith a Christian in the midst of all his worldly delights, comforts, and contents, oh these are not the delights, the comforts, the contents that my soul looks for, that my soul expects and hopes to enjoy. I look and hope for choicer delights, for sweeter comforts, for more satisfying contents, and for more durable riches.

Ah, saints! ah, souls! Shall the great heirs of this world live upon their hopes, and keep up their hopes, that their inheritances shall in time be settled respectively upon them? and will not you, will not you live upon your hopes, and keep up your hopes of enjoying all the treasures, pleasures, and glories that are reserved in heaven for you? A Christian's motto always is, or always should be, *Spero meliora*, I hope for better things; I hope for better things than any the world can give to me, or than any that Satan can take from me. A Christian is always rich in hope, though he hath not always a penny in hand. But,

(7.) Seventhly, If there be such great and glorious things reserved for you in heaven, then *do nothing unworthy of your dignity, nor of that glory that is laid up for you*.[2] Your calling is high, your honour is great, your happiness is matchless; you have so much in promises, so much in expectation, and so much in reversion, as cannot be conceived, as cannot be expressed; therefore, do not you stoop to sin, nor bow down to Satan, nor comply with the world.

When Alexander was moved to run with some persons of inferior rank, he refused, saying, It was not fit for Alexander to run in a race with any but princes and nobles.

Ah, Christians! are you not more nobly born? are you not better bred? have you not more royal hopes than to stoop to lust, or to do as the men of the world do?

Antigonus, being invited to dinner where a notable harlot was to be present, asked counsel of Menedemus, his tutor, what he should do, and how he should carry himself? His tutor bade him remember that he was a prince, that he was the son of a king, and this would preserve him.[3]

[1] οὐρανοσκόπος, the heaven-gazer. Cf. Pliny, xxxii. 7, 24, sec. 69; xi. 52, sec. 146.—G.

[2] Heb. xi. 38; Philip. iii. 14; Isa. lxiii. 4; 1 Cor. ii. 9.

[3] Diog. Laërtius, ii. 125–144; Athen. l. c.—G.

Ah! Christians! nothing will preserve you from being base, like the remembrance of your present dignity, and of that future glory that is laid up for you.

Ah, Christians! you are kings elected, you are heirs-apparent of a crown, of a glorious crown, of a weighty crown, of an incorruptible crown, of an everlasting crown of glory! Oh why then should you be crowning yourselves with rosebuds? why then should you take up in the low enjoyments and poor contentments of this world?[1]

It was a generous speech of that heathen Themistocles, who, coming by a thing that seemed to be a pearl in the dark, scorned to stoop for it, but bade another stoop, saying, Stoop thou for this pearl, for thou art not Themistocles. Oh let the men of the world stoop and take up the world, oh let them whose practice speaks them out to be of the world, and to be worshippers of that golden calf, the world, let these dance about it, bow down to it, and take up in it; but let the heirs of heaven divinely scorn to bow down to earth, or to take up in it, or to be much taken with it. It was a good saying of Seneca, *Major sum et ad majora natus, quam ut mancipium sim corporis mei,* I am too great, and born to greater things than that I should be as a slave to my body.[2]

Ah, Christians! you are too great, and born to greater things, than that you should be slaves to your bodies, or slaves to your lusts, or slaves to the world; can you seriously consider of the great things that are reserved in heaven for you, and not set your feet upon those things that the men of the world set their hearts upon? Can you look up to your future glory, and not blush to be taken with the glory of this world?

What Alexander the Great said to one of his captains that was called Alexander, *Recordare nominis Alexandri,* remember the name of Alexander, and see, said he, that you do nothing unworthy of the name of Alexander.[3] So say I, Remember, O Christian thy name; remember thy dignity and glory, and see that thou dost nothing unworthy of the one or the other. But,

(8.) Eighthly, If the best and greatest things are reserved for the saints till they come to heaven, then *let them desire and long to be possessed of those blessed things that are reserved in heaven for them.*[4] Oh, how do the heirs of this world long to have their estates in their own hands! how do they long to have their inheritances settled upon them! some of them wishing their relations dead that stand between them and their inheritances; and others, of a little better nature, wishing them in the bosom of Abraham, that they might come to inherit, and that they might suck the sweet, and take up their rest, in their worldly inheritances. And shall not the saints desire and long to be in a full and happy possession of that crown, of that inheritance, of those jewels that are reserved in heaven for them? O Christians! how is it, why is it, that your heavenly Jerusalem, your mansions above, your glorious treasures, suffer not an holy violence, in respect of your earnest wishes and burning desires after them?

[1] Oh, say not of this world as Peter of his little heaven, *Bonum est esse hic,* it is good to be here. [2] Sen. Epist. lxvi. [3] Plutarch, *Alexander.*—G.

[4] *Tota vita boni Christiani, sanctum desiderium est,* the whole life of a good Christian is an holy wish, saith one. [Bernard Serm. Canticles.—G.]

The primitive Christians did so hunger and thirst, look and long, wish and desire after this heavenly kingdom,[1] this glorious inheritance, that the Roman State had a jealousy of them, as if they had affected their kingdom and their worldly glory. But where is that spirit now to be found? Most men live now as if there were no heaven, or else as if heaven were not worth a seeking, worth a desiring; as if heaven were a poor, low, contemptible thing.

But ah, Christians! you have learned better; and therefore be you much in desiring and longing to get into that glorious city, where streets, walls, and gates are all gold, yea, where pearl is but as mire and dirt, and where are all pleasures, all treasures, all delights, all comforts, all contents; and that for ever. This word 'for ever' is a bottomless depth, a conception without end; it is a word that sweetens all the glory above, and that indeed makes heaven to be heaven. I can hardly call him a Christian that doth not long more after spirituals, and after the great things that are reserved in heaven for the saints, than Ulysses did for the smoke of his house after ten years' absence.[2] But,

(9.) Ninthly, If the best and greatest things are reserved for the saints till they come to heaven, then, Oh *let not the men of the world envy the saints, whilst they are here in this wilderness.*

Ah! sinners, sinners, the people of God have but little in hand; though they have much in hope; they have but little in the bag whatever they may have in the bank; they have but little in the cistern whatever they may have in the fountain; they have but little in possession whatever they may have in reversion; and therefore do not envy them, James ii. 5. Who but monsters will envy the child in his cradle, or in the arms, or in his non-age, though he be an heir to a great estate, inasmuch as it is out of his hand, and he is not in the possession of it? and yet such monsters this world affords, who are filled with envy against Christ's precious ones, though their estates are out of their hands. Old Jacob speaking of his son Joseph, saith, that 'the archers have sorely grieved him, and shot at him, and hated him,' Gen. xlix. 23; and Jerome, expounding the words, noteth, *Hic invidiam cum arcu et sagittis introduci ad sagittandum quod immaculatum est,* that here envy is brought in with bow and arrows shooting at that which is immaculate, and where there is no spot to be a mark for it! or else, as an archer doth set up some white thing to be the mark at which he shoots, so it is the whiteness of some good thing or other, against which envy shoots.[3] Such is the wrath, the rage, the hatred, the envy of wicked men against the saints, that they will still be envying of them upon one score or another. Such was Saul's envy to David, that David chooses rather to live under king Achish, an enemy, than to live under Saul's envy; nay, such was Saul's envy against David, that when David played on his harp, to cure him of the evil spirit that haunted him, that he threw his spear at him to destroy him, *malens a malo spiritu torqueri, quam Davidem vivere,* choosing rather to be tormented with an evil spirit, than that David should live.[4] And such was Cain's envy to Abel, that though he had but one brother, nay, though there was but one

[1] Justin Martyr, *Apol.* ii.

[2] Odyssey, i. 57.—G.

[3] Jerome *in quæstionib. Hebræ.*

[4] Bern *de inter domo. c.* 2.

brother in all the world, yet enraged envy will wash her hands in that brother's blood.

Chrysologus noteth of the rich glutton, who would have Lazarus to be sent to him, that being still cruel and envious towards Lazarus, he would have him to be sent *Ad infernum de gremio, de solio sublimi ad profundissimum chaos, ad tormentorum stridorem, de sancta quiete beatorum*, to hell from the bosom of Abraham, to the bottomless gulf from the highest throne of glory, to the gnashing and grinding of torments from the holy rest of the blessed. The truth is, envy sticks so close to the heart of wicked men, that courtesies provoke it;[1] offices of love and respect swell it, and an eminency in gifts and graces enrages it; no man of worth hath ever escaped it. Neither mine accusers, nor my crimes, saith Socrates, can kill me, but envy only, which hath, and doth, and will destroy the worthiest that ever were; and therefore, the same person wishes that envious men had more eyes and more ears than others, that so they might be tormented more than others, by beholding others' happiness. Well! sinners, if, notwithstanding all that hath been said, you will still be envious against those gracious souls that have but little in hand, though they have much in hope; if you will be envious against those who stand between you and wrath, between you and hell; if you will be envious against those to whom, as instruments, you are beholding for all the mercies, comforts, and contents, that you enjoy in this world, then know, that your envy will torture you,[2] your envy will slay you, your envy will prepare the hottest, darkest, and lowest place in hell for you. But,

(10.) Tenthly, If the best things are reserved for believers till they come to heaven, then *let not any outward losses trouble you, nor deject you.* What is thy loss of a house made with hands to one eternal in the heavens? what is thy loss of rags to the royal robes above? what is thy loss of earth to the gain of heaven? what is thy loss of husband, wife, child, friends, to the enjoyment of God, Christ, angels, and the spirits of just men made perfect? 2 Cor. v. 1; Rev. vi. 11, vii. 9, 13, 14.

When Paulinus Nolanus his city was taken from him by the barbarians, he prayed thus to God: Lord! let me not be troubled at the loss of my gold, silver, honour, &c.; for thou art all, and much more than all, these unto me.[3]

When Demetrius asked Stilpo[4] what loss he had sustained when his wife, his children, and country were all burned, he answered, that he had lost nothing, counting that only his own which none could take from him, to wit, his virtues. What an unlovely, what an uncomely, thing would it be to see a rich heir, upon the loss of a ribbon out of his hat, or upon the loss of a glove from his hand, &c., to stand sighing and grieving, vexing and lamenting; or to see a prince, upon the burning up of his stables and outhouses, to stand wringing his hands and beating his breasts, and to cry out, Undone, undone! when his royal palace is safe, his crown safe, his treasures safe! As unlovely, yea, a more unlovely and uncomely, thing it is to see a saint upon the account of losing

[1] Envy is like certain flies called cantharides, who light specially upon the fairest wheat, and most blown roses.

[2] Prov. xiv. 30; Job v. 2; Mat. xxiii. 13–15. [3] Cf. *ante*.—G.

[4] A philosopher of Megara.

wife, child, friend, &c., to cry out, Undone, undone! no sorrow to my sorrow! no loss to my loss! when his great all is safe; when his crown, his heaven, his happiness, his blessedness, is safe. Basil, bringing in Job comforting his wife under all their sad losses and calamities, makes him speak thus:[1] *Semper prospere agere solius est Dei; bibisti liquidum vitæ laticem et turbidum jam toleranter bibe,* it belongeth to God only always to enjoy contentment. Thou hast drunk of the clear waters of this life; now drink of them patiently when they are troubled. But,

(11.) Eleventhly, If the best things are reserved for believers till they come to heaven, then *let believers live cheerfully and walk comfortably up and down in this world.*[2] Ah! how cheerfully and merrily do many great heirs live! Though for the present things goes hard with them, the hopes of a good inheritance makes them sing care and sorrow away. It is not for the honour of Christ, nor for the glory of the gospel, to see the heirs of heaven look so sadly and walk so mournfully and dejectedly, as if there were no heaven, or as if there was nothing laid up for them in heaven. It becomes not the sons of glory, with Rachel, to give so much way to weeping as to refuse to be comforted, Neh. viii. 10. Dost thou not remember, O Christian, that the joy of the Lord is thy strength, thy doing strength, thy bearing strength, thy prevailing strength. What! hast thou forgotten that 'the joy of the Lord is thy strength' to live, and thy strength to die? If not, why with Cain dost thou walk up and down with a dejected countenance, with a cast-down countenance? A beautiful face is at all times pleasing to the eye, but then especially when there is joy manifested in the countenance. Joy in the face puts a new beauty upon a person, and makes that which before was beautiful to be exceedingly beautiful; it puts a new lustre upon beauty; so doth joy put a lustre and a beauty upon a Christian; and upon all his words, his ways, his works. It was this that made the faces of several martyrs to shine as if they had been the faces of angels. One observes[3] of Chispina, that she was cheerful when she was apprehended, and joyful when she was led to the judge, and merry when she was sent into prison; so when she was bound, when she was brought forth, when she was lifted up in a cage, when she was heard, when she was condemned. In all these things she rejoiced; so that they who were miserable thought her to be miserable, who indeed was happy under a spirit of joy. When Cæsar was sad, he used to say to himself, *Cogita te Cæsarem esse,* think thou art Cæsar. Ah, Christians! when you are sad and dejected, think of your dignity and glory; think of all those precious and glorious things that are reserved in heaven for you.

It becomes not Christians, who have so much in reversion, to be like Angelastus, grandfather to Crassus, who never laughed in all his life save once, and that was when he saw a mare eating of thistles; nor like Anaxagoras [of] Clazomenæ, who was never seen to laugh or smile from the day of his birth to the day of his death. Christians, I desire to leave that serious and sad word upon your hearts: Deut. xxviii. 47, 48, 'Because thou servest not the Lord thy God with joyfulness and with

[1] Basil, Homil. xxiii.
[2] Ps. xxxiii. 1, lxxix. 12; Isa. xli. 16; Joel ii. 23; Zech. x. 7; Philip. iii. 1, iv. 4.
[3] Augustine in Ps. cxxxvii.

gladness of heart, for the abundance of all things; therefore shalt thou serve thine enemies, which the Lord shall send against thee, in hunger, and in thirst, and in nakedness, and in want of all things: and he shall put a yoke of iron upon thy neck, until he hath destroyed thee.' Sad souls! it will be your wisdom to make this scripture your daily companion, and to ponder it seriously in your hearts, as Mary did the saying of the angel. God takes it so unkindly at his people's hands that they should be sad, and sighing, lamenting, and mourning, when they should be a-rejoicing and delighting themselves in the Lord for the abundance of his mercies, that he threatens to pursue them with all sorts of miseries and calamities to the very death. A sad, dejected spirit opens many foul mouths that God would have stopped, and sads many precious souls that God would have gladded, and discourages many weak Christians and young beginners whom God would have encouraged and animated; and therefore we need not wonder if God should deal so sadly and severely with such sad souls, who make little of sadding many at once, viz., God, Christ, the Spirit, and many precious ones, 'of whom this world is not worthy.' Surely there is infinitely more in the great and glorious things that are reserved for believers in heaven, to joy and rejoice them, than there can be in all the troubles and trials, afflictions and temptations, that they meet with in this world, to sad, grieve, and deject them. Ah, Christians! the great and glorious things that are reserved in heaven for you, will afford you such an exuberancy of joy, as no good can match, as no evil can overmatch. Witness the joy of the martyrs, both ancient and modern. Oh how my heart leapeth for joy, saith one, that I am so near the apprehension of eternal bliss![1] But,

(12.) Twelfthly, If the best and greatest things are reserved for believers till they come to heaven, why then *let not believers be unwilling to die; yea, let them rather court it, and when it comes, sweetly welcome it,* 1 Cor. v. 1, 2, 7, Philip. i. 21, There is no way to paradise but by this flaming sword; there is no way to those heavenly treasures, but through this dark entry; there is no way to life, immortality, and glory, but by dying; there is no coming to a clear, full, and constant fruition of God, but by dying. Augustine upon those words, Exod. xxxiii. 20, 21, 'Thou canst not see my face and live,' makes this short but sweet reply, 'Then, Lord, let me die, that I may see thy face.' 'Shall I die ever?' saith one.[2] 'Yes; or shall I die at all? yea, why then, Lord, if ever, why not now, why not now!' So St Andrew, saluting the cross on which he was crucified, cried out, 'Take me from men, and restore me to my Master.' So Lawrence Sanders, when he was come to the stake at which he was to be burnt, kissed it, saying, 'Welcome the cross of Christ, welcome everlasting life.'[3]

Ah, Christians! can you read over those instances, and not blush,

[1] See [Fox.] Act. and Mon. 1668–70, &c.

[2] Monica, mother of Augustine.—G.

[3] So Moses, Jacob, and old Simeon. So Cowper, Nazianzen, Faninus, Cyprian, young Lord Harrington, and others, &c. *Præcipit ut quisque vitam suam futuri desiderio laboret, præsentium tædio.*—Bernard. [The 'funeral' sermon of 'young' Lord Harrington was preached by Richard Stock, and contains some touching sayings of above kind. Cf our Memoir, prefixed to Stock on Malachi, in the series of 'Commentaries' issued by the present Publisher.—G.]

and not be troubled that these worthies should be so ready and so willing to die, that they might come to a happy fruition of those glorious things that were reserved in heaven for them, whilst you are unwilling to die; whilst your desires are rather, with Peter, to build tabernacles here, than to be in a full fruition of God, and in a happy possession of your heavenly mansions, Mat. xvii. 4, John xiv. 2, 3. Cyprian tells of a bishop, who, being near his death, and unwilling to die, and praying to God for a longer life, an angel appeared unto him, and, with an angry countenance in reproving him, said, *Pati timetis, exire de vita non vultis, quid faciam vobis?*[1] Ye fear to suffer, ye will not go out of this life, what shall I do unto you? Ah, Christians, Christians! how justly may that father be angry with his child that is unwilling to come home, and that husband with his wife who is unwilling to ride to him in a rainy day, or to cross the seas to enjoy him? And is not this your case? is not this your case? I know it is. Well, Christians! let me a little expostulate the case with you, that if it be possible I may work your hearts into a willingness to die, yea, to desire death, to long for death, that so you may come to a full fruition of whatever is reserved in heaven for you: and that I may, I beseech you, Christians, tell me,

[1.] First, *Can death dissolve that glorious union that is between you and Christ?* No; Rom. viii. 35–39. Why, why then are you unwilling to die, as long as in death your union with Christ holds good? As in death Saul and Jonathan were not parted, 2 Sam. i. 23, so in death a believer and Christ is not parted, but more closely and firmly united. That is not death, but life, that joins the dying man to Christ; and that is not a life, but death, that separates the living man from Christ. As it is impossible for the leaven that is in the dough to be separated from the dough after it is once mixed, for it turneth the nature of the dough into itself; so it is impossible, either in life or death, for the saints ever to be separated from Christ; for Christ, in respect of union, is in the saints as nearly as the leaven in the very dough, so incorporated one into another as if Christ and they were one lump, John xvii. 20, 21; xv. 1–6. But,

[2.] Secondly, For I shall but touch upon things, tell me, O Christian, who art unwilling to die, *Whether death can dissolve or untie that marriage-knot that by the Spirit on Christ's side, and by faith on thine, is knit between Christ and thy soul?* No. Death cannot untie that knot, Hosea ii. 19, 20. Why, why then, O Christian, art thou unwilling to die, as long as the marriage-knot holds fast between Christ and thy soul? Mat. xxv. 1, 2; Rom. vii. 1–4. I readily grant that death dissolves that marriage-knot that is knit between man and wife; but death nor devil can never dissolve the marriage-knot that is knit between Christ and the believing soul. Sin cannot dissolve that marriage-knot that is knit between Christ and a believer; and if sin cannot, then certainly death, that came in by sin, cannot. Though sin can do more than death, yet sin cannot make null and void that glorious marriage that is between Christ and the soul; therefore a Christian should not be unwilling to die: Jer. iii. 1–5, 12–14, compared. But,

[3.] Thirdly, *Can death, O Christian, dissolve that glorious covenant that God hath taken thee into?* No; Death can never dissolve

[1] Cyprian, *de immortalitate.*

that covenant: Jer. xxxii. 40, 'And I will make an everlasting covenant with them, that I will not turn away from them to do them good; but I will put my fear in their hearts, that they shall not depart from me.' Though Abraham be dead, yet God is Abraham's God still, Mat. xxii. 30–32. By covenant, and by virtue of this everlasting covenant, Abraham shall be raised and glorified. Oh! then, why shouldst thou be afraid of death? why shouldst thou be unwilling to die?

When David was upon his dying bed, he drew his strongest consolation out of this well of salvation,—the covenant: 2 Sam. xxiii. 5, 'Although my house be not so with God, yet he hath made with me an everlasting covenant, ordered in all things, and sure; for this is all my salvation, and all my desire, although he make it not to grow.' Dear hearts! the covenant remains firm and good between you and the Lord, both in life and in death; and therefore there is no reason why you should be unwilling to die. There are three things that are impossible for God to do, viz. to die, to lie, or deny himself, or that gracious covenant that he hath made with his people; and therefore death should be more desirable than terrible to gracious souls. But,

[4.] Fourthly, *Tell me, O Christian, can death dissolve that love that is between the Lord and thy soul?* Ps. cxvi. 15; Deut. vii. 7, 8. No, death cannot; for his love is not founded upon any worth or excellency in me, nor upon any work or service done by me, but his love is free; he loves because he will love. All motives to love are taken out of that bosom that is love and sweetness itself. His love is everlasting, it is like himself: Jer. xxxi. 3, 'I have loved thee with an everlasting love; therefore with loving-kindness have I drawn thee;' John xiii. 1, 'Whom he loved, he loved to the end;' Isa. liv. 8–10, 'In a little wrath I hid my face from thee for a moment; but with everlasting kindness will I have mercy on thee, saith the Lord thy Redeemer. For this is as the waters of Noah unto me: for as I have sworn that the waters of Noah should no more go over the earth; so have I sworn that I will not be wroth with thee, nor rebuke thee. For the mountains shall depart, and the hills be removed; but my kindness shall not depart from thee, neither shall the covenant of my peace be removed, saith the Lord that hath mercy on thee.' The love of Jesus Christ was to Lazarus when dead (John xi. 11), 'Our friend Lazarus sleepeth.' By all which it is most evident that death cannot dissolve that precious love that is between the Lord and his children. Oh! why then are they afraid to die? Why then do not they long to die, that they may be in the everlasting arms of divine love? The love of the Lord is everlasting; it is a love that never dies, that never decays, nor waxes cold. It is like the stone albestos,[1] of which Solinus writes, that being once hot, it can never be cooled again. Death is nothing but a bringing of a loving Christ and loving souls together. Why, then, should not the saints rather desire it, than fear it or be dismayed at it? But,

[5.] Fifthly, *Can death, O thou believing soul, dissolve those gracious grants, or those grants of grace that the Lord hath vouchsafed to thee?* as the grant of reconciliation, the grant of acceptation, the grant of justification, the grant of adoption, the grant of remission, &c., 2 Cor.

[1] 'Asbestos.'—G.

iii. 21–23. No; death cannot dissolve any of these gracious grants. Rom. xi. 29, 'for the gifts and calling of God are without repentance.' Why then, O Christian, art thou unwilling to die? Indeed, were it in the power of death to make void any of those noble and gracious grants that God hath vouchsafed to thee, thou mightest be afraid and unwilling to die; but that being a work too great, and too hard for death to accomplish, why shouldst thou not, in a holy triumphing way, say with the apostle, 'O death, where is thy sting? O grave, where is thy victory? The sting of death is sin, and the strength of sin is the law. But thanks be to God, which giveth us the victory, through our Lord Jesus Christ,' 1 Cor. xv. 55–57. A Christian, upon the account of what is laid up for him, may and ought divinely to out-brave death, as this precious saint did. A little before she breathed out her last into the bosom of Christ, she called for a candle; Come, saith she, and see death; and this she spake smilingly, out-braving death in a holy sense. Being free both from the pains of death, and from the fear of death, she knew him in whom she had believed, 2 Tim. i. 12. She knew right well that death could not dissolve those gracious grants that God had vouchsafed to her; and therefore when she came to it, she made no more of it to die than we do to dine. But,

[6.] Sixthly, *Tell me, Christians, did not Christ come to deliver you from the fear of death?* Yes; he did come into the world, and did take our nature upon him, that he might deliver us from the fear of death, Heb. ii. 14, 15. Why, then, should you be unwilling to die? Tell me, hath not Christ disarmed death of all its hurting power, and taken away its sting, that it cannot harm you? Yes, he hath, 1 Cor xv. 55–57. Why then should you be unwilling to die? Tell me, souls, will not Christ be with you in that hour? will he not stand by you, though others should desert you? Yes; we have it under his own hand that he will be present with us, and that he will neither, living nor dying, leave us, nor forsake us, Ps. xxiii. 4, Heb. xiii. 5, 6. Why then should you be unwilling to die? Tell me, O trembling Christians, shall death be any more to you than a change? a change of place, a change of company, a change of employment, a change of enjoyment?[1] No, certainly! Death to us will be but a change; yea, the happiest change that ever we met with, Job xiv. 14, John xi. 26, 1 Thes. iv. 14; why then should you be unwilling to die, seeing that to die is nothing but to change earth for heaven, rags for robes, crosses for crowns, and prisons for thrones, &c.? But tell me once more, Christians, hath not Jesus Christ, by his lying in the grave, sanctified the grave, and perfumed and sweetened the grave? Hath he not, by his blood and death, purchased for you a soft and easy bed in the grave? Yes; we believe he hath done all this for us. Oh why then should you be unwilling to die? Once more, tell me, Christians, will not Jesus Christ raise you out of the grave after you have taken a short nap? Will he not cause you to hear his voice? Will he not call you out of that withdrawing-room, the grave, and bring you to immortality and glory? Yes; we believe he will, John vi. 39, 40, 1 Cor. i. 5, 1 Thes. iv. 14–18. Oh why then should you be unwilling to die? Oh why should you not, upon

[1] *Ejus est timere mortem qui ad Christum nolit ire*, Let him fear death that is loth to go to Christ—*Cyprian.*

all these accounts, long for it, and whenever it comes, readily and willingly, cheerfully and sweetly, embrace it? O Christians, Christians! let but your hopes and your hearts be more fixed upon the things that are reserved in heaven for you, and then you will neither fear death, nor feel it when it comes. But,

[7.] Seventhly, *Death will perfectly cure you of all corporal and spiritual diseases at once:* as the aching head and the unbelieving heart; the ulcerous body and the polluted soul.[1] Now your bodies are full of ails, full of aches, full of diseases, full of distempers, so that your wisest physicians know not what to say to you, nor what to do with you, nor how to cure you. It is often with your bodies as it was with the civil and ecclesiastical body of the Jews, which from 'the sole of the feet, even to the crown of the head, was full of wounds, bruises, and putrefying sores,' Isa. i. 6. But now death will perfectly cure you of all; death will do that for you that you could not do for yourselves; death will do that for you that all your friends could not do for you; death will do that for you that the ablest and wisest physicians could not do for you. It will cure you of every ache, of every ail, &c. At Stratford-Bow, in Queen Mary's days,[2] there was burnt a lame man and a blind man at one stake. The lame man, after he was chained, casting away his crutch, bade the blind man be of good comfort, for death, said he, will cure us both: thee of thy blindness, and I of my lameness.

Ah, Christians! death will cure you of all your infirmities, of all your distempers; and why, then, should you be unwilling to die? Mæcenas in Seneca had rather live in many diseases than die; but I hope better things of you, for whom Christ hath died.

And as death will cure all your bodily diseases, so it will cure all your soul-distempers also. Death is not *mors hominis,* but *mors peccati,* not the death of the man, but the death of his sin; *peccatum erat obstetrix mortis, et mors sepulchrum peccati,* sin was the midwife that brought death into the world, and death shall be the grave to bury sin.[3] Death shall do that for a Christian that all his duties could never do, that all his graces could never do, that all his experiences could never do, that all ordinances could never do. It shall at once free him fully, perfectly, and perpetually from all sin, yea, from all possibility of ever sinning more.

The Persians had a certain day in the year in which they used to kill all serpents and venomous creatures; such a day as that will the day of death be to their sins who are interested in a Saviour. When Samson died, the Philistines also died together with him; so when a believer dies, his sins die with him. Death came in by sin, and sin goeth out by death. As the worm kills the worm that bred it, so death kills sin that bred it, Heb. xii. 23, Rom. vi. 7, 1 Cor. xv. 26.

And why, then, should Christians be afraid of death, or unwilling to die, seeing death gives them a writ of ease from infirmities and weaknesses, from all aches and pains, griefs and gripings, distemper and diseases, both of body and soul?

Homer reports of his Achilles, that he had rather be a servant to a

[1] *Ultimus morborum medicus mors.*

[2] [Foxe] Act. and Mon. fol. 1,773.

[3] *Quid est mors nisi sepultura vitiorum?* What is death but the burial of vices?—Ambrose *de bono mortis,* c. 4.

poor country clown here in this world, than to be a king to all the souls departed;[1] and the truth is, the most famous heathens have preferred the meanest life on earth above all the hopes they had of a better life; but I hope better things of you, Christians; and that upon this very ground, that death will certainly and perfectly cure you of all bodily and soul distempers at once. But,

[8.] Eighthly, *Is not your dying day an inevitable day?* Why, yes, yes. Why, then, should you be afraid to die? Why should you be unwilling to die, seeing that your dying day is a day that cannot be put off? The daily spectacles of mortality which we see before our eyes clearly evince this truth, that all must die.[2] It is a statute-law in heaven that all must die. All men and women are made up of dust, and by the law of heaven they must return to dust. All have sinned, and therefore all must die. The core of that apple which Adam ate sticks in the throats of all his children, and will at length choke them all one by one.[3]

Masius,[4] out of *Jacob Ediscenus Syrus*, saith that when Noah went into the ark, he took the bones of Adam with him, and that when he came out of the ark, he divided them among his sons, giving the head, as the chiefest part, unto his first-born, and therein as it were saying unto them, Let not this delivery from the flood make you secure; behold your first parent, and the beginning of mankind; you must all, and all that come from you, go unto the dust to him. What day is there that passes over our heads wherein the Lord doth not, by others' mortality, preach many sermons of mortality to us? and therefore why should we be unwilling to pay that debt that all owe, and that all must pay, and that so many daily pay before our eyes? But,

[9.] Ninthly, *A believer's dying day is his best day*,[5] and why then should he be unwilling to die? Eccles. vii. 1, 'A good name is better than precious ointment; and the day of death than the day of one's birth.' In respect of profit, pleasure, peace, safety, company, glory, a believer's last day is his best day; and when then should a believer be unwilling to die? In a printed sermon on this very text, I have proved this truth at large, and to that I refer you, who desire further satisfaction about this truth.[6] But,

[10.] Tenthly, *A believer's dying day is his resting day;* it is his resting day from sin, from sorrow, from affliction, from temptation, from desertion, from dissension, from vexation, from persecution, and from all bodily labour.[7] And therefore why should a believer be unwilling to die, seeing that for him to die is no more but to rest? But of this rest I have spoken largely before; and therefore a touch may be enough in this place. But,

[11.] Eleventhly, *The saints' dying day is their reaping day.* Now they shall reap the fruit of all the prayers that ever they have made, and of all the sermons that ever they have heard, and of all the tears

[1] Odyssey, xi. 488.—G.

[2] Eccles. ii. 16; Zech. i. 5; Heb. ix. 27; Gen. iii. 19; Rom. vi. 23.

[3] See Brooks's Will in Appendix to Memoir.—G.

[4] Masius *in ult. cap. Josh.*, ver. 32. [Andrew Masius, a learned writer, died 1573. His 'Commentary' on Joshua (1574) was reprinted in the 'Critici Sacri.'—G.]

[5] Ambrose, *de fide resurrectionis*, speaks of some who lamented men's births and celebrated their deaths, &c.

[6] His 'Believer's Last Day is his Best Day,' 1657.—G.

[7] Rev. xiv. 13, xxi. 4; Job iii. 13–16; Isa. lvii. 1, 2.

that ever they have shed, and of all the sighs and groans that ever they have fetched, and of all the good words that ever they have spoke, and of all the good works that ever they have done, and of all the great things that ever they have suffered; yea, now they shall reap the fruit of many good services, which themselves had forgot, 2 Cor. ix. 6; Gal. vi. 7–9. 'Lord, when saw we thee hungry, and fed thee; or thirsty, and gave thee drink; or naked, and clothed thee; or sick, or in prison, and visited thee?' Mat. xxv. 34–41. They had done many good works and forgot them, but Christ records them, remembers them, and rewards them. Sabinus in Seneca could never in all his lifetime remember those three names of Homer, Ulysses, and Achilles; and as bad memories have many Christians in spirituals. But our Lord Jesus, as he hath a soft and tender heart, so he hath an iron memory; he remembers not only the best and greatest services, but also the least and lowest services that have been done by his people, and he remembers them to reward them. A bit of bread, a cup of cold water, shall not pass without a reward. Therefore it is good counsel one gives,[1] *Nunquam quum veniat Dominus, inveniat imparatos, sed semper vultus suspensos expansosque sinus habentes, ad largam Domini benedictionem*, Let the Lord when he cometh never find us unready, but always with our faces looking up towards him, always having our bosoms open, our laps spread abroad, as looking to receive a large blessing from him. Christians, however Christ may seem to forget your labour of love, and to take no notice, or but little, of many good services that you have done for him, his name, his gospel, his people, yet when you die, when you come to heaven, you shall then reap a plentiful, a glorious crop, as the fruit of that good seed, that for a time hath seemed to be buried and lost, Prov. xi. 25; Ps. cxxvi. 5, 6. When mortality shall put on immortality, you shall then find that bread which long before was cast upon the waters, Eccles. xi. 1–6. Therefore be not, O Christian, afraid to die! be not, O Christian, unwilling to die! for thy dying day will be thy reaping day. But,

[12.] Twelfthly, *Thy dying-day, O believer! will be thy triumphing day*, John xi. 26. Now thou shalt gloriously triumph over sin, Satan, the world, thy own base heart, yea, and over death itself. I readily grant, that if you consider believers in Christ, as he was a public person, they have then already triumphed over principalities and powers; what Christ did in his greatest transaction, he did as a public person, representing all his chosen ones; he suffered as a public person, representing all his elect; he died as a public person, representing all his precious ones; he rose, he ascended, and now he sits in heaven as a public person, representing all his children: Eph. ii. 6, 'And hath raised us up together, and made us sit together in heavenly places in Christ Jesus.' Christ hath taken up his children's rooms in heaven aforehand; Christ hath already taken possession of heaven in their names, in their steads, they do now sit together in heavenly places in Christ Jesus.[2] And so when Jesus Christ spoiled 'principalities and powers, and triumphed openly over them on the cross,' he

[1] Bernard. Ser. xvii. *in Cant.*

[2] Eph. iv. 8; Col. ii. 14, 15; a plain allusion to the Roman triumphs; 1 John ii. 13, 14; Rom. viii. 37; 1 John iv. 4, 5.

did this as a public person, representing all his children who triumphed in his triumph over all the powers of darkness; and therefore, in this sense, believers have already triumphed; yea, and I readily grant, that believers, even in this life, by virtue of their union and communion with Christ, and by virtue of his gracious presence, influence, and assistance, they do always triumph, as the apostle speaks: 2 Cor. ii. 14, 'Now thanks be unto God, which always causeth us to triumph in Christ.' Believers now are more than conquerors, they are triumphers over the world, the flesh, and the devil. Christ so routed Satan upon the cross, saith Ignatius, that he never since either hears or sees the cross, but he falls a-shaking and trembling. Believers, by holding forth to Satan the cross of Christ in the arms of faith, and by their laying hold on his cross and pleading his cross, they do easily, they do frequently overcome him and triumph over him. But notwithstanding all this, ah! how often doth the best of saints find the world, the flesh, and the devil triumphing sadly over them? Now a Christian triumphs over Satan, Rom. vii. 14-25; by and by Christ withdraws, and then Satan triumphs over him. Now the believer leads captivity captive; anon the believer is led captive; this day a saint gets the wind and the hill of Satan, and beats him quite out of the field; the next day Satan draws forth and falls on with new forces, with new arguments, with fresh strength, and then puts a Christian to a retreat, ay, too often to a rout. In many a battle a Christian is worsted, and much ado he hath to come off with his life. Oh but now death, that brings a Christian to a full, perfect, complete, absolute, and perpetual triumph over the world, the flesh, and the devil. Now a Christian shall for ever have the necks of these enemies under his feet; now these enemies shall be for ever disarmed, so that they shall never be able to make resistance more, they shall never strike stroke more, they shall never affront a believer more, they shall never lead a believer captive more, &c. Oh why then should believers be afraid to die, be unwilling to die, seeing that their dying day is their triumphing day?[1] But,

[13.] Thirteenthly, As a believer's dying-day is his triumphing-day, so a believer's dying-day is *his marriage-day*, Hosea ii. 19, 20. In this life we are only betrothed to Christ; in the life to come we shall be married to Christ. Here Christ and the believer is near, but death will bring Christ and the believer nearer; here Christ and the believer is asked, and all things are agreed on between them, only the marriage-knot must be tied in heaven, the marriage-supper must be kept in heaven, Rev. xix. 5-10. And, therefore, several of the martyrs on their suffering-days, on their dying-days, they have invited several to their marriage, as they have phrased it, knowing right well, that their dying-days would be their marriage-days to Christ; the very thoughts of which hath so raised and cheered, so warmed and inflamed their hearts, that they have made nothing of death, that they have outbraved death, that they have, to the great joy of their friends, and to the amazement and astonishment of their enemies, more resolutely, friendly, and sweetly embraced death, than they have their nearest and dearest relations. But in the

[1] The Romans used in all their battles to lose at first, to win at last; it is so with Christians.

(14.) Fourteenth place, A Christian's dying day is his *transplanting-day*. Death transplants a believer from earth to heaven, from misery to glory, Job xiv. 14. Death to a saint is nothing but the taking of a sweet flower out of this wilderness, and planting of it in the garden of paradise; it is nothing but a taking of a lily from among thorns, and planting of it among those sweet roses of heaven which God delights to wear always in his bosom. Death is nothing but the taking off of a believer fully from the stock of the first Adam, and the planting of him perfectly and perpetually into that glorious stock, the second Adam, the Lord Jesus, who is blessed for ever. Death is nothing but the taking off the believer from a more barren soil, and planting of him in a more fruitful soil. Here some Christians bring forth thirty, others sixty, and others a hundred-fold, Mat. xiii. 8. 23; but heaven is so fruitful a soil, that there are none there but such as abound in the fruits of righteousness and holiness, but such as bring forth a thousand-fold, yea, many thousand-fold. Here our hearts are like the isle of Patmos, which brings forth but little fruit; but when they shall by death be transplanted to heaven, they shall be like the tree in Alcinous's garden, that had always blossoms, buds, and ripe fruits, one under another.[1]

In the island of St Thomas, on the back side of Africa, in the midst of it is a hill, and over that a continual cloud, wherewith the whole island is watered and made fruitful. Such a cloud will Jesus Christ be to all those precious souls that shall be transplanted from earth to heaven.

Oh! why, then, should believers be unwilling to die, seeing that their dying day is but a transplanting day of their souls from earth to heaven, from a wilderness to a paradise? But in the

[15.] Fifteenth place, As a believer's dying day is the day of his transplantation, so his dying day is *the day of his coronation*. Here believers are kings elected, but when they die, they are kings crowned; now they have a crown in reversion, but then they have a crown in possession; now they have a crown in hope, but then they shall have a crown in hand, James i. 12, Rev. ii. 10. Death will at last bring the soul to a crown without thorns, to a crown without mixture, to a righteous crown, to a glorious crown, to an everlasting crown. Though a crown be the top of royalty,[2] and though beyond it the thoughts and wishes of mortal men extend not, yet most may say of their earthly crowns as that king said of his: O crown! more noble than happy! But death will set such a crown upon a believer's head as shall always flourish, and as shall make him happy to all eternity. Here the believer, as his Saviour before him, is crowned with thorns, but death will turn that crown of thorns into a crown of pure gold, Ps. cxxxii. 18, xxi. 3.

Upon a triumph, all the Emperor Severus his soldiers, for the greater pomp, were to put on crowns of bays on their heads, but there was one Christian among them that wore this crown on his arm; and it being demanded why he did so, he answered, *Non decet Christianum in hac vita coronari*, it becomes not a Christian to wear his crown in this life. The truth is, a Christian's crown never sits so fast, nor never so well

[1] Homer *Od.* vi. 12, &c., 62, &c.; and cf. Hyginus. Fab. 125, 126.—G.
[2] Still another Shakesperian word, 'The round and *top* of sovereignty:' Macbeth, iv. 1, &c., &c.—G.

becomes him, as when it is put on by a hand of death. Here most princes' crowns are the fruits of unrighteousness, but death will at last put upon the believer a crown of righteousness, or a righteous crown, 2 Tim. iv. 7, 8; and so it is called, not only because it is purchased by the righteousness of Christ, but also to difference it from those unrighteous crowns, or crowns of unrighteousness, that the princes of this world put upon their own heads. Earthly crowns are corruptible, but death will put on the heads of believers an incorruptible crown, 1 Cor. ix. 25.

Worldly crowns are fading and withering. Though king William the Conqueror was crowned three times every year, during his reign, at three several places, viz., Gloucester, Winchester, and Westminster, yet how soon did his crown fade and wither?

But death will put such a crown upon the believer's head as shall never fade nor wither, 1 Pet. v. 4. Worldly crowns are tottering and shaking; most princes' crowns hang but on one side of their heads, and all their interest, power, and policy cannot make them sit fast on both sides. But death will put upon the heads of believers an immortal crown, an unmoveable crown, an everlasting crown, an eternal crown, a crown that none can shake, that none can take, that none can conquer or overcome, 2 Cor. iv. 14–18, Rev. ii. 10.

Oh, why then should Christians be afraid to die, or unwilling to die, seeing that their dying day is but their coronation day? Who would be unwilling to ride to a crown through a dirty lane or a rainy day? But in the

[16.] Sixteenth place, *A gracious soul shall never die till his work be finished, and he prepared to die:* and why then should he be unwilling to die when his work is done, and he prepared to go home? When God hath no more work for you to do in this world, why then should you be unwilling to die, to go home? Now, till your work be finished that God hath cut out for you in this world, no power nor policy shall ever be able to cut off the thread of your lives; in despite of all the world, and all the powers of hell, you shall do that work, be it more or less, that God hath appointed you to do in this world. The life of Christ was very often in danger, both among pretended friends and professed foes, but yet he still escapes all the snares that they had laid for him, and all the pits that they have digged for him, and that upon this very ground, 'That his time was not yet come, his hour was not yet come:' John vii. 30, 'Then they sought to take him: but no man laid hands on him, because his hour was not yet come;' viii. 19, 20, 'Then said they unto him, Where is thy Father? Jesus answered, Ye neither know me, nor my Father: if ye had known me, ye should have known my Father also. These words spake Jesus in the treasury, as he taught in the temple: and no man laid hands on him; for his hour was not yet come.'[1] God can and will secure his people from the rage and malice of their enemies by a secret and invisible hand of providence, till they have finished the work that he hath set them about in this world. David was surrounded with enemies on all hands, but yet, in spite of them all, he keeps up till his work was done: Acts xiii. 36, 'For David, after he had served his own generation by the will of God, fell

[1] God often bridles wicked men's malice and fury invisibly.

on sleep.' Though many thrust sore at him, yet he did not fall asleep, he did not die till he had served his generation. Bonds and afflictions waited on Paul in every city, Acts xx. 23; so in that 2 Cor. xi. 23–28, 'In stripes above measure, in prisons more frequent, in deaths often. Of the Jews, five times received I forty stripes save one' (the Lord commanded that the number of strokes should not exceed forty, Deut. xxv. 3, and therefore the Jews, that they might not transgress that law, gave one less); 'thrice was I beaten with rods, once was I stoned, thrice I suffered shipwreck, a night and a day I have been in the deep, in journeying often, in perils of waters, in perils of robbers, in perils by mine own countrymen, in perils by the heathen, in perils in the city, in perils in the wilderness, in perils in the sea, in perils amongst false brethren. In weariness and painfulness, in watchings often, in hunger and thirst, in fastings often, in cold and nakedness,' Acts xvi. 23, xiv. 17. And yet notwithstanding all these hazards, hardships, dangers, deaths, Paul lives, and bravely bears up till his work was done, his course finished: 2 Tim. iv. 7, 8, 'I have fought a good fight, I have finished my course, I have kept the faith;' and so in that Rev. xi. 7, The beast that ascended out of the bottomless pit, and that made war against the two witnesses, could not overcome them, nor kill them, till they had finished their testimony. Christians shall live to finish their testimony, and to do all that work that God hath cut out for them to do, in spite of all the beasts in the world, in spite of hell or antichrist.

It was so with Ambrose; a certain witch sent her spirits to kill him, but they returned answer, that God had hedged him in, as he did Job, so that they could not touch him. Another came with a sword to his bedside to have killed him; but he could not stir his hand, till repenting, he was by the prayer of Ambrose restored to the use of his hands again. No means, no attempts, could cut him off till his work was done.

So for Luther, a poor friar, to stand so stoutly against the pope, this was a great miracle; but that he should prevail against the pope as he did, this was a greater; and that after all he should die in his bed, notwithstanding all the enemies he had, and the several designs they had to have destroyed him, this was the greatest of all; and yet for all that the pope or the devil his father could do, Luther, when he had finished his testimony, dies in his bed. Oh! why then should any Christian be unwilling to die, seeing he shall not die till his work be done, till his testimony be finished?

And as a believer shall not die till his work be done, so he shall not die till he be prepared to die. A believer is always habitually prepared to die; ay, even then when he is not actually prepared; yet then he is habitually prepared to die, for he hath not his ark to build, nor his lamp to trim, nor his oil to buy, nor his pardon to seal, nor his peace to make, nor his graces to get, nor his interest in Christ to seek, nor divine favour to secure, nor a righteousness to look after, &c. That promise is full of honey and sweetness that you have in Job v. 26, 'Thou shalt come to thy grave in a full age, like as a shock of corn cometh in in his season.' The husbandman brings not his corn into his barn till it be full ripe, no more will God take his children out of this world till they are fit for another world; he will not transplant them from earth till they are fit, till they are prepared for heaven. It is with Christians as it is with the fruits of the earth; some are ripe sooner, some later; but as we, so God will gather none till they are ripe for glory. Some souls, like some fruits, are ripe betimes; other Christians, like other fruit, are a longer time of ripening; and so God gathers his fruit in as they ripen, some sooner, some later, but none till they are in a measure ripe for heaven. And why, then, should Christians be unwilling to die, seeing they shall not die till they are prepared to die? I do not say they shall not die till they think they are fit to die, or till they say they are prepared to die; for they may be graciously prepared and sweetly fitted to die, and yet may judge otherwise, by reason of Satan's sleights, or some spiritual distemper that may hang upon them, or from a natural fear of death, and some great unwillingness to die; but they shall not die till they are either actually or habitually prepared to die, till they are ripe for glory; and therefore be not, oh be not, Christians, unwilling to die. But in the

[17.] Seventeenth place, *When a righteous man dies, he shall leave a sweet savour behind him, his name shall live when he is dead*, Heb. xi. Are not the names of the patriarchs, prophets, apostles, martyrs, and other saints, a sweet savour to this very day? We know there is no sweet savour to that they have left behind them: Ps. cxii. 6, 'The righteous shall be had in everlasting remembrance.' Prov. x. 7, 'The memory of the just is blessed:' the Septuagint thus translates it, 'The memory of the just is with praises.' Many are the praises that wait on the name of the just when their bodies are in the dust; no scent so sweet as that which the just man leaves behind him: Eccles. vii. 1, 'A good name is better than precious ointment.'[1] He doth not say a great name, a name arising from outward greatness, but a good name, a name arising from inward goodness, and manifested by outward holiness; that is the name that is better than precious ointment. Ointment only reaches the nostrils, but a good name reaches to the cheering and the warming of the heart. The Chaldee reads this verse thus: *Melius est nomen bonum quod comparabunt justi in hoc sæculo, quam unguentum unctionis, quod fuerit inunctum super capita regum et sacerdotum*: better is the good name which the just shall obtain in this world, than the ointment of anointing which was poured upon the heads of the kings and priests. Though a believer may not leave great sums of money behind him, nor yet thousands nor hundreds a-year behind him, yet he shall leave a good name behind him, which answers to all, nay, which outweighs all the riches, gallantry, and glory of this world. That heathen [Plautus] hit right who said, *Ego si bonam famam servasso, sat dives ero.* If I may but keep a good name, I have wealth enough. It is a greater mercy to leave a good name behind us than to leave the riches of a kingdom, yea, of a world, behind us. But in the,

[18.] Eighteenth place, *Death is nothing but the believer's inlet into glory.* Death is the gate of life, it is the gate of paradise; it is the midwife to bring eternity to bed. When Jacob saw the chariots that were to bring him to Joseph, his spirit revived, Gen. xlv. 27. Ah, Christian!

[1] The initial letter ט of the Hebrew word *tob*, that is, for good, is bigger than ordinary, to shew the exceeding excellence of a good name.

death is that chariot that will bring thee not only to a sight of Jacob and Joseph, but also to a blessed sight of God, Christ, angels and 'the spirits of just men made perfect, Heb. xii. 23, 24. Here we meet with many inlets to sin, to sorrow, to affliction, to temptation; but death, of all inlets, is the most happy inlet; it lets the soul into a full fruition of God, to the perfection of grace, and to the heights of glory; and why, then, should a gracious soul be unwilling to die? But I must hasten to a close; therefore in the,

[19.] Nineteenth place, *Was Jesus Christ so willing to leave heaven, his Father's bosom, his crown, his dignity, his glory, his royal attendance, to come into this world to suffer the saddest and the heaviest things that ever was thought of, that ever was heard of, for thy sins, for thy sake? and wilt thou be unwilling to die, and to go to him who hath suffered so much, who hath paid so much, who hath prepared so much for thee?*[1] Ah, Christian, Christian! why dost thou not rather reason thus with thy own soul: Did Christ die for me, that I might live with him? I will not therefore desire to live long from him. All men go willingly to see him whom they love, and shall I be unwilling to die, that I may see him whom my soul loves? Oh, I will not! oh, I dare not! oh, I may not! Others venture through many dangers and many deaths to see their friends and relations, and why then shouldst not thou, O Christian! be willing to venture through death to the Lord of life, to him that is thy crown, thy comfort, thy head, thy husband, thy heaven, thy all? &c. But, in the

[20.] Twentieth and last place, *Consider, O believer! that thou always standest before God in the righteousness of Jesus Christ, who is called the Lord our righteousness, and who, of God, is made unto thee wisdom, righteousness, sanctification, and redemption,* Jer. xxiii. 6; 1 Cor. i. 30. Whilst thou livest thou standest before God, not in the righteousness of thy duties, nor in thy gracious dispositions, which are but weak and imperfect, but in the pure, perfect, matchless, and spotless righteousness of Jesus Christ. And when thou diest thou appearest before God in the same glorious righteousness, so that thou mayest appear before God's unspotted justice and holiness with the greatest boldness and comfort that is imaginable, upon the account of that righteousness with which thou art clothed: Ps. xlv. 13, 'The king's daughter is all glorious within' (there is her inward glory; grace makes the soul glorious within); 'her clothing is of wrought gold.' Some read it purled work, or closures of gold, enamelled with gold; such as precious stones were set in, which were exceeding splendid and glorious, and which shadowed forth the glorious righteousness of our Lord Jesus, Exod. xxviii. 11, 14; xxxix. 1–5, &c. This clothing of wrought gold is the glorious righteousness of our Lord Jesus. Now, in life and in death, the believer stands before God in the glorious golden robes of Christ's righteousness; and hence it is that believers are said to be all fair and without spot, and to be without spot or wrinkle, and to be complete in Christ, and to be without fault before the throne of God;[2] and why then should a believer be unwilling to die and appear before God? By reason of this clothing of wrought gold, you stand spotless,

[1] One of the fathers longed to die, that he might see that head that was crowned with thorns.

[2] Cant. iv. 7; Eph. v. 27; Col. ii. 10; Rev. xiv. 4, 5.

blameless, and faultless before God. This golden clothing, this glorious righteousness of Christ, is as truly and really the believer's, and as fully and completely the believer's, as if it were his very own. Ah! no clothing to this. The costly cloak of Alcisthenes, which Dionysius sold to the Carthaginians for a hundred talents, was indeed a mean and beggarly rag to this embroidered mantle that Christ puts upon all believers. And therefore a Christian, both living and dying, should say with the psalmist, 'I will make mention of thy righteousness, of thy righteousness only,' Ps. lxxi. 15, 16, 19. Let them be afraid to die, let them be unwilling to die, who must appear before God in their sins, and in their own righteousness, which at best is but as filthy rags, Isa. lxiv. 6. But as for thee, O Christian, who shalt always appear before God in clothing of wrought gold, be not thou afraid of death, be not thou unwilling to die, but rather desire it, rather long for it, 1 Cor. xv. 55–57, because thou art clothed with such righteousness as will bear thee up sweetly in it, as will carry thee bravely through it, and as will make thee triumph over it. Christ's righteousness is a Christian's white raiment, in which he stands pure before God, Rev. iii. 18, and Rev. xix. 7, 8, 'Let us be glad and rejoice, and give glory to him: for the marriage of the Lamb is come, and his wife hath made herself ready. And to her was granted that she should be arrayed in fine linen, clean and white: for the linen is the righteousness of saints.' By the fine, clean, white linen which is here called the righteousness, or, as the Greek hath it, the righteousnesses of saints, most understand the glorious righteousness of Christ.[1] Righteousness is an Hebraism, noting that most perfect absolute righteousness which we have in Christ; white is a natural colour, it is a colour of purity, ornament, and honour. It was the habit in times past of nobles, saith Drusius, and others. Now in this pure, clean, white linen all the saints are clothed, and so presented to God by Jesus Christ; and why then should they be unwilling to die? Here is not a speck, not a spot, to be found upon this white linen, which is the righteousness of saints, which should make saints rather to pursue after death, than to fly from it, or to be unwilling to welcome it when it comes.

I am not ignorant that this unwillingness to die most usually springs from those low and dark apprehensions men have of God, and from weakness of faith, and from coldness of love, and from laying the creatures too near our hearts, and from our little communion with God, and our rare taking of turns in paradise, and from our not treasuring up a stock of promises, and a stock of experiences, &c. I have also considered what a dishonour to God, a reproach to Christ, a grief to the Spirit, a scandal to religion, a blot to profession, a mischief to sinners, and a wrong to saints, it is, for Christians to be unwilling to die, or to be afraid of death, which hath occasioned me to muster up these twenty considerations to work you to be willing to die; and if these will not prevail with you, I profess I do not know what will.

Obj. I would be willing to die, if I had but assurance: but that is the jewel I want; and therefore I am unwilling to die.

(1.) First, I answer, *It may be thou hast assurance, though not such a measure of assurance, such a plerophory or full assurance, as thou*

[1] δικαιώματα, *i. e.* say some, imputed and imparted righteousness.

desirest. A perfect, complete, absolute, and full assurance is very desirable on earth, but I think few attain to it till they come to heaven. This sparkling diamond God hangs in few saints' bosoms till they come to glory. But,

(2.) Secondly, I answer, *The least grace, if true, is sufficient to salvation*, Mat. v. 3, 10; and therefore the sense of the least grace, or of the least measure of grace, should be sufficient to assurance of salvation. But,

(3.) Thirdly, *The time of death is one of the most usual seasons wherein God gives his children the sweetest and fullest assurance of his love, of their interest in him, and of their right to glory.* When there was but a step, a stride, between Stephen and death, then he saw heaven open, and Christ standing at the right hand of his Father, Acts vii. 55–60.

Mr Glover, though he had been long under clouds and much darkness, yet when he came near the fire, he cried out to his friend, O Austin, Austin, he is come, he is come! meaning the Lord, in the sweet and glorious discoveries of his love and favour to him; and so he died, with a heart full of joy and assurance.[1]

Mr Frogmorton, a precious godly minister, lived thirty-seven years without assurance, after the Lord had wrought savingly upon him, and then died at Master Dod's, having assurance but an hour before he died.[2]

I could here give you divers examples, of a later date, of many precious Christians who have lived close with God many years, and have been much in seeking of assurance, and the Lord hath held them off till a few years before their death, and then he hath filled their souls so full of the sense of his love, and the assurance of their everlasting welfare, that they have died under the power of their joys. Assurance is a free gift of God, and God loves to give his gifts to his children when they may most cheer them, and be of greatest use and service to them; and when is that, but at the day of death? And therefore Christians should not be unwilling to die for want of assurance, because that is a special season wherein God usually gives assurance to his children. But,

(4.) Fourthly and lastly, *Thou mayest die and go to heaven without assurance.* This truth, with several others of the like import, that may further satisfy such as are unwilling to die, I have made good in that treatise of mine called 'Heaven on Earth,'[3] and to that I refer the reader for further satisfaction, if what is said do not satisfy.

The next inference, then, that I shall make, and so hasten to a close, is this:

[1] Clarke, *as before.*—G.

[2] The above incident is strikingly told in Brooks's favourite folio, and may here be given:—Mr Frogmorton was a man of high reputation, and a pious and zealous preacher of the word; but labouring, in the decline of life, under a consumption, and being oppressed with melancholy apprehensions about the safety of his state, he removed to Ashby, near Fausley, in Northamptonshire, to enjoy the counsel and advice of the venerable Mr John Dod. A little before he died, he asked Mr Dod, saying 'What will you say of him who is going out of the world, and can find no comfort?' 'What will you say of our Saviour Christ?' replied Mr Dod, 'who, when *he* was going out of the world, found no comfort, but cried, "My God, my God, why hast thou forsaken me?"' This administered consolation to Mr Throgmorton's troubled mind, and he departed soon after, rejoicing in the Lord.'—Clarke's 'Martyrologie, as before, p. 172.—G.

[3] See this treatise in Vol. II.—G.

If the best things are reserved for believers, then let not Christians mourn immoderately, 1 Thes. iv. 13, 14. Oh! be not over-much afflicted and grieved for the death of husband, wife, child, sister, friend, who dies in the Lord; for they are but gone to take possession of those great and glorious things that are reserved in heaven for them. This deceased saint is now gone to her home, to her heaven, to her God that hath loved her, to her Christ that hath died for her, and to her crown that was prepared for her. Abraham mourned moderately for his dear deceased Sarah, Gen. xxiii. 2, as is imported by a small *caph* in that Hebrew word that signifies to weep; and that not because she was old and over-worn, as some Rabbins say, but because death to her was but an inlet into glory: death did but bring her to a happy fruition of all those glorious things that God hath laid up for them that love him. Death, that seems to dispossess a Christian of all, puts him into a possession of all; of all joys, of all comforts, of all delights, of all contents, of all happiness, of all blessedness; and why then should our sorrow, our tears overflow the banks of moderation? Sorrow is good for nothing but for sin. Now that the child is dead, wherefore should I fast and weep? said David. Grief preceding evil, if it be used for a remedy, cannot be too much; but that which follows an evil past, cannot be too little.

When Ezekiel lost his wife, the delight of his eyes, he must not weep, Ezek. xxiv. 15–17. When Mary the mother of Jesus stood by the cross of her only dear Son, she wept not, as Ambrose saith, John xix. 25–27. We may say of our deceased friend, as the Jews of their father Jacob, *Non est mortuus*, he is not dead; or as our Saviour of Lazarus, 'He is not dead, but sleepeth,' John xi. 11; and the maid, 'Why trouble you yourselves? they are not dead, but sleep.' To die, in the prophet Isaiah's phrase, is but to lie down in our beds, Isa. xliii. 17; lvii. 1, 2. So Asa the king's coffin is called a bed, 2 Chron. xvi. 14. And when 'thy days shall be fulfilled,' saith Nathan to David, 'and thou shalt sleep with thy fathers;' or, as the original hath it, 'and thou shalt lie down with thy fathers,' 2 Sam. vii. 12. Death is nothing but a sleeping with our fathers, or a lying down in the bed with our fathers and friends, who have lain down before us. And, therefore, when a friend, a wife, a child dies, and leaves this world, we are to bid them but good night, as the primitive Christians used to do, in sure and certain hope to meet them in the morning of the resurrection.

The ancients were wont to call the days of their death *natalia*, not dying days but birth-days. It hath been the custom, saith *Haymo*,[1] when a child of God departed this life, to call it not the day of his death, but the day of his nativity. The Jews to this day stick not to call their Golgothas *Batte Cajim*, the houses or places of the living.

The Jews' ancient custom was, by the way as they went with their corpse, to pluck up every one the grass, as who should say, they were not sorry for the death of their friends and relations, as men without hope, for they were but so cropped off, and should spring up again in due season.[2] Ah, friends! if you will needs mourn, then mourn for

[1] Bishop of Halberstat: see list of writings in Watt's Bib. Brit., *sub nomine*.—G.

[2] The Persian kings would have no mournings, nor mourning apparel worn in their presence.

yourselves, mourn for your sins, mourn for the barrenness and baseness of your own hearts; but do not mourn, at least excessively, for the death of any Christian friend or relation, seeing that death gives them a quiet and full possession of all that glory and happiness that is reserved in heaven for them.

The next use is cause of comfort and consolation to all the people of God. If it be so that the best things are reserved for believers till they come to heaven, then this may serve to comfort the people of God, and that,

(1.) First, against *their poor, low, and mean condition in this world.* Ah! poor Christians, what though you have little in hand, yet you have much in hope; though you have little in possession, yet you have much in reversion. He that hath but little in present possession, yet if he hath a fair estate in reversion, he comforts himself, and solaces his spirit in the thoughts of it, that there will come a day when he shall live like a man, when he shall live bravely and sweetly; and this makes him sing care and sorrow away. Why! Christians, do you do so: you have a fine, a fair estate in reversion, though you have but little in possession; and therefore bear up bravely and live comfortably, James ii. 5; 2 Tim. iv. 7, 8; Ps. xvi. 6.

Christ, who was the heir of all, yet he lived poor and died poor, Mat. viii. 20. As he was born in another man's house, so he was buried in another man's tomb. When Christ died he made no will; he had no crown lands; only his coat was left, and that the soldiers parted among them. If thy outward condition be conformable to his, there is no reason why thou shouldst be discouraged, for thou hast a rich and royal revenue that will shortly come into thy hand, and then thou shalt never know what poverty and penury means more: and for thy comfort, know, that though men may for thy poverty despise thee, yet the Lord doth highly prize thee. It was a good saying of Basil, *Placet sibi Deus abstrusam in despecto corpore margaritam conspicatus.*[1] God pleaseth himself, beholding a hidden pearl in a despised and disrespected body. The truth is, Christians, if there were any real happiness in the things of this life, you should have them, but it is not in all the wealth and glory of this world to make up a happiness to you; and therefore, as the enjoyment of them should not swell the rich, so the want of them should not trouble the poor. The angels and saints departed in heaven are happy, and yet they have neither silver nor gold; they are blessed and yet they have none of the gay things of this life, they have none of the gallantry and glory of this world. You have now your worst, your best days are to come; it will not be long before you shall have your portion in hand; therefore live sweetly and walk comfortably up and down this world. But,

(2.) Secondly, If the best things are reserved for believers till they come to heaven, then *this may serve to comfort them against all outward abasements from the malignant world.*[2] What though you are counted as the scum, the dirt, the filth, the scraping, the offscouring of the world, by men that know not, that see not, that believe not what great and glorious things are reserved in heaven for you? Yet at last you

[1] Basil, *Selu oratione* 15.

[2] No man is able to bear so much contempt as Christ bears daily, saith Luther.

shall be advanced to that dignity, and be made partakers of that felicity and glory, which shall work amazement and astonishment in those that now despise you and vilify you. Those that now count you the troublers of their Israel, shall be troubled with a witness, when they shall see you with crowns upon your heads and the royal robes of glory upon your backs, and two-edged swords in your hands, to execute the vengeance written, Ps. cxlix. 4–9. Men that know their future greatness, are not troubled at reproaches; they think themselves above reproaches; they can divinely scorn scorns and contemn contempts. Ah, Christians! how can you seriously consider of your future greatness, happiness, and glory, and not bear up sweetly and comfortably against all the contempt that you may meet with in this world?

And thus I have done with this subject, which of one sermon is multiplied into several, by a good hand of heaven upon me. I shall follow this poor piece with my weak prayers, that it may be a mercy to hearers, readers, and writer.

AN ELEGY

Upon the Death of Mrs MARY BLAKE, the Wife of Mr NICHOLAS BLAKE, of London, Merchant.

WHERE virtue, seated in the heart,
Shining forth in suiting acts of life,
Oh! what delight doth it impart
To pious minds! Experience rife
  Of thee we have, as otherwise,
  So in this godly woman's guise.

Her sweet endowments, pregnant wit,
And holy graces from above,
How made they her an object fit
No less for wonder than for love!
  Such precious fruit, so ripe, though green
  In so few years, is seldom seen.

They who enjoyed the sight and sense
Of her dear converse, to her close,
Oh! what contentment did from thence
To them arise! chiefly to those
  Who nearest to her did relate,
  In blood, in grace, or married state.

Parents' dear comfort, husband's glory,
Kindred's honour, friendship's praise,
To after-times a fair writ story
For a pattern to their ways:
  All these in her did meet, as one
  That suited all and failed none.

Thus, while we her enjoyed, she was
A precious cordial to us all;
But now, being taken hence, alas!
From joys unto laments we fall.
  Thus sith her loss to all extends,
  Sorrow doth seize on all her friends.

It doth indeed; nor do we find
That God Almighty doth dislike
Good nature's working in this kind,
When us in ours he thus doth strike.
  Their deathbeds, while in this sad trim,
  We may besprink, but not make swim.

Tears from our eyes like precious dew,
As from a lymbeck may drop out,
Not flow, as usually we view,
Like common water from a spout.
  Why should they? sith to our relief
  We have cause no less of joy than grief?

This friend of ours for whom we weep
Is safely come unto the shore;
She is not dead, but fall'n asleep,
And only gone to bed before.
  And we, when ended is our pain,
  Shall sleep with her, and wake again.

Mean season, as for her, we know
Where, aud with whom, and how she dwells,
In heaven with Christ, and myriads mo,
Whose presence all delight excels;
  And there she sings with high desire
  Her hallelujahs in full choir.

All this she studied here, but never
Could fully tell what it should be,
Till God did soul from body sever,
And took it up these joys to see:
  There let her rest, until we meet
  Each other in that place to greet.

MART. BLAKE.

END OF VOL. I.